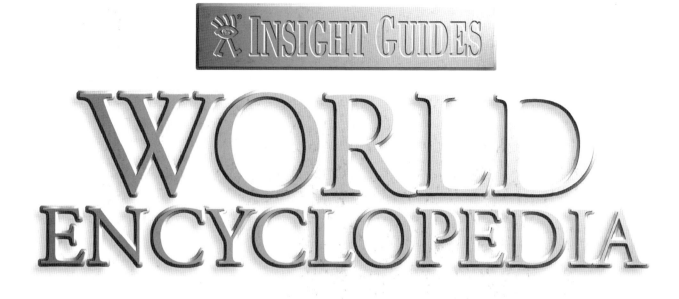

INSIGHT GUIDES

WORLD ENCYCLOPEDIA

Second Edition

Table of Contents

Europe

Europe has a total area of 10.5 million sq. km. More than 700 million people, slightly more than one-tenth of the world's population, live on the Earth's most densely populated continent. Europe's wide variety of landscapes include vast plains and lowlands extending over most of the north and east, while the terrain of southern Europe consists largely of low mountains, plateaus and hills. A chain of high mountain ranges, dominated by the Alps (highest peak: Mont Blanc: 4,807 m) and the Pyrenees, stretches from west to east across the continent. Islands and peninsulas constitute no less than one-third of Europe's total land area. The Volga and the Danube are the longest rivers and Russia's Lake Ladoga is the continent's largest inland body of water. Many of the countries of Europe have existed as nation-states for centuries and each one has a wealth of historic and cultural attractions. For centuries, European scientists, scholars and artists contributed to the continent's reputation as the cultural centre of the world.

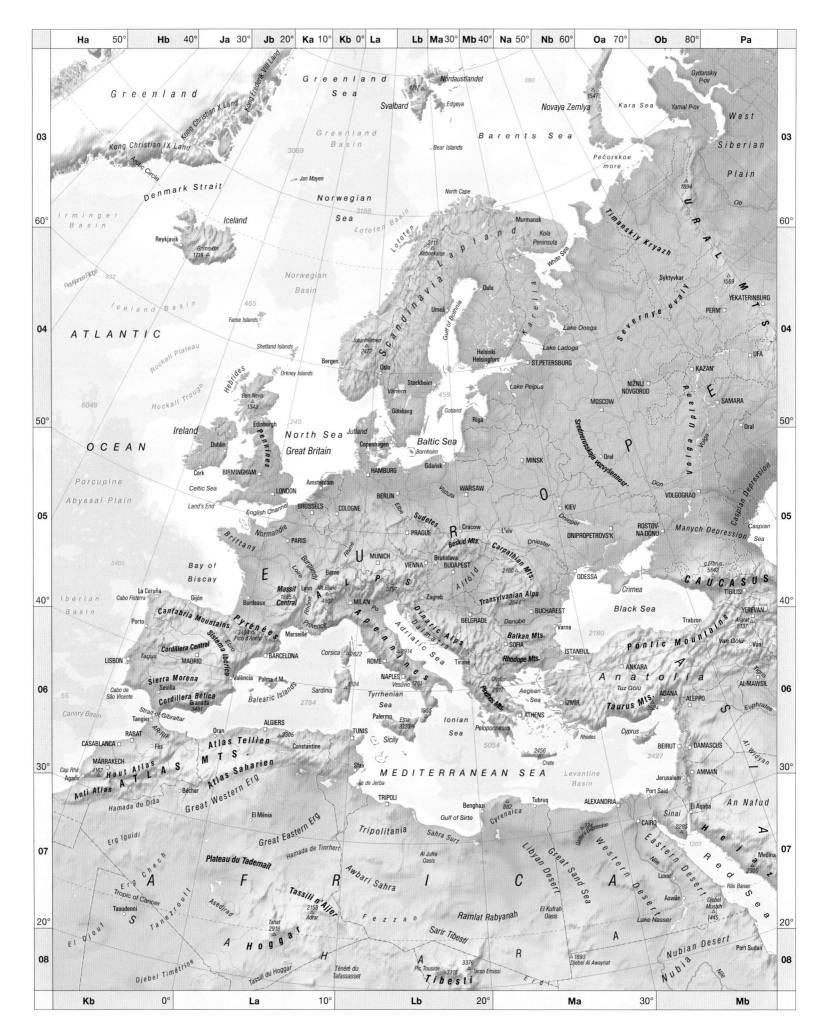

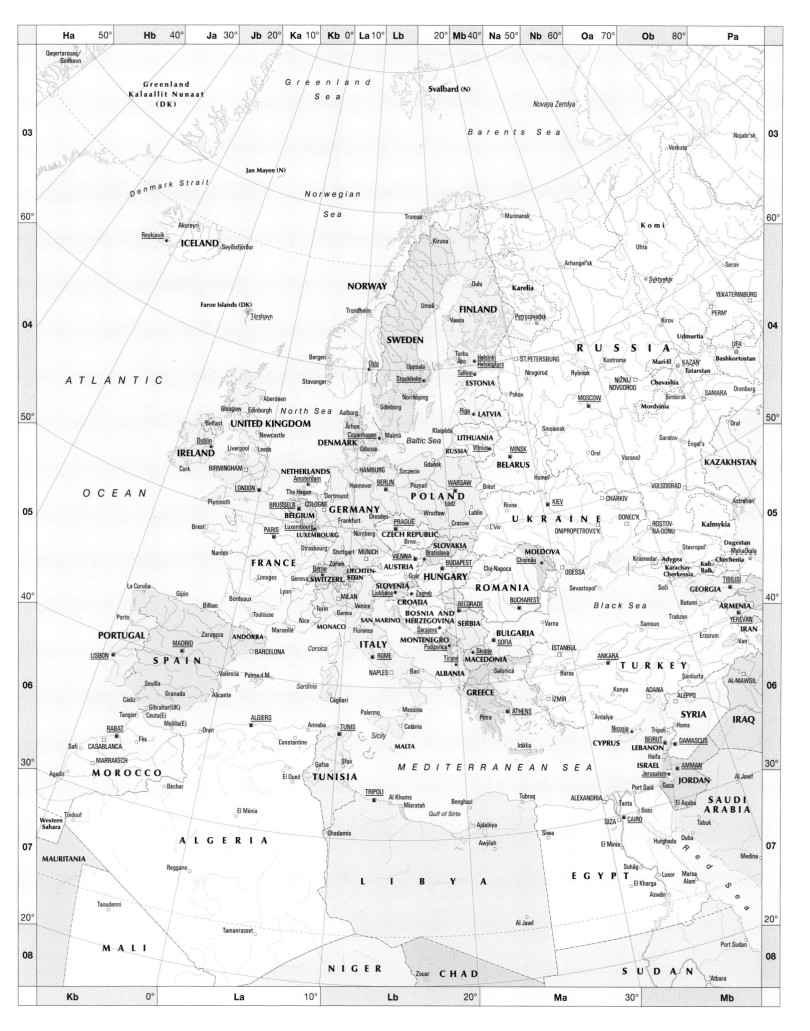

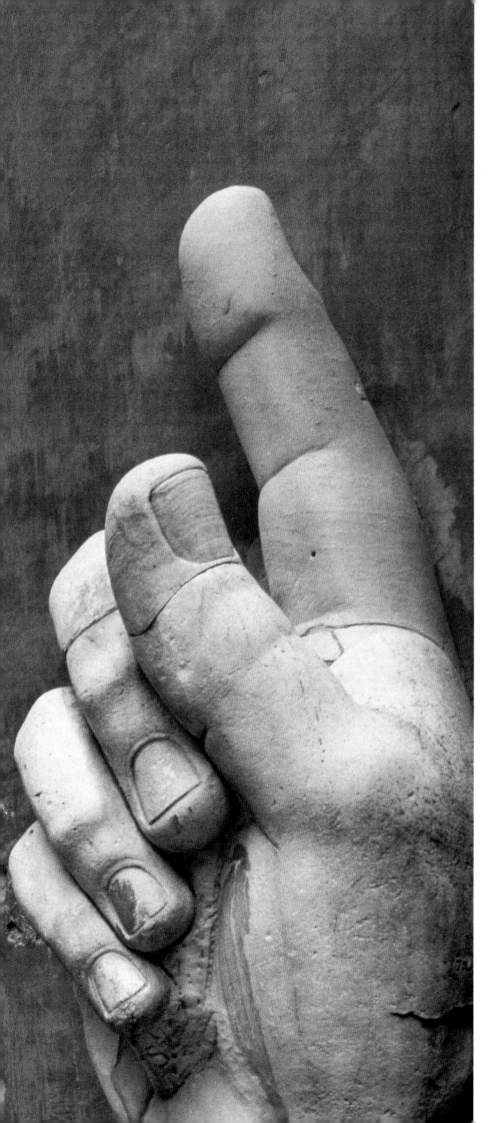

The remains of a colossal statue of the Roman Emperor Constantine the Great at the Palazzo dei Conservatori in Rome. Constantine changed the course of European history when he declared Christianity to be the official religion of the Roman Empire.

The History of Europe

Early Bronze Age cultures were followed in turn by the Greeks, Etruscans, Romans, the Holy Roman Empire, absolute monarchies, the Enlightenment, the rise of the middle classes and finally the democratic, fascist and socialist

Venice was once known as the 'Queen of the Seas'.

Trafalgar Square, London, a reminder of Britain's naval power.

systems of the twentieth century. Great discoveries and the industrial revolution enabled European expansion, and European colonies throughout the world have significantly shaped world history over many centuries. The rise of the USA, Japan and other non-European nations has meant that the Old World has lost some of its global power, yet twenty-first century Europe remains of great cultural, economic and political importance.

Early European History

Charlemagne (747–814). The Frankish king played an important role in the history of medieval Europe. Charlemagne founded the first major empire in Europe since the fall of Rome, laid the foundations for the French nation state and initiated important reforms throughout his realm. Medieval Frankish culture combined influences from Germanic, Latin, and Christian traditions.

Ancient history

Europe was first settled by hunter-gatherer cultures more than 1.5 million years ago. The first urban settlements emerged between 3000 and 2000 BC. The name 'Europe' probably originated from Ancient Greek mythology in which Europa was a Phoenician princess abducted by the god Zeus and taken to the island of Crete where she gave birth to King Minos. Crete was an important bridge between the cultures of Mediterranean Europe and western Asia. Around 1100 BC, Greek culture had spread to Asia Minor and the first Greek city-states were founded. In the turbulent centuries between 800 and 500 BC, the aristocracy replaced monarchs as local rulers as the Greeks established colonies around the Mediterranean. The major political centres of this period are Athens, Sparta, Thebes, Corinth, Argos and Miletus.

Despite the internecine wars between the Greek colonies they shared a cultural identity which celebrated in the Olympic Games and at religious ceremonies such as those held in Delphi.

Greek history between 500 and 336 BC was dominated by conflicts between Athens and Sparta and attacks by foreign nations. Athens became the dominant naval power in Greece and leader of the Delian League after the Athenians led the battle against a Persian army commanded by Xerxes I and helped to end the Carthaginian attacks on Greek colonies in Sicily. Sparta supplanted Athens as the dominant power after its victory in the Peloponnesian War but lost influence after the Delian League was restored.

Rivalries and conflicts between the Greek city-states gave the Macedonian king Phillip II the opportunity to bring the whole of Greece under his control. Phillip II's son, Alexander the Great, led a series of military campaigns and conquests that initiated the Hellenistic Age. Greece, Egypt and most of the Middle East were united in one vast empire by Alexander but after his sudden, early death , his empire was fragmented. His legacy was the spread of Helenistic culture throughout the region, leaving a lasting impact. After a succession of dynasties and Hellenistic empires, including

the Ptolemaic dynasty and the Seleucid Empire, in 146 AD, Greece finally lost its independence and fell to a rapidly expanding new power – the Republic of Rome.

According to legend, the city of Rome was founded in 753 BC and ruled by seven kings before it was declared a republic. The Romans defeated the last Etruscan kingdom in 509 BC and by 272 BC had gained control over the whole of Italy south of the Po Valley. Yet, Carthage rather than Rome, was the most powerful naval force in the western Mediterranean during this period. In 146 BC, the Romans finally defeated Carthage after waging three Punic Wars. Despite the Republic's expansion and

Germanic invasions became a serious threat to the empire during the reign of Marcus Aurelius. Within the empire, the spread of Christianity was also a threat to traditional social order and the new religion was brutally suppressed. The Emperor Constantine themade Constantinople into the a second capital and declared Christianity the official religion of Rome in 379 AD. The Roman Empire was split into a western and an eastern empire in 395. The weak Western Empire with Rome as its capital quickly lost control over much of its territory; the last western emperor, Romulus Augustus, was deposed in 476. The Eastern Roman (Byzantine) Empire

as Germanic and Slav tribes moved westwards. The Vandals, Visigoths, Ostrogoths and Lombards all established kingdoms but it was the Franks who created the first major empire in Western Europe since the fall of Rome. The Frankish Merovingian dynasty was succeeded by the Carolingians in 751, under Pippin the Younger, the son of Charles Martel, who led a Christian army to victory over Muslim forces at the Battle of Tours in 732. Charlemagne, the Frankish king who was crowned Emperor of Rome in 800, established a powerful realm, known as the Holy Roman Empire, that covered most of Western Europe.

The western Frankish realm, under the control of the Capetian dynasty, was weakened by internal strife and political disputes. The Eastern Franks appointed Otto I Holy Roman Emperor. He was able to defeat a Magyar invasion and expand his territory. During his reign, the Czechs, Danes and Poles were forced into alliances with the Holy Roman Empire.

The relationship between the popes and Europe's most powerful monarchs was an important factor in the early Middle Ages. In 1076, Pope Gregory VII excommunicated the Holy Roman Emperor Henry IV during one of the many conflicts between the church and Europe's rulers. The Concordat of Worms, signed in 1122, brought only a temporary respite to the political struggles between the popes and the Holy Roman emperors.

Conflicts between Christians and Muslims, including several major wars, also played an important role. In 1492, the last Muslim kingdom in Spain was conquered by Christians. The conquest of the Holy Land and 'liberation' of Jerusalem were the primary goals of the Crusades, which took place between 1095 and 1275.

The growing cultural differences between Western Europe and Byzantium led to the Great Schism of 1054, which divided European Christianity into the Roman Catholic and Eastern Orthodox rites. Several city-states in northern Italy became powerful economically and politically and challenged the power of the Byzantine Empire in the Mediterranean.

In western Christendom, the papacy and Roman Catholicism faced increasing criticism and challenges from new reformist sects; many of these movements were brutally suppressed by the Inquisition. Conflicts, rivalries and wars between European kingdoms lead to political instability and curtailed the power of many secular rulers.

The feudal societies of medieval Europe experienced a dramatic transformation after the fourteenth century, although this process began at different times in different places. France and England gradually emerged as modern nation-states after the Hundred Years' War. Spain and Portugal also emerged as unified nation-states during this period.

1 Religious reformer Martin Luther (1483–1546). **2** Holy Roman Emperor Charles V (1500–1558). **3** Queen Elizabeth I (1533–1603). **4** King Louis XIV of France (1638–1715). **5** Peter the Great, Tsar of Russia (1672–1725). **6** Frederick II of Prussia (1712–1786).

military successes Rome was plagued by internal conflicts that led to several civil wars.

By the time Julius Caesar was assassinated in 44 BC, the Roman senate had lost most of its political influence. Officially, Rome was still a republic but support for an empire ruled by an hereditary monarch continued to grow.

managed to survive in an increasingly weakened state until the Ottoman Turkish conquest of Constantinople in 1453.

The Middle Ages

After the collapse of the Western Roman Empire, Europe experienced a period of mass migrations

England was ruled by Anglo-Saxons monarchs until William of Normandy's victory at the Battle of Hastings in 1066. The Normans were descendants of the Vikings who had established new kingdoms in areas far from their Scandinavian homelands, including Russia and Southern Italy.

*The colourful imagery of the Bayeux Tapestry tells the story of **William of Normandy's** invasion of England and his victory at the Battle of Hastings. The oldest remaining medieval pictorial work of its kind, the Bayeux Tapestry was probably made in the eleventh century and is some 70 m long. The embroidered linen cloth is full of beautiful artistic details.*

The development of banking and the growth of shipping as a source of wealth were signs of the changes taking place in Europe. The effects of the Black Death on the demographics, the discoveries of the New World by Spanish and Portuguese explorers, the Humanist revival of the Renaissance and the Protestant Reformation all marked the end of the Middle Ages in the sixteenth century.

The Early Modern Era

The European exploration of the New World and the revolutionary discoveries of scientists such as Galileo and Copernicus marked the beginning of a progressive new era in the history of Europe. Spain and Portugal, followed by England, France and the Netherlands, explored the world's oceans and established the first colonies in the New World. The influence of the pope and the Catholic Church were significantly weakened by a series of religious wars. The Protestant Reformation and the Catholic Counterreformation led to the devastating Thirty Years' War that ended in 1648 with the Peace of Westphalia.

Europe was divided between Protestant and Catholic rulers. In 1534, the English king Henry VIII founded the Church of England, a new Protestant established church. While Germany and Italy remained patchworks of small kingdoms and city-states, England became a naval power after the defeat of the Spanish Armada in 1588. The Netherlands were liberated from Spanish rule and rapidly became one of the wealthiest nations. The wars of the seventeenth century enabled the Continent's most powerful nations to expand their influence and military domination.

After centuries of invasions, the Ottoman Turks were defeated in Central Europe. France's desire for hegemony was challenged by the other powers. The War of Spanish Succession (1710–1714) proved that at the time no one nation was capable of dominating Europe. Most of Europe's rulers were absolute monarchs throughout the eighteenth and nineteenth centuries. The Russian Empire emerged as a new power under Tsar Peter the Great.

Two powers struggled for control of Germany in the nineteenth century, Prussia in the north and the Hapsburg Austrian Empire in the south.

Poland found itself at the mercy of its more powerful neighbours who divided the country up them three times between 1772 and 1795. The extravagance of European aristocracy and the absolutist rule of the monarchs were challenged during the Age of Enlightenment. Prussia and Britain initiated important political reforms to grant their citizens more rights. Elsewhere, however, the limited reforms were not enough to contain the people's demands for greater political and personal freedoms.

1 The Roman Forum was once the centre of the Roman Empire. Government offices, temples, shops and banks filled this small district in the heart of ancient Rome.

2 Florence was one of the wealthiest cities in Europe in the Middle Ages and today has a wealth of Renaissance art and architecture.

3 Paris, The Louvre was the first royal palace, built around 1200. French kings lived there for centuries, but it was eventually replaced by the Palace of Versailles. It was finally converted into a museum in 1793.

World War I (1914–18) claimed over 9 million human lives. Tanks, aircraft and weapons of mass destruction, such as poisonous gas, were used for the first time. World War II (1939–45) was the bloodiest conflict ever, causing around 60 million deaths, mainly among the civilian populations. An exploding tank

in Flanders (left, top) and Canadian soldiers in the trenches at Verdun (left, below) illustrate the horror of World War I. The course of World War II changed

Modern Europe

The **French Revolution** began when the **Bastille** was stormed on 14 July, 1789. The old Parisian prison was virtually empty and was slated for demolition when crowds of Parisians stormed it. Nevertheless, this symbolic act had a major political impact; Louis XVI was forced to listen to the demands of the Third Estate. For the common people the Bastille was a symbol of royal tyranny and despotism.

The French Revolution

A guarantee of basic rights, a democratically elected government and limits on government power-were demanded of the French monarchy in 1789. The calls for 'liberty, equality, fraternity' became even more urgent after the Bastille was stormed by the mob. A newly created National Assembly granted a series of basic human rights to all citizens, created a constitutional monarchy and limited the power of the clergy.

A republic was declared in 1792 leading to the French Revolutionary Wars, which began with a series of military successes. Foreign threats radicalised France's revolutionary rulers. Louis XVI and his family were executed and the Jacobins under Robespierre initiated the Reign of Terror.

The Thermidorian Reaction was a revolt against the excesses and brutality of the revolution and resulted in the creation of a new constitution. The army fell under the control of a Corsican general with political ambitions called Napoleon Bonaparte. Bonaparte had himself proclaimed emperor in 1804. His *code civil* and his many other reforms showed his skills as a military and political leader. By 1810, Napoleon had reached the peak of his power. Europe's existing rulers stirred up resistance to Napoleon's conquests as fear of French hegemony increased. The British navy defeated Napoleon's forces at sea and his army suffered a devastating blow during the Russian campaign of 1812.

Paris was occupied by troops of the nations allied against Napoleon in 1813. The French emperor was forced into exile and the Bourbon dynasty restored, Louis XVIII being made king.

A new order in Europe

In 1815, the great powers of Europe gathered in Vienna to redraw the continent's boundaries under the guidance of the Austrian politician Prince Metternich. The Congress of Vienna was interrupted by Napoleon's escape from exile. His return was short-lived, however, and he suffered a final defeat at the Battle of Waterloo in 1815. In Vienna, the representatives of the European powers supported a return to the social order that had existed prior to the French Revolution. Despite this conservatism, many of the legal and social reforms, of the Napoleonic era were left in place.

The region known as the Austrian Netherlands and the United Provinces were merged to form the Kingdom of the Netherlands. Germany was consolidated into 39 states united in a loose confederation. Support for a united Germany increased significantly in the early ninteenth century, despite political differences and the rivalry between the two most powerful German states, Prussia and Austria.

The nineteenth century

The Industrial Revolution, which began in England, and the emergence of liberalism and nationalism dominated the development of Europe throughout the nineteenth century. Many of the conservative regimes were successful in resisting or suppressing the demands of the emerging liberal middle classes. Throughout Europe, calls for social reform and national and ethnic unity grew louder. Ottoman rule of Greece ended in 1829 with foreign aid. In Ireland, the nationalists demanded independence from Great Britain and the Poles itemporarily expelled the Russian army from Warsaw. In 1830, the Bourbon dynasty was again deposed in France and the country became a constitutional monarchy under King Louis-Philippe. In Italy, Giuseppe Mazzini formed the 'Giovine Italia', an organization that advocated a united and independent Italian state. Even in the Austro-Hungarian Empire, the Hungarians and Slavs increasingly resisted the domination of the German-speaking Habsburgs.

In Germany, the rise of liberal and nationalist ideals culminated in the 1848 revolution; this inspired a series of uprisings in that year in other countries. Louis-Philippe was deposed in France, Metternich fled Vienna, Prussia's king Frederick was forced to grant a constitution, and a constitutional assembly in Frankfurt began discussing plans for a democratic, united Germany. Eventually most of the revolutions of 1848 were defeated and in many countries the ruling classes were able to successfully resist meaningful reforms. Switzerland and Sardinia were the only countries to ratify reformed liberal constitutions.

Napoleon Bonaparte had himself crowned Emperor of France by Pope Pius VII in 1804.

Conflicts between the Great Powers

After the mid-nineteenth century, Europe experienced a period of growing national rivalries that led to several wars involving the Continent's dominant powers. Russia exploited the obvious weakness of the Ottoman Empire to expand its influence in Eastern Europe. The British and the French, together with their Turkish and Italian allies, defeated the Russian Empire in the Crimean War (1853–1856). Austria lost control of its territories in northern Italy and Italian nationalists, including Cavour and Garibaldi, led the struggle for the country's unification. Germany was also on the road to national unity during this period. The Prussian prime minister Bismarck supported the nationhood in the form of a 'small Germany'; this called for a united German nation-state that excluded Austria. The birth of the German Empire was officially proclaimed at Versailles in 1871.

Europe's industrialization

The living conditions of Europe's impoverished urban working class reflected the dark side of the Continent's technical advances. The German philosopher Karl Marx advocated radical social change and revolutionary workers' parties emerged throughout Europe. During the same period, the rivalries between the European powers intensified as the countries of Europe became increasingly industrialized. Great Britain, France, Russia and later Italy and Germany were drawn into a race for regional and global influence.

World War I

After the resignation of Chancellor Bismarck in 1890, Emperor Wilhelm II took personal control of Germany's government and armies. His aggressive foreign policy and determination to challenge Great Britain's naval superiority increased the tensions that culminated in World War I, which began in August, 1914. When Ottoman domination ended in south-east Europe, the region experienced a series of brutal wars and suffered political instability. In 1914, the heir to the Austro-Hungarian throne and his wife were assassinated by a young Serbian nationalist in Sarajevo. This caused the Austro-Hungarian Empire to declare war on Serbia.

A complicated web of defence treaties and alliances meant that Austria's declaration of war was quickly followed by military mobilization and numerous declarations of war throughout Europe. Germany, Austria-Hungary, Bulgaria and the Ottoman Empire were ranged against the *Entente*, an alliance of Great Britain, France and Russia.

The war, which many predicted would not last long, quickly turned into a series of bloody battles and dragged on for years. In Russia, the Tsar was deposed and replaced by a moderate government that chose to continue the war until it was overthrown by Lenin's Bolsheviks after the October Revolution in 1917.

The United States' entry into the war on the side of the Entente led to the defeat of Germany and Austro-Hungary in 1918. The military government that ruled Germany distanced itself from any blame for the defeat and the Emperor abdicated, along with all of Germany's other monarchs. Workers' and veterans' councils assumed power in many parts of Germany until the Weimar Republic restored political order throughout the country.

*The German philosopher **Karl Marx** (1818–83) was one of the most radical critics of capitalism and greatly influenced European workers' movements. His political ideology advocating a system of **socialism** led to the development of several new political systems during the twentieth century. **Vladimir Lenin** (1870–1924) adapted Marx's theory for Russian society. His Bolshevik movement was instrumental in overthrowing the Tsar in the Russian Revolution of 1917.*

The Treaty of Versailles (1919–20) was drafted without input from the defeated nations and imposed huge fines on them. When the treaty process was completed very little remained of the fair post-war world order that United States' president Woodrow Wilson had strongly advocated. Germany was forced to surrender territory in the east and west. The Austro-Hungarian and Ottoman empires were dissolved, while Poland, Czechoslovakia, Finland and the Baltic States were granted independence. The League of Nations was created to preserve world peace.

The Post-war era and World War II

In the early post-war era it seemed as if parliamentary democracy had been accepted throughout Europe but an increasing number of authoritarian regimes emerged in the 1920s. Mussolini, leader of the Fascist movement, seized power in Italy in 1922. The situation was made worse by the Wall Street Crash of 1929, which plunged the Western world into a lasting depression. At the height of the economic crisis, in 1933, Adolf Hitler was appointed Chancellor of Germany and Francisco Franco became the dictator of Spain in 1939, after a destructive civil war. In the Soviet Union, Stalin instituted a brutal dictatorship and had his political opponents executed or exiled. Hitler's aggressive foreign policy was largely successful in the early years of his reign. Despite the brutal repression of political opponents and Germany's Jewish population Hitler was allowed to achieve many of his aims with relatively little opposition from the other powers of Europe. It was only after Nazi Germany invaded Poland on 1 September, 1939 that France and Great Britain finally declared war on Germany. It took the German army only a few weeks to conquer Poland. After a successful campaign in Western Europe and North Africa, the German army controlled much of Europe by 1940. The tide of the war turned against Germany as Britain successfully defended itself in the air in the Battle of Britain and the German army was defeated at Stalingrad in 1942–43. German defeat was almost certain after the

United States entered the war in 1941. The racist policies of the Nazis resulted in the death of 6 million Jews, most of them in extermination camps, and the death of another 6 million members of races deemed 'inferior', such as gypsies, Poles and Russians.

Europe after 1945

The German Army surrendered in May 1945, ending the war in Europe. Germany was divided into four occupation zones and later into two states. In 1945, much of Europe was in ruins and the political picture had changed dramatically. Western Europe oriented itself towards the USA while Stalin established a series of communist satellite states in Eastern Europe. The North Atlantic Treaty Organization (NATO) and the Warsaw Pact confronted each other in a Cold War armed with an arsenal including nuclear weapons.

In the 1960s, the Vietnam War triggered student riots in Europe and the United States. In Prague, attempts at political reform were crushed by Soviet tanks, as had happened in the 1950s in Poznan, Budapest and East Berlin.

In the 1970s, several Western European politicians, including Germany's Willy Brandt and Sweden's Olof Palme, worked to improve the relationship between the two Cold War factions.

The military dictatorships in Portugal, Spain and Greece were overthrown in the 1970s and the colonial empires all but disappeared. At the same time, however, organised terrorism became a problem in several European countries as so-called liberation movements such as ETA and the IRA used violence to bring about political change and socialist terror groups such as the Red Brigade in Italy and RAF in Germany targeted their declared enemies.

The European Community began with the signing of the Treaty of Rome in 1957 and has been expanding ever since

The Fall of Communism

During the 1980s, the communist regimes of Eastern Europe were challenged by demands for political change. In Poland, the Solidarity movement led to strikes and Mikhail Gorbachev struggled to reform the

Soviet Union with his policies of *glasnost'* and *perestroika*. In 1989, the border between East and West Germany opened and Germany was reunited 1990–92. The Communist regimes were toppled in 1990–92 and both the Soviet Union and the Warsaw Pact were dissolved. Hopes for a new era of peace were dashed by a series of wars in Yugoslavia.

1 The European powers met at the Congress of Berlin in1878 to discuss the influence of Russia and Turkey in southeast Europe.

2 Stalin, Roosevelt and Churchill agreed to the postwar division of Germany and the creation of the United Nations at the conferences held in Potsdam and Yalta in 1945.

3 In 1970, West German chancellor Willy Brandt knelt in remembrance of the Nazis' victims in the former Warsaw Ghetto.

The City of London is the historic heart of the capital. Covering almost exactly one square mile, it contains the head offices of many of the UK's leading financial companies. Far right is the striking 'Gherkin', or Swiss Re Tower, designed by Norman Foster.

The Countries of Europe

Europe at the start of the twenty-first century is more than just the name of a land mass. After a hundred years of nationalist wars and political division, the old dream of a united Europe has become a reality. The European Union had 15 members at the start of the twenty-first century but was greatly expanded

La Grande Arche is a highlight of modern Parisian architecture.

Twenty-first century art: The Guggenheim Museum in Bilbao, Spain.

in 2003 when ten new members, including many former Communist nations of Eastern Europe, joined the organisation. With the entry of Romania and Bulgaria in 2007, the EU has now grown to 27 member states. The ultimate goal of the European Union is to unite the diverse countries and cultures of Europe in a close alliance capable of preserving peace and spreading prosperity across the Continent.

United Kingdom

Oxford: *Situated at the junction of the Cherwell and Thames rivers, Oxford is the historic capital of the English county of Oxfordshire. The site of the English-speaking world's oldest university, the city has played an important role in the development of British scholarship, philosophy, literature and the arts. The 34 colleges of England's most beautiful university town continue to attract gifted scholars and students from all over the world.*

United Kingdom

Area:	244,820 sq. km
Capital city:	London

Form of government:
Constitutional Monarchy
Administrative divisions:
England: 34 two-tier counties, 36 metropolitan counties, 46 unitary authorities, Greater London. Northern Ireland: 26 district council areas. Scotland: 32 unitary authorities. Wales: 22 unitary authorities.
External territories:
Channel Islands, Isle of Man, Anguilla, Bermuda, British Virgin Islands, Falkland Islands, Gibraltar, Cayman Islands, Montserrat, Pitcairn Island, St Helena, Turks and Caicos Islands, South Georgia and South Sandwich Islands
Population:
60.8 million (248 inhabitants/sq. km)
Languages:
English (official), Welsh, Gaelic
GDP per capita: US$39,600
Currency:
1 pound Sterling (£) = 100 pence

Natural Geography

Separated from mainland Europe by the North Sea and the **English Channel**, the **United Kingdom** is a **group of islands** consisting of the main island **Great Britain**, several smaller islands and the north of the island of Ireland. England, the largest of the United Kingdom's constituent countries, is dominated by flat coastal plains and **rolling hills** as well as several **low mountain ranges** such as the **Pennines** in the north and the **Cumbrian Mountains** in the north-west. Wales and Scotland are mountainous. Like England, Northern Ireland is largely hilly and mountainous.

Ben Nevis, the United Kingdom's highest mountain, is situated in the **Grampians** in Scotland's Highlands and rises 1343 m above sea level.

Climate

With the exception of south-east England with its mildly **continental climate**, most of the United Kingdom has a **maritime climate** with mild, wet winters and cool summers.

Population

The United Kingdom stands out as one of the most **ethnically diverse** nations in Europe. While the majority of Britons have **English**, **Welsh**, **Scottish** or **Irish** ancestry many others are the descendants of recent immigrants from other parts of Europe and former British colonies in Africa, Asia and the Caribbean. In terms of faith, 44 per cent of the population is affiliated to one of the two established **Protestant churches** in Britain and 8.7 per cent (40 per cent in Northern Ireland) are **Roman Catholic**. In addition to Christians, the United Kingdom is also home to 1.5 million **Muslims** and to large **Hindu, Jewish** and **Sikh** communities. English is the country's de facto official language, while Welsh has official status in Wales but is spoken by only a fifth of the Welsh population. Other significant minority languages are Scots, Scottish Gaelic, Irish and Cornish.

History and Politics

Centuries of **Roman control** over most of Britain was followed by a period of invasion and migration as northern European tribes, including the **Saxons**, **Angles** and **Frisians**, gained control and colonized most of what was to become England. In 1066, the Normans, under **William the Conqueror**, successfully invaded southern England. The Anglo-Norman kings who followed William I expanded English territory into large parts of France. After a series of wars, Edward I brought **Wales** under the control of the English crown in 1282. **Scotland** remained an independent kingdom until 1603. It was only in 1707 after the union of the English and Scottish crowns that Great Britain was united under one government.

The United Kingdom is not only one of the world's oldest **kingdoms** but it is also considered to be one of the world's oldest **democracies**. In 1215, the English king John I was forced to sign the **Magna Carta** which

primarily **Catholic nationalists** and predominantly **Protestant loyalists** erupted into the Troubles, a period of violent conflict between unionist and Irish nationalists that claimed thousands of lives. In recent years, the Northern Ireland Peace Process has led to a dramatic reduction in sectarian violence, although ethnic tensions remain.

The English victory over the **Spanish Armada** in 1588 opened the way for England to gradually become the world's pre-eminent naval power. It was also during the sixteenth century that England's **empire** began to emerge as new **colonies** and trading outposts were founded on several continents. Eventually, the British Empire would develop into the largest empire in history and encompass vast territories in Africa, south Asia, North America and the Caribbean.

The **decline** of Britain's global empire started after **World War I**. The founding of the **Commonwealth of Nations** in 1931 ushered in a period that would see

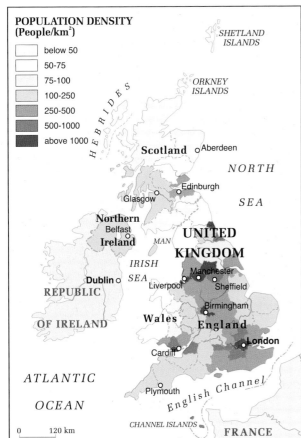

POPULATION DENSITY (People/km²)

	below 50
	50-75
	75-100
	100-250
	250-500
	500-1000
	above 1000

SHETLAND ISLANDS
ORKNEY ISLANDS
HEBRIDES
Scotland ○ Aberdeen
NORTH
○ Edinburgh
Glasgow ○
SEA
Northern Ireland
Belfast ○
MAN
UNITED KINGDOM
IRISH SEA
Dublin ○
Manchester ○
Liverpool ○ ○ Sheffield
REPUBLIC
Birmingham ○
Wales **England**
OF IRELAND
Cardiff ○ ● London
ATLANTIC OCEAN
Plymouth ○
English Channel
0   120 km
CHANNEL ISLANDS
FRANCE

A view of the Thames and St Paul's: London is the United Kingdom's economic and political centre.

Elizabeth II

*London, 21.4.1926

After the death of her father, King George VI, Elizabeth ascended the throne in 1952 and was crowned Queen of Great Britain and Northern Ireland in 1953. She has four children from her marriage to Prince Philip. She celebrated 50 years on the throne in 2002. She has been unable to quell debate about the future of the British monarchy.

increased the rights of the aristocracy and limited the power of the crown. England's first parliament was held shortly afterwards in 1230, an event which eventually led to the creation of British parliamentary democracy. After 1171, **Ireland** which had previously been dominated by the Vikings, came under Anglo-Norman rule. After centuries of conflict between the Irish and British, the whole of Ireland was united with Great Britain in 1801. In 1921, most of Ireland became independent with only six predominantly Protestant northern counties remaining in a union with Great Britain. The conflict in Northern Ireland between

most British colonies being granted independence. With the Chinese takeover of **Hong Kong** in 1997 Britain lost control of the last of its heavily populated overseas territories.

The United Kingdom still retains several **small territories** scattered around the globe including the Isle of Man and the Channel Islands near the British mainland as well as more distant territories including **Bermuda** and **Saint Helena** in the Atlantic Ocean, the peninsula of **Gibraltar** at the southern tip of Iberia, **South Georgia** and the **Falklands** in the South Atlantic, and **Pitcairn Island** in the Pacific. Almost half of Britain's overseas territories are small islands in the Caribbean – **Anguilla**, **Montserrat**, the **British Virgin Islands**, the **Turks and Caicos Islands** and the **Cayman Islands**.

The United Kingdom's political system is based on an unwritten constitution and other significant legislation, including the Magna Carta and the 1679 Act of Habeas Corpus Act. Britain is governed by a **bicameral parliament**. The **lower house**, the House of Commons, is the more influential chamber and consists of members who are directly elected by electoral constituencies. The **upper house**, the House of Lords, draws its unelected members from a variety of sources, including bishops of the Church of England, hereditary peers from the British aristocracy, and representatives chosen by the country's leading political parties. In recent years, the British government has undertaken steps to reform the House of Lords and transform it into a more representative body. The British **monarch** is the official head of state of the United Kingdom and the Dominions, the countries of the Commonwealth as well as head of Church of England. As a result of government reforms, both Scotland and Wales have been granted greater local political autonomy in recent years. In 1999, Scotland was granted its own parliament for the first time in almost 300 years.

Economy

In 2006, GDP was US$ 2.4 trillion. the United Kingdom's economy is predominantly based on **industry** and **services**. Almost one-half of the land is **agricultural**, used for the cultivation of wheat, barley, oilseed rape and sugar beet, as well as for livestock. Although agriculture makes up only one per cent of GDP, the **export** of cattle and food forms a significant proportion of export revenue.

Traditionally, the **fishing** industry also plays an important economic role. Industry makes up 24 per cent of GDP, but while the importance of the traditional British industries – iron and steel, machine construction, shipbuilding and mining – declined in the 1980s, the **chemical and electronics industries** have gained in significance. The UK has the largest **coal and crude oil reserves** in Western Europe, as well as significant supplies of natural gas.

The service industries, which now make up some 75 per cent of GDP, have been the driving force behind the upswing that started in the 1990s in the UK, which is not part of the European Monetary Union. The rate of unemployment is almost five per cent, with economic growth lying between two and three per cent.

Transport Infrastructure

The world's first public **railway** was opened in 1825 in England, the birthplace of the industrial revolution. Britain's rail network now encompasses more than 18,000 km of railways, including the **Channel Tunnel** between England and France. Britain's **road network** covers 370,000 km of roads and is one of the densest in the world. Of its 140 **airports**, 21 are international. London's Heathrow Airport is the busiest in Europe. The main **ferry and passenger ship terminals** are Dover, Newhaven, Plymouth, Harwich, Hull, Newcastle, Liverpool, Aberdeen and Holyhead.

Elizabeth II is both the queen of the United Kingdom of Great Britain and Northern Ireland, and the formal head of state of the following Commonwealth countries: Antigua and Barbuda, Australia, the Bahamas, Barbados, Belize, Grenada, Jamaica, Canada, New Zealand, Papua New Guinea, the Solomon

Islands, St Kitts and Nevis, St Lucia, St Vincent and the Grenadines, and Tuvalu. As the head of state of the United Kingdom, she has a purely ceremonial role, reading the annual speech given by the government to the House of Commons at the State Opening of Parliament.

United Kingdom, Ireland

Tourism

The United Kingdom attracts more than 25 million foreign tourists each year. The **Lake District**, **Northumberland National Park** near the Scottish borders, **Snowdonia National Park** in Wales and the **Scottish Highlands** are some of the most beautiful landscapes. Other attractions include **cathedrals** and **churches**, **castles** and **stately homes**, the **coastline** and the major cities. London remains the most popular destination in the country and one of the world's most visited cities.

Winston Churchill

(Winston Leonard Spencer C.)
*Blenheim Palace, 30.11.1874,
†London 24.1.1965

Member of parliament for the Liberal and later the Conservative Party, Churchill held ministerial positions in several governments. He was the First Lord of the Admiralty between 1911 and 1915, the year of the disastrous Battle of Gallipoli. He returned to this office again in 1939 before becoming Prime Minister in 1940. His moving speeches were a vital boost to British morale during World War II and his conduct of the war is highly praised by historians. After the war the Conservative party lost control of government but he was re-elected as Prime Minister in 1951 and 1955.

Margaret Thatcher

*Grantham, 13.10.1925

Margaret Thatcher made history in 1979 when she was elected the first woman Prime Minister of the United Kingdom. Her term as PM was both the longest of any British head of government in the twentieth century and one of the most controversial periods of government in the country's recent history. Her economic policies brought inflation under control but led to a rise in unemployment. Supporters argue that these policies ended economic stagnation, while critics claim they sharpened social divides and devastated British industry. She left office in 1991 and has held the title Baroness Thatcher since 1992.

Ireland

Area:	70,280 sq. km
Capital city:	Dublin/Baile Átha Cliath
Form of government:	Parliamentary Republic
Administrative divisions:	29 counties and 5 cities
Population:	4.1 million (58 inhabitants/ sq. km)
Languages:	Gaelic, English
GDP per capita:	US$52,000
Currency:	1 euro = 100 cents

Natural Geography

Ireland is an **island** in the Atlantic Ocean west of the Great Britain, at the western edge of northern Europe. Much of the island's terrain is **hilly** with **low mountains** (Carrauntoohill, 1041 m) rising in the north and south of the country. The **Great Shannon Basin** is a large low-lying plain covering much of the island's interior.

Ireland has numerous lakes, heaths, bogs and moors. The south-west of the island, primarily County Cork and County Kerry, has a particularly mild climate and lush vegetation due to the effects of the Gulf Stream.

Only one per cent of Ireland is forested, the smallest area of woodland of any country in Western Europe. Due to its fertile **green meadows** and fields the island is popularly known as 'the Emerald Isle'.

Climate

The island of Ireland has a **mild maritime climate** due largely to the Gulf Stream and other ocean currents. Heavy rainfall throughout the year is common in many parts of the island, especially in the west. Summers are generally cool, while winters tend to be mild and wet.

Population

The Republic of Ireland has a largely homogeneous population, 94 per cent being of **Irish** ancestry. Around 96 per cent of the population is Christian, 93.1 per cent of the population identifying as **Roman Catholics**. In recent years, the country's strong economic growth has attracted an increasing number of migrants, including many from Eastern Europe. The official languages of the Republic of Ireland are Irish and English, though just five per cent of the Irish speak **Irish** as their first language. The Irish school system, and many other institutions, are similar to those of the United Kingdom, a legacy of the union that once existed between the two nations.

History and Politics

Archaeological evidence indicates that Ireland has been settled for thousands of years. **Celtic** peoples are believed to have arrived no later than in the third century BC. The people converted to Christianity in the fourth century AD. Celtic Ireland was divided into small kingdoms, and it was not until the tenth century that a united **Irish kingdom** emerged. By the time of St Patrick and his successors, culture and education flourished and the island had become a base for the

POWER SOURCES

- Main oil fields
- Main natural gas fields
- Main coal fields
- Oil pipelines
- Natural gas pipelines
- Main refineries
- Hydroelectric power plants
- Thermoelectric power plants
- Nuclear power plants

Edinburgh Castle: once the home of Mary Stuart, Queen of Scots.

IRISH EMIGRATION

Poblacht Na h´Eireann, *an Irish village: After centuries of poverty, famine, and emigration Ireland has recently undergone a dramatic economic transformation. None the less the Irish have held on to many of their cherished traditions and native culture. Although English remains the dominant language in the republic, Irish is affirmed in the constitution as the first official language.*

spread of Christianity to Great Britain and to parts of mainland Europe. In 795, the **Vikings** reached the coast of Ireland and began a period of invasion and conquest that lasted until the eleventh century. By the time the great High King Brian Boru finally drove them out, Ireland had become impoverished.

Much of Ireland was conquered by England's Norman king **Henry II** after 1169. This marked the beginning of a long period of English domination and eventually outright control. Under the rule of the English kings, farmers and soldiers from Britain were granted large landholdings at the expense of the native landowners. Attempts to impose **Protestantism** on the Catholic population of Ireland were largely ineffective, although the Catholic upper classes and gentry were largely replaced by Protestants from Scotland and England. A series of Irish revolts against British rule led to reprisals and increased persecution of Catholics. In the nineteenth century, the Potato Famine led to a massive wave of emigration from Ireland. Most went to the United States, while large numbers also settled in Great Britain, Canada and Australia. After decades of political struggle and years of violence most of Ireland's counties separated from the United Kingdom to form the **Irish Free State** in 1922. Six largely Protestant counties in the north chose to remain part of the United Kingdom and became the British province of **Northern Ireland**.

Ireland has a **bicameral parliament** consisting of a directly elected lower house called the Dail Eireann and a Senate whose members are not directly elected but are instead chosen through a variety of methods. The Republic of Ireland's head of state is the directly elected president.

Economy

In 2006, GDP was US$ 220 billion, of which three per cent came from **agriculture**, 41 per cent from industry and 56 per cent from **services**. With a rate of growth of around five per cent, Ireland has become a major player in Europe. The main agricultural export products are live cattle, meat, dairy products and eggs – Ireland can supply 86 per cent of its domestic food requirements. Membership of the **EU** has played a decisive part in Ireland's positive economic development; about one-quarter of direct **investment by American companies** in Europe is in Ireland. The economic upswing experienced, primarily from the computing, high-tech, pharmaceutical and chemical industries, has been considerable – the combination of low wages, low taxes and a highly qualified workforce has provided a continuous boom in employment in a country that has traditionally had high rates of unemployment. A member of the

EU since 1973, Ireland caused controversy by rejecting the Lisbon Treaty in a referendum in June 2008.

Transport Infrastructure

The **rail network** consists of only about 2,000 km of track. The dominant form of transport is the **car**. Like their British neighbours, the Irish drive on the left. Ireland has four international **airports** and a national airline, Aer Lingus.

Tourism

The Republic of Ireland's most popular tourist attractions are its sparsely populated countryside and historic sights. More than **five million foreign visitors** visit 'the Emerald Isle' each year, providing a major source of income. The centre of the tourist industry is the country's capital and largest city, **Dublin**. The natural attractions include the jagged coastline with its beaches,

cliffs and quaint fishing villages. The **numerous lakes** are ideal destinations for anglers, hikers, and for those who enjoy aquatic sports. Ireland also has a wealth of both **cultural and historic attractions**, including prehistoric archeological sites as well as medieval forts, monasteries, and cathedrals.

1 A coastal lookout: Danluce Castle in Northern Ireland.

2 The crosses at Clonmacnoise monastery are the oldest Christian relics in Ireland.

3 Irish folk music is performed live in public houses throughout Ireland. Many songs deal with the country's history of foreign domination, poverty and emigration.

4 London: Brightly-lit advertisements have been a feature of Piccadilly Circus since 1890. The famous intersection was planned by John Nash in the early nineteenth century.

***Norway:** The enormous oil and gas reserves in the North Sea account for a large part of Norway's gross domestic product. The undersea natural resources are exploited by large offshore oil platforms, which are equipped with drilling equipment, storage tanks and living quarters. Many of the more modern oil rigs are anchored to the seabed. Once extracted oil and gas is transported by pipeline or tanker to onshore refineries.*

Norway

Area: 323,802 sq. km
Capital city: Oslo
Form of government:
Constitutional Monarchy
Administrative divisions:
19 provinces
External territories: Svalbard, Jan Mayen, Bouvet Island, Peter I Island
Population:
4.6 million
(14 inhabitants/sq. km)
Languages: Norwegian, Sami
GDP per capita: US$72,500
Currency:
1 Norwegian krona = 100 øre

Natural Geography

Norway extends from Cape Lindesnes in the south to the North Cape, a distance of 1725 km and covers much of the western half of the **Scandinavian Peninsula**. The coastline is 2650 km long, while several **fjords** are up to 200 km long, running deep into the country's interior. There are numerous **islands** off Norway ragged coastline. The interior is largely **mountainous** with **glacial plateaus**, high plains, and fairly high mountains. Only the relatively densely populated southwest of Norway contains large areas of **flat land**.

The south-east of Norway is covered in vast **forests** extending up to the treeless **tundra** that covers the north much of which lies inside the Arctic Circle. The country's many **lakes** are rich in fish and other marine life. Northern Norway is home to fascinating wildlife, including elk, reindeer and bear.

Climate

The effects of the **Gulf Stream** give coastal Norway a relatively **mild maritime climate**, the mildest on earth for such a northern country. The port of Narvik, remains open all year round, the most northerly year-round harbour in the world. The interior and highlands tend to have a much cooler climate than the coast.

Population

More than 96 per cent of the country's population consists of ethnic **Norwegians**. In addition, Norway also has a **Sami** (Lapp) minority which is concentrated in the north (Lapland), as well as established communities of **Swedes, Danes** and **Russians**.
The official national language is Norwegian which has two written forms, Bokmål and Nynorsk. Many Sami people speak dialects of the Sami language. Norwegians enjoy one of the highest standards of living in the world. The government spends around 35 per cent of national income on **social services** and **health care.**

History and Politics

United and converted to Christianity in the reign of Harald Fairhair in the ninth century, Norway fell under **Danish rule** in 1387. The union with Denmark lasted more than 400 years and only ended when Denmark ceded Norway to **Sweden** in 1814. In 1905, Norway was granted independence after a referendum. The Norwegian sovereign is the official head of state under the country's constitutional monarchy. Norway, one of the founding members of **NATO**, abandoned its policy of strict **neutrality** after the German occupation during World War II. The constitution, which has been amended several times since it first passed into law in 1814, gives the task of government to the national parliament and assigns the monarch largely symbolic powers.
The 169 members of the country's **parliament**, the Storting, are elected directly every four years. In 1994, the Norwegians voted in a referendum against joining the **European Union**. Norway has several **territories,** including the **Svalbard** archipelago and the uninhabited **Bouvet Island, Peter I Island**, and **Jan Mayen Island.**

Economy

In 2006, GDP was US$ 335 billion, of which two per cent was derived from agriculture, 39 per cent from industry and 59 per cent from services. The rate of unemployment is consistently below five per cent. Only about three per cent of the land can be used for agricultural purposes. The Norwegian **fishing** and **fish farming** industries are an important source of **export** income. Norway is one of the biggest fishing nations, and this includes **sealing and whaling**. It is also a large producer of paper, timber and foodstuffs and has important aluminium and iron and steel industries.
The main income stems from the reserves of **oil and natural gas** in the North Sea, most of which belong to Norway and which make it one of the world's largest exporters of heavy crude oil.

Norway: The craggy mountains on the Lofoten make most of the island uninhabitable.

Sven Olof Palme

*Stockholm, 30.1.1927,
†Stockholm, 28.2.1986

Chairman of the Swedish Social Democratic Party between 1969 and 1986, Sven Olof Palme served as Prime Minister of Sweden for seven years until 1976. His firm opposition to the Vietnam War and nuclear armament during the 1970s brought him respect from outside of his native country. Sven Olof Palme was assassinated in 1986 on a Stockholm street after a visit to a local cinema. His murder, which remains unsolved, was a major shock for the Swedish society.

Transport Infrastructure

Norway's mountainous terrain means that the country has no significant **rail network**.
Three-quarters of the **road network** of the country is surfaced. Norway has two international **airports**, one in Oslo and one in Stavanger.

Tourism

Norway is an expensive but nonetheless popular holiday destination. The country's attractions include **winter sports** facilities in the mountains as well as the stunning landscapes of the country's **fjords** and inland national parks. Other popular sights include the historic stave churches found throughout the country and the old warehouses in **Bergen**, Norway's second city. Oslo has a sculpture park, the Oseberg Viking ship, the national museum and the Kon-tiki.

Sweden

Area: 449,964 sq. km
Capital city: Stockholm
Form of government:
Constitutional Monarchy
Administrative divisions:
21 districts
Population:
9 million (20 inhabitants/sq. km)
Languages:
Swedish (official), Finnish
GDP per capita: US$42,200
Currency:
1 Swedish krona = 100 öre

Natural Geography

Sweden covers the eastern and southern half of the **Scandinavian Peninsula**. More than half of the country is afforested and **lakes** occupy more than a tenth of Sweden. In addition to the mainland, Sweden also includes the islands of **Gotland, Öland,** and countless **islets** near the coast. Northern Sweden, which lies between the **Scandinavian mountains** and the **Gulf of Bothnia**, contains numerous rivers, lakes and waterfalls, many of which are used to generate electricity. Southern Sweden consists largely of rolling hills, wide plains and moorland.

Climate

The climate of Sweden varies from south to north and is greatly affected by the **Gulf Stream**, especially along the coast. Much of Sweden's interior, however, has the harsher **continental climate** with summers that are often very warm and bitterly cold winters.

Population

Around 95 per cent of the population consists of ethnic **Swedes**. Significant minorities include the **Sami** (Lapps) and **Finns**. At least 83 per cent of the population lives in the cities. The official language is Swedish, but Finnish and Sami (a group of Uralic languages spoken in Northern Europe and northeast Russia) are also spoken. The Swedes have access to excellent **social services** and **health care** as well as the highest levels of **taxation** in the world. **Education** is highly valued in all sectors of Swedish society and no fewer than 95 per cent of all adults have had some form of higher education or training. Sweden has more than 30 universities, including the University of Uppsala, Scandinavia's oldest.

History and Politics

The oldest settlements in Scandinavia appeared before 10,000 BC. The **Vikings**, Scandinavian warriors, raided and conquered territories throughout Europe starting in the eighth century AD. The trading routes of the Vikings stretched as far as the Arab world. **Christianity** did not reach Scandinavia until after the eleventh century AD. From 1389 to 1520 Sweden was united with **Norway** and **Denmark** in the Kalmar Union. By the seventeenth century, Sweden had emerged as an important European power and played a significant role in the **Thirty Year's War** (1618 to 1648). However, a devastating defeat in the Second Northern War (1697–1718) led to the end of the Swedish Empire and Swedish dominance of the Baltic

Sea. Sweden declared neutrality during World Wars I and II. Between 1932 and the 1970s, it developed one of the world's most progressive welfare states. The constitution of 1975 defines Sweden as a constitutional monarchy with the sovereign as its head of state. It has a directly elected parliament, the **Riksdag.** The political map of Sweden has remained unchanged

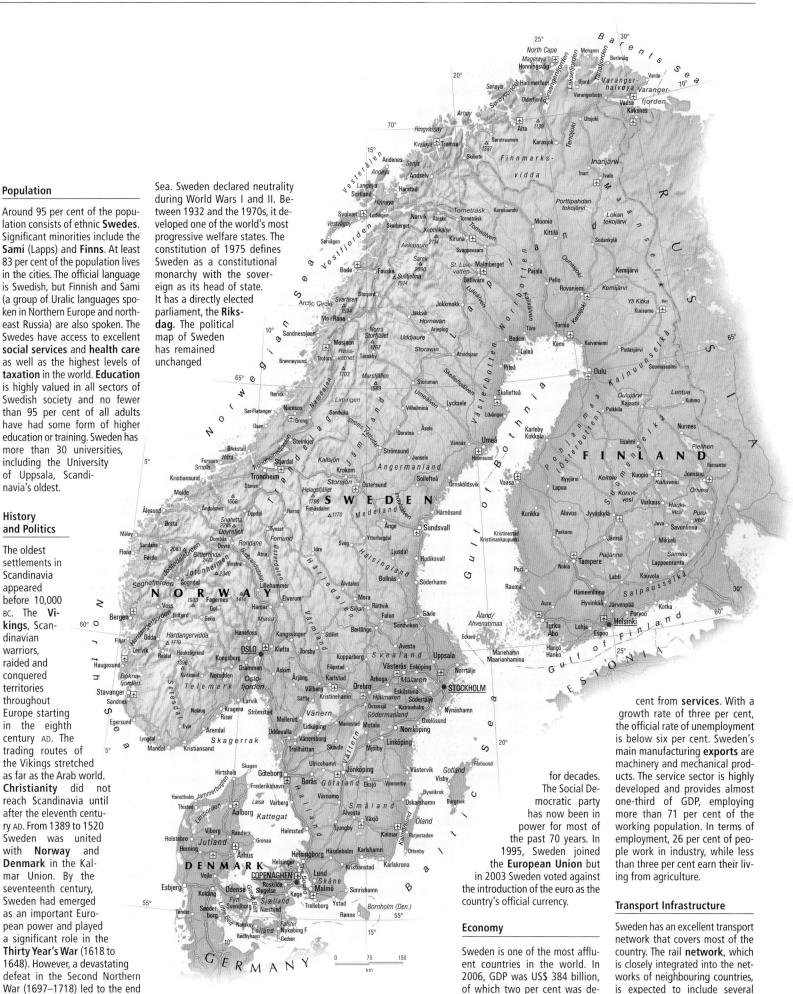

for decades. The Social Democratic party has now been in power for most of the past 70 years. In 1995, Sweden joined the **European Union** but in 2003 Sweden voted against the introduction of the euro as the country's official currency.

Economy

Sweden is one of the most affluent countries in the world. In 2006, GDP was US$ 384 billion, of which two per cent was derived from **agriculture**, 29 per cent from **industry** and 69 per

cent from **services**. With a growth rate of three per cent, the official rate of unemployment is below six per cent. Sweden's main manufacturing **exports** are machinery and mechanical products. The service sector is highly developed and provides almost one-third of GDP, employing more than 71 per cent of the working population. In terms of employment, 26 per cent of people work in industry, while less than three per cent earn their living from agriculture.

Transport Infrastructure

Sweden has an excellent transport network that covers most of the country. The rail **network**, which is closely integrated into the networks of neighbouring countries, is expected to include several **high-speed train routes** in the near future. The completion of the

Stockholm: *The Swedish capital is one of the wealthiest and most beautiful cities in Europe. Stockholm is situated on a group of islands and peninsulas between the Baltic Sea and Lake Mälaren. The historic city centre covers the islands Riddarholmen, Helgeandsholmen and Staden. Drottingholm Palace, the residence of Sweden's royal family is near the city centre. King Carl XVI. Gustav is the current reigning monarch of Sweden.*

impressive 16 km long **Oresund bridge** connects Malmö, the largest city in southern Sweden, to the Danish capital of Copenhagen. Sweden has three international **airports** and is one of the owners of the Scandinavian airline, SAS. The largest **commercial shipping and ferry ports** are Stockholm, Helsingborg and Göteborg.

Tourism

The capital city, **Stockholm, Göteborg,** Sweden's second city and **Malmö** are the most important centres of tourism. Southern Sweden attracts visitors with its beaches, countless lakes, small islands and forests. Central Sweden also has lakes and vast forests as well as the historic university city of **Uppsala**. In northern Sweden, **Lapland**, the home of the Sami people, has pristine, sparsely populated landscapes that are ideal for hiking trips.

Population:
5.5 million
(127 inhabitants/sq. km)

Language:	Danish
GDP per capita:	US$50,900
Currency:	1 euro = 100 cents

Natural Geography

Situated between the North and Baltic seas, Denmark encompasses the peninsula of Jutland and more than **474 islands,** of which only about a quarter are inhabited. **Zeeland**, the largest island, is home to more than 40 per cent of the country's population. The other large islands are **Funen, Lolland, Bornholm** and **Falster**. Only three of Denmark's many islands are situated in the North Sea, **Rømø, Fanø,** and **Mandø**. The landscapes of Jutland include forests, moorlands and heaths as well as coastal wetlands in the west and sands dunes in the north. Nature reserves and conser-

Population

Ethnic **Danes** of Nordic ancestry make up 96 per cent of the population. Significant minorities include **Germans** in Jutland, **Swedes, Norwegians** and **Greenlanders**. Recent immigrant communities account for at least five per cent of the Danish population, the majority being from **Turkey** (16 per cent). In addition to Danish, the national official language, German has official status as a minority language in **North Schleswig** on Jutland. The modern Danish **welfare state** guarantees the country's population a high standard of living and excellent social services and health care.

History and Politics

The history of the Danish nation began around 800 AD with the **Viking** warriors who raided the coasts of Europe for generations.

Sweden and to give the island of Heligoland to the British. The country was then forced to cede the duchies of Schleswig and Holstein to Prussia after the Danish-Prussian War of 1864. Denmark became **a constitutional monarchy** in 1849 and during the nineteenth century developed into one of the world's most prosperous nations. It declared its neutrality in both **world wars** but was invaded and occupied by German forces in 1940. Denmark has a **unicameral parliament** whose members are elected every four years. The Danish sovereign is the official head of state but the powers granted to the monarchy are largely symbolic. Despite their distance from the Danish mainland, the **Faroes,** a group of 18 rocky islands, 17 of them inhabited, lying between Scotland and Iceland, belong to Denmark. The official language of the islands is Faroese, a Northern Germanic language closely related to Norwegian and Icelandic.

Norway and Denmark ended in 1814, the Faroes remained a part of the Danish kingdom. The Faroes have been an **autonomous province** of Denmark since 1948 and send members to the Danish parliament. Unlike Denmark, the Faroe Islands are not part of the **European Union**. **Deep-sea fishing** is the islands' most important industry and it has one of the world's largest fishing fleets.

Fishing and **mining** are the two most important industries of **Greenland**, an island in the North Atlantic which was a Danish **colony** from the fourteenth century until 1953 and is now a Danish autonomous province. With just 56,000 inhabitants Greenland, the world's largest island, is also one of the most sparsely populated areas on Earth. That is because more than 80 per cent of Greenland is covered by an ice cap throughout the year. The official languages are Greenlandic and Danish. In recent

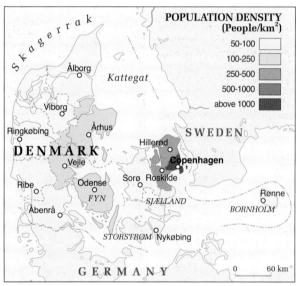

POPULATION DENSITY
(People/km²)

	50-100
	100-250
	250-500
	500-1000
	above 1000

Skagerrak

Ålborg — *Kattegat*

Viborg

Ringkøbing — Århus — **S W E D E N**

D E N M A R K — Hillerød

Vejle — **Copenhagen**

Ribe — Odense — Sorø Roskilde

Åbenrå — *FYN* — *SJÆLLAND* — Rønne
BORNHOLM

STORSTRØM Nykøbing

G E R M A N Y — 0 ___ 60 km

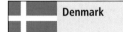

Area: 43,094 sq. km;
Greenland 2.166 million sq. km,
Faroe Islands 1,398 sq. km

Capital city:	Copenhagen
Form of government:	Constitutional Monarchy
Administrative divisions:	5 regions
External territories:	Faroe Islands, Greenland

vation areas cover around one-third of the land mass.
Unlike the rest of Scandinavia, Denmark is generally flat.

Climate

Denmark's regions all have a **temperate** climate, although the weather along the Baltic coast tends to be milder than in western Denmark. The average temperature in January, the coldest month, is 0° C rising to 17°C in July, the warmest month.

By the eleventh century, Vikings dominated most of the Baltic and North seas. The rise of the **Hanseatic League** in the late fourteenth century brought Viking control of the Baltic to an end. During the fifteenth century, Denmark was again able to assert its control over much of the Baltic and the surrounding regions. **The Kalmar Union** united the Scandinavian nations under the rule of the Danish crown for more than a century. In 1814, Denmark was forced to surrender control of Norway to

Danish, however, plays an important role in the education system. The first settlers in the Faroes arrived from Norway in the early ninth century. Established around 825 AD by early settlers, the Faroese parliament, the **Løgting,** is one of the oldest parliaments in the world. Its members are elected every four years. In 1035, the Faroes came under the control of the Norwegian crown and in 1380 the islands, together with Norway, entered into a union with Denmark. After the union between

decades, the island has become increasingly self-governing and autonomous.

Economy

In 2006, the GDP of this highly developed industrial country was US$ 276 billion. Five per cent of those employed work in what is highly specialised **agriculture** (primarily dairy products and pork). Significant export revenue also comes from the fishing industry and fishery products.

The once nomadic Sami people have inhabited the grassy moors and tundra of **Lapland** in northern Norway, Sweden, Finland and Russia for at least 2,000 years. The Sami, who have their own languages, divided into several dialects, are now largely integrated into the dominant cultures of their respective home countries.

Denmark must import all of its raw materials for industrial production, and due to its small domestic market, it is heavily dependent upon exports. Major Danish **exports** include agricultural produce, processed foods and drink, shipbuilding, chemicals and machinery as well as products of the country's burgeoning high tech industries. The **industrial sector** accounts for around 25 per cent of the country's economy. The Danish **service sector**, which accounts for 70 per cent of economic activity, has grown rapidly in recent years, with tourism now playing a central role.

Transport Infrastructure

Denmark's **rail network** is extensive and well integrated into the country's **shipping and ferries** that connect the various islands and link Denmark to other countries. The largest islands are connected by a series of **bridges**. Zeeland and Funen, the country's largest and most populous islands are connected by the world's second-longest suspension bridge at the time of writing.

Tourism

Millions of tourists visit Denmark each year. In addition to its many **beautiful beaches** and **sailing facilities**, Denmark also has numerous cultural and historic attractions to offer. The major tourist destinations include the vibrant capital city, **Copenhagen** and the historic town of **Roskilde** on the island of Zeeland. **Svendborg** on Funen as well as **Aalborg**, **Aarhus** and **Esbjerg** on the Jutland peninsula are also tourist attractions, **Odense**, as the birthplace of Hans Christian Andersen, is of particular interest.

Finland

Area:	338,145 sq. km
Capital city:	Helsinki
Form of government:	Republic

Administrative divisions:
6 administrative provinces and 20 regions

Population:
5.2 million
(15 inhabitants/sq. km)

Languages:
Finnish (official), Swedish

GDP per capita:	US$40,000

Currency:
1 euro = 100 cents

Natural Geography

Sparsely populated Finland has a long jagged **coast** that stretches along the Gulf of Bothnia in the west and along the Baltic Sea and Gulf of Finland to the south. Finland owns countless off-shore **islands**, including the largest group, the **Aaland Islands**. Around one-tenth of the country is covered by **lakes**, many of which are interconnected by an extensive network of streams

1 Ålesund, one of the most important fishing towns in Norway, is situated at the entrance to the Storfjord.

2 An important harbour for centuries, Copenhagen is Denmark's capitals and one of Northern Europe's most modern cities.

3 The Swedes cherish their holiday homes. Clusters of these homes are built along most of the coast of Bohuslan province, a region on the shores of the Kattegat.

Finland

Finland: a country often called 'the land of a thousand lakes' because of the more than 55,000 inland bodies of water scattered across its territory. The region around Lake Saimaa in south-eastern Finland is a popular and ideal destination for tourists. Lappeenranta, a small city in southern Finland, is a major centre of the tourist industry in Finland.

and rivers. With the exception of the hilly areas east of the centre of the country, Finland is largely flat. The north includes sections of Lapland's **tundra** and the **Norwegian coastal mountains**. The highest mountain in the region, Haltiantunturi, rises 1,328 m. Large sections of the country are covered by bogs and moors from which peat is harvested in the summer months.

Climate

Most of Finland belongs to the vast belt of coniferous forests that stretches across northern Europe as far as Siberia, while the south-west and the southern islands have a more temperate climate with deciduous vegetation. Finland's **sub-polar continental climate** is characterized by long cold winters with abundant snowfall and warm summers. Helsinki has an average temperature of 6°C in winter 17°C in summer.

Only eight per cent of Finland is farmland and agriculture plays only a minor role in the nation's economy.

POPULATION DENSITY (People/km²)

- below 25
- 25-100
- above 100

Population

Ethnic **Finns** constitute 93 per cent of the country's inhabitants. Minorities with Finnish nationality include a large ethnic **Swedish** community (six per cent) and small minorities of **Lapps** and **Roma**. **Russians** and **Estonians** make up the largest groups of foreigners. Finnish and Swedish are the **two official national languages** of Finland, and Russian and Sami are widely spoken in certain regions. Some 86 per cent of the Finns are Protestant and one per cent are Greek Orthodox.

History and Politics

The ancestors of the Finns settled the land around 800 BC. Finland was under **Swedish rule** between the twelfth and eighteenth centuries, during which time **Christianity** was introduced. After numerous wars between Russia and Sweden, the Swedes surrendered control of Finland to the **Russian Empire** in 1809. Finland was declared a grand duchy of the Russian empire but retained a great deal of local autonomy. The country declared its independence during the **Russian Revolution** of 1917. During the **World War II**, Finland fell within the sphere of influence of both the Soviet Union and Nazi Germany. After a brief war with the Soviet Union, the country was forced to surrender the province **Karelia** to Russia. During the Cold War era Finland adhered to a policy of **neutrality** but maintained close economic ties to the Soviet Union. The country joined the European Union in 1995. Finland's **constitution**, ratified in 1919, was last altered in 1991. The country has a **unicameral parliament** whose members are elected for four year terms. The president is directly elected by the public for six-year terms.

Economy

In 2006, GDP was US$ 210 billion, of which three per cent came from **agriculture**, 30 per cent from **industry** and 67 per cent from **services**. Finland's most significant period of **industrialisation** took place after World War II, when progress was particularly rapid. However, the economy subsequently became more service based during the 1980s when, as a result of a restructuring, the economy successfully made the transition from manufacturing to being more **services oriented**. Important segments of Finland's industrial sector include the metals, electronics, chemicals and foodstuffs industries. Finland's major **exports** include **paper**, wood, electronics, and machinery.

Oil and natural gas reserves in northern Finland are currently being exploited in cooperation with Russia. Finland has been a **European Union** member since 1995 and one of the founding members of the EU's currency union.

Transport Infrastructure

Helsinki is the hub of the Finnish **railway system** which encompasses almost 6,000 km of rail. The country's motorway network is well developed and includes numerous bridges to span the country's many lakes and rivers. Regular **ferry services** travel from Finland to Russia, the Baltic States, and the other Nordic countries. The country's most important international airports are located in Helsinki, Turku, and Tampere.

Tourism

As well as the capital **Helsinki**, Finland's leading tourist destinations include its numerous **lakes** as well as the Aaland Islands with their mild climate. The cities of **Turku** and **Tampere** have many cultural and historic attractions.

Finland's capital, Helsinki, has many historic buildings.

Iceland: The island of ice and fire was created by volcanic activity. Iceland is situated on the Mid-Atlantic Ridge in an area of frequent seismic and volcanic activity. The numerous geysers and solfataras scattered around the island are vivid reminders of the island's geological activity. Iceland's geothermal energy is now used to generate power and warmth for the island's people.

Iceland

Area:	103,000 sq. km
Capital city:	Reykjavík
Form of government:	Republic
Administrative divisions:	
8 regions	
Population:	
300,000 (3 inhabitants/sq. km)	
Language:	Icelandic
GDP per capita:	US$53,000
Currency:	
1 Icelandic krona = 100 aurar	

Natural Geography

Iceland is a large and ancient volcanic **island** in the North Atlantic situated just below the **Arctic Circle**. Most of the population inhabits the coastal region, while most of the largely **barren interior** is uninhabited. Numerous **fjords** run inland from the coast. Iceland is situated on a so-called 'hot spot', an area of volcanic activity. Consequently, it has no fewer than 27 **active volcanoes**, many of which are buried beneath glaciers and ice caps.

The island is covered in **geysers**, hot springs and lava fields which give Iceland a continuously changing landscape.

Iceland emerged from the ocean around 16 million years ago at the junction of the North American and Eurasian tectonic plates. More than a tenth of the island's surface is covered by glaciers, including the largest glacier in Europe, the **Vatnajökull**. Occasional volcanic eruptions beneath the surface of the glaciers can cause massive streams of water to be released and pour out from the interior to the coast. Around half of the country's territory consists of **tundra** covered in sub-arctic vegetation.

Climate

Thanks to the **Gulf Stream,** Iceland is situated in a transition area between a **sub-arctic** and a **cool temperate** zone. The air masses that pass over it have a major effect on the weather of distant parts of western and central Europe.

Winters in Iceland are long and bitterly cold. The summers are relatively short and cool but temperatures above 20°C are not uncommon. In the highlands of the interior snow can fall at any time of year, even in summer. Strong winds blow across Iceland throughout the year.

Population

Icelandic, a Germanic language closely related to Norwegian, is spoken by all of the relatively small population. The country has no significant ethnic minority communities other than some American army personnel, Scandinavians and guest workers from Eastern Europe. The Icelanders are the descendents of Norse and Celtic settlers who arrived from the British Isles and Scandinavia. In terms of religion, 96 per cent of Icelanders are **Protestant**, although church attendance is low. The standard of education is one of the highest and the illiteracy rate the lowest in the world. In rural districts, **travelling teachers** ensure that even children in the most remote regions have access to **education**. The country's only university is located in Reykjavik, the capital, where almost half the population lives.

The public health and welfare systems of Iceland are among the best in the world; some 45 per cent of government revenues are invested in them.

History and Politics

Roman sailors may have reached the islands in the third century AD and ancient chronicles tell of Irish monks who lived on the island in the sixth century. The first permanent settlers were **explorers from Norway** who arrived in the ninth century. In 930 AD, the Norse settlers on Iceland founded the **Althing**, a **parliament** which is now the oldest in the world.

Christianity wa introduced to Iceland around 1000. The island was ruled by Norway in the thirteenth century and Denmark in the fourteenth century. An **independence movement** emerged in the nineteenth century, so that Iceland had achieved much **autonomy** by 1918. During World War II, the island was occupied by the British and Americans, preventing a German invasion. In 1944, the island's leaders declared **independence** from Denmark.

Iceland was a founding member of **NATO**. It maintains no army of it own but is home to large American army bases.

Economy

In 2006, GDP was US$ 16 billion, of which 11 per cent came from agriculture, 28 per cent from industry and 61 per cent from services. **Fishing and fish processing** remains the backbone of the economy, employing a quarter of the labour force. Animal husbandry, especially horse and cattle breeding, remains important. Iceland's potentially vast **mineral resources** (aluminium, diatomite) will be increasingly exploited. The most important natural resource is its enormous **geothermal and hydroelectric power**. These renewable energy sources come from the geysers and hot springs that have been harnessed to heat greenhouses in which fruit and vegetables are grown. The **tourism industry** has grown in importance in recent years, thanks to the island's natural wonders and has played a large part in economic growth of over five per cent.

Transport Infrastructure

The only major road is the 1600-km **ring road** around the island only around one-tenth of which is paved. There is a bus service runs between the country's main population centres, but no **railway**. Regular direct flights connect Iceland to several major cities in North America and Europe. The only international **airport** is in Reykjavik. **Passenger ferries** ply between Greenland, Norway, Great Britain and the Faroes.

Tourism

Iceland is an increasingly popular tourist destination. The rivers are ideal for rafting and the landscapes of the interior appeal to hikers. **Reykjavik**, the northernmost capital in the world, is the starting point for tours of the island. Iceland's political history began in **Thingvellir National Park** near Reykjavik more than a thousand years ago. **Skaftafell National Park** covers the southern half of the Vajnajökull glacier. A series of islands off the west coast are home to large colonies of **birds**.

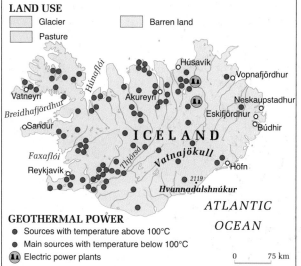

LAND USE
- Glacier
- Pasture
- Barren land

GEOTHERMAL POWER
- Sources with temperature above 100°C
- Main sources with temperature below 100°C
- Electric power plants

0   75 km

Estonia, Latvia, Lithuania

Riga and Tallinn: Both northern Baltic capitals feature a wealth of historic architecture including medieval and art nouveau buildings. The cities were major Hanseatic ports during the Middle Ages.

Estonia

Area:	45,226 sq. km
Capital city:	Tallinn

Form of government:
Parliamentary Republic

Administrative divisions:
15 regions

Population:
1.3m (29 inhabitants/sq. km)

Languages:
Estonian (official), Russian

GDP per capita:	US$12,400

Currency:
1 Estonian Kroon = 100 senti

Natural Geography

The northernmost of the three Baltic republics is bounded by the **Gulf of Finland** to the north and the Baltic Sea to the west. Estonia is a largely flat country with countless rivers, lakes, moors and marshes as well as more than **1500 islands** and islets.

Climate

Estonia has a **cool temperate climate**, although the weather in the interior tends to be warmer in summer than at the coast.

Population

Some 64 per cent of the population are ethnic **Estonians**. The largest minorities are **Russians** who constitute 29 per cent of the population and there are smaller communities of **Ukrainians, Belarusians** and **Finns**. Estonia's official language is Estonian, although Russian is widely spoken. The integration of the large Russian minority remains one of the country's major social challenges. Estonia has **two universities**, in Tallinn and in Tartu.

History and Politics

This small country on the Baltic coast fell to the **Danes** in 1219 and remained under **foreign domination** for long periods of time; in 1561 it became a territory of **Sweden** and in 1721 part of the Russian Empire. In 1918, Estonia declared **independence** but it was occupied by the Soviets under Stalin in 1941. After five decades of Soviet rule, Estonia gained **independence** in 1991 and became a member of the EU in 2004. The unicameral parliament, the Riigikogu, is elected every four years.

Economy

In 2006, GDP was US$ 16.6 billion, of which four per cent came from **agriculture**, 28 per cent from **industry** and 68 per cent from **services**. In recent years, Estonia has experienced a high economic growth rate of seven per cent. Trade in raw materials and part-finished products (wood, wooden goods, metal products and textiles) is of primary importance. Estonia is currently ranked twentieth in the list of most competitive countries.

Transport Infrastructure

Estonia's only international **airport** is located near the capital, Tallinn. Regular **ferry services** connect Tallinn with Helsinki and Stockholm as well as other cities on the Baltic Sea.

Languages: Latvian (official), Russian

GDP per capita:	US$8,700

Currency: 1 Lats = 100 santimas

Natural Geography

The country is bordered by the **Baltic Sea**, into which extends the **Courland peninsula**. The interior is mainly fertile lowland. The **Western Dvina** flows through the country before draining into the eastern marshes. This region is dotted with numerous **lakes**, and conifers cover 40 per cent of the land.

Population

The population is 56 per cent **Latvian** and 30 per cent **Russian**, with smaller groups of Belarusians, Ukrainians and Poles. Latvia is 55 per cent **Protestant** and 24 per cent **Catholic**. Nine per cent of the population belong to the **Russian Orthodox** church.

The old town district of Belarus' capital city Minsk.

Tourism

Tallinn is the centre of the tourist industry. Several lakes are situated in the region around **Tartu**. The Baltic Sea islands **Saaremaa** and **Hiiumaa** are also popular.

Latvia

Area:	64,589 sq. km
Capital city:	Riga

Form of government:
Republic and 7 cities

Administrative divisions:
26 districts and 7 cities

Population:
2.3m (35 inhabitants/sq. km)

History and Politics

The **Teutonic Knights** and merchants of the **Hanseatic League** dominated Latvia in the Middle Ages. Latvia came under the control of Tsarist **Russia** in the eighteenth century. It declared **independence** in 1918, but became part of the Soviet Union in 1939. In 1991, **Latvia** and the other two Baltic states declared independence. The last Russian military base in Latvia was closed in 1998. Latvia has been a member of the EU since 2004.

Economy

In 2006, GDP was US$ 20 billion, of which four per cent came from **agriculture**, 22 per cent from **industry** and 74 per cent from **services**. The economy is growing at a good eight per cent. Its industry is competitive, manufacturing machinery, railway freight cars and electronic components. The trans-shipment of goods in Baltic ports plays an important role in the economy and the **privatisation** of state companies is being driven forward.

Transport Infrastructure

Latvia's only international airport, **Riga International Airport** is situated several miles outside the capital city.

Tourism

Latvia's **national parks** and the historic old city of **Riga** on the Baltic Sea coast are the most popular tourist attractions and have become increasingly popular since independence.

Lithuania

Area:	65,200 sq. km
Capital city:	Vilnius

Form of government:
Parliamentary Republic

Administrative divisions:
10 districts

Population:
3.6m (55 inhabitants/sq. km)

Languages:
Lithuanian (official), Russian

GDP per capita:	US$8,700

Currency: 1 Litas = 100 centas

Natural Geography

Situated between the **Baltic Sea** and **Belarus**, Lithuania is the southernmost Baltic nation. Marshlands, **plains** and thick forests cover most of the land mass.

Climate

Lithuania's coast has a **cool maritime climate**; the interior has a **continental climate** with greater seasonal temperature variation.

Population

Lithuanians constitute at least 80 per cent of the country's population, with significant minorities of ethnic **Russians, Ukrainians, Belarusians** and **Poles**.

History and Politics

The first Lithuanian **kingdom** stretched from the Baltic to the **Black Sea**. Lithuania joined **Poland** to form the Polish-Lithuanian Commonwealth in 1385. The country fell to the **Russian Empire** in 1772. In 1918, Lithuania was declared an **independent republic** but was invaded and annexed by the **Soviet Union** in 1940. In 1990, Lithuania became the first **republic** of the Soviet Union to declare independence. The 141 members of the country's parliament, the **Sejm**, are directly elected for five years. Lithuania became an EU member in 2004.

Economy

In 2006, GDP was US$ 30 billion, of which seven per cent came from **agriculture**, 30 per cent from **industry** and 63 per cent from **services**. In recent years, the economy has grown at well over six per cent. Privatisation is to a large extent complete and, in July 2005, the World Bank ranked Lithuania as a 'donor country', as its economy is now considered to be in a relatively good condition.

Transport Infrastructure

Lithuania has two international **airports**, at Vilnius and Kaunas. The main **port** is Klaipeda.

Tourism

The **Courland Spit** is a nature conservation area, and the many **national parks** and capital city, **Vilnius,** are great tourist attractions.

Belarus's cultural roots stretch back to the time of the first settlements by non-Christian Slavic groups. Elements of these cultures survive in the country's traditional culture, including local music *and poetry. Brightly coloured paintings are typical of region's traditional art. This influence is clearly apparent is the works of the region's most famous painter, Marc Chagall.*

Belarus	
Area:	207,600 sq. km
Capital city:	Minsk
Form of government:	Republic
Administrative divisions:	
6 regions, 1 district (capital city)	
Population:	
9.7m (47 inhabitants/sq. km)	
Languages:	
Belarusian, Russian (official)	
GDP per capita.:	3,800 US$
Currency: 1 Belarusian Rouble = 100 kapiejkas	

Natural Geography

Situated on the vast **lowland** that expands through most of **Eastern Europe**, Belarus is an extraordinarily flat country covering wide plains. In addition to plains, the Belarusian landscapes are characterised by numerous rivers, lakes and large marshy forests. The **Pripjat marsh** in southern Belarus is one of the largest marshes and moor lands in Europe.

Climate

Belarus has a **continental climate** with cold winters.

Population

Seventy-eight per cent of the population consists of **Belarusians**. **Russians** are the country's largest minority, constituting 14 per cent of the total population. Like many other former members of the Soviet Union, Belarus is experiencing significant demographic changes, including a declining and ageing population.

History and Politics

Because of the relative isolation, the Slavs who inhabited Belarus in the middle ages were able to preserve their distinct culture and language, despite periods of **Polish** and **Lithuanian** domination. The union with **Russia** in the late eighteenth century led to a revival of the country's culture and traditions. In 1919, Belarus was declared a sovereign communist state but joined the **Soviet Union** just three years later. Although

officially a democratic republic, Belarus has an **authoritarian government** dominated the president.

Economy

In 2006, GDP was US$ 37 billion. At 11 per cent, **agriculture** contributed a relatively large proportion, while at 49 per cent the service sector is only developing slowly. The main focal points of **industrial production** (40 per cent) are machine building, chemicals and light industry, although industry is rapidly losing significance in the economy through obsolete plant and machinery and a lack of investment. The government continues to

follow an economic policy of steering the markets from the centre, which has led, among other things, to restraint on the part of foreign investors.

Transport Infrastructure

The capital city Minsk is the hub of the **rail network** and is situated along the main rail route connecting Moscow and Warsaw. Minsk International Airport is the country's most important air transport hub.

Tourism

Minsk, the capital and its largest city, is the most popular tourist destination, as are the country's many **lakes** and forests.

London

London, the capital of the United Kingdom of Great Britain and Northern Ireland, lies in the south of England on the River Thames. It is home to the British royal family at Buckingham Palace, their official London residence, and the Prime Minister at 10 Downing Street. London is a world financial base, an international transport hub and the most populous city in the European Union with over 7.5 million inhabitants from a wide range of origins. This multicultural characteristic has its roots in the British Empire – over 300 languages are now said to be spoken in the city. London was founded as Londinium by the Romans in AD 43. London will play host to the summer Olympic Games in 2012.

Area:
1,579 sq. km (city)
Inhabitants:
7,520,000 (city, 2006)
8,520,000 (urban area, 2006)
Population density:
4,763 inhabitants/sq. km (city)

Tradition versus modernity: The giant wheel of the London Eye and the Palace of Westminster.

Paris

Paris, the capital of France, lies on the River Seine in the Paris Basin. Numerous international organisations such as UNESCO and the OECD are based here. Today's cityscape with its wide boulevards was created in the mid-nineteenth century. Impressive structures (such as Notre Dame Cathedral, the Eiffel Tower and the Arc de Triomphe) and important museums (like the Louvre and the Pompidou Centre) have made their mark on the city. Its origins can be traced back to Roman Lutetia, built on an earlier Celtic settlement. Paris was the seat of the French kings until Louis XIV moved his court to Versailles in 1682. Even after the move, Paris remained the focal point of France; the French Revolution started here in 1789.

Area:
105 sq. km (city)
Inhabitants:
2,167,994 (city, 2005)
9,928,000 (urban area, 2001)
Population density:
20,648 inhabitants/sq. km (city)

The heart of France: A view from Pont Alexandre III towards the Eiffel Tower.

Madrid

Madrid, the capital of Spain, is the largest city on the Iberian Peninsula. Situated in the centre of Spain, on the Manzanares River, Madrid is the seat of the Spanish royal family and the government. The city has six universities and is home to over 50 different museums of note (such as the Prado, the Centro de Arte Reine Sofia for contemporary arts, and the Palacio Villahermosa with the Thyssen-Bornemisza Collection). Madrid is also the transport focal point of Spain, with all motorways and railway lines leading to it. The city was first documented in 939 and was appointed the seat of government in 1561 by Philip II. It was the European City of Culture in 1992.

Area:
605,770 sq. km (city)
Inhabitants:
3,093,000 (city, 2003)
Over 4,000,000 (conurbation, 2003)
Population density:
5,106 inhabitants/sq. km (city)

The Plaza de Cibeles with its spectacular fountain, in the heart of Madrid.

Rome

Rome, the capital of Italy, is also known as 'the eternal city'. According to legend, it was founded by Romulus in 753 BC. Today, Rome is the seat of the Italian government and parliament. It is also home to the Vatican City and its head of state, the Pope. The cityscape of Rome is characterised by historic buildings dating back over two millennia. The Forum Romanum lies at the heart of the city but there are several other Imperial Forums from the time of the Roman Empire. Other important buildings are the Capitol and the Colosseum and St Peter's Basilica. In 1890, Rome became the capital of the Kingdom of Italy. The city withstood World War II without suffering great damage and has been the capital of the Italian Republic since June 1946.

Area:
1,508 sq. km (city)
Inhabitants:
2,710,000 (city, 2007)
Population density:
1,797 inhabitants/sq. km (city)

'La dolce vita' Roman style: The Piazza della Rotonda with the Pantheon.

Cities of Europe

Berlin

The capital of Germany, Berlin is the largest city in the country. The seat of government and parliament are based here. After the German Reich was founded in 1871, as the capital of the empire and the Weimar Republic (from 1918/19) Berlin was at the centre of German history. It became the Nazi dictatorship's capital in 1933. After World War II, two focal points developed in the city as a result of the division of Germany: in the West around the Ku'damm and the Bahnhof Zoo; in the East around Alexanderplatz. Extensive building work following the dissolution of East Germany in 1989, such as in the government area, the new central station and Potsdamerplatz, changed the cityscape considerably.

Area:
892 sq. km (city)
Inhabitants:
3,414,000 (city, 2007)
Population density:
3,829 inhabitants/sq. km (city)

The Brandenburg Gate is the symbol of the reunified city of Berlin.

Prague

Situated on the Vltava River in the the Prague Basin, Prague is the capital of the Czech Republic. It is the seat of government and parliament and also the scientific heart of the country thanks to Charles University, founded in 1348. The central district of Hradcany is dominated by Prague Castle, which can be traced back to the ninth and tenth centuries. The ornate Charles Bridge, built in 1357, has become an emblem of the city. The city has seen turbulent times – it was occupied by the Germans in 1939 and the Russian Red Army in 1945, while in 1968 the ultimately unsuccessful Prague Spring took place, and in January 1989 Prague became the starting point for the 'Velvet Revolution', which led to the overthrow of the Communist government.

Area:
496 sq. km (city)
Inhabitants:
1,210,000 (city, 2008)
Population density:
2,439 inhabitants/sq. km (city)

A superb view from Letna Park over the old town and the bridges crossing the Vltava.

Moscow

Moscow has been the capital of the Russian Federation since 1991. It lies on the Moskva River in the European part of Russia. Housing the seat of government, Moscow is the largest city in Russia and its most important base for banking, trade and finance. With nine terminal stations and four airports, it is also Russia's most important transport hub. The city was first documented in 1147. Around 1480 it became the capital of the State of Moscow. Although the court was moved to St Petersburg in 1712, Moscow remained an important administrative metropolis. After being conquered by Napoleon I in 1812, it was virtually razed to the ground. Between 1922 and 1991, Moscow was the capital of the USSR.

Area:
1,081 sq. km (city)
Inhabitants:
10,470,000 (city, 2008)
About 12,500,000 (conurbation, 2008)
Population density:
9,685 inhabitants/sq. km (city)

The centre of Russian power: Red Square, the Kremlin and St Basil's Cathedral in Moscow.

Istanbul

Situated on the Sea of Marmara at the southern outlet of the Bosporus, Istanbul is the capital of the province of the same name and the largest city in Turkey. Important trade routes intersect here – the sea route from the Mediterranean to the Black Sea, and the land route from Asia Minor to the Balkan Peninsula. With its natural port the Golden Horn, Istanbul is the point through which most goods enter and leave the country. Istanbul can be traced back to Byzantium, founded in around 660 BC. Constantine the Great renamed it Constantinople in the fourth century AD and made it the imperial capital of the Byzantine Empire. The city was conquered by the Ottomans in 1453, and it remained the capital of the Ottoman Empire until 1923.

Area:
1,538.77 sq. km (city)
Inhabitants:
10,300,000 (city, 2007)
12,300,000 (conurbation, 2007)
Population density:
6,994 inhabitants/sq. km (city)

Sultan Ahmed Mosque or the Blue Mosque: Istanbul's principal mosque and landmark.

Netherlands, Belgium

The Netherlands: *The Dutch have reclaimed a large portion of their country from the sea over many centuries. Former beaches and salt marshes have been transformed into fertile fields producing important crops such as flowers and cereals. The historic windmills scattered around the country were once used to grind wheat and barley and pump water from the fields.*

Netherlands

Area:	41,526 sq. km
Capital city:	Amsterdam
(Seat of government: The Hague)	
Form of government:	
Constitutional Monarchy	
Administrative divisions:	
12 provinces, 2 overseas regions	
Population: 16.6 million	
(399 inhabitants/sq. km)	
Language: Dutch	
GDP per capita:	US$41,000
Currency:	1 euro = 100 cents

Natural Geography

More than a quarter of this flat country beside the North Sea on the **Northern European Plain** lies below sea level. Low-lying areas are protected by an extensive network of **dykes**, canals and pumps. The only significant elevations (up to 321 m) are in the south-east. The islands of West Friesland are also Dutch. Almost one-sixth of the country consists of lakes and rivers. Land is still being reclaimed from the sea.

Climate

The temperate **maritime (warm, damp) climate** of the Netherlands is affected by the Gulf Stream.

Population

Citizens of the **Netherlands** with Dutch ancestry comprise 96 per cent of the country's population. Significant minorities include communities of Turks, Moroccans and German-speakers as well as those whose trace their ancestry to the former Dutch colonies such as Suriname and Indonesia.

More than a third of the Dutch people have no religious affiliation. About 59 per cent identify as Christians; 36 per cent of the population is **Catholic** and at least 25 per cent are members of **Protestant** churches. Dutch is the official language and Frisian is a recognised minority language in the province of Frisia.

History and Politics

The Low Countries finally threw off the yoke of **Spanish** domination in 1648. By the next century, it had become the **most powerful naval and trading power** in Europe. In 1831, the Austrian Provinces (today's Belgium), declared independence from the Netherlands, but the newly created **Kingdom of the Netherlands** remained a strong world power, thanks to its overseas territories. Despite declaring neutrality in **World War II**, the Netherlands were occupied by Germany. After the war, the Netherlands became a the founding member of **NATO**. The capital, the Hague is the home of the International Courts of Justice.

Since the 1986 constitution, the Carribean Island of **Aruba** has enjoyed a special status. The neighbouring **Netherlands Antilles,** whose main island is Curaçao, have belonged to the Netherlands since 1634, and have been **self-governing** since 1954.

Economy

In 2006, GDP was US$ 671 billion, of which three per cent was derived from **agriculture**, 25 per cent from **industry** and 72 per cent from **services**. Thanks to its location, the country has always been an important **international trading centre**.

The **agricultural sector** is highly developed. Major exports include tomatoes, cucumbers, peppers and flowers, most of which are now grown in hi-tech greenhouses. The Netherlands are the world's third largest exporter of agricultural produce (after the United States and France). **Fishing** was once a leading export, and remains an important source of income and jobs along the coast. The **industrial sector** is diverse and advanced; important exports from this sector include machinery, cars and trucks, technology and chemicals.

Tourism

The Netherlands' leading tourist destinations include the **North Sea coast** with its beaches and islands as well as the country's main cities, **Amsterdam, The Hague,** and **Leiden,** all of which contain many historical and cultural attractions, including museums housing paintings by the Dutch Old Masters. The **tulip fields** remain a great attraction.

Belgium

Area:	30,528 sq. km
Capital city:	Brussels
Form of government:	
Constitutional Monarchy	
Administrative divisions:	
3 regions (Flanders, Wallonia, Brussels)	
Population:	
10.4 million	
(340 inhabitants/sq. km)	
Languages:	
French, Flemish, German	
GDP per capita:	US$37,300
Currency:	1 euro = 100 cents

Natural Geography

The dunes of the **North Sea coast** protect a series of fertile plains and sandy heaths over most of the north and west, while fertile **low hills** extend throughout most of southern Belgium. East of the Meuse (Maas) river, Belgium's terrain is dominated by the rolling hills of the heavily forested Ardennes and the High Fens (Hautes Fagnes).

Population

The Belgians are a nation divided by language; around 57 per cent of the Belgian people are **Dutch-speakers** and 32 per cent are **Francophone Walloons**. There is a German-speaking community in the east near the German border. More than three-quarters of the population is Roman Catholic and some 2.5 per cent are Muslims. Smaller communities of Jews and Protestants have a long history in Belgium.

History and Politics

During the late middle ages, the cities of **Flanders** were among the greatest centres of trade and commerce in Europe. However, most of Belgium remained under foreign control for centuries. The **Spanish** controlled most of Belgium in the sixteenth and seventeenth centuries, followed by the **Austrians** and eventually the **French** and the **Dutch**. The country finally became an **independent kingdom** in 1831. Radical changes to the constitution lead to the kingdom's restructuring as a **federal national** with autonomous regions and a complicated political structure. Modern Belgium is now comprised of three culturally and linguistically distinct **regions** (Flanders, Wallonia, and Brussels); each region possessing a great deal of political **autonomy** with their own regional parliaments and courts. Belgium's head of state is the country's **monarch**. The defence alliance **NATO** and the **European Union** both have their headquarters in Brussels.

Economy

In 2006, GDP was US$ 395 billion, of which one per cent came from **agriculture**, 25 per cent from **industry** and 74 per cent from **services**. Economic growth lies just above that of the Eurozone, with chemical products, manufactured materials and machines being the principal Belgian exports.

Transport Infrastructure

Belgium has one of the world's most extensive **railway networks**. In addition to Brussels International Airport, the country also has four other international airports. **Antwerp** in Flanders has one of the world's busiest harbours and important **inland harbours** include Brussels, Ghent, and Liége.

Tourism

The historic cities of **Bruges** and **Ghent** as well as metropolises of **Brussels** and **Antwerp** are popular tourist destinations. Belgian seaside resorts continue to draw visitors. **Hautes Fagnes National Park** is popular with hikers.

Historic buildings on the Grand Place in Belgium's capital city Brussels.

Alkmaar: Until World War II, agriculture dominated the economy of the Netherlands. Even now the country has a strong agricultural sector, producing hothouse fruits and vegetables as well as excellent cheeses. Alkmaar has the country's oldest and most traditional cheese market which is a tourist attraction.

Luxembourg	
Area:	2,586 sq. km
Capital city:	Luxembourg City
Form of government:	
Constitutional Monarchy	
Administrative divisions:	
3 districts with 12 cantons	
Population:	
480,000 (186 inhabitants/sq. km)	
Languages: Luxembourgish,	
French, German	
GDP per capita:	US$89,000
Currency:	1 euro = 100 cents

Natural Geography

Luxembourg, one of Europe's smallest nations, shares borders with Germany, Belgium, and France. The **hills and forests** of the **Ardennes** dominate the northern part of the country. The south, like neighbouring areas in Germany, has several river valleys. Much of the country is covered by forests and many river valleys are devoted to **wine cultivation**.

Population

At least 30 per cent of Luxembourg's population consist of foreign workers, mostly from other European nations, including a significant number from Portugal (36.9 per cent), Italy (13.5 per cent), France (11.2 per cent), Belgium (8.9 per cent), and Germany (6.8 per cent).

History and Politics

Luxembourg became a **duchy** in the fourteenth century and was a member of the German confederation between 1814 and 1866, when it finally become a completely **independent nation**. Luxembourg abandoned its policy of neutrality after its **occupation by German forces** during the World War II. The small nation was a founding member of **NATO** and the **European Union**. Luxembourg head of state is the **Grand Duke**, who has considerable reserve powers. The 60 members of this small nation's parliament are directly elected for five-year terms.

Economy

In 2006, GDP was US$ 42 billion, of which four per cent came from **agriculture**, 28 per cent from **industry** and 68 per cent from **services**. The per capita income is one of the highest in the world.

The **service sector**, especially the **financial and banking sectors**, is now the backbone of the economy and accounts for 70 per cent of all jobs in Luxembourg. The European Court of Auditors and several other EU institutions have offices in Luxembourg.

Tourism

The lovely countryside and the architecture of the historic cities are tourist attractions. **Luxembourg City** with its well preserved architecture and royal palace is the most popular destination.

France

Savoir vivre: France is one of the world's leading producers and consumers of wine with the average Frenchman consuming 63 l of wine annually. Several French regions are well known for their high quality local wines.

Area:	547,030 sq km
Capital city:	Paris

Form of government:
Parliamentary Republic

Administrative divisions:
22 regions, 96 départements,
9 independent territories

External territories:
French Guiana, Guadeloupe, Martinique, Réunion, Mayotte, Saint Pierre and Miquelon, French Polynesia, New Caledonia, Wallis and Futuna

Population: 60.9 million
(111 inhabitants/sq km)

Languages: French (official), and many dialects, including Alsatian, Breton, Basque, Occitan and Languedoc

GDP per capita:	US$36,700
Currency:	1 euro = 100 cents

Natural Geography

The hexagon-shaped country stretches between the **English Channel** in the north and the **Mediterranean Sea** in the south and borders the Atlantic Ocean as well as the **Bay of Biscay** in the west. Most of France is largely hilly or consist of flat fertile plains. High mountain ranges on the country's periphery form natural borders to several of France's neighbours; in the south the **Pyrenees** and in the east the **Alps**. River basins encompass much of northern and western France, while the plateaus and mountains

of the **Massif Central** extend through large parts of southern and central France. Several important rivers flow through including the **Loire, Rhone**, and the **Seine** rivers.

Climate

The regions along the English Channel and Atlantic Coast, including the provinces of Normandy and Brittany, share a **temperate maritime climate** with abundant precipitation. The interior has a **mild continental climate** with warm summers and cool winters. Southern France has a **Mediterranean climate** with dry and hot summers and mild rainy winters.

Population

Ninety-four per cent of the population are of French descent. The country, however, has one of the most diverse populations in Europe. A large percentage of

The Arc de Triomphe: a monument to the glory of Napoleon's army.

French citizens are the descendants of recent immigrants, including many people of **Italian, Spanish, East Asian, North African, Caribbean**, and **West African** descent. Around 81 per cent of the French people identify as **Roman Catholics**, although levels of church attendance are relatively low. In addition to Catholics, around 3 million **Muslims**, at least 1 million **Protestants**, and more than 700,000 **Jews** live in France. In addition to French, **regional dialects** are widely spoken, including Breton, Corsican, Basque

and Alsatian.
The French **educational system** is considered to be one of the best in the world. Many students attend one of the country's more than 90 universities and institutions of higher education, including the elite 'grandes ecoles'.

History and Politics

Once the Roman province of Gaul, invaders from the East

overran France in the fifth century AD. **Clovis I**, who converted to Christianity in the early fifth century, founded the Merovingian Dynasty that ruled much of France for centuries. The Frankish king **Charlemagne** united France with Saxony and Bavaria and had himself declared emperor. France only emerged as a distinct nation with after the division of the Frankish

Palace of Versailles: *The grandiose palace complex was designed by the architects Le Vau and Harouin-Mansart at the behest of Louis XIV, France's absolutist monarch. Connected to the impressive garden Le Nôtre,* *the palace was constructed in the late seventeenth century. Between 1682 and 1789, the year of the French Revolution, Versailles as the home of the king was the centre of political power in France.*

centuries, a form of government that reached its peak during the reign of **Louis XIV** during the seventeenth century. The **French Revolution** which began in 1789 was an important development for the emergence of democracy in Europe but ended in the **Reign of Terror**, a period of brutal repressions that left thousands dead. **Napoleon Bonaparte**, a Corsican general, was declared emperor of France in 1804. The **Napoleonic Code**, which influenced legal systems around the world, was introduced during his reign. After many spectacular **victories** Napoleon's armies were defeated at the **Battle of Waterloo** in 1815. The **Congress of Vienna** led to a short-lived **restoration** of the French monarchy. This period ended in revolution in 1848. In 1871, the **Second Empire** of Napoleon III was toppled after France's defeat in the Franco-Prussian War. France fought against Germany during **World War** I; most of the bloodiest battles being fought on French soil. After the war, Alsace and Lorraine were restored to France after almost five decades of German rule. Northern France and the Atlantic coast were occupied by German troops during the **World War II** and a collaborationist regime known as

Empire in 888. The country was divided into rival **duchies** and **principalities**, while **Normandy** was conquered by the Vikings. In the 987 the **Capet** dynasty united large areas of France and would rule the country on and off until 1848. France emerged victorious from the long **Hundred Years War** (1338–1453) with England. **Joan of Arc** who led to march to expel the English out of Paris is still revered as a French national heroine. The French **nation-state** was ruled by an **absolutist** monarchy for

Vichy France ruled the south. General **Charles de Gaulle** dominated the politics and development of France in the post-war decades. Most of France's **colonies** began to demand their independence and the process of decolonisation began. In 1952, Algeria became the last major French colony to be granted independence after a demoralising war of liberation. The current constitution, ratified in 1958, defines France as democratic presidential republic. France has a **bicameral parliament** that consists of a senate and a **national assembly**. The heads of state are the **president**, who is

1 Located on the coast of Normandy in northern France, the historic abbey built atop Mont-Saint-Michel.

2 The Eiffel Tower, Paris' most famous landmark, rises 320 m high, taller than all of the modern office towers built along the Seine in recent decades.

3 The seaside resort town of Menton is built on a group of coastal hills near the Italian border. The French Riviera (Côte d'Azur) is popular destination.

The South of France: Provence's colourful fields of lavender are not only beautiful but also play an important role in southern France's historic perfume industry. Lavender oil from the region is used to produce soaps, cosmetics, and perfumes. During the Middle Ages Christian pilgrims passing through the region on their way to Santiago de Compostela found shelter in the many local monasteries.

elected for a five-year term, and the **prime minister** who heads the Council of Ministers.

The Mediterranean island of **Corsica** was purchased from the Italian city-state Genoa in 1768 and is now the largest French island. After decades of local agitation, Corsica now has a unique political status and enjoys greater local political autonomy than most other French regions.

France's numerous overseas territories are a legacy of the country's history as a colonial empire. These territories include **French Guiana** in South America, the small islands of **Saint-Pierre and Miquelon** off the Newfoundland in Canada, the Caribbean islands of **Martinique** and **Guadeloupe** and the Indian Ocean island **Reunion** near Mauritius as well as **New Caledonia, Wallis and Futuna**, and the islands of **French Polynesia** in the South Pacific.

Charles de Gaulle

*Lille, 22.11.1890,
†Colombey-les-deux-Eglises, 9.11.1970

Charles de Gaulle fought in World War I and achieved the rank of general. After the defeat and occupation of France in 1940, he led the Free French resistance from exile in London. In 1944 de Gaulle returned to France and was appointed leader of the country's provisional government. As founder of the RPF party (Reassemblement du people Francais), he dominated French politics in the early 1950s, but dissolved the party in 1953. After the military revolt in Algeria, he was appointed prime minister and soon after became the first president of the fifth French Republic. Granted wide ranging powers by the new constitution, he ended the war in Algeria and played a major role in the reconciliation between post-war France and Germany. De Gaulle remained president until his resignation in 1969.

Economy

In 2006, GDP (including overseas *départements*) was US$ 2.2 trillion, putting France sixth in the world. Its growth, which has been weak of late, should be strengthened through structural reforms in tax and labour laws. It was one of the founding members of the European Economic Community. Fifty-four per cent of mainland France is devoted to **agriculture**, mainly grain, sugar beet, potatoes, fruit and wine. Thanks in part to EU subsidies, France is now the world's second biggest **exporter of agricultural produce**, after the USA. The most important **manufacturing sector**, accounting for 22 per cent of GDP, include machine and textile production. The **service sector** now constitutes 75 per cent of France's total economic activity and 68 per cent of the French workforce is now employed in this sector.

The old town and harbour of Cannes in southern France.

Valéry Giscard d'Estaing

*Koblenz, 2.2.1926

He occupied several ministerial posts during the 1960s and founded the National Centre for Independent Republicans in 1966. Giscard was elected president in 1974 but was defeated at the polls by Francois Mitterrand in 1981. He was selected to head the Convention for a European Constitution in 2001 and was admitted to the Académie francaise in 2003.

Transport Infrastructure

The **TGV**, France's high speed train system, is the most popular symbol of France's excellent **railway network**. The train connects the country's largest cities at speed up to 300 km per hour. Completed in 1994, the **Channel Tunnel** made high speed train connections between France and Great Britain possible. The country's **network of roads** has a total length of 1.5 million km, more than of which are paved. Charles de Gaulle international airport near Paris is the most important of France's ten **international airports**. A network of historic canals, including many which were built in the Middle Ages, spans France. Rouen and Bordeaux are the country's most important **inland ports** for traffic along the country's rivers and **canals**. The most important **sea ports** in France are Marseilles on the Mediterranean coast and Le Havre on the northern coast.

Tourism

France is often ranked as the most popular tourist destination in the world and each year tens of millions of foreign tourist visit the country.

Paris is both the country's capital and its most popular tourist destination. The city has a wealth of sights including countless historic and cultural attractions such as the Louvre and the Eiffel Tower. The section of the **Loire Valley** between Angers and Orléans contains beautiful landscapes and is famous for its many châteaux and gardens in France. The **French Riviera**, the coastline between the Spanish and the Italian border, has fashionable resorts such as Cannes, Nice and St. Tropez, charming fishing villages and beautiful beaches. Winter sports and breathtaking views lure many visitors to the **Pyrenees** and the **French Alps**. Important ski resorts in France include Albertville, Val-d'Isère and Chamonix. Other popular rural destinations are Britanny, Provence and Périgord, with their unspoiled countryside.

François Mitterrand

*Jarnac, 26.10.1916,
†Paris, 8.1.1996

The socialist president occupied various ministerial posts during the 1960s. He was elected secretary of the French Socialist Party in 1971 and was only narrowly defeated in 1974 presidential elections. He was elected President in 1981 and served in that office until 1995, making him the longest serving French President.

Monaco

Area:	1.95 sq. km
Capital city:	Monaco City
Form of government:	
Constitutional Monarchy	
Administrative divisions:	
Principality	
Population: 32,700	
(16,750 inhabitants/sq. km)	
Languages: French (official),	
Monegasque, Italian	
GDP per capita:	US$60,000
Currency: 1 euro = 100 cents	

Natural Geography

Bordered by **France**, the small principality sits in a small bay on the **Mediterranean**, surrounded by **limestone hills**. Monaco is the world's second smallest independent nation but the country's land area has been significantly expanded through land reclamation in recent decades. Monaco, one of the world's most densely populated states, consists of four districts; Monte Carlo (with beaches and the famous casino), La Condamine (the port), Monaco-Ville (the historic fortified city) and the new district Fontieville, a commercial area created on reclaimed land.

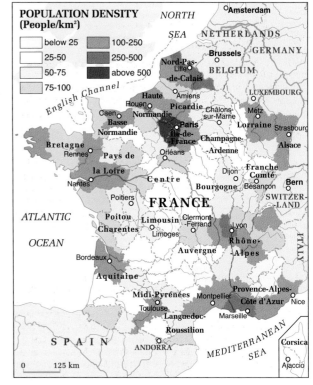

POPULATION DENSITY (People/km²)

below 25	100-250
25-50	250-500
50-75	above 500
75-100	

*Monte Carlo: Monaco's most glamourous district lures visitors with its beach and famous historic casino. Because of its low taxes, many wealthy Europeans choose to reside in **Monaco**.*

Native Monegasques now constitute only 17 per cent of the country's population. Several new areas have been reclaimed from the sea to accommodate the demand for building space.

Climate

Monaco has a **Mediterranean climate** with mild winters and warms often dry summers.

Population

Native **Monegasques** now form only around 17 per cent of the principality's population. The rest of the population consists largely of foreign residents including significant numbers of French citizens, who now constitute more than half of the country's population. Many of the more affluent foreign residents move to the principality to take advantage of the Monaco's **low tax levels**. Monaco abolished its income tax laws in 1865. French and the indigenous Monegasque language are both taught in school although French is now the dominant language in the country.

History and Politics

Founded in the thirteenth century as a **Genoese colony**, Monaco first came under the control of the **Grimaldi** dynasty in 1297. The dynasty, one of the longest reigning in Europe, still rules today. Monaco gained **full independence** in 1861 after centuries as a Spanish and later a French protectorate. In 1918, the principality signed a treaty with France that committed the French to defend Monaco against foreign military threats. Monaco also has a customs and currency union with **France** and the Euro is the common currency of both countries. **Constitutional reforms** in 1911 and 1962 shifted the country's government away from a system of absolute monarchy to one of **constitutional monarchy** with a strong parliament. Members of Monaco's National Council are directly elected for five-year terms. All Monegasque citizens above the age of 21 are eligible to vote. The head of government, who is required by law to be a French citizen, is appointed by the country's **reigning monarch**. Until 2002, a historic agreement between Monaco and France stipulated that should the Grimaldi dynasty fail to produce a male heir sovereignty over Monaco would be given to

France. Albert II, the son of Prince Rainier III and Grace Kelly, has reigned as Prince of Monaco since his father's death in 2005.

Economy

In 2005 GDP was estimated to be about US$ 2 billion, of which 25 per cent came from **industry** and 75 per cent from **services**. The economy is based on banking, property dealing and tourism, which flourishes all year round. A significant contribution to GDP is made by small and medium-sized businesses in the processing industry, which primarily manufacture cosmetics and electrical appliances.

Transport Infrastructure

Public transport in Monaco consists of several bus and mini-bus routes. Taxis are also available throughout the principality. Only locally registered **cars** are allowed into Monaco's old town, but the district is connected to the rest of city by five **public elevators**. Monaco's train station is integrated into the French **rail network**. The nearest **international airport** is in **Nice**.

Tourism

Monaco's first **casino** opened in 1861 and the current Belle Époque-style building was completed in 1878. Monaco is one of the most popular tourist destinations in Europe. Millions of tourists visit each year, mostly on day trips. Sights include Saint Nicholas cathedral, the **Prince's**

Palace, the small **old town** of Monaco-Ville, and the famous **Oceanographic Museum**. In addition Monaco also offers several **beaches** and facilities for **aquatic sports**. Monte Carlo hosts two of the world's most famous **auto racing events**, the Monaco Grand Prix and Monte Carlo Rally.

1 The mountain village Eze is situated in a breathtaking natural setting on the Côte d'Azur (French Riviera). A small narrow path leads up to the village.

2 During the fourteenth and fifteenth centuries, Avignon was an important cultural centre as the residence of the Popes.

3 Sisteron, the 'pearl of Haute Provence' between the Durance River and the craggy mountains of the coastal Alps.

4 Corsica's interior is a fascinating region with stunning mountainous landscapes and traditional small villages.

The owner of the Pommery Estate regards a bottle of champagne with an expert's eye. This sparkling wine is manufactured under strict regulations in the Champagne region near Reims in France. The regulations include the cultivation of the grapes in an officially identified area of cultivation, adherence to

certain cultivation regulations, immediate pressing of the grapes after the harvest, in-bottle fermentation and a minimum storage time. Each year, about 2.5 million hectolitres of sparkling wine are produced, equivalent to 300 million bottles of champagne, 60 per cent of which are drunk in France itself.

Spain

The Way of St James: Christian pilgrims have been taking the famous *Camino de Santiago* since the Middle Ages. Travellers from many nations have journeyed along the various routes that lead to the cathedral of Santiago de Compostela which according to tradition contains the tomb of the apostle Saint James.

Spain

Area:	504,782 sq. km
Capital city:	Madrid
Form of government:	
Constitutional Monarchy	
Administrative divisions:	
17 autonomous regions,	
50 provinces	
Population: 40.4 million	
(80 inhabitants/sq. km)	
Languages: Spanish (Castillian),	
Catalan, Basque, Galician	
GDP per capita:	US$28,000
Currency:	1 euro = 100 cents

Natural Geography

Spain occupies four-fifths of the **Iberian Peninsula**, separated from the rest of Europe by the **Pyrenees** (Pico de Aneto, 3,404 m). **Mesetas**, large arid plateaus, occupy much of the country's land area, including most of central Spain. The **Andalusian plain** stretches from the south coast to the mountains of the **Sierra Nevada** (Mulhacén, 3,478 m). Spain's national territory includes the **Balearic Islands** in the Mediterranean and the **Canary Islands** off the coast of West Africa.

Climate

Northern Spain has a **cool, maritime climate** with **abundant rainfall**. Central Spain is a largely arid region with a **continental climate** and **steppe vegetation**. The mountains of the Sierra Nevada shield the south coast from cold north winds.

Population

People who consider themselves to be **Spaniards** constitute 74 per cent of Spain's population. Other important ethnic groups in the country include **Catalonians** (17 per cent), **Galicians** (six per cent) and **Basques** (two per cent). The British and the Moroccans are the two largest foreign communities in Spain. Some 98 per cent of Spain's population are **Roman Catholics**. The official languages include Spanish, also known as Castillian, and several regional languages including Basque, Catalan and Galician. In recent decades, many areas in Spain have witnessed a resurgence of regional identity. Despite having one of the lowest birth rates in Europe, Spain is experiencing a period of steady population growth due to immigration.

History and Politics

Originally inhabited by several **Celtic** and **Iberian** tribes, Spain came under the control of the **Roman Empire** in the first century BC. In the fifth century AD, most of Spain was conquered of the **Visigoths** who then lost control of the country to the Moors, Muslim Arabs and North Africans, in the year 711. For almost the next 800 years, the Moors controlled most of Iberia and a unique new culture was created. Starting in the eleventh century, the Christian kingdoms of northern Spain expanded their territory southwards. After centuries of conflict, **Granada,** the last bastion of Moorish power, fell to Christian forces in 1492. In the same year, **Christopher Columbus** discovered America and opened the door for Spain's emergence as a **world power**. Spanish explorers and adventurers brought enormous wealth from the New World to their home country and conquered vast territories in the name of the Spanish monarchy. During this era, Catholic clergy led the persecution of Spain's non-Christian population, Muslims and Jews. The Jews were expelled in 1492. There followed the **Spanish Inquisition**, designed to root out Christian heretics. The *Moriscos,* the Spanish Muslims, were expelled in 1568, and in 1579, the Low Countries threw off the Spanish yoke. The defeat of the **Spanish Armada** against England in 1588 marked the end of Spain's domination of Europe. The **War of Spanish Succession** (1701–14) lead to an international crisis that involved most of Europe's major powers. Spain lost most of its colonies, after a series of revolutionary uprisings in countries of South America in the early nineteenth century.

In 1936, the Spanish king went into exile and Spain was declared a **republic**. Francisco **Franco**, an army general, initiated a coup d'état that lead to the Spanish Civil War Spain and the ultimate victory of Franco's reactionary nationalist forces. Franco supported Mussolini and Hitler, though Spain declared neutrality in World War II. The monarchy was restored in 1975 and **Juan Carlos** became King. The country

The fort of the ancient city Toledo towers above the old town and the Rio Tajo.

Francisco Franco

*Ferrol, 4.12.1892,
†Madrid, 20.11.1975

Franco was a general in the Spanish Foreign Legion, stationed in Morocco. He seized power in 1936, causing the Spanish Civil War which he won, thanks to his allies, Nazi Germany and Fascist Italy. His neutrality during World War II, his shrewd Cold War policies, and suppression of all opposition in Spain enabled him to maintain his authoritarian rule until his death.

Juan Carlos I

*Rome, 5.1.1938

Juan Carlos was the son of Don Juan de Bourbon and was named by Franco as his successor to re-establish the monarchy. Juan Carlos acceded to the throne in 1975, after Franco's death. An attempted military coup was thwarted in 1981 when the King made a public television broadcast, and this was a turning point for Spain's move towards democracy and a constitutional monarchy.

*A traditional **Spanish** bullfight usually ends with the death of the bull. In Portugal and southern France the animals are not killed during the fights.*

Mallorca, Ibiza and **Gran Canaria**, which are visited by millions of foreign tourists each year. Northern Spain's attractions include the spectacular coasts of the **Basque country**, **Asturias**, and **Galicia**. Catalonia's capital Barcelona, is one of Europe's most visited cities and the seaside resorts of the Costa Brava sand Costa Blanca are popular with foreign tourists. **Valencia** has become increasingly popular and visitors to **Andalusia** can discover the region's Arab heritage in **Seville, Malaga,** and **Granada**. The **Pyrenees** and the **Sierra Nevada** offer winter sports.

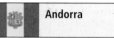

Andorra	
Area:	468 sq. km
Capital city:	Andorra la Vella
Form of government:	
Constitutional Monarchy	
Administrative divisions:	
7 districts	
Population:	
72,000 (153 inhabitants/sq. km)	
Languages:	Catalan (official)
Spanish, French	

The Basque separatist movement, **ETA**, was founded in 1959 to challenge the Franco regime's suppression of Basque nationalism. ETA led a violent campaign for Basque independence causing the deaths of hundreds and leaving thousands injured. After decades of violence, the organisation declared a unilateral ceasefire in 2006, which has since been broken. Spain's last **overseas territories** are Ceuta and Melilla, both enclaves surrounded by Morocco on the north coast of Africa.

Economy

In 2006, GDP was US$ 1.2 trillion – the eighth highest in the world. Spain's economy has experienced a continuous boom in recent years. **Agriculture**, which comprises some four per cent of GDP, forms a significant part of exports, as does Spain's **fishing industry**. Major agricultural production includes vegetables and fruit (including citrus), grain and wine. **La Rioja** in the interior is one of the leading centres of wine production. Spain's **manufacturing industry** is concentrated in the country's northern regions and the capital Madrid. This sector contributes around 30 per cent of the country's gross domestic product. Spain's **service sector** is the most dynamic and largest in the economy and accounts for some 67 per cent of economic activity. **Tourism** is also an important industry in most Spanish regions.

Transport Infrastructure

Spain has an excellent **train and motorway network**. The country has more than 20 international **airports** and is the base for dozens of medium-sized and small private airlines, many catering to tourists. Spain's most important **ports** are Barcelona, Gijon, and Bilbao. Numerous **ferry services** connect the Spanish mainland to the Balearic and Canary Islands.

Tourism

Spain is one of the most popular destinations in the world. Its attractions include the islands of

made a successful transition from dictatorship to constitutional monarchy. The king is now the head of state. Spain's **parliament**, the Cortes, has a lower house and a senate, both elected directly every four years. The senate represents the country's 17 **autonomous regions**. Spain is one of the founding members of the European Economic and Monetary Union.

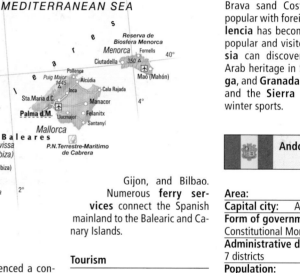

El Escorial: The enormous complex of El Escorial lies north-west of Madrid at the foot of the Sierra de Guadarrama mountain chain. Designed by Juan de Toledo, it was built between 1563 and 1584 during the reign of King Philip II.

In addition to several churches and monasteries, the complex houses Spain's royal mausoleum and the summer residence of the country's monarchs. Its architecture and design inspired many monasteries throughout Europe.

GDP per capita: US$28,000
Currency: 1 euro = 100 cents

Natural Geography

The tiny mountain principality of Andorra covers three mountain valleys in the eastern **Pyrenees** and is surrounded by mountains rising to 3,000 m above sea level. The **Valira River** and other smaller rivers flow through the country's deep valleys. Andora's elevation ranges between 840 m above sea level in the south to 2946 m in the north. Andorra la Vella is Europe highest capital.

Climate

The climate in Andorra varies **depending on elevation**, the mountainous areas being distinctly cooler than the valleys. Andorra is one of the **sunniest regions** in the Pyrenees. Average monthly temperatures in the capital range between 5°C in the winter and 22°C in summer.

Population

Native Andorrans who are closely related to their neighbours in **Catalonia** form only a minority of their country's population

(30 per cent). Most of the country's residents are citizens of **Spain** (50 per cent) or **France** (ten per cent). Around 94 per cent of the population are **Roman Catholics**. Resident foreigners are only eligible for Andorra citizenship after 25 years. The country is a tax haven in which permanent residents pay no direct income tax. This has led to some acrimony in recent years, as French and Spanish citizens have sought refuge in the mountain principality from their respective taxation regimes.

History and Politics

According to a popular legend, Andorra was founded by **Charlemagne**, who granted this tiny

The Alhambra in Granada: former residence of Spain's Moorish rulers.

country independence as a reward for its loyalty to the Holy Roman Empire in his wars against the Moors. Andorra has two official heads of state, the **Bishop of Séo de Urgel** in Spain and the **president of France**, who took over from the French monarchy after the French Revolution. These traditional heads of state now perform purely ceremonial roles. In practice, the country is ruled by its own elected parliament and has a modern constitution. The government is led by a council elected every four years that represents the country's various municipalities.

Economy

In 2006, GDP was around US$ 2 billion. In spite of the introduction of value added tax in 2006, Andorra has extremely low rates of tax, mainly for companies. The economy is dominated, however, by the service sector and invisibles, as befits a tax haven, and these account for 80 per cent of the gross domestic product. **Tourism** is one of the most important industries in the service sector. The country has traditionally been a popular destination for shoppers from neighbouring regions in France and Spain thanks to the tax-free goods on offer, but it also has excellent skiing and other winter sports facilities. Andorra has used the currencies of France and Spain for centuries and when these countries switched to the **euro** it followed suit by adopting the euro as a standard currency.

Transport Infrastructure

Andorra can be easily accessed by road from the **French** and **Spanish** frontiers. The nearest international **airports** are Barcelona in Spain and Toulouse in France.

Tourism

The **landscapes** and tax-free shopping opportunities lure millions of visitors each year. In winter, tourists come for the **skiing**. Andorra's hiking trails guide visitors through the country's mountainous landscapes. The hot springs in **Les Escaldes** health spa are also popular with tourists.

	Portugal

Area:	92,391 sq. km
Capital city:	Lisbon
Form of government:	Republic
Administrative divisions: 18 districts, 2 autonomous regions (Azores and Madeira)	
External territory: Macao (until 1999)	
Population: 10.6 million (115 inhabitants/sq. km)	
Language:	Portuguese
GDP per capita:	US$18,400
Currency:	1 euro = 100 cents

Natural Geography

Portugal is a relatively narrow strip of land on the **Atlantic coast of Iberia** with an average width of only 150 km. The foothills of the **Cantabrian Mountains** rise in the country's north and the mountains of **Serra de Estrela** (highest peak: Torre, 1,991 m) extend through central Portugal. The basin of the **Tagus (Tejo) River**, which flows into the Atlantic near Lisbon, extends south to the hot and arid **Alentejo region**. The **Algarve** is the country's southernmost region.

Climate

The **Mediterranean climate** of Portugal is strongly influenced by the winds and currents of the **Atlantic Ocean**. In summer, temperatures in the interior range between 25°C and 27° C. The winter temperature is mild at around 11°C during the coldest months. Portugal's mountainous regions experience the heaviest rainfall.

Population

People of **Portuguese** descent constitute more than 98 per cent of the country's population. Only a third of the population lives in towns and cities. The largest immigrant communities are from former Portuguese colonies, such as Angola and Brazil, and there are growing numbers of Eastern Europeans. Portugal is an overwhelmingly **Catholic** nation, almost 95 per cent of the population professing Roman Catholicism. The **social and education system**s have been improved dramatically since Portugal joined the EU in the 1986.

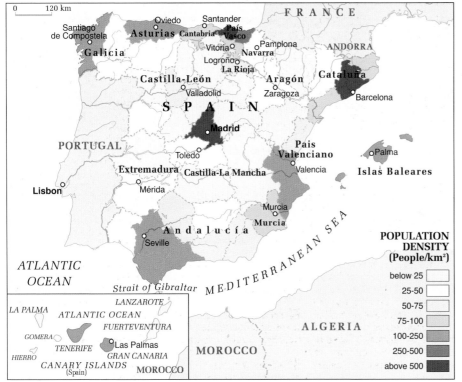

POPULATION DENSITY (People/km²)

below 25	
25-50	
50-75	
75-100	
100-250	
250-500	
above 500	

When the Moors lost their final battle against Spain's King Ferdinand and Queen Isabella in 1492 they left a cultural legacy of beautiful architecture.
*The former mosque of **Cordoba** is one of the most impressive Moorish structures.*

History and Politics

Dominated by Muslim rulers between the eighth and thirteenth centuries, Portugal was able to secure its **independence** from the **Spanish kingdom of Castille** during the fourteenth century. In the fourteenth and fifteenth centuries, Portuguese **explorers** became the first Europeans to circumnavigate the globe. They sailed down the west coast of Africa, rounded the Cape of Good Hope, and built up tradings relationships in Asia and Africa. The **Treaty of Tordesillas** between Spain and Portugal In 1494, granted Portugal a vast territory in the **South America**. By the sixteenth century, however, Great Britain and the Netherlands had surpassed Portugal as a naval power and the country was ruled by **Spain** between 1580 and 1640. **England** captured most Portugal possessions in East Asia in the seventeenth century and Brazil, the country's largest colony, became independent in 1822. In 1911, Portugal became the first European country to depose its **constitutional monarchy.** The new republic suffered from instability and only lasted 15 years before it was toppled by a military coup in 1926. The military **dictatorship** supported Franco's nationalists during the Spanish Civil War but remained neutral during **World War II**. Portugal's remaining **colonies** began to demand greater freedom in the 1960s and after several wars, the country granted independence to its last major colonies in 1976. Portugal's decades of dictatorship, under Salazar, came to an end in 1974. The country experienced dramatic changes in the years following the return to democracy; many companies were nationalised and the wealthiest landowners lost many of their properties. The political situation stabilised after Portugal joined the **European Union** in 1986. The parliament is **unicameral,** the members and the country's **president** being directly elected for five-year terms of office. The president is granted considerable powers under the country's **constitution**.
In addition to the mainland, Portuguese territory includes the **Madeira archipelago** and the **Azores**, a group of islands 1,700 km from the mainland in the Atlantic Ocean.

Economy

In 2006, GDP was US$ 195 billion. The Portuguese economy is struggling to combat limited growth (just 0.3% in 2005) due to a large extent to the disappearance of low-paid jobs. **Agriculture**, which forms three per cent of the overall economy, is experiencing low productivity and is also suffering from structural problems; the main crops are maize, wheat, potatoes, olives, tomatoes and grapes for wine. The **industrial sector**, which processes agricultural products and manufactures

textiles and shoes, is gaining in significance; it makes up 27 per cent of GDP. At 69 per cent of GDP, the **service sector** is the most important area of the country's economy.

Transport Infrastructure

Portugal has a well developed **rail network** and services are especially extensive between the cities and towns on the coast. There is also a good network of **motorways**. The 17-km-long **Vasco da Gama Bridge** in Lisbon, over the River Tagus, built in 1998, is one of the longest bridges in Europe.

Tourism

Portugal is a popular tourist destination for people from all over Europe. The country's 850-km-long coastline with its coastal resorts, as well as the cities of **Lisbon** and **Porto**, are popular destinations, and Northern

Portugal and the **mountainous interior** offer excellent hiking and angling. The **Algarve** is especially popular, attracting visitors with beaches, picturesque fishing villages and rocky coastal landscapes. Portugal's **historic towns**, such as Coimbra, are becoming increasingly popular destinations.

1 The region and province of Alentejo lies between the River Tagus and the Algarve region.

2 Porto was the major port for many centuries; ships left from here for the Americas.

3 Alfama, the oldest district of Lisbon, was spared destruc-

tion during a devastating earthquake in 1755. Lisbon was largely rebuilt by the Marquès de Pombal whose statue dominates the city.

4 Tourism is the leading industry in the Algarve, a warm coastal region with beaches and rocky seaside landscapes.

Germany

*The Bundestag, the lower chamber of Germany's parliament, moved into the renovated **Reichstag** in April, 1999. The spectacular new dome was designed by British architect Norman Foster and has become a landmark of the new Berlin.*

Germany

Area:	357,021 sq. km
Capital city:	Berlin
Form of government:	
Parliamentary Federal Republic	
Administrative divisions:	
16 federal states	
Population: 82.4 million	
(230 inhabitants/sq. km)	
Language:	German
GDP per capita:	US$35,400
Currency:	1 euro = 100 cents

Natural Geography

Germany is bordered by the **North Sea** and the **Baltic Sea** in the north and the **Alps** in the south. The country extends 840 km from north to south and 620 km from east to west. A vast plain of **extensive coastal wetlands** stretches throughout most of north-western Germany, and several archipelagos lie off of Germany's flat North Sea coast. These islands include the **East and North Frisian Islands** as well as a collection of tiny islets called **Haligen**. Germany's Baltic Sea coast has a mixture of **rocky and sandy beaches** as well as

Gustav Stresemann

*Berlin, 10.5.1878,
†Berlin, 3.10.1929

Berlin-born Stresemann held radical national views throughout the World War I but in his later career as German chancellor worked hard for peace in Europe and for reconciliation between Germany and France. He managed to bring some stability to the weak Weimar Republic and was awarded the Nobel Peace Prize in 1926.

numerous **cliffs**. Several large islands, including **Usedom** and **Rügen**, are located along the country's Baltic coast.
Northwestern Germany's landscapes include a mixture of barrens moorlands and fertile heaths, including the famous **Lüneberg Heath**. Northeastern Germany, like the country's northwest, is a largely **flat region**. Mecklenburg's

Lake District contains numerous bodies of water, including Lake Müritz, the second-largest lake in Germany. The southern and central regions of eastern Germany are dominated by the basins of several **major rivers**, including the **Elbe, Havel** and **Oder** Rivers. The plains in the centre of eastern Germany are bounded by several low mountain ranges, including the **Harz Mountains** (Brocken 1142 m) and the hill country of **Weserbergland**. To the east of this region lies the largely flat **Thuringian Basin** as well as the hills and low mountains of the **Thuringian Forest**, the **Ore Mountains** and the **Elbe Sandstone Mountains**. Central Germany is a diverse region including

the **Rhineland,** as well as the rolling hills of the **Sauerland**, the **Westerwald** and the **Taunus Mountains**. The scenic valley of the **Moselle** river is bounded by the **Eifel** and **Hunsruck**, two areas of hills and low mountains. Southwest Germany contains such diverse landscapes as the **Rhine** basin, the **Black Forest** (Feldberg, 1493 m), and the **Swabian Alb**, a

high limestone plateau. **Lake Constance,** lies on the border between Germany, Austria and Switzerland. Germany's largest state by area, **Bavaria,** covers most of southeast Germany. The landscapes of this region include the hills of the **Franconian Alb** and the **Bavarian Forest**. Southern Bavaria is a diverse region with hilly areas, plains, river valleys and the foothills of the **Alps** which extend south to the Austrian border. Germany's highest mountain, the Zugspitze, rises to 2962 m above sea level.

Climate

Germany has a **temperate climate** with significant regional

Berlin old and new: above, Berlin cathedral and the Charlottenburg Castle, below Potsdamer Platz.

variations. In northern Germany the climate is distinctly **maritime and temperate**, while the eastern and southern regions of the country have a **continental climate**. Northern Germany's climate is greatly affected by ocean currents which give the region its **maritime climate** with mild summers and cool, rainy winters. In the coastal north German city

of Hamburg, the average temperature is 4°C in summer and 17°C in winter. In Berlin, the capital, situated inland in eastern Germany, the average summer temperature is 19°C and it is -1° C in winter. The Alpine regions of southern Germany have cold winters, the average winter temperature in Munich is -2°C. The warmest areas in the country are located in the south-west, including the Black Forest and in the Rhine basin.

Population

Ethnic **Germans** form more than 91 per cent of the population. Traditional minority communities with long histories in the country include the Slav **Sorbs** in eastern Germany, the **Danish-speaking minority** in the North German region of Schleswig, the **Frisians** along the North Sea coast and the **Sinti** and **Roma** who lived throughout the country. Traditional minorities form only a small percentage of the country's population and are far less numerous than more recent minority

communities. Former 'guest workers' and their descendants form the vast majority of Germany's minority population. Other recent migrants have arrived in Germany as asylum-seekers and economic migrants. **Turks** and **Kurds** form the largest foreign ethnic group in Germany, at least 2.2 million of them. Other important immigrant communities include **Italians, Greeks, Russians, Poles, Spaniards, Portuguese** and those from the former **Yugoslavia**. The population of Germany is overwhelmingly Christian with almost equal numbers of **Protestants** and **Roman Catholics**. Around a quarter of Germans are not affilitated to a religious community. **Muslims,** the largest non-Christian group in Germany, form around 3.3 per cent of the population and **Jews** around 0.1 per cent of the population. Germany has extensive and well-funded **public welfare, pension and healthcare systems**. Almost one-tenth of the German national GDP is invested in the national healthcare system. The male **life expectancy** of 77 years is relatively high, while **infant mortality** in Germany is among the lowest in the world. Chronically **high levels of unemployment** and slow economic growth have posed a major threat to the standard of public services in Germany since the 1990s, due to the reunification. Germany's **public education system** has one of the world's largest and best funded school and university systems. Education is compulsory between the ages of 6 and 18. Adult illiteracy is estimated at less than one per cent. The 337 **higher education institutions** in Germany include 84 universities, 7 polytechnics, 147 institutes of higher education, as well as colleges of art and theology.

History and Politics

When the Roman Empire collapsed in the fifth century, the area that is now modern Germany was home to various **Germanic, Celtic,** and **Latin-speaking peoples**. At the start of the ninth century, most of Germany was conquered and incorporated into the domain ruled by the Frankish king, **Charlemagne**. The **Holy Roman**

*The fairy tale castle of **Neuschwanstein** was one of those built at the behest of Ludwig II, the so-called 'mad King of Bavaria'. Once a drain on the budget of the Bavarian state, the castle is now one of Germany's most popular attractions.*

Empire, which encompassed mostly German-speaking kingdoms, was founded in 962 and lasted, until the early nineteenth century, although for most of its history, it was little more than a loose collection of kingdoms, constantly plagued by iternecine conflict and rivalries.

Religious divisions played a critical role in the history of Germany in the late Middle Ages. **Martin Luther's** teachings led to the Protestant Reformation and the division of Germany into predominantly Protestant and Catholic regions. During the devastating **Thirty Years' War,** as much as half of Germany's population perished from Plague and violence. The **rivalries and divisions** in the Holy Roman Empire continued for centuries as various kingdoms vied for domination of the empire and Germany. **Prussia**, with its capital Berlin, had emerged as the most powerful German state by the early nineteenth century.

The **Congress of Vienna** in 1814–15 radically changed the political picture of Germany. Hitheto, it had consisted of more than 200 kingdoms, principalities and 'free cities'; these were now replaced by 36 kingdoms which united to form the **German Confederation** led by Austria and Prussia. Rivalry between Austria and Prussia, the most powerful kingdoms in the confederation, weakened the alliance greatly and it finally disbanded in 1866 after the Austro-Prussian War.

Adolf Hitler

*Braunau, 20.4.1889,
†Berlin, 30.4.1945

Born in the Austro-Hungarian Empire near the Bavarian border, Adolf Hitler fought in the German army in World War I. After the war, Hitler was jailed by the Bavarian authorities following a failed coup attempt in Munich. By the late 1920s, he had become leader of the National Socialist (Nazi) party. In 1933 he became Chancellor of Germany. The fascist ideology and fanatical racism of his dictatorship resulted in World War II and the Holocaust.

Under the leadership of the Prussian chancellor von **Bismarck,** most of the German kingdoms joined the Prussian-dominated **North German Confederation**, which was dubbed the **German Empire** in 1870. The Empire experienced a rapid economic transformation and emerged as one of the world's leading **industrialised countries**. Germany, however, became increasingly **isolated** as a result of its aggressive push for international influence and rapid expansion of its military forces.

Germany entered **World War I** in 1914 in alliance with the Austro-Hungarian Empire and the Ottoman Empire. The country's defeat in 1918 led to widespread social unrest and forced Kaiser Wilhelm II into exile. With the ratification of a new **constitution** in 1919, Germany became a republic for the first time. The new state, often known as the **Weimar Republic**, was created during a time of major social and economic instability.

In 1933, there began the darkest chapter in Germany's history. The **National Socialist (Nazi) party** under the leadership of Adolf Hitler seized power and created a brutal totalitarian and racist regime known as the **Third Reich**. Germany's **invasion of Poland** in 1939 marked the beginning of **World War II**, the deadliest war in history. The Nazi regime in Germany initiated a brutal programme of murder and genocide now known as the **Holocaust** that resulted in the death of millions of civilians, including the majority of Europe's Jewish population. Germany was occupied by the four major allied powers following its surrender in 1945. Post-war disputes between the wartime allies led to Germany's division into two states. The capital city, Berlin, was also divided into sectors. In May 1949, the occupation zones of the United States the United Kingdom, and France were united to form the Federal Republic of Germany, a democratic republic covering most of Germany. Five months later, in October 1949, the western portion of the Soviet occupation zone was declared the **German Democratic Republic** (East Germany). The rest of the Soviet occupation zone had been annexed by the Soviet Union or handed over to Poland.

In 1949, **West Germany** comprised ten federal states and about half of Berlin (West Berlin). The smallest states were the two city-states of the North German port cities of Hamburg and Bremen. Bavaria, the largest German

The car is synonymous with Germany. The inventors of the modern automobile in 1886 were Carl Benz in Mannheim and Gottlieb Daimler in Cannstatt. Today, more than 1 million people work in the German automotive industry, producing almost 6 million vehicles, 4 million of which are for export.

The largest car manufacturer in Europe is Volkswagen, providing mid-range models. However, public interest focuses on luxury brands such as Mercedes Benz, BMW and Porsche, attracting legions of visitors at the International Motor Show in Frankfurt, the largest automotive trade exhibition in the world.

Germany

*Pfalzgrafstein Castle near the town Kaub sits on a small island in the river **Rhine**, Germany's longest river. The river is both a vital economic resource for the country and a popular tourist attraction.*

state, was granted the largely ceremonial status of a free state. In addition to these historic entities, several new states were created by the allies, including Schleswig-Holstein, Hesse, North-Rhine Westphalia and Lower Saxony. The original states of Württemberg-Baden, and Württemberg-Hohenzollern merged in 1952 to form the state of Baden-Württemberg. Saarland became the last of the West German states to join the Federal Republic in 1957. Though the residents of West Berlin were granted West German citizenship, the city itself remained officially under the control of the allies until German reunification in 1990 when it became a single city state once

communist countries in Eastern Europe lead to calls for greater political freedom for East Germany. The Berlin Wall, the most visible symbol of Germany's division, was opened on 9 November, 1989. During negotiations the two German states and the four World War II allied powers agreed to the **reunification** of Germany. In 1990, the West German currency, the Deutschmark, was introduced into East Germany. On 3 October, 1990, the German Democratic Republic was dissolved and five new states joined the **Federal Republic of Germany**; Thuringia (16,171 sq. km), Saxony (18,413 sq. km), Saxony-Anhalt (20,446 sq. km), Brandenburg (29,449 sq. km), and Mecklen-

level of government in Germany, the individual states are granted wide-ranging powers and responsibilities by the German constitution. The country's official head of state is the **federal president**. Each president is elected for a five-year term by a federal assembly consisting of members of the Bundestag and delegates from the 16 states. Despite being granted important reserve powers, the post of federal president is a largely representative position. Germany's most powerful political official is the **federal chancellor** who appoints **ministers** and leads the federal government. The highest body in the judicial branch of the German government is the **federal**

accounts for less than one per cent of Germany's economy. Germany imports a large percentage of its food consumption.

The German **industrial sector**, one of the world's most technologically advanced, accounts for 30 per cent of the country's economy. Thanks to high wages and manufacturing costs, however, the German industrial sector concentrates on the production of high-tech and specialised manufacturing. Major **exports** include machinery, the aviation, aerospace and electronics industry, chemicals and motorised vehicles. Germany is the third largest car-maker in the world. In addition, the electronics and food industries make a signifi-

Since reunification, the German federal government has invested large sums of money in improving the infrastructure and economy of eastern Germany.

Transport Infrastructure

Germany's **road network** is one of the world's most extensive with 644,000 km of surfaced roads, 90 per cent of which are asphalted. The **motorway** (autobahn) network is 11,250 km long. With more than 538 cars for every 1,000 inhabitants, Germany also has one of the world's highest levels of **private vehicle ownership**. More than 99 per cent of the country's railways are owned by the national rail com-

---

Dresden has some of Germany's most beautiful historic monuments.

---

more. East Germany joined the **Warsaw Pact** (a group of European communist states) in 1955, while West Germany joined **NATO** in the same year. West Germany became a founding member of the **European Economic Community**, a predecessor of the EU, in 1957. The construction of the **Berlin Wall** in 1961 led to years of tension between the two Germanies. During the 1970s, West German chancellor **Willy Brandt's** *Ostpolitik* (foreign policy concerning the Eastern bloc) greatly improved relations between the two countries, leading to greater cultural exchanges and easier travel conditions. During the 1980s, political **reforms** in the Soviet Union and other

burg-Western Pomerania (23,171 sq. km). The two parts of Berlin were reunited to form one federal state and the city was designated the capital of the reunited republic by the German parliament in 1991. Germany is a democratic federal republic with a **bicameral parliament** in accordance with the country's constitution. Members of the German parliament (**Bundestag**) are elected for four-year terms. The interests of the 16 states are represented at the federal level by the 69 members of the federal council, the **Bundesrat**. Representation in the Bundesrat is based on the population of each state.

Although the federal government is the highest and most powerful

constitutional court. Its panel of judges is appointed by parliament and the federal council for one twelve-year term.

Economy

In 2006, Germany ranked third in the world, with a GDP of US$ 2.9 trillion. Germany is one of world's **wealthiest nations** and has the largest economy in Europe. The country is a leading exporter of agricultural produce, including cereals, fruit, vegetables, potatoes and wine. Meat and dairy products are also important in the **agricultural sector**. Less than three per cent of the German labour force is employed in agriculture and the sector

cant contribution to GDP, while several historically important industries such as shipbuilding, steel production and coal mining have declined dramatically in recent decades.

The **service sector** now accounts for almost two-thirds of economic activity in Germany and is expanding. Germany's banks and insurance companies are among the largest in the world. Germany's retail, media and trade sectors have all expanded in recent decades.

Tourism is an important industry in several regions. Although the country has been reunited, there remains a considerable **economic gap** between eastern German states and the rest of the country.

pany Deutsche Bahn. In total, the **rail network** covers 43,586 km of track, of which 18,192 km are electrified. **High speed trains** connect many of Germany's largest cities. In addition to Deutsche Bahn, there are also a growing number of small train companies operating on regional and commuter routes.

The **navigable waterways** of Germany have a total length of 7,467 km. At least 20 per cent of the all commercial goods transported through Germany are carried on the country's waterways. Major **canals** include the North Sea-Baltic canal in northern Germany and the Rhine-Main-Danube canal. Duisburg in western Germany and Magdeburg in

Hamburg is the location of Germany's busiest **harbour**. The busy port relies on modern equipment and large container ships are swiftly loaded and unloaded.

eastern Germany are the most important **inland ports**. Important **coastal habours** include the cities of Hamburg, Bremen, Rostock, Lübeck and Wilhelmshaven. Germany's **commercial fleet** has 1,645 ships, at least half of which sail under flags of convenience. **Ferry services** connect several ports in northern Germany with ports along the Baltic and North Sea coasts. The extensive network of **airports** includes 150 national and 14 international airports. **Frankfurt am Main** has one of the world's busiest airports and is the leading air transport hub for central Europe. Lufthansa, once a state enterprise, now privatised, is one of the world's leading airlines.

Tourism

Germany has diverse tourist attractions and is visited by millions of foreign tourists each year. Major destinations include the country's larger cities, such as **Munich, Berlin**, and **Cologne**. **Bavaria** is the country's most visited region. The **Bavarian Forest** is popular with hikers. **Alpine lakes**, historic towns and **fine castles**, such as Neuschwanstein, bring large numbers of tourists to the region and the **Bavarian Alps** have excellent tourist facilities. **Baden-Württemberg** has several major tourist destinations including the historic towns of **Freiburg** and **Heidelberg**, the **Black Forest** and **Lake Constance**. Medieval castles, terraced vineyards and picturesque towns line the banks of the **Moselle** and the **Rhine** in western Germany. **Trier**, the oldest city in Germany, has some of the most impressive Roman structures north of the Alps.

Weimar, Dresden and **Leipzig** are major historic cities. The Ore Mountains, stretching through western Saxony along the border to the Czech Republic, are popular with walkers and climbers. **North Rhine-Westphalia** is Germany's most populous state and contains several interesting cities, including **Cologne, Düsseldorf** and **Münster**. **Lower Saxony's** attractions include the **Lüneberg Heath**, the **Harz Mountains** and the **Weserbergland**. Mecklenburg-Western Pomerania is the most sparsely populated state

and, perhaps for this reason, one of the most popular destinations. The seaside resorts and beaches on the islands of **Rügen, Hiddensee**, and **Usedom**, off the East German coast attract their share of visitors. Schleswig-Holstein boasts the beautiful port city of **Lübeck**, a world heritage site. Naturally, the capital, Berlin,

at the historic heart of central Europe attracts many tourists, since it combines important cultural attractions with a scenic landscape of lakes and meadows. Germany is fortunate in having a relatively low population density in the rural districts, so that it has some of the most unspoiled countryside in Europe.

1 The market square of Bremen is surrounded by historic merchants' houses, the St. Petri cathedral, a statue of the city's symbol, the Roland, as well as the famous town hall, one of the finest examples of North German Renaissance architecture.

2 Heidelberg: The Old Bridge crosses the Neckar River into the city's well-preserved old town district.

3 Bavaria: The pilgrimage church of St. Koloman stands near the castle of Hohenschwangau at the foot of the Bavarian Alps.

Switzerland

Local culture and traditions are cherished throughout the cantons of **Switzerland**. Due to their relative isolation from the rest of Europe, the most mountainous regions have been especially successful at preserving many of their unique traditions. But even the lowlands take pride in preserving their regional identities, including local dialects, traditional costumes and festival days.

Switzerland

Area:	41,290 sq. km
Capital city:	Bern
Form of government:	
Democratic Confederation	
Administrative divisions:	
26 cantons	
Population: 7.6 million	
(183 inhabitants/sq. km)	
Languages: German, French, Italian, Rhaeto-Romansh	
GDP per capita:	US$53,000
Currency:	
1 Swiss franc = 100 centimes	

Natural Geography

Switzerland has three major distinct geographical regions; the **Swiss Alps**, the **Swiss Plateau** and the **Jura Mountains**.
The Swiss part of the Jura Mountains stretches over the north-western part of the country, from the French border, and covers around one-tenth of the country's total land area. The Swiss Plateau, a high plain situated at between 400 and 1000 m above sea level, covers the area between the Alps and the Jura Mountains. **Lake Geneva** and **Lake Constance**, the country's two largest lakes, are located between the two mountain chains. The Alps and Alpine valleys account for most of the rest of the land mass. The northern and southern branches of the Swiss Alps are demarcated by the Rhine and Rhône river valleys. Switzerland has many other waterways, including sections of the **Italian lake** district as well as countless beautiful **Alpine lakes**.

Climate

The Swiss climate varies from a **temperate continental** climae throughout most of the country to an **alpine** climate in the most mountainous regions. In general, the summers are warm with plentiful rainfall, while winters are often bitterly cold; the capital, Bern, occasionally experiences temperatures of -30°C. The Swiss canton of the Tessin (Ticino) near the Italian border is the warmest part of the country.

Population

Around 80 per cent of the population are **Swiss** citizens and the remaining 20 per cent, resident foreigners. Switzerland is ethnically linguistically divided into **Swiss-German-**, **French-**, **Italian-**, and **Rhaeto-Romanish-speaking** regions. All four of them have an official status in the country.
Forty per cent of the population identify themselves as **Protestants** and 46 per cent are **Roman Catholics**. The wealth of the country is reflected in its excellent public health care and social services, which account for about one-third of the national budget.
The well-funded Swiss **education system** is largely the responsibility of the individual cantons. Switzerland's **universities** and other institutions of higher education and research have an excellent reputation, especially in the fields of medicine, pharmaceuticals, medicine and molecular biology.

an alliance that would eventually grow into the **Swiss Confederation**. In the centuries that followed, the first three canton's declaration of an 'eternal alliance', many new cantons joined the Confederation.

states, which represents the cantons. Both houses of the parliament have equal powers and both are responsible for electing the federal council, a seven-member commitee which functions as the country's executive branch.

History and Politics

In 1291, the small states of **Uri**, **Scwyz** and **Unterwalden** formed Switzerland became a **federal union** in 1848 and the current constitution has been in effect since 1874. Foreign policy, national defence, postal services, telecommunications, monetary policy, customs as well as energy and transport are all the responsibility of the federal government. Most other areas of governance are regulated by the country's 20 cantons and six half-cantons. One of the most distinctive aspects of Swiss democracy is the role that **referendums and petitions** play in the country's system of government.
Switzerland's **bicameral parliament** consists of a **national council** and the **council of** The parliament appoints a member of the federal council to hold the office of **federal president**. Unlike in most other countries however, the federal president is only the presiding member of the federal council and not the country's head of state.

Economy

In 2006, GDP was some US$ 388 billion, making Switzerland one of the richest countries in the world. **Agriculture**, mainly the production of cereal, fruit, vegetables and wine, makes up just one per cent of the economy. In spite of its inland position and dependence on raw materials,

The Matterhorn (4,478 m) in the Valais Alps in one of Switzerland's most famous mountains.

The United Nations (UN) was formed in 1945 as a successor to League of Nations, an international organisation created in 1920. The League of Nations was headquartered in **Geneva** and today many of the organisation's buildings are occupied by bodies of the UN, including the Palais des Nations.

Switzerland's extremely efficient **industrial sector** (mechanical engineering and precision mechanics, chemicals and pharmaceuticals) makes up 30 per cent of GDP. Banks, insurance and tourism dominate the

trails. The **Bernese Oberland** is one of the most beautiful regions, with its pristine lakes and high mountains. **Valais** and **Grisons** offer **skiing**.

	Liechtenstein
Area:	160 sq. km
Capital city:	Vaduz
Form of government:	
Constitutional Monarchy	
Administrative divisions:	
11 municipalities	
Population: 34,200	
(214 inhabitants/sq. km)	
Language:	German
GDP per capita:	*c.* US$100,000
Currency:	
1 Swiss franc = 100 centimes	

Natural Geography

Situated high above sea level in the **Alps**, the tiny, land-locked country of Liechtenstein is surrounded by **Austria** and **Switzerland**. The **Rhine** forms the country's northern and western borders.

As the fourth smallest state in Europe, Liechtentstein measures only 25 km from north to south and extends only 6 km from east to west. The area along the Rhine is situated almost 1,000 m lower than the western districts around the country's capital, Vaduz.

service sector, which forms the backbone of the Swiss economy with a 69 per cent share of GDP.

Tourism

Because of its **landscapes** and well-preserved **historic cities** Switzerland has long been a popular tourist destination. There are no less than 50,000 km of **hiking**

Transport Infrastructure

The Swiss **rail network** is widely acknowledged to be one of the world's best. Switzerland also has an excellent network of **motorways**, funded largely through petrol taxes. The 17-km-

long **St Gotthard Tunnel** running through the Alps is one of the longest road tunnels in the world. The country has three international **airports** (Basle, Geneva, and Zurich) and several smaller, regional airports.

Zurich: A view of the historic buildings along the Limmat River.

Vienna is a great Baroque city, but modern architecture still has its place here, as demonstrated by the many Art Nouveau buildings, the clean lines of Adolf Loos, and the fantastic houses of Friedensreich Hundertwasser.

Climate

Liechtenstein has a **continental climate**. Temperatures in the capital can reach a low of -15°C in January, and can climb as high as 28°C in July, the warmest month.

Population

One-third of the population of Liechtenstein is **Austrian, Swiss, Italian** or **German**, and the proportion of foreign residents is even higher among the labour force. Almost two-thirds of people working in Liechtenstein come from abroad and many are cross-border commuters from Switzerland and Austria. Like their neighbours in Switzerland, the Liechtensteiner speak an Alemannic dialect of German. **Roman Catholics** constitute 82 per cent of the population, and seven per cent are **Protestant**.

History and Politics

The **principality** was founded in 1719 and became a sovereign state within the **Confederation of the Rhine** in 1806. Liechtenstein maintained a strict policy of neutrality during both World Wars.
Since 1923, the country has shared currency, customs and a postal system with its neighbour **Switzerland**, and Liechtenstein has been represented on the international arena by Switzerland since 1919. The country has been a constitutional hereditary principality with a parliamentary system since 1921. The parliament, known as the **Landtag**, consists of 25 members, elected every four years to advise the Prince.

Economy

No other country in Western Europe has seen such radical changes since World War II. Liechtenstein has moved from a purely agricultural economy to one of the most highly **industrialised** countries – considering the size of the population – in the world. **Agriculture**, mainly animal husbandry and milk production, today represents just one per cent of GDP, estimated at US$ 3.5 billion in 2005. Half of the population works in the **service sector**, while the other half works in **industry** (machine construction, transport and ceramics). The service sector contributes to 50 per cent of GDP and is dominated by trade and the highly developed **banking and trust company** sectors. Other important sources of revenue are postage stamps and **tourism**.

Transport Infrastructure

There is an open border to Switzerland, and the border to Austria is manned by Swiss border guards. Liechtenstein has no airports, the nearest airport is in Zurich, Switzerland.
The railway station at Schaan provides a connection to the international **rail network**. Liechtenstein's 11 districts are connected by a good internal **bus network**.

Tourism

Liechtenstein offers good year-round **skiing and hiking**. The winter sport resorts are **Malbun** (altitude 1,600 m) and **Steg** (altitude 1,300 m). The capital city, **Vaduz**, has many cultural attractions, including an excellent Postal Museum and an impressive royal art collection. Other cultural highlights are Gutenberg Castle in **Balzers**, Church Hill in **Bendern** and the castle ruins in **Schellenberg**.

Austria	
Area:	83,870 sq. km
Capital city:	Vienna
Form of government:	
Federal Republic	
Administrative divisions:	
9 provinces	
Population:	8.2 million
(98 inhabitants/sq. km)	
Language:	German
GDP per capita:	US$39,200
Currency:	
1 euro = 100 cents	

Vienna: the Gothic St. Stephen's Cathedral dominates the city.

Natural Geography

The massive peaks of the **Alps**, including the Grossglockner, which reaches a height of 3,797 m, dominate more than half of Austria's land mass. In the east, there is the **Pannonian basin** and the **Hungarian lowlands**, including the **Neusiedler See**, a large lake.
The **Danube** river flows through Austria for a length of 350 km; the river and its tributaries are flanked by various water-meadows and fields. The mountain regions are covered in dense forest. Wildlife at these high altitudes (ibex, chamois, marmots) are endangered, to the extent that some 24 per cent of the country is protected as a nature reserve.

Climate

Austria has a **continental climate**, but the weather varies depending on **altitude**. Winters are mostly bitterly cold, while summers, particularly in the south and east of the country, can be moderately warm. Average temperatures in the capital, Vienna, are -2°C in January and 20°C at their warmest in July.

Franz Joseph I
*Schönbrunn, 18.8.1830, †Schönbrunn, 21.11.1916
Franz Joseph I of Austria was the last great Emperor of the Habsburg Dynasty. He ascended to the throne in 1848 and reigned for 68 years. During this time, he was forced to deal with several personal and national tragedies. In 1859, Austria lost control of northern Italy, and in 1866 it lost a war against Prussia. The Empire collapsed and was replaced by the Austro-Hungarian Empire. Franz Joseph's son committed suicide, his brother, Emperor Maximilian I of Mexico, was executed and both his wife, Empress Elisabeth, and his heir, Archduke Franz Ferdinand, died violent deaths.

Population

Austria's population consists of over 90 per cent German-speaking **Austrians**, with minority groups of Croatians, Slovenians, Hungarians, Czechs and Rom (gypsies). **Foreigners** make up roughly nine per cent of the population, of whom the largest groups are from the former Yugoslavia (more than 35 per cent), Turks (20 per cent) and Bosnians (ten per cent). The population is 78 per cent Catholic, five per cent **Protestant** and two per cent **Jewish**. Nine per cent of the population have no religious affiliation. Austria's social welfare, pension and health systems are exemplary, but the burden on the state is heavy, with 17 per cent of GDP spent on the **welfare state**. The country has 19 **universities**, of which the most famous is the University of Vienna, founded in 1365.

History and Politics

During the time of the great **tribal wanderings** before the Roman conquest, the area covered by modern-day Austria was at the crossroads of Europe. It was in this region that the **Celts** established the Hallstatt culture, and for the **Romans**, the Danube in

Bruno Kreisky
*Vienna, 22.1.1911, †Vienna, 29.7.1990
Bruno Kreisky was a lawyer and journalist who was active in Austria's Social Democratic Party even during the time of the First Republic. Under Nazi rule of Austria, Kreisky lived in exile in Sweden. After World War II, he entered the diplomatic service, and from 1959 to 1966 he was Foreign Minister. From 1967, he was chairman of the Socialist Party. He became Chancellor in 1970 and introduced far-reaching reforms. He was greatly involved with solving international problems. After the Socialist Party lost its absolute majority in 1983, Kreisky resigned from all offices.

the province of Noricum represented the north-east border of their Empire. From the twelfth century AD, Austria became the heart of the **Habsburg Dynasty**, which at times ruled the German Empire and which had a decisive impact on the history of Europe. The rule of the Habsburgs extended from the Netherlands to Sicily, and after the war against the **Ottoman Empire** in the seventeenth century, it extended ever further eastward. The **Aus-**

*High society in **Vienna** revolves around the Opera Ball and the coffee houses, made famous as a meeting place for the artists, politicians and businessmen from the nineteenth century until today.*

trian **Empire** was founded in 1804, and from 1815 became an ever stronger power in the **German Confederation**. A union with Hungary in 1867 formed the **Dual Monarchy** of the Austro-Hungarian Empire, but this union was often troubled by internal nationality conflicts. The assassination of Archduke Ferdinand, heir to the Emperor, and his wife, in **Sarajevo** in 1914 was one of the triggers for the outbreak of **World War I**. When the war came to an end, the great empire was dismantled and was reduced to a fraction of its former size. A **republic** was founded in 1918, bringing an end to the hierarchical social structure and removing the imperial dynasty. A **constitution** was introduced in 1920, creating a federal state.

In 1938, Austria was annexed by the German **Third Reich**. In 1945, former Austria was divided into four occupied zones until 1955, when an **international treaty** forced the country to declare a policy of 'perpetual neutrality'. The 1920 constitution, which was reintroduced in 1945, provides for a **bicameral parliament**, constituting a lower house, the Nationalrat, and an upper house, the Bundesrat. The nine provinces (Burgenland, Carinthia, Lower Austria, Upper Austria, Salzburg, Styria, Tyrol, Vorarlberg and Vienna) send representatives to these houses. The **President** is directly elected by the people every six years.

Austria has been a member of the **European Union** since 1995, and is one of the founder members of the Economic and Monetary Union. Vienna is the headquarters of several United Nations organisations and of the Organisation for Petroleum Exporting Countries (OPEC).

Economy

In 2006, GDP was US$ 324 billion. Growth was running at 6 per cent. Austria's **agricultural sector** is based on the cultivation of cereal crops, vines and potatoes. It accounts for only 1.5 per cent of GDP but provides 90 per cent of the country's food. Excess production, mainly of milk and dairy foods, is exported.

The most important raw material is **iron ore**. The **manufacturing**

sector accounts for 31 per cent of Gross Domestic Product and the sector employs 30 per cent of the country's labour force. The **Main exports** are machinery, metalworking, electronics, timber and paper, clothing and textiles and vehicles.

Tourism alone accounts for eight per cent of GDP and this makes it one of the most important areas of the **services sector**, which accounts for as much as 67 per cent of GDP.

Transport Infrastructure

Austria is an important **transit country** to and from eastern Europe and has excellent **transport links**. The **road network** extends for 130,000 km, including the **Brenner motorway** across the **Alps** to Italy, one of the best known routes across the numerous alpine passes. Motorways and express roads are toll roads. The **rail network** covers 5,600 km. The entire length of the **Danube** in Austria is navigable, and the most important ports are Linz and Vienna. The country's main **international airport** is **Vienna-Schwechat**.

Tourism

Austria is one of the most popular **tourist destinations** in Europe, especially for its winter sports. The alpine regions of **Salzburg, Tyrol, Carinthia** and **Vorarlberg** provide countless opportunities for **skiing, hiking and climbing**. The numerous alpine lakes in the **Salzkammergut** and **Carinthia** are very popular, as is the Neusiedler See in **Burgenland**, which has an exceptionally mild climate.

Austria also has many important cultural attractions, including the world's oldest salt mine in **Hallstatt**. The country has numerous monasteries, convents and churches which are well worth a visit. **Linz, Klagenfurt** and **Innsbruck** are picturesque old towns, full of character, and the baroque buildings of **Salzburg** are particularly impressive.

The highlight of a trip to Austria is a visit to the capital, **Vienna**, with its rich culture, important theatres, museums and art collections, and the numerous palaces and castles in the historic centre,

which are a lasting monument to the Habsburg Empire. There is plenty of nightlife, and especially the quaint little inns in the Vienna woods, known as **heurigen**, little inns where the Viennese go in summer to drink new Austrian wine and eat onion bread, while being entertained by musicians, dancing and comedians.

1 The stunning Alpine landscape in the province of Tyrol makes it Austria's number one destination for tourists.

2 Salzburg's skyline contains a wealth of classical and Baroque architecture. The city is a centre of classical music, thanks to its most famous son, Mozart.

3 The Schönbrunn Palace in Vienna was built to match the grandeur of the Palace of Versailles. It was designed by the architect Johann Bernhard Fischer von Erlach, and construction work commenced in the 17th century. It was later rebuilt by the Empress Maria Theresa of Austria.

The annual Vienna Opera Ball, which takes place in the city at carnival time, is the society event of the year. More than 4,000 people attend the 'ball of balls' each year, half visiting from other countries. The history of the Opera Ball began with dance events organised by members of the court opera at

the time of the Congress of Vienna. The ball in its current form has been held since 1935. One hundred and eighty 'debutant' couples ceremonially enter the Vienna State Opera and lead off the dance. Then, on the call of 'Alles Walzer' (all waltz), the dance floor is opened up to the guests.

Italy

Italy	
Area:	301,230 sq. km
Capital city:	Rome
Form of government:	Republic
Administrative divisions:	
20 regions; 103 provinces	
Population: 58.1 million	
(193 inhabitants/sq. km)	
Language:	Italian
GDP per capita:	US$31,800
Currency:	1 Euro = 100 cents

Natural Geography

The **Alps** form the northern border of this predominantly mountainous country with the Ortler as the highest peak (3899 m). The **Apennines** are joined in the south to the long **Po Valley**. In the north, the Apennines surround the hilly landscape of **Tuscany** and the valley of Umbria.

The Apennines split the Italian 'boot' down the centre for about 1100 km to the extreme sout, with one side facing the **Adriatic Sea** and the other facing the **Tyrrhenian Sea**.

The western coastal plains with their numerous bays show clear traces of volcanic activity (**Vesuvius, Etna, Stromboli**). The **Adriatic Coast**, on the other hand, is rather flat. In addition to the larger islands of **Sardinia** and **Sicily** in the southern Mediterranean. Other islands off the coast such as **Ischia, Elba** and **Capri** also belong to the national territory.

Climate

With the exception of the area encompassing the high mountains of the **Alpine region**, the climate is predominantly **Mediterranean** with **dry, hot summers** and **mild, rainy winters**, particularly in the southern regions – although in the south occasional snow showers are also possible in a bad winter. The average temperatures over the whole country are 4–8°C in January and 25–28°C in July.

region and in the Aosta Valley **French** is spoken. **Friulian** and other **local dialects**, which often owe their individuality to Italy's eventful history, are also spoken. Well over 90 per cent of theItalian population are **Roman Catholic**.

History and Politics

From the fourth century BC until the mid-fourth century AD, the **Roman Empire** was the dominant power in Europe. After the decline of the Roman Empire, Rome – and thus Italy – was the centre of the **Papacy**. The political influence and constant conflicts between the Popes and European sovereigns significantly determined the history of the Middle Ages in Europe.

Cultural and political centres in the late Middle Ages became independent **city republics** such as **Venice** and **Milan**. From the sixteenth to the nineteenth century, the regions of today's Italy – which had lost much of their influence – were

fication was finally achieved and in 1861 Victor Emmanuel II ascended the Italian throne as the first **King**.

Domestic crises after World War I led in 1922 to a **Fascist** coup and,18 years later, to the accession of the country to the Axis pact. After the fall of **Mussolini** in 1943 and the abdication of the king in 1946, Italy was proclaimed a **republic**. The bicameral parliament consists of the **House of Representatives**, whose members stand for election every five years, and the **Senate**, which consists of about 315 directly elected members and a further ten senators who are elected for life. Both chambers have equal rights and political decisions are made jointly. The **President** of the Republic, who is elected for seven years, has far-reaching power.

In the mid-1990s, numerous cases of **corruption** were uncovered which led to extensive restructuring of the political landscape.

reflects the long period during which Italy's economy was marked by **great state influence**. Just under three per cent of the country's GDP derives from **agriculture** – which is highly modernised in the north, and organised into smallholdings in the south – with the cultivation of fruits, vegetables, wine and grains. Italy is Europe's largest **rice producer**. In order to meet the demand for the production of **pasta**, Italy imports wheat from North and South America. Industry contributes a total of 29 per cent to the GDP. As Italy has few raw materials, mining has traditionally made no important contribution to GDP. Nevertheless, the main industrial emphasis of the Italian economy is in **metal work**. In addition to motor **vehicles**, chemicals, textiles and clothing are among the main exports. **Tourism** is one of the most important economic sectors and makes a large contribution to the **service sector** (68 per cent of GDP). The standard of Italy's tourist facilities and services is

Benito Mussolini

*Predappio, 29.7.1883,
†Como, 28.4.1945

Mussolini was originally a socialist, but in 1919 he founded the radical right-wing party Fasci di Combattimento. In October 1922, he marched on Rome and took power. Over a three-year period, he got rid of all his opponents and in 1925 he established a single-party rule that Hitler later copied to establish his regime in Germany. Mussolini aimed at a Mediterranean kingdom ruled by Italy, and this dream was only abandoned after the first defeats of the German Army in World War II. In 1943, he was deposed and arrested by the Fascist Grand Council. He was rescued by German troops and established the Republic of Saló, but he was a puppet of his liberators. At the end of the war, he fled to Switzerland, but was executed by Italian Communist Partisans.

The Pantheon in Rome was initially a Roman temple, but was later used as a church and mausoleum.

Sandro Pertini

*Stella (Savona), 25.9.1896,
†Rom, 24.2.1990

Pertini joined the Italian United Socialist Party at an early age. As a vocal opponent of Mussolini, he was imprisoned and exiled. When released in 1943, he founded the Italian Socialist Party with Pietro Nenni and Giuseppe Saragat, and organised the resistance against the Fascist regime and German occupation. He was a senator from 1948 to 1953 and a Deputy from 1953 to 1978. From 1968 to 1976, he was president of the Italian Chamber of Deputies, and was President of the Italian Republic from 1978 to 1985.

Population

As many as 95 per cent of the population speak **Italian** as their mother tongue, and five per cent speak minority languages. **German** is widely spoken in the Trentino-South Tyrol

fought over by all the European powers and fell alternately under **Spanish, Austrian and French rule**. Military opposition to foreign power is inseparably linked with the name of the hero of Italian emancipation, Giuseppe **Garibaldi**. Uni-

Economy

In 2006, GDP was US$ 1.8 trillion, ranking seventh in the world. The large **gap** between the industrialised **north** and the predominantly rural **south**, in which high unemployment predominates,

corresponding high. The country was a founder member of the **European Common Market** (EC).

Transport Infrastructure

The **road network** stretches over 317,000 km; major roads

*The Spanish Steps in **Rome**: the stairway to the Trinità dei Monti, constructed by Alessandro Specchi and Francesco de Sanctis from 1723 to 1726.*

sportsmen. Here, nature-lovers find hiking routes and beautiful natural landscapes. The best known centres are **Meran** and **Cortina d'Ampezzo**.

The national parks in the **Abruzzi** and the Pollino National Park in **Calabria** are among the many **national parks** in Italy – a country in which eight per cent of the land mass is protected.

Bathing and beach holidays are spent on the western **Mediterranean coasts**, the islands and on the **Adriatic**. The resorts are on the Adriatic coast and in the town of **Rimini** and along the world famous **Ligurian** coast. In addition, the islands of **Elba**, **Ischia**, **Capri** and **Sardinia** are popular holiday destinations. Italy has always been the classic holiday destination for culture lovers: the country is steeped in history from Antiquity to recent times. The most popular attractions are the 'eternal city' of **Rome** which, in addition to impressive buildings from pre-Christian times, such as the Roman Forum and the Colosseum has countless churches, and Renaissance and baroque architectural masterpieces.

are on the whole, subject to a toll charge. In spite of the extensive **rail network** almost 20,000 km long, more than two thirds of all goods are transported by road.

The **inland navigation** system is operated on routes with a length of approximately 2,400 km. **Coastal shipping** is of great importance – a regular ferry service is maintained to the large islands. The largest **ports** in the country are Genoa, Venice, Naples and Leghorn (Livorno). Italy has over 96 **airports**, including eight international airports.

Tourism

Italy is one of the most popular holiday destinations in Europe, not only because of its famous **cuisine** or the pleasant year-round **climate**. The eastern **Alps**, for example the **South Tyrol** and the **Dolomites**, the about the western Alps – the rather remote **Val d'Aosta** – as well as many areas in the Apennines offer numerous opportunities for mountain climbers and winter

The centres of Renaissance art are found in **Tuscany**, especially in the cities **Florence**, **Sienna** and **Pisa**.

Venice, the city built on a lagoon – and sinking fast – is considered the most romantic. The cities of **Milan** and **Naples** also attract countless tourists. Southern Italy is not just for sunbathing, it also has archeological remains, especially in the **Naples** area and in **Sicily**.

Although in terms of GDP the agricultural industry is comparatively insignificant for Italy, it plays an important part in the appearance of the landscape. Around 60 per cent of the land area is used for agricultural purposes, principally by over 2 million small farms, which grow mainly grain and potatoes.

as well as fruit and vegetables. These pictures show a Piedmont wine grower during the harvest, and Calabrian farmers sorting red onions, and harvesting olives and tomatoes, staples of Italian cuisine.

Vatican City, San Marino

A view of San Gimignano: as a symbol of power and wealth, influential families in the medieval town of San Gimignano built high towers to be used as living space and fortresses. The living space provided by these towers meant that the town walls did not need to be extended. Only 13 of the 77 original towers remain today. Similar towers were once common in Tuscany, but San Gimignano provides the best preserved example.

Vatican City

Area:	0.44 sq. km
Capital city:	Vatican City
Form of government:	
Elective Monarchy	
Population: 820	
(1,860 inhabitants/sq. km)	
Languages:	Italian, Latin
Currency: 1 euro =	
100 cents and own currency	

Natural Geography

The smallest sovereign state in the world is surrounded by the Italian capital, **Rome**. The national territory is disjointed: next to the area about St Peter's Basilica, the Apostolic Palace and the well-tended gardens, there are some **extraterritorial churches** and palaces in Rome as well as the Pope's summer residence at **Castelgandolfo**, which is considered to be part of the Vatican.

Pope John Paul II

born Karol Woityla
*Wadowice, 18.5.1920,
†Rome, 2.4.2005

In 1978, the former Archbishop of Cracow became the first non-Italian Pope since Hadrian VI. He was the most-travelled Pope in history and supported the opposition in the countries of the Soviet bloc, particularly in his native country Poland. He was severely injured in an assassination attempt in 1981 in St Peter's Square.

Climate

Has a **Mediterranean climate**: in summer, the average temperature is 25°C, and in winter 7°C.

Population

The Vatican has about 450 citizens, who do not pay any taxes. There are also about 400 residents who have no civil rights as well as approximately 3000 employees and 90 Swiss guards, who enjoy civil rights during their period of their service. The fact that all the residents of the city are **Roman Catholics**, goes without saying.

History and Politics

The Vatican City dates back to the **Donation of Pippin** (Rome, Ravenna, the Adriatic coast), which was made to the Roman Catholic church by the French King Pippin in 754. In European history, the Vatican was always a power base to be taken seriously. In 1929, the Lateran Treaties, made with the Italian state, promised the Vatican City its sovereignty. Today, the political and religious **centres of the Catholic church** are here. The Apostolic Constitution of 1968 was amended for the first time in 1997. The **College of Cardinals** is the highest governing body, whose members – who come from over 60 states – elect the **Pope** from their midst and afterwards function as his advisers. The actual executives of the small country, and at the same time of the whole of the Roman Catholic church throughout the world, are the various departments of the **Roman Curia**, which consist of the Secretariat of State, the Congregations, tribunals, senior officials and other offices; these can be compared to the ministries of a secular government. The pope of the day, who is elected for a lifetime, is their president.

Economy

The Vatican is mainly financed from the running of its enormous **treasury** and the so-called **Peter's pence**, which is raised worldwide. Other sources of income are the contributions from the dioceses spread throughout the world, as well as the returns from **tourism** and the sale of postage stamps (income in 2004: about 200 million Euros). Moreover, the Vatican mints its own coins, which are valid as currency in addition to the euro; The Vatican publishes its own newspaper and operates a radio station, which broadcasts in all the major languages of the world. It also has a news agency.

Tourism

The majority of visitors are **pilgrims**. **St Peter's Basilica** and **St Peter's Square**, the Vatican museums and the galleries with their immense **art treasures**, the **Stanze** containing Raphael's frescoes as well as the **Sistine Chapel** with its world famous frescoes by Michelangelo are the main attractions. The Vatican library contains one of the world's greatest collections of ancient manuscripts and early books and has great attraction for scholars.

Natural Geography

The smallest republic in Europe lies between the Italian regions of **Emilia-Romagna** and **Marche**. San Marino is cut in two by the mountain ridge of **Mount Titano** (739 m) which is the location of the ancient capital. The mjor rivers are the **Ausa** in the north and the **Marano** in the south east.

Climate

As in central Italy, the **mild climate** has extremes of temperature of +30°C to -2°C.

Population

Eighty-seven per cent of the population are **Sammarinese**, 13 per cent being **Italian**. The inhabitants are almost without exception **Roman Catholics**.

History and Politics

The **constitution** (the Arengo) of San Marino dates from 1600 but

In spring, the charming green hills of Tuscany are covered in a blanket of red poppies.

San Marino

Area:	61.2 sq. km
Capital city:	San Marino
Form of government:	
Republic	
Administrative divisions:	
6 Castelli	
(municipalities)	
Population: 29,600	
(485 inhabitants/sq. km)	
Languages: Italian (official),	
Emiliano-Romagnolo	
GDP per capita:	US$22,000
Currency: 1 euro = 100 cents	

was revised in 1939 and 1971. San Marino is among the **oldest republics** in the world. Inhabited for the first time about 600, today's republic was a **protectorate**, ruled by a count and later a duke, between the ninth and the thirteenth centuries. In 1400, it became an independent state under the protection of the **Dukes of Urbino**. The republic, which was neutral in World War II, was occupied by Germany and then by allied troops in 1944. The post-war years were marked by fundamental agricultural reform and largely state control of politics. In 1968, Italy's status as the protecting power ended. San Marino joined the **Council of Europe** in 1988 and the United Nations four years later. This brought San Marino into the European as well as the world politics.

The **parliament** is newly elected every five years; citizens of San Marino who live abroad are also entitled to vote. Two so-called 'captains-regent', who are elected by parliament for a period of office of every six months function as **head of state**.

Economy

In 2005, GDP was around US$ 650 million. The sale of San Marino **stamps and coins** forms the most significant economic sector for this small country, comprising more than 10 per cent of the total economic turnover, along with a significant **tourist industry**. Cereal crops and grapes for wine are cultivated, and cheese and olive oil are produced. Industrial production and the craft industry are gaining in importance.

Transport Infrastructure

San Marino has international connections via the **railway station** and **airport** of the seaside resort of Rimini in Italy.

Tourism

The centre of tourism is the **capital**, San Marino, with its historic fortifications, government buildings and famous basilica.

*In the mid-sixteenth century, Crusaders successfully defended the island of **Malta** against the advancing Turkish armies. After the retreat of the Muslims, the foundation stone for a new capital was laid on 28 March 1566.*

*The city was planned by Jean de la Valette and Francesco Laparelli. The result was the city of **Valetta** on the Sciberras peninsula, now the capital, with its grid-like network of streets and a surrounding defensive wall.*

Malta

Area:	316 sq. km
Capital city:	Valletta
Form of government:	Republic

Administrative divisions:
6 districts

Population:
400,000 (1,271 inhabitants/sq. km)

Languages:	Maltese, English
GDP per capita:	US$16,000

Currency:
1 Maltese lira = 100 cents

Natural Geography

The **island republic in the Mediterranean** consists of the main island of **Malta** and the neighbouring islands of **Gozo** and **Comino**. The main island consists of a limestone plateau, which has neither mountains nor rivers. There are remains of land bridges which existed millions of years ago linking Malta to Italy and north Africa. The country's forests fell victim to ship-building in Antiquity.

Climate

A **Mediterranean climate** prevails with mild air and water temperatures all year round. In Valletta, the average temperature in January is 13°C, rising to 26°C in July.

Population

As many as 96 per cent of the population are **Maltese**; there is also a small **British community**. Malta is among the most densely populated countries in the world. Divorce is prohibited by law in this almost exclusively **Roman Catholic** country.

History and Politics

The areas of **Megalithic Culture** in Gantija and Mnajdra testify to the neolithic settlements that once flourished in the islands. The surrounding naval powers of **Phoenicia**, **Carthage** and **Rome** in pre-Christian times and later the **Saracens** and **Normans** invaded the island but also passed on their skills to the inhabitants over the centuries. As a possession of the knights of the **Order of St John of Jerusalem** (**Knights Hospital-**

iers), whose Grand Master founded the capital, Valetta, between 1530 and 1798, Malta became a bastion of the western world against the **Turks**. In 1800, the islands were conquered by the British and remained a **British colony** until 1964. In 1974, Malta became an independent **Republic**. In 2004, accession to the **European Union** followed.

Economy

In 2006, GDP was US$ 6.4 billion. **Agricultural production** is too small for self-sufficiency. Wheat, barley, potatoes, tomatoes, onions, grapes, citrus fruits and figs are cultivated (two per cent of GDP), mainly with the help of artificial irrigation. About a quarter of the GDP derives from shoes, clothing, food and metal industries. Malta has important **harbour and shipyard repair facilities**. The most important economic sector is **tourism**.

Transport Infrastructure

Valetta has an international **airport**. Additionally there are **regular passenger ship connections** between Italy and most of the rest of Europe. A busy **ferry service** shuttles between the islands, which have a dense, fully developed **road network**.

Tourism

The centre of tourism is the **capital city**, Valetta, with its old part of the town, Fort St Elmo, palaces and churches. The medieval old town of **Medina** attracts many visitors. **Gozo**, on the other hand, in comparison to Malta. is largely untouched. Megalithic temples and charming fishing villages are found between remote bathing bays. **Como** which is only some 2,75 sq. km in area, is a real paradise for divers with its rocky bays.

1 St Mark's Square contains the Doge's Palace, St Mark's Campanile, St Mark's Basilica and the Biblioteca Marciana, and is the grand entrance to the city of Venice.

2 The Amalfi coast surrounding Naples is one of the most beautiful in the world.

3 Preserved by the ash falling from the eruption of Mount Vesuvius in 79 AD, Pompeii gives a fascinating insight into the lives of the Ancient Romans.

4 Baroque architect Gianlorenzo Bernini surrounded the square in front of St Peter's in Rome with grand colonnades.

Gdansk: *The port was an autonomous city from the sixteenth to the eighteenth century, bringing great prosperity to the nation. This trading post on the Baltic coast enjoyed a higher turnover than the famous British East India Company. Imposing buildings designed by Flemish and Dutch architects were symbols for the citizens of Gdansk (Danzig) of their wealth, prosperity and education.*

Poland

Area:	312,685 sq. km
Capital city:	Warsaw
Form of Government:	Republic
Administrative divisions: 49 provinces	
Population: 38.5 million (123 inhabitants/sq. km)	
Language:	Polish
GDP per capita:	US$8,900
Currency: 1 zloty = 100 groszy	

Natural Geography

The **Baltic Sea** forms the northern border of Poland. The country consists predominantly of lowlands divided by glacial valleys. The **Baltic Ridge** with the **Great Masurian Lakes** and the **Pomeranian Lakelands** are linked in the south with the **Polish mountains** which are actually rolling hills. They are separated from the **Sudeten** range and the **Carpathians** (Rysy: 2,499 m) by the Upper Silesian Basin on the southern border.

Climate

The **temperate climate** assumes a continental character towards the south. The summers are mild and rainy, the winters severe and very snowy. **Average temperatures** in Warsaw are 4°C in January and 19°C in July.

Population

Almost 98 per cent of the population is **Polish**. There are a few **minority** communities of Ukrainian, Belarusians, Roma and Sinti (gypsies). Germans are the largest minority at 1.3 per cent, of the population. In terms of religious affiliation, 95 per cent of the Polish population is Roman Catholic; there are also Eastern Orthodox and a small group of Protestants.

History and Politics

Polish tribes settled the territory in the ninth century. In the Middle Ages and Renaissance period, Poland was among Europe's great powers, but it was divided three times between 1772, 1793 and 1795 among Prussia, Austria and Russia. Poland did not regain its independence until 1918. The 1921 **constitution** formed the basis for a **parliamentary democracy**, whose timid beginnings came to an abrupt end with the German invasion in 1939. Poland's current borders were established in 1945, when it lost part of its eastern lands to the Soviet Union and extended its western borders up to the **Oder-Neisse line**. This Soviet satellite state was repeatedly unsettled by unrest and rebellion, which culminated in the major strike of 1980 led by the union leader **Lech Walesa**. The freedoms achieved were abolished soon afterwards and **martial law** was imposed. In 1989, Poland threw off the communist yoke and became a democratic republic, creating a **bicameral legislature**, consisting of the Sejm (parliament) and the Senate. Parliament elects the prime minister, while the president is elected directly. Poland has been a **member of NATO since 1999**. A further milestone was the acceptance of Poland into the European Union in 2004.

Economy

Since democratisation and the radical economic reforms which followed entry to the EU, Poland has experienced something of an **economic miracle**. In 2006, GDP was around US$ 341 billion, and in recent years Poland has even achieved double-digit rates of growth. While the industrial sector has fallen to one-third of GDP, today the service sector dominates Poland's economy at 64 per cent. The leading European producer of organic products, agriculture accounts for just three per cent of GDP. Small farmers own 70 per cent of the farmland on which potatoes, sugar beet, grains, rapeseed, linseed, hops and fruit are grown. Livestock also makes an important economic contribution, pork products being a major export. Although the country's coal, copper and sulphur deposits are considerable, the **mining industry** is still state-owned and is a heavy burden on the budget. **Foreign investment** in Polish industry has reached record levels, and 70 per cent of all employed Poles work in the largely privatised businesses. Polish industrial **exports** consist of metalwork, building materials, electrical items and vehicles. The service sector contributes 64 per cent to the GDP.

Transport Infrastructure

Poland has a well developed infrastructure. The **railway network** covers 24,313 km, of which about 9,000 km of track is electrified. The **road network** is more than 375,000 km long, and includes 550 km of motorways. There is **inland shipping** on the Vistula, Oder and Neisse rivers for 3,812 km. The major sea ports are Gdansk (formerly Danzig), Gdynia and Szczecin. There are 68 **airports**, including three international – Warsaw, Cracow and Gdansk.

Tourism

In addition to the **the Baltic Sea**, the **Great Masurian Lakes** and the mountainous region of the **High Tatras**, south of **Cracow**, **Warsaw** and **Wroclaw** as well as the former free state of **Gdansk** are popular tourist destinations. The **Slowinski national park** on the Pomeranian Lakelands and **Bialowieza** national park on Poland's border with Belarus attract hikers. Czestochowa is a site of pilgrimage to the shrine of the Black Madonna. Cracow, the former capital has a magnificent citadel, the Wawel, in which the kings were crowned and many baroque monuments, evidence of its former prosperity. It is also famous for its proximity to the Auschwitz concentration camp, now preserved as a memorial, which attracts visitors.

Czech Republic

Area:	78,866 sq. km
Capital city:	Prague
Form of government:	Republic
Administrative divisions: 72 regions	
Population: 10.2 million (130 inhabitants/sq. km)	
Languages: Czech (official), Slovak	
GDP per capita: US$13,900	
Currency: 1 Czech koruna = 100 haleru	

Natural Geography

The hilly landscape of the heartland, the densely populated **Bohemian Basin**, is surrounded by **the Ore mountains, the Bohemian Forest** and the **Sudetenland**. Rolling hills are also characteristic of the **Moravian Basin** in the east of the country. the highest peak is the **Snezka** (1,602 m). The most important rivers are the **Elbe** and **Vltava**.

Climate

The Czech climate is **continental** with warm summers and cold, damp winters. The average temperature in the capital, Prague, is 20°C in summer and freezing point in winter.

Horse-drawn carriages in the square of Warsaw's old town.

KATOWICE'S INDUSTRIAL CONURBATION IN SILESIA

Mineral
- Fossil coal
- Lead and zinc
- Rock salt

Industry
- Iron metallurgy and metallurgy
- Mechanics industry
- Electronics and electrotechnics
- Chemicals
- Urban and industrial areas

Zawiercie
Tarnowskie Góry
Bytom
Dabrowa Górnicza
Chorzów
Gliwice
Ruda Śląska
Sosnowiec
Katowice
Jaworzno
Chrzanow
Rybnik
Tychy
Oświecim
Zory
Pszczyna
Wodzisław Śląski
Jastrzebie-Zdrój
Jez Goczalkowickie
Wisla
Bielsko-Biała
RUSSIAN FED.
POLAND
CZECH REP.
0   10 km

Lech Walesa

*Popowo, 29.9.1943

Lech Walesa was an electrician who assumed leadership of the strike committee of the Lenin shipyard in Gdansk. He became a leading Polish opposition figure and successfully fought for legal, free trade unions in Poland. In 1980, he became chairman of the Solidarity trade union. He was awarded the Nobel Peace Prize in 1983, and served as President of Poland (1990–95).

Population

Of the population 95 per cent is **Czech**, three per cent **Slovak**, 0.6 per cent **Polish** and 0.5 per cent **German**. Other minorities are **Sinti and Roma** (gypsies) and **Hungarian**. Around 40 per cent of the Czech population do not belong to a religious denomination; 39.2 per cent are Roman Catholic, 4.6 per cent are Protestants, three per cent Orthodox and a further 13.4 per cent belong to other religions. The excellent social system, a legacy from Communist times, is undergoing a radical change.

History and Politics

The ninth century saw the rise of the **Great Moravian Empire**. Eventually, Bohemian became part of the German-dominated Holy Roman Emperor. After the **Hussite rebellion** in the early fifteenth century, and subsequent Protestant kings, the country was conquered by the Habsburgs and absorbed into the Austro-Hungarian empire. The first Czechoslovak republic was founded in 1918 but ended with the German invasion that triggered **World War II**. In 1948, the **Czechoslovak People's Republic** arose, known as the Socialist Republic from 1961, became Communist. The 1968 uprising, known as the '**Prague Spring**' was quashed by Soviet troops. The Czech Republic has been an independent **Republic**, since 1 January 1993, after the split of Czechoslovakia into two states. The Czech Republic has a **bicameral legislature**. One third of the **Senate** is elected every two years, while members of parliament are elected every four years. In 1999, the Czech Republic joined **NATO**, and in 2004, it joined the European Union.

Edvard Benes

*Kozlány, 28.5.1884,
†Sezimovo Ustí, 3.9.1948

Edvard Benes was an advocate of Czechoslovak independence from Austro-Hungary. Foreign Minister of Czechoslovakia from 1918 to 1935, and Prime Minister from 1921 to 1922, he became president in 1935, but resigned in 1938. During World War II, he led the government-in-exile, and became president again from 1945 to 1948.

Alexander Dubček

*Uhronec, 27.11.1921,
†Prague, 7.11.1992

First secretary of the Central Committee of the Communist Party of Czechoslovakia, he attempted to reform the Communist regime during the famous Prague Spring. His aim was 'Communism with a human face'. This led in 1968 to an invasion by Warsaw Pact troops. After 1989, he became speaker of the Federal Assembly of Czechoslovakia.

Economy

Since the **privatisation** of the economy most sectors have prospered. In 2006, GDP was US$ 142 billion. Agriculture provides potatoes, grains, sugar beet and hops and contributes four per cent to the GDP. There is mining of brown coal, hard coal, iron, silver, copper, uranium and lead; manufactured goods include metal, glass, textiles and paper and contributes 39 per cent of the GDP. Of the labour force, 44 per cent work in the service sector, which contributes 55 per cent of the GDP.

Czech Republic, Slovakia, Hungary

The historic heart of **Prague** is located on a bend on the Vltava River. The city is now a UNESCO world heritage site. The area of the city known as the Malá Strana (literally the 'small quarter') has many medieval buildings, dominated by Prague Castle. Many of the city's buildings are of great artistic, cultural and historical interest, including St Vitus Cathedral, located within Prague Castle, and the Old Town and the Nove Mesto, the 'new' town'.

Transport Infrastructure

The **railway network** covers over 9,440 km, of which 2,688 km is electrified. The **road network** is 55,000 km long but only partially surfaced. The international **airport** is in Prague.

Tourism

Tourist centres include the **Bohemian spas** of Karlovy Vary (Carlsbad) and Marianske Lazne (Marienbad), the Bohemian forests and the **Giant Mountains**. The historic cities are **Prague** and **Brno**.

Particularly important regions are the outer arch of the **White Carpathians** and the **West Beskids**, the central zone of the Lesser Carpathians, the Small and High **Tatras** as well the southern volcanic peripheral zone. The small **Danube Lowlands** form the gateway to its Hungarian neighbour.

Climate

The **continental climate** produces cold winters and hot summers. The average temperatures in Bratislava are -3°C in January and 20°C in July.

1918, Slovakia gained **autonomy status** within the framework of the Munich Agreement. During World War II, Slovakia was a Nazi puppet state whose dictator was a Catholic bishop, Father Tiso. In 1948, Slovakia became part of the **Czechoslovak Socialist Republic** following the Communist takeover of Czechoslovakia. In 1969, it became part of the Federation of the Czech and Slovak Republic. In 1989, successful **attempts at reform**, which weakened the leadership of the Communist Party, followed the failure of the reform policy of the 1968 'Prague Spring'. Following the

Four per cent of GDP derives from **agriculture**, and 31 per cent from industry. **Heavy industry** is dominant, including iron, steel and non-ferrous metal processing and heavy machinery. Other exports are chemicals, rubber, man-made fibres and pharmaceuticals, contributing 31 per cent of the GDP. The **service sector** (65 per cent) is increasing in importance.

Transport Infrastructure

The **railway network** extends over 3,665 km, of which about one third is electrified. The **road network**, with 215 km of motor-

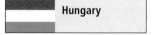
Area:	93,030 sq. km
Capital city:	Budapest
Form of government:	
Parliamentary Republic	
Administrative divisions:	
20 regions	
Population:	
10 million	
(107 inhabitants/sq. km)	
Language:	
Hungarian	
GDP per capita: US$11,200	
Currency:	
1 forint = 100 filler	

Václav Havel

*Prague, 5.10.1936

This famous Czech dramatist wrote several books as well as plays in the 'Theatre of the Absurd' style. He was spokesman for the Czechoslovak opposition movement 'Charter 77' and was imprisoned several times. After the collapse of Communism in 1989, he was elected President of Czechoslovakia. He resigned in 1992, but when Czechoslovakia split in January 1993, Havel became the first President of the Czech Republic. He retired in February 2003, after exactly ten years as President.

Late baroque buildings from the reign of Maria Theresa of Austria in the centre of Bratislava.

Imre Nagy

*Kaposvár, 7.6.1896, †16.6.1958

Imre Nagy was a locksmith by trade. He joined the revolutionary Hungarian workers' movement and had to emigrate to the Soviet Union in 1929. After the end of the German occupation of Hungary, he became Minister for Agriculture in 1944. He became Hungarian Prime Minister in 1953, but was forced to resign by Stalinists in 1955. He returned to office in 1956 and led great reforms. After some initial hesitation, he aligned himself with the uprising against the USSR, which was brutally suppressed. He was executed in 1958.

Area:	48,845 sq. km
Capital city:	Bratislava
Form of government:	Republic
Population: 5.4 million	
(112 inhabitants/sq. km)	
Languages: Slovak (official),	
Hungarian, Czech	
GDP per capita:	US$10,200
Currency:	
1 Slovak koruna = 100 halierov	

Natural Geography

Slovakia lies in the mountain system of the **West Carpathians** and consists of numerous valleys between the mountain ranges.

Population

Of the population, 86 per cent are **Slovak** and 11 per cent **Hungarian**; 1.5 per cent are **Sinti and the Roma** (gypsies). There are other minorities. In terms of religion, 61 per cent of Slovaks are Roman Catholic, 8.4 per cent Protestants and less than ten per cent non-denominational.

History and Politics

The area has been inhabited by **Slavs** since the sixth century. It passed to Hungary in 908 and subsequently became part of the Austro-Hungarian **empire**. After the proclamation of the **Czechoslovak Republic** in

break-up of the Communist states, an independent constitution came into force in September 1992 and the Slovak Republic was set up on 1 January 1993 as successor to the Czech and Slovak federation. The **unicameral parliament**, the National Council, is elected every four years. In 2004, Slovakia joined the **EU**.

Economy

In 2006, GDP reached around US$ 55 billion, a good 15 per cent higher than the previous year. **Structural reforms** carried out since separation from the Czech Republic and through alignment to the EU have proved fruitful but have led to high unemployment.

ways, covers some 36,000 km. The **Danube**, navigable for 172km, connects the interior with the surrounding countries. The two **ports** are Bratislava and Komarno. Slovakia has eight **airports**, five of them international, Bratislava being the biggest.

Tourism

The most popular tourist destinations are the western Slovakian **spas**, the best known of which is probably Trenãianske Teplice. The **historical cities** of East Slovakia and the Tatras are popular. There are **18 national parks** including the outstanding 'Slovak Paradise'. Bratislava, the capital, has important historical monuments.

Natural Geography

The **Hungarian Lowland Plains** to the east of the Danube cover the largest part of Hungary. In the north, lies the **Hungarian Mountain Range** of which the highest peak is Kékes (1,015 m); in the south, there is the hilly region of **Pécs**. The **Puszta steppe**, once very extensive, has remained unchanged in few places. The **Danube**, navigable throughout its length in Hungary flows southwards through the country. The longest river is the **Tisza**. **Lake Balaton**, the largest inland stretch of water in Central Europe, is close to Budapest. Hungary is land-locked, like its Czech and Slovak neighbours.

The Gellért Baths: The natural hot springs on Gellért Hill in Budapest have been used as baths since the thirteenth century. Since the early twentieth century, visitors have been able to relax beneath the huge copper dome.

Climate

The **continental climate** manifests itself in cold, very rainy winters and very warm summers. In winter, the temperatures are near freezing, in summer they can rise to 22°C and above.

Population

Hungary's population is composed predominantly of **Magyars** (90 per cent) with minorities of **Sinti and Roma** (gypsies) (four per cent), **Germans** (2.6 per cent), **Serbs** (two per cent), **Slovaks** and **Romanians**. Two-thirds of Hungarians are Roman Catholic, 20 per cent Calvinists and there are other small religious groups.

History and Politics

In the ninth century, the **Magyars** invaded Hungary, which was a leading power in Europe until the thirteenth century. In the sixteenth century, most of Hungary came under **Ottoman rule**; western Hungary became part of the Austro-Hungarian Empire, which ruled the whole country after the Ottomans were defeated in the seventeenth century. Powerful national movements lead to **independence** in 1867; however, the country remained in the Habsburg **Austro-Hungarian Dual Monarchy** until 1918.

After World War II, in which fascist Hungary fought on the side of Germany, the **Republic of Hungary** was proclaimed in 1946. The people's democracy became a Soviet satellite under a one-party Communist system. In 1989, a peaceful reform process replaced the socialist system of government with a democratic one. In 1990 the first ever democratic elections were held.

The **unicameral parliament** of the National Assembly is elected every four years. Hungary joined **NATO** in 1999 and joined the **European Union** in 2004.

Economy

As a consequence of the privatisation and investment programmes that began in 1995/1996, the economy has experienced a remarkable upturn. In 2006, GDP was US$ 113 billion, corresponding to a good two per cent growth. A large part of the farmland is used to grow fruit, vegetables, vines and cereals as well as for breeding cattle. The **agricultural sector** contributes only three per cent, however, to the GDP; the extensive bauxite deposits are of particular economic significance.

In the highly developed **industrial sector** (31 per cent of the GDP), the main emphasis is on metal smelting as well as machinery and motorised vehicles; these are now Hungary's main exports. Chemicals, in particular **pharmaceuticals**, are an important export. **Services**, above all

tourism, are areas of growth and importance, contributing as much as 66 per cent to the GDP.

Transport Infrastructure

The **railway network** stretches over a length of 7,606 km; the connection to Austria is managed with Austrian Railways.

The **road network** covers 158,000 km, inclusive of 420 km of motorway, of which around 70,000 km are surfaced. **Inland navigation** is mainly on the Danube and Tisza rivers.

Hungary has over 15 **airports**, including two international airports in Budapest and on Lake Balaton.

Tourism

The centres of tourism are the capital, **Budapest** (once the twin cities of Buda and Pest) with its lovely location on the Danube and numerous historic monuments. **Lake Balaton** is a summer resort where the temperature can reach as high as 30°C. Fishing on Lake Balaton is an important industry. The famous pike-perch (fogas), found only in the lake, being a national delicacy. The largest national park is the **Puszta Hortobágy (Hungarian Puszta)** which covers 52,000 ha. The wine country, where the famous Tokay is grown and vinified, is also popular.

1 The sculptures along the Charles Bridge lead through the bridge towers and into Prague's old town, the Stare Mesto.

2 The Danube divides Buda on one side from Pest on the other. The twin cities were amalgamated in 1873 to form the Hungarian capital, and are joined by the 375-m-long Széchenyi Chain Bridge, built between 1838 and 1849.

3 The parliament building on the Danube in Budapest was built in the Gothic Revival style in the late nineteenth century. The National Assembly has its seat in the southern wing.

Romania

Dracula: Bran Castle in Transylvania has a gruesome history. It was the residence of Count Dracula, the vampire-hero of Bram Stoker's famous novel. The real Count Dracula was known as Vlad the Impaler for his habit of impaling his victims on stakes.

Romania	
Area:	237,500 sq. km
Capital city:	Bucharest
Form of government:	Republic
Adminsitrative divisions:	
41 regions	
Population:	
22 million (94 inhabitants/sq. km)	
Languages: Romanian (official), Hungarian, German	
GDP per capita:	US$5,600
Currency:	1 leu = 100 bani

Natural Geography

The **Carpathians** (Moldoveanu: 2,544 m) surround the centre of the country and the **Banat and Apuseni Mountains** join the west **Highlands of Transylvania**. In the west lies part of the **Tisza lowlands**; in the south, the land stretches to the **Danube Delta** and the **Black Sea Coast** with the fertile lowlands of **Walachia**. The hill country of **Moldova** is bounded in the east by the River Prut.

Climate

The climate is predominantly **continental**. The Black Sea coast is mild, with cold winters and hot summers inland. Average temperatures in Bucharest are -3°C in January and 23°C in July, with heavy rainfall in spring and autumn.

Population

Of the population, 90 per cent are **Romanians**, but there are also

Nicolae Ceauşescu

*Scornicesti, 26.1.1918, †Târgoviste, 25.12.1989

The self-appointed 'Conducator' ('Leader') became an absolute ruler in 1965. His refusal to drag Romania into the 1968 invasion of Czechoslovakia demonstrated that he was not controlled by his Moscow allies, but he was a despotic tyrant who led the country to ruin. At the end of 1989, the uprising against him gained strength and intensity, and he and his wife were eventually executed.

Hungarians and the descendants of German immigrants (Transylvanian Saxons), **Ukrainians, Serbs, Croats**, Russians, as well as around 400,000 **Roma** (gypsies). Some 70 per cent of the population are Romanian-Orthodox Christian, six per cent are Roman Catholic and six per cent are of the Protestant faith.

History and Politics

The principalities of **Walachia, Moldavia** and **Transylvania** which were formed in the fourteenth century lost their independence under the Ottoman Empire. The decline of the **Ottoman Empire** brought freedom to Bessarabia, Transylvania and Bukovina. In 1859, the principalities of Moldavia and Walachia joined them and Romania became a **sovereign state** in 1881. After World War II, during which Romania collaborated with the Nazis, it had to cede a part of its territory.

The **People's Republic,** proclaimed in 1947 existed until 1960, as a satellite of the Soviet Union. This led to 20 years under the **dictator Nicolae Ceausescu**. Following his fall in 1989, Romania became a **Republic** in 1991. The **bicameral legislature** consists of a senate and parliament, whose members are elected for a term of four years. The head of state, the **President**, is chosen directly by the people for a five-year term. Romania joined the EU in 2007.

Economy

Romania is in a transitional phase to a **market economy**. Farming still accounts for 64 per cent of land use. Cereals, maize, fruit and wine contribute 14 per cent of the GDP. In 2006, GDP was US$ 122 billion. The country's **mineral resources** (coal, oil and gas, iron, lead, copper and manganese) form the basis of the chemicals industry and the **metal processing industry**, contributing 36 per cent of GDP. The main manufactured exports are textiles, machinery and metal products. The

*Winding streets through villages lined with brightly painted houses are a feature of **Transylvania**, the historic region where most of Romania's German and Hungarian minorities live. Their ancestors were brought here in the twelfth century in order to secure national borders. German and Hungarian are still spoken here.*

Population

85 per cent are **Bulgarian** and Romanian Orthodox and 13 per cent profess Islam. In addition, there are 8.5 per cent Turks, 2.6 per cent **Sinti and Roma** (gypsies), as well as other **Slav minorities**.

History and Politics

The first Bulgarian state was founded in 681 by the nomadic Huns. Around 200 years later, Christianity was adopted. Ottoman **Turkish rule**. which lasted a good 500 years. ended in 1878 when Bulgaria became a kingdom. During World War II, Bulgaria was occupied by the Nazis and in 1947, became a **People's Republic**, and Soviet satellite. It has been a **parliamentary republic** since the fall of Communism in 1991. The **national assembly** is elected every four years. The **head of state** is directly elected by the people every five years. Bulgaria entered the EU in 2007.

Todor Zhivkov

*Pravets, 7.9.1911,
†Sofia, 5.8.1998

In World War II, Zhivkov was a leading figure in the People's Liberation Insurgent Army, fighting against the German occupation of Bulgaria. He then led a successful career in the Communist Party, becoming First Secretary in 1954. He was head of state for Bulgaria from 1971 until his downfall in 1989.

Natural Geography

The Danube plains form the northern border of the country. In the south, there is the fertile North Bulgarian lowlands. Southern Bulgaria is mountainous: the Balkans, Rhodope, Rila (Musala: 2,925 m), Pirin and Vitosha Plateau cover a good third of the land mass.

Climate

The **continental climate**, marked by harsh winters and hot dry summers, is attenuated by the influence of the **Black Sea**.

growing **service sector** provides 50 per cent of Romania's GDP.

Transport Infrastructure

The **railway network** stretches over 11,365 km, of which around 3,800 km is electrified. Only half of the 153,000-km-long **road network** is surfaced. The **inland navigation routes** are 1,724 km long and mainly serve the **Black Sea port** of Constanta.

Tourism

The principal **winter sports facilities** are in the **Carpathians**.

The best known resorts are the towns of **Brasov** and **Poiana**, 1,000 km above sea level. Sulina and Tulcea stand at the gateway to the **Danube Delta conservation area**, which stretches across the border with the Ukraine and contains unique flora and fauna.

The **Black Sea Coast** is the best known holiday destination. The **port of Constanta** dates from pre-Roman times and the nearby **seaside resorts of Mamaia** and **Eforie** offer water sports and spa facilities. The capital city **Bucharest** and **Bukovina** with its famous fifteeenth

and sixteenth-century painted churches are also well worth visiting. The Romanian countryside and rural way of life is stil largely unspoilt, and has proved a magnet to tourists.

Bulgaria	
Area:	110,910 sq. km
Capital city:	Sofia
Form of government:	Republic
Administrative divisions:	
8 regions, 1 district (capital city)	
Population: 7.4 million	
(67 inhabitants/sq. km)	
Language: Bulgarian	
GDP per capita:	US$4,100
Currency:	
1 Ley = 100 stotinki	

The Alexander Nevsky Cathedral in Sofia was completed in 1912.

Influenced by the decades of atheistic ideology of Bulgaria's communist regime, just 52 per cent of Bulgarians consider themselves religious. Yet around 85 per cent of the population belongs to the Bulgarian Orthodox Church; 13 per cent are for the most part Muslims originating from Turkey. The tradition

of Bulgarian Orthodoxy goes back to the year 927, when their independence and liturgical autonomy was recognised by the Ecumenical Patriarchate in Constantinople. The picture shows the faithful in St Nicholas's Church in Melnik and an icon of the Virgin Mary covered with prayer requests.

Bulgaria, Moldova, Ukraine

*The Roma and Sinti (gypsies) were originally nomads and there are large concentrations of them in **Romania, Bulgaria** and the rest of the Balkans. They have now settled across all of Europe. The Roma express their culture mainly through music. 90 per cent of Roma are professing Roman Catholics. Although most Roma communities are no longer nomadic, many Roma live apart from the general population.*

Economy

In 2006, GDP was US$ 31 billion. In spite of high rates of growth in recent years, the country's level of affluence still lies far behind that of the EU. Privatisations have been completed to a large extent but there continues to be a lack of legal security. **Agriculture** – which contributes 11 per cent to the GDP – provides tobacco, fruit, wine, vegetables and attar of roses; animal husbandry is important in the mountain regions. There is an important **mining industry** producing brown coal, iron, lead and zinc. **Industry** contributes a total of 31 per cent to GDP, and includes heavy machinery and metal processing as well as chemicals and textile production. The **service sector**, which accounts for 58 per cent of GDP, is becoming important as Bulgaria modernises and became a member of the EU.

Transport Infrastructure

The **railway network** stretches over 4,292 km and is as well planned as the **road network**, which is surfaced over its total length of 36,720 km. **Inland navigation** is of relatively low significance; the major **ports,** in addition to Burgas and Varna– which are also international **airports** – are Lom and Ruse on the **Danube**. Sofia, the capital, also has an international airport.

Tourism

The resorts of the **Black Sea Coast** include Varna with its 'Golden Sands' and the **seaside towns** of Burgas and Nesebar. The **Pirin National Park** welcomes hikers and ramblers. The capital city, **Sofia** whose cathedral is the largest in the Balkans, has many other historic monuments. Winter sports facilities are close to the capital. In addition, the **Rila Monastery** in the mountain range of the same name, as well as the numerous archeological sites, particularly at **Nesebar** and **Kazanlak,** are of great tourist importance. Unquestionably, Bulgaria's most famous attraction is the Valley of the Roses, where attar of roses has been cultivated since early antiquity and is one of Bulgaria's major exports.

Moldova	
Area:	33,843 sq. km
Capital city:	Chisinau
Form of government:	Republic
Administrative divisions: 40 districts, 10 municipal districts	
Population: *c.* 4 million (128 inhabitants/sq. km)	
Languages: Moldovan (official), Bulgarian, Gagauz, Russian	
GDP per capita:	*c.* US$900
Currency: 1 Moldovan leu = 100 bani	

Natural Geography

The country of Moldova consists of various rolling hills with peaks

Bulgaria: Frescoes adorn the walls of the Rila Monastery.

of up to 430 m (Balanesti). They are crisscrossed by beautiful river valleys. The northern border of the country forms the **River Dniester**, the western border, the **River Prut**. The largest part of the area is taken up by steppe; there are some stretches of unspoiled deciduous forest.

Climate

The climate of Moldova is **continental**, with warm summers and cold winters. The average temperature in the capital Chisinau is -5°C in January, and 23°C in July.

Population

The majority of the population consists of **Moldovans** (64.5 per cent), followed by **Ukrainians** (13.8 per cent), **Russians** (13 per cent) and minorities of **Gagauzians** (3.5 per cent), **Jews** and **Bulgarians**.
Furthermore 98.5 per cent belong to the **Eastern Orthodox Church**, 1.5 per cent are of the **Jewish faith**. There is a small group of **Baptists**. **Moldovan**, the official language, is very similar to Romanian. There have been demands for independence from the predominantly Russian-speaking population of the **Transnistria** region (east of the River Dniester).

History and Politics

In the fourteenth century, the area that is now Moldova was a part of the autonomous **principality of Moldavia**, which was conquered by the **Ottomans** in the sixteenth century. The eastern part, **Bessarabia**, was annexed by **Tsarist Russia** in 1812 and by Romania in 1918. In 1947, the whole of Moldavia was annexed by the **Soviet Union**. The Republic of Moldova declared its **independence** in 1991. A plebiscite was held in 1994 with a proposal to merge Moldova with **Romania,** but this was rejected.

Economy

In 2006, GDP was US$ 3.4 billion (or less, taking into account Moldavians living abroad who transfer money into the country), of which 22 per cent came from **agriculture**, 24 per cent from **industry** and 54 per cent from **services**. Over half of GDP comes from the cultivation of tobacco and plants for the production of essential oils, as well as table wines and sparkling wines, canned fruit and vegetables.
Of the labour force, 46 per cent work in agriculture, which is increasingly producing goods for export. In the **heavy industries**, which are mainly located on the banks of the Dniester, heavy machinery predominates. A considerable obstacle to changing the formerly planned economy to a market economy remains the irresolute progress of **privatisation** of collective farms.

Transport Infrastructure

The 12,300-km-long road network is extensively surfaced. There are excellent international coach services linking Moldova with Russia, the Ukraine and Romania. The interior of Moldova has access to the **Black Sea** via the Dniester and access to the **Danube** via the Prut. The most important **river**

ports are Bender and **Ribnita** as well as **Ungheni**. Moldova's international airport is in the capital, **Chisinau,** which is also a stop on the international railway line that links land-locked Moldova to Romania and Russia.

Tourism

Tourism is not well developed but currently centres on **capital city, Chisinau**. The **fortresses and castles** throughout the country, including the **Soroca fortress** on the Dniester, are sites of great historical interest. The best time to visit Moldova is during the **grape harvest** in October when numerous wine festivals are held.

DNEPR-DONBASS INDUSTRIAL AREAS

0   150 km

⊘ Hydroelectric power plants   ▨ Industrial areas
⚙ Thermoelectric power plants   ☐ Oil fields
☢ Nuclear power plants   ☐ Natural gas
⛏ Main refineries
— Oil pipelines
— Natural gas pipelines

RUSSIA

Saratov

Kursk

Kharkiv

Volgograd

Kiev   U K R A I N E

Luhans'k

Vinnytsya   *Dnieper*

Dnipro-petrovs'k   Juzovka

Donbass

Kryvvy Rih   Mariupol'   Rostov-na-Donu

Mykolayiv   *Dniester*

Chişinău   *Dnieper*   SEA OF AZOV   Stavropol'

Odesa   Krasnodar

Galaţi   Simferopol'   Novorossiysk

Sochi

BLACK SEA

Ukraine	
Area:	603,700 sq. km
Capital city:	Kiev
Form of government: Republic	
Administrative divisions: 25 regions, autonomous Republic of Crimea	
Population: 46.3 million (77 inhabitants/sq. km)	
Languages: Ukrainian (official), Russian	
GDP per capita:	US$2,300
Currency: 1 hryvnia = 100 kopiykas	

Bulgaria's Black Sea Coast makes it an attractive tourist and holiday destination. After the collapse of the Soviet Union in 1989, foreign visitor numbers fell dramatically, but the region is now enjoying renewed popularity.

Natural Geography

The landscape of the Ukraine along the **Black Sea** is characterised by an undulating, fertile plain, which gradually flattens to the south. The **black earth area** is extremely fertile. The country's main rivers are the **Dnieper**, with its tributaries, the **Pripjat** and the **Desna**, as well as the **Dniester**. Mountains are found in the south-west, with the foothills of the **Carpathians** and the in the **Crimean Peninsula** (Roman-Kosh: 1,545 m) in the south.

Climate

The climate has **continental** characteristics, only Crimea has a **Mediterranean** climate. The rainfall tails off towards south-eastern Ukraine. The average temperatures in the capital, Kiev, in the north are between -5°C in January and 19°C in July.

Population

Some 73 per cent of the population are **Ukrainians**, 22 per cent **Russians** with minorities of **Crimean Tatars** and **Jews**. The Ukrainians are predominantly Christian and profess allegiance to the Eastern Orthodox or to the Greek-Catholic church. There are also Muslims and Jews.

History and Politics

The area covered by the Ukraine was a part of the Slav kingdom centred on Kiyv (Kiev) between the ninth and thirteenth centuries. Falling first to the **Mongols**, it was then incorporated into the **Polish-Lithuanian Commonwealth**. In the seventeenth century, the eastern part fell to **Russia**. After further divisions in the eighteenth century and as a consequence of World War I, in 1922 the Ukraine became a **Republic of the Soviet Union**. The centuries-old culture of the Ukrainian Jews was destroyed with the occupation by the **German armed forces** from 1941. After the dissolution of the Soviet Bloc and the **Declaration of Independence** by the Ukraine, the country became a member of the **CIS** in 1991. Dissatisfaction within the population led to the peaceful 'Orange' Revolution in 2004. Members of parliament are

elected every four years. The **President** is elected directly by the people for a five-year term. The **autonomous Republic of Crimea**, whose population is predominantly Russian, was first ceded to the Ukraine in 1954. The Ukraine aspires to join the EU, but its economy and political structure are not yet considered suitable.

Economy

Within the former Soviet Union, the Ukraine was the most important **economic power** after Russia. It was the 'granary' of the Soviet Union (72 per cent of the land is cultivated) and this, along with its mineral wealth and highly diversified **industry** made the Ukraine one of the richest Soviet Republics. In 1992, the Ukraine, which was **economically isolated** when the Soviet Union dissolved, adopted a **liberalisation** approach to the economy, but this was continuously blocked by bureaucracy. After an impressive 12.1 per cent in the previous year, only 2.6 per cent could be achieved in 2005 – certainly also due to the anticlimax after the 'Orange' revolution. Around 12 per cent of today's GDP (2006: US$ 106 billion) derives from **agriculture**, of which only a small part has been privatised. The **manufacturing sector** is based on heavy industry. There are rich coal and iron ore deposits. Other exports are **machinery and armaments**, which account for most of the profits. While industry accounts for 36 per cent of GDP, the growing service sector contributes 53 per cent.

Transport Infrastructure

The **railway network** covers 23,350 km, of which 8,600 km is electrified. The 172,565-km **road network** is largely surfaced. **Inland navigation** is used on the 4,400 km of the Pripyat and the Dniester. The network of **air routes** includes 163 airports; Kiev's Borispil is an international airport.

Tourism

The capital city, **Kiev**, is steeped in history and has numerous tourist attractions, including a ski run and a magnificent cathedral. Lviv (formerly Lvov or Lemburg) also has a picturesque old town. The northern

Black Sea Coast and **Crimea** were the Riviera of the former Soviet Union and their **spa resorts**, such as **Yalta**, and the extensive vineyards are reminiscent of Italy. The historic port of **Odesa** with its classical buildings is a port of call for cruise ships. The Crimea also has sites of archaeological interest from the **Byzantine period**.

1 The Kiev Monastery of the Caves overlooks the Dnieper River and the city.

2 The crenellated towers of Swallow's Nest Castle in Yalta. This part of the Black Sea coast welcomes large numbers of tourists and has a particularly mild climate.

3 A two-storey arcade surrounds the courtyard and the medieval Hrelyu Tower (fourteenth century) at Rila Monastery in Bulgaria. The complex was begun in the ninth century when the hermit St John of Rila moved there and lived in a cave nearby.

*The church St Mary of the Lake is one of the landmarks of **Bled**, a picturesque **Slovenian** spa town in a narrow valley in the Karawanken mountains. Bled is not far from the Austrian and Italian borders, the place attracts thousands of foreign tourists from neighbouring countries.*

Slovenia

Area:	20,273 sq. km
Capital city:	Ljubljana
Form of government:	Republic
Population: 2 million	
(99 inhabitants/sq. km)	
Language:	Slovenian
GDP per capita:	US$19,000
Currency:	1 euro = 100 cents

Natural Geography

Predominantly mountainous Slovenia is characterised by very different landscapes. The **Julian Alps** in the north with the 2,863 m high Triglav as well as the **Karavanke chain**, adjoin the Trnovac and the Franconian forests, which merge into the **Karst field** of Inner Carniola. In the west, there is the Triestine Karst and the 42 km long Adriatic Coast. In Lower Carniola, in the south east there is the **hill country** farmland, bordering in the north with the Sava mountainous district.
The **Sava**, the largest river in Slovenia, crosses the country from the north-west to east.

Climate

Like the landscape, the climate is also varied; it is **Mediterranean** on the coast changing inland to a **continental and Alpine climate**. Around half of the country is afforested.

Population

Slovenia is 92 per cent **Slovenian** and predominantly Roman Catholic. The standard of living is the highest in Eastern Europe thanks to an excellent **social security system**.

History and Politics

Over the long period from 1283 until 1918, the area of Slovenia was ruled by the **Habsburg Empire**. Some parts of the country were then combined with **Croatia**, **Serbia** and **Montenegro** into a **kingdom** while the other parts were ceded to **Italy** and **Austria**. Following the German-Italian occupation of 1941, Slovenia was divided between Germany, Italy and Hungary. Slovenia was recreated in 1945 when it became a constituent of the republic of **Yugoslavia**. In 1991, Slovenia declared its **independence**. The constitution of 1991 defined Slovenia as a **parliamentary republic** based on the model of Western European democracies. The country was largely spared during the **wars** that so damaged the other former regions of Yugoslavia because of its position at the periphery. Its historic ties to Austria make Slovenia the most 'westernised' of the countries of former Yugoslavia. Slovenia has been a member of the **European Union** since 2004; the Euro was introduced in 2007.

Economy

In 2006, GDP was US$ 38 billion, of which three per cent came from **agriculture**, 37 per cent from **industry** and 60 per cent from **services** (including tourism). Growth, based principally on exports, has reached approximately eight per cent.

Transport Infrastructure

Slovenia has three **ports** (Koper, Izola and Piran) as well as three **airports** (Ljubljana, Maribor and Portoroz). The Slovenian airline is called Adria Airways.

Tourism

Slovenia's tourist destinations, including **winter sports and health resorts** in the Slovenian Alps, **spas** in the Slovenian Styria, and the famous **caves in Karst** and the **Adriatic Coast**. Ljubljana, hosts a major international art show, the Biennale.

Croatia

Area:	56,542 sq. km
Capital city:	Zagreb
Form of government:	Republic
Administrative divisions:	
20 regions, 2 districts	
Population: 4.5 million	
(79 inhabitants/sq. km)	
Language:	Croatian
GDP per capita:	US$9,600
Currency:	1 kuna = 100 lipa

Natural Geography

In the west, the country is bounded by the **Adriatic Sea**; the **Dalmatian Coast**, which narrows towards the south-east, ends at the Bay of Kotor. More than **600 islands** lie off the Adriatic Coast to the northeast and have always belonged to Croatia. The largest, Krk, has its own airport. To the north-east, the Dinaric Mountains gradually give way to lowlands between the **Sava, Danube** and **Drava** rivers.

Ljubljana: buildings from the reign of the Habsburgs give the city a distinctly Austrian appearance.

Climate

The **Mediterranean climate** of the Adriatic Coast turns increasingly continental inland.

Population

Of the population, 78 per cent are **Croats**, 12 per cent **Serbs** and there are also Bosnian, Slovenian, Hungarian and other **minorities**. The majority of Croats are **Roman Catholic** (around 77 per cent). In addition to small groups of Muslims and Protestants, about 11 per cent of **Serbs are Orthodox Christians**.

History and Politics

After the **southern Slavs** settled in the seventh century, the **Croatian Dynasty** was founded in the ninth century. In 1527, part of the country was ruled by the **Habsburgs**, and the rest became part of the **Ottoman Empire**. Between World War I and 1941, Croatia was part of **Yugoslavia**. It became a puppet of the Nazi regime after the invasion, and rejoined Yugoslavia in 1945. The **Declaration of Independence** (the first Constitution of 1990 was amended in 1997) led to a bloody **war**, which ended in 1995.

Economy

The Croatian economy is slowly but steadily recovering from the consequences of **war** and has reached a growth rate of about four per cent. In 2006, GDP was US$ 43 billion, of which eight per cent came from **agriculture**, 30 per cent from **industry** and 62 per cent from **services**. Industry is based on food production, textile products, chemicals, wood and machinery, among others. The traditionally strong **tourism** sector has now exceeded the level it reached before the war and provides about one-fifth of GDP.

Tourism

The most attractive destinations are **Zagreb, the capital,** the picturesque sea ports of **Rijeka, Dubrovnik** and **Split**, the famous **Dalmatian coast** and the Krka and Plitvice lakes **National Parks** in Croatia's mountains.

Bosnia and Herzegovina

Area:	51,129 sq. km
Capital city:	Sarajevo
Form of government:	Republic
Population: 4 million	
(78 inhabitants/sq. km)	
Languages: Bosnian, Croatian, Serbian	
GDP per capita:	US$2,900
Currency:	
1 convertible mark = 100 fening	

Natural Geography

Most of the land is forested, partly karst and partly **upland regions**. The soil is mostly barren; only a small part of the country – the loess soil of the **Sava** Valley – is suitable for agriculture. The country gets its name from the **Bosna River**, which flows through Sarajevo into the River Sava.

Climate

An **alpine continental climate prevails**, but the coast has a **Mediterranean climate**.

Population

The population of the country is composed of around 40 per cent **Serbs** and **Bosnians**, 17.3 per cent **Croats** and other smaller groups. As to religious faith, 40 per cent are **Muslims**, and 30 per cent **Serbian Orthodox**. The Civil War caused around one million inhabitants to flee abroad. A further one million people became **refugees** in their own country.

History and Politics

The **Kingdom of Bosnia and Herzegovina** was created in the fourteenth century but was conquered in 1463 by the **Ottoman Turks**. It was part of the Ottoman Empire for about 400 years. During this time, many Bosnian Christians converted to Islam. In 1878, the country was incorporated into the **Austro-Hungarian Empire**; in 1918, Bosnia became part of the **Kingdom of Serbia, Slovenia and Croatia**. In 1929, this country was renamed the **Kingdom of Yugoslavia** by King Alexander I.

*The architecture of many **Slovenian** cities is a record of the country's eventful history: some places are built in the baroque style of Austro-Hungary, while others are very Italianate in design – for example, the market square in Piran.*

Following disputes between the Slovenians and Croatians, and despite increasing ethnic problems, Alexander I restructured the country from the ground up. In 1941, the Germans invaded Yugoslavia and forced a large part of the country into the state of **Croatia** which was a puppet state of the Nazis.

In 1945, Bosnia became one of the six republics of the **People's Federal Republic of Yugoslavia**. When this diffuse state broke up in 1991, the majority of Muslim and Croats declared Bosnia to be **independent**. In 1992 Bosnian Serbs proclaimed the 'Serbian Republic' and there followed a bitter **ethnic cleansing war** against the Croats and Muslims. After several fruitless efforts to achieve peace, a plan was only successfully drawn up in 1995 separating the country into a Serbian Republic and a Muslim-Croat Federation.

NATO Peace Forces are permanently stationed in Bosnia-Herzegovina, in order to monitor the peace process.

Economy

Production and trade were completely destroyed in the **civil war** and are recovering slowly. In 2006, GDP was US$ 11.4 billion, of which 12 per cent came from **agriculture**, 29 per cent from **industry** and 59 per cent from **services**. However, as unofficial and unauthorised trade (the 'grey market') plays a significant part in economic life, the real performance data may be much higher. With economic growth at over five per cent in recent years reconstruction has been gaining momentum. Hopes are pinned particularly on electrical, construction and wood-processing industries, as well as agriculture.

Transport Infrastructure

Road and rail networks were largely destroyed by acts of war and the state railway was destroyed in three attacks. Only recently have the main road arteries through the country come back into use. The roads and bridges, of which around 40 per cent were also destroyed in the

war, are now slowly being rebuilt. Sarajevo is the only international **airport**.

Tourism

Despite the fact that Bosnia and Herzegovina still has many problems, the country continues to attract visitors. The unspoiled uplands and alpine forests are a hiker's paradise. The capital Sarajevo has a picturesque Turkish quarter. In the summer, there is a folk festival and an arts festival

held by the walls of the Kastel, the ancient fortress in the old town.

	Serbia
Area:	77,474 sq. km
Capital city:	Belgrade
Form of government:	Republic
Population: 8 million (100 inhabitants/sq. km)	
Languages: Serbian (official), Albanian	
GDP per capita:	US$4,000
Currency: 1 new dinar = 100 para	

Natural Geography

Serbia is largely mountainous country with the exception of the **Vojvodina** province and several areas in the Danube and Sava river basins.

Climate

Serbia has a continental climate in its interior and a mediterranean climate on the coast.

Population

Serbs are the largest ethnic group, constituting 83 per cent of the population (excluding Kosovo); in addition there are minorities of Hungarians (four per cent) and **Bosnians** (two per cent).

History and Politics

The first Serbian kingdom was founded in the twelfth century and eventually came under Ottoman control. Serbia gained its independence in the nineteenth century and was the most populous republic in the socialist Yugoslavia founded after World War II. The collapse of Yugoslavia began in 1990–91 and ushered in a decade

of wars and ethnic conflict that culminated in genocide. The Bosnian War, in which Serbia supported Bosnian Serb secessionists, ended in 1995 with the Dayton Peace Treaty. Conflicts between Kosovo Albanians and the Milosevic regime lead to a wave of repression in the province and finally a NATO bombing campaign against Yugoslavia in 1999. Kosovo was placed under UN control. In 2000, Milosevic was forced from office. Yugoslavia was replaced by a union of states called Serbia-Montenegro lasting until 2006,

when Montenegro declared its independence. In 2008, Kosovo declared independence.

Economy

In 2006, GDP was US$ 35 billion (including Montenegro and Kosovo), with 20 per cent coming from **agriculture**, 37 per cent from **industry** and 43 per cent from **services**. Serbia is battling the consequences of an economic crisis.

Transport Infrastructure

The road network and public transport system are both well developed. Belgrade has an **international airport**.

Tourism

The tourism industry almost disappeared during the 1990s but is now beginning to recover.

Religion in the Balkans: far left, mosque in Tirana, Albania. Two-thirds of Albanians are Muslims, most of the Christians are in the north. Left, the Euphrasius Basilica in the Croatian city of Poreč dates from the sixth century.

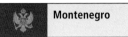
Montenegro

Area: 13,812 sq. km
Capital city: Podgorica
Form of government: Republic
Population: around 650,000
(47 inhabitants/sq. km)
Languages:
Serbian (official), Albanian
GDP per capita: US$3100
Currency: 1 euro = 100 cent

Natural Geography

The interior is mountainous with 2,500-m-high summits.

Climate

The climate is mainly **continental** in the interior and **Mediteranean** along the Adriatic coast.

History and Politics

The largest ethnic groups are **Montenegrins** (43 per cent)

Serbs (32 per cent) and **Bosnians** (8 per cent).

History and Politics

United with Serbia for almost 90 years, Montenegro declared independence in 2006. A new constitution came into force in 2007.

Economy

In 2006, GDP was US$ 2 billion. Detailed economic data is not yet available for this young country, which is currently undergoing intense economic transformation.

Transport Infrastructure

The road network is relatively well developed. Podgorica has an international airport.

Tourism

Montenegro's pristine coast is its major attraction. The tourism industry is now on the rise again.

Kosovo

Area: 10,887 sq. km
Capital city: Pristina
Form of government: Republic
Population: approx. 3 million
Languages: Albanian, Serbian
GDP per capita: US$1,300
Currency: 1 euro = 100 cents

Natural Geography

In the centre of the Balkan Peninsula, Kosovo is a terrain characterised by high valleys with surrounding mountains and no outlets to the sea. Its capital Pristina is located in the heart of Kosovo. The country borders Albania, Serbia, Macedonia and Montenegro.

Climate

Temperatures vary considerably in Kosovo's continental climate, depending on season and altitude.

History and Politics

After the Battle of Amsfeld in 1389, Kosovo became an Ottoman province and was occupied by Albanians. After World War I, it became part of the Kingdom of Yugoslavia and then an autonomous province in 1974. Conflict between Albanians and Serbs led to the Kosovo War and NATO's intervention in 1999. Kosovo became a UN protectorate before declaring independence in 2008, though it is not recognised by all countries, including Serbia.

Economy

Just over half of Kosovo's land is classed as **agricultural** with natural resources including **brown coal**. The weak economy is supported by **money transfers** from international organisations and Kosovar residents abroad.

Macedonia

Area: 25,333 sq. km
Capital city: Skopje
Form of government: Republic
Administrative divisions:
38 municipalities
Population: 2 million
(81 inhabitants/sq. km)
Languages: Macedonian (official), Albanian, Turkish, Serbian
GDP per capita: US$3,100
Currency:
1 Macedonian denar = 100 deni

Natural Geography

Macedonia is a **mountainous country** with wide **valleys**. Some of the peaks rise to heights of over 2,000 m. More than a third of the country is forested.

Climate

In the south, and in the large Vardar basin in the south-east, a

---

THE ETHNIC MOSAIC IN THE EX-YUGOSLAVIA

Majority of
- Serbs
- Muslims
- Croatians
- Slovenes
- Montenegrins
- Bulgarians
- Hungarians
- Macedonians
- Albanians
- Mixed areas

The old harbour of Dubrovnik with its cluster of medieval buildings.

Tito, Josip

*Kumrovec 25.5.1892,
†Ljubljana 4.5.1980

As Secretary-General of the CPY, in 1941 Tito organised partisan armed resistance against the German occupiers in the Yugoslav **People's Liberation War**. He became Prime Minister of the People's Republic of Yugoslavia after the end of the war and President in 1953. After the break with the USSR in 1948 he followed a separate socialist path.

Mediterranean climate predominates; in the rest of the country, a **continental climate** prevails.

Population

The largest population group is Macedonian at around 68 per cent, followed by **Albanians** (22 per cent), **Turks** and **Serbs**. About 67 per cent of the inhabitants are of **Christian Orthodox belief**; almost 30 per cent, mostly Albanians, are **Sunni Muslims**.

History and Politics

From the fourteenth century until 1913 the country was under Ot-

The archeological and ethnographic museum in the Albanian capital of **Tirana** *has wonderful exhibits from the Illyrian, Greek, Roman and medieval periods, illustrating Albania's fascinating and eventful history. The building itself is built in the Italian, monumental style of the twentieth century, a perfect example of its type, and demonstrating the Italian influence in Albania.*

toman rule. The Serbian part of Macedonia was split into three in 1913 but became an independent state structure after the founding of the **People's Republic of Yugoslavia**. In 1991, this former province of Yugoslavia declared independence as the **Republic of Macedonia**. In the same year, the **constitution** was passed. Macedonia has faced major hostility from Greece which has its own province of Macedonia and insists that Macedonia call itself FYROM – the Former Yugoslav Republic of Macedonia – to avoid confusion.

Economy

Agriculture contributes a total of 14 per cent to the GDP (2006: US$ 6.3 billion). Iron ore is **mined**. The **industrial sector** contributes 27 per cent of GDP. The capital, Skopje, has iron and steel foundries and important leather and textiles industries. The **services sector** is gaining in importance (57 per cent of GDP).

Transport Infrastructure

The **road network** has been extended by a new **motorway**, connecting Istanbul and Albania through Macedonia. There are two international **airports**.

Tourism

The charming city of **Ohrid** and the **lake** of the same name on the Albanian border has numerous medieval orthodox **monasteries in its vicinity**. The **national park** on Lake Prespa as well as the old town of **Skopje** with its Turkish quarter, are the main tourist centres.

Albania	
Area	28,748 sq. km
Capital city:	Tirana
Form of government: Republic	
Administrative divisions: 27 provinces	
Population: 3.3 million (125 inhabitants/sq. km)	
Language:	Albanian
GDP per capita:	US$2,900
Currency: 1 lek = 100 qindarka	

Natural Geography

This mountainous country has over 40 mountain peaks over 2,000 m high, part of the **Dinaric** and **Albanian Alps**. Unnavigable rivers cut deep channels through the gorges of the mostly rough karst mountains.

Climate

The **Mediterranean climate** on the coast gives way to a **continental and alpine climate** in the interior.

Population

Albanians constitute 98 per cent of the population. Two-thirds are **Muslims**. Economic reforms have dragged large sections of the population into poverty.

History and Politics

In 1272, **Charles of Anjou** proclaimed the **Kingdom of Albania**. Albania was originally part of the **Roman Empire** and subsequently the **Byzantine Empire**. In 1502, the country became part of the **Ottoman Empire**, but finally achieved its **independence** in 1912–13 as the Ottoman Empire collapsed. Following vain attempts at democratic order and first **Italian**, then **German occupation** in World War II, Albania became a kingdom under King Zog, then a **People's Republic** in 1946 under Enver Hoxha, a ruthless dictator. The Communist regime was the most radical in the West, Religion was totally banned! Since 1990 the country embarked on a policy of reform. In 1991, the first free **elections** were held. Albania still attempts to integrate into the international community.

Economy

Albania is currently the **poorest country** in Europe. **Agriculture** contributes to over 25 per cent of GDP, including the production of grains, cotton and tobacco. In 2006, GDP was around US$ 9 billion, of which 20 per cent came from **industry** and 55 per cent from **services**. Restructuring for a market economy is progressing, but a lack of legal security is restricting investment.

Transport Infrastructure

Only approximately one third of the Albanian **road network** is surfaced , so donkey-carts represent the main form of transport in many areas. There is one European **rail service** and the only **international airport** is located in the capital, Tirana.

Tourism

Even today, very few tourists visit Albania, despite the fact that the country has numerous **cultural monuments** from the ancient world and the Middle Ages that are well worth seeing and a way of life in the country that is soon to disappear.

1 Paklenica national park, Croatia and Slovenia.

2 Houses cling to the cliffs on the picturesque coast of Istria.

3 Macedonia: Lake Ohrid, the largest and deepest lake in the Balkanst.

Greece

Selling fruit and fish: In Greece, the cultivation of citrus fruit, wine grapes and olives contributes considerably to the economy. The fishing industry is in danger due to over-fishing in the Mediterranean.

Greece

Area:	131,940 sq. km
Capital city:	Athens
Form of government:	
Parliamentary Republic	
Administrative divisions:	
13 regions and the autonomous region of Agion Oros (Mt. Athos)	
Population: 10.7 million	
(81 inhabitants/sq. km)	
Language:	Modern Greek
GDP per capita:	US$28,000
Currency: 1 euro = 100 cents	

Natural geography

Greece is located at the tip of the Balkan Peninsula. It is bordered to the north by **Albania, Macedonia, Bulgaria** and **Turkey**, and to the south by the **Aegean Sea**. Roughly one-fifth of the land mass consists of widely scattered islands. To the west are the **Ionian Islands**, the best known of which are Corfu and Ithaki. The **island of the Aegean** include Evvoia, the Northern Sporades, Lesbos, Khios, Samos, the Cyclades, the Dodecanese, Rhodes, Cythera and Crete. There are a couple of islands, Bozcaada and Imbros, that belong to Turkey. The largest island in the southern Aegean is Crete. The southern tip of mainland Greece is known as the **Peloponnese**. Almost half of the Greek mainland is covered by upland forest. The **Pindus** mountain chain extends along the west coast;

the mountains in the east are dominated by **Mount Olympus** (2,911 m). The mountain chains surround the fertile plain of **Thessaly**. Even the Peloponnese and many of the Aegean islands are mountainous. There are alluvial flood plains on the coast. Mainland Greece and the Greek islands have a total of some 14,000 km of coastline, much of it consisting of sheer cliffs. Despite numerous bays, many of which extend deep inland, Greece has very few natural harbours.

Climate

The mountains have a **central European climate**, while the rest of the country enjoys a **Mediterranean climate**. Summers on the coast are dry and hot, and the winters mild and wet. In the mountains to the north, winters are bitter but summers are comparatively mild. Summer temperatures in southern Greece can often rise as high as 45°C.

Population

Approximately 95 per cent of the population is **Greek**. There are relatively small communities of **Macedonians, Turks** and **Bulgarians**, mainly in the north, as well as some **Roma** (gypsies). The majority of the population (98 per cent) belong to the **Greek Orthodox Church**. Muslims comprise two per cent of the population. More than half of all Greeks (58 per cent) live in towns of more than 10,000 inhabitants. About one third of the population resides in the Athens and Piraeus conurbation alone.

Rural areas are suffering increasingly as more and more people move to the towns and cities. Under the Greek health system, all citizens have national insurance cover.

History and politics

The **Mycenaean civilisation** dominated in Greece from 1900 BC but collapsed in the early **Classical period**, ca. 800 BC.

Ancient Greece was the **intellectual and cultural centre of the western world**. **Athens** and **Sparta** emerged as leading powers and rivals. The two cities fought each other frequently for control of the land.

Alexander the Great, who was from Macedon, founded a **world empire** and spread Greek civilisation as far as India. After his death in 323 BC, this empire quickly disintegrated.

Greece was a **Roman province** from 148 BC until 396 AD, after which it became part of the **Byzantine Empire**. In 1356, Greece was conquered by the Ottomans. It was not until 1832, after a lengthy **War of Independence**, that Greece gained its independence, and became a kingdom. A **Republic was declared** in 1924.

During the **Balkan Wars** of 1912 to 1913, Greece managed to extend its territory, and after **World War I** Greek forces attempted to annex parts of Turkey. Greece was occupied by Germany during **World War II**, causing great suffering. The **monarchy** was reintroduced in 1946.

There was a **military coup** by right-wing generals in 1967, and the monarchy was finally abolished in 1973. The conflict with neighbouring **Turkey** over the status of the island of **Cyprus**, which continues to this day, began with the fall of the military dictatorship. A **democratic republic** was established in 1974. The 1975 constitution provides for a **unicameral parliament**, whose members are elected every four years. A new **President** is elected every five years.

Economy

In 2006, GDP was US$ 308 billion, of which seven per cent was derived from agriculture, 22 per cent from industry and 71 per cent from services. Greece is currently converting from an

Santorini: The Cyclades are the perfect destination for those who love picturesque villages that blend into the landscape. Cube-shaped houses painted brilliant white stand out against the brilliant blue sky, and scattered, isolated churches break the skyline. The island of Santorini is a perfect example. It is actually part of the crater of an undersea volcano that erupted around 1500 BC. The fertile volcanic soil is ideal for wine cultivation.

agrarian economy to one based on trade and services. Roughly one-third of **exports** are of typically Mediterranean agricultural produce, including citrus fruits, olives, wine, currants, cotton and tobacco. There are mineral reserves of iron ore, bauxite, manganese and oil. The **manufacturing sector** still consists mainly of small businesses. Only two per cent of Greek companies have 30 or more employees.

Main exports are food, shoes, clothing and leather goods. The **service sector** is becoming increasingly important. The high percentage is mainly due to shipping and to tourism, which has a long history in Greece. Despite decreasing numbers of ships and tonnage, shipping remains one of the country's most important economic activities. Greece has the fourth largest **merchant navy** in the world. Main trading partners are other member states of the European Union and the USA. In recent years, the country has managed to curb its high levels of national debt and high inflation, and in 2000 successfully met the criteria for entry into the **European Monetary Union.**

Transport infrastructure

The tracks of the **rail network** are only two-thirds the width of the international gauge, and only a very small part is electrified. The whole network is in need of modernisation and renovation. The **road network** is relatively well constructed.

Nine of the country's 36 **airports** are served by international airlines. Greece also has a dense network of flight connections between the various islands and the mainland. The most important **shipping and passenger ports** are **Piraeus, Patrai, Volos** and **Salonica (Thessaloniki)**. Naturally, there is a network of ferries that ply between the islands, and from the islands to the mainland.

Tourism

Greece is a major holiday destination. Its culture and Mediterranean climate attract more than

7 million tourists annually, all year round. The **Ionian** and **Thracian** islands, the **Cyclades**, the **Dodecanese** and **Crete** are the most popular holiday islands. Obviously, Greece is a favourite destination for amateur archaeologists and anyone interested in antiquities. The best-known Ancient Greek archaeological sites are the capital city **Athens** and especially its **Acropolis, Thebes** and **Delphi, Corinth** and **Olympia**. The palace of King Minos on Crete, offering a glimpse of the ancient Minoan civilisation, is another major attraction. Magnificent **Byzantine** architecture can be seen in the orthodox monasteries and churches of Mount Athos on the Chalcidice (Haldidiki) Peninsula. Mount Athos is a self-governing enclave within Greece, and the only territory in Europe which forbids entry to women. Another group of Greek Orthodox monasteries, the impressive **Meteora monasteries,**

are perched inaccessibly on the top of high rocky outcrops in the centre of Greece. Winter sports facilities are enjoyed on **Parnassus** and on **Mt. Olympus.**
Athens, the capital city, suffers from pollution due to its heavy traffic which is affecting the Acropolis, already damaged due to war and plunder.

1 The picturesque island of Mykonos in the Cyclades, and the town of the same name, is a popular tourist destination.

2 The Parthenon, a marble temple dedicated to the goddess Athena, built in the Doric style in 447 to 438 BC tops the Acropolis in Athens.

3 Crusaders stormed the island of Rhodes in the fourteenth century and converted the town of the same name into a fortress.

4 Narrow alleys wind through Oya on Santorini, one of the islands of the Cyclades.

The Byzantine church **Hagia Sophia** in Istanbul was completed during the reign of the Roman Emperor Justinian in 537, but when the city was conquered by the Ottomans, it was converted into a mosque. In 1935, the building became a museum and national monument. The church's dome has a surface area of 7,570 sq. m and for a long time it was the largest dome in the eastern world, inspiring generations of Muslim and Christian architects.

Turkey

Area:	780,580 sq. km
Capital city:	Ankara
Form of government:	Republic
Administrative divisions: 81 provinces	
Population: 71 million (91 inhabitants/sq. km)	
Languages: Turkish (official), Kurdish	
GDP per capita:	US$5,600
Currency: 1 Turkish Lira = 100 kurus	

Natural Geography

Turkey is split in half by the **Bosphorus**, the **Sea of Marmara** and the **Dardanelles**. European Turkey (known as **Thrace**) is the smaller land mass, the **Anatolian Peninsula** in Asia accounting for most of the land mass. Turkey extends to the **Pontic Mountains** and the **Black Sea** coast in the north, and the **Taurus Mountains** in the south. Between the two lie the country's broad, high plateaus. The **Aras Mountains** (Mt Ararat, 5,137 m) lie to the east of the **Tigris** and **Euphrates** rivers.

Climate

Both, the Mediterranean and the Aegean coasts have a **subtropical climate**, while the Black Sea coast has a rather **humid climate** with year-round heavy rainfall. Eastern Anatolia's high plateaus have a **continental steppe climate**.

Population

The country's population is 80 per cent **Turkish**, of whom almost all (99.8 per cent) are **Muslim**. Roughly 20 per cent of the population are **Kurds**.

History and Politics

Turkey has been ruled by the Hittites, Greeks, Persians and finally the Romans. The first state in the region of modern Turkey was established in 552 AD.

Turkey first began to flourish in the late thirteenth century under the rule of the Sultan Osman I. His successor quickly extended the rule of the **Ottoman Empire** as far as the Balkans. In 1453, the fate of the Eastern Roman Empire was sealed when Sultan Mehmet II seized **Constantinople** (modern-day Istanbul). Constantinople then became the capital city of the Ottoman Empire, and the subsequent years were the most glorious in Turkey's history. Ottoman rule extended from **Hungary**, right across the **Balkans**, Ottomans' plans were foiled by when the **Siege of Vienna** failed in 1683, marking the end of their conquest of Europe. The corruption of the sultanate caused a revolution by the **Young Turks** in 1909. In World War I, Turkey sided with the Germans and Austro-Hungarians and there were terrible battles against the British, notably in the Dardanelles and Gallipoli. The **Turkish Republic** was founded in 1923 with **Kemal Ataturk** as its president. The new regime attempted modernisation. Turkey opted for neutrality in World War II. After a **military coup** in 1980, Turkey received a new constitution. Current internal political problems include human rights abuses, the increasing influence of radical Islam and the conflict with the Kurdish minority. Turkey is currently seeking **EU membership**.

Economy

In 2006, GDP was US$ 400 billion, of which 12 per cent came from **agriculture**, 21 per cent from **industry** and 67 per cent from **services**. Traditionally subject to heavy state influence, the Turkish economy has been liberalised in recent years. Important branches of industry have been deregulated and transparency in public investments and in the the whole of the **Middle East** including **Mesopotamia** (modern-day Iraq), and as far south as **Egypt**.

In 1526, Sultan Suleiman I (Suleiman the Magnificent) defeated King Lajos I of Hungary, opening the way for the Ottoman onslaught on central Europe. The banking sector has been increased. Privatisation of what have been in part very inefficient state-owned enterprises has so far been sluggish but continues to be pushed forward, not least in view of possible entry to the EU. There is a striking east-west divide.

Transport Infrastructure

Turkey has an excellent transport infrastructure, but **rail and road connections** become fewer the further east one travels. Istanbul, Izmir and Ankara have **International airports**. The major **ports** are Istanbul, Trabzon and Izmir.

Tourism

Istanbul has many tourist attractions, including the Blue Mosque and the Topkapi Palace. The main Mediterranean resorts are Izmir and **Antalya**. **Ankara** and Trabzon on the **Black Sea** are also important tourist destinations.

Cyprus

Area:	9,250 sq. km
Capital city:	Nicosia
Form of government: Presidential Republic	
Administrative divisions: 6 districts	
Population: 790,000 (85 inhabitants/sq. km)	
Languages: Greek, Turkish (both official), English	
GDP per capita:	US$23,700 (Republic of Cyprus)
Currency: 1 Cyprus pound = 100 cents	

In the European part of Istanbul, the 'Golden Horn' divides the districts of Galata and Beyoglu from the Ottoman old town.

Natural Geography

Cyprus is the third largest **island** in the Mediterranean, lying at the intersection of Europe, Asia and Africa. The south of the island is dominated by the **Troodos Mountains** whose highest peak is Mt Olympus (1,953 m). The Mesaoria plain covers the interior bounded in the north by the **Kyrenia Mountains**.

Climate

The country has a **Mediterranean climate** with hot, dry summers and mild, wet winters.

Kemal Ataturk

born Mustafa Kemal Pasha
*Salonica, 12.3.1881,
†Istanbul, 10.11.1938

After the defeat of the Ottoman Empire in World War I, Mustafa Kemal organised the national resistance to the Greek occupation and liberated modern Turkey. After the abdication of the Sultan in 1923, he became the first President of the Turkish Republic. In terms of domestic issues, he enforced monogamy, female equality, the separation of state and church, the introduction of Latin script for Turkish and fostered closer ties with the West. In 1934, he was awarded the honourary title of Ataturk ('Father of the Turks') by the Turkish National Assembly.

*Meticulous archeological excavation and restoration has restored the city of **Ephesus,** on the west coast of **Turkey**. In ancient times, the city was of immense importance due to its harbour and the Temple of Artemis, one of the Seven Wonders of the Ancient World. Other important monuments include the **Temple of Hadrian**.*

Average temperatures in Nicosia range from 10°C in January to 29°C in July.

Population

The largest proportion of the inhabitants of Cyprus are **Greek Cypriots**, representing 78 per cent of the population, of whom 99.5 per cent live on the Greek part of the island. **Turkish Cypriots** comprise 18 per cent of the population, and 98.7 per cent live in the Turkish part of the island. Cypriots are 78 per cent **Greek Orthodox**, and 18 per cent Sunni **Muslim**.

History and Politics

The island has been ruled by a series of nations, from the Egyptians, the Phoenicians, the Persians, Romans, Arabs, Crusaders and the Venetians. In 1925, it became a **British colony**. Cyprus declared itself an independent **republic** in 1960, but the United Kingdom continues to maintain military bases on the island.

The **conflict** between the Greek and Turkish populations errupted into civil war in 1963. After the Turkish invasion of 1973, the island was partitioned in 1974. The **Turkish Republic of Northern Cyprus** is only internationally recognised by Turkey. The **Republic of Cyprus** is governed by a house of representatives, in which only the seats for Greek Cypriots are occupied. Northern Cyprus has its own parliament. Cyprus joined the European Union in 2004, despite the unresolved problems of partition. Shortly after the signing of the accession treaties in the spring of 2003, the Turkish-Cypriot government opened the border between the two sides of the island.

Economy

After a 25-year upswing with rates of growth of 5.5 per cent on average, the economy has recently cooled somewhat. In 2006, GDP was US$ 18 billion, of which four per cent came from **agriculture**, 19 per cent from **industry** and 77 per cent from **services**. The most important source of income for the country continues to be tourism. Financial and corporate services have been flourishing due to beneficial tax laws.

Transport Infrastructure

There is no longer a railway on the island. The **road network** covers 12,500 km. There are **international airports** in Nicosia and Paphos. Cyprus has the fourth-largest merchant navy in the world.

Tourism

One of the many attractions is the old city of **Nicosia**. The **Troodos Mountains and the Kyrenia Mountains** contain numerous churches of the Byzantine period. The most popular coastal resorts are Limassol, Kyrenia and Larnaca. There is skiing in Troodos in the winter and one can swim in the Mediterranean on the same day.

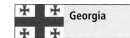

Georgia		

Area:	69,700 sq. km
Capital city:	Tbilisi
Form of government:	
Republic	
Administrative divisions:	
79 districts and cities,	
3 autonomous regions	
Population: 4.6 million	
(67 inhabitants/sq. km)	
Languages: Georgian (official),	
Russian, Armenian	
GDP per capita:	US$1,700
Currency:	
1 lari = 100 tetri	

Natural Geography

Georgia is bordered by the **Black Sea** in the west. which becomes the **Plain of Colchis**. The northern border is defined by the southern slopes of the **Greater Caucasus** (Mt Kazbek: 5048 m). The south of the country covers part of the Lesser Caucasus. East of Tbilisi, dry forest gives way to grassy steppes. Up to 80 per cent of the land is mountainous, and the population lives mainly around the river basins.

Climate

The Black Sea coast has a **humid sub-tropical climate**. Average temperatures in Tbilisi range from 6°C to 23°C, but east of the capital city, the climate becomes increasingly **continental**.

Population

Georgians constitute 70 per cent of the population, with eight per cent **Armenians**, 6.3 per cent **Russians**, 5.7 per cent **Azerbaijanis**, three per cent **Ossetians** and 1.7 per cent are **Abkhazians**. Three-quarters of the population are Christian orthodox, ten per cent of them Russian Orthodox. Muslims represent 11 per cent of the population and eight per cent

*Today, the traders in **Istanbul's** covered bazaar mainly trade with tourists. The bustling atmosphere is typical of souks and markets all over the Middle East. The oldest part of the original bazaar, the Old Bedesten, dates from the time of Mehmed the Conqueror. From here uncovered streets lead to the so-called Egyptian Bazaar.*

belong to the Armenian Apostolic Church. Georgia has some 250,000 internal refugees as a result of the struggles for independence in the region.

History and Politics

Georgia in mentioned in ancient **Greek myths**. The land was occupied by the **Romans** from 65 BC, and in the fourth century AD became part of the **Byzantine Empire**. The Georgian kingdom reached the height of its glory in the twelfth and thirteenth centuries, until the land was conquered by the **Mongolians** in the fourteenth century. The country was **divided** between the **Ottomans, Persians and Russians** in 1555, and in the eighteenth century, a kingdom of East Georgia was created, which became part of Tsarist Russia between 1801 and 1810. Georgia declared its independence in 1918, and the

Georgian Socialist Soviet Republic was formed in 1921. Since **independence** in 1991, the predominantly Islamic republics of **Abkhazia** and **South Ossetia** have fought to separate from Georgia. The **Autonomous Republic of Adjara** is 54 per cent populated by Georgian Muslims. In 1994, Georgia joined the **Commonwealth of Independent States** (CIS). The 'Velvet Revolution' took place in 2003, resulting in a new generation of young politicians coming to power.

Economy

In 2006, GDP was US$ 7.8 billion, of which 17 per cent came from **agriculture**, 24 per cent from **industry** and 59 per cent from **services**. Beet, potatoes and cereals are cultivated on the vast majority of agricultural land. In addition, citrus and tropical fruits, tea, tobacco, grapes and wine are cultivated. On the coast, eucalyptus, bamboo and bay laurels are also grown and harvested.

Mining includes ores, coal, copper, manganese, barite, diatomite and semi-precious stones. The processing industries produce foods and textiles and make up some 31 per cent of GDP. The main exports are raw materials and foods. The main focus of the service sector continues to be tourism, as it was during Soviet times.

Transport Infrastructure

The **infrastructure** has suffered badly from recent civil wars and economic problems. The **rail network** covers 1,583 km but is in poor condition. There are 20,700 km of **roads, however,** much of which are surfaced, though they can be impassable in the winter in the mountains. The **international airport** is in Tiflis (Tbilisi), and the major sea **ports** are Batumi, Poti and the Abkhazian capital city of Sokhumi.

Tourism

The country has 15 **nature conservation areas** and extensive **winter sports and hiking** facilities. **Sokhumi** and **Batumi** on the **Black Sea** coast are popular resorts. There are many **spas and hot springs** in the mountain regions. Important cultural centres are **Tbilisi, Kutaisi** and **Mtskheta**. Georgia's unique cultural heritage is a major attraction for tourists from the West.

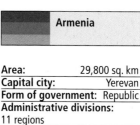

Armenia	
Area:	29,800 sq. km
Capital city:	Yerevan
Form of government:	Republic
Administrative divisions: 11 regions	
Population: 3 million (100 inhabitants/sq. km)	
Languages: Armenian (official), Russian, Kurdish	
GDP per capita: around US$2,000	
Currency: 1 dram = 100 luma	

Natural Geography

The **Armenian Highland** extends across the western reaches of the country. The north is dominated by the peaks of the **Lesser Caucasus**. The highest mountain is Mount Aragats (4,090 m).

Armenia lies at an average elevation of 1,800 m. The most fertile areas are found in the southern **Aras Valley**, where climate and soil are favourable for agriculture. Powerful earthquakes are common in Armenia and the country often suffers from prolonged **droughts**.

Climate

Armenia has a **continental climate** and steppe and semi-desert vegetation. Summers are hot, with temperatures in the capital, Yerevan, reaching an average of 25°C, but winters are bitterly cold.

Population

Armenians constitute some 96 per cent of the population, and there are also minority populations of **Kurds** and **Russians**. Christianity was introduced in the third century AD, making Armenia the oldest **Christian nation** in the world. Despite being under former Soviet rule, 94 per cent of the population belongs to the Armenian Apostolic Church. The people of Armenia suffer from the effects of an economic crisis and have a poorly developed **health care and social system**. Their plight is also intensified by natural disasters, such as earthquakes, and extreme air and environmental pollution.

History and Politics

The country was conquered in turn by the **Persians, Arabs** and **Mongols**. In 1828, the northern part of Armenia was conquered by Tsarist **Russia**. The first Armenian Republic was founded in 1918, but was then divided in 1922, one part becoming a Soviet republic of the USSR, and the other part ceded to **Turkey**. Armenia declared independence in 1991.

Armenia is demanding autonomy for the **Nagorno-Karabakh**, exclave which is located within the borders of **Azerbaijan** but whose population is overwhelmingly Armenian Christian. This has led to many conflicts. Azerbaijan, in turn, lays claim to the enclave of **Nakhichevan**, which is situated within Armenia's borders.

Economy

In 2006, GDP was US$ 6.4 billion, of which 24 per cent derived from **agriculture**, 39 per cent from **industry** and 37 per cent from **services**. Growth of 13.9 per cent was also reported in the same year – although starting from a very low level (official per capita income: US$ 1,439). Armenia's strong agricultural sector cultivates cereals, tea, tobacco and grapes for wine. The main exports are jewellery and metal products. However, trade is hampered due to closed borders with Turkey and Azerbaijan.

Transport Infrastructure

The country's **rail network** covers 825 km, but both the rail and **road network** are in a poor condition. There is an **international airport** in Yerevan.

Tourism

The capital city, **Yerevan**, contains several important museums and is the country's cultural centre. Armenia's greatest treasures are, without doubt, the numerous early Christian monuments. There are magnificent **churches and cliff top monasteries** in the mountains around Yerevan. **Lake Sevan**, at an altitude of 1,600 m, is popular with hikers.

The Blue Mosque in Istanbul gets its name from the blue Iznik tiles covering its walls.

*Much of **Turkey** is farmland, but many farmers have to survive without modern equipment – so the donkey is a very important pack-animal. Agriculture has only been modernised in the fertile lowlands.*

Azerbaijan

Area:	86,600 sq. km
Capital city:	Baku
Form of government:	Republic
Administrative divisions: 54 districts, 9 cities, 2 autonomous regions	
Population: 8.1 million (94 inhabitants/sq. km)	
Languages: Azerbaijani (official), Turkish, Russian	
GDP per capita:	US$2,400
Currency: 1 Manat = 100 gepik	

Natural Geography

The **Greater Caucasus** in the north (4,466 m), the **Lesser Caucasus**, the **Karabakh** in the west and the mountain chain in the south, which extends into Iran, cover over half of Azerbaijan's land mass. In the east lie the start of the plains of the **Kura** and **Aras** rivers, bordered in the south by the **Caspian Sea**. Parts of this region lie up to 28 m below sea-level. The **Nakhichevan** enclave is separated from the rest of the country by the Sangesur mountains.

Climate

Azerbaijan has a **semi-desert climate**, meaning that agriculture is only possible through the irrigation of large tracts of land. Average temperatures in the capital , Baku, range from 1°C to 34°C.

Population

The population is 90 per cent **Azeri**, 2.5 per cent **Russian** and two per cent **Armenian**. All the Armenians live in the **Nagorno-Karabakh** region. The vast majority of the population is **Muslim**, but there are small groups of **Orthodox Christians**.

History and Politics

The region has been inhabited for millennia, and was once a **Roman province**. It has been a **Muslim country** since the seventh century. After 300 years of **Mongolian** rule, the country first had to defeat the **Ottoman Turks** then deal with attack from **Tsarist Russia**. It was then divided between Russia and Persia in 1813. The **Soviet Republic of Azerbaijan** was

established in 1920. Ethnic conflicts in the dispute over the Nagorno-Karabakh region and its union with Armenia in 1988 led Azerbaijan to declare **independence** in 1991 and revived Islamic fundamentalism, although it has not allied itself with other Muslim countries and maintains good relations with Israel and the West.

Economy

In 2006, GDP was US$ 20 billion, of which 12 per cent came from **agriculture**, 54 per cent from **industry** and 34 per cent from **services**. Azerbaijan's economy is based

primarily on its oil deposits, which, with the help of foreign investors, is currently leading to enormous rates of growth (26.4 per cent in 2005). However, almost one-third of the population lives below the poverty line and derives no benefit from this natural resource.

Transport Infrastructure

The public **rail network** covers 2,125 km and the mostly surfaced **road network** covers 57,700 km. The main **port** and **international airport** are located in Baku which is also an important **oil terminal**.

Tourism

Baku is Azerbaijan's cultural centre with numerous mosques, palaces and an interesting old town. The **Seki caravanserai**, in the foothills of the **Caucasus**, is an ancient hostel for travellers, now converted into a delightful hotel. There are ancient **Babylonian monuments** in the south.

1 At 5,165 m high, Mt Ararat rises above the disputed border region between Turkey, Armenia and Iran. According to the Old Testament, Noah's Ark came to rest on top of this extinct volcano when the Flood subsided.

2 Turkey is not a well-known wine producer, but the regions around the Sea of Marmara and the Aegean yield excellent red and white wines.

3 Bodrum is an historic town, whose narrow streets are filled with tourists in the summer. In antiquity, the town was known as Halicarnassus and was the site of the tomb of King Mausolus – one of the seven wonders of the Ancient World. The castle on the headland dates from the time of the Crusades (fourteenth century).

4 The thirteenth century Metechi Church sits atop a craggy peak above the Georgian capital city of Tbilisi.

Russia

St Petersburg: one of the world's greatest art collections is housed in the Hermitage. Since the collapse of the Soviet Union, foreign tourists are once again flocking to the city (formerly Leningrad) which has a long tradition of attracting visitors. In the mid-nineteenth century, Leo von Klenze, court architect of Bavarian King Ludwig I, designed the buildings that surround the Winter Palace.

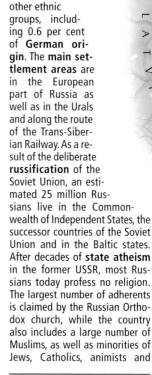

Russia	
Area:	17,075,200 sq. km
Capital city:	Moscow
Form of government: Federal Presidential Republic	
Administrative divisions: 89 territories of the federation	
Population: 141 million (8 inhabitants/sq. km)	
Languages: Russian (official), more than 100 other languages	
GDP per capita:	US$6,900
Currency: 1 Rouble = 100 kopecks	

Natural Geography

Russia is the **largest state** on Earth in terms of area, covering some 11 per cent of the surface of the planet. It extends from the **Baltic** and the **Black Sea** in the south to the **Pacific** and the **Bering Straits** and from the **Arctic Ocean** to the inner Asian east by hills and mountains. In the north and north-east the gigantic afforested regions of the **Taiga belt** covering large parts of Siberia merge into the **Arctic Tundra**; there are peninsulas off the north-east **coast,** such as Kola and Kamchatka and islands such as Sakhalin, which is part of the Japanese archipelago. To the south-east, the wide **steppes** give way to **desert**.

In total, more than one-fifth of the **afforested areas** of Earth are situated within the territory of the Russian Federation. They include the great mixed woodlands of western Russia as well as the huge coniferous forests (boreal forests) of the Taiga in the north.

The **Kamchatka** peninsula on the Pacific and the **Kuril Islands** at the extreme east of the country are full of seismic activity. Of the 3,000 **volcanoes** on Kamchatka, thirty are still active; the highest of these peaks is Klyuchevskaya Sopka (4,750 m). Ten making it the deepest freshwater lake on Earth.

Climate

The Russian climate is as varied as the enormous extent of the country. It ranges from the **steppe climate** in the central-south through the **dry continental climate** of most of the European part of Russia, with very hot summers and snowy winters, to the **sub-Arctic and Arctic** temperatures of Siberia. The whole of the north is characterised by a **tundra and polar climate**.

The **coldest place on** Earth is at Oimyakon, Eastern Siberia. Temperatures of -69.8°C have been recorded here. Just under half of the total land mass of Russia is under permafrost. The Black Sea coast and south-central Asia, however, are typically **sub-tropical**, with temperatures of between 6°C in the winter and an average of 23°C in the summer. Temperatures in Moscow in

other ethnic groups, including 0.6 per cent of **German origin**. The **main settlement areas** are in the European part of Russia as well as in the Urals and along the route of the Trans-Siberian Railway. As a result of the deliberate **russification** of the Soviet Union, an estimated 25 million Russians live in the Commonwealth of Independent States, the successor countries of the Soviet Union and in the Baltic states. After decades of **state atheism** in the former USSR, most Russians today profess no religion. The largest number of adherents is claimed by the Russian Orthodox church, while the country also includes a large number of Muslims, as well as minorities of Jews, Catholics, animists and

Josef Stalin

born Dzhugashvili, J.
*Gori, 21.12.1879,
†Moscow, 5.3.1953

Stalin led the Communist Party of the Soviet Union from 1929 until his death. His Great Purges and policy of collective farming cost the lives of millions of people. Before the outbreak of World War II, Stalin initially signed a pact with Germany, but later joined the Allies and helped defeat Germany. In so doing, he brought large parts of eastern Europe under Soviet influence.

Monument to Nicholas I and St Isaac's Cathedral in St Petersburg.

Vladimir Lenin

born Uljanov, V. I.
*Simbirsk, 22.4.1878,
†Gorky, 21.1.1924

Lenin was a Russian revolutionary who was imprisoned several times in Tsarist Russia. He was exiled but continued to fight against the House of Romanov. After the March 1917 revolution, he returned to Petrograd and organised a Bolshevik coup, known as the October Revolution of 1918. The founder of the Soviet Union resigned after the civil war in 1922 due to illness.

History and Politics

As early as the first millennium BC the **ancient Slavs** came from the East and settled in the area around the Dnieper. On the **trade route** between the Baltic and the Black Sea, there developed **Kievan Rus**, a country that was christianised as early as 988. It was to become the largest state in Europe until it was overrun by the **Mongols** in 1230. Before this, it gained in standing and influence through its trade with Byzantium. **Novgorod** remained for a long time the only city-state to withstand the onslaught of the Mongols. It was the principality of Moscow, obscure hitherto, that in 1380 vanquished the Golden Hordes and unified the existing **Russian city-states**. In 1547 the Grand Duke of Mus-

uplands. There is a time difference of more than ten hours between the Bering Straits and the Baltic. The **Urals** (Mount Narodnaya: 1895 m) divides the interior of Russia into the **Eastern European Uplands** and the **Western Siberian Lowlands**, an enormous wetland area about the size of Central Europe, fed by the rivers **Ob** and **Yenissey**.

The **Caucasus** (Mount Elbrus: 5633 m) forms the south-eastern border of the country, which is enclosed in the east and south-

rivers more than 2,200 km in length flow through Russia, of which the longest is the **Ob** with its tributary the **Irtysh**, which rises in the Altai mountains and flows into the **Karal Sea**. The two rivers combined are 5,410 km long.

At 3,351 km, the **Volga** is Europe's longest river. The largest lake, which lies close to the **Caspian Sea**, is the 600-km-long **Lake Baikal**, south of the Central Siberian mountain range. It has a maximum depth of 1,620 m,

January are -9°C on average, and temperatures of -30°C and below are by no means uncommon. In July, the temperature rises to an average of 20°C.

Population

The majority of the population, of whom only 20 per cent live in the Asian part of Russia, are **Russians** (81.5 per cent); minorities include **Tatars** (3.8 per cent), **Ukrainians** (three per cent), **Chuvashes** and hundreds of

Buddhists. **Sects** (such as Mun and Aum) are also widely represented. The **health, pensions and social security systems**, were built up under the Soviet Union and until recently were heavily subsidised. They are now in a state of flux, and as a result there is great difficulty in achieving effective adjustment to the fundamentally altered social and economic conditions. About one-fifth of the population, particularly old people, live below the national **poverty line**.

covy, Ivan IV, had himself crowned the **first Tsar** of all the Russias, the ruler of a 'Third Rome'. He initiated ambitious **expeditions of expansion and conquest**, which led his troops far to the east, beyond the Urals and as far as the Caspian Sea. **Peter I** (Peter the Great) (1682–1725) pushed for **Europeanisation**, defeating Sweden

in 1709 and, through his **new capital St Petersburg,** secured the influence of the Russian Empire in the Baltic states. It was that parts of Karelia, Latvia and Estonia were annexed to the Russian Empire. Thereafter, Russia, became a **major power**, playing a decisive part in European politics, and gradually extended its influence as far as the Far East and the Balkans, and conquering the lands of Central Asia. Russia's internal situation, however was bleak. There was serfdom, the peasants and city-dwellers endured **appalling living conditions**, resulting in constant **uprisings** between peasants and landowners, as well as **nationalist rebellions**. The revolutions

Russia

Moscow: the underground is an important method of transport in the capital city of the **Russian Federation**. Since 1935 it has guaranteed speedy connections between different parts of the city. Many of the stations are spectacularly decorated, as seen here at Komsomolskaya. This is yet another sign of Moscow's importance as the political, economic and cultural centre of the former USSR.

of 1825, 1860 and 1905 culminated in the **February Revolution** of 1917 and led to the deposition of the last tsar, Nicholas II, who was executed with his family in 1918.

In the **October Revolution** of 1917, the Provisional Government was replaced in a coup by the Workers' Councils, the Bolsheviks, who seized executive power under the leadership of **Vladimir Ilyich Lenin** and **Lev Davidovich Trotsky**. The Communist Party set up a **'dictatorship of the proletariat'**. After the the Red Army won back numerous provinces that had used this opportunity to secede from Russia, the **Union of Soviet Socialist Republics (USSR)** was founded in 1922. Nationalities were officially granted the

defended its territory making great sacrifices until it was finally victorious, entering the German Reich and occupying Berlin in 1945. After World War II, the Soviet sphere of influence extended over the whole of Eastern Europe through Finland and as far as Manchuria. The Berlin blockade of 1948 marked the beginning of the **Cold War** with the USA; in 1949 the USSR became an **atomic power**. On Stalin's death, the process of **destalinisation** was begun, and limited co-operation with the USA started. In spite of several crises, such as the Cuban Missile Crisis of 1962, a raprochement with the West continued. **Leonid Ilyich Brezhnev** suppressed the **struggle for independence** of the satellite states such as Czecho-

West Germany and, only a year later, the mighty **Warsaw Pact**, an alliance of Communist countries to counter that of NATO, was dissolved. Within the USSR, **nationality conflicts** soon broke out and the first republics asserted their independence (Latvia in 1990, Estonia in August 1991, the Ukraine in 1991, Lithuania and Tajikistan in September 1991 and Kazakhstan in December 1991).

With the **resignation of Gorbachev** at the end of 1991, the old USSR was finally dissolved. Its successor was the **Russian Federation**, consisting of 21 autonomous republics: Adygea, Altai, Bashkortostan, Buryatia, Khavkassia, Dagestan, Ingushetia, Kabardino-Balkaria, Kalmykia, Karachay-Cherkessia,

Kaliningrad, between Poland and Lithuania. The 1993 agreement, which was rejected by the republics of Chechnya and Tatarstan, envisages a federated democratic republic.

Russia's **bicameral parliament** consists of the **State Duma**, whose representatives are directly elected every four years, and the **Federation Council**, to which each of the total of 89 administrative regions (republics, regions and districts) sends two deputies. The **President**, directly elected by the people is accorded extensive authority.

A **potential for conflict** in the future lies in the aspirations to independence of some republics which have led in recent years to violent military clashes in Chechnya, Ossetia and Tatarstan. In the

seven per cent, which is to a large extent based on immense deposits of raw materials (one-third of global natural gas deposits, 12 per cent of crude oil and one-third of coal deposits, as well as the world's largest mineral deposits and enormous forest stands). The continuously high prices of oil and gas compensate for continued serious problems in transferring from a planned to a market economy. In addition, the government has increasingly protected itself in recent years – sometimes using questionable means – by exerting substantial influence on strategically important branches of industry, particularly the energy sector, which along with insufficient legal security has frightened off many investors.

Other significant branches of industry are foodstuffs, iron and steel, machine construction, chemicals and transportation equipment. Agriculture, with its cultivation of potatoes, cereals, sugar beet and cabbage, the rearing of livestock and dairy farming, is no longer of any great macroeconomic significance, but makes a major contribution to the subsistence economy in rural areas. The informal sector still plays a large part in the Russian economy.

There is great inequality in the distribution of assets: while Moscow, St Petersburg and some oil-producing regions are booming, the majority of the rural population continues to live in conditions of poverty.

Nikita Khrushchev

*Kalinovka, 17.4.1894,
†Moscow, 11.9.1971

After Stalin's death in 1953, Khrushchev joined the internal power struggle. At the Twentieth Party Congress in 1956, he exposed Stalin's crimes and became premier of the Soviet Union in 1958. His attempt to produce a 'thaw' in the Cold War was overshadowed by the Berlin Ultimatum, the Hungarian Uprising, the Berlin Wall, the Cuban missile crisis and the split with China. He was deposed by Brezhnev in 1964.

Ice statues in front of St Basil's Cathedral in Moscow.

Mikhail Gorbachev

*Privolnoje, 2.3.1931

After being named General Secretary of the CPSU, Gorbachev led a process of democratisation of the Soviet Union under his 'perestroika' and 'glasnost' programmes. He also ended the atomic arms race. The collapse of the political and economic systems of the Eastern Bloc also led to the breakup of the USSR, of which he was president until 1991. He received the Nobel Peace Prize in 1990.

---

right to self-determination. Under the USSR's next ruler, **Josef Vissarionovich Stalin**, industrialisation was driven forward from 1924 on a massive scale, and agriculture was collectivised, but at the same time the government also set up labour camps to which dissents were deported and ordered millions of executions of alleged enemies of the state.

In 1939, Stalin concluded a **non-aggression pact** with Germany using this opportunity to gain time and to annex the Baltic states and eastern Poland. When the German Wehrmacht eventually attacked the Soviet Union in 1941 Russia entered the **World War II**. The Red Army valiantly

slovakia, Poland and Hungary, and made efforts to secure the post-war borders. The enormous cost of the **arms race** took its toll, and the economy suffered a downturn. Gradually, a **movement** took shape, which finally led in 1985 to the election of **Mikhail Sergeyevich Gorbachev** as General Secretary of the Communist Party.

His slogans of **'glasnost'** and **'perestroika'** introduced the 'politics of change' which involved Russian renunciation of pretensions to the d omination of its neighbours. This also produced **political upheavals** in the satellite states of central and eastern Europe. The year 1989/90 saw the reunification of East and

Karelia, Komi, Mari El, Mordova, North Ossetia, Sakha, Tatarstan, Chechnya, Chuvashia, Tuva and Udmurtia. Added to these were Birobidjan, the Jewish autonomous region on the Chinese border, the autonomous region of the Nenets on the Barents Sea, the autonomous region of the Chukchi on the Bering Strait, and the autonomous region of the Evenks in Central Siberia. Plans to set up an autonomous republic for **Germans** living in Russia were postponed for the time being, but the republic of Altai includes administrative districts with self-government by German residents. Part of the territory of the Russian Federation is the **exclave of**

Commonwealth of Independent States (CIS), founded in 1991, the union of the twelve former Soviet republics of Armenia, Azerbaijan, Georgia, Kazakhstan, Kyrgyzstan, Moldova, Russia, Tadjikistan, Turkmenistan, Ukraine, Uzbekistan and Belarus, Russia, as the successor to the Soviet Union, plays a leading role.

Economy

In 2006, GDP was almost US$ 1 trillion, of which five per cent derived from agriculture, 37 per cent from industry and 58 per cent from services. In recent years, Russia has experienced stable rates of growth of about

Transport Infrastructure

Russia's **railway network** covers 154,000 km mainly in the south-western part of the country. Some 40 per cent of the system is reserved for freight. The most important long-distance connection is the **Trans-Siberian Railway**, which covers more than 9,311 km and runs from Moscow to Vladivostok. There is also an extension to China, as far as Beijing.

Russia's **road network** extends over a length of 948,000 km, of which 416,000 are not public, but reserved exclusively for military and industrial purposes. Only 336,000 km are surfaced, another 201,000 are only passable

Russian Orthodox churches: Despite the great iconoclasm of the eighth and ninth centuries, holy icons are still central to the rituals of Russian Orthodoxy, which has survived throughout 80 years of atheist, Communist rule.

during a few months of the year. Russia has more than 630 **airports**, meaning that even remote areas of Siberia can be reached by air.

The two international airports are Sheremtevo in **Moscow and St Petersburg**. The national airline **Aeroflot**, which is still largely state-owned, serves 100 cities in 47 countries. **Inland navigation** on the waterway whose total length is 101,000 km, of which 16,900 km are canals, is also an important means of transport. The country's most important **ports**, the gateways to the Pacific, Atlantic and North Sea, the Black Sea and the Baltic, are at Archangel (Arkhangelsk), St Petersburg, Kaliningrad, Vladivostok, Okhotsk and Rostov.

Tourism

Russia continues to attract mainly **group travel**, because since the dissolution of the state tourist organisation, when individual travel was actually forbidden the tourist sector has been in a state of flux. **Individual tourists** encounter obstacles such as an inadequate infrastructure and an occasionally crippling bureaucratic system. In addition, many areas are still forbidden to tourists. This gigantic country has innumerable attractions to offer, from **beautiful landscapes** to superb evidence of its long **cultural history**.

The main centres of tourism are the two great cities of **St Petersburg and Moscow**. Among the most important sights of St Petersburg, capital city of the tsars, are the 125 museums, including the **Church of the Resurrection**, the **Hermitage**, one of the greatest art museums of the world, and the **Peter and Paul Fortress**. Most visitors to this city in the far north come for the famous 'white nights' in July, when the sky never gets dark.

Further attractions are the **palaces of the tsars** in the surrounding area, **Pavlovsk** with its unique **Park, the Peterhof** and **Tsarskoe Selo**. The main attractions of **Moscow** are **Red Square** with the **Kremlin**, **St Basil's Cathedral** and the **GUM department store**.

Among the tsars' residences in and around Moscow are **Arkhangelskoye, Kolomenskoye, Kuskovo** and **Ostankino**. About 200 km south of St Petersburg lies the city of **Novgorod** with its mighty sixteenth-century Kremlin as well as two monasteries and 47 churches, of which the Cathedral of St Sophia is the most important. The Ring of Golden Cities contains monuments from a period covering more than 1000 years: **Rostov** on the Don, the old capital of **Vladimir** with its magnificent mansions, **Susdal** with its monasteries and churches, as

well as the former royal residence of **Kideksha** are the most important of the many notable sights.

Barely four per cent of the area of the country is an official conservation area. The **Komi forest** in northern Russia is one of the world's largest national parks. Polar animals inhabit the vast, untouched forests and **Tundra**. Parts of the **Taimyr peninsula** in northern Siberia are protected areas. The still largely unexplored peninsular of **Kamchatka** contains the Kronotsky National Park whose geysers and hot springs have given the peninsula the soubriquet of 'Land of Fire and Ice'. There is also great variety of animal and plant life. The island of **Wrangel** in north-eastern Siberia, inside the Artic Circle, is home to polar bears, seals, walruses and numerous species of Arctic birds.

Lake Baikal, in the mountains of central Siberia, has also been declared a protected area. It

has unique flora and fauna, including the Baikal seal. Surrounding this inland stretch of water are health resorts and mineral springs. Other popular holiday destinations are the **Baltic** resorts near Kaliningrad, the **northern Caucasus** and the **seaside towns** of the Black and Caspian Seas.

1 Moscow is the seat of government of the Russian Federation: the palace in the Kremlin is overlooked by the 'Ivan the Great' clock tower.

2 Huts for storing straw stand on stilts to protect them from the waters of the Kamenka River.

3 The brightly-coloured domes of Russian orthodox churches originate in the Byzantine tradition. This is the Pereslavl-Zalessky-Goritsky Monastery.

4 The Stalinist architecture of Moscow State University on the banks of the Moskva River.

Russia's wealth lies in the expanses of Siberia. In addition to petroleum, pumped through giant pipelines to China and Japan, Siberia has the world's largest natural gas reserves. Other mineral resources include coal, uranium, diamonds, gold and other precious metals. The pictures to the left show the

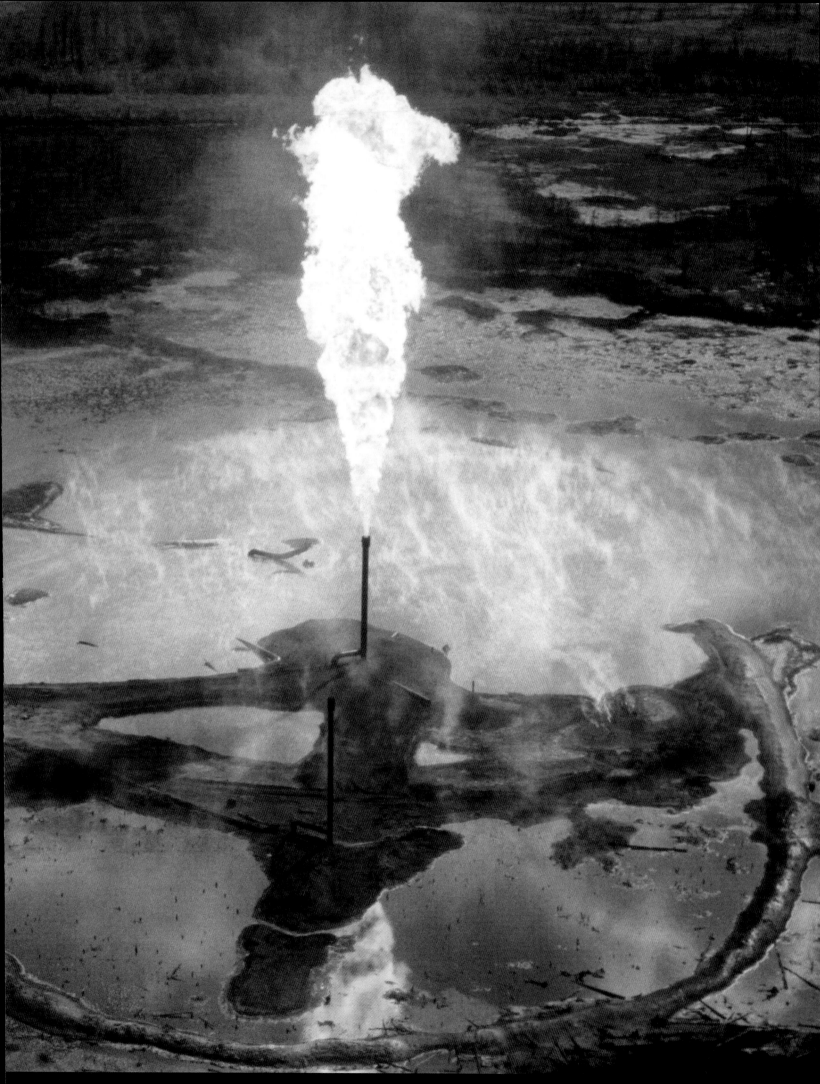

extreme conditions experienced by those extracting deposits of natural gas on Jamal, a peninsula in Western Siberia on the Arctic Ocean, and nickel smelting at Norilsk. The image on the right shows the flares above an oil field at Nizhnevartovsk, the fourth largest in the world.

Peoples of Europe

In terms of surface area, Europe is the world's second smallest continent – but with approximately 725 million inhabitants spread across 44 countries (including Russia), in terms of population it is second only to Asia. The population

Europe meets Asia in the features of this young Russian girl.

density of Europe is equally high, and has been the cause of countless wars fought over land and raw materials throughout its history.

Europe's ethnic diversity can be traced back to the first great waves of migrating Indo-Europeans from Central Asia 5,000 years ago. Later, peoples from Egypt and the Near East settled on the island of Crete, from where the Minoans – the most ancient civilization of Greece and therefore also of Europe – spread out across the entire Mediterranean region.

From around 1500 BC, Greece became Europe's cultural hub. Along with the expansion of the Roman empire 2,000 years ago, it was the Greek civilization that shaped the entire Western world.

Northern Europe

*The friendly and perpetually laid-back **Icelanders** enjoy a similar high standard of living to that of the other Scandinavian countries – Norway, Sweden, Denmark, Finland, the Faroes and Lapland. The numerous small and large geysers found all over Iceland are testament to the fact that this is still a highly volcanic island. At regular intervals, jets of boiling hot water shoot up into the air from deep inside the earth, before settling in steaming pools of water.*

The Icelanders

The Icelanders are descended from the Norwegian **Vikings** and **Scottish Celts** who settled **Iceland** at the beginning of the ninth century. For many centuries Iceland belonged to various Scandinavian kingdoms, until finally gaining political and economic independence in 1944. Today the island has a population of about 280,000 inhabitants, most of whom live in the capital, **Reykjavik**.

With its origins dating back to the beginning of the eighth century, the great mythological work known as the **Edda** marked the birth of an Icelandic **literature** that became the foundation of Nordic literary heritage. The Edda is a collection of poems and songs whose authorship is largely unknown. It includes epigrams, magic spells and tales of wisdom about the creation of the earth, featuring the deeds of gods, giants and dwarfs, as well as other mythical creatures.

Two traditional Icelandic musical instruments, used to accompany singing, are the **langspil**, resembling the Norwegian **langeleik** string zither, and the **fidla** (a fiddle with no similarity to the modern violin). Both instruments are played with a bow.

Today Iceland boasts a higher proportion of writers than any other country.

The Faroese

Like **Iceland**, the **Faroe Islands** (or, in Faroese, 'Sheep Islands') were also settled by Scandinavian **Vikings** during the ninth century. However, it is possible that Irish monks had already set foot upon the Faroes in the seventh century. The islands have belonged to **Denmark** since 1380 and since 1948 have been an autonomous province.

Thanks to the islands' remote location, the lives of the **Faroese**, a population some 50,000 strong, are still heavily influenced by old traditions. Alongside countless old legends and myths, the islands' medieval chain dances and some 70,000 sung ballads – passed down orally through the generations – lie at the heart of Faroese tradition. The **Faroese language** has its roots in Old Norse, and is spoken alongside **Danish** – the islands' second official tongue.

The Laplanders (Sami)

Originally from **Siberia**, the Sami (the term '**Laplander**' is considered pejorative) settled the northern European countries long before the Vikings. Today, the 65,000-strong **Sami** population is spread across the northern regions of **Norway** (40,000), **Sweden** (6,000) and **Finland** (17,000), as well as the Russian **Kola Peninsula** (2,000).

The Sami are sub-divided by both geography and traditional occupation: **Sea Sami** live in **northern Norway** and live by sea fishing and agriculture, **River Sami** live mostly in **Sweden** and **Finland** and make their living from hunting, river fishing and agriculture, while the **Forest Sami** – whose settlements are mostly in **northern Sweden** – survive by hunting and fishing. **Mountain Sami**, meanwhile, make up about ten per cent of the Sami population and lead a nomadic existence, moving between two or three fixed grazing lands with their herds of reindeer.

In reality, the boundaries between the **Sami** and the general population have become increasingly blurred, and today only a small minority still live according to the old Sami way of life. Even in the traditionally nomadic reindeer-breeding communities – where the Sami still live in **gammen** (a type of tent) – cell phones and motorised sleighs have long since become part of everyday life.

The Sami language is of the Finno-Ugric family and bears similarities only to Finnish. The nine Sami dialects can be so different from each other that northern and southern Sami can only communicate via the native tongue of their respective countries.

The bright Sami national costumes are an important part of Sami tradition, albeit one that is now mostly confined to folk festivals. Traditional Sami craft skills are displayed in beautifully made objects carved from wood and reindeer horn, and there is also a strong silversmithing tradition. Sami music is characterised by the **joik**, an unusual overtone song whose roots go back to prehistoric times. Also passed down through generations of Sami is the belief in the healing powers of the shamans, although it is only in the most remote regions that the shaman are still accorded any real influence.

The Norwegians

Like all Scandinavians, the 4.5 million **Norwegians** are directly descended from the Vikings and belong to the Germanic group of peoples. Norway's close ties to the other Scandinavian countries have a long history. In the fifteenth century, Norway was united with **Denmark**, then – from 1814 until its independence in 1915 – with **Sweden**. This history has given rise to a vigorous cultural interchange between the Norwegians and its fellows.

Old Nordic legends provide the foundations of Norwegian literature. Passed down from the eighth century in the **Edda**, they tell of **Odin**, the father of the gods, his wife **Frigga**, the realm of mankind **Midgard**, and the mythical **Yggdrasil** tree. There is also an extensive body of Norwegian folk music. The different regions' local identities are reflected in their individual traditional costumes, which are worn on feast days.

The Swedes

Europe's 9 million **Swedes** almost certainly get their name from the **Svear**, who lived in central Sweden from around 300. Their places of worship and grave mounds at **Uppsala** date from the fifth and sixth centuries, and mark what was once the heart of their region. By the tenth century, the Svear had also brought the area occupied by the north Germanic **Geats** as well as **Gotland** and **Öland** under their control. Around 1100, this became the basis of Sverige – modern-day Sweden. Between

Young girls and women wear bright garlands of flowers at the midsummer's eve festival.

*Making use of all that nature has to offer is a way of life for the traditional nomadic **Sami**, as can be seen from their folk costumes and elaborately embroidered felt caps. In common with many other nomadic peoples, the Sami boast a long tradition of felting. The dense woollen cloth provides protection from the elements, and is also highly decorative. The embroidered patterns on the felt signify the particular Sami tribe to which the wearer belongs.*

the ninth and eleventh centuries, Swedish **Vikings** sailed across the **Baltic** to the **Volga** river and on as far as **Hungary**, **Byzantium** and **Baghdad**. By the end of the fourteenth century, Sweden had been brought under the rule of the Norwegian-Danish crown, but the country became independent again in 1523.

In 1814, **Sweden** was united with **Norway**, a union that was to last until 1905. The **Sami** people of northern Sweden were granted a number of special privileges in order to safeguard their culture.

The **Julfest** – an old Germanic celebration marking the birth of the sun in homage to the god Odin – is the most important ancient Swedish tradition. People believed that between 25 December and 6 January, Odin soared through the skies on his eight-legged horse, and during these twelve nights they left an oak log to char in their fireplaces and so protect their houses from evil curses. Farmers would also leave sheaves of corn out for birds, giving rise to the Scandinavian tradition of hanging a straw wreath above the Christmas table. Another old Swedish tradition takes place on December 13, when the festival of light in homage to **Saint Lucia** marks what is considered to be the shortest day of the year. According to the tradition, a girl in every family plays the role of the bride Lucia. She dresses in white and dons a crown decorated with burning candles before offering sweet pastries to the rest of the family as they wake up.

The Finns

Finno-Ugric peoples began to settle in southern Finland around 1300 BC, driving the indigenous **Sami** ever further north. By the end of the thirteenth century, three distinct Finnish tribes had emerged: the **Finns** proper (the **Suomi** people) lived in the southwest, the **Tavastians** lived in the inland lake regions, and the **Karelians** inhabited the east of the country. From the thirteenth century, **Finland** belonged to Sweden, and from 1809 to 1917 it was part of **Russia**.

The main difference between the approximately 5.2 million Finns and the Scandinavians is the Finnish language, which – like Estonian and Hungarian – belongs to the Finno-Ugric linguistic family. The Finns are also distinguished by their unique culture, most notably their traditional folk music and the Kantele – the Finnish national instrument, with which Finnish folk music is intimately entwined.

The most important Finnish epic poem is the **Kalevala** (22,795 verses) – some 3000 years old, it continues to be performed on Finnish feast days.

The Danes

The **Danes** have been traced back to the sixth century BC. It is thought that their original homeland was probably **southern Sweden**, from where they spread to the islands south of the Kattegat all the way to **Jutland**. Danes from different groups first came together to form a state in the tenth century. In the eleventh century, Danish **Vikings** conquered the entire **North Sea region**, occupying **England** and forming a Danish North Sea empire consisting of **Denmark**, **Norway**, **England** and **Scotland**, which disintegrated within 50 years.

The next incarnation of the Danish empire was the thirteenth-century Baltic Sea empire, comprising – among other places – **Holstein**, **Hamburg**, **Lübeck**, **Mecklenburg**, **Pomerania**, the island of **Rügen** and **Estonia**. Approximately 5.3 million people live in today's Denmark. Mem-

ories of the Vikings are kept alive by the many surviving examples of their craftwork, while the last remaining ruins of early wooden churches bear witness to old Danish culture.

As in the traditions of Sweden and Norway, Danish folk literature is rooted largely in the Old Nordic Edda.

1 Icelandic fisherman are well used to a frugal existence. Fishing and fish processing are the backbone of the Icelandic economy, and fish products account for 75 per cent of the country's exports.

2, **3** and **4** The Sami of Lapland originally lived to the south of their current settlements. In the face of hundreds of years of Viking and Finnish advancement, the Sami gradually retreated north to the area around the Arctic Circle. Pictured: herding reindeer in spring, cooking fish over a traditional wood fire, and making shoe soles from blades of grass.

Western and Central Europe

Ireland – slightly smaller in area than the US state of South Carolina – has one of Europe's highest child population rates. It also has the greatest number of redheads, bucking the global trend since redheads elsewhere in the world are in rapid decline. Northern Ireland has *suffered long-standing ethno-political conflict between Catholics and Protestants, but since the 1998 Good Friday Agreement, the situation has been improving. Many schools are segregated by faith, although integrated schools are now gaining in popularity.*

The Irish

Ireland was settled by the **Gaelic Celts in** around 500 BC. The Celts repressed the native tribes and, in the period up to the fifth century AD, founded five empires on the island. Knights and druid priests, in particular, enjoyed great power and influence.

After 795, **Vikings** settled on the island, where they built trading posts and ports. But the Vikings were driven out again in 1014, and in 1169 large parts of Ireland were conquered by the **Anglo-Normans**. In 1601, Ireland came completely under English rule.

The United Kingdom, made up of **Great Britain** (comprising England, Wales and Scotland) and **Ireland,** was declared in 1801. Southern Ireland (**Eire**) became independent in 1949, but **Northern Ireland** remains a part of the United Kingdom. Today, the

Numerous Irish customs and festivals have been passed down from ancient, pre-Christian times. One of these festivals, **Samhain** – a precursor of the modern-day **Halloween** – has been celebrated in **Ireland** for 5000 years and is probably one of the oldest festivals in the world.

The word '**Samhain**' is believed to derive from '**sam-fuin**', which roughly translates as '**the end of summer**' and therefore marks the end of the year, since the Celtic calendar is divided into only two seasons – summer and winter. Samhain served as a deadline for the year's agricultural work to be completed, so that the family could gather for an evening of celebration, during which they would ask the oracle about the year ahead. Six months later, at the beginning of May, they would celebrate the awakening of nature with the **Beltane** festival, when the cattle were put out to pasture.

The Scots

Pictish people began to settle in **Scotland** in the fifth century BC, but it was not until around AD 450 that the first Irish **Celts** landed there. The Romans called the Irish settlers '**Scoti**'. Conflict between the **Gaels** and **Picts** went on for hundreds of years before a united '**Alba**' (the **Gaelic** term for Scotland) was established in 843. Subsequently, the rich Gaelic culture spread across the entire country, and **Gaelic** became its primary language.

In around 800, Scandinavian **Vikings** settled on the west coast of Scotland and on the **Hebrides** islands. The **Union of Scotland and England** was declared in 1707, although it continues to be rejected by a significant proportion of **Scotland**'s contemporary population of approximately 5.1 million.

great importance to their traditions. Scotland's many fortresses and castles bear witness to the former glory of the Scottish clans, each of which had its own **tartan kilt**. Some Scots still speak the Celtic dialect, and the **Highland Games** – in which the country's strongest men compete at tug-o-war, tossing the caber and the hammer throw – are known throughout the world.

The Welsh

The **Welsh** peninsula (Cymru) forms the western part of mainland Great Britain. Settled during the Roman period by Celtic tribes, Wales received Germanic **Angle** and **Saxon** immigrants during the fifth century. A constituent country of the United Kingdom, Welsh legislature and government was devolved in 1999.

contemporary Welsh identity. One of the year's particular highlights is the **eisteddfodau** in the first week of August, a festival that provides an opportunity to see indigenous craftwork alongside music, dance and theatrical performances. As used to happen during the festivals of old, the Welsh language poets and singers compete against each other for the prestige of being declared the best performer.

The English

The area occupied by modern-day England was settled by Celtic tribes around 500 BC, and became a Roman province in AD 85. After the Romans had withdrawn around AD 450, the Celtic **Britons** joined forces with the Germanic **Angles** and **Saxons** to fight the **Picts** and **Scots**. Soon, however,

The Vikings

The Vikings, also known as Norsemen or Normans, lived in what are now the countries of Scandinavia – Denmark, Norway and Sweden. Outstanding seafarers – their distinctive longboats were propelled by sixty rowers – and ruthless warriors, the Vikings spread fear and terror wherever they went. Between the eighth and eleventh centuries, the Vikings' ships carried them on pillages to Russia, northern Germany and England, and to the north-west past Iceland and Greenland as far as north America, which the Viking Leif Ericson had already 'discovered' some 500 years before Christopher Columbus.

The bagpipes are synonymous with Scotland.

The Flemish and the Walloons

Since the Belgian state was founded in 1830–31, the Flemish movement has developed to counterbalance the economic and cultural dominance of the French-speaking Walloons. Dutch became the second official language, and Flanders the hub of the Belgian economy. These Flemish achievements set the scene for the formation of the Walloon Movement in the twentieth century. In the 1960s, the Flemish Movement – weakened by its collaboration with the Germans in World War II – stirred up a new round of conflict with the Walloons, which was only relieved when Belgium became a federal state.

The Bretons

Known as Armorica in Roman times, Brittany has belonged to France only since 1532. The Bretons are descended from Celtic Britons who fled from the Anglo-Saxons to the French Atlantic coast in the fifth and sixth centuries. The Celtic Breton language ('Brezhoneg') is still spoken by about half the population – mostly fishermen, seamen and farmers – and many Bretons take great pride in their cultural traditions. The folk costumes with their tall, white bonnets, the festivals ('pardons') of patron saints and the 'Calvaires' – granite crucifixes depicting scenes from the Passion – are well-known.

Republic of Ireland has a population of around 3.8 million, while that of Northern Ireland is 1.7 million. There are a further 10 million Irish living elsewhere in the world (most of them in the **USA**, **Canada**, **Australia** and **New Zealand**).

The majority of the overwhelmingly Catholic population still speaks the Gaelic language, the roots of which are Celtic.

Traditional folk music continues to be an important part of Irish culture to this day. It is played on typical Irish instruments such as the **fiddle** (like a violin, but played in a more sprightly style), the **uilleann pipes**, various flutes, and the Celtic harp. Irish folk music boasts a considerable body of often slightly melancholy songs, many of which are hundreds of years old.

The heyday of Scottish Gaelic culture lasted from around 1000 to 1500. At court, **bards** sang accompanied by the traditional Celtic violin and harp, while society at large benefited from the achievements of the country's doctors, scientists, jurists, wrought iron smiths and stonemasons. Today, bagpipes and whisky are synonymous with the Scots, who continue to attach

Most of **Wales**' 3-million-strong population are **Anglicans**, and some 500,000 still speak **Welsh** (Cymric). The language has Celtic roots, but the name 'Wales' in fact derives from the Anglo-Saxon word '**woel**', which roughly translates as 'slave' or 'foreigner'. Wales' many old fortresses and castles are evidence of its rich cultural tradition, which continues to play an important role in

the Angles and Saxons drove back the Celts. In the early eleventh century, the **Anglo-Saxons** were defeated by the Danish and, at the Battle of Hastings in 1066, Britain fell to descendants of the Scandinavian **Normans**. After 1588, England became a dominant naval power, and, in the centuries that followed, the riches of its global colonies secured its rise to become one of the world's leading

In **England**, as in some other European countries, school uniform is often compulsory and serves to express a sense of belonging and unity among the pupils. A similarly strict dress code is in force at the ancient English universities of Oxford and Cambridge, whose numerous faculties and institutes have been educating the country's academic elite since the tenth and eleventh centuries. Many of the older 'Oxbridge' colleges were endowed by English monarchs.

trading nations and economic powerhouses. In the twentieth century, however, the British empire began to crumble. In its place, the **Commonwealth** became the loose union of Great Britain and its former colonies.

Religion is diverse, though many of England's 50 million citizens belong to the Anglican Church, England's state church. England is also home to 2.5 million immigrants, most of whom originally came from Commonwealth states. The famous stone circles at **Stonehenge** and **Avebury** betray the existence of an earlier **megalithic culture** dating back to around 2000 BC. Later, Celtic and Norman influences made themselves felt – notably in the form of traditional dances such as the **Morris Dance**, whose roots are Celtic, and above all in the legends of **King Arthur** and the **Knights of the Round Table** and the wizard **Merlin**.

The French

The rich cultural and linguistic heritage enjoyed by today's approximately 60-million-strong **French** population is firmly rooted in the history of the French people. Celts from south-east and central Europe first settled the area occupied by modern-day France around 900 BC. Roman rule over the **Gauls** (as the **Romans** called the **Celts**) began in 58 BC and lasted for over 500 years, until the invasion of Germanic tribes (the **Franks**, **Saxons**, **Burgundians** and **Visigoths**) in the fifth century put an end to Roman rule.

Modern Normandy was settled by Scandinavian **Vikings** in the ninth century. Western France was occupied by the English from the twelfth century until the mid-fifteenth century. The ejection of the English prompted a new sense of national feeling, which climaxed in the seventeenth century in the absolutist rule of the **'Sun King' Louis XIV**. In 1789, however, the **French Revolution** put paid to the power of the aristocracy. The revolutionary motto of **'liberty, equality, fraternity'** became an aspiration against which all modern democracies would be measured.

In the Middle Ages, as Celtic, Norman, Anglo-Saxon, Roman and Christian influences mixed together, France, alongside Italy, became the cultural heart of the Western world, its scholars, architects and artists setting the standard of cultural progress for almost all of Europe.

In some parts of France, strong regional identities developed, notably among the 1.2 million once German-speaking inhabitants of **Alsace Lorraine** to the east, and among the 300,000 **Catalans** and 60,000 **Basques** to the south. Southern France is considered to belong to the occitan linguistic region, and there is an estimated 2 million active speakers. Further, there are almost 1 million **Bretons** in **Brittany**.

The Belgians

Predominantly Catholic, Belgium was one of the most important trading hubs of medieval Europe. The country is divided by a linguistic border that runs south of Brussels. **Flanders**, the northern, Flemish (Dutch-speaking) region, has a population of around 5.6 million and was shaped by the influence of the Germanic tribes that settled here in the fifth century. By contrast, the 3.4 million **Walloons** who live in the south are closely related to the French by both language and culture. There is also a small German-speaking minority in the east.

Both Flemish and French are spoken in **Brussels**. The city was founded in the tenth century as 'Bruoscella' ('city on the stream'), and became the Belgian capital in 1830, ending an era of alternating Burgundian, Spanish, French and Dutch rule.

The medieval townscapes of the former Hanseatic cities of **Ghent** and **Bruges** – with their imposing churches and gabled houses, and their picturesque canals, streets and lanes – bear witness to the wealth of old **Flanders**. Many traditional festivals and customs have been preserved in both parts of the country. The medieval **Ducasse festival** takes place every year in the Walloon town of Ath, during which the battle between David and the giant Goliath is re-enacted. The roots of

the **Laetare festival**, held on the third Sunday before Easter in the Walloon town of Stavelot, go back to 1502. The famous competition between teams on stilts that takes place every August in the Walloon capital, **Namur**, is older still – mentioned in documents dating back to the fourteenth century.

1 The easy-going Irish like nothing more than a relaxed discussion of the big and not so big questions life throws at them.

2 East of Bordeaux, many farmers in the Périgord area of France also grow tobacco, which thrives in this region.

3 For centuries, the winegrowers of French Burgundy have lived off the cultivation of grapes and their transformation into top quality wines.

4 Scene at the horse market in Brussels. The Belgian capital has been a lively trading city since ancient times.

Johanna Spyri's popular children's novel Heidi *confirmed the popular perception of idyllic,* **Alpine Switzerland** *as the epitome of unspoilt nature in all her glory. In reality, life for the mountain farmers was anything but easy. One of* *them was the Swiss national hero William Tell, a simple farmer from Uri canton. Legend has it that, around 1300, Tell succeeded in a challenge to save his son's life by shooting an apple off the top of his head with a crossbow.*

The Dutch

Until the fifth century AD, the area that is now the **Netherlands** was settled by Germanic **Friesians** and **Saxons**. It fell to the kingdom of Middle Francia after the division of France in 843. From 1363, most of **Holland** belonged to **Burgundy**, and from 1477 to the **Habsburgs**. In the sixteenth century, **Friesland, Flanders, Overijssel, Gelderland** and **Utrecht** were added, and by 1555 Holland was part of Habsburg Spain. In the seventeenth century, Dutch naval and colonial power, combined with the pre-eminence of the Netherlands in global trade, secured the country's European supremacy, a position it would soon lose to England. Today, the population is some 16 million.

The **Friesians**, who until the **Viking** invasion, and perhaps up to the foundation of the Hanseatic League, were the leading traders in the entire North Sea and Baltic region, now form a minority of about 350,000. They have their own West Friesian dialect.

The Friesans' high quality wools were already recognised as desirable commodities in the ninth

The Friesians

Originally a Germanic tribe living on the North Sea coast, the Friesians were absorbed into the Roman empire and Christianised as early as AD 750. Since then, Friesland has been conquered frequently. The region is divided into West, Middle and Eastern Friesland (from Lake Yssel to the river Weser), each with its own Friesian (North Sea Germanic) language. These languages are, to a certain extent, still spoken today.

century. They were exported as far afield as Baghdad and, as the 'Fries', were even used as currency. Characterised by their love of liberty, the Friesians are still proud of their centuries-old traditions. Two notable examples are the sport **Fierljeppen** – jumping over water using a long pole – and **Skûtsjesilen**, a race between traditional sailing boats.

The Germans

The area between the **Danube, Vistula** and **Rhine** rivers was settled by Germanic tribes from **Denmark, southern Sweden** and **Schleswig** during the first millennium BC. In the eighth century AD, the 'Holy Roman Empire of the German Nation' was created through the union of the **Alemanni, Thuringians, Friesians, Franconians** and **Saxons** under **Charlemagne**. Today, some 82 million people live in Germany, including immigrants from many different countries, as well as a 50,000-strong **Danish** ethnic minority in **Schleswig-Holstein**, around 15,000 **Friesians** in North and East Friesland and about 60,000 **Sorbs** in **Brandenburg** and **Saxony**.

The marked differences between Germany's various regions have given rise to a great variety of cultural traditions and customs, especially in rural areas. Many of these traditions are rooted in pre-Christian times and reflect the changing of the seasons. In the **Black Forest**, for example, the beginning of spring was marked with the symbolic **drowning of**

Men in traditional costume in the Allgäu region of Bavaria.

the winter bear. Today, many Germans still light **bonfires** to celebrate **Walpurgis Night** on the eve of May 1, and put up a maypole the next morning. **Midsummer** is also marked with a bonfire in many regions. In autumn, the **harvest festival** is celebrated, followed in winter by the **Raunächte** (the twelve nights after Christmas).

The Swiss

The area occupied by modern **Switzerland** was settled by Celtic **Helvetians** in the first century BC and conquered by the **Romans** around 58 BC. Two hundred years later, the western part of the region was occupied by the **Burgundians** and the eastern part by the **Alemanni**. After the division of France in the ninth century, the border between Burgundy and the Alemanni also marked the division of the French West Franconians and German East Franconians.

The first Swiss confederation was formed in 1281, and the neutral confederation of 22 **cantons** (states) whose borders we know as contemporary Switzerland was declared in 1815. The population of modern Switzerland is around 7.2 million. Since World War II, the country's political and economic life has been closely intertwined with that of neighbouring Liechtenstein.

Wedged between Italy, Austria, Germany and France, Switzerland has three official languages as well as a small **Rhaetian** minority in the south-eastern canton

of **Graubünden**. Accordingly, Switzerland's rich culture bears the signs of both **Romance** and **Germanic** influences.

Always determined to assert its independence, this small country has preserved many of its folk traditions, notably **alphorn blowing**, the **rifle match in Rütli** (Uri canton), and the **Basel Fasnacht** carnival.

The Austrians

Austria has a population of around 8.1 million. From 60 BC, the area occupied by today's Austria formed the **Noricum** province of the Roman empire. After the empire's dissolution, the area was settled by Germanic tribes, who arrived from the north during the sixth century. They were joined from the east by **Slovenians, Avars, Franconians** and **Bavarians**, who quickly established their rule.

In the ninth century, the Bavarian area was integrated with Franconia and some time after 955 the Bavarian Eastern March, **Ostarrîchi**, was formed. **Habsburg** rule of Austria began in 1278. By 1526, the Habsburgs' reach extended to **Bohemia, Hungary** and – through politically motivated marriage – to the Spanish Netherlands and most of **Burgundy**. The **Austro-Hungarian** empire (Dual Monarchy) spanned the period 1866–1918. In 1919, Austria lost South Tyrol to Italy, but gained **Burgenland** from western Hungary.

A common language and a long, intertwined political history explain the close relationship of

The Sorbs

Evidence of the west Slavic Sorb group around upper and lower Lusatia (in modern-day Saxony and Brandenburg) goes back to AD 631. The Sorbs survived the establishment of German settlements in the east, and today some 60,000 descendents of the Sorbs maintain the Sorb language and culture there. Since 1991, the overwhelmingly Catholic Sorbs have received state subsidies to protect their linguistic and cultural heritage.

Austrian and German culture; the same is true of their traditions, among them **Scheibenschlagen** (hitting burning wood blocks into the valleys) and the **Leonhardi-Ritt** (a procession with horses in homage to St Leonard of Limoges). The traditional costumes are also similar, their differences reflecting less national than regional distinctions.

The Czechs

The modern **Czech Republic** has a population of around 10.2 million and is formed of **Bohemia, Moravia** and parts of **Silesia**. Bohemia gets its name from the Celtic Bojer who migrated there around 400 BC and were later driven out again by the Germanic **Marcomanni**. In the sixth and seventh centuries, the first Slavic tribes arrived. From the thirteenth century onward, many towns were founded, often settled by Germans. By 1278, **Bohemia** already reached far into **Austria**, and in the fourteenth century it was expanded further when **Silesia** and **Lusatia** were added. The almost 400-year-long reign of the Habsburgs over the region began in the fifteenth century, with Bohemia and Moravia both belonging to the Dual Monarchy from 1867. **Czechoslovakia** was created at the end of World War I, while the end of World War II saw some 3 million **Sudeten Germans** expelled from Bohemia. The area sustained relatively little war damage, and many historic buildings – such as those in the southern Bohemian village of **Holasovice** –

The Rhaetians

The Rhaetians, descended from an early mountain people related to the Etruscans, were among the first peoples to be Romanised. Today, around 1 million Rhaetians still live in the Alpine region. Their various Romance languages are sub-divided into several dialects, and the relationship between the different groups – despite their geographical separation – was only recognised in the nineteenth century.

have been preserved. Folk customs have also survived, particularly in Moravia and among the **Vlach** living in the northern part of the Western Carpathians. In **Prague**, traces of the city's Jewish past are also in evidence. Until the Holocaust, Prague was for centuries one of the most important hubs of the **eastern European Jewry**.

The Jews – at home in Europe

Since the early Middle Ages, the eventful history of the European Jewry has been characterised by both social integration and a thriving cultural life on the one hand, and intolerance, exclusion and persecution on the other – culminating in the unspeakable horrors of the Holocaust during the Third Reich.

In the middle of the tenth century, the heart of Jewish secular and religious life was Islamic Moorish Spain, where Jewish statesmen, bankers, scholars and doctors enjoyed great influence in public life. In 1215, however, a council convened by Pope Innocent III condemned Jews to the ghetto and forced them to identify themselves in public. Many Jews died when plague ravaged Europe in the fourteenth century, and others – held responsible for the scourge – were driven from their homes. Jews were forced to leave Spain in 1492, and in 1497 Portuguese Jews also had to emigrate. Most of the Jews driven out of England, France and

Germany settled in Poland and Russia (these were the Ashkenazim), and by 1648 there were over 500,000 central European Jews in Poland alone.

The Spanish and Portuguese Jews (the Sephardim), meanwhile, mostly settled in Constantinople, which by the sixteenth century had become home to Europe's largest Jewish community. The persecution of the Jews began in the Ukraine after 1648, and Polish Jews were next to fear for their lives. In western Europe, however, the Reformation ushered in an atmosphere of increasing political and social liberation, from which the Jews also benefited. The Jewish community

became ever more integrated in wider society, a trend that continued up to the mid-nineteenth century. Meanwhile, in eastern Europe pogroms and persecution had made life unbearable for Jews. In the period after 1890, some 2 million Jews emigrated to both North and South America, as well as to Palestine.

By the end of the nineteenth century, central European politics had given rise to growing anti-Semitism, focusing on what were held to be typical racial characteristics of the Jews, one of the Semite peoples. New political groups made it their goal to prevent Jews from occupying positions of high office. After World

War I, anti-Semitic feeling was strongest in Germany, where it culminated in the rise of National Socialism. The Nazis murdered 6 million Jews between 1933 and 1945, most of them in the concentration camps or in the German occupied territories. In the early Soviet Union, anti-Semitism – whose roots lay in the Tsarist period – remained virulent long

European life: a young Jewish boy outside a Berlin synagogue (top); trading diamonds in Brussels (middle); a shop in the Jewish quarter of Paris (bottom).

after the end of World War II. For most Soviet Jews, however, emigration only became a realistic possibility with the fall of the Iron Curtain in the 1980s.

Since the fall of the Iron Curtain, the 'golden city' of Prague – with its splendid architecture and maze of intriguing little streets and alleyways – has become a popular destination for tourists and artists from all over the world.

Visitors are attracted to Prague by both its unique, almost Parisian charm and its long, rich history, in which – until World War II – the Jewish community and literary figures such as Franz Kafka played an important part.

The Poles

The Polish name for Poland, *Polska*, is derived from the Slavic **Polans** ('field dwellers') who, together with the Slavic branches of the **Lechians**, **Kuyavians**, **Masovians** and **Jazyges**, settled the area between the **Oder** and **Vistula** rivers from the sixth century. Poland was first unified in the mid-ninth century, and its borders were expanded by the addition of **Silesia**, **Krakow** and **Bohemia** in the tenth century. Polish autonomy ended in 1795, but in 1918 the **Republic of Poland** was formed. Modern Poland is home to some 39 million inhabitants, including 100,000 Germans and – in the north of the country – the **Kashubian** ethnic group.

Poland is a Catholic country and Christian traditions are taken very seriously. The most important festival of all is **Easter**, celebrated with *pisanki* (decorated eggs). On Easter Monday, Poles also celebrate *Smigus Dyngus* ('Wet Monday') – a tradition dating back to 966. In the Tatra region of southern Poland, folk culture bears the signs of Hungarian and Slovakian influences – most obviously in the region's traditional costumes, rich folk music and painted glass.

Here too, traditional customs and festivals are an important part of life, most notably the annual Goralian wedding procession of decorated horse-drawn coaches in **Zakopane**. *Wycinanki*, the beautifully painted cut paper designs used to decorate Polish homes, are another local tradition.

The Slovaks

Slovakia has a population of 5.5 million. Its original inhabitants were **Celts**, who were driven out of the area by the **Suebi**, **Vandals**, **Quadi**, **Marcomanni** and **Langobards** around 300 AC. The Slavic **Slovaks** arrived in the sixth century, and in the ninth century their settlements formed part of the Greater Moravian Empire. From 907 to 1918, Slovakia, as Upper Hungary, belonged to Hungary. Then, from 1918 to 1993, it was part of Czechoslovakia. Many Slovaks still speak **Hungarian** and **Czech** today.

Unlike the adjacent **Czech**s, the overwhelmingly Catholic **Slovaks** continue to attach great importance to Christian traditions. Traditional costumes are regularly worn at folk festivals and weddings, where the men sport dark woollen suits and knitted caps while the women wear embroidered skirts and blouses with bright scarfs. Folk music and traditional dancing are also alive and well.

The Russians

Contained by the Ural mountains to the east, European **Russia** has a population of approximately 120 million. The area around the **Dnieper River** was settled by early Slavs, who came from the Carpathian Mountains some time during the first millennium BC. The **Kiev empire** established in the ninth century was, by area, the largest state in Europe. After the **Mongol invasion** of 1240, it was home to Ukrainians, Russians and Belorussians. From 1547, the Volga region up to the **Caspian Sea**, the eastern regions beyond the **Urals**, and the area that makes up the modern-day **Ukraine** were all conquered. In the eighteenth century, the empire expanded again, reaching down to the **river Don** and up as far as **south-east Finland**. The annexion of the **Crimea** followed shortly afterwards. Parts of **Poland** and **Georgia** were next to be conquered, followed by the rest of **Finland** and **Bessarabia**. By the end of the nineteenth century, Russia's borders stretched as far as they do today – touching **China** and **Iran**. Following the October Revolution of 1917, the **Union of Soviet Socialist Republics** (USSR) was born in 1922. Today, the former Soviet countries are – with the exception of the Baltic states – bound together in the Commonwealth of Independent States (**CIS**), which was created in 1991 by **Russia**, **Belorussia** and the **Ukraine**.

Russian folk culture has developed over hundreds of years. It is a mixture of eastern Slavic traditions combined with Germanic, Finnish, Mongolian and Turkic influences, but western European and oriental cultures have also made their mark. The vast majority of Russians belong to the Russian Orthodox Church. The church year follows the **Julian calendar**, so Christmas falls on January 7. Long suppressed by the Soviet regime, Christmas is celebrated with church services and folk festivals, at which fortune-tellers and tealeaf readers are notable attractions. But the new year festivities are the most important family celebration. Pine trees are put up and **Father Frost** distributes presents, assisted by his **snow maiden** (*Snegurochka*).

Russian folk culture is defined first and foremost by its music. Traditional instruments include

Fishing through a hole in the ice is a tradition in Kiev.

the **balalaika**, **kalyuki**, **zhaleika**, **gusli** and Russian **lyre**.

The Ukrainians

For centuries, nomadic peoples like the **Huns**, **Bulgars**, **Hungarians** and **Mongolians** moved through what is now the **Ukraine**. Between the ninth and twelfth centuries AD, the **northern** and **western Ukraine** formed the backbone of the Kiev empire. After the fall of the empire, the Ukraine belonged at different times to **Poland**, **Lithuania**, **Austria** and **Russia**. It became part of the new **USSR** in 1922, and gained its independence following the collapse of the Soviet regime in 1991, when it joined Russia and other ex-Soviet republics to form the **CIS**.

Once also known as **Little Russians** or **Ruthenians** (*Rusyny*), there are about 45 million Ukrainians. Some 36 million live in the Ukraine itself, while the rest live in **Poland**, **Slovakia**, **Rumania**, **Serbia** and **North** and **South America**. Most Ukrainians belong to the **Russian Orthodox Church** and – like the Belorussians – are descended from the **old Russian peoples**. Key trade routes to northern and western Europe have always run right through the Ukraine, resulting in a very early **cultural interchange** between **Christian Slavs** and **nomadic groups** from the east. The best-known example of Ukrainian craftsmanship is the traditional embroidery of the **Kiev**, **Chernigov** and **Poltava** regions. It is used to decorate fabrics and shirts, usually depicting scenes from nature and mythology or reproducing ornaments associated with traditional Ukrainian customs.

The Balts

Today, the term '**Balts**' refers to **Lithuanians**, **Latvians** and **Estonians**. It once also included the Baltic Prussians, Livs and Curonians, as well as other peoples of the **Baltic linguistic group**. While Latvian and Lithuanian are both **Indo-European** languages, only Estonian belongs to the **Finno-Ugric** linguistic family.

The Lithuanians

Lithuanian tribes began settling the area between the **Memel** and **Western Dvina** rivers during the eleventh century. Lithuania is the biggest and most southerly of the three Baltic states. More than 80 per cent of its population are **Lithuanian**, eight per cent **Russian**, seven per cent **Polish** and one per cent **Belorussian**. Almost all are **Roman Catholics**. Since the dissolution of the USSR, traditional crafts have enjoyed a resurgence throughout the Baltic states, and the 400-year-old art of Lithuanian **wood carving** (such as *stogastulpis* or *koplytstulpis*) is a prime example.

The Latvians

Eastern **Baltic tribes** (specifically the Latgalians, Selonians, Semigallians, Curonians and Livs) settled the area that is modern-day Latvia in the ninth century. Today, Latvia is the second largest of the three Baltic states. Two-thirds of its population are **Latvians**, while the remainder are mostly **Russians**, with **Polish** and **Ukrainian** minorities. The **Lutheran**, **Roman Catholic** and **Russian Orthodox churches** are the biggest religious denominations. Despite their turbulent

In Mother Russia – as the Russians affectionately call their homeland – traditional costumes are again being worn with pride. For Russians, the story of their country in the twentieth century is one of relentless and all-embracing social transformation. The traditional costumes – from tunics, fur and felt caps to embroidered shirts and pleated skirts – are made to old patterns and worn at festivals organised by the newly revived folk music and dance groups.

political history, Latvians have preserved a rich oral tradition of **folk music** (*daina*). Passed down over hundreds of years, it boasts more than a million songs and some 30,000 melodies.

The Estonians

The area that forms modern Estonia was once home to **Finnish ethnic groups**. Today, the Estonian population is in rapid decline. Today, two-thirds of the country's inhabitants are **Estonian** and one quarter **Russian**, while **Ukrainian**, **Belorussian** and **Finnish minorities** make up the rest. Most of the population are **Lutheran Protestants**. Estonian culture has been shaped over the centuries by **Swedish** and **German** influences.

The Slovenians

Most of the world's 2.2 million **Slovenians** live in Slovenia itself, but there are also minorities in the Austrian provinces of **Styria** and **Carinthia**, as well as in **Croatia** and **Italy**. The roots of this **southern Slavic** people go back to the sixth century, when peoples from the upper **Dnieper** region migrated to the lower **Danube**, **Panonia** and **eastern Alps**. Their progress was stemmed by the Bavarians, who would later exert great cultural influence over them. Today, most Slovenians are **Catholic**. The country has a rich tradition of **religious art**, while its secular art is heavily influenced by adjacent Austria. Slovenian is one of the **southern Slavic languages**, whose literary heritage goes back to the Middle Ages.

The Croatians

The area that forms modern-day **Croatia** was inhabited by **Illyrian** and Thracian settlers around 1000 BC, and it was not until the seventh century AD that southern Slavic **Croatians** settled here. From 1098, the region came under **Hungarian** rule and from 1526 to 1699 it was ruled by the

Turks. **Croatia** became part of Yugoslavia in 1918, gaining its independence again in 1991. Today, the **Croatian** population stands at some 6.5 million, around a third of which live outside Croatia itself.

Though Croatian culture owes much to Christian festivities such as Christmas, Lent and Easter, the *Badnjak* or **winter solstice celebrations** have their roots in the pre-Christian era.

In rural Croatia, the traditional **circle dance** (*kolo*) is still occasionally performed at folk festivals. Dancers wear traditional black and white costumes.

The Serbs

Most **Serbs** belong to the Serbian Orthodox Church, and around a quarter of the 8.5-million-strong population live outside the Republic of Serbia itself. The area occupied by modern Serbia was first settled in pre-Christian times by Illyrians from northern Italy. As the province of Moesia, it became part of the Roman empire in AD 44 and, from AD 395, part of the Byzantine empire. In the seventh century, the area west of the **Morava** River was occupied by the Slavic Serbs. They established the first Serbian kingdom (Rascia) around 1168 and by 1355 ruled large parts of Serbia and Montenegro as well as Albania and Greece. Serbia came under Ottoman rule from 1459 to 1817. **Yugoslavia** – the 'Kingdom of Serbs, Croats and Slovenes' – was established in 1918. The Serbs dominated Yugoslav political life, and, when Yugoslavia fell

apart between 1991 and 2006, the independent republic of Serbia emerged from the remnants. The roughly 600,000 Montenegrins of Serbia and **Montenegro** have their own language.

There are also around 2 million Muslim Albanians in Kosovo and 350,000 Hungarians in the northern province of Vojvodina.

1 Visitors to Vitoslavlitsy, the open-air museum in Novgorod, learn about Russian peasant life.

2 Life for the rural population of Poland's Masuria region has barely changed over the years. In the villages, everyone knows everyone else.

3 In rural Slovakia, too, people are largely self-sufficient, surviving on the produce of their own land.

4 Far from the crowded tourist resorts of the region, this Black Sea shepherdess herds her animals across the pastures of the Crimean.

The Sinti and Roma of Europe

The global population of Sinti, Roma and other related minorities is estimated to be around 12 million. Around half live in Europe, mostly to the east and south-east of the continent in Serbia and Montenegro, Hungary, Romania and Bulgaria. In the south-west, Spain's 500,000 Calé are a significant minority.

Roma (Romany for 'man' or 'human') is a generic term used throughout the international Romany community to describe a series of related ethnic groups. It applies to communities that have often been referred to as 'gypsies', although the Roma themselves regard this term as derogatory. The Sinti, meanwhile, are a sub-group of the Roma who have lived in central Europe since the Middle Ages. The Indo-European Romany language is a cornerstone of this ethnic minority's cultural identity, and is still spoken by around 1 million Roma. The language also serves as a reminder of the Roma's Indian roots. The Roma started to leave India in the face of Arab

attack during the ninth and tenth centuries, and they were later forced to emigrate. Between the fourteenth and seventeenth centuries, most of the emigrants settled in the Balkans, the Middle East and eastern Europe, but it was not long before they were forced to leave their newly adopted homelands.

In Europe, Roma and Sinti are broadly divided into three groups: the eastern European Roma, the central European Sinti and Manush and the south-west European Calé. Many Roma settled in Spain, Hungary and Romania, where – despite their contribution to local folk art – they met with suppression. In Spain and

Hungary, the wandering Roma – who were experienced ironworkers – were forced to produce weapons and instruments of torture. Hungarian and Romanian princes even kept Roma as slaves. The church too was complicit in anti-Roma discrimination, using the Roma's decorative ironwork as evidence of their connection with the devil.

All this, however, was but a prelude to the atrocities committed by the Nazi regime during World War II – crimes to which some 500,000 Sinti and Roma across Europe fell victim. After the war, especially in the communist Eastern bloc countries, Roma were forcibly assimilated into main-

stream society. Yet they never forgot their unique heritage, and – while absorbing the language and culture of the countries in which they lived – maintained a great body of stories and songs. Today, Roma and Sinti continue to face discrimination. Towards the end of the 1970s, they formed pressure groups to campaign for official recognition of their statelessness and win the right to move freely through the states of Europe, as well as the right to remain wherever they choose.

Top: In an environment of rejection and exclusion, the legendary solidarity of Sinti and Roma families was one of their most important survival strategies – even if it did feed mistrust of the so-called 'gypsy clans'.

Bottom: For many Roma and Sinti, their culture's rousing music represented the only way of earning the recognition of respectable society.

Crete has only belonged to **Greece** since 1912. Nowadays, old men wearing the island's traditional baggy black trousers (*vraka*) are a rare sight. The trousers date back to the sixteenth century. Traditionally worn with high boots (*stivania*) and a frayed, black headscarf (*sariki*), they are thought to derive from garments once worn by North African pirates. Unlike Cretan costume, Cretan music – and the classical lyre, lute and tambouras on which it is played – is omnipresent.

Over a third of the Serbian population is rural, and in some areas the men of the family still lead their kin into a form of economic commune known as a *zadruga*. Another traditional social unit is the *vamilija*, a clan descended from the same male ancestor and united by the same name as well as a common patron saint. The *vamilija* can be as small as a few families and as big as 50 people, sometimes with more than 300 members.

The Hungarians

In the ninth century, **Magyars** (meaning 'the sons of the earth') came from the area that lies between the **Volga** and the **Urals** and settled the land that forms modern-day Hungary. In the fourteenth century, the country was united with Poland and ruled by the house of Luxembourg. Hungary fell to the Turks in 1526, but was liberated by the Habsburgs in 1699 and absorbed into the Danube monarchy, precipitating the arrival of ethnic German **Danube Swabians**.
The Austro-Hungarian Dual Monarchy was created in 1867 and Hungarian independence followed in 1918. In 1920, however, the new country lost two-thirds of its territory to Yugoslavia, Czechoslovakia, Romania and Austria. The Republic of Hungary was founded in 1946.
The most notable difference between the Hungarians (with a population of approximately 10 million) and the adjacent Slavs is the Hungarian language. Hungarian is a distant relative of Estonian and Finnish, and belongs to the Ugric branch of the **Finno-Ugric linguistic family**. Hungary is an overwhelmingly Catholic country, but secular as well as religious festivals play an important role in Hungarian life – in the **Palóc** community, for example, wedding festivities can attract some 300 guests and celebrations often continue for several days. The distinctive traditional Hungarian folk costume – notably comprising bright ribbons and layered skirts elaborately embroidered with pearls – is still routinely worn for the occasion.

The Romanians

Romanians make up 90 per cent of the approximately 23-million-strong Romanian population. **Hungarians** account for a further seven per cent, followed by **Roma** (some 500,000), **Serbs**, **Croatians**, **Slovaks**, **Turks**, **Ukrainians**, **Bulgarians** and **Tatars**. Two further ethnic minorities are Transylvanian Germans, descended from the **Mosel Franconian farmers** and craftsmen who settled in Transylvania in the twelfth century, and Banat Swabians, who settled in the **Banat** region in the eighteenth century. Romanian, a Romance language, borrows plenty of Slavic vocabulary. Hungarian, German, Romany, Turkish, Serbian and Yiddish are also spoken. Nearly 90 per cent of Romanians belong to the Romanian Orthodox Church. Catholics (Germans and Hungarians), Protestants (Germans), Jews and Muslims (Tatars and Turks) form the next biggest religious groups. Though heavily influenced by Slavic, Turkish and Greek culture, Romanian culture is quite distinctive. Legends like that of Count Dracula of **Transylvania** ('beyond the forest') are its most important component, but folk dance and music is also a significant element. The *hora* and *calusari* are two Romanian dances, accompanied by traditional folk instruments.

The Bulgarians

The **Bulgarians** are descended from immigrant Slavs, Romanised Thracians and **Turkic-speaking Bulgars**. The population numbers around 10 million, of which over a million live in Romania, Russia, the Ukraine and Turkey. Bulgarian is of the south-Slavic linguistic family and uses the Cyrillic alphabet. Approximately 85 per cent of the population belongs to the Bulgarian Orthodox Church, while the **Pomaks** (who make up 13 per cent of the population, mostly in the **Rhopode** region) are Muslims.
Many old traditions still survive, especially in rural areas. Most revolve around religious and seasonal festivals. These include the **Kukerov Den** festival in February, a procession to signal Lent; **Lazaruvane**, a fertility festival the week before Easter; and the **Kazanlak** Rose Festival in June. The **Koprivshtitsa Folklore Festival** is a celebration of traditional music and dance. Held every five years, it is an opportunity to wear traditional folk costume.

1 In modern Romania, the Transylvanian German ethnic minority group is a fraction of its former size.

2 Even the smallest of Greek villages has at least one *kafenion*, where the local men while away the hours over coffee or an ouzo.

3 Hungarians love a good party and seize every opportunity for a celebration. In the country, weddings and other festivities are still an occasion for wearing traditional costume. Friends and family join in wishing the happy couple good fortune, and set about enjoying all that life has to offer.

South-Eastern and Southern Europe

*Legend has it that the Guanches – the tall, blond and blue-eyed indigenous people of the **Canary Islands** – are descended from the inhabitants of the sunken continent of Atlantis, and that they valiantly fought Spanish conquest.*

However, ethnologists now believe that the Guanches (Guan Chenech means 'man from Chenech' or 'man from Tenerife') were in fact the descendants of North African Berbers, who gradually integrated with their Spanish colonisers.

The Greeks

As well as the roughly 10 million **Greeks**, 300,000 **Albanians** and 100,000 **Turks** living in Greece, about another 700,000 Greeks live in **Cyprus** and some 2 million elsewhere (notably in the **USA**, **Russia** and **Turkey**). The Greeks are descended from **Indo-European peoples** (the Ionians, Dorians, Achaeans and Aeolians). Their culture was shaped first by over 400 years of Roman influence, then by **Byzantine rule** from AD 395, and above all by **Slavic immigration** in the sixth century. After an influx of Albanians, by the fourteenth-century the population of Greece had become **very diverse**, the result of both Venetian and **Turkish occupation**, the latter lasting for 500 years. Greece became independent in 1830, and in 1922 Greeks living along Turkey's west coast were driven back to their homeland.

Numerous monuments and buildings dating from the early Christian and Byzantine periods have been preserved, including the monasteries on **Mount Athos** – when Greece was the cultural and intellectual capital of the contemporary Western world, and the country's achievements in fine arts, language, architecture, science, mathematics, philosophy, literature and theatre would set the course of Europe's cultural development. Democracy (government by the people) also has its roots in classical Hellas.

The Macedonians

Nearly two-thirds of the population of Macedonia are **Macedonians**, around a quarter **Albanians**, five per cent **Turks**, and the remainder are **Roma** and **Serbs**. The official language, Macedonian, is closely related to Bulgarian. Most Macedonians belong to the Macedonian Orthodox Church, but the Albanian and Turkish communities are Muslim.

Macedonia came under Greek rule from the seventh century BC, and from 359 to 323 BC **Alexander the Great** established a vast empire that stretched all the way to India. Macedonia became a tines. Turkish rule lasted from the fourteenth to the nineteenth century. In 1912–13, Macedonia was divided between Greece, Serbia and Bulgaria and in 1929 it became part of the kingdom of Yugoslavia. Macedonia declared its independence in 1991.

Macedonia's architecture bears witness to the Greek, Roman, Byzantine and Islamic periods of its history. Other important elements of its rich cultural heritage are its old religious icons and frescoes, and its traditional regional dress, such as the lavishly embroidered **boljar costume** dating back to Byzantine times.

The Bosnians

Bosnia and Herzegovina was until 1992 a constituent republic of the former Yugoslavia. Now independent, the country has a population of about 4 million.

The region currently inhabited by the **Bosnians** was settled by the Illyrians around 800 BC. From 156 BC it formed the Roman province of Illyricum, and from Serbia and Bosnia in 1377. From the fifteenth to nineteenth centuries, Bosnia and Herzegovina belonged to the **Ottoman empire**, prompting many Bosnians to become Muslims. After 1878, the country was briefly part of the **Austrian Dual Monarchy** before becoming part of Yugoslavia in 1918. Bosnian culture bears strong Islamic influences, and in rural areas folklore also continues to be accorded considerable significance. Typical folk instruments include the accordion, the tamburica (a type of small guitar) and the cibuk (Turkish pipes).

The Albanians

The Albanian population numbers some 5.5 million, of which 2 million live in **Kosovo**, **Macedonia**, **Italy** and **Greece**. More than 70 per cent of Albanians are Muslim. Descended from the Indo-Germanic **Illyrians** who settled the country in the fifth century, Albanians are one of the world's most ethnically homogenous peoples. They are divided into occupation, Albanian culture was suppressed and the teaching of the Albanian language remained forbidden until the end of the nineteenth century. Nevertheless, remnants of an autonomous Albanian culture have been preserved, especially in the north of the country. Notable examples are the country's fortified houses and the old refuge towers (**kula**).

The Italians

The name Italy is derived from the 'Italics', the Roman name for the peoples of the Apennine peninsula. After the end of the Roman empire in AD 476, the region was ruled first by the **Ostrogoths** and then by the **Byzantines** in the south and the **Langobards** in the north. In 774 the Langobards were conquered by the **Franks** under **Charlemagne** and northern Italy became part of the Holy Roman Empire until 1250, while Southern Italy continued to belong to the Byzantine empire. In the ninth century, **Sicily** and **Calabria** were conquered by Arabic **Saracens**. In

The Basques

The Basques are a pre-Indo-European people who live around the Bay of Biscay. They call themselves 'Euskaldunak', and there are around 1 million in the Basque region, as well as a further 200,000 in France. Basque borrows from Celtic, Germanic and Romance languages, as well as from Latin, and is now the only pre-Indo-European language spoken in Europe. It is also an important part of the Basque people's distinct sense of ethnic identity, which is expressed in folk culture and in aspirations to political autonomy – a goal that ETA has pursued through terrorism.

A Portuguese woman at the annual festival of Senhora da Agonia.

The Catalans

The Catalans are one of the Romance peoples. The Catalan language – as distinct from Castilian Spanish – is spoken by some 6 million people, mostly in the autonomous north-eastern province of Catalonia, but also in parts of the province of Valencia, on the Balearic Islands (Majorca, Minorca and Ibiza), Roussillon, Andorra (where it has official status), and in the Sardinian city of Alghero. The Catalans' struggle to preserve their unique identity has sustained many regional customs, notably the traditional sardana circle dance.

The Corsicans

The Mediterranean island of Corsica, which belongs to France, is home to nearly 200,000 Corsicans. The island's indigenous inhabitants were probably descended from immigrant Ligurians and Iberians, who over time mixed with the Carthaginians, Etruscans, Romans, Moors, Italians and French. Corsican is one of the Iberian languages, but since the eleventh century it has been eclipsed by the languages of the island's successive rulers. Though France granted Corsica special status in 1982, terrorist attacks by separatist organizations are still making headlines.

historically open only to men – and those in **Meteora**. Countless remains of classical Hellas also survive, notably the Acropolis and Pantheon in Athens, the ancient city of Epidauros, the site of the **Oracle of Delphi** and the ruins at **Olympia**. They date from a time province of the Roman empire in 148 BC and part of the Byzantine empire from AD 395. In the sixth and seventh centuries, southern Slavic tribes settled Macedonia, and from the eleventh century it was variously ruled by Bulgarians, Serbs, Greeks and Byzan- AD 530 became part of the Byzantine empire. From the seventh to the twelfth centuries, rule over the Bosnian region passed first to the Slavs and then to the Hungarians, who also conquered the area occupied by modern-day Serbia and established the kingdom of **Ghegs** (in the north) and **Tosks** (in the south), although the cultural and linguistic differences between the two groups are minor. Albania has at different times come under the foreign rule of Serbs, Bulgarians and Turks. During the 400-year-long Ottoman the eleventh century, they were conquered again, this time by the **Normans**, who created a single state in 1130. The fourteenth and fifteenth centuries saw the establishment of the republics of Genoa and Venice as well as the rise of the **Medici** dynasty in Florence. The

*Just off the coast of north-west Africa, the **Canary Islands** (Tenerife, La Palma, Hierro, Gran Canaria, Fuerteventura, Lanzarote and Gomera) are autonomous provinces of Spain. On the streets of the Gomeran town San Sebastián, fantastic costumes, music and dancing mean it is carnival time again. Afterwards, Ash Wednesday marks the beginning of a fast that continues until the 'Semana Santa' (Holy Week), which concludes with festive Easter processions.*

Medici would make Italy the capital of European cultural life.

Today, some 58 million people live in Italy, including around 1.5 million Sardinians. It is a Catholic country in which religious festivals play an important part. Notable festivals include the **Feast of San Gennaro** in September in Naples; the July **Feast of Forgiveness** in Assisi; and the traditional **Festa de Noantri** in Rome, in homage to the Madonna. Numerous secular festivals are also celebrated, among them the **Venice Carnival** and the **Palio**, a medieval horse race held in Siena. **Sicilians** boast their own culture, born of the various influences left by the region's successive conquerors – Greek, Byzantine, Arab, Norman, Spanish, Habsburg, Savoy and Bourbon. It mostly revolves around religious festivals.

The Sardinians

Sardinians are descended from a pastoral people whose roots can be traced back to the **Romans** and **Arabs**. Sardinian, which shares many characteristics with the **Catalan**, **Spanish** and **pre-Roman** languages, is still spoken by roughly 80 per cent of the population. In rural **Sardinia** in particular – where blood feuds still rage – Sardinian is the language of everyday life. Many of the island's religious and secular traditions have been preserved, among them the flamboyant **carnival** parades and festive Easter processions like the one that takes place in **Valledoria**.

The Spanish

Settled by Celts in around 600 BC, Spain came under Roman rule from 200 BC. Germanic **Alan**, **Suebic** and **Vandal** settlers arrived around AD 400, the Visigoths following shortly afterwards. In 711, the Visigoths were driven out by North African **Moors**, but the sustained expansion of the northern Spanish kingdoms from 1031 led to the Moors' retreat. Modern Spain dates from 1479. Under Habsburg rule, Spain's extensive colonies secured its position as a major world power. At the end of the

sixteenth century, Spain's naval power began to decline, and from the seventeenth and eighteenth centuries most of its overseas territories were lost. The diverse Spanish population numbers nearly 40 million today, comprising **Castilians**, **Catalans**, **Andalucians**, **Galicians**, **Basques** and **Gitanos**.

Spoken by around 2.5 million inhabitants of north-west Spain, **Galician** is similar to Portuguese. That Galician culture can be traced back to the Celts should be obvious from one of its traditional instruments: the bagpipes.

The Portuguese

Originally home to Ibero-Celtic tribes, **Lusitania** – the area that is modern Portugal – was occupied by the Romans in 72 BC. It was settled by Germanic **Alans** and **Suebi** in the fifth and sixth centuries AD, coming under Arab rule from 711. In the thirteenth century, Portuguese explorers became the first Europeans to sail the oceans: **Henry the Navigator** claimed the **Azores** and **Madeira**; **Diaz** discovered west Africa; **Vasco da Gama** ventured to the Indian Ocean; and **Magellan** was the first sailor to circumnavigate the globe. In 1494, Portugal and Spain divided Latin America between themselves. Brazil became a Portuguese colony, but declared independence in 1822.

Modern Portugal has a population of nearly 10 million. Its culture bears strong Spanish-Arabic influences, visible both in its architecture and in the Moorish

patterns on painted ceramic tiles. Portuguese folk tradition dates back to the Middle Ages, incorporating music, song and dance as well as the traditional costume. Accompanied by the **guitarra portuguesa** (Portuguese guitar), the melancholy **fado** song, with its roots in the poorest districts of Lisbon, is uniquely Portuguese.

1 Dressed in their highly decorative traditional costumes, even these young Portuguese girls take their country's folk festivals very seriously.

2 The flamenco was born of the music and passion of the Andalucian Gitano gypsy community.

3 In devout Catholic Sicily, no community is without its patron saint, and the saint's name day is celebrated with a lively procession for which the entire local population turns out. Carrying a statue of their patron saint through the streets, these young men are no exception.

Asia

Asia is the largest and most populous continent, with an area of some 44.5 million sq. km – over a third of the Earth's total land surface – and a population of approximately 4 billion.

Towering mountain ranges – the Pamirs, the Karakorums, Hindu Kush and the Himalayas, the last containing the world's highest summit (Mt Everest: 8,850 m) – form a natural barrier between northern Asia, with its sub-arctic and continental climates, and tropical or sub-tropical south Asia. The continent's wildlife is as varied as the climate. Vegetation ranges from the mosses and lichens of the tundra, to the world's oldest rainforest in Malaysia. The range of peoples, cultures, languages and religions is remarkable. Judaism, Christianity, Islam, Buddhism, Hinduism and the philosophies of Confucius and Lao Tse all originated here.

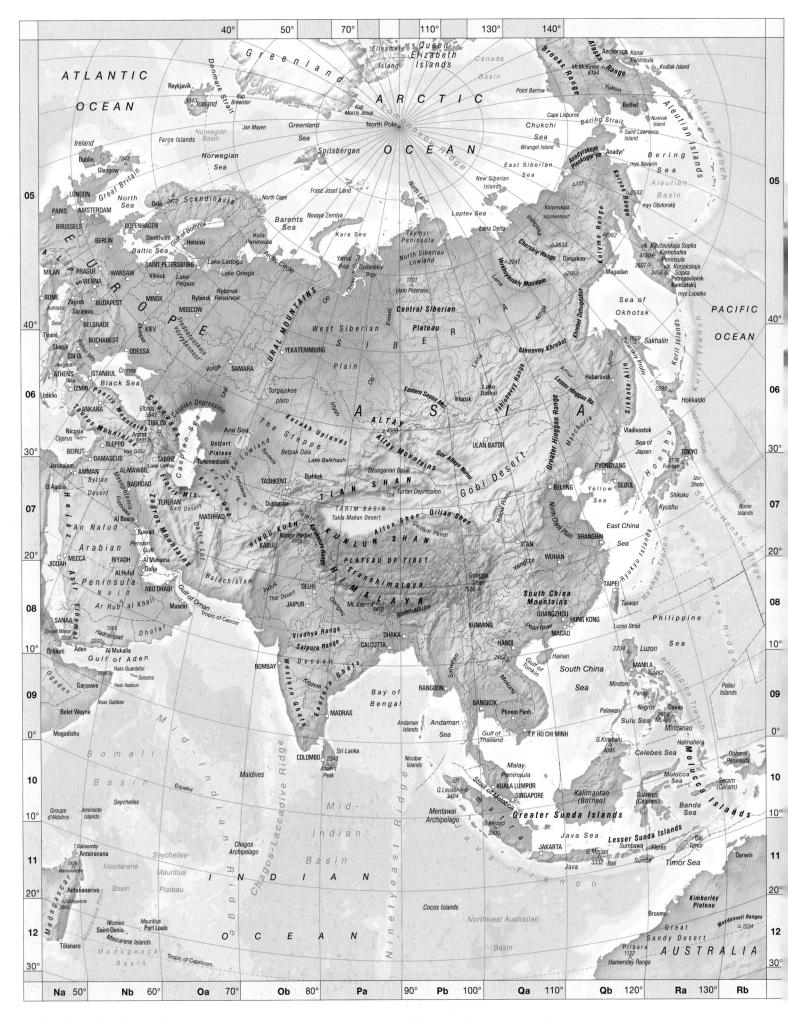

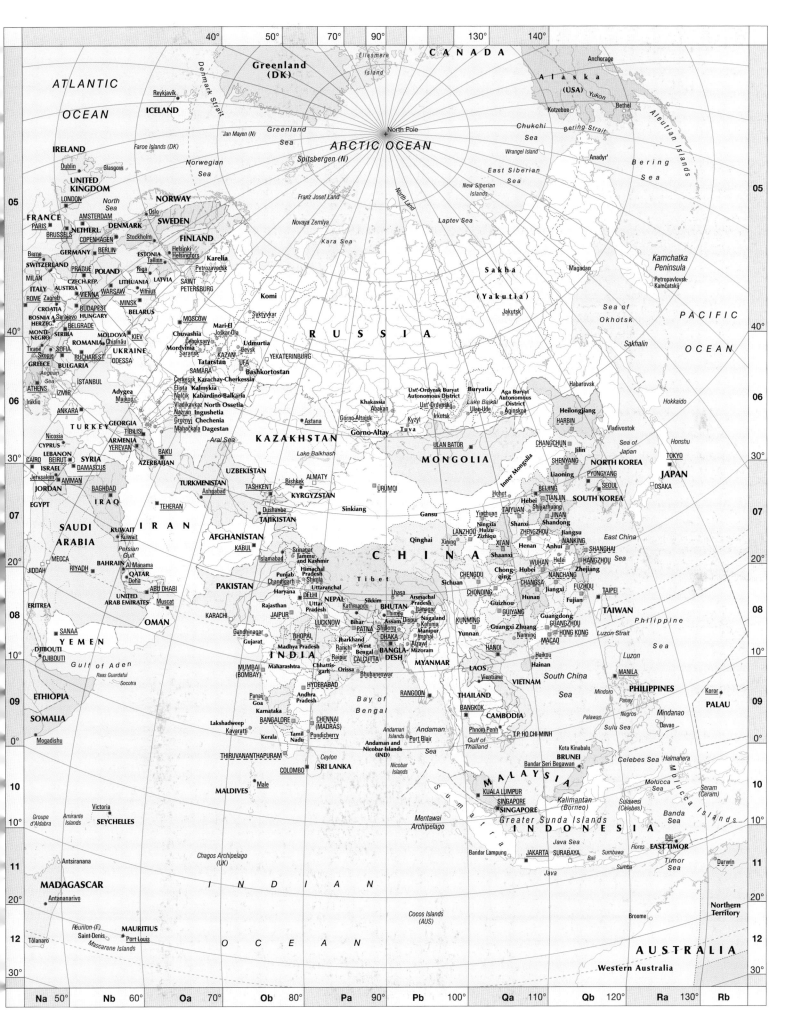

The History of Asia

So many of humanity's greatest innovations first appeared in Asia. The continent saw the foundation of the world's first cities, and it is here that writing was invented. Most importantly, all of the major world religions

A statue of Buddha Amitabha in Kamakura, Japan.

originated in Asia. While people in Europe were still at subsistence level, great cultures were flourishing in Asia, with formidable power structures and extensive trade routes. The stone remains of these lost kingdoms, of which two examples are the ruins of Persepolis and the Forbidden City, clearly show that the rulers saw themselves as governing the whole world. In modern times, after centuries of Western domination, the world is again looking east. Today, China has the potential to become the world's greatest economic power.

Anatolia and the Near East

*The **Babylonian Exile** was a popular theme in mediaeval illuminations. These two thirteenth-century examples depict the conquest and destruction of Jerusalem and the exile of the Jewish people.*

Prehistory and early history

Evidence has been found of settlements in Asia as early as the Palaeolithic Age. Neolithic cultures developed in Mesopotamia, the Levant and Iran. Settlements based on agriculture were formed in north-western India in the fourth millennium BC.

In China, Neolithic cultures have been found mainly in Henan and Gansu. The Yangshao culture is considered to be the nucleus of the country that became China.

The earliest Asian cities were founded in the Bronze Age, first along the Indus, then in China. Bronze Age cultures developed in Mesopotamia, Anatolia and Syria in the second millennium BC, and the first Iron Age cultures followed in the ninth century BC.

Anatolia

The first important Anatolian culture was that of the Hittites, who invaded Anatolia around 2000 BC, and, after violent clashes with the indigenous population, established a kingdom of their own whose capital city was Kussar. The Old Hittite Kingdom, extending as far as Babylon, came into being between 1640 BC and 1387 BC Under king Suppiluliuma, the New Hittite kingdom grew into a great power from 1380 BC. The Mitani kingdom was destroyed and Hittite frontiers were extended ever further. A combined attack by the sea-faring nations ca. 1200 BC eventually destroyed the Hittites.

In the thirteenth century BC, Urartuan kingdoms were formed in Eastern Anatolia. From about 825 BC the Urartu were the dominant power in Eastern Anatolia, until the Assyrians conquered the region in 714 BC. Around 620 BC, the Scythians from southern Russia traversed the land, as did the Indo-European Armenians from 600 BC. In 610 BC, Urartu was part of the kingdom of the Medes. Gordion was the capital of the Phrygian kingdom, which was founded around 800 BC, and collapsed in the seventh century BC with the invasion of the Cimmerians. The way now lay open for the rise of the Lydian kingdom, which gradually conquered almost all the Greek cities on the Aegean coast. Together with Sparta,

Egypt and Babylon, the Greeks planned to counter the Persian threat in a preventive war. After the defeat of Pteria, Lydia became a Persian province in 546 BC. The invention of coinage is considered to be Lydia's great contribution to civilisation.

The uprising of the Greek cities against the Persians was defeated in 494 BC with the destruction of Miletus. A further punitive expedition against the Greeks failed at Marathon. A subsequent Persian campaign against Greece was postponed on the death of King Darius I, but failed when finally launched in 479 BC. It was not until 387 BC that Western Anatolia fell again to Persia in the King's Peace. After the victory of Alexander the Great over the Persian king Darius III, Asia Minor became part of Alexander's

gigantic empire, which was divided after his death into the three Kingdoms of the Diadochi (successors), with Antigonus becoming ruler of Lycia and Phrygia. At the battle of Ipsus in 301 BC, Antigonus suffered a crushing defeat and Anatolia came under the control of Lysimachus. After his death and the victory of Seleucus at Kourupedion in 281 BC, the Seleucids dominated the whole of the Near East. The Celts and Galatians invaded the region in 279 BC, making it possible for Nicomedes to found the kingdom of Bithynia with its capital of Nicomedia.

In 74 BC, this kingdom passed by inheritance to the Romans. The rule of Pergamon lasted from 263 BC until 133 BC, when Attalus III bequeathed it to the Romans.

In 247 BC the Parthian empire was formed, representing a constant threat to the Seleucids as well as, later, to the Romans. The power of the Seleucids reached its height under Antiochus III, but after his defeat at the battle of Magnesia in 190 BC, their rule began to decline, and in 64 BC, the region was finally captured by the Roman general, Pompey. The whole of Anatolia now became the Roman province of Asia, and after the division of the nations it fell to Byzantium. In 1453 AD, Constantinople fell to the Turks and Anatolia was Islamised and became the capital

of the Ottoman Empire, remaining so until after World War I.

After the Armistice of Mudros, the Allies occupied Istanbul, the Italians the regions of Antalya and Konya, the Greeks the region around Smyrna (Izmir), and the French, Cilicia. The Turkish nationalist movement (the Young Turks) that had begun as early as 1898, staged an uprising under General Mustafa Kemal (Kemal Attaturk) demanding a Turkish state within the original borders. In 1923, the Treaty of Lausanne established the frontiers of Turkey more or less in their present form.

The Near East

The first advanced cultures in Asia developed in Mesopotamia, the land between two rivers, the Tigris and the Euphrates. Between 3200 and 2800 BC, the Sumerians built city states, containing monumental temples, developed cuneiform script, constructed irrigation systems and used a sophisticated calendar. The city-states including Uruk, Ur, Lagash and Kish developed the Sumerian culture, backed by a well-organised priesthood and officialdom, and governed events in the third millennium BC. The Sumerians experienced their final cultural heyday under Rimsin of Larsa in the eighteenth century BC. Hammurabi (1728–1686 BC) made Babylon into the power centre of Mesopotamia. His rule

was succeeded by that of the Cassites, who immigrated from Iran. From the thirteenth century to 612 BC, the Assyrians dominated the Middle East. Under Esarhaddon ca. 670 BC, their empire covered the whole of Mesopotamia, the Levant and Egypt. The Assyrians were defeated in 612 BC and were replaced by the Babylonians, whose most famous ruler, Nebuchadnezzar, built the Tower of Babel, exiled the Jewish people from their land and destroyed the Temple in Jerusalem. In 539 BC, the Babylonians were overthrown by the Medes and Persians. The Persian

King Cyrus II made Babylon into a Persian province and allowed the Jews to return to their land. The Israelite tribes conquered Canaan ca. 1500 BC and made it the Land of Israel. Around 1010 BC, King Saul was defeated in his war against the Philistines. Under Saul's successor, King David, Israel became a major power which split, after the death of King Solomon in 926 BC, into the kingdoms of Israel and Judah. The conquest and destruction of Jerusalem by Nebuchadnezzar II was followed by the Babylonian Exile. After Cyrus II's conquest of the New Babylonian Kingdom, Israel and Judah became part of the Persian empire.

Judaism could now be actively practised again, since the Persians were themselves monotheists (Zoroastrians) and this was not altered by the conquest of Alexander the Great. In 63 BC, the Romans conquered the country and called it Judaea. From 39 to 4 BC, Herod the Great was a Jewish puppet king; it was under his reign that Jesus Christ was crucified. The Jewish Revolt of 70 AD resulted in the destruction of Jerusalem by the Romans, and in 133 AD the Emperor Hadrian again expelled the Jews from their land which the Romans dubbed Palæstina.

In Persia, the rule of the Medes was followed by that of the Persians, which in the course of the sixth and fifth centuries BC absorbed Lydia, Israel and Judah, Egypt. Nubia, Libya and Anatolia. After the murder of Darius III the Persian empire fell to the forces of Alexander the Great.

The Near East experienced a decisive change through the advance of Islam from the seventh century onwards. By the time its founder, Muhammad, died in Medina in 632 AD, the new teaching had already conquered the whole of Arabia. Under Omar, the Arabs conquered Syria, Persia, Palæstina and Egypt. Under the Umayyads, in the seventh and eighth centuries, the Arab kingdom was extended to include the whole of North Africa, Spain, Kabul, Bokhara, Samarkand, Transoxiana and the Indus region.

Under the Abbasids, the kingdom disintegrated. The Arabs lost their position of supremacy, and the Persians now took control. After

Impressive reliefs adorn the palace complex of Persepolis, founded by Darius the Great, ca. 518 BC.

One of **Yasser Arafat's** greatest political successes was his speech before the United Nations General Assembly in 1974. This led to the international recognition of the Palestine Liberation Organization (PLO) as the official representative of the Palestinians. In the 1990s, the Gaza-Jericho agreement and the Oslo Accords were further important steps for the Palestine-Israel peace process, though resolution of the conflict is still a long way off.

the death of Haroun al-Rashid in 809, the Caliphate became politically insignificant. The Mongols invaded Persia in 1256 and destroyed Baghdad in 1258.

Repeated attacks on the Byzantine Empire, the heir to the eastern half of the Roman Empire, were at first ineffectual, but the Crusaders, in spite of the temporary conquest of Jerusalem, were once again driven out of the area after a total of seven crusades.

In 1301, Sultan Osman I founded the Ottoman Empire, which at various times ruled North Africa, Syria, Mesopotamia, Arabia, the Caucasus, Anatolia, the Balkan peninsula and parts of Hungary. Starting in the late eighteenth century, the Ottoman Empire showed signs of collapse, and in 1875 it had to declare national bankruptcy.

Further to the east, the conquest of Persia was completed in 1736 by the Turkmen leader Nadir. Since the mid-nineteenth century liberal ideas had been spreading through Persia, and in 1906 a constitution was proclaimed. At the instigation of St Petersburg, the country was divided into zones representing Russian and British interests respectively, until the constitution again came into effect in 1909.

Afghanistan, on the north-west frontier of India, founded in 1747, was the subject of British colonial aspirations, but the Afghan rulers were largely successful in preserving their independence.

The French occupied Syria in 1920 and expelled the Emir Faisal its ruler. France was granted a mandate for Syria by the League of Nations in 1923 while Britain was given the mandate for Palestine. Great Britain separated Transjordan from the rest of Palestine and installed the Hashemite Abdallah ibn Hussein. In 1926, Lebanon was separated from Syria and the regions of Hejaz and Najd were combined to form the kingdom of Saudi Arabia. In 1919, Iraq became a British mandated territory. In 1925 a constitutional monarchy was proclaimed but was later overthrown.

On 14 May 1948, after the British withdrawal from Palestine, the Jewish National Council proclaimed the state of Israel. It was immediately invaded by all its Arab neighbours, Jordan, Egypt,

Lebanon and even Iraq with which it had no borders. After four wars – in 1948, 1956, 1967 and 1973 – a process of détente began in 1974, which was continually endangered by terrorist activities. Nevertheless, a peace treaty was signed with Egypt in 1979, and with Jordan in 1994, though a solution to the conflict with the Palestinians is still a remote prospect.

In 1979, Shah Reza Pahlevi was forced to flee Iran, and the Shi'ite leader, Ayatollah Khomeini, proclaimed the Islamic Republic. Iraq's president Saddam Hussein took advantage of his neigh-

bour's military weakness in 1980 to invade Iran. The war ended in 1988 with no clear victory for either side. Iraqi troops invaded Kuwait in 1990. Following a UN ultimatum, an international army under US leadership liberated the emirate. In 2003, Iraq having failed to implement the post-Kuwait UB resolutions, the USA and its allies initiated a war against Iraq. Saddam Hussein's regime was overthrown, but the country remains embroiled in bitter sectarian fighting.

The history of Yemen is also tumultuous. In 1990, an agreement was reached for the peaceful unification of the People's Democratic Republic of Yemen (formerly Aden) and the Yemen Arab Republic to form the Republic of Yemen.

In Afghanistan, the monarchy was toppled in 1973. Soviet troops invaded in 1979. Gorbachev ended Soviet intervention in 1988, but the war against the Islamicists continued. In 1994,

the radical Taliban brought most of the country under their control. After the terrorist attacks of 11 September, 2001, for which the USA held the terrorist organisation Al Qaeda, operating in Afghanistan, responsible, the USA began a military offensive. Elections were held in 2004, but fighting and terrorism continue.

1 Palestinians staging a protest in Nablus.

2 Iran: on 12 February 1951, Shah Muhammad Reza Pahlevi married Princess Soraya. He later divorced her and married Farah Diba. In 1979, the Shah was deposed and forced to flee the country.

3 Celebrating the 'Islamic Revolution' in Tehran, overshadowed by the portrait of Ayatollah Khomeini, who until his death in 1989 was Iran's political and spiritual leader.

4 Operation Desert Storm, in 1991, liberated Kuwait from the Iraqi invaders.

Central and Southern Asia

*Maharajas reigned over the Indian kingdom of **Rajasthan** until 1847. Jodhpur Fort was built by the ruling Rajputs in the seventeenth century. It is constructed from yellow sandstone blocks, that are not held together by mortar.*

*The **Vietnam War** against the United States cost the lives of some 2 million Vietnamese. Around another 3 million were injured. The U.S. used carpet bombing and chemical weapons such as napalm and the defoliant Agent Orange*

Central Asia

The thinly populated steppe and desert landscapes of Central Asia and Siberia were hardly conducive to the formation of urban cultures. The Mongol Empire, united by Genghis Khan in 1206, was of supreme importance in terms of world history. In the fourteenth century, Mongol rule in Iran collapsed, and in 1368 it ended in China with the beginning of the Ming dynasty. Tamburlaine's new Mongol Empire, extending over wide regions of Inner Asia and the Near East, lasted only briefly after his death in 1405. Babur's kingdom of the Great Mughals in India survived until 1857, while the Golden Horde was defeated in 1502 in southern Russia, and the states of Kashan and Astrakhan fell in 1552 and 1557. In 1911, Outer Mongolia separated from China. Since 1990, Mongolia has been a parliamentary democracy.

In the fifteenth century, Tibet became a theocracy, with the Dalai Lama as its spiritual and political leader. In 1950, the country was occupied by Chinese troops and incorporated into China in 1951. Nepal has succeeded in preserving its independence since 1769, and in 1990 replaced the autocratic rule of the king with a constitutional monarchy, the latter being finally abolished in 2007. After the dissolution of the USSR, several former Soviet republics declared their independence. While the process of separation was peaceful in Kyrgyzstan, Tajikistan, Kazakhstan, Turkmenistan, Georgia and Uzbekistan, Azerbaijan and Armenia went to war over the Armenian Christian exclave of Nagorno-Karabakh. The aspirations to independence of the Republic of Chechnya (part of the Russian CIS, whose inhabitants are Muslims) were forcibly suppressed in two wars from 1994 to 1996 and 1999 to 2005 by the Russian army. A diplomatic solution is currently unlikely.

The Indian sub-continent

The excavations at Mohenjo-Daro and Harappa in the Indus valley provide evidence of an advanced civilisation in the third and fourth millennia BC, which possessed a script, planned towns and cities, sewerage and ventilated granaries. Around 1000 BC, the Aryans immigrated from Central Asia and founded the caste system. The new religions, Jainism and Buddhism, emerged in the sixth century BC. In 327 BC, Alexander the Great advanced as far as the Punjab, but had to halt his campaign there.

The first Indian empire was the Maurya dynasty founded by Chandragupta, whose domination extended through Afghanistan, Baluchistan, Sind, Kashmir, Nepal, the Ganges valley and the most of the Deccan Plateau.

After the fall of the regime no one power was able to establish itself permanently, until India experienced its Golden Age under the Gupta dynasty from 320 to 480 AD, with the flourishing of industry, art, architecture and literature. At this time, Buddhism was

Gradually the British were able to assert themselves in the face of Portuguese and French competition and subjugate the local rulers. Through the East India Company, the British gradually conquered India and Queen Victoria adopted the title of 'Empress of India' in 1876, appointing a viceroy to rule the country. From the late nineteenth century, a resistance movement was formed by the indigenous Muslims and Hindus with the foundation of the Indian National Congress. A massacre ordered in 1919 by a British general at a peaceful demonstration in Amritsar was the trigger for the first campaign of non-violent resistance organised by Mahatma Gandhi in 1920–1922. A further campaign of civil disobedience in 1930–32 led to the arrest of several hundred thousand Indians.

Laos: imposing temple statues at Wat Xieng Khwan in Vientiane.

already retreating as Hinduism advanced. Until 1000 AD, several dynasties set up various more or less short-lived regimes, when Islamic invaders first occupied northern India and then established smaller Islamic states throughout the country.

In the sixteenth century, the Great Mughals founded a vast empire which had its heyday under Akbar. Afghan invasions, increased involvement by Europe and the fall of the Mughal empire dramatically changed the power relationships during the seventeenth and eighteenth centuries.

The British government was now ready to make concessions, but the solution of the Indian question was delayed until after the end of the World War II.

The 'Transfer of Power', by which India attained independence, in August 1947, however, culminated in a bloody conflict, due to the demand for autonomy by the mainly Muslim regions in the north. As Pakistan they also achieved independence in 1947. Millions were resettled, but the resulting disturbances cost the lives of more than a million people and the two states are in

continual conflict due to border disputes.

India has had a troubled history since independence. Several prominent politicians were assassinated, including Mahatma Gandhi, Indira Gandhi and Rajiv Gandhi. The conflict over Kashmir led in 1965 to war with Pakistan. In the Tashkent Agreement, both sides renounced further use of force, but there were repeated small skirmishes and some sabre-rattling, since both India and Pakistan are believed to have atomic weapons. In 1961, India forcibly annexed the Portuguese colony of Goa, and in 1962 China annexed some border territory.

In 1971, India helped East Pakistan gain independence. The new state called itself Bangladesh and incorporated the semi-independent state of Sikkim in 1975. The Indian government intervened several times, on occasion with armed forces, in the civil conflict in its neighbouring state Sri Lanka, to the south. The conflict between Muslims and Hindus, as well as the aspirations to independence of the Sikhs in the Punjab continues to cause unrest.

South-Eastern Asia

The kingdom of Lan Xang, which had existed since 1335 in Laos, divided into three parts in 1707. It was conquered by Siam in the nineteenth century. In the sixth century, the Khmer conquered the kingdom of Funan and in the twelfth and thirteenth centuries they ruled the greater part of Indo-china. It was they who built the temple cities of Angkor Wat and Angkor Thom.

In 207 BC, the Lak-Viet conquered the kingdom of Au-Lak, which they called Nam-Viet. In 111 BC, Vietnam came under Chinese rule, which lasted until the mid-tenth century. In 1802, the country, ruled by rival families, was successfully united by the Vietnamese emperor Gia-Long. In 1887, the French seized the areas of the present states of Cambodia, Laos and Vietnam calling them French Indochina. During World War II, the whole of Indochina was occupied by the Japanese. When they capitulated, the country's desire for self-determination was at first thwarted by the return of their former colonial

rulers from France. Supported by Pathet Lao and the Khmer Issarak, the communist Vietminh fought the French and their anti-communist Vietnamese allies.

The bombing of Haiphong and the Vietminh attack on Hanoi triggered the Indo-Chinese war in 1946. After the intervention of China and several military defeats, France withdrew from Indo-China in 1954. Cambodia and Laos were now independent states; Vietnam was divided, until the time when elections were due to be held, into a Communist zone in the north and a non-Communist zone in the south.

In Laos, independence was marked by continual changes of government and civil wars. During the Vietnam war, North Vietnam moved some of its supplies through the Communist-controlled regions of Laos. The South Vietnamese attacked the country in 1971. In 1975, Laos became a Communist people's republic and it was not until 1996 that the impoverished country began to free itself from its isolation in terms of foreign affairs.

In Cambodia, Prince Norodom Sihanouk at first succeeded in keeping the country out of the Vietnam war. But the communist supply routes through Cambodia led to tensions with South Vietnam and internal conflicts. Sihanouk was toppled, General Lon Nol declared a republic and actively supported the South Vietnamese and the USA.

In 1975, the communist Khmer Rouge conquered the city of Phnom Penh and Sihanouk briefly resumed his leadership of the state. The brutal terrorist regime of Pol Pot ruled between 1976 and 1978, and more than two million people fell victim to his extremist brand of communism. In 1979, Communist opposition groups achieved power with the military support of Vietnam.

Pol Pot again retreated underground and carried on guerrilla warfare. The fall of the Khmer Rouge was not officially recognised by the UN until 1981. After the departure of the Vietnamese in 1989, Sihanouk returned from exile, and became king in 1993. It was not until 1998 that the Khmer Rouge abandoned their guerrilla warfare, but after the promise of an amnesty, some

leading to terrible and largely irreversible environmental damage. After the war, thousands of Vietnamese 'Boat People' left the country.

leaders of the organisation were given leading positions in the legitimate government. From 1957, the Vietcong guerrillas fought in the south of Vietnam for national unity under a socialist banner, and with the support of North Vietnam, China and the USSR. From 1960, the USA supported the south, at first with military advisers, then with troops. Neither napalm, chemical weapons, B-52 bombing of the major cities of the north, nor the deployment of elite troops could bring about victory over Ho Chi-Minh's Viet Cong guerillas. Under pressure, from their own population too, the US troops withdrew in 1973. In 1975, the south surrendered and Vietnam was officially reunified in 1976. The mass flight of the 'Boat People' and skirmishes on the Chinese border again brought the country back into the headlines. In 1978, Vietnamese troops toppled the Pol Pot regime in Cambodia. Since 1987, the government has followed a course of reform, bringing about the lifting of the American trade embargo in 1994 and achieving diplomatic recognition in 1995.

Burma, today officially called Myanmar, came into being in the eighteenth century as a result of the union of the kingdoms of Arakan and Ava. In 1885, the last king was taken into custody by the British and the country was annexed to British India, but liberated again in 1937. It achieved independence in 1947 after occupation by the Japanese in the World War II. Since then, it has been ruled by a succession of military dictators, claiming a bizarre combination of socialist and Buddhist objectives.

The kingdom of Siam was the only south-east Asian country to escape colonialisation, even though King Chulalongkorn was forced to cede large territories to France and Britain. In 1939, the Fascist government under Pibul Songgram renamed Siam as Thailand. In World War II, Thailand allied itself with Japan and annexed French and British colonies which it had to hand back at the end of the war. Since then, the political scene, in which only the figure of the king remains a constant element, has been typified by a series of coups d'état, dissolutions of parliament and disturbances,

including calls by Muslims in the south for an independent state. The country's industrial ambitions as a so-called Tiger State proved to be of only short duration in the Asian crisis.

The kingdom of Malacca was conquered by the Portuguese in 1511. In 1641 it was captured by the Dutch and from the eighteenth century the British became the leading power in the region. Malacca, Sarawak and North Borneo (later Sabah) were occupied by the Japanese in 1941, and in 1945, they were again ruled by the British. In 1957, the Federation of Malaya gained independence

and in 1963, with Singapore, Sarawak and Sabah, was extended to become Malaysia. Singapore left the Federation in 1965. Indonesian claims on the area led in 1965 to military conflict which was settled peacefully.

Indonesia and the Philippines

The Buddhist and Hindu regimes in the islands of Indonesia were succeeded from the thirteenth century by Islamic sultanates. In the sixteenth century, the Portuguese founded trading posts and Christian missions, but were driven out by the Dutch East India Company. In 1799, the Netherlands officially incorporated the islands into their colonial possessions as the Dutch East Indies, and, with one short interruption, ruled the land until 1942, when it was occupied by Japanese troops. After the Japanese surrender, Sukarno and Hatta declared the Independent Republic of Indonesia, but in two military actions in

1947 and 1948, the Dutch re-occupied their former colony, but were forced to recognise its independence at the Hague Conference in 1949. The federated United States of Indonesia were replaced in 1950 by a centralised system, while the new democracy was shaken by repeated uprisings. In 1959 Sukarno went over

1 In 1969, President Ho Chi Minh of North Vietnam was laid to rest in a grand mausoleum in Hanoi.

2 Mahatma Gandhi's personal dedication made him into a worldwide figure of peaceful resistance.

3 Jawaharlal Nehru was the first Prime Minister of independent India and followed a policy of non-alignment.

4 In 1998, protests against the Indonesian government escalated, mainly in the capital Jakarta. On 21 May, Suharto was forced to resign.

to a 'guided democracy' and led the country into a severe economic crisis and political isolation. In 1966, he was forced to give way to Suharto's 'New Order', whose liberal economic policy led to a distinct upturn in the economy, though all opposition was brutally suppressed. After the Asian crisis, Suharto could no longer hold out and was replaced by Habibie. The year 1999 also saw an end to the occupation of East Timor, which had been annexed by Indonesia after the departure of the Portuguese. In 2002, East Timor became a sovereign state.

When the Spanish took possession of the Philippines in 1521, they named the islands after their king. Colonial rule there ended when the rebel freedom fighters turned for support to the USA, which declared war on Spain in 1898. Madrid then handed over the Philippines to the United States for the sum of twenty million US dollars. The US proceeded to quell the uprisings with military force and took possession of the islands. After Japanese occupation during the World War II, the Philippines were granted their independence in 1946. In 1965, Ferdinand Marcos became president and ruled from 1972 under martial law, until he was toppled in 1986. Since then, the Philippines has had a new constitution and democtratic rule.

China

After the early Xia (twenty-first to sixteenth centuries BC) and Shang (sixteenth to eleventh centuries) dynasties, the Zhou dynasty came to power around 1050 and ruled until 256 BC. Under the Zhou, the country was organised as a feudal state and greatly extended in the years that followed. The 'Warring States' period end in 221 BC with the unification of the kingdom by King Zheng of Qin, who took the imperial title Shi Huangdi, 'First Emperor', and created a united, centrally administered state.

After his death in 210 BC Liu Bang emerged as victor of the many uprisings, and founded the Han dynasty, which lasted until 220 AD. The Han dynasty saw the invention of paper, the partial reintroduction of feudalism and the

start of trade on the Silk Road. National and civil wars repeatedly divided the country, and it was only under the Tang emperors of 618–907 that the vast Chinese empire experienced its greatest prosperity.

China was united under the foreign domination of the Mongol Yuan dynasty. In 1386, the Mongols were toppled by national uprisings and were succeeded by the twenty emperors of the Ming dynasty, in which the middle classes rose to prominence. In 1644, the Manchurians occupied the capital, Peking (Beijing) and founded the Qing dynasty.

The Mongol leader Genghis Khan practising falconry.

A phase of prosperity was followed in the eighteenth and nineteenth centuries by explosive growth in the population and the economic decline resulting from a succession of wars. The European powers did not succeed in colonising China, but in the Opium War of 1839–42 Britain enforced the opening of some ports to foreign trade, and acquired the island of Hong King which China considered to be of little economic importance. Further hostile action enabled the French and British to open Chinese markets even further. After

its defeat in war against Japan, China was forced to cede Taiwan and recognise the independence of Korea.

A series of agreements forced China to cede various regions to Russia, France and Britain. The German Empire leased the Bay of Jiaozhou. In 1911, the revolutionary movement deposed the imperial government and in January 1912, Sun Yat-sen became the first president of the Chinese Republic. During World War I, in which China was on the side of the Allies, various provincial warlords contended for military supremacy, causing anarchy.

In 1921, the Chinese Communist Party was founded in Shanghai. Under the leadership of Chiang Kai-shek the Kuomintang succeeded in restoring national unity. The Japanese occupied Manchuria and set up a puppet government under emperor Puyi This led to war, in which Mao Zedong's Communist partisan army only narrowly avoided defeat in the Long March of 1934/1935.

In 1937, the Japanese occupied extensive areas of the country in open war. After the Japanese surrender in 1945, the Communist People's Liberation Army, with

Soviet support, gained the upper hand in a civil war, and on 1 October 1949 Mao declared the People's Republic of China. Chiang Kai-shek fled to Taiwan and continued as president of the Republic of China on the island.

But order still did not prevail throughout the gigantic nation. Mao's 'Hundred Flowers' movement was followed by the merciless persecution of all opposition. The 'Great Leap Forward', an ambitious programme of industrialisation, resulted in the deaths from starvation of 30 million people. In 1960, the battle for leadership in the Communist camp ended with China's break with the Soviet Union. In 1964, with the explosion of its first atom bomb, China established its claim as the fifth world power.

In the 'Great Proletarian Cultural Revolution' of 1966, Mao once again destroyed internal opposition. The country's relationship with the West eased with China's membership in the UN, from which Taiwan was excluded, and the state visits of US President Nixon in 1972 and German Chancellor Helmut Schmidt in 1975. After the deaths of Chou En-lai and Mao in 1976, a power struggle broke out, which resulted in the victory of Hua Guofeng over the so-called Gang of Four. But the new 'strong man' proved to be Deng Xiaoping, who introduced basic industrial reforms and a cautious liberalisation programme.

A burgeoning democratic movement was suppressed in June 1989 on Tiananmen Square and a countrywide wave of arrests and executions aroused international protest. Anti-corruption campaigns, further liberalisation of economic life by means of the 'Socialist market economy' and the smooth return of Hong Kong and Macao led China further out of its political isolation.

The relationship between the People's Republic of China and Taiwan remains problematic, with a strong potential for conflict.

Japan

According to legend, the first Japanese emperor was descended from the sun goddess Amaterasu and founded the uninterrupted line of the ruling house.

In the fourth century, Japan came into contact with Buddhism by way of Korea, and around 550 AD it adopted Chinese characters for its language. China was also the model for the absolute bureaucratic state created in 664 by Emperor Kotuku. At the end of the twelfth century Shogun Yoritomo created a feudal state and brought in a military nobility at the cost of the loss of power of the court nobles. Henceforward, the emperor (Tenno) was merely a puppet of the powerful warlords.

In violent battles, the Shoguns and their feudal knights, the samurai, continued to strengthen their position of power. In 1600 Shogun Tokugawa Ieyasu ended the internal turmoil of the country, unified it and by means of a strict new order ensured internal peace for more than 250 years. During the time of the Shogunate, Christianity was outlawed and from 1637 Japan was almost hermetically sealed off from the outside world. Only very limited trade with the Dutch and Chinese was maintained.

As a result of US pressure, after 1854 Japan was forced to open several of its ports and agree to trade agreements with the USA and some of the European powers. The resulting xenophobic movements led to a civil war that ended with the fall of the last Shogun. In 1863, the old feudal system was abandoned and Japan was transformed into an absolute monarchy, which became a constitutional monarchy in 1889. At the same time, the army and industry were modernised, and Japan slowly advanced to the status of a regional great power.

In the war against China of 1895, Japan was able to assert its interests in Korea and gained the island of Taiwan. In 1904–05 Japanese ships sank the Russian fleet in the Russo-Japanese War; at the Peace of Portsmouth, Japan secured for itself the area around Port Arthur and the southern half of Sakhalin island.

In 1910, the Japanese annexed Korea, and in 1914 they entered World War I against the Central Powers, conquered Jiaozhou and the German South Sea Islands. In 1921, under pressure from Britain and the USA, Japan had to

*On 6 August 1945, the first **atomic bomb** fell on **Hiroshima**. Three days later, a second fell on Nagasaki. The devastating effects forced Japan to capitulate, and the ceasefire was signed on 2 September on board the USS Missouri.*

*Tenzin Gyatso is the 14th **Dalai Lama** of Tibet. After the occupation by China in 1950, he was forced to emigrate to India in 1959. His peaceful struggle for independence for Tibet earned him the Nobel Peace Prize in 1989.*

renounce supremacy in China, and an industrial crisis, a severe earthquake and battles for a universal suffrage weakened Japan's position further. In 1931, Japanese troops occupied Manchuria and created the puppet state of Manchukuo.

As a result of international protests, Japan left the League of Nations in 1933 and in 1934 announced its withdrawal from the Washington Naval Agreement, which provided for a ratio of 3 : 5 : 5 in relation to the fleets of the USA and Britain. In 1936, Japan entered the Anti-Comintern Pact with Hitler's Germany, and in 1937 abruptly initiated the Sino-Japanese War, in the course of which extensive areas of China were occupied.

On 7 December 1941, without any declaration of war, Japanese bombers attacked the American fleet at Pearl Harbor. After initial military success, Japan was forced to surrender on 2 September 1945, following the dropping of atom bombs on Hiroshima and Nagasaki.

Until 1951, General MacArthur, who was commander of the US military government, forced the emperor to renounce his divinity in a radio broadcast. Japanese war criminals were tried at the Tokyo international military tribunals and there was a thorough reform of industry. At the San Francisco Peace Treaty of 1951, Japan lost all the territories it had acquired in the previous 80 years, as well as the Kuril Islands.

Korea

The history of Korea is closely bound up with Japanese foreign policy, but despite all the attempted advances made to the country by China and Japan, it has been able to preserve its own ethnic and cultural identity and independence.

In 1876, Japan enforced trading rights with Korea. In 1895, after the Sino-Japanese war, Korea became a Japanese protectorate, and in 1910 it was annexed. After World War II, the country was divided into two zones, one Soviet-influenced and one American-influenced. North of the 38th parallel, the (Communist) Democratic People's Republic of Korea (known as North Korea) was

formed, and south of it the Republic of Korea (or South Korea), which looked to the West. In 1949 the occupying troops moved out. On 25 June 1950, North Korean troops crossed the demarcation line and conquered almost the whole of South Korea. The United Nations decided to send in a task force, which consisted chiefly of American troops under the command of General MacArthur. The North Koreans were eventually driven back as far as the Chinese border, but China intervened with a counter-offensive which pushed the UN troops back beyond Seoul. MacArthur, for his

part, was able to beat off the Chinese-North Korean units as far as the 38th parallel, and demanded expansion of the war into Chinese territory and the use of atomic weapons. As a result, he was dismissed from his post. With the armistice agreement of 1953, the 38th parallel was reinstated as a border. South Korea now changed from an agricultural nation to a prosperous industrial one, while ruled politically by military dictatorships and authoritarian regimes. Only since 1993 has Korea had a freely elected president and parliament. The country's relationship with North Korea remains tense though North Korea was ruled up to his death in 1994 by Kim Il Sung with the support of China and the Soviet Union. At present, despite talks with the South, the country, ruled by his son Kim Jong Il, is politically isolated and struggling with a disastrous economic situation of intense poverty and there are rumours of famine among the

population. This has not stopped North Korea from attempting to develop nuclear weapons with which it is threatening South Korea, and other countries, including Japan. There is an alleged alliance between North Korea and Iran in the development of these lethal weapons. North Korea remains politically isolated.

1 In July 1953, in Panmunjeom, the 38th parallel was fixed as the border between North and South Korea.

2 Mao Zedong and Lin Biao were the political leaders of the People's Republic of China, which was officially proclaimed on 1 October 1949.

3 Propaganda for the People's Liberation Army of China in the 1960s and 1970s depicting the iconic soldier-worker, Lei Feng.

4 Demonstrations for political reform began in Tiananmen Square in Beijing in 1989, but were violently suppressed.

Since 1997, Hong Kong has once again been restored to Chinese sovereignty as a special administrative region. It is one of the world's most important financial centres and a hub of merchant shipping.

The Countries of Asia

The countries of Asia, inhabited by somewhere in the region of 4 billion people, cover one-third of the Earth's landmass. This makes Asia both the largest and most populated continent in the world. All those who cross the Bosphorus with the intention of discovering Asia will be fascinated by the variety of natural geography. The continent is

The heart of the Middle East Conflict: the holy city of Jerusalem.

The Wat Phra Kaeo temple, part of the Royal Palace in Bangkok.

divided in two by impressive mountain ranges such as the Himalayas, the so-called 'roof of the world'. Further north lie the endless grassy steppes of Mongolia and the moss-covered tundra of Siberia. To the south sprawl ever-green rainforests. The peoples are as varied as the land. Asia contains a wider variety of cultures and religions than any other continent.

Syria

Petra, in southern Jordan, is one of the most fascinating and mysterious ruined cities in the world. In the middle of the desert, elegant pillars and bridges appear to grow out of the cliff face. This monumental piece of architecture was built by the Nabataeans, nomadic traders who combined Greek and Arabic elements in their architecture. The city dates from 300 BC and was the residence of the Nabataean King until the Romans occupied the land.

Syria

Area:	185,180 sq. km
Capital city:	Damascus
Form of government:	
Presidential Republic	
Administrative divisions:	
13 provinces, 1 district (capital city)	
Population:	
19.3 million	
(104 inhabitants/sq. km)	
Languages:	
Arabic (official), Kurdish,	
Armenian	
GDP per capita:	US$1,800
Currency:	
1 Syrian pound = 100 piastres	

Natural Geography

Syria's land mass consists of 90 per cent steppe and desert terrain. The north and north-east are dominated by **steppes** and flat **plateaus** and the **Syrian Desert** covers the south-east. The **Jabal al-Nusayriyah mountain range in the west** runs parallel to the Mediterranean coast. South and east of the Anti-Lebanon lie the **Golan Heights** which have been occupied by Israel since 1967. The **Euphrates** and its tributaries flow through the north-east.

Climate

Syria is affected by two different climates. The west of the country has a **Mediterranean climate** while the east has a **dry continental climate.**

Population

Syria's population is relatively **homogeneous** in terms of ethnic origin, 90.3 per cent being **Arabs.** There are also small communities of **Kurds** and **Armenians.** The population is 90 per cent **Sunni Muslim,** but there are also minority **Alawite, Christian** and **Druze** populations. The country has a poor education system, with the result that the literacy rate is only 70 per cent.

History and Politics

The country was the centre of some of the Earth's **oldest civilisations,** being ruled consecutively by the Romans, Byzantines, Arabs and Ottomans. These various occupying powers have left wonderful archaeological remains. In 1922, the League of Nations granted France a mandate over Syria. The country first became fully **independent** in **1946.** During the unstable years leading up to 1970, Syria was ruled by **military governments.** Other important events include the **Union with Egypt** (United Arab Republic 1958–1961) and the **Six Day War** in 1967, when Syria attacked Israel causing it to lose the Golan Heights. The constitution of 1973 caused Syria to declare itself a **Socialist Democracy.** Hafez al-Assad was the country's leader from 1971 until his death in 2000. He was followed by his son Bashar al-Assad. In 2004, he announced negotiations with Israel but no further steps were taken. In 2005, after the murder of the former Lebanese prime minister Hariri, Syrian troops withdrew from Lebanon. Syria's behaviour remains decisive for development in the Near East.

Economy

The state regulates large parts of economic life, but in recent years there has been a careful opening up to a market economy and competition. In 2006, GDP was US$ 35 billion, of which 22 per cent came from agriculture, 28 per cent from industry and 50 per cent from services. Oil production provides 70 per cent of export earnings. However, it is in decline and reserves are fast becoming exhausted. The construction of alternative branches of industry is therefore given priority in Syrian policies. The trade deficit is a hindrance to the economy, and one cause of this is that there has been serious inflation, now around ten per cent. The economy has been hit in recent years by the huge increase in population. In 1972 it was only 6.6 million but by 2008 it was close to 20 million.

Transport Infrastructure

Syria's **road network** covers 40,000 km. Roads in the interior are often in poor condition. There are international airports in **Damascus** and **Aleppo,** and the main port is in **Latakia.**

Tourism

Syria's tourist infrastructure remains underdeveloped. The **historic cities** of Damascus, Aleppo and Hama and Palmyra in central Syria, are all testament to the country's varied history.

Omnipresent in Syria: a portrait of the the late President Assad.

Hafez al-Assad	King Hussein of Jordan
*Qardaha, 6.10.1930, †Damascus, 10.6.2000	*Amman, 14.11.1935, †Amman, 7.2.1999
Al-Assad joined the Ba'th Party in 1946 and became Minister of Defence in 1966. From 1971 onwards, he was President of Syria. During the Six-Day War of 1967, he cooperated with Egypt against Israel, but refused to sign a peace treaty in the 1970s, unlike Egypt, which is why the territories lost by Syria have not been regained. After the collapse of the Soviet Union, Assad worked towards a better relationship with the West.	King Hussein of the Hashemite dynasty, was crowned in 1952. During the Six-Day War against Israel in 1967, Jordan lost East Jerusalem and the West Bank. Hussein's efforts for a political solution of the Middle East conflict earned him recognition in the West, but led to tensions with the PLO. In 1974, he renounced claims to the West Bank. In 1998, he was involved in the drawing up of the Wye Treaty and in 1994 signed a peace treaty with Israel.

*The **bazaars of the Middle East** date back to the days of the caravanserai. They are the market quarters of middle-eastern cities. Open or covered alleys are lined with stalls. Some shops have several storeys, with large internal courtyards.*

Lebanon

Area:	10,452 sq. km
Capital city:	Beirut
Form of government: Republic	
Administrative divisions: 5 provinces	
Population: 3.8 million (375 inhabitants/sq. km)	
Languages: Arabic (official), French	
GDP per capita:	US$6,000
Currency: 1 Lebanese pound = 100 piastres	

Natural Geography

Lebanon is a **mountainous** country (with peaks rising to 3,087 m) on the eastern Mediterranean seaboard. It has a very narrow, but fertile coast.

Climate

The mountain regions have a **continental climate** with snowy winters, but the coastal areas have a climate with **Mediterranean influences**.

Population

Arabs form the majority of the population, and there is a small **Armenian** minority. 70 per cent of the population belongs to one of the 11 recognised branches of **Islam**. 30 per cent belong to one of five **Christian denominations**.

History and Politics

After the collapse of the Ottoman Empire in 1920, Lebanon became part of the **French mandate of Syria,** until it gained independence in 1943. The Muslim and Christian populations have since been engaged in numerous **disputes** including a civil war which lasted from 1975 to 1990 and was ended in 1991 by a **peace treaty.** Since then, the country, which had been **heavily damaged by the war.** The Syrians occupied the country until early 2005. In the summer of 2006, the radical Islamic Shiite Hezbollah militia provoked Israeli military action by attacking an Israeli military patrol on the border with Israel, which quickly developed into war.

Economy

More than **1 million foreigners** work in Lebanon. The **agricultural sector** is unable to supply the country's needs. A complex irrigation system enables cultivation of fruit and vegetables. The **manufacturing sector** (paper, food) accounts for 20 per cent of GDP. The **services sector** (trade, banking) has a long history and contributes 73 per cent of GDP, making it the most important sector of the economy. Lebanon's economy is significantly in debt, though it receives funding from other Arab states.

Transport Infrastructure

The majority of the road network is surfaced. **Beirut** has an international airport.

Tourism

Main points of interest are the historic cities of **Byblos** and **Baalbek,** and **Beirut**. The beaches of the Mediterranean offer many attractions.

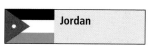

Jordan

Area:	92,300 sq. km
Capital city:	Amman
Form of government: Constitutional Monarchy	
Administrative divisions: 12 provinces	
Population: 6 million (65 inhabitants/sq. km)	
Languages: Arabic (official), English	
GDP per capita:	US$2,400
Currency: 1 Jordanian dinar = 1000 fils	

Natural Geography

Jordan lies on the north-west corner of the Arabian Peninsula and is divided by the 400-km-long and 10-km-wide **Great Rift Valley**.

1 The Bedouin are a nomadic people who travel with their camels across the desert regions of the Middle East.

2 Syria contains sites that are holy to both Muslims and Christians. A view of the town of Saydnaya with its famous convent.

3 Beirut: the Corniche, the world-famous beach promenade, lined with high-rise blocks of shops, offices, hotels and restaurants.

4 Damascus: mosaic in the Rugaiya Mosque, built by the Iranian government for the Shi'ite community.

Jordan

To the west, the land is **hilly**, with peaks of 600–800 m. In the east there are sheer **mountains** of up to 1,745 m, which descend to the **Arabian desert**. The **Jordan River** flows along the valley floor and into the **Dead Sea**, but it is **not navigable**, due to numerous bends. A small stretch of coast on the Gulf of Aqaba connects Jordan to the **Red Sea**, and this is Jordan's only coastal region.

Climate

Most of the country has a **desert climate** (temperatures up to 50°C in summer) with low rainfall. The **Mediterranean climate** in the west of the country means that the land there can be used for agriculture. Farm produce include grapes and olives.

Population

The population is 98 per cent **Arab**, the majority of whom are nomadic or semi-nomadic **Bedouin**. Palestinians make up 40 per cent of the population, and there are also some **1.4 million Palestinian refugees**.

History and Politics

The country was formerly known an **Transjordan** and became a British mandate in 1923. According to the **constitution,** which has been in place since 1952, the King has sole executive powers and shares legislative decisions with the national assembly. In 1994, King **Hussein** (1935–1999) concluded a **peace treaty** with Israel. Jordan's foreign policies remain a **balancing act** between the interests of the Arab countries and the West. In 1999, Hussein's son Abdullah Ibn Hussein II inherited the throne.

Economy

Up to 90 per cent of Jordan's land mass is **desert** and **mountain terrain** and unsuitable for agriculture. The country has only small oil reserves, making it one of the poorer Arab countries. The lack of development opportunities in **agriculture** (three per cent of GDP) and **industry** (30 per cent, potash, phosphorus) has meant the the economy centres on the **services sector**, which contributes 67 per cent of GDP.

Transport Infrastructure

Jordan's road network is well constructed. There are international airports in **Amman** and **Aqaba**. Aqaba is the only port.

The Dome of the Rock in Jerusalem has a 31-m-high golden dome.

David Ben-Gurion	Yitzhak Rabin
*Plonsk, 16.10.1886, †Tel HaShomer, 1.12.1973	*Jerusalem, 1.3.1922, †Tel Aviv, 4.11.1995
The leader of the Zionist movement worked in Palestine from 1906 as a union leader and chairman of the Jewish Agency. In 1944, he took over the leadership of the World Zionist Organization and proclaimed the State of Israel on 14.5.1948. As Prime Minister and Minister for Defence in the years 1948 to 1953 and 1955 to 1963, he remains an important figure in the history of the State of Israel.	Israel owed its convincing victory in the Six Day War to its General Chief of Staff, Yitzhak Rabin, who became Washington ambassador from 1963 to 1973 and Prime Minister from 1974 to 1977. From 1984 to 1990, he was Minister for Defence. He returned to office as Prime Minister in 1992 until his assassination in 1995. He received the Nobel Peace Prize in 1993 for his peace work.

Tourism

Tourism is one of the most important sources of income. The main attractions for most visitors, apart from the cities of Amman and Aqaba, are the ruins of **Petra** made famous in legend and poetry as 'The Rose Red City half as old as Time'. There are other archaeological remains, especially at Jerash, and Amman, once the Roman city of Philadelphia. Aqaba on the Red Sea has many tourist attractions in the form of sandy beaches and the coral reefs offshore which can be explored by scuba divers.

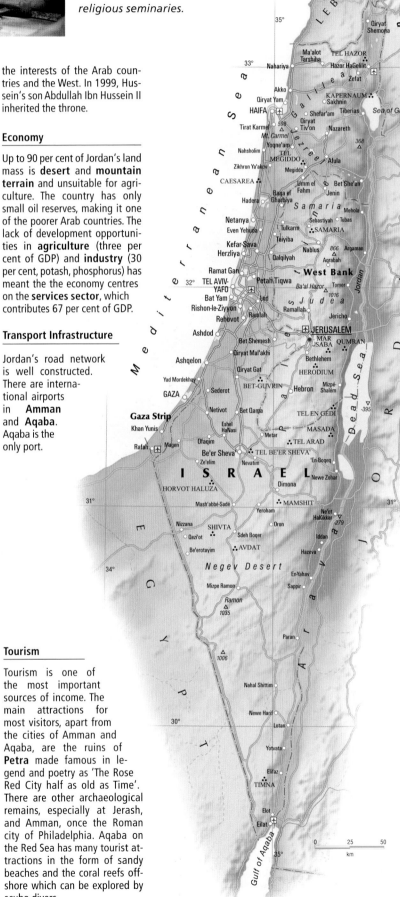

*Israel is home to some 150,000 **Christians**. The largest denomination is the Greek Orthodox Church, followed by the Greek Catholics. The holiest site in Jerusalem is the Church of the Holy Sepulchre containing the Tomb of Christ.*

	Israel
Area:	20,766 sq. km
Capital city:	Jerusalem
Form of government:	Republic

Administrative divisions:
6 districts, occupied and semi-autonomous territories
Population:
6.5 million (290 inhabitants/ sq. km), including the West Bank, Golan and East Jerusalem
Languages:
Hebrew, Arabic (both official), English
GDP per capita: US$21,000
Currency:
1 new shekel = 100 agorot

Natural Geography

In the north, the **hills of Galilee** stretch from the Mediterranean to the river Jordan. South of this is a narrow and fertile coastal plain. To the south is the **Negev desert,** which covers most of Israel's land mass. To the east, the country is bordered by the **Dead Sea** and the **Jordan Valley.**

Climate

Coastal areas have a Mediterranean climate, while the south has a **desert climate**. The summers are dry and warm, and the winters are mild and wet. Winters in the desert and mountain regions are cold.

Population

Israel has a multi-ethnic population, many of whom are **immigrants. Jews** make up some 82 per cent of the population, of whom 32 per cent are immigrants from Europe, America, Asia and Australia. Amongst the non-Jewish population, **Arabs** form the majority, with 14 per cent, but there is also a minority of **Druze**.

History and Politics

The **parliamentary republic** of Israel was proclaimed by the **Jewish National Council** in **1948** at the end of the British mandate in Palestine. A large proportion of the 700,000–900,000 Arabs living in mandatory **Palestine,** left the country when Israel's Arab neighbours invaded in an attempt to destroy it from the

outset. There have been four wars and many skirmishes and terrorist attacks between Arab states and Israel. The legalisation of the Palestine Liberation Organization (PLO) in 1993 marked the beginning of the **Middle-East Peace Process,** which ultimately aims for **Palestinian self-rule.** The peace process has had many stumbling blocks, due to Israeli settlements on the **West Bank** and Palestinian bombings. Since 2001, conflicts have escalated, with **suicide bombings** by Palestinian extremists and reprisal attacks by the Israeli army hindering a peaceful resolution. Israel

unilaterally withdrew from the Gaza Strip in 2005, but in 2006, Israel was attacked by Hezbollah, the guerilla army occupying Southern Lebanon, sparking a fifth war.

Economy

Israel's economy used to be predominantly agricultural but the country has developed into a modern **industrialised nation** with an important services sector accounting for 75 per cent of GDP. The **manufacturing sector** consists mainly of foodstuffs, metal and steel production. **Kibbutzim** and **moshavim** (collective farms) on the mainly state-owned land produce most food needs.

Transport Infrastructure

Israel has a very good road network. Shipping is important for **exports,** and the **ports** of Haifa, Ashdod, Ashkelon and Eilat are well-developed. The international airport is Ben-Gurion airport.

Tourism

Israel has sites sacred to three world religions, including the Temple ruins, early Christian and Byzantine churches, Jewish and Roman remains and Crusader relicts. Important Muslim sites include the Dome of the Rock and the Al-Aqsa mosque in Jerusalem Old Town, a UNESCO World Heritage Site.

1 Jerusalem: The twelfth-century Church of the Holy Sepulchre is the holiest church in Christianity. It is built on the site of the tomb of Christ.

2 Laid-back Tel Aviv: Locals relax on the beach. Hotels and bars line the promenade.

3 Dignified Tel Aviv: The port in the 7,000-year-old twin city of Jaffa retains much of its Arab architecture and past.

4 The Palestinians have developed a new self-confidence. This young woman in Bethlehem is proudly wearing traditional dress.

Iraq

The **Kurds** live in an autonomous region in the mountainous northeast of Iraq. They represent over 15 per cent of the population and are the largest minority group in the country. Here, women take up weapons to fight alongside the men for an autonomous Kurdish state. This land was promised to them in 1920 by Turkey and the Allies, but the promise still remains unfulfilled, despite 80 years of fighting. Meanwhile, the Kurdish independence movement has splintered.

Iraq

Area:	437,072 sq. km
Capital city:	Baghdad
Form of government:	
Presidential Republic	
Administrative divisions:	
18 provinces	
Population:	
27 million (60 inhabitants/sq. km)	
Languages:	Arabic, Kurdish is
the official language in the northern provinces	
GDP per capita:	US$1,800
Currency:	
1 Iraqi dinar = 1000 fils	

Natural Geography

The fertile **flood plains** of the **Euphrates** and **Tigris** rivers form the heartland of this state in the north eastern Arabian peninsula. Even in pre-Islamic times, artificial **irrigation systems** were built along the course of the rivers, which has produced a wide green belt parallel to both rivers. These often ended abruptly at the edge of the desert in the north east **Kurdish highlands**. In the west and south-west, semi-desert and desert predominate. In the south, east of Kuwait, there is a narrow access to the **Persian Gulf** where the Tigris and the Euphrates meet at the **Shatt Al-Arab**. The Iran-Iraq war of 1980 to 1988 and the Gulf War of 1991 caused great ecological damage to the area, as did Saddam Hussein's policy of draining the marshes, from which the environment is only slowly recovering.

Climate

The arid regions have a **desert climate** with cold winters and hot, dry summers. In the northern **mountains**, whose peaks rise to 3,600 m, the winters are cold and snowy. In the capital city, Baghdad, which is in the plains, the average temperatures are 10°C in January and 35°C in July. This is temperate in comparison with other parts of the country.

Population

The majority of Iraqis are **Arabs**, of whom 97 per cent profess **Islam**, 60 per cent belonging to the **Shi'ite branch**. The largest minority is the **Kurds** (20 per cent) who live predominantly in an autonomous region in the mountains. There are also **Turks** and **Turkmens**. The population suffers seriously from a **shortage** of basic commodities. This can largely be attributed to the dictatorship of Saddam Hussein and the **UN Sanctions** of 1991 to 2003, the effects of which are also noticeable in the poor infrastructure (hospitals and public transport).

History and Politics

The alluvial land on the lower reaches of both rivers, one of the oldest settlements on Earth, forming the heart of the **Mesopotamian kingdom**, which the Sumerians founded in the third millennium BC. Among the great achievements of this people is the invention of the **cuneiform script**, one of the earliest forms of writing. The Sumerian civilisation was followed by that of the **Babylonians** and the **Assyrians who** ruled in the second and first millennia BC. Babylon, the capital of the powerful kingdom, was a magnet for the sciences and arts.

Saddam Hussein

*Tikrit, 28.4.1937
†Baghdad, 30.12.2006

After the Ba'ath Party seized power in 1968, Saddam Hussein became head of state and government in 1979 and commander-in-chief of the armed forces. He established a totalitarian regime, brutally eradicating any opposition. His interference with UN weapons inspectors led to conflict with the UN and USA, resulting in the 2003 Iraq War. Captured by US forces in 2003, he was sentenced to death by a Special Tribunal in 2005 and was hanged 30 December 2006.

One of the achievements of this period, **The Hanging Gardens of Babylon**, was among the Seven Wonders of the World. In the sixth century BC, Mesopotamia was conquered by the **Persians**. The **Greeks** and later the **Romans** moved into the region at the beginning of the common era and increasingly repressed the Babylonian kingdom. In the seventh century AD, it fell to the Abbasids whose capital was **Baghdad**, at the heart of the **Islamic Empire**. This period ended with the city's conquest and destruction by the **Mongols** in the thirteenth century. In the sixteenth century, Mesopotamia became a province of the **Ottoman Empire** who ruled it for more than 300 years.

When the Ottoman Empire disintegrated at the end of **World War I**, Mesopotamia became the British mandate of Iraq. The British installed a **monarchy** in 1921 which was eventually toppled in 1958 after rioting. Since 1961, there have been **violent conflicts** with the **Kurdish minority** who, together with the Kurds from Turkey and Iran are demanding an autonomous **Kurdistan**. Fulfilment of this demand was promised in 1920 by Turkey and its allies under the Peace Treaty of Sèvres but the promise has never been kept. Under Saddam Hussen, Kurdish settlements were attacked with **poison gas**.

The monarchy was succeeded by a series of dictators, ending with **Saddam Hussein,** who waged a long and bloody war (1980–1988) against Shi'ite **Iran**. In the **First Gulf War** (1990–1991), international armed forces, led by the USA, freed **Kuwait**, which had been annexed by Iraq under Saddam Hussein.

Following the war, no-fly zones were set up for the protection of the Kurdish minorities in the north and the Shi'ites in the south. Iraq was required to fulfil various UN Resolutions, for example, recognition of the sovereignty of Kuwait and the abandonment of nuclear, biological and chemical weapons. However, the **UN weapons inspectors** were continually deceived and obstructed by the Iraqi regime. This led to air raids on Iraq by the USA and Britain, and to an extension of the **economic sanctions**, of which the general population were the principal victims. In 2002, the conflict with the USA intensified after Iraq was accused of having weapons of mass destruction. On 20 March 2003, US and British forces attacked Iraq and toppled Saddam Hussein's

Baghdad: this Iraqi shopkeeper displays his wares with a smile.

The Great Mosque of Kadhimain is a Shi'ite pilgrimage centre.

[Map of Iran and surrounding region, with labels including: AZERBAIJAN, TURKMENISTAN, AFGHANISTAN, PAKISTAN, IRAN, SAUDI ARABIA, KUWAIT, BAHRAIN, QATAR, UNITED ARAB EMIRATES, OMAN, Caspian Sea, Persian Gulf, Gulf of Oman, Strait of Hormuz, Salt Desert, Eiburz Mountains, Zagros Mountains, Baluchistan. Cities include TABRIZ, Ardabil, Rasht, Qazvin, Karaj, TEHERAN, Qom, Hamadan, Kermanshah, Arak, Kashan, ISFAHAN, Yazd, Kerman, Zahedan, Shiraz, Bandar-e Abbas, AL BASRA, MASHHAD, Sabzevar, and many others.]

regime within a matter of weeks. In January 2005, the first free elections in over 40 years were held and a coalition government formed from the various, disparate winning factions, including Kurds. A high degree of insecurity prevails, however, and the political situation remains unstable. There are brutal terror attacks and suicide bombings, mainly from foreign militants, on a daily basis.

Economy

Iraq has the **third largest oil reserves** in the world. The country is only recovering slowly from **wars that have lasted for decades** and the **economic sanctions** imposed by the West after the Gulf War. Reconstruction will only succeed with the help of international aid. Currently, industry contributes 69 per cent to GDP, including **oil**-refining, processing and construction. Before the Iraq War, the oil economy contributed 45 per cent to GDP, industry seven per cent, agriculture 20 per cent and the services sector 28 per cent. Only 12 per cent of the land can be cultivated and 60 per cent of this is irrigated. Cereals, tomatoes, melons and dates are the main crops.

Transport Infrastructure

Iraq's **rail network** is 2,032 km long, the **road network** is 47,000 km long, The major ports are Chur el-Amja, Basra and Umm Qasr. The Tigris, Euphrates and the Shatt al Arab are navigable. Baghdad and Basra have international airports.

Tourism

Since the wars, tourism in Iraq has come to a standstill.

Iran

Persepolis, built in approximately 400 BC, was for centuries a symbol of power of the first Persian empire of the Achaemenids, until it was burned down by Alexander the Great. Archaeological digs have not resolved the enigma of the purpose of this fortress-like residence. Some believe that it was a shrine for celebrating the Persian New Year on 21 March. However, the grandeur of the construction suggests that it may have been a royal palace.

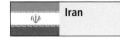
Iran

Area:	1,648,195 sq. km
Capital city:	Tehran
Form of government:	
Islamic Republic	
Administrative divisions:	
28 provinces	
Population:	68.6 million
	(42 inhabitants/sq. km)
Languages:	
Farsi (official), Kurdish, Turkish languages	
GDP per capita:	US$3,200
Currency:	1 rial = 100 dinars

Natural Geography

The country which lies between the **Caspian Sea** and the **Persian Gulf** is bounded in the north by the **Alborz mountains** which rise up to 5,604 m above sea level and in the south by the **Zagros mountains**. In the south-west, the country is part of the **Mesopotamian Lowland Plains**. The arid highlands in the interior of the country are riven with deep valleys. In the east, the land becomes the **Lût desert**. In the north there is the **Dasht-e-Kavir**, the **Great Salt Desert**.

Climate

Iran is a country of extremes: hot summers (up to 50°C) alternate with extremely cold winters. Generally an **arid** or a **semi-arid** climate predominates, with subtropical traces along the **Caspian seaboard**. **Rainfall** is confined mostly to the edges of the mountain ranges; subtropical vegetation is found in the north on the Caspian Sea coast.

Population

In addition to the 51 per cent **Persians**, 24 per cent **Azeris** live in the centre and in the north-west of Iran, and seven per cent of the population are **Kurds**, as well as minorities of **Lurs, Turkmens, Baluchis** and **Armenians**. Of the population, 99 per cent are **Muslims**, consisting of 89 per cent **Shi'ite** and ten per cent **Sunni**. There are also two million **refugees**, mainly from Afghanistan and Iraq. In addition to the official language of **Farsi**, Kurdish, Azerbaijani, Arabic and Armenian are also spoken. The population of Iran is very young, with an average age of 25 years. The state has set up a **national insurance system** for cases of illness or unemployment. The proportion of spending on social insurance and health amounts to 15 per cent. The country has 36 universities but the **illiteracy** rate is over 20 per cent , mainly among women; there is over 30 per cent **unemployment**.

History and Politics

In 600 BC, the Persians founded an empire that extended throughout the Middle East as far as Egypt. The **Iranians** first settled the area in the second millennium BC.

Islamisation began in the seventh century AD when Arabs overthrew the **Sassanid Dynasty**. This introduced a period of cultural prosperity, which came to a sudden end in the thirteenth century with the **Mongol invasion**. The **Safavid-Dynasty** replaced foreign rule in the sixteenth and seventeenth centuries. In the following period, under the **New Persian Empire** whose capital was Isfahan, the economy and culture flourished, as is evidenced by the fact that many surviving buildings are regarded as the finest examples of Persian architecture.

In the nineteenth century, the country was drawn into the conflict of interests between Russia and Great Britain. **Rebellions** against the influence of the foreign powers led in 1906 to the first constitution and to the establishing of a parliament. **Shah Pahlavi**, who considered himself to be the successor to the legendary Cyrus II, ascended the Peacock throne following a coup d'etat in 1925 and founded the first Iranian kingdom. He ordered the complete reshaping of the country along **western** lines carrying out **reforms** in the educational system, modernising agri-

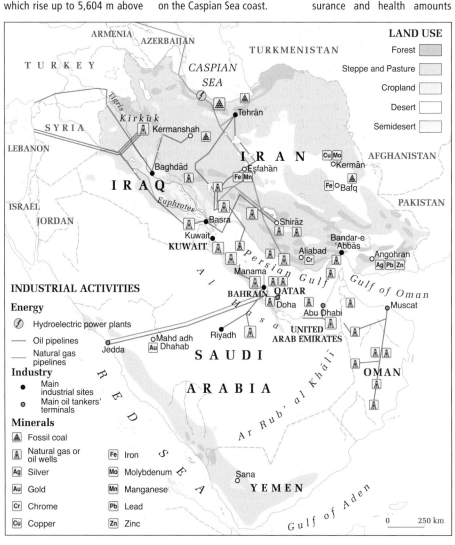

Mullahs on a PC: the computer age has reached Iran.

Mohammad Reza Pahlevi	Ruhollah Khomeini
*Tehran, 26.10.1919, †Cairo, 27.7.1980	*Khomein, 17.5.1900, † Tehran, 3.6.1989
After his father was forced to abdicate by the Allies in 1941, the young heir to the throne was made Shah. Reza Pahlevi began a process of modernisation in Iran. His frequent disregard of Islamic traditions and brutal style of government, supported by the secret police, the SAVAK, led to massive protests and increasing opposition. In 1979, he was overthrown and forced into exile.	This Iranian philosophy professor and cleric was the spokesperson of anti-government demonstrations and was banished from the country in 1964. After the abdication of the Shah, he returned from exile in 1979 and founded the Islamic Republic, a fundamentalist state ruled by mullahs. During his time in office, he also fought an eight-year war with Iraq. He remains a revered religious and political figure in Iran.

Map labels:

ARMENIA, AZERBAIJAN, TURKMENISTAN, TURKEY, CASPIAN SEA, SYRIA, Tigris, Kirkūk, Kermanshah, Tehrān, LEBANON, IRAN, AFGHANISTAN, Baghdād, Esfahān, Kermān, IRAQ, Bafq, PAKISTAN, Euphrates, ISRAEL, JORDAN, Basra, Shirāz, Kuwait, Bandar-e Abbās, KUWAIT, Aliabad, Angohran, Manama, BAHRAIN, QATAR, Persian Gulf, Gulf of Oman, Doha, Abu Dhabi, Muscat, Mahd adh Dhahab, Jedda, Riyadh, UNITED ARAB EMIRATES, SAUDI ARABIA, OMAN, Ar Rub' al Khali, RED SEA, Sana, YEMEN, Gulf of Aden

LAND USE

- Forest
- Steppe and Pasture
- Cropland
- Desert
- Semidesert

INDUSTRIAL ACTIVITIES

Energy
- Hydroelectric power plants
- Oil pipelines
- Natural gas pipelines

Industry
- Main industrial sites
- Main oil tankers' terminals

Minerals
- Fossil coal
- Natural gas or oil wells
- Ag Silver
- Au Gold
- Cr Chrome
- Cu Copper
- Fe Iron
- Mo Molybdenum
- Mn Manganese
- Pb Lead
- Zn Zinc

0   250 km

*The **shrine** of the Iranian Shah Nematollah Vali is the religious focal point of south-east Iran. Islamic burial shrines serve as a remembrance of great rulers, but are also a place where the faithful can come in isolation to contemplate and pray because they are open every day. In the great Friday mosques, by contrast, people come in great numbers to pray on what, for Muslims, is the most important day of the week.*

culture and putting the state budget back on its feet. A plan to settle the nomadic tribes and to create a balance between the upper echelons of society and the masses was unsuccessful. These reforms, soon led to serious **conflicts** with the country's ruling classes, although these were subdued by force.

In 1978, the **Islamic Revolution** unsettled the country. **Ayatollah Khomeini** organised this coup from his French exile. In 1979, the second Shah was forced to flee the country and Iran was proclaimed an **Islamic Republic**. Since then, Shi'ite Islam, under Khomeini has caused a political and social transformation dominating all areas of life from the media to the judiciary. The President is elected by **Parliament** but the real rules are the twelve-man **Council of Guardians**, a team of six religious representatives and six parliamentary elected representatives. Reforms introduced by the liberal president **Sayyed Mohammed Khatami** were slow and mitigated by the strong **ultra-conservative opposition** who, with the help of the Council of Guardians, successfully opposed innovation under the religious leader **Khamenei**. The feeble attempt at reform ended with the parliamentary elections of June 2005, which was won by hardliners. The intensification of the **Iranian nuclear programme** is a central goal of the new rulers and has put the country at odds with the West, and especially the United States.

Economy

Although 38 per cent of the country's land is used for agricultural purposes, **farming** is only possible thanks to the largely underground, irrigation systems. In addition to wheat, barley, citrus fruits and sugar beet, **tobacco, tea, pistachios** and **dates** are grown for **export**.

Whitefish and skate, as well as sturgeon that are so important for **caviar,** are fished from the Caspian Sea. The huge **oil and gas reserves** on the Persian Gulf, the coast of the Caspian Sea as well as in the north-eastern border areas form the basis for Iran's heavy industry. The country is rich in other natural resources, including coal, copper, nickel and chromium deposits. Heavy industry contributes 85 per cent of exports; it is almost exclusively controlled by the state. Traditional industries such as **carpet-making** and also the making of copper and silver artefacts receive state support; nevertheless they are in increasing decline.

Transport Infrastructure

The country's road network covers 162,000 km. Half of the network is surfaced.

The most important **ports** are Bushehr, Bandar Imam Khomeini

and Bandar Abbas. Many remote areas are only reachable by **train**, while the **inland domestic network of air routes** is comparably well developed and extensive, due to the mountainous terrain.

Tourism

The **unstable political conditions** make the construction of a tourist infrastructure difficult. There are also strict **clothing restrictions**, which are imposed as soon as tourists land in Tehran if they have entered the country on the Iranian airline, **Iran Air**. All women are required to wear headscarves and long dresses at all times, and since men are not allowed to shave under Islamic law, razors are banned!

All of these strict measures have been a strong deterrent to tourism, despite the fact that Iran has a rich heritage, from impressive archaeological and architectural sites to hot springs in

the Zagros Mountains. In addition to the Shi'ite relics in the holy cities of **Qom** and **Mashhad,** the ancient ruined, pre-Christian cities of **Persepolis** and **Pasargadae** are world cultural treasures. The **royal mosque** in **Isfahan** with its wonderful mosaics, is an impressive example of Persian Islamic architecture.

1 Nomadic tribes still live in Iran. They wander with their flocks across the mountains. Attempts to make them settle have failed.

2 Women are required to keep themselves covered. Here they prepare for Friday prayers at the King's Mosque in Isfahan.

3 Isfahan is a trade and cultural centre in which elegant restaurants serve the finest food.

4 An elegant structure: the mausoleum of Ayatollah Khomeini – the founding father of the 'Islamic Republic'.

Although the war against Saddam Hussein's army was won from a military point of view, the American and British-led assault on Iraq did not succeed in achieving its aims of a democratised society, peaceful cooperation between the faith communities and economic prosperity. On the contrary; political and

religiously motivated bombings brought this Islamic country to the brink of civil war (left, below right). House searches by the US Army and an increased use of Iraqi police have not yet been able to calm the situation (top right).

Cities of Asia

Dubai

Dubai is the capital of the emirate of the same name, which is part of the United Arab Emirates. It lies on the Arabian Peninsula on the Persian Gulf near the Strait of Hormuz. A sea inlet called the Dubai Creek runs through the city. The spectacular 'Burj-al Arab' luxury hotel, built in the shape of the sail of a dhow on an artificial island, has become the city's emblem. In 2005 work was begun on the 'Burj Dubai', which will be the world's tallest building when it is completed in 2009. Founded in 1833, today Dubai is one of the fastest growing economic locations in Arabia, bolstered by the city's free trade zones. A stock exchange was opened in 2007.

Area:
3,885 sq. km (city)
Inhabitants:
1,670,000 (city, 2008)
Population density:
430 inhabitants/sq. km (city)

The Burj al-Arab in Dubai is the world's only seven-star hotel to date.

Delhi

Delhi lies in northern India in the western Doab, the area of land between the Ganges and the Yamuna. Delhi's district of New Delhi has been the capital of India since 1947. Delhi is the third largest industrial location in the country. It has four universities and is the most important transport interchange in northern India. The Red Fort in the old town, completed in 1648, is a UNESCO World Heritage Site, as is Qutb Minar and its monuments, including the ruins of the Qutb-ul-Islam mosque and the Qutb-uddin-Minar tower, dating from the twelfth and thirteenth centuries, and Humayun's Tomb in New Delhi dating from the sixteenth century. Delhi was the seat of government of British India from 1911 until 1947.

Area:
491 sq. km (city)
Inhabitants:
10,930,000 (city, 2005)
13,780,000 (conurbation, 2001)
Population density:
22,261 inhabitants/sq. km (city)

The traffic chaos on Delhi's streets is part of everyday life in the capital.

Mumbai

Mumbai (formerly known as Bombay), the largest city in India, lies on the western coast on Bombay Island, which covers 68 sq. km. The city includes the island of Salsette and new residential areas on the mainland. Mumbai is India's largest port and the centre of the country's textile industry. It is also home to the large studios of the Indian film industry known as 'Bollywood'. As Bombay, the city was held by the Portuguese in 1534, but in 1661 it was ceded to English king Charles II as dowry, who leased it in 1668 to the British East India Company. The company's main base from 1703 until 1773, Bombay was the most important trading location on the west coast of India.

Area:
438 sq. km (city)
Inhabitants:
13,600,000 (city, 2008)
17,400,000 (Greater Bombay, 2008)
Population density:
31,071 inhabitants/sq. km (city)

The Gateway of India is the symbol of Mumbai, as Bombay was renamed in 1997.

Bangkok

Bangkok, the capital of Thailand, lies about 30 km to the north of the mouth of the Menam Chao Praya, which flows into the Gulf of Thailand. The seat of government and the king's palace are located here. Since the end of World War II, the former 'Venice of the East' (due to its network of canals) has turned into a booming industrial metropolis, although almost all of the canals have now been replaced by wide streets. Bangkok is today suffering under an almost uncontrollable volume of traffic, with all the predictable negative consequences for the environment. In addition, the city area, which lies just a few metres above sea level, is sinking further year by year.

Area:
1,565 sq. km (city)
Inhabitants:
5,770,000 (city, 2008)
11,571,000 (conurbation, 2006)
Population density:
3,686 inhabitants/sq. km (city)

The view from the Lebua State Tower over Chao Phraya River and the Oriental Hotel.

Saudi Arabia, Yemen, Oman

*Arabian mocha coffee, here being enjoyed by three men in **Bahrain**, is black, strong and sweet. In the Islamic world, the tradition of coffee-drinking, which probably originated in Ethiopia, developed much earlier than in Europe.*

Caffeine has been known and enjoyed throughout Arabia since the thirteenth century. The traditional method of preparation has changed little – coffee is brewed in a special pot from very fine grounds and poured into tiny cups.

Saudi Arabia

Area:	2,240,000 sq. km
Capital city:	Riyadh
Form of government:	
Islamic Absolute Monarchy	
Administrative divisions:	
13 regions	
Population:	
27.5 million	
(12 inhabitants/sq. km)	
Language:	Arabic
GDP per capita:	US$14,700
Currency:	
1 Saudi riyal = 20 qurush =	
100 hallalah	

Natural Geography

Saudi Arabia covers most of the Arabian peninsula and the entire country is made up of **rocky** and **sandy desert**, traversed by **wadis**. The only natural vegetation can be found in the oases.

Climate

The country has a hot and extremely dry **desert climate**. The average temperatures are 2°C in January, and 31°C in July.

Population

Approximately 90 per cent of the population is **Arab**, but there are also large numbers of **foreign workers, mainly** from the Indian sub-continent and the Philippines, as well as many from the West. The native population is exclusively Muslim, and three-quarters of the population lives in the country's cities. The standard of living is high, at least for Saudi nationals.

History and Politics

The history of Saudi Arabia begins with the Prophet **Muhammad**, who not only founded the new religion of **Islam** in the seventh century AD but also united the various Arab tribes. The region was conquered by the Mamelukes in 1269 and became part of the Ottoman Empire in 1517. After the **Ottomans**, the **al-Saud Dynasty,** which still reigns today, conquered the region, then known as Hejaz-Nejd, and created an Islamic state. The **Kingdom of Saudi Arabia was**

founded in 1932. Under the political system, the king is also the head of government and 'Guardian of the Holy Places'.

Economy

The **agricultural sector** accounts for just under ten per cent of GDP. The vast petroleum reserves have made Saudi Arabia the world's **largest exporter of crude oil**.

Transport Infrastructure

The **road network** is well developed. There are three international airports. The country's **oil terminals** are of great importance.

Tourism

The state of Saudi Arabia is a strictly Islamic country, and the

Mecca, the birthplace of the Prophet Mohammed, is an important pilgrimage site for Muslims.

only tourists permitted to enter the country are millions of **pilgrims** to the holy places of **Mecca** and **Medina**.

Yemen

Area:	527,970 sq. km
Capital city:	Sana'a
Form of government:	Republic

Administrative divisions:
17 provinces

Population: 22.2 million	
(42 inhabitants/sq. km)	
Languages:	
Arabic (official), English	
GDP per capita:	US$930
Currency:	
1 Yemen rial = 100 fils	

Natural Geography

Yemen is located on the south-western edge of the Arabian peninsula. In the north, a sandy, flat coastal strip borders the **Red Sea**, but behind this the landscape rises to form a craggy **upland**. This develops into the Rub al-Khali (Empty Quarter) one of harshest deserts in the world. South Yemen has a narrow, rainy coastal plain where most of the population lives, bordered to the north by a **plateau,** which in turn descends into a sandy desert.

Climate

Yemen's uplands receive abundant **monsoon rains**, but the southern part of the country has a **tropical desert climate**.

Population

The country is mainly populated by Yemeni **Arabs,** but one per cent of the population consists of guest workers from the Indian

sub-continent. **Islam** is the state religion, no other is permitted.

History and Politics

In pre-Christian times, this was the Empire of the **Minaeans** and then the **Sabaeans**, who were overthrown by the **Abyssinians** in the seventh century. Parts of the country fell under **Ottoman** rule during the sixteenth century. The Kingdom of Yemen came into being in Northern Yemen in 1918 and became a **republic** after a **military coup** in 1962. South Yemen, formerly the British colony of Aden, became a **Socialist Republic** in 1967. **The two Yemens were eventually unified,** taking four years from 1990 to 1994.

Economy

Agriculture is restricted to the north of the country and crops include coffee, citrus fruits and dates. It contributes 13 per cent of GDP. The country's economy is based on the **export of crude oil**.

Transport infrastructure

Only ten per cent of the roads are fully made, making economic development very slow. In Yemen, there are six international **airports**.

Tourism

Main attractions for tourists include the numerous **Islamic sites** and some fascinating ancient remains of the **Sabaean kingdom**.

Oman

Area:	309,500 sq. km
Capital city:	Muscat
Form of government:	
Sultanate (Absolute monarchy)	
Administrative divisions:	
59 provinces	
Population:	
3.2 million	
(10 inhabitants/sq. km)	
Languages:	
Arabic (official), Farsi, Urdu	
GDP per capita:	US$13,800
Currency:	
1 Omani rial = 1000 baizas	

Natural Geography

The **Sultanate** is bordered to the north-east by the **Gulf of Oman**, to the east and the south by the **Arabian Sea** and to the west by the **barren Empty Quarter** (Rub al-Khali). The north-east coast ends in a fertile **coastal plain** about 15 km wide and the **Oman mountains**, a range of more than 600 km from the north to the south-east. The **exclave of Musandam** on the Straits of Hormuz also belongs to Oman.

Climate

Oman has an **extreme desert climate**, and temperatures in summer can soar to 50°C. The climate in the **highlands** has subtropical influences. The south and west of the country are affected by **monsoon rains**.

Population

Native **Omanis** are 74 per cent of the population. The huge **migrant worker** population includes 21 per cent from **Pakistan**. The education, social and healthcare systems were completely modernised in the 1970s, and the literacy rate has risen to 80 per cent. The **state religion** is Islam.

*Yemen's capital **Sana'a** is an impressive example of an intact Arab city. The brick decoration and the whitewashed filigree work on the facades of the clay brick buildings are very characteristic and unique.*

History and Politics

Oman's territory has been settled since 2500 BC. and came under Islamic rule in 634 AD. Oman has been an **independent** state since 751. After Portuguese **colonisation** in the sixteenth century, **Ahmed bin Said** founded a dynasty in 1744 that still rules today. **Sultan Qaboos,** who rules the country as an absolute monarch, came to the throne in 1970. Since then, great advances have been made in all areas, and the Sultanate has on the whole been **stable** and **liberal** over the recent period. The country has friendly relations with the West.

Economy

Only five per cent of the land mass is used for agriculture (dates, fish, frankincense). The **crude oil sector** is the dominant branch of the economy, contributing 70 per cent to the state income. Thanks to increasing prices for crude oil, there has been an increase in the rate of economic growth in recent years. Since the crude oil reserves will run dry within three decades, the state is making attempts to **diversify** the economy.

Transport infrastructure

There are many important roads in the **north**, in the **hilly regions** and near **Salalah** in the south.

Tourism

There are several medieval **forts** scattered throughout the country which are well worth a visit for tourists. On the coast there are diving and water sports facilities. A particular attraction are the **turtle colonies.** Tourism is likely to be encouraged as other sources of income are sought to replace oil.

Kuwait

Area:	17,820 sq. km
Capital city:	Kuwait
Form of government:	
Emirate	
Administrative divisions:	
5 provinces	
Population: 2.5 million	
(140 inhabitants/sq.km)	

Language:
Arabic
GDP per capita: US$31,000
Currency:
1 Kuwaiti dinar = 100 dirham = 1000 fils

Natural Geography

Kuwait is an **emirate** on the Persian Gulf. Ten offshore islands are also part of Kuwaiti territory. The land consists of **dry steppes** and **sandy deserts,** with some **saltwater lagoons.** Vegetation in the country is extremely sparse, consisting mainly of thorn bushes. Fauna is similarly rare. The **Gulf War** of 1991 caused severe **environmental damage.**

Climate

Summers in the country's interior are **extremely hot** (with average temperatures of 36°C) and dry – even the comparatively humid coastal regions are among the driest parts of the world, and see almost no precipitation.
Temperatures in winter can sink as low as 14°C, and there is occasional ground frost.

Population

62 per cent of those living and working in Kuwait come from neighbouring **Arab** and **Asian** countries. Kuwaitis pay no taxes and make no social security

contributions. Islam is the state religion and no other is permitted.

History and Politics

Until 1716, the land was mainly uninhabited. It became a **British Protectorate** in 1899 and gained its **independence** once more in 1961.
The executive power lies in the hands of the **Emir,** who is elected from the **Al-Sabah dynasty** that has ruled since 1756. A **National Assembly** has existed since 1996, but it only has very restricted legislative influence. In May 2005, the parliament decided that from 2007, women would have the active and passive right to vote.

Economy

Only 0.2 per cent of the land mass is suitable for agricultural

use, and cultivation is only possible in these areas by using artificial irrigation techniques. Most of the country's food has to be imported. Since 1946, **crude oil** has been extracted from Kuwait, and this alone is responsible for making Kuwait **one of the richest nations in the world.**

Transport Infrastructure

The road network is extensive. There is an international airport in the capital **Kuwait City** and the country has large **oil ports.**

Tourism

The **old town** of Kuwait is an attractive travel destination, as is the offshore island of **Faylakah** with its holiday resorts and beaches. Tourism may develop if the situation improves in Iraq.

Bahrain

Area:	665 sq. km
Capital city:	Al-Manama
Form of government:	Emirate
Population:	
700,000 (1050 inhabitants/sq. km)	
Language:	Arabic
GDP per capita:	US$20,500
Currency:	
1 Bahrain dinar =	
1000 fils	

Natural Geography

Bahrain is an **island state** in the Persian Gulf consisting of a total of 33 islands, of which only 13 are inhabited. The main island, Bahrain, is connected to the islands of Al Muharraq and Sitrah by causeways. The desert landscape consists of **salt marshes** and **sand dunes.**

Camel racing is very popular in the land of 'black gold'. The camels are often ridden by child jockeys, specially selected from poorer neighbouring countries – their dangerous careers are cut short as the children grow in size.

Climate

The **desert climate** is slightly modified by Bahrain's position as an island. In winter, the average temperature is 19°C, and winters are warm with abundant rainfall. Summers are **extremely hot and humid** and temperatures reach an average of 36°C.

Population

Only 63 per cent of those living in Bahrain are **Bahraini** nationals. The rest of the population consists of **Arabs** from other countries in the region as well as 30 per cent of other **Asians**. There is also a substantial minority of Iranian nationals. Some 60 per cent of Bahrainis are Shi'ite **Muslims**, and 40 per cent are Sunni. Inhabitants of Bahrain pay no contributions towards the health and education systems, subsidised by the vast oil revenues.

History and Politics

As early as the third millennium BC, the city of **Dilmun** was a major trading centre between Mesopotamia, Southern Arabia and India, until it was conquered by the **Babylonians**. The Portuguese occupied the area in the sixteenth century, and this was followed by **occupation** by the **Ottomans**. Since 1783, the country has been ruled by the Sunni **Al-Khalifa** family, though it was a British protectorate from 1816 to 1971. The **Emirate** declared itself **independent** from Britain in August 1971. Bahrain introduced a **constitution** in 1973, making it the second Arab country in the Gulf to have a **Parliament**. The **Emir** abolished this constitution as well as the parliament in 1975, however, and since then, he ruled Bahrain as an **absolute** monarch.

Economy

Rich **crude oil reserves** were found in 1932, and this has long been a solid basis for the country's economy. The agricultural sector accounts for only one per cent of Gross Domestic Product.
The **manufacturing sector** accounts for 37 per cent of GDP. Since Bahrain's own oil reserves will soon run out, the country is increasingly developing its **services sector**, mainly off-shore banking services. The service sector makes up 62 per cent of GDP.

Transport Infrastructure

The road network is well constructed; causeways link the main islands to the mainland of Saudi Arabia. **Bahrain International Airport** is one of the most modern in the Middle East.

Tourism

The tourism industry is rapidly expanding and centres on the capital **Al Manama**. Bahrain is a relatively liberal country, and attracts tourists. Attractions include numerous archaeological sites, such as the **Temples** and **tombs** of **Barbar** and the **Qal'at al-Bahrain (Bahrain Fort)**.

A Kuwait landmark: the Kuwait Towers are used for storing water.

Qatar	
Area:	11,437 sq. km
Capital city:	Doha
Form of government:	
Emirate (Absolute Monarchy)	
Administrative divisions:	
9 districts	
Population:	
900,000	
(79 inhabitants/sq. km)	
Language:	Arabic
GDP per capita:	US$63,000
Currency:	
1 Qatar riyal = 100 dirham	

Natural Geography

Qatar is a peninsula with off-shore **coral islands** extending from the east coast of the Arabian peninsula into the **Persian Gulf**. The lowland plains are interrupted on the east coast by **low hills** roughly 100 m high. Of the islands, only **Halul** is inhabited.

Climate

Qatar has a hot and **dry climate**. The sparse desert vegetation grows only in some northern **wadis**.
Average temperatures are 17°C in January and 37°C in July. Apart from the varied **sealife**, very few animal species live in Qatar.

Population

Only 20 per cent of the population is **Qatari**. The rest are **Indians** and **Pakistanis** (35 per cent), **Arabs** from other countries (25 per cent) and **Iranians**. The social welfare, health and education systems are good and subsidised by the oil revenues. The

*The wealth of the **United Arab Emirates** is very obvious. Oil millionaires from around the world come to buy jewellery and expensive clothing here. In public, however, local women must remain completely covered and cannot go out alone.*

state religion, of 90 per cent of the population, is **Islam**.

History and Politics

The peninsula has been settled since prehistoric times. It has been ruled by the **Al-Thani family** since the eighteenth century. Qatar was conquered by the **Ottomans** (1872–1916) and was then ruled by the **British** (until 1971), but now the head of the Al-thani family rules as an **absolute monarch**.

Economy

The entire economy is based on **crude oil**. The **natural gas reserves** are supposedly the largest in the world.

Transport Infrastructure

There is a well-constructed road network between the cities and neighbouring countries. **Doha** has an international airport.

Tourism

The country is only visited by business travellers, and is not particularly accessible to tourists. It does not have many attractions for the casual visitor.

United Arab Emirates

Area:	83,600 sq. km
Highest altitude:	
Jabal Yibir (1,572 m)	
Capital city:	Abu Dhabi
Form of government:	
Federation of Independent Sheikhdoms	
Administrative divisions:	
7 emirates	
Population:	
4.5 million	
(53 inhabitants/sq. km)	
Language:	Arabic (official)
GDP per capita:	US$38,600
Currency:	
1 dirham = 100 fils	

Natural Geography

The country consists of a flat coastal strip along the Persian Gulf, behind which lies a **salty clay plain** and the Rub al-Khali desert. On the eastern border,

the Al-Hajar mountains rise to 1,100 m.

Climate

The **extremely hot** and **dry climate** (in summer the average temperature is 42°C) means that vegetation can only grow with intensive irrigation.

Population

Over 80 per cent of the residents are **migrant workers** from the Indian sub-continent. The native population enjoys a **high standard of living**.

History and Politics

The sheikhdoms of Abu Dhabi, Dubai, Sharjah, Ajman, Umm al-Qaiwain, Fujairah and Ras' al-Khaimah became **British protectorates** in the nineteenth century. After the withdrawal of the British, the Emirates joined together in 1971 to form a **federation** of Arab states. According to the constitution, which was drawn up in 1975, the seven Emirs form the **supreme council** and choose the **president** from among themselves.

Economy

Since 1962, when **crude oil** was discovered in the Persian Gulf, oil has become the main source of national income. The industry contributes some 56 per cent of GDP. The **services sector** has come to account for 42 per cent of GDP, while only two per cent of GDP in the United Arab Emirates derives from agriculture.

Transport infrastructure

The road network is well constructed. There are six international airports.

Tourism

The country offers luxury hotels, shopping and water sports.

1 Traditional and modern: The so-called 'black gold' has made Kuwait one of the richest countries in the world.

2 Omani men carrying the *khanjar* – these proud men will not be seen without their highly ornate daggers.

3 The Jumeirah Mosque in Dubai is one of the most important places of worship in the United Arab Emirates.

4 The old and the new in Dubai, the trading capital of the U.A.E. The palace of Sheikh Al Makhtum and the modern buildings reflected in the water.

Kazakhstan, Kyrgyzstan

Kazakhstan is, after Russia the second largest country in the CIS. Steppes dominate the terrain which is roamed by red deer, roe deer and bears. Many Kazakhs are hunters or nomadic herdsmen, who still enjoy the traditional sport of falconry. The Kazakhs are descendants of Turkic and Mongolian nomadic tribes, who established a very influential Khanate in the fifteenth century.

Kazakhstan

Area:	2,717,300 sq. km
Capital city:	Astana
Form of government:	Republic
Administrative divisions: 19 regions, 2 municipalities	
Population: 15.3 million (6 inhabitants/sq. km)	
Languages:	Kazakh, Russian
GDP per capita:	US$5,400
Currency:	1 tenge = 100 tiin

Natural Geography

The country includes **steppe** and **desert areas** and part of the **Tianshan Mountains** (highest peak: Khan-Tengri, 6,995 m) in the south-east. The Caspian Sea forms the south-east border. The siphoning off of water from the

Population

Kazakhstan has the **most multiracial population in the CIS**: 46 per cent are Kazakhs, 34 per cent Russian, five per cent Ukrainian, three per cent of German origin, 2.3 per cent Uzbeks, together with Tatars and other ethnic groups. **Muslims** make up 47 per cent of the population, while most of the **Christians** (46 per cent) are Russian Orthodox.

History and Politics

In the mid-eighteenth century, Kazakhstan placed itself under **Russian sovereignty**, and in 1873, it was annexed by **Russia**. In 1920 it was declared an **Autonomous Socialist Republic**, which became a **Soviet republic** on joining the Soviet Union in 1925. When the Soviet Union was

irrigation systems. Agriculture accounts for eight per cent of the country's GDP. One of the **world's richest deposits of copper and iron ore**, together with the large **reserves of petroleum and natural gas**, form the basis for heavy industry.
The pollution of the environment by chemicals and high levels of radioactivity resulting from the USSR's nuclear testing programme represent a major threat to the population as does the shrinking of the Aral Sea, a vast lake whose waters were used to irrigate cotton fields.

Transport Infrastructure

The thinly populated country is made accessible by a **rail network** 13,500 km in length. The 141,000 km road network is mostly surfaced. There are ap-

Kyrgyzstan

Area:	198,500 sq. km
Capital city:	Bishkek
Form of government: Presidential Republic	
Administrative divisions: 6 regions, 1 district (capital city)	
Population: 5.3 million (27 inhabitants/sq. km)	
Languages: Kyrgyz (official), Russian	
GDP per capita:	US$550
Currency: 1 Kyrgyzstan som = 100 tyin	

Natural Geography

Most of Kyrgyzstan lies in the **Tianshan mountains**. Three-quarters of the land area is over 1,500 m above sea level, half of which is over 3,000 m high.

Alpine-polar climate in the high mountain areas. Average temperatures in the capital range between -18°C in January up to 28°C in July.

Population

The multinational population is composed of **Kyrgyz** (52 per cent), **Russians** (18 per cent), **Uzbeks** (13 per cent), as well as Ukrainians, Germans and other ethnic groups. Three-quarters of the Kyrgyz are **Muslim**, 20 per cent are Russian Orthodox.
Since 1996, **Russian** has again become the second official language in the areas in which mainly Russians live and work.

History and Politics

Under oppression from the **Mongols** in the thirteenth century, the Kyrgyz people withdrew into the mountains. They were subsequently ruled by the **Manchus** and finally by the **Russians**.
In 1876, Kyrgyzstan was incorporated into the Russian empire. The modern state emerged for the first time after the October Revolution of 1917. In 1936, it became a **Socialist Soviet Republic** and in **1991** declared its **independence** from the Soviet Union. In 2005, there was unrest during new elections, which led to the resignation and flight of the previous president Akayev.

Economy

Kyrgyzstan is a small mountainous country in which **agriculture** is only practicable over seven per cent of the land mass but represents the most important branch of the economy. Apart from grain and fodder plants, fruit, vegetables, cotton, hemp and poppies, as well as oil-bearing plants and tobacco, are cultivated. In addition, **silkworms** are bred. The **agricultural sector** represents 38 per cent of the country's GDP. **Light industry** is of great importance. Kyrgyzstan possesses substantial reserves of gold and precious **metals**, which have yet to be exploited. The country exports its **hydro-electric power** to the neighbouring states. The services sector and tourist industry are relatively underdeveloped at present.

ARAL SEA DISAPPEARENCE

1960

Syrdarja

1985

Amudarja

1992

0   100 km

Uzbekistan: modern buildings in the ancient oasis city of Tashkent.

numerous rivers and lakes for the irrigation of the land has led to **severe ecological damage**, especially the rapid shrinking of the Aral Sea.

Climate

Kazakhstan has a **continental arid climate**. Average temperatures in the capital city, Astana, range from 0°C in January to 29°C in July.

disbanded, the country declared its **independence in 1991**, and a **constitution** was drawn up in **1993**. The **bicameral parliament** consists of the **Senate** and the **Lower House**, whose representatives are directly elected.

Economy

The cultivation of **grain** and **sugar beet**, **tobacco** and **fruit** is only possible through the

proximately 4,002 km of **inland waterways**. The international airports are at Alma-Ata and Astana.

Tourism

Alma-Ata ('Father of Apples') is the centre of the country's **infant tourism industry** and a major transport hub. **Winter sports** and **trekking** in the Altai mountains are possible.

The highest peak is **Mount Pobedy** (7,439 m). At 3,000 m, the landscape changes from **desert** and **semi-desert** to **mountain steppes, meadows** and **forest**. The mountain tundra adjoins the **glacier zone**, which feeds the country's lakes.

Climate

The climate is predominantly **dry and continental**, with an

*Isolated in their small, mountain republic, the people of **Kyrgyzstan** were able to escape the forced collectivisation of agriculture imposed by the Soviets. Within the protection of the 7000-m-high mountains, even their religion, Sunni Islam, managed to survive the Soviet ban. Traditional dress is still worn. The characteristic bulky headcovering of the women consists of a tightly wound white cloth; the men wear coarse felt hats.*

Transport Infrastructure

The 18,500-km-long **road network** is mainly surfaced. In addition a very dense network of buses makes access fairly easy, even to remote areas. Inland navigation is possible over about 600 km of the waterways; **Issyk-Kul** is the largest body of water in this land-locked country.

Tourism

The nature reserves and health resorts around **Issyk-Kul**, one of the world's largest inland lakes, at a height of 1,609 m, and the capital city of **Bishkek**, are the chief tourist attractions. Hiking, rambling and mountaineering will no doubt attract tourists as the country gradually develops its services sector.

Uzbekistan

Location:	Central Asia
Area:	447,400 sq. km
Capital city:	Tashkent
Form of government:	
Presidential Republic	
Administrative divisions:	
12 regions, 1 autonomous republic	
Population: 27.8 million	
(62 inhabitants/sq. km)	
Languages:	
Uzbek (official), Russian	
GDP per capita:	US$640
Currency: 1 Uzbekistan sum =	
100 tijin	

Natural Geography

Uzbekistan includes the centre of the **Turan Basin** with the southwest of the **Kyzylkum desert**, an area 600 km long, 350 m wide.

On the south-west border, the **Amu Darya** river flows through the desert and into the Aral Sea. This makes Uzbekistan the country with the best water resources in the region. In the east, the country is bordered by the foothills of the Tianshan and Altai mountains.

Climate

The **continental climate** ensures long, hot summers with an average temperature of 32°C as well as short, extremely cold winters, during which a temperature of -38°C is not unusual. Throughout the year there is **very little precipitation**; desert and steppe areas are very extensive.

Population

The population consists of a majority of **Uzbeks** and minorities including Russians (5.5 per cent), Tajiks (five per cent), Kazakhs (three per cent), Tatars and other groups. The **Karakalpaks**, who represent 2.5 per cent of the population, were granted an autonomous republic. Of the Uzbeks, 88 per cent are **Muslims**, the majority of them of the Sunni denomination.

History and Politics

The cities of Samarkand, Bukhara and Khiva were three of the most important stages on the Silk Road. The first independent state came into being in the fourteenth century. Its **enforced incorporation** into the Autonomous Soviet Republic of Turkestan was a result of the **Russian waves of conquest** that began in 1864. On the collapse of the Soviet Union in 1991, Uzbekistan declared its independence. Its **constitution of 1992** admittedly envisages political pluralism, but the opposition is suppressed. The single-chamber parliament admits only parties that support the **president**, who alone rules the land, and has extensive authority. Displeasure with those in power culminated in May 2005 in mass demonstrations, which were ruthlessly suppressed, resulting in the deaths of several hundred people.

Economy

Uzbekistan is an agricultural country with little industry. The cultivation of **cotton** plays a central role. Uzbekistan is currently one of the largest exporters of cotton. The agricultural sector's share of GDP is 30 per cent. The country's manufacturing sector is equally geared towards

Uzbekistan is home to a mixture of people from over a dozen ethnic groups, of which just under 90 per cent are Sunni Muslim. Although the different groups share the same religion, the country has seen many internal conflicts since 1989.

agriculture: the largest share, apart from the manufacture of **cotton harvesting machines**, is taken up by the production of fertiliser. Of the labour force, 44 per cent are employed in farming, 20 per cent in manufacturing and 36 per cent in trade or in the services sector. A changeover from a planned economy to a competitive market economy has been the goal ever since independence was declared, but is proving difficult to achieve. There are rich reserves of **raw materials** (oil, gas, gold, silver and precious metals).

Transport Infrastructure

The majority of the 81,600 km of road network is paved. The partially navigable rivers, **Amu Darya** and **Syr Darya,** are important inland waterways. The rail network is only 3,500 km long and is awaiting development. The air transport network, with an **international airport** at Tashkent, is being expanded.

Tourism

The country is as yet barely developed for tourism, but the cities of **Bokhara, Khiva, Samarkand** and **Tashkent** are centres of interest with many archaeological remains and magnificent mosques that are sure to attract tourists who will want to take 'the Golden Road to Samarkand'.

Turkmenistan	
Area:	488,100 sq. km
Capital city:	Ashgabat
Form of government:	
Presidential Republic	
Administrative divisions:	
5 regions	
Population:	5.1 million
	(10 inhabitants/sq. km)
Language:	Turkmen
GDP per capita:	US$4,300
Currency: 1 manat = 100 tenge	

Natural Geography

The territory extends from the **Caspian Sea** in the west to the border with Uzbekistan in the east, which is bounded by the **river Amu Darya**. The flatlands of the **Karakum desert** account for 80 per cent of the land area. Striking features of the landscape include the **Kopet Dag** mountain range, which rises to 2,942 m at the border with Iran in the south, the **Ustyurt Plateau** in the north and the adjacent **Plateau of Turkmenbashi**.

The coastal strip beside the Caspian Sea is flat and sandy. The only major river is the **Amu Darya** in the north-east of the country. Since Turkmenistan includes vast **nature reserves** (for example a 260,000-ha-large bird sanctuary), there is a great variety of wildlife.

Islam since the seventh century, Turkmenistan came under **Russian rule** as a result of Russian expansion into Central Asia from 1877 to 1881.

In 1918, it became part of the Autonomous Soviet Republic of Turkestan, and after the dissolution of the Soviet Union in 1991 an independent member of the CIS. After the adoption of a new **constitution in 1992,** the autocratic President Niyazov, who established a bizarre personality cult, ruled until his death in 2006.

Economy

In 2006, GDP was US$ 22 billion, of which 21 per cent came from

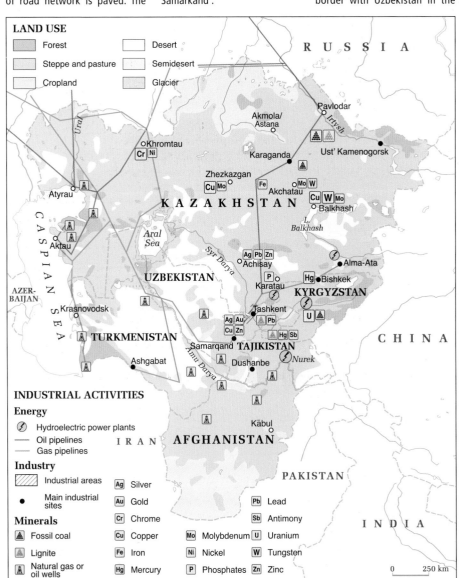

LAND USE

	Forest		Desert
	Steppe and pasture		Semidesert
	Cropland		Glacier

INDUSTRIAL ACTIVITIES

Energy

- ⚡ Hydroelectric power plants
- — Oil pipelines
- — Gas pipelines

Industry

- ▨ Industrial areas
- ● Main industrial sites

Minerals

- ▲ Fossil coal
- ▲ Lignite
- ▲ Natural gas or oil wells

Ag	Silver
Au	Gold
Cr	Chrome
Cu	Copper
Fe	Iron
Hg	Mercury

Pb	Lead
Sb	Antimony
Mo	Molybdenum
Ni	Nickel
U	Uranium
W	Tungsten
P	Phosphates
Zn	Zinc

0   250 km

Samarkand's Islamic buildings are among the most beautiful in the world.

Climate

Turkmenistan has a **continental desert climate** with very hot summers (average temperature 30°C) and cold winters (average temperature -33°C).

Population

The largest population group is represented by the **Turkmens** at 77 per cent. Of the rest, nine per cent are Uzbeks, six per cent Russians, with Kazakhs and other groups representing small minorities. Islam is the religion of 90 per cent of the population. Health and social security systems are well developed.

History and Politics

Settled by **Turkic peoples** since the fifth century, and mainly

agriculture, 44 per cent from industry and 35 per cent from services.

There are rich natural **resources** including natural gas, petroleum, sulphur and various mineral salts. While the desert landscape, which fortunately lacks costly and ecologically harmful irrigation, allows no farming to speak of, the most important areas of the processing industry apart from **petrochemicals** and **chemicals** are **metalworking** and the **textile industry**.

Transport Infrastructure

The 24,000-km-long road network is largely surfaced. **Air connections** are of great importance even in remote areas. Ashgabat lies on an important railway line that leads to the **Trans-Siberian Railway**. The **Amu Darya** river is

*The ancient oasis city of **Bukhara** in Uzbekistan is famous for its arts and crafts: many of the goldsmiths, and silk and carpet weavers produce high-value goods, which are sold throughout the world. Bukhara was founded as a trad-ing post on the caravan route; it was a centre of art and culture in the tenth century and attracted people from many lands. Today the city has a university and is home to more than 70 different ethnic groups.*

the most important navigable waterway.

Tourism

The centre of the country's somewhat underdeveloped tourist industry is the capital city, situated in an oasis, with **archeological sites** to be found in the surrounding area.

Turkmenistan is now being discovered by adventurous tourists.

Tajikistan

Area:	143,100 sq. km
Capital city:	Dushanbe
Form of government:	
Presidential Republic	
Administrative divisions:	
2 regions,1 district (capital city), 1 autonomous republic	
Population:	
7 million (49 inhabitants/sq. km)	
Language: Tajik (official), Russian	
GDP per capita:	US$440
Currency:	
1 Tajik somoni = 100 diram	

Natural Geography

90 per cent of this mountainous country is **over 1,000 m** above sea level, and 70 per cent of it consists of **high mountains**. The north includes the extensive Fergana Valley; mountain ranges such as the Turkestan, Zeravshan and Gissar ranges characterise the centre of the country, and the High **Pamirs** lie to the southeast.

The mountainous regions in the west, include the 7,495-m-high **Mount Communism** and the 7,134-m-high **Mount Lenin**, the highest peaks in the CIS.

Climate

The **continental climate** is marked by dry summers (27°C) and cold winters (-20°C), replaced by a **polar climate** in the high mountainous regions.

Population

Almost the entire population lives in narrow mountain valleys, which cover barely seven per cent of the land mass. **Tajiks** represent 65 per cent of the population,

with a 25 per cent minority of Uzbeks and groups of Russians and others. A total of 85 per cent of the country's inhabitants are Muslims, 80 per cent of these being of the Sunni denomination.

History and Politics

The region, which has been settled since the first millennium BC, belonged to the great kingdoms of the Persians, Greeks and Macedonians and Arabs. In the ninth century, it fell to the **Mongols, and later to the Tatars and Uzbeks.** The north of the region came under **Russian rule** around 1870, and in 1918, Tajikistan became part of the Autonomous Soviet Republic of Turkestan. From 1929, the Tajik Socialist Soviet Republic continued to be an independent republic of the USSR.

After the fall of the Soviet Union in 1991, the country emerged as an independent state and member of the CIS. Since then, the multinational state has seen **three changes of government** and one **civil war**; the political situation has now somewhat stabilised.

Economy

War has had a severe effect on the nation's economy. As a result of the impenetrable mountain landscape, a poor infrastructure, and the **cultivation of cotton**, for so long the single source of revenue due to Soviet policy, Tajikistan remains the **poorest republic in the CIS** and is heavily dependent on foreign aid.

In the processing industry, apart from **wool processing** only the **foodstuffs and textile industries** are of significance. Farming still brings in 24 per cent of the GDP. The important raw materials are uranium and gold, and to a lesser extent petroleum, natural gas, lead, zinc, tungsten and tin. Up to the present day, the political regime continues to hinder economic reform.

Transport Infrastructure

The 32,000-km-long **road network** is mostly surfaced. Buses connect the remote areas. There are **international airports** at Dushanbe and Khudzhand.

Tourism

Tourism is still comparatively undeveloped. The unstable political situation means that travel is not without danger. The starting-point for tourism is the capital city, Dushanbe, from which trekking tours to the high mountain areas are organised.

1 Uzbekistan: the old town of Bukhara is the most beautiful in the Near East. Wide squares containing impressive mosques dominate the heart of the city.

2 A Kyrgyz family gathers to share a meal. Family life is of great importance in Kyrgyzstan, where many people still live a nomadic existence and travel with their clans through the country.

3 The Registan with its historic madrasah (Islamic religious school) gives the impression of stark simplicity. It is the central square in Samarkand.

By 2006 already the twelfth largest economy in the world, India is currently profiting both from the policy of internal privatisation and the opportunities of globalisation. Yet in spite of good economic growth, India continues to remain a developing country. These images show the different layers of

development in the Indian economy: on the one hand, tiny workshops such as this welding shop on the edge of the road, and a child workforce in a match factory (left); on the other, complex software development in Bangalore and modern machine technology in a cotton mill (right).

In Pakistan, Sharia Islamic law based on religion is also sometimes applied in criminal law. The mosques are important social centres, such as this one, the Badshahi in Lahore, where holy men rule on matters of justice and injustice.

Afghanistan

Area:	652,000 sq. km
Capital city:	Kabul
Form of government:	Islamic Republic
Administrative divisions:	
31 provinces	
Population:	
30 million (45 inhabitants/sq. km)	
Languages:	Pashto, Dari
GDP per capita:	US$300
Currency:	1 Afghani = 100 puls

Natural Geography

The mountainous interior is partly comprised of the **Hindu Kush mountain range** in which there are passes of heights up to 4,000 m. These areas are mainly **steppe terrain** and **stony deserts** with sparse vegetation.

The south of the country is dominated by mountainous uplands that extend into wide desert expanses. The Hindu Kush mountains are often shaken by powerful **earthquakes**.

Climate

There are **great variations in climate** ranging from an arid climate to a sub-tropical climate, and even a high-alpine climate in the mountain regions.

The capital city, Kabul, has average temperatures of -3°C in January and 24°C in July.

Zulfikar Ali Bhutto

*Larkana, 5.1.1928,
†Rawalpindi, 4.4.1979

The founder of the Pakistan People's Party held many ministerial posts in the 1960s but he was imprisoned from 1968-9 after conflicts with the president of the time, Ayub Khan. From 1972 to 1973 he ruled Pakistan as President and was Prime Minister, Minister of Foreign Affairs and Minister of Defence from 1973 to 1977. He was toppled by a military dictatorship in 1977. He was condemned to death and executed in 1978.

Population

Afghanistan's population is 38 per cent **Pashto**, 25 per cent **Tajik**, 19 per cent **Hazara** and six per cent **Uzbek** with a sprinkling of other ethnic minorities.

As many as 99 per cent of the population is **Muslim**, of which the **Sunnis** are the majority (84 per cent). Afghanistan is in general an underdeveloped country. A massive 68 per cent of the population is **illiterate**, the literacy rate among women being a mere 15 per cent.

After many years of war and Taliban rule, the education, health and social systems are still in a rudimentary state. **The public health** situation is appalling with only a minority of the population having access to clean drinking water. As a result, the average life expectancy is just 43 years. Since the **war began** in 1979, almost two million people have died in direct combat. Between three and four million children have died from **malnutrition**. Over a third of the population were forced to flee the country and live in refugee camps, mostly in Iran and Pakistan.

History and Politics

The region was settled by **Persian tribes** in 2000 BC but has been under constantly changing **foreign rule** ever since. The **Emirate of Afghanistan** was founded in 1747 but later fell under of the British sphere of influence, though the British found it impossible to control these tribes on India's North-west Frontier. In 1919, Afghanistan became a kingdom. The **republic** was founded in 1973. In order to support the Communist-leaning regime, the Red Army invaded in 1979, fighting the **Mujaheddin** guerillas for ten years, and being ultimately unsuccessful. After the last Soviet soldiers left 1989, the Afghan president, who had been installed by the Soviets, was overthrown, but the rebels then began fighting amongst themselves. In 1994, the radical Muslim **Taliban militia** joined the war and soon controlled 90 per cent of the territory, which then proclaimed an Islamic religious state ('**Islamic Emirate of Afghanistan**'). They introduced Sharia law: **television was banned** and **women** were denied education and placed under virtual **house arrest**. Conflict with the USA was triggered by Afghanistan's tolerance of the Islamic extremist Osama Bin Laden and his terror organisation, Al Qaeda. After the attacks on the World Trade Center and the Pentagon in September 2001, the USA named Bin Laden and Al Qaeda responsible and launched a military attack on Afghanistan. With the support of the Northern Alliance, they were able to bring down the Taliban regime in just under two months. From the end of 2001, the country was ruled by a transitional government under Hamid Karzai, who was confirmed president in 2002 by the Loya Jirga, a gathering of tribal and ethnic leaders. He also won recognition in the presidential elections of October 2004.

Economy

Afghanistan is one of the poorest countries in the world. Its economy is based on agriculture. Cereals, fruit and nuts are cultivated in the irrigated valleys, and livestock is reared in the mountain regions. There is also illegal cultivation of the opium poppy on a large scale. **Agriculture** accounts for 50 per cent of GDP.

Transport Infrastructure

The country has no rail network and the 21,000-km-long **road network** is poor. There are two international airports in Kabul and Kandahar.

Tourism

Afghanistan is **not a tourist destination**, although it was in the past. It has **historic mosques** in **Kabul**, **Kandahar**, **Herat** and at **Mazar-e Sharif**. **Bamiyan** is where the Taliban destroyed two third- and fifth-century Buddha statues in the year 2001.

The Blue Mosque in Mazar-e-Sharif, Afghanistan: doves of peace in a troubled land?

Pakistan

Area:	803,940 sq. km
Capital city:	Islamabad
Form of government:	
Islamic Republic	
Administrative divisions:	
4 provinces, 1 district (capital city), 2 territories	
Population:	
165 million	
(205 inhabitants/sq. km)	
Languages:	
Urdu (official),	
English, Punjabi, Sindhi	
GDP per capita:	US$800
Currency:	
1 Pakistani Rupee = 100 paisa	

Natural Geography

The north of Pakistan contains sections of the **Himalayas**, the **Hindu Kush** and the **Karakoram ranges** (K2: 8,611 m). The west of the country has mountainous borders with Iran and Afghanistan. The east is dominated by the **Indus Basin**, which stretches for more than 2,000 km to the south, and ends in the **Arabian Sea**. This is where 80 per cent of the population live. Parts of the country are subject to frequent earthquakes. The Pakistani section of Kashmir was struck by a major earthquake in October 2005 in which some 80,000 people died.

Climate

The climate of Pakistan is as varied as the landscape. The mountain chains in the north-west and the north of the country have a **high-altitude climate**, while the Indus Basin has a **dry, hot climate**, which also dominates in the **steppe and desert regions**. Only four per cent of the country's land is forested.

Population

Half of the population is **Punjabi**, but there are also many **Pashtun**, **Sindhi**, **Baloch**, **Muhajir** (of Indian origin), and other ethnic minorities, including Afghans.

The official language, **Urdu**, is only the mother tongue of some eight per cent of the population, while 48 per cent speak **Punjabi**. In total, more than 20 different languages and dialects are spoken

*The radical Islamic group the **Taliban** initiated a reign of terror in Afghanistan. Mass executions, and human rights abuses, particularly in relation to women, were part of daily life.*

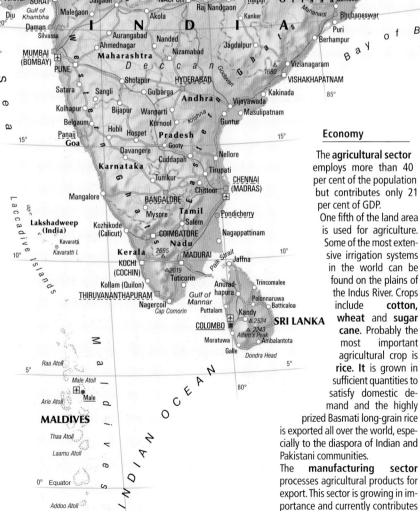

in the country. English is the language used in government and administration. Pakistan is currently home to some one million refugees from Afghanistan. The majority of the Pakistani population are **Sunni Muslims**, but there are also minorities of Shi'ites, Christians and Hindus.

The health system is very poorly developed. **School is not compulsory**, as a result only 38 per cent of the population is literate.

History and Politics

In 1947, British India was divided into **India** and the mainly Muslim **Pakistan**. Later, in 1971, after a bloody civil war, the eastern territory of Pakistan split away and became **Bangladesh**. Since gaining its **independence**, the islamic republic has been plagued by **ethnic conflicts**, **coup attempts** and **military dictatorships**.

Even the first free elections in 1988 did not free the country from political, religious and ethnically motivated acts of violence. The **constitution** provides for a bicameral parliament, consisting of a Senate and a National Assembly. The head of state has extensive powers. For as long as Pakistan has existed, it has fought India for control of the **Kashmir region**. The country has **one of the largest armies in the world**, and much of the state budget is used to fund it. Pakistan is also a **nuclear power**.

Economy

The **agricultural sector** employs more than 40 per cent of the population but contributes only 21 per cent of GDP.

One fifth of the land area is used for agriculture. Some of the most extensive irrigation systems in the world can be found on the plains of the Indus River. Crops include **cotton**, **wheat** and **sugar cane**. Probably the most important agricultural crop is **rice. It** is grown in sufficient quantities to satisfy domestic demand and the highly prized Basmati long-grain rice is exported all over the world, especially to the diaspora of Indian and Pakistani communities.

The **manufacturing sector** processes agricultural products for export. This sector is growing in importance and currently contributes 25 per cent of GDP. The other main export apart from **wool** are textiles, clothing and **carpets**. Pakistanis living abroad make a substantial contribution to the economy by sending money home.

Transport Infrastructure

The country has good transport connections, with a **rail network** and a **road network** covering some 220,000 km, up to 60 per cent of which is surfaced. Part of

Pakistan, India

*In **Pakistan** and **India,** the markets offer a highly colourful range of products, from numerous varieties of the finest herbs to tea and exotic fruits, carpets and textiles and even livestock.*

the **Karakoram Highway** along the historic **Silk Road** leads to the Chinese border. The domestic **flight network** is also important. The main international port is in **Karachi**, the former capital.

Tourism

After **Lahore** and **Karachi**, the main places of interest are the ancient sites of **Mohenjo-Daro** and the **Hyderabad** with its relics from the colonial era.

India	
Area:	3,287,590 sq. km
Capital city:	New Delhi
Form of government:	Republic
Administrative divisions: 28 federal states, 7 union territories	
Population: 1.130 billion (343 inhabitants/sq. km)	

Mohandas Karamchand Gandhi

*Porbandar, 2.10.1869, †New Delhi, 30.1.1948

Until 1914, Gandhi was a lawyer and a prominent member of the Indian minority in South Africa. He returned to India after World War I and organised passive resistance against British colonial rule. As president of the Indian National Congress he tried to lead India to independence through civil disobedience. He was not able to make peace between Hindus and Muslims, and India was divided into three parts. In 1948, Ghandi was assassinated by a Hindu fanatic.

Languages:
Hindi, English and 17 others
GDP per capita:	US$780
Currency: 1 Indian Rupee = 100 paise	

Natural Geography

The Indian sub-continent extends from the foothills of the **Himalayas** (Nanda Devi, 7,816 m) in the north, to the pointed triangular peninsula in the Indian **Ocean** to the south. India is divided into three different landscape zones: the mountainous zone of the Himalayas gives way to the plains of the **Indus** and **Ganges** rivers. The plains then rise in the south to form a plateau traversed by rivers. This plateau is called the **Deccan**, and has broad plains along the coasts of the peninsula.

The country's vegetation is correspondingly diverse: the north and north-east are dominated by **rain forests** and **plantations**. The plains around the Indus and Ganges have sub-tropical vegetation. The **Ganges delta** has many **mangrove swamps**.

The uplands are covered in wide savannas, and there are broad steppe and desert areas in the west. India's sovereign territory also includes the **Lakshadweep Islands** and the **Andaman and Nicobar Islands**. The country has an astounding rage of fauna, including tigers, lions and many poisonous snakes. Some species are now endangered due to heavy **deforestation** and encroaching human habitation.

An under-sea earthquake in the Indian Ocean in December 2004 triggered a tsunami which caused great damage, mainly to the Andaman and Nicobar islands.

Climate

India has a **sub-tropical to tropical climate**, with a monsoon period. The climate in the north becomes more temperate, and mountain regions have an **alpine climate**. Average temperatures in the capital New Delhi range from 14°C in January to 31°C in July.

Population

India's population includes approximately 72 per cent **Indo-Aryan**-language speakers and 25 per cent **Dravidian-language speakers**. There are also some Himalayan and south-east ethnic groups. **Hindus** form the largest religious majority (80 per cent); **Muslims** account for 14 per cent of the population. There are also **Christian** (2.4 per cent), **Sikhs** (two per cent) minorities and groups of Buddhists, Jains and others.

Hindi is the official administrative language and the mother tongue of 30 per cent of the population and there are also 17 regional languages with official status. Since 24 languages are spoken by more than 1 million people and there are also many regional dialects, **English** remains a language of communication throughout the country. Despite the numerous colleges and the **204 universities**, the **literacy rate** is still very low at 52 per cent.

History and Politics

The **Indus valley civilisation**, one of the earliest advance soci-

India: the ornamental Char Minar gate in Hyderabad.

eties, flourished in northern India between 3300 and 1000 BC Although knowledge of this ancient culture is limited, many believe the people spoke a proto-Dravidian language. The **caste system**, an important part of Indian society today, may have been introduced by Indo-Aryan settlers after the fall of the Indus valley civilisation. The region saw the development of several great religions, including **Buddhism** in the sixth century BC, which spread through much of the **Indian empire**, first established two or three hundred years BC. In the twelfth century AD, the country became increasingly **Islamic under Mughal rule**, which reached its peak with the establishment of the **Delhi sultanate**. In 1858, after a series of battles, India became directly ruled by the **Great Britain**. **Struggles for independence** began as early as the late nineteenth century, and after World War I this movement gained momentum. A key figure was **Mahatma Gandhi**, who lived and preached passive resistance and civil disobedience. India was finally granted independence in 1947 at the same time as mainly Muslim Pakistan. Since then, India and Pakistan have fought several **wars** over the region of **Kashmir,** which is today divided. In 1971, India supported the creation of **Bangladesh**. Since gaining independence, India has been enjoyed relative political stability, but ethnic and religiously motivated **conflicts** between the Hindu majority and the Sikh and Muslim minority has led to internal unrest.

Under the 1950 **constitution**, India is ruled by a bicameral parliament, which consists of an upper house with delegates from the parliaments of the 25 federal states and seven union territories, and the lower house, whose representatives are elected for five-year terms. The head of state is the **president**.

Jawaharlal Nehru

*Allahabad, 14.11.1889, † Delhi, 27.5.1964

Nehru campaigned with Gandhi for India's independence. He became General Secretary in 1923 and President of the National Congress in 1929. He fought in all resistance movements against British rule and was imprisoned several times. After India gained independence, he became Prime Minister from 1947 until his death. On domestic issues, he followed a moderate socialist course; on an international level he advocated non-alignment.

Economy

India is the **second most populous country** in the world, after China, but it is also one of the countries with the **lowest incomes per capita**. Despite this, the country has highly developed armaments, nuclear and aerospace industries.

India's economy is very wideranging, from traditional village **agriculture,** to handicrafts and a range of modern **industries**. The vast majority of the workforce lives directly from agriculture, which contributes 22 per cent of GDP. India is one of the world's **largest tea exporters**. Jute, herbs and pulses are also cultivated. Although most Indians are vegetarians for religious reasons, the country has the largest number of head of cattle in the world and is the second largest exporter of dairy products.

Extensive estuaries make India one of the largest **fishing nations** on Earth. The plentiful **natural resources** (coal, titanium, bauxite, iron ore, manganese, chrome), which are mined in small quantities, form the basis of the **heavy industry sector,** (steel and aluminium smelting, ship building and heavy machinery) which is largely in state hands. The **services sector** accounts for 51 per cent of GDP, and much of this comes from tourism.

Transport Infrastructure

India's **rail network** is a relic of the colonial era. It covers more than 62,000 km, making it the most extensive in the world. It remains to this day the country's **main form of transport**.

The **road network** covers more than two million km, half of

Mumbai, formerly known as Bombay, is the gateway to India. Some 50 per cent of India's foreign trade passes through Mumbai's huge port. The city is spread over several islands and has more than 13 million inhabitants.

which is surfaced, but it still does not connect all of the populated areas. The country has 16,180 km of **inland waterways**, which are of great economic importance. The major **ports** for India's massive merchant fleet are in Kolkata (formerly Calcutta), Mumbai (formerly Bombay), Jawaharlal Nehru and Kandla. There are numerous regional airports, served by both the national airlines, and five **international airports** in New Delhi, Mumbai (formerly Bombay), Chennai (formerly Madras), Kolkata and Bangalore.

Tourism

After **nature reserves** – the most important being the Kaziranga National Park in the northeast, which still has some 100 rare Indian rhinoceros – India offers an enormous number of **cultural attractions and places of interest**. These include the temple complexes of Khajuraho, Madurai and Mahabalipuram, and the world renowned **Taj Mahal** in Agra. The most popular holiday destinations are the beaches of **Goa** and **Kerala** and the area around **Chennai**, as well as Rajasthan's forts and desert.

up to 1,000 m (Reng Tlang: 957 m). The south-west, on the Indian border, contains part of the **Sundarbans region,** and the deltas of the **Ganges** and the **Brahmaputra** rivers.

Climate

Bangladesh has a **monsoon climate** with abundant rainfall. There are three seasons: a cool, dry winter between October and March with an average temperature of 19°C, a hot and humid summer from March to June, and the relatively cool rainy season from June to October, during

Bangladesh

Area:	144,000 sq. km
Capital city:	Dhaka
Form of government:	Republic

Administrative divisions:
6 provinces, 64 districts

Population:
150 million
(1040 inhabitants/sq. km)

Languages:
Bengali (official), Urdu, Hindi

GDP per capita:	US$400
Currency:	1 Taka = 100 poisha

Natural Geography

Bangladesh's land mass consists entirely of **fertile lowlands**, but the unprotected, port-free coast is constantly at risk of inundation, and is often affected by severe **floods**, sometimes with catastrophic consequences.
In the east and south-east, **mountain chains** rise in the border regions, with a height of

which many thousands die in massive flooding.

Population

The vast majority of the population is **Bengali** (98 per cent) but there are also minorities of **Biharis** and other groups.
Bangladesh has **one of the highest population densities in the world**. More than 80 per cent of the population lives in rural areas, which are only partly connected by the road network and have almost no access to electricity. Social welfare is the responsibility of the family and **child labour** is very common. Public health and state provision of medical care are also seriously under-developed. The **education system** is neglected, with the result that only one third of the population can read and write. This also accounts for the huge amount of emigration, many Bangladeshis living abroad, especially in the United Kingdom.

History and Politics

Bangladesh was originally the Indian province of **East Bengal** and was part of India from its early history. Between 1757 and 1947 it was part of **British** India. As part of the division of India following independence, West Bengal became part of India,

 Jodhpur Fort is as impregnable as a cliff wall. It is one of the most striking buildings in the 600-year-old city.

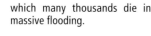 The Taj Mahal is a marble mausoleum for the favourite wife of Emperor Shah Jahan. At dusk and dawn, the whole structure turns a striking pink.

3 The Golden Temple of Amritsar is the centre of the monotheistic Sikh faith.

4 Dasaswamedh Ghat in Varanasi is a holy place for Hindus on the banks of the Ganges. The faithful gather here for ritual bathing.

*The people of **Bangladesh** call their country 'golden Bengal' – but the country is anything but blessed. Thousands of people drown every year in floods, and the people are forced to endure terrible poverty.*

while East Bengal became part of Pakistan.

During a period of bloody unrest after the great flood of 1970, East Bengal split from Pakistan, and proclaimed the **Republic of Bangladesh** in 1971.

After 15 years of authoritarian rule by presidents, the **first democratically elected government** took power in **1991**. The national parliament has 330 members. The **head of state** is chosen every five years by the parliament and has largely ceremonial powers.

Economy

Bangladesh has **one of the poorest national economies in the world**. **Agriculture** forms the basis of the economy and employs 63 per cent of the working population, mainly in very small operations. The sector is responsible for roughly a quarter of GDP.

Rice and **jute** are the most important agricultural exports. The **fishing industry** mainly exports shellfish. The **manufacturing sector** employs 18 per cent of the working population, but consists largely of small operations, which mainly process agricultural products (jute, cotton, sugar and tea) and textiles. Manufacturing accounts for approximately 27 per cent of GDP. **Heavy industry** is currently experiencing some growth, and major activities are the processing of **raw materials** (natural gas, crude oil, coal, vitreous sand and other minerals).

The **services sector** is also of increasing importance and contributes 48 per cent of GDP.

Transport Infrastructure

The 223,891-km-long **road network** is only partially paved, and the **rail network** is poorly developed. Both are of negligible importance.

The **inland waterways** consisting of a network of rivers and canals, with a length of more than 8,400 km, are the country's main transport arteries and connect to the major sea port of **Chittagong**. The only international airport is in **Dhaka**.

Tourism

Bangladesh is yet to be really discovered by tourists. Important destinations are the capital city with its interesting old town, numerous **mosques** and the city of **Chittagong**. Bathing and watersports are available in Cox's Bazaar.

Part of the **Sundarbans National Park** is located in Bangladesh. The unique collection of mangrove swamps is a refuge for many rare species of tropical fauna. The best time to visit is between December and February during the dry season.

Sri Lanka

Area:	65,610 sq. km
Capital city:	Colombo

Form of government:
Socialist Presidential Republic in the Commonwealth
Administrative divisions:
9 provinces, 25 districts
Population:
21 million
(319 inhabitants/sq. km)
Languages: Singhalese, Tamil
GDP per capita: US$1,350
Currency:
1 Sri Lankan Rupee = 100 cents

Natural Geography

Separated from India by the **Palk Strait** and the **Gulf of Mannar**, Sri Lanka lies on the southern tip of the sub-continent. In the north and the east, the coastal strip is bordered by lowland regions, dotted with isolated hills.

In the centre of the island, there are the **Central Mountains**, that gradually rise to the 2,238-m-high **Adam's Peak** (Sri Pada) and the 2,524-m-high **Pidurutalagala**. Sri Lanka's territory also includes a further 22 smaller surrounding **islands**. The tsunami of December 2004, caused by a massive under-sea earthquake, left behind a massive swathe of destruction.

Climate

The **tropical climate** means that the country has year-round high temperatures of about 30°C. Precipitation varies according the the seasonal monsoon rhythm. With the exception of some wetlands in the south-west of the country, Sri Lanka has an extended **dry season**, which lasts for eight months.

Population

Sri Lanka's population is 74 per cent **Singhalese** and 18 per cent **Tamil**, who are further divided into Ceylon Tamil (12.6 per cent) and Sri Lankan Tamil (5.5 per cent). Since the mid-1980s, hundreds of thousands of Tamils have left the island.

The population also consists of seven per cent Moors (Muslims) and minorities of Burghers

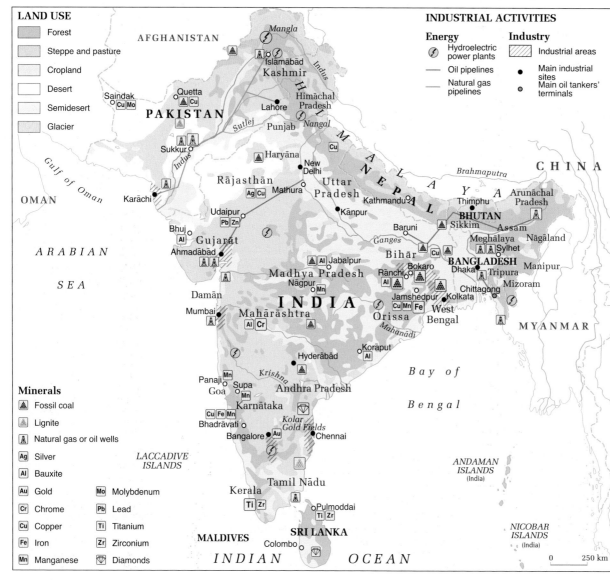

LAND USE

- Forest
- Steppe and pasture
- Cropland
- Desert
- Semidesert
- Glacier

Minerals

- Fossil coal
- Lignite
- Natural gas or oil wells
- Ag Silver
- Al Bauxite
- Au Gold
- Cr Chrome
- Cu Copper
- Fe Iron
- Mn Manganese
- Mo Molybdenum
- Pb Lead
- Ti Titanium
- Zr Zirconium
- Diamonds

INDUSTRIAL ACTIVITIES

Energy
- Hydroelectric power plants
- Oil pipelines
- Natural gas pipelines

Industry
- Industrial areas
- Main industrial sites
- Main oil tankers' terminals

*The name **Sri Lanka** means 'venerable island'. Ceylon tea, cultivated here, is famous throughout the world. The island suffers from some serious problems, including rapid population growth, internal tensions and widespread poverty.*

(descendants of the Portuguese and Dutch) and Malay. In terms of religion, 69 per cent are **Buddhist**, 15 per cent Hindu and eight per cent each Christian and Muslim. Singhalese is spoken by 74 per cent of the population, and 18 per cent speak Tamil. The education and healthcare systems are well organised.

History and Politics

After settlement in the first millennium by the forefathers of the modern **Veddas**, the **Portuguese** discovered the island of Ceylon in 1505. In 1656, the Portuguese were replaced by the Dutch, who were in turn expelled by the British in 1795/1796. The island was proclaimed a British crown colony in 1802. Sri Lanka has been **independent** since 1948.

The country suffers from political instability caused by the as yet unresolved **minority problems** of the Sri Lankan Tamils and the Indian Tamils, who were in a dominant position under British rule, and who now feel disadvantaged in relation to the Singhalese. The Tamil tigers have been fighting a **civil war** in the north and east of the country in order to assert their rights. The introduction of a republican constitution in 1972 changed the country's name from Ceylon to Sri Lanka. The 1978 **constitution** is still in force today and provides for a unicameral parliament, whose representatives are elected for six -year terms and appoint the Prime Minister.

The **President** is directly elected and is both head of state and head of government. The President has wide-reaching powers.

Economy

Despite the long-running civil war, Sri Lanka's national economy shows stable **growth**. In comparison to **agriculture** (rubber, tea, coconuts), which accounts for 19 per cent of GDP, the **manufacturing sector** is growing and contributes some 26 per cent to GDP. The main sector of Sri Lanka's economy is the **trade** and **services sector** with 54 per cent of GDP. The most important exports are textiles and foodstuffs, especially tea. Cigars

(cheroots) are the traditional export of Trincomalee.

Transport Infrastructure

The island has a good transport infrastructure, with 1,501 km of **rail network** and 100,000 km of **roads**, one third of which are surfaced. The major airport and international port is in Colombo.

Tourism

The favourite tourist destinations are **Negombo**, **Trincomalee** and **Hikkaduwa**. Sri Lanka has many important cultural and historic

sites, including Kandy, once the capital, with its **'Temple of the Tooth'**, **Anuradhapura** and **Polonnaruwa**, the **cave temples** of Dambulla and the old fort of **Sigiriya**. A whole 12 per cent of Sri Lanka is a **nature conservation area**. The island has superb flora and fauna and if it were not for the unrest, it would be a favourite tourist destination.

The Maldives

Area:	298 sq. km
Capital city:	Malé

Form of government:
Presidential Republic in the Commonwealth

Administrative divisions:
19 districts (atolls) and the capital municipality

Population: 370,000
(1,238 inhabitants/sq. km)

Languages:
Dhivehi (official), English

GDP per capita:	US$2,600
Currency:	1 rufiyaa = 100 laari

Natural Geography

The Maldives consist of **1,190 coral islands** grouped together both north and south of the equator to form **26 atoll groups**. The territory extends 800 km in

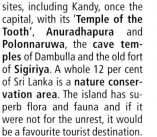

1 A film poster and the wares of small traders compete for attention in the streets of Colombo.

2 Elephants are vital for clearing the dense jungles. In Sri Lanka, they have been tamed for millennia, and in some places they are worshipped.

3 Buddhists, Hindus and Moslems make pilgrimages to the perahera of Kataragama in Sri Lanka. Dances accompany the celebrations, during which the gods are asked for luck.

4 Sri Lanka: the important Buddhist temple complex of Raja Maha Vihara in Kelaniya.

The Maldives, Nepal, Bhutan

*The **Sadhu**, the holy men of Nepal, spend their lives in strict asceticism. The ascetic tradition is common in the many branches of Hinduism. Through abjuration, the Sadhu attempt to go beyond their connection to worldly possessions and their own mortality, and so become closer to nirvana. This is rooted in the belief that through its connection with material objects, the soul forgets its eternal being.*

one direction and 130 km in the other. The average elevation of the islands is between one and two metres above sea level and the highest point is near Wilingili (24 m). None of the islands is larger than 13 sq. km, and the main island, Malé, measures just 1.7 km by 1 km. The country has no rivers or raw materials.

Climate

The **hot, tropical climate** means that the year-round average temperature is 30°C. The two **rainy seasons** last from November to March (north-east monsoon) and from June to August (south-west monsoon).
Land animals (tortoises, geckoes and rats) are not very varied, but there is a fascinating range of **sea life** in the coral reefs.

Population

The **Maldivians**, descendants of Malay, Singhalese and Arab settlers, live on some 200 islands. One quarter of the population lives in the capital city alone.
The national language, **Dhivehi** is a dialect of Sinhala, which uses the **Arabic script**.
Since 1153, the national religion has been **Islam** and 99.9 per cent of Maldivians are **Sunni Muslims**.

History and Politics

The Maldives became a **British protectorate** in 1887, gaining **independence in** 1965. British rule in the islands was less rigid than in other parts of the empire, and the British powers respected the country's internal autonomy. The Sultanate was replaced by a republic in 1968.
The **constitution of 1975** provides for a president with extensive powers directly elected by the people. There are no political parties and no parliament.

Economy

Due to the quality of the land, **agriculture** in the Maldives is only important in terms of subsistence. Coconuts, betel nuts, cassava, onions and chilli peppers are cultivated on 13 per cent of the country's land mass.
Fishing is the most important export and is, after **tourism,** the most lucrative sector of the economy. The country obtains over a third of its wealth from tourism alone, and a quarter of the population lives from the tourist industry. Roughly three-quarters of the visitors come from **Europe**.

Transport infrastructure

There is no rail network, and motorised vehicles are only permitted on Malé and Gan. The **main forms of transport** are ox-**carts** and **bicycles**. The islands are connected to each other via small craft, mainly yachts, sailing boats and motor boats. The only **international airport** is in Hulule. Domestic flights between the country's three airports are of increasing importance.

Tourism

Of the 200 inhabited islands, more that 70 are used exclusively for tourism, and this number is increasing. The **diving spots** in the Maldives are some of the most beautiful in the world, and there are diving schools on every island. The capital city Malé is also of **cultural importance**, due to its seventeenth-century mosque.

A beach on the Maldives: one of the country's many beautiful places.

Administrative divisions:
14 regions
Population: 28 million
(190 inhabitants/sq. km)
Languages:
Nepali (official), Maithili, Bhojpuri
GDP per capita: US$370
Currency:
1 Nepalese rupee = 100 paisa

Natural Geography

Nepal consists of a narrow strip of land 853 km long and 160 km wide on the southern slopes of the **Central Himalayas**.
The **plains of the Terai region** in the far south border the **Shivalik mountains** and the foothills of the **Lesser Himalayas**. The north of the country ends in the Great Himalayas, where **eight of the ten highest mountains in the world** are situated. Several mountains are over 8,000 m high, including **Mount Everest,** the **world's highest mountain**, in the extreme north of the country on the border with Tibet.
The economic and social heart of the country is the **Kathmandu Valley**, 30 km long and 25 km wide, located in the Lesser Himalayas.

Climate

In the north, the **summers are cool** and the **winters** very **severe** due to the high altitudes. In the Terai and the plains of the Ganges, as well as in the Kathmandu Valley, the climate is **subtropical.** The temperatures in Kathmandu reach an average of 0°C in January, and 24°C in July.

Population

Many different ethnic groups live in Nepal. These include the Newar, Indians, Gurung, Magar, Tamang, Bhutia, Rai, Limbu and Sherpa peoples. The population also includes refugees from neighbouring Bhutan and Tibet. **Nepali** is the official language, but a **further 20 languages** are spoken.
Ninety per cent of the Nepali people profess to be of the Hindu faith. There are also **Buddhist** and **Muslim minorities**.

History and Politics

A single state consisting of the various principalities and clan communities of the Katmandu Valley first came into being in 1756 in the form of a **Gurkha Kingdom**. In 1792, Nepal concluded a treaty with the representatives of Great Britain.
The year 1951 saw a change in the ruling dynasty and a constitutional monarchy was introduced. The **democratic constitution** of **1959** was updated in **1962** and greater powers were assigned to the monarchy. Since the constitution of 1990, political parties have been permitted, and representatives of these parties are voted into the country's National Assembly for five-year terms.
A civil war between the government and Maoist rebels lasted for several years and resulted in the loss of more than 10,000 lives. A ceasefire was agreed in early 2003, but this was broken by the Maoists in August of the same year. In 2006, the powers of the king were to a large part withdrawn and a new peace agreement was reached. In January 2007, a transitional constitution dismantled the monarchy.

Economy

Nepal's terrain and landscape has made it one of the most underdeveloped countries in the world. The basis of the economy is **agriculture** – mainly livestock – which employs approximately 75 per cent of the population and contributes some 40 per cent of GDP.
The rich gold, copper, iron ore, slate and limestone reserves are mined for **export**. The modest **manufacturing sector** mainly processes agricultural products, including jute, sugar cane, tobacco and cereals. Other exports are **textiles** and **carpets**.

Transport Infrastructure

The **rail network** only covers a stretch of 101 km near the Indian border. Less than half of the 7,700 km of **road** is surfaced. There are irregular flight connections to the isolated high valleys. Katmandu has the only **international airport**.

Tourism

Apart from **the Himalayas**, the main attractions are the Royal Chitwan National park (Bengal tigers, rhino) and the Katmandu valley, with its **temples, monasteries** and medieval forts.

Nepal	
Area:	147,181 sq. km
Capital city:	Kathmandu
Form of government: Federal Democratic Republic	

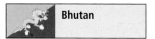

Bhutan	
Area:	47,000 sq. km
Capital city:	Thimphu
Form of government: Constitutional Monarchy	
Administrative divisions: 18 districts	
Population: 800,000 (20 inhabitants/sq. km)	
Languages: Dzongkha (official), Tibetan dialects	
GDP per capita:	US$1,200
Currency: 1 Ngultrum = 100 chetrum	

*The **Sherpa**, a Himalayan people, are the pathfinders across the roof of the world. They have developed survival techniques to cope with their hostile environment and have even managed to grow crops in the most unlikely places.*

Natural Geography

The small kingdom on the southern slopes of the eastern Himalayas is largely inaccessible to the outside world. Vast **mountain chains** (Jomolhari: 7,314 m) surround the high plateau, which descends gradually into the foothills at the Indian border.

Climate

Bhutan's climate is mainly a **high altitude climate**. In the capital city, Thimphu, the average temperature in January is 4°C, and it is only 17°C in July.

Population

Buddhists comprise 75 per cent of the inhabitants of Bhutan, and a further 25 per cent are **Hindu**. The population is 63 per cent **Bhutanese**, but there are also **Gurung** and **Assamese** peoples. In 1985, a **campaign of 'Bhutanisation'** was introduced, with the intention of strengthening the traditional Buddhist culture of the population. Even today, religious and ethnic diversity is frowned upon by the majority of the dominant Buddhist population of Bhutan.

History and Politics

Though archeological exploration of Bhutan is limited, evidence of civilisation in the region dates back to at least 2000 BC. The original Bhutanese, known as Monpa, are believed to have migrated from Tibet. Since the seventeenth century, the land has been known to its own people as Drukyul, Land of the Dragon People, a reference to the dominant branch of Tibetan Buddhism that is still practiced here. The territory was initially ruled by **Indian princes**, but **Tibetan conquerors** established a **Tibetan Buddhist state** in the ninth century AD. The British invaded in 1865 and established control. A **monarchy** was established in 1907 under **British influence**, and continues to rule to this day, with a national assembly (the Tshogdu). Bhutan is represented by **India** in respect of its foreign and defence policies. The country's self-imposed **isolation** can be seen by the fact that only 6,000 visitors cross the border

each year. On his 25th jubilee on 2 June 1999, the reigning monarch, King Jigme Singye Wangchuck, introduced **television** as a gift to his people.

Economy

Almost half of GNP derives from **agriculture,** which employs over 90 per cent of the working population. The country is self-sufficient in terms of food. Only very few crops (maize, wheat, cardamom) are exported. **Wood** from the extensive forests is one of the main exports. The manufacturing sector is poorly

developed and consists of small **crafts** (weaving, metal work, carvings). Technology and machinery are traditionally looked down upon.

Bhutan has only been open to **tourism since 1974,** and remains **restricted**, despite the fact that tourists bring by far the most money into the country.

Transport Infrastructure

The **first surfaced road** between India and the hitherto almost completely isolated capital city was only built in **1962**. Today, some roads connect Bhutan's larger centres of population. The mountainous landscape makes **transport connections difficult**, if not impossible. The only **international airport** is in **Paro**.

Tourism

Entry visas to Bhutan are only permitted for **group travel.** Tourists are only allowed to stay

for ten days and must pay a **daily fee** of US$200. The religious and cultural centre is **Thimphu**, but **Punakha** and **Paro** also have numerous historical sites. There are also **dzongs**, ancient monastic fortresses, which seem to cling to precariously to the mountainsides like birds' nests.

1 Those who climb to the summit of Mt Everest (8,850 m) find themselves truly on the roof of the world.

2 The eyes of the Buddha survey the four corners of the Earth: the Stupa of Swayambhunath in Kathmandu is one of the holiest Buddhist temples.

3 The atmosphere of Kathmandu's Durbar Square illustrates how religion fills the daily lives of the Nepali people.

4 Bhutan's monasteries are not just for prayer: they also play an administrative role – this is the seventeenth-century Paro Dzong.

*The **Mongolians** are a people of the steppes and live in extended families or clans. Their livestock forms the basis of their nomadic lives. Traditionally, they herded sheep, cattle, yaks and goats as well as horses, pack animals and camels.*

Mongolia

Area:	1,564,116 sq. km
Capital city:	Ulan Bator
Form of government:	Republic

Administrative divisions:
21 provinces, 1 district (capital city)
Population: 2.9 million
(2 inhabitants/sq. km)
Languages:
Mongolian (official),
Kazak, Russian, minority languages
GDP per capita: US$1,200
Currency:
1 tugrik = 100 mongo

Natural geography

Mongolia is dominated in the west by the **Altai Mountains** with altitudes of up to 4,300 m and the **Khangai Mountains** with altitudes of over 3,500 m. Highlands 1,000–1,500 m above sea level occupy the eastern part of the country, at the border with China. In the north-east, these highlands are characterised by **Kerulen rivers**, vital for irrigation in this arid land.

Climate

The climate is **continental** and extremely **dry**: During the long winters, the average temperature ranges from -26°C to -18 °C; during the short summers, average temperatures of 17°C to 23°C are attained. In the desert the temperature can reach 50°C. The country enjoys an exceptionally high proportion of clear, **sunny** days; approximately **260** per year.

Population

Mongolians account for 90 per cent of the population. They still lead a traditional nomadic way of life to a great extent. There are also Kazakhs and Russians in addition to a small Chinese minority. The predominant religion is **Tibetan Buddhism**. There is also a minority of Muslims (four per cent). The majority of Mongolians have no professed religion.

Mongol Yuan Dynasty in 1368, the country became an insignificant territory ruled by **China**.
In 1911, **Outer Mongolia** separated from China and in 1924, the **People's Republic of Mongolia** was formed. In contrast, Inner Mongolia continued its association with China.
Following massive demonstrations, a multi-party system was introduced in 1992, during the collapse of the Soviet Union, and the **Republic of Mongolia** came into being.
Mongolia is ruled by a **unicameral parliament** whose members are re-elected every four years. The president is directly elected as head of state every four years.

Economy

The transition from a socialist planned economy to a market economy seems to have been a success. In **agriculture, traditional animal husbandry** continues to predominate (especially sheep, goats, cattle, camels and horses).

In total, the **manufacturing sector** accounts for 29 per cent of the Gross Domestic Product, whilst the **services sector** accounts for 50 per cent.

Transport

Ulan Bator is connected to the **Trans-Siberian Railway** via the country's 1,928-km-long rail network. Only a small percentage of the road network (46,470 km) is paved, predominantly around the capital city, Ulan Bator. The majority of roads are cart tracks and are mainly used by buses and HGVs.
A total of eight **airports** interconnect the populated areas which lie great distances apart. There is an international airport at Ulan Bator.

Tourism

Mongolia is hardly opened up to tourism at all. There are **few hotels** or comparable facilities. Tourists come here first and foremost to experience the **desert and go on hunting expeditions** which start out from Ulan Bator.
The capital and the ruins of the city of **Karakorum**, founded in the thirteenth century, are among the few important **historic and cultural sites**. The Mongolians themselves, many of whom still live in yurts and follow a traditional way of life are an attraction in themselves, especially as the country is rapidly modernising.

China

Area:	9,598,000 sq. km
Capital city:	Beijing/Peking

Form of government:
Socialist People's Republic
Administrative divisions:
23 provinces, 5 autonomous regions, 3 municipalities; 147 autonomous districts
Population:
1.3 billion
(138 inhabitants/sq. km)
Languages:
Mandarin Chinese (official),
dialects and minority languages
GDP per capita: US$2,000
Currency: 1 renminbi yuan =
10 jiao = 100 fen

Natural geography

As the world's **third largest country in land mass**, China contains a wide range of landscapes. From the fertile **lowlands** in the east, the landscape rises to the **Tibet Highlands** in the west and the Himalayas in the south-west. Western China is dominated by **plateaus** and **steppes** that turn into desert in the north-west and north of the country (Takla Makan, Gobi).
In the west, the Tibetan Plateau, the 'roof of the world', reaches an average altitude of 4,500 m. It is the southerly range of the Himalayas and contains **Mount Everest** (8,850 m), the world's highest mountain. The densely populated east has the **characteristics of a range of hills**. The Yellow Sea coast is flat; both of China's major rivers, the **Huanghe** (4,875 km) and the 6300-km-long **Yangtze Kiang** flow into it.
There are over 5,000 islands off the coast which is 14,500 km

Horses are very important for riding and as pack animals for the nomadic people of Mongolia.

taiga vegetation. The **mountainous desert** and **steppe vegetation** that occupies the rest of the country turns into the **Gobi Desert** in the south which lies about 1,000 m above sea level.
Four-fifths of the country consists of **grassy steppes** used as grazing land for sheep, goats and cattle. The most important stretches of water are the **Selenga** and

Social services, the health service and the education sector are all well developed.

History and Politics

Mongolia, which was long populated by nomadic horsemen, was **united** in **1206** and became the centre of a great empire which stretched **from China to Eastern Europe**. After the downfall of the

A mere one per cent of the country's land mass is usable as arable land for growing maize, wheat, fruit and vegetables. Agriculture accounts for 21 per cent of GDP.
The **rich resources** of coal, oil, copper, molybdenum, gold and tin which were exploited in Soviet times are being phased. They still form the basis for manufacturing industry. Foodstuffs and cashmere wool are exported.

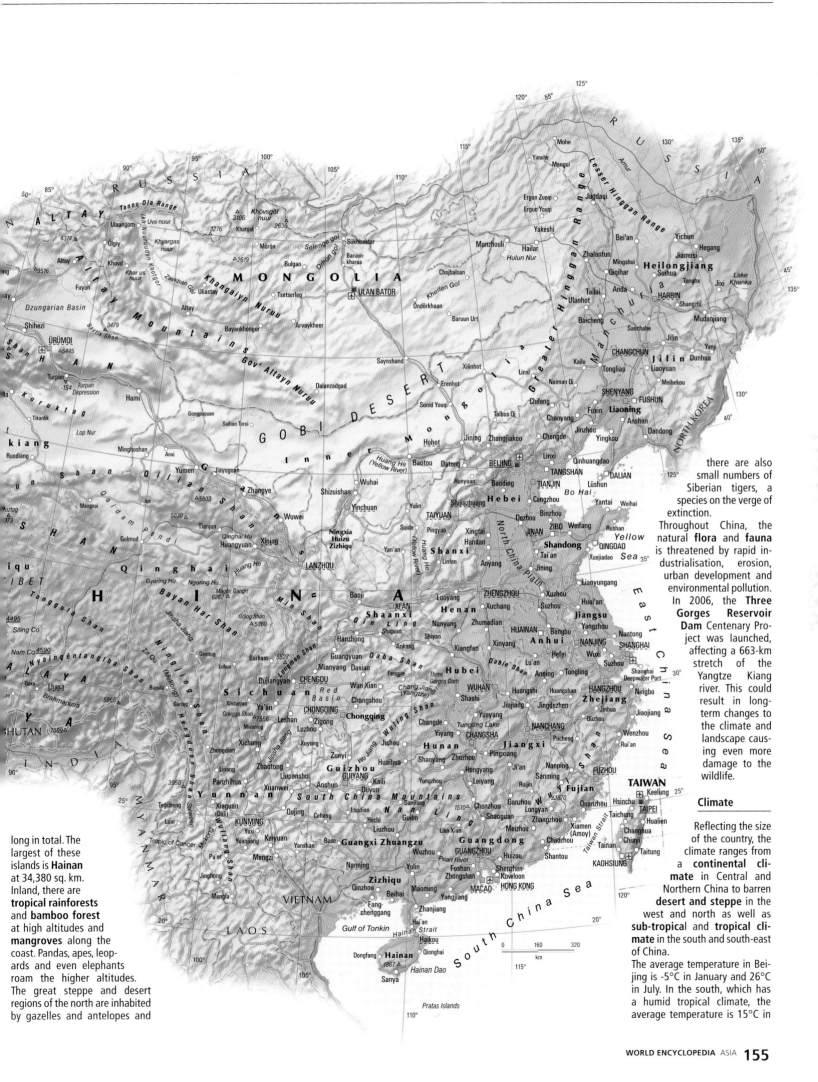

there are also small numbers of Siberian tigers, a species on the verge of extinction.

Throughout China, the natural **flora** and **fauna** is threatened by rapid industrialisation, erosion, urban development and environmental pollution. In 2006, the **Three Gorges Reservoir Dam** Centenary Project was launched, affecting a 663-km stretch of the Yangtze Kiang river. This could result in long-term changes to the climate and landscape causing even more damage to the wildlife.

Climate

Reflecting the size of the country, the climate ranges from a **continental climate** in Central and Northern China to barren **desert and steppe** in the west and north as well as **sub-tropical** and **tropical climate** in the south and south-east of China.

The average temperature in Beijing is -5°C in January and 26°C in July. In the south, which has a humid tropical climate, the average temperature is 15°C in

long in total. The largest of these islands is **Hainan** at 34,380 sq. km. Inland, there are **tropical rainforests** and **bamboo forest** at high altitudes and **mangroves** along the coast. Pandas, apes, leopards and even elephants roam the higher altitudes. The great steppe and desert regions of the north are inhabited by gazelles and antelopes and

China

The **Great Wall of China** stretches for a total lenghth of 10,000 km. The immense defensive structure began as a series of walls from as early as 400 BC. The wall in its current form dates from between the 13th and 16th centuries AD.

January and 25°C in July. The heavy rainfall decreases significantly further inland.

Population

The world's **most populous country** has no less than 40 **cities containing over one million inhabitants**. Yet over 80 per cent of Chinese still live in rural areas.

The vast majority (92 per cent) are **Han Chinese**. The most important of the approximately 50 official **ethnic groups** are Zhuang, Yi and Miao in Southern China, Hui, Manchu and Mongolian in the north and north-east and Tibetan and Uighur in the west and north-west.

It is estimated that only **15 per cent** of the population of China professes a religion. **Buddhism** and **Islam** predominate, while the proportion of Christians is approximately one per cent.

In addition to the Chinese **official language (Putonghua or Mandarin)** which is taught in the schools and used in the media, numerous Chinese dialects and minority languages are spoken. Comprehension difficulties are overcome thanks to the fact that all share the **Chinese script**.

In China, only the inhabitants of large cities or employees of large public companies are **covered by social security**. In rural areas, in particular, the provision of social security is the responsibility of the family and village community. The **health service** is organised by the state and serves the cities predominantly. Severe environmental and air pollution is a considerable problem for public health. In vast areas of the country the quality of drinking water is poor. The soil is contaminated with chemicals and heavy metals. The **education system** is strictly organised and well developed. Primary school is attended by 98.8 per cent of children. In future, it will be compulsory for all children to attend school for nine years. China has over 600 universities and institutions of higher education. There is a charge for attendance at these institutions, however, and a political appren-

ticeship year must first be completed. In 1979, the government was decided to introduce the One Child Policy. This has led to a considerable deceleration in population growth.

History and Politics

Archaeological finds indicate that there were settlements in what is now China in the early Palaeolithic era. It is believed that Yuanmou Man lived over 600,000 years ago. Of the multiplicity of strongly regional cultures of the late Neolithic period, the **Yangshao culture** (which existed in ca. five to three millennia BC, in the province of Shaanxi) and the **Longshan culture**

(which existed in ca. 2400–1900 BC, in the province of Shandong) are among the best known due to their characteristic coloured and black ceramics.

The first historically ascertained dynasty is the **Shang** (sixteenth to the eleventh century BC) from which the first written records originate. The **Zhou** Dynasty was organised into fiefdoms. The last period of the 'Battling Empires' was that of the classical **philosophical schools**.

The Qin Dynasty began with the **unification of the empire in 221 BC.** by the king of the Qin feudal state who was the first Chinese ruler to name himself **emperor**. He unified the system of weights and measures and the

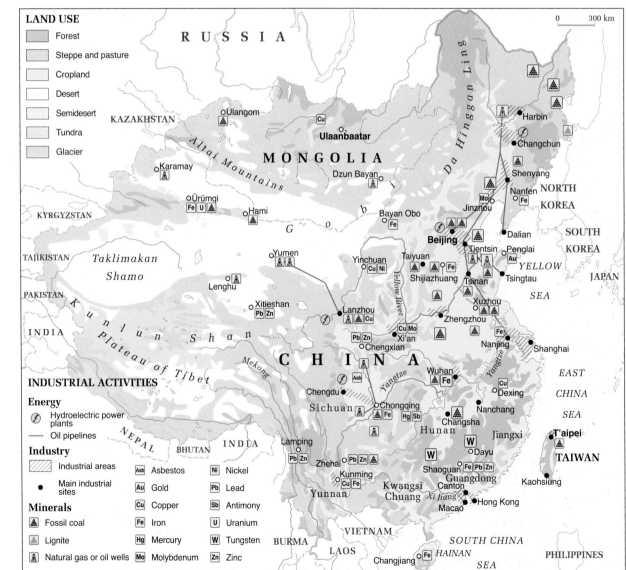

LAND USE

- Forest
- Steppe and pasture
- Cropland
- Desert
- Semidesert
- Tundra
- Glacier

INDUSTRIAL ACTIVITIES

Energy
- Hydroelectric power plants
- Oil pipelines

Industry
- Industrial areas
- Main industrial sites

Minerals
- Fossil coal
- Lignite
- Natural gas or oil wells

Asb	Asbestos	Ni	Nickel
Au	Gold	Pb	Lead
Cu	Copper	Sb	Antimony
Fe	Iron	U	Uranium
Hg	Mercury	W	Tungsten
Mo	Molybdenum	Zn	Zinc

0   300 km

Sun Yat-sen

*Cuiheng, 12.11.1866, †Beijing, 12.3.1925

After a coup attempt in Guangzhou, Sun Yat-sen went into exile, but returned to China in 1911 after the fall of the Manchu Dynasty and became provisional President of the Chinese Republic. He was the founder of the Kuomintang, which he formed into a potiical party with the help of the Soviets. He led a military government in 1917 and became President of Canton in south China in 1921.

Mao Zedong

*Shaoshan, 26.12.1893, †Beijing, 9.9.1976

Mao was the son of a farmer and an assistant librarian but founded the Chinese Communist Party and was its undisputed leader after the Long March. The Communists won the civil war against the Kuomintang troops, and Mao proclaimed the People's Republic of China in 1949. As president (1954–1958), he made radical changes to China. The Cultural Revolution became an example to many Communist movements in the Third World.

*The Gate of Heavenly Peace marks the entrance to the **Forbidden City** in Beijing. The palace complex was reserved for the family of the Emperor until 1911. It was from here in Tiananmen Sqaure that Mao Zedong proclaimed the People's Republic in 1949.*

system of writing. A **central government** was formed and the empire protected by the first Great Wall. The **Han Dynasty** which followed immediately afterwards (206 BC–220 AD) began with the colonisation of the neighbouring peoples and expansion of the empire. **Paper was invented** during this period.

The empire's contacts with India and Persia flourished under the **Tang Dynasty**. In subsequent centuries, China was twice ruled by foreign invaders. The Mongolian **Yuan Dynasty** reigned from 1280 to 1368 and the Manchus of the **Qing Dynasty** ruled from 1644 to 1911.

European and American enclaves were created following the **Opium War** of 1842 when Great Britain enforced the **opening** of the **ports** that had been closed by the Chinese to foreign trade.

As a result of the Japanese Empire's victory in the **Sino-Japanese War** from 1894 to 1895, Japan annexed parts of Manchuria in 1905. Formosa (Taiwan) was also ceded to Japan.

In 1900, the **Boxer Rebellion** attacked the enclaves of foreigners but resulted in forcing further concessions from China to western countries.

In October **1911,** there was a **revolution** against the imperial government and in December 1911 the **Republic of China** was proclaimed under a military regime which was rocked by **civil war** from 1916 onwards.

The **Communist Party of China**, founded in **1921**, remained associated with the **Kuomintang**, founded in 1912, until 1927. In 1928 the **Kuomintang** established a **national government** and then fought the Communists. On the **Long March** of 1934 to 1935, the **Red Army** was compelled to retreat to the northwest. When open war broke out in 1937 against the Japanese who had founded the **puppet state of Manchukuo** in Manchuria in 1931, the two groups formed a united front.

The battles between the Kuomintang and the Communists flared up again following the capitulation of the Japanese in 1945. They did not end until 1949 with the retreat of the Kuomintang to the island of Formosa where the National Republic

of China (Taiwan) was installed. In October 1949 the **People's Republic of China** was formed under Mao Zedong. It fostered a close relationship with the **Soviet Union** until 1960. Internal battles led to the **Great Proletarian Cultural Revolution** in the 1960s which culminated in well-planned purges and civil war-like conditions.

Since 1978, the Communist leadership has been operating an **economic liberalisation policy**. However, the political system remains untouched by economic opening strategies and tolerates no opposition.

The **National People's Congress** is an indirectly elected parliament. It has in excess of 2900 members who are elected every five years; the National People's Congress appoints the **country's president** and which legislates in conjunction with a **standing** committee. The executive authority is the responsibility of the **state council** which is led by the prime minister. The state council is, in turn, elected by the **National People's Congress**. The only hitherto significant party is the **Communist Party of China** whose leaders fundamentally determine policy guidelines. The party congress elects the **Central Committee** and the **Politburo** which has 22 members and its standing committee which consists of seven members. The People's Republic of China has a seat in the **United Nations Security Council**. It also possesses **atomic weapons**.

Hong Kong and Macao have **special** political and economic

status within the People's Republic as they were the last European colonies to be restored to their mother country in 1997 and 1999 respectively.

Hong Kong and its offshore islands cover an area of 1080 sq. km. The former **British crown colony** was returned to China on 1 July 1997 after over 150 years.

1 Shanghai, the second largest and most westernised city in mainland China has a huge sea port. Foreign trade is booming, as is the leisure industry.

2 Tiantan, the 'Altar of Heaven' in Beijing: until 1911, only the Emperor, the 'Son of Heaven' was permitted to enter. Today, the complex and the surrounding park are a favourite spot for residents of the capital to spend their leisure.

3 Hong Kong's skyline is constantly expanding. The trade and services centre is thriving, even after its return to China.

China

*The **cookshops**, tiny food stalls located in every back street and alley, are a favourite place for the Chinese to eat at any time of day – the choice is large, and the food is freshly prepared and very good value.*

As early as 1842, following the First Opium War, the British acquired the island of **Hong Kong Island** from China. At the time it was inhabited by 5,000 fishermen and farmers. The British acquired **Kowloon** in 1860. In 1898, Britain also leased the **New Territories** which lie to the north for a 99-year period. Hong Kong flourished under British rule in the decades that followed and became one of Asia's **most important trading centres**.

Today, Hong Kong has roughly seven million inhabitants, **95 per cent** of whom are **Chinese**. In the modern city, dominated by business and finance, the services sector contributes ca. 84 per cent of GDP, in contrast to the manufacturing sector which contributes only 16 per cent. **Agriculture** is insignificant in this densely populated region.

Macao is only separated from Hong Kong by the Pearl River es-

after, in 1887, under Dutch rule, Portugal's claims to Macao were finally recognised by the Chinese. The city had given up its dominance to Hong Kong a long time previously.

Over half of Macao's revenue today comes from **gambling** in casinos and hotels and on racecourses. The stream of visitors from neighbouring countries and regions where gambling tends to be prohibited accounts for approximately 25 per cent of GDP, whilst the manufacturing and agricultural sectors contribute little.

China has committed itself to maintaining the existing **capitalist economic system** in both regions for a further 50 years. Both have received the status of **special administration zones** with a high degree of internal autonomy and democracy.

The regions are represented by China in matters of foreign af-

companies were partially privatised by allowing them to be responsible for their own budgets. Enormous growth spurts originate predominantly from **commercial initiatives** which are gaining in significance through the creation of new jobs in the manufacturing and services sectors. The result is a **'Socialist market economy'** in which the key industries remain under state control, but more leeway is given to the commercial sector. The economy is hampered by **corruption** and **arbitrariness**.

As a whole, 53 per cent of the country's surface area is used for agriculture. China is the **world's largest rice producer;** Southern China is the most important centre for **rice farming**. Considerable volumes of maize, potatoes, sorghum, nuts, oilseeds, tea and cotton are also cultivated in China.

ment is rising due to the extensive restructuring of the economy. Another social problem is internal migration. It is estimated that approximately 100 million migrant workers have relocated to the boom cities in the last few years.

Transport

The **rail network** which is just 65,000 km long connects all the major cities and provinces and is the country's **main means of transport**, despite the fact that only ten per cent of the network has been electrified.

The **road network** in China is over 1,118,000 km long and a fifth of it is paved. China still belongs to the least developed countries as far as private car ownership is concerned. There are only 10 private cars per 1,000 inhabitants.

of the country's 206 which are served by 40 Chinese airlines. The most important are located in Beijing, Shanghai, Guangzhou and Hong Kong.

Tourism

The numerous testimonies to a 5,000-year-**old culture** and a varied and **fabulous landscape** throughout China offer manifold attractions which are becoming increasingly geared towards tourism.

There are numerous sites which are worth a visit in this great empire, meaning that only the most important can be mentioned. The starting point for most visitors to China is the capital city **Beijing** which offers many historic attractions such as the **'Forbidden City'**, the Heavenly Temple, the Summer Palace and Tiananmen Square. In the vicinity are the graves of the Thirteen **Emperors** of the Ming Dynasty. The most-visited section of the **Great Wall** is near Badaling and it is the most complete. Elsewhere, parts of the Great Wall have completely disappeared and other parts are only a few feet high.

The gigantic **Yungang Grottos** and the **Hanging Monasteries** near Datong tare worth a visit. Shenyang in Manchuria was formerly called Mukden; it has the palace of Ching, the second-largest after the emperor's palace in Beijing.

Qufu, the birthplace of Confucius, honours the scholar with China's largest **Confucius Temple**. The scholar is allegedly buried here in the Kong Forest.

The **ports** of Qingdao and Tianjin, contain many relics of European and Japanese colonialisation as does Shanghai which has become China's largest city.

Hangzhou and Suzhou are located on the **Grand Canal**. Hangzhou is a unique site worth a visit with its **beautiful West Lake** famous throughout China. Neighbouring Suzhou is known as the **'Venice of the East'** because of its many bridges and canals. The city is also famous for its **Literati Gardens**.

Other important destinations include the old imperial cities of Kaifeng, Luoyang with its imposing **Longmen Grottos**, **Shaolin Monastery**, Chengde with its

Deng Xiaoping

*Xiexing, 22.8.1904,
† Beijing, 19.2.1997

This senior party member was stripped of his rank during the confusion of the Cultural Revolution, was rehabilitated in 1973, and again deposed in 1976. He regained office in 1977. As acting Chairman of the Central Commission and the military, he was a strong figure until his death. His legacy includes the bloody suppression of the democratic movement that culminated in the protests in Tiananmen Square, Beijing in 1989.

A Zhuang woman surveys the irrigated terraced paddy-fields in the province of Guangxi.

tuary. The islands of Taipa and Coloane and the peninsula on the mainland are part of the region which covers an area of only 18 sq. km.

On **20 December 1999**, Macao was given back to China. The region, whose Chinese name is Aomen, has approximately 400,000 inhabitants, **95 per cent** of whom are Chinese.

The oldest European settlement in East Asia was founded as early as 1557 by the **Portuguese** who monopolised Chinese trade through this trading post. Shortly there-

fairs. The Beijing government also has a great influence in major matters of internal policy.

Economy

China's economic system has been in a period of upheaval since 1978. The significance of the rigid planned economy has been officially scaled down since 1993 in favour of China's **opening** up to the **global marketplace**. The collectivisation of agriculture was weakened. In the manufacturing sector, many

Massive deposits of raw materials form the basis of the manufacturing sector which accounts for 46 per cent of GDP. The mining sector (coal, graphite, iron ore, mineral oil, industrial minerals) employs seven per cent of the labour force. Finished goods account for the highest proportion of **exports**, mostly machinery and electronics, as well as textiles (especially cotton), finished clothing and toys.

Although the per capita income of the population has increased massively since 1978, unemploy-

The significant **inland navigation network** is operated on waterways with a total length of 110,600 km. This includes the **Grand Canal**, the largest man-made waterway, which runs for over 1,782 km from Beijing to Hangzhou. China has approximately 2,000 **ports**, approximately 80 of which are open to international trade. China maintains one of the world's **largest merchant fleets**. The **domestic flight network** is also well developed. There are approximately 19 **international airports** out

China

Shanghai is China's boom town: in a few short years, a completely new residential and business quarter has sprung up on the east bank of the Huangpu River, and the skyscrapers here can compete with anything in Hong Kong. Numerous infra-structural measures, for example the new underground, the city motorway and the new Pudong Bridge should solve the city's travel problems.

magnificent imperial **summer palace** and Nanjing.

At the eastern end of the historic **Silk Road** lies the old capital city of Xi'an. The city has become world-famous thanks to the discovery of the **grave** of China's **first emperor**, and the nearby massive **Terracotta Army**, part of which can be visited today.

Further sites in the city worth visiting include the museum, the **Wild Goose Pagoda** and the graves of numerous emperors.

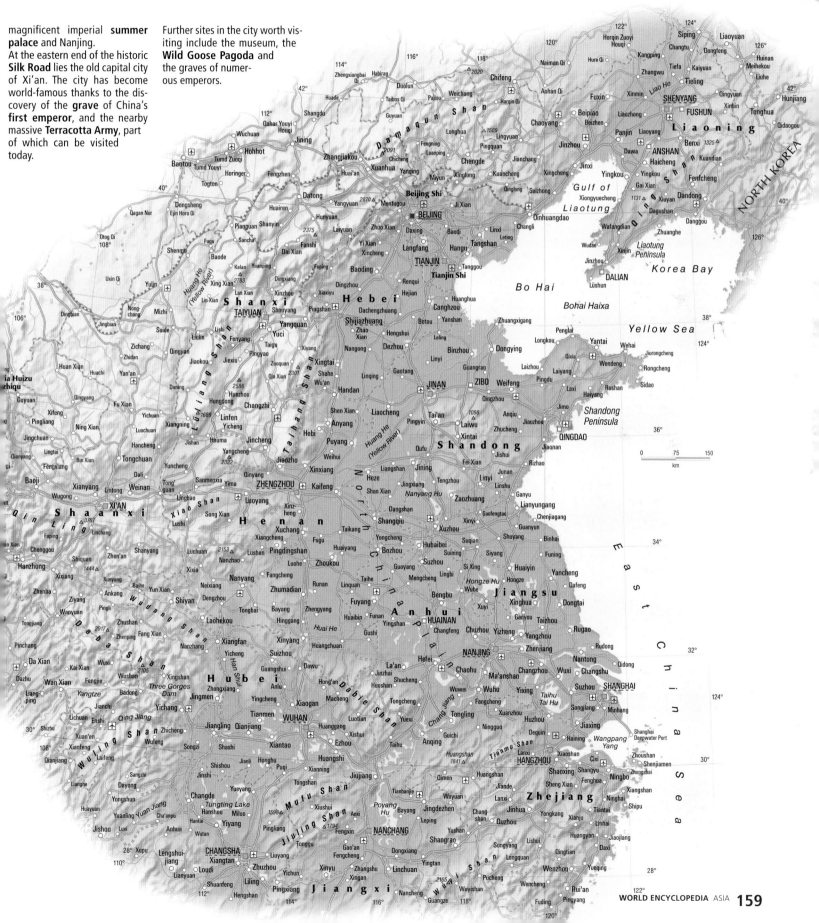

Hong Kong was handed back to the Chinese on 1 July 1997 in a grand ceremony. Under the motto 'One Country, Two Systems', the region has been turned into an economic and political free zone for the next 50 years.

The oasis city of **Dunhuang**, the legendary hub of the **Silk Road**, lies along the approximately 3,500-km-long historic route which takes about two-and-a-half days to cover by train. The **452 Mogao grottos** in the middle of the desert are a unique testament to **Buddhism**. The cities of Tulufan, Gaochang, Wulumuqi and Kashi were shaped by strong **Muslim** cultural influences. Kashi has an old quarter which contains the largest mosque in the province. It is worth a visit.

The main tourist centres of southern China are **Guangzhou** (formerly Canton) and the former British crown colony of **Hong Kong**, whose glittering facades attract millions of tourists annually. Haikou, the capital of the tropical island **Hainan**, has a unique western colonial architecture. Sanya has developed into a tourist centre with opportunities for **watersports** and **seaside holidays**.

Lhasa is the capital city of what is now the autonomous region of Xinjiang but was formerly the country of **Tibet**. In addition to the **Winter Palace**, the former seat of the Dalai Lama, the capital city boasts numerous temples and shrines. Once totally inaccessible, except over the Himalayas from Nepal, Tibet is now slowly opening up to tourism. The country is gradually being populated by Chinese brought in to colonise it and eventually outnumber the native Tibetans.

Other worth visiting tourist destinations are the six **Gelugpa Monasteries**, the monastery town of Ganden and the town of **Rikaze**. Lhasa is the starting point for **expeditions** to the high mountains which last several weeks.

The **Yangzi** ravines and their secondary channels are among China's numerous scenic highlights. These picturesque landscapes take several days to **travel through**.

The extraordinary **craggy landscape** on the Lijiang River around **Guilin** and **Shilin** and a **strange landscape** of **limestone formations** in Yunnan are among the wonders of China.

The mountainous landscape of Wuyishan with its 36 summits and 99 rocks, Emeishan, Wutaishan and Taishan are among the **holy mountains** of China which also offer unique scenic attractions. The **world's largest statue of Buddha** is in Leishan.

Further tourist destinations include the Jiuzhaigou and Huanglong nature reserves where small colonies of **giant pandas** have found refuge and those of **Wulingyuan** and **Lushan**.

Taiwan

Area:	35,980 sq. km
Capital city:	Taipei
Form of government:	Republic

Administrative divisions:
16 counties, 5 city counties, 2 special city counties
Population:
22.8 million
(635 inhabitants/sq. km)
Languages: High Chinese (official), Taiwanese, Hakka

GDP per capita:	US$16,000

Currency:
1 new Taiwanese dollar = 100 cents

Natural Geography

Situated off the south-east coast of the Chinese mainland, Taiwan belongs to the arc of islands in the South China Sea south of Japan. Densely **forested mountain** ranges with summits of over 3000 m can be found in the centre of the island. Taiwan's highest peak is **Yushan**, known as 'Jade Mountain', which is 3997 m high.

This extremely volcanic area levels out in the east, whilst in the west it turns into an 8 to 40-km-wide **coastal plain** following terraced graduations.

The Pescadors, a group of volcanic islands, belong to Taiwan but are located close to the Chinese mainland.

Climate

The climate is **sub-tropical** in the north with a good deal of precipitation. In contrast, there is a **tropical** climate in the south-west which is characterised by the winter monsoon. The average temperatures in Taipei are 15°C in January and 29°C in July.

Population

Eighty-four per cent of the population is **Taiwanese**. There are also people originating from the **Chinese mainland** (14 per cent) and Aborigines (two per cent). The **country's** official **language** is Standard Mandarin (Guoyu).

China, Guilin: Cormorant fishermen at dusk.

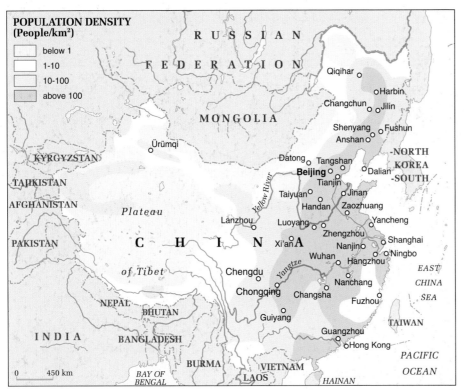

POPULATION DENSITY (People/km²)

- below 1
- 1-10
- 10-100
- above 100

Dalai Lama

*Taktser, 6.7.1935

The religious and political leader of Tibetan Buddhism is the reincarnation of Bodhisattva Avalokitesvara, who, after the death of one Dalai Lama ('Ocean Teacher'), is reincarnated into the body of a boy born at exactly the same time. The current 14th Dalai Lama, Tenzin Gyatso, was enthroned on 17 November 1940 in Lhasa aged five. China invaded Tibet in 1950/51. When the Chinese quelled Tibetan uprisings in 1959, the Dalai Lama fled to India, where he has since lived as head of the Tibetan government-in-exile. From India he has led a peaceful struggle against Chinese occupation. He received the Nobel Peace Prize in 1989.

Macao, once a Portuguese colony, is the Las Vegas of China. Since December 1999, the city is once again part of the People's Republic, but the Chinese come here to gamble as fervently as the seven million tourists who flock to Macao from around the world. The Casino Lisboa is a glamourous and often ruinous centre of the action. Every year, 5 million people come to this casino alone in the hope of making some quick and easy money.

Min (Taiwanese) and Hakka dialects are also spoken. Taiwan has a well-developed **social security system** and **health service**. Over 13 per cent of the state's budget is spent on them. The country's universities and institutes of higher education, of which there are approximately 130, are the pride of the **education system**.

History and Politics

Following the first **Chinese settlement** in the ninth century and various forays from the European colonial powers – **Portugal**, which discovered the island of Formosa in 1590, **Spain** and subsequently **the Netherlands** – Taiwan again became part of the Chinese empire in 1683.

In 1895, China was obliged to relinquish the island to **Japan** in the **Treaty of Shimonoseki**. In 1945, it became the territory of the Republic of China following the surrender of the Japanese.

After defeat in the civil war on the mainland the **Chinese Nationalist government** relocated its headquarters to Taiwan in 1949 in order to continue the battle against its Communist rivals from there with the **protection of the USA**.

Relations with the People's Republic of China, which views Taiwan as its twenty-third province, remain extremely tense up to the present day. Due to pressure from mainland China, the Republic of China finds itself internationally isolated from a diplomatic viewpoint, its citizens have difficulty obtaining visas from foreign countries for travel.

The **1947 Constitution** envisages a combination of **a parliamentary** and a **presidential system**. However, the **president** has extensive powers.

Economy

Taiwan has a predominantly **capitalist** economy in which **state control** of investments, foreign trade and important branches of industry are being increasingly **privatised**. Before Taiwan was **rapidly industrialised** in the 1960s with the assistance of the USA, agriculture traditionally dominated life on this densely populated island which has a shortage of raw materials. The contribution of **agriculture** (rice, maize, soya beans, fruit, vegetables, fish and meat) to GDP is now only about three per cent.

The **highly productive manufacturing sector** is central to the Taiwanese economy (29 per cent of GDP). The majority of goods are manufactured for **export**. This applies, in particular, to the manufacture of electronic and high-tech goods but also to chemicals, textiles, clothing, cars and machines.

The **services sector** contributes 69 per cent to GDP and employs approximately one half of the

working population. Thanks to significant investment in neighbouring countries such as Indonesia, Thailand, the Philippines and Vietnam, labour-intensive manufacturing is increasingly being relocated abroad.

Transport

Part of the 4,600-km-long **rail network** is for freight only. The island has a dense **road network** which is mainly surfaced with asphalt. The country's **air links** are good. International airports are located in Taipei and Gaoxiong.

Tourism

Taipei is the tourist centre. It has an **old town** and numerous **temples**. The **National Palace Museum** houses the largest collection of Chinese paintings, artefacts and objets d'art in the world, now unique, since so much Chinese art was destroyed in mainland China during the Cultural Revolution and the Great Leap Forward. There are relics from colonial times in Gaoxiong and Tainan in the south. The mountains of Central Taiwan offer **hiking and mountain climbing**. **Gending National Park** in the south and **Yushan National Park** in the centre are the important national parks.

1 A high pass in Tibet: Tibetan Buddhists hang out colourful prayer flags in this remote region.

2 The Potala Palace, the former residence of the Dalai Lama, perches on a cliff in Lhasa. The 14th Dalai Lama has lived in exile in India since 1959.

3 Representation of a laughing Buddha in Gyantse, the third largest city in Tibet.

4 People from Taipei perform Qigong breathing exercises near the Chiang Kai-shek monument, built in remembrance of the first President of Taiwan.

In spite of the introduction of the market economy and increasing Westernisation, the memory of the 'Great Leader' Mao Zedong is omnipresent in China. His larger-than-life portrait continues to adorn the Tiananmen Gate on the Square of Heavenly Peace. His image is still to be found in countless offices

and his books, such as the famous 'Little Red Book', and the Mao-inspired grey uniforms are on sale at markets and bazaars. His mortal remains are at rest in the Mao Mausoleum at the southern end of the Square of Heavenly Peace in the centre of Beijing.

Cities of Asia

Beijing

Beijing, the capital of China, lies to the north of the lowland plains of northern China. The city's origins go back over 3,000 years. It became the capital city of China in 1644 and still retains this function, apart from a short interlude between 1927 and 1949.

There are many historic monuments in the city, such as the Forbidden City and the Temple of Heaven, which have been designated UNESCO World Heritage Sites. Development in recent years has been substantially determined by the 2008 Olympic Games. The most significant structure, the Olympic Stadium, was designed by the Swiss architects Herzog & de Meuron.

Area:
16,808 sq. km (city)
Inhabitants:
15,800,000 (city, 2007)
Population density:
940 inhabitants/sq. km (city)

The Gate of Divine Might: One of several entrances into Beijing's Forbidden City.

Shanghai

Shanghai lies in eastern China on the estuary delta of the Yangtze Kiang. It is the largest industrial city in China. Since 1984, Shanghai has been an 'open city' where foreign investment is possible. The special economic zone of Pudong was set up in 1990, and the Transrapid maglev train link was built in 2003 to connect Pudong international airport with the city. The rapid modernisation of Shanghai has been to the detriment of its historic areas, which are still being eroded. The old trading city of Shanghai was captured by the British in 1842 and was occupied by the Japanese from 1937 until 1945. Shanghai is the city of 'Expo 2010'.

Area:
6,340 sq. km (city)
Inhabitants:
18,150,000 (city, 2007)
Population density:
2,863 inhabitants/sq. km (city)

View over the Huangpu River to Pudong with the Jin Mao Tower (right).

Hong Kong

Situated on the coast of southern China, today Hong Kong is a Special Administrative Region (SAR) of the People's Republic of China. The city consists of the island of Hong Kong, the Kowloon peninsula, the New Territories, the island of Lantau, and around 240 smaller islands. Hong Kong came under British rule in 1842 under the Treaty of Nanking and became one of Asia's major trading bases. On 1 July 1997, Hong Kong was returned to the People's Republic of China, which was contractually obliged to grant the city almost full autonomy ('one country, two systems') and not to fundamentally change its legal or economic system for 50 years.

Area:
1,014 sq. km (city)
Inhabitants:
6,680,000 (city, 2006)
Population density:
6,051 inhabitants/sq. km (city)

Victoria Harbour and the city skyline: A view from Wanchai over the centre of Hong Kong.

Seoul

Founded in the eleventh century, Seoul, the capital of South Korea, lies on the Hangang River near the western coast of the Korean peninsula. Along with the 17 surrounding cities, Seoul forms the second largest conurbation in the world after Tokyo. In the 1970s the city began to develop into a modern administrative, economic and trading metropolis. Today, the image of modern Seoul is characterised by more than 2,000 high-rise buildings. The Seoul Tower, built in 1980, has become the symbol of the city, while two of its historic monuments, the Jongmyo Shrine and the Changdeokgung Palace Complex, have been included in the list of UNESCO World Heritage Sites.

Area:
606 sq. km (city)
Inhabitants:
10,350,000 (city, 2005)
20,400,000 (conurbation, 2000)
Population density:
17,093 inhabitants/sq. km (city)

A view over Seoul's nighttime skyline with the mountains that encircle the city in the background.

Cities of Asia

Jakarta

Jakarta is the capital of Indonesia. It lies at the mouth of the Ciliwung River as it enters the Java Sea, on the north-west coast of the island of Java. Along with the cities of Bogor, Tangerang and Bekasi, Jakarta – the tenth largest city in the world – forms the metropolitan area of Jabotabek, which has a population of over 18 million people. Under the name of Batavia, Jakarta was the Dutch East India Company's most important Asian base. In recent decades, unrestricted immigration has led to straggling settlements in the outer regions of the city. An additional problem is posed by massive flooding (most recently in 2002 and 2007).

Area:
664 sq. km (city)
Inhabitants:
Approx. 10,000,000 (city, 2007)
18,300,000 (Jabotabek, 2007)
Population density:
15,060 inhabitants/sq. km (city)

High-rise buildings continue to spring up in much of this prosperous Indonesian city.

Kuala Lumpur

The capital of Malaysia, Kuala Lumpur lies on the Kelang River on the Malay Peninsula. It was founded in 1857 as a settlement for Chinese mine workers. The modern city is symbolised by the Petronas Twin Towers, the world's tallest buildings until 2004. Kuala Lumpur's modern constructions are in stark contrast to many older buildings in different styles, such as the Victorian Selangor Club of 1910, or the Moorish-style main station, built in 1911. The city is a major location for industry and tourism. Opened in 1998, Kuala Lumpur International Airport at Sepang to the south of the city, is one of Asia's major aviation interchanges.

Area:
243 sq. km (city)
Inhabitants:
1,450,000 (city, 2002)
4,060,000 (conurbation, 2002)
Population density:
5,967 inhabitants/sq. km (city)

The Petronas Twin Towers in Kuala Lumpur. Petronas is Malaysia's national oil company.

Singapore

Singapore is an independent island state located off the southern tip of the Malay Peninsula. About three-quarters of its 4.5 million inhabitants are Chinese. Singapore has undergone breathtaking levels of development in recent decades and now boasts world-class transport, industry, trade, finance and services. The port of Singapore is the largest seaport in the world in terms of the movement of goods. The city has evolved from its humble origins as a Malay fishing village where, in 1819, the British East India Company established a trading post. Singapore was occupied by the Japanese between 1942 and 1945, when British rule was restored. It became an independent republic in 1965.

Area:
693 sq. km (city)
Inhabitants:
4,600,000 (city, 2005)
Population density:
6,638 inhabitants/sq. km (city)

Boat Quay on the south bank of the Singapore River, the heart of the city's nightlife.

Tokyo

Tokyo is the capital of Japan and the seat of the imperial family. It lies on the eastern side of the island of Honshu on Tokyo Bay on the Pacific Ocean. The city is the most significant industrial base and the most important transport hub in the country. After New York, Tokyo, with the Tokyo Stock Exchange, is the most important financial metropolis in the world. With around 35 million inhabitants, the Greater Tokyo Area is the most populous metropolitan area in the world. With millions of commuters every day, transport systems are regularly at their limits of capacity. The former fishing village of Tokyo became the base of the Shogun in the sixteenth century, and since 1869 it has been home to the imperial palace.

Area:
581 sq. km (city)
Inhabitants:
8,670,000 (city, 2008)
About 35,000,000 (conurbation, 2003)
Population density:
14,923 inhabitants/sq. km (city)

Tokyo Tower, in Shiba Park in the municipal district of Minato, was completed in 1958.

North Korea

*The cult around Kim Il-Sung, who died in 1994, survives to this day in the 'Dictatorship of the Proletariat' in **North Korea**. A constitutional amendment in 1998 made him 'Eternal President'. His son Kim Jong Il acts as president.*

North Korea	
Area:	120,538 sq. km
Capital city:	Pyongyang
Form of government:	
People's Republic	
Administrative divisions:	
9 Provinces, 2 city districts	
Population:	
23m (190 inhabitants/sq. km)	
Language:	Korean
GDP per capita:	US$1,000
Currency:	1 won = 100 chon

Natural Geography

In the north, the country forms part of **mainland Asia**; the east coast falls steeply to the **Sea of Japan**. North Korea is largely **mountainous** with heights of up to 2,541 m (Kuanmao): it flattens, however, in a south-westerly direction. The country's flora and fauna, which at one time were very diverse, have suffered severe damage from **massive industrialisation and pollution**.

Climate

A **cool temperate monsoon climate** predominates, with low temperatures in winter and **large amounts of rainfall** in the summer months. The temperatures in the capital city are on average -8°C in January and 24°C in July.

Population

Almost **100 per cent** of the population is **Korean**. There is a small Chinese minority.

Kim Il Sung, born Kim Song Ju

*Mangyongdae, 15.4.1912,
†Pyongyang, 8.7.1994

The Korean general led the Korean People's Revolutionary Army in 1932 against the Japanese occupying powers and became General Secretary of the Korean Workers' Party in 1946. He was Prime Minister from 1948 to 1972 and President of the Democratic People's Republic of Korea from 1972 until his death.

Religious practice is officially tolerated in North Korea, but it barely plays a role in public life. 68 per cent of the population practice no religion.

Since 1994, North Korea has been afflicted by severe **famines** as a result of crop failure, flooding and the lack of relief programmes. According to estimates from foreign relief organisations, up to three million people have starved to death in recent years. The health service is also in a disastrous condition as a result of lack of supplies. In contrast, there is **massive expenditure on weapons** (around 25 per cent of GDP), which makes North Korea one of the world's **most heavily armed countries**. There is hardly a country in the world as isolated as the Democratic People's Republic of Korea.

History and Politics

The history of both North Korea and South Korea has always been strongly influenced by the tense relationship between the neighbouring powers **Japan** and **China**. After the **occupation** of the country by Japan until 1945 and subsequently by Soviet and US troops, northern Korea was declared a **Democratic People's Republic** in 1948. A surprise invasion of South Korea by North Korean troops in 1950 started the **Korean War**. UN troops, under the leadership of the USA, launched a counter-attack. During the clashes, the North was supported by Chinese and Soviet weapons and troops.

The **armistice of 1953** set the present borders. Since then, after initial alliances with the People's Republic of China and the Soviet Union, the country has isolated itself and insisted on political, ideological and economic **independence**. Along the military buffer zone, which has existed since 1953, there have been repeated clashes with South Korea. A first historic North-South **summit** took place between the President of South Korea, Kim Tae Chung, and the President of the North Korea, Kim Jong Il in June 2000 in Pyongyang. However this resulted in further bitter clashes. North Korea's confession in 2002, that it was pursuing a nuclear weapons programme, has put pressure on the country's

relations with the US, which considers North Korea to be a 'rogue state'. This position has been reinforced by recent threats from North Korea to unleash atomic weapons on Japan and by alleged Korean cooperation with Iran in nuclear technology.

Economy

The economic policy is based on a socialist **planned economy**. In the **collectivised agricultural system**, in which 36 per cent of all those employed produce approximately 27 per cent of GDP, principal crops are rice, maize and potatoes. North Korea cannot supply its own domestic food requirements and even **feeding** the population can currently only be guaranteed by expensive

international relief action. A good 40 per cent of GDP derives from **heavy industry**, which is based on the country's **mineral resources** (coal, graphite, iron, gold, silver, lead and zinc) and the iron and **steel industry**. **Machinery** and **armaments are manufactured** for export. According to estimates, only 20 per cent of the labour force work in industry because of a energy shortage.

*Korean Buddhism, which contains many elements of shamanistic piety, is not a single religious entity. In **South Korea** there are 20 different schools and sects.*

developed tourist industry are the capital city, Pyongyang, which has palaces and museums. There is also the ancient capital of Kaesong close to the border with South Korea. As a result of North Korean government's isolationist policies, contact with foreigners tourism is unlikely to develop in the foreseeable future.

South Korea

Area:	98,480 sq. km
Capital city:	Seoul
Form of government: Presidential Republic	
Administrative divisions: 15 provinces	
Population: 49 million (498 persons per sq. km)	
Language:	Korean
GDP per capita:	US$18,400
Currency:	1 won = 100 Chon

Natural Geography

The terrain of the Republic of Korea, which lies in the **southern part** of the **Korean Peninsula**, is predominantly **mountainous**. The highest summit in the **Taebaek Mountain range** reaches a height of 1,708 m. In contrast with the flat east coast, the south and west coasts are strongly mountainous. In the south, there is a hilly, **fertile** basin through which the **Nakdong River** flows.

There are also mountain ranges on the **3500 islands,** of which around 600 are inhabited. The west of the country is covered by a 50 to 100-km-wide **coastal plain**.

The largest **rivers** in South Korea, the Han, the Pukhan, the Kum and the Nakdong, all flow into the **Yellow Sea**. Their navigability is limited.

Extensive **deciduous** and **coniferous forests** dominate the landscape. The volcanic island of **Cheju** in the **South China Sea** south of South Korea is also part of the national territory. Its highest peak, which rises to 1,950 m, is called Hallasan.

Climate

With the exception of the extreme south which is characterised by a **sub-tropical** climate, the climate is **continental** and **temperate-cool**.

In the capital city, average temperatures are 25°C in July and -5°C in January

Population

The only **minority** in South Korea is a small community of **Chinese**. Approximately half of the South Koreans are **Christians**, 47 per cent **Buddhists** and a further four per cent belong to no religious denomination.

Over **80 per cent** of the **population** live in the **cities**; of these, over a third live in the capital city, **Seoul**, one of the **largest cities** in the world with **over ten million inhabitants**.

The standard of living is high. Around 11 per cent of the state budget is spent on the **health service**. **Education** is also highly developed. Almost all **children** of school age start school; approximately half of those of the right age group is enrolled at one of more than **130 universities** in the country.

History and Politics

According to legend, the founding of a **Korean Empire** goes back to the year 2333 BC Historical support exists for 57 BC as the beginning of the era of the three **rival kingdoms** Silla, Koguryo and Paekche. In the seventh century, **Silla**, the largest of the three kingdoms, with support from the Chinese, united the whole peninsula. The **Goryeo Dynasty, founded in** 918 AD, brought the entire peninsula under its rule in 936 AD.

Following the **Mongolian conquest** of 1259 AD to 1392 AD came the **Joseon Dynasty** which was to last until 1910. During this time an administrative system was established in accordance with the Chinese model and **Confucianism** was introduced as the official state creed.

North Korea: statues protect the Emperor's tomb in Kaesong.

The Kim Il Sung Stadium in Pyongyang can seat 100,000 people.

Transport

The **rail network** covers a length of approximately 5,000 km of which 3,500 km is electrified. There are international rail connections with Russia and China. Very little of the **road network** which covers 31,000 km is surfaced; all the important cities are, linked to each other by frequent **bus services**. There are hardly any private cars. The country's domestic flight network is of little significance. The **international airport** is in Py. The

most important **sea ports** are Namp'o, Ch'ongjin and Wonsan.

Tourism

Individual trips to North Korea are not permitted. Centres of the barely

*Near the small town of **Gyeongju** lies the Solluram Grotto, in the dense forests of a national park. Built in the eighth century, it contains a 3.4-m-high granite statue of Buddha Shakyamuni, which is regarded as an important piece of Buddhist art. The surrounding temple was constructed from giant granite blocks, which together form an artificial hill.*

Invasions by **Japan** in 1592 and 1597 were fended off with Chinese support. In the seventeenth century, the country began to cut itself off from the outside world, keeping contact only with China. Through its victory in the **Sino-Japanese** war of 1894/1895 Japan increased its influence, culminating in 1910 in the **annexation of Korea**.

In **World War II**, hundreds of thousands of Korean labourers were deported to Japan as forced labour and Korean women were forced into prostitution for the Japanese troops. After the capitulation of Japan in 1945, the Red Army occupied the part of Korea north of the 38th parallel.

In the south, which was controlled by the **US, the Republic of Korea** was set up in 1948. After the **Korean War** (1950–1953), South Korea's politics were characterised for decades by a **dictatorial regime** mainly run by generals. From the mid 1980s, however, the **democratic opposition**, which had been brutally repressed until then, gained increasing influence. The democratisation process culminated in democratic elections and the **constitution** of 1988.

The members of the **National Assembly** serve four-year terms and the **President** who has extensive powers is elected by direct popular vote for a single five-year term of office.

Due to the political troubles of the past, there is a large Korean diaspora, living mainly in the United States, especially in California. Some overseas Koreans have prospered greatly, many owning small businesses.

Economy

Over the last 30 years, economic development has been characterised by an intensive, export-orientated **industrialisation**. South Korea has developed from a producer of labour-intensive **cheap goods** in the foodstuffs, textiles and clothing industries to a supplier of its own **technologies** and proprietary goods – above all in the **motor vehicle and electronics industries**, but also in ship-building and in iron and steel production.

Industry contributes 40 per cent of GDP. The fishing industry which is intensively operated by one of the world's largest fishing fleets (fish, seafood, algae) is also a major source of exports. The **agricultural sector**, with the cultivation of cereals, as well as canimal husbandry and poultry farming, is of relatively little importance, contributing four per cent to GDP. The **services sector,** meanwhile, contributes 56 per cent.

Transport

South Korea has an excellent, fully developed infrastructure with an extensive **rail network** (3,081 km) and a well developed **road network** (83,000 km).

The most important **sea ports** are Pusan, Ulsan ch'on. South Korea also has a busy domestic flight network and **three international airports** in Seoul (Gimpo/Kimpo Airport), Incheon (Incheon) and Busan.

Tourism

The main tourist attractions are to be found in the modern capital city of Seoul with its many places of interest, royal palaces and gardens. Other cultural and historical sites are the old **imperial cities of Kyongju** and **Suwon** and their grounds which contain numerous cultural treasures as well as the **Haeinsa Temple**. **Songnisan Park** and **Seoraksan-Park** are among the best known of the country's **national parks** which cover approximately ten per cent of the country's land mass and offer excellent mountaineering, walking and hiking opportunities in addition to magnificent landscapes.

The island of **Cheju** which has a much milder climate than the mainland and wonderful scenery

Population:	127.4 million
	(337 inhabitants/sq. km)
Language:	Japanese
GDP per capita:	US$34,000
Currency:	1 yen = 100 sen

Natural Geography

The country consists of around **4,100 islands**, in an arc about 2,600 km long. The four main islands are **Kyushu** (42,073 sq. km), **Honshu** (230,862 sq. km), **Shikoku** (18,792 sq. km) and **Hokkaido** (83,511 sq. km). The **Ryukyu Islands** in the south includes **Okinawa**. The largest of the smaller islands are **Sado** (857 sq. km) and **Amamioshima** (709 sq. km).

The islands consist of approximately 75 per cent **wooded low mountain ranges**. The highest mountain is the volcanic peak of **Mount Fuji** at 3,776 m above sea level. There is massive volcanic and seismic in the land mass, due to its position at the juncture of two tectonic plates.

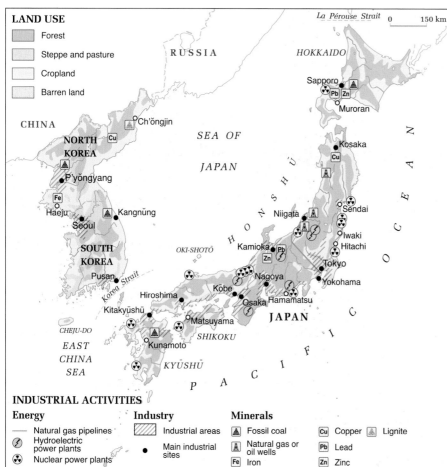

LAND USE

- Forest
- Steppe and pasture
- Cropland
- Barren land

INDUSTRIAL ACTIVITIES

Energy
- Natural gas pipelines
- Hydroelectric power plants
- Nuclear power plants

Industry
- Industrial areas
- Main industrial sites

Minerals
- Fossil coal
- Natural gas or oil wells
- Iron
- Copper
- Lead
- Zinc
- Lignite

Seoul, capital of South Korea, against its backdrop of mountains.

around the **Hallasan** volcano is another attraction for foreign visitors and the Koreans alike.

Japan	

Area:	377,835 sq. km
Capital city:	Tokyo
Form of government:	
Constitutional Monarchy	
Administrative divisions:	
47 prefectures	

The islands of Japan are actually a row of peaks in an underwater mountain range. It has hundreds of **volcanoes**, of which as many as 40 are active. In addition, there are over 10,000 **hot springs**. Japan is rocked daily by **earthquakes** and **seaquakes** of varying intensities.

The densest areas of population are in the wide coastal plains around Tokyo and in the area of **Kyoto** and **Osaka**.

The once rich **animal and plant world** has been almost com-

*Fish and seafood are important elements in the **cuisine** of South Korea, as it is in many of the coastal areas of south-east Asia. Ullung Island is famous for its dried cuttlefish; live fish and frogs are sold in the market in Busan.*

pletely destroyed by industrialisation and extensive use of the few areas of arable land; only a few conservation areas have been spared.

Today, over **350 Natural parks** and **27 National Parks** occupy a total of 7.5 per cent of the land. Apart from these, **paddy-fields**, **unirrigated crops**, forests of **cedar** and **bamboo** predominate in the countryside.

Climate

Japan lies in the pressure field between **continental artic air** and **maritime tropical air**. Due to the long north-south axis along which the country lies, it is subject to extremes of climate. The **south** is predominantly **subtropical and hot**, the **north** has **a temperate cool climate**.

Annual rainfall increases significantly in the southern most islands. While in Hokkaido, the average temperature drops in January to -3°C – against 22°C in July – the average temperature in the Okinawa prefecture is almost always 22°C.

The main island, **Honshu**, is **climatically divided**: on the side facing the Sea of Japan there are snowy winters and tropical hot winters, and on the side overlooking the Pacific Ocean, mild but dry winters alternate with hot rainy summers. In **Tokyo** the temperature in January is on average 5°C, and in July 25°C.

Population

99 per cent of the population is **Japanese**; there is also a small minority of **Ainu** (aborigines) on Hokkaido. Among the foreigners living in Japan, **Koreans** form the greatest proportion, followed by **Chinese** and **Brazilians**. The Japanese frequently belong to different religious communities at the same time: over 80 per cent are both **Buddhist** and **Shinto**, around four per cent are **Christians**. Average **life expectancy** is 80 years, the highest in the world.

In view of the corresponding **fall in the birth rate**, the increasingly **ageing population** is a major problem for Japan's **social welfare and healthcare systems**, which are amongst the most advanced on earth. Reforms, such

as the introduction of nursing care insurance and improvements in state and company pension schemes should address the problem. Japan's economic recession, which has been exacerbated by the continuing **financial crisis**, could also have an effect on the social situation in the future: the traditional rigorous **work ethic**, until now rewarded by the guarantee of **lifetime employment**, automatic promotion and closely knit company community, could eventually be replaced by the western model, based on individual performance, which will be a painful conversion.

History and Politics

Archaeological evidence indicates very early **settlements** in Japan over 20,000 years ago. However only in 350 BC when the **Yamato-Province** was formed from hundreds of small principalities did traditional history begin. In the sixth and seventh centuries AD, during the Yamato era, Chinese influence was evident in the introduction of a **bureaucratic government**, the introduction of **Buddhism**, and the adoption of Chinese cultural and technological achievements such as **Chinese script** and agricultural technology. With the **Taika-Reform** of 645 AD, a fully developed, institutionalised **empire** arose.

From the twelfth century, powerful warlords, the **Shoguns**, assumed power in the kingdom. Under the rule of the **Tokugawa-Shogun** dynasty who ruled from the sixteenth to the nineteenth centuries, the country isolated it-

self until **1853**, when the US fleet forced the **opening of the ports**. With the abolition of the last Shogun in 1868 and the restoration of the rule under a now **'divine' emperor (Tenno)**, the country was to a large extent opened up to the west and was intensively industrialised. Both the **constitution** of 1889 and

1 Red wooden torii in front of the island of Miyajima. the symbolic and spiritual entrance to the famous Itsukushima Shrine.

2 Unique aesthetic unity: the Golden Pavillion of 1398 and the landscaped gardens in the old imperial city of Kyoto.

3 Tokyo: one of the most important shrines in Japan is that of Emperor Meiji, who died in 1912, after ending the rule of the Shoguns.

4 The bright lights of the Shibuya district in Tokyo illustrate Japan's love of everything hi-tech.

Japan

Mount Fuji *rises majestically above Lake Kawaguchi. The symmetrical shape of the 3,776-m-high volcano has inspired countless poets, painters and architects. The sacred mountain is surrounded by Japan's largest area of lowland.*

the reorganisation of the military were directly **modeled on the organization of the German kingdom Prussia**. Soon after that, Japan, poor in mineral resources, began to extend its sphere of influence to the whole of east Asia, defeating the forces of **China** in 1895 and **Russia** in 1905; five years later it **annexed Korea**.

In 1931, the Japanese army occupied **Manchuria** approving the last Chinese Emperor, **Puyi**, as ruler of the puppet kingdom Manchukuo. Beginning in 1937, the **Sino-Japanese War** lasted until 1945. At the same time, Japan tried to protect and extend its conquests by entering the **Axis Pact** with **Germany** and **Italy**. With the attack on **Pearl Harbour** in 1941, the **Pacific War** began and large parts of southeast Asia were conquered. In August 1945, after the US dropped **atomic bombs** on **Hiroshima** and **Nagasaki**, the emperor announced Japan's unconditional surrender. In **1947**, with support from the USA, a new **constitution** was proclaimed which planned for **parliamentary government** under an **emperor** who had merely ceremonial functions, as a symbol of the state and the unity of the people.

The members of the House of Representatives – the **lower house** (Shugiin) – are elected every four years; the leader of the parliamentary majority in this house becomes **Prime Minister**. The House of Councillors – the **Upper House** (Sangiin) consists of delegates from regional constituencies, who each serve six year terms.

In foreign affairs, Japan maintains a **policy of pacifism**, in spite of its enormous economic strength and since 1992, has taken part on a small scale in UN peace missions.

Economy

Japan has the second **largest economy** in the world after the United States. **Agriculture** (cereals, rice and green tea grown on terraces, fruit and vegetables) is mostly a secondary occupation; Hokkaido is the centre of the extensive beef **cattle breeding industry**. As one of the world's largest **fishing nations** (fish, seafood, sea grass and seaweed), Japan maintains one its biggest fishing fleets. The fleet is partly stationed overseas and accounts for nearly **15 per cent** of the **entire world catch**.

The **country which is poor in natural resources** is industrially highly developed and strictly organised, particularly in the **metal-processing** sector. The most important **exports** are in the **ship-building and motor vehicle manufacturing industries**, the **chemicals industry**, iron and **steel** as well as the **computer industry** (telecommunications, vending machines, industrial robots and machine tools). Although all raw materials – and the majority of foodstuffs – are imported, Japan has a **positive trade balance**. The country's modern infrastructure offers employment to around 60 per cent of the labour force in the **services sector** (trade, banks, invisibles), which accounts for 67 per cent of total GDP.

Japan, which is among the world's largest creditor nations, has experienced a **major economic slowdown** since 1997 whose effects have been largely mitigated by the state but which has had a seriously detrimental effect on neighbouring countries.

Transport Infrastructure

In spite of its mountainous terrain, Japan has an excellent, fully developed infrastructure.

All four of the main islands are connected to each other by **tunnels** and **bridges**. The Seikan-Tunnel, which at 53.9 km is the **longest underwater railway tunnel in the world**, connects Hokkaido with Honshu; the Akashi-Kaikyo-Bridge which at 3.9 km is the world's **longest suspension bridge**, stretches from Honshu to the Awaji Island. The country's **rail network** covers a length of 23,670 km, of which 11,952 km is electrified. The 7,000 km long **Shinkansen-Network**, which links the major cities by high speed ('bullet') trains, is of great importance for

JAPANESE MEGALOPOLIS

The landmarks of Kobe under a full moon: the red port tower.

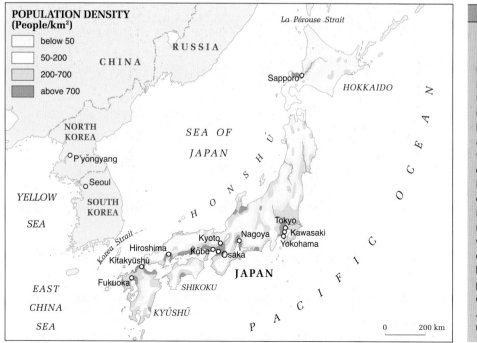

*The art of seduction that is never passionate: Japanese **geishas** are by no means submissive coutesans, but professionals of the disciplined and highly cultured art of entertaining men.*

individual travellers. The **road network** covers more than 1.14 million km, of which over 60,000 km are arterial roads and motorways. It is surfaced for two-thirds of its length.

The **vehicle density** of 552 vehicles per 1,000 inhabitants is among the largest in the world. In addition to numerous airports within the densely connected inland flight networks, there are three international **airports** in **Tokyo**, **Narita** and **Osaka**.

While the inland navigation routes with a total length of 1,770 km are of secondary importance, Japanese sea **ports** are among those with the **world's highest volume** of shipping. The most important international sea ports are Kobe, Hiroshima, Nagoya, Chiba, Tokyo and Sakai.

Tourism

Japan's attractions range from culturally and historically unique sites to charming landscapes and draw millions of visitors from abroad every year, despite the high cost of living and correspondingly high cost of hotel rooms and tourist facilities. There are also language difficulties; the Japanese often do not speak foreign languages and street signs are exclusively in Japanese.

The **capital city** and the **Osaka** region are regarded as the centres of tourism. Tokyo has a wealth of important museums and cultural sites; in the vicinity, there are the coastal town of **Kamakura** (famous for its large bronze Buddha) and the ancient town of **Nikko** set amidst charming mountain landscapes.

Osaka is the starting point for tours to the **old imperial cities of Kyoto** and **Nara**, which are among the highlights of touring Japan, especially the former with its important museum of Japanese artefacts and objets d'art. Kyoto also contains countless Buddhist and Shinto buildings and shrines; Nara has some of the **oldest Buddhist temples** in East Asia.

On the **Ise Peninsula**, there is the most important **Shinto relic**, along with the **Shrines of Ise**. Other towns worth seeing are Himeji, Hiroshima and Nagasaki. Opportunities for skiing, mountain-climbing and walking can be

found in the **'Japanese Alps'**. Among Japan's many areas of outstanding natural beauty, which range from landscapes, formed by lava flows and other volcanic action, there is the flora ranging from alpine to sub-tropical. Examples of such landscapes include the **Fuji-Hakone-Izu National Park**, south of Mount Fuji,

with its lakes and volcanic landscapes as well as the largely untouched **Shirakami-Sanchi mountain range** in northern Honshu. Equally charming, but less developed touristically, is **Kyushu** Island with its numerous active volcanoes, **hot springs** and well known spas such as **Beppu**.

1 Yokohama Bay is the gateway to Japan. The city of the same name has one of the world's largest harbours. Tokyo, Kanagawa and Yokohama have grown together to form one strip of urban development.

2 Imperial Kyoto: the steps lead up to the Kibune Shrine,

one of the most beautiful holy places of Shintoism.

3 A warren of streets: Tokyo is home to some eight million people, and there is a great lack of space. As a result, the face of the city is always changing. The skycrapers and motorways mirror this dynamism.

Thailand

Area:	513,115 sq.km
Capital city:	Bangkok
Form of government:	
Constitutional Monarchy	
Administrative divisions:	
73 provinces	
Population:	
65 million	
(126 inhabitants/sq.km)	
Languages:	
Thai (official), English, Chinese	
GDP per capita:	US$3,100
Currency:	1 baht = 100 stangs

Natural Geography

The west of the country is defined by extensions of the south-east Asian mountain range, which extends down into the **Malay** peninsula.
Rainforests cover the fertile lowlands which run from north to south. The delta of the **Menam** river is the most populated area. The **Korat plateau** in the east, gradually descends to the river **Mekong**.

Climate

Thailand has a **tropical climate** with year-round high temperatures and high humidity. The **rainy season** lasts from June to October.

Population

Up to 80 per cent of the populace lives in the countryside. The population consists of 80 per cent **Thais** with smaller groups of

Following independence, the country descended into **civil war** from which the military emerged victorious. Military dictatorship since 1962 has prevented any attempts at democratisation. Since 1993, a **national assembly** controlled by the military, has ruled the country.

Economy

The dominant economic sector is **agriculture** (rice, pulses, beans). The forests are good sources of hardwoods, such as **teak,** which are a profitable export. The highest export income derives from **diamonds** and **natural gas reserves**. The **opium plantations** in the 'Golden Triangle' are a not insignificant sector of the economy.

Transport Infrastructure

The road network is only developed around the main cities. The main form of transport is the **train**; some of the rolling stock dates from the pre-war era but is still used to reach many parts of the country. In contrast, the air travel network is very good. The only international airport is in **Yangon** (formerly Rangoon).

Tourism

The main points of interest for tourists are the **Buddhist monuments** in the capital Yangon (formerly Rangoon) and the temple city of **Pagan. Mandalay** is also worth a visit. The Shan Plateau in the central north-west has particularly attractive landscapes. Tourists are only allowed a 14-day visa.

History and Politics

The **Burmans** settled and established an empire in the eighth century. The region was later conquered by the **Mongols** in the thirteenth century. The power struggles between the ruling houses ended with the country being united under a Burmese dynasty in the year 1752. Between 1866 and 1948, Burma was under **British rule**.

and the minorities mainly live on the border and in remote areas.

Myanmar (Burma)

Area:	678,500 sq. km
Capital city:	Yangon
Form of government:	Republic
Administrative divisions:	
7 states, 7 districts	
Population:	55 million
(80 inhabitants/sq.km)	
Languages:	
Burmese (official), local languages	
GDP per capita:	US$230
Currency:	1 kyat = 100 pyas

Natural Geography

The country is surrounded by high mountains in the border regions, but the land becomes more open towards the coast. The **Arakan Mountains** in the southwest are covered in primeval forest, and here is the country's highest point, the 5,881-m-high **Hkakabo Razi**. In the east lies the **Ayeyarwaddy basin**, that ends in a delta on the Gulf of Martaban. This river is used to irrigate one of the largest rice growing areas in the world.

Climate

Myanmar has a variety of different climates in different regions. Near the coast, the climate is **equatorial**, but in the north it has more **sub-tropical** features. The average temperature on the plains is approximately 27°C.

Population

Myanmar is populated by a variety of different peoples, including **Burmans** (71 per cent) **Karen** (6.2 per cent), the **Shan** people (8.5 per cent), who live in a partially autonomous region, the **Rakhine** (4.3 per cent),the **Mon** (2.4 per cent) and other small ethnic minorities.
Roughly 90 per cent of the population is **Buddhist**, but there are also communities of Christians and Sunni Muslims. The Burmans live in the centre of the country,

Myanmar: royal barge on the Lake Inle in Ywama.

'The Golden Triangle': the border region between Myanmar, Thailand and Laos on the central Mekong plain was for a long time one of the largest opium cultivation regions of the world. While Thailand has been able to eradicate the cultivation of opium poppies, the plant is still grown in Myanmar, where the local population funds its fight against the military regime by selling the drug. After Afghanistan, Myanmar is the second largest opium producer in the world.

Chinese, Indians and Malays, and some mountain people. Some 95 per cent of the Thai people follow the **Buddhist** faith.

History and Politics

The **Thai empire** began to form in the thirteenth century, and its capital city was moved to **Bangkok** in 1782. In the nineteenth century, this empire ceded large areas to France and Great Britain. A coup d'état in 1932 led to the establishment of a **constitutional monarchy**. For many years, the formation of a modern state was hindered by repeated **attempted coups** and **unrest**, most recently in 2006.
Since 1998, a new constitution has been in effect, under which legislative decisions are the responsibility of a unicameral parliament. The head of state is the **monarch**.

Economy

Agriculture employs over 50 per cent of the working population. The main crops are rice, maize, cassava, sugar cane and rubber. The **manufacturing industry** mainly produces foodstuffs, but also motor vehicle and computer components, and contributes 44 per cent of GDP. Tourism represents most of the **service sector**, which accounts for 47 per cent of GDP.

Transport Infrastructure

Thailand has extensive and modern rail and road connections. Internal flights are also of great importance; the international airports are in **Bangkok** and **Chiang Mai**.

Tourism

Since the 1980s, Thailand has become a favourite holiday destination, despite problems with drugs, prostitution and the spread of AIDS.
In addition to **Pattaya** on the Gulf of Thailand and the southern island of **Phuket,** there are numerous tourist attractions such as the ruins of **Ayutthaya** and **Sukhothai** and the Khao-Yai national park. The Thais are also famous for their delicious cuisine and luxury hotels.

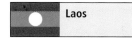

Laos	
Area:	236,800 sq.km
Capital city:	Vientiane
Form of government:	
People's Republic	
Administrative divisions:	
16 provinces and 1 prefecture (capital city)	
Population:	
6.5 million (27 inhabitants/sq. km)	
Languages:	
Lao (official), minority languages	
GDP per capita:	US$570
Currency:	1 kip

Natural Geography

The country is surrounded by the **Xiangkhoang Plateau** (2,817 m) to the north and the 2,000 m-high **Boloven Plateau** to the south. The **Mekong** flows through the country for a distance of 1,865 km. Forests cover 40 per cent of the land area.

Climate

Laos has a **tropical monsoon climate**. The rainy season lasts from May to September; in this period, the average temperature in the capital city is 27°C.

Population

The population consist mostly of ethnic **Lao**, who can be further divided into 70 ethnic groups. There are also ethnic minorities of **Vietnamese** and **Chinese**. The population is 60 per cent **Buddhist**. Three-quarters of the people live in rural areas and only the major cities and their surrounding areas have an electricity supply.

History and Politics

In the fourteenth century, the first Laotian kingdom was formed and Buddhism was introduced. After occupation by **Thailand** in the nineteenth century, Laos became

1 Thailand: the statues on the Grand Palace of Bangkok are demonic in appearance and are there to protect the precious Emerald Buddha inside.

2 The Buddhist leader of Laos resides in a modest residence in the former government city of Luang Prabang.

3 The grand Shwedagon Pagoda in Yangon, Myanmar is 450 m in circumference, 116 m high, coated with pure gold, and inlaid with 4,000 diamonds.

4 Thailand's capital, Bangkok: skyscrapers light up the skyline along the Chao Phraya River.

Laos, Cambodia, Vietnam

*Angkor was the former capital of **Khmer Empire**, whose influence spread far beyond Cambodia. The Angkor Wat Temple contains the mausoleum of King Suryavarman II, the glorious ruler of the Khmer in the twelfth century.*

a French protectorate, but regained **independence** in 1954. The Vietnam War spilled over into large parts of the country and Communist **revolutionary troops** conquered extensive tracts of land. In 1974, these revolutionaries became the government of the country. The **People's Democratic Republic of Laos** was proclaimed in 1975.

Economy

Laos was once a very isolated country, but since 1986, the economy has taken a successful course. **Agriculture** accounts for 80 per cent of the labour force mainly working in the paddy-fields, and farming contributes 50 per cent of GDP. The forests are excellent sources of **exotic woods** (teak, ebony, rosewood) for export. The forests are endangered, however, by the slash-and-burn clearances for **the cultivation of the opium poppy**. The **manufacturing sector** is very underdeveloped. The **services**

Vietnam: magnificent gate leading into the Dai Noi citadel in Hue.

sector is increasing in importance, in particular in the area of **tourism,** which has been permitted since 1988.

Transport Infrastructure

The road network is still very rudimentary, and roads are often barely passable during the rainy season. There is no rail network. The main transport artery is the **Mekong River**. The only

international airport is in **Vientiane**, the capital.

Tourism

Attractions include the former royal city of **Luang Prabang** and Vientiane. Cruises on the **Mekong** are particularly popular.

Cambodia	
Area:	181,035 sq.km
Capital city:	Phnom Penh
Form of government:	
Constitutional Monarchy	
Administrative divisions:	
21 provinces	
Population:	
14 million	
(77 inhabitants/sq.km)	
Languages:	
Khmer (official),	
Vietnamese	
GDP per capita:	US$510
Currency:	
1 riel = 10 kak = 100 sen	

Natural Geography

The lowlands of the **Tonle Sab basin** and the **Mekong delta** are enclosed by the Dangrek mountain chain in the north and in the south and south-west by the Cardamom mountains. The Mekong divides the lowlands into east and west. While the upper reaches are densely forested, further downstream there are many large areas

under cultivation. The Tonle Sab in the central plain is the largest inland waterway in south-east Asia and also has the largest fish stocks.

Climate

The country has a humid **tropical climate** with an average temperature of 27°C. The vegetation in coastal areas is mainly **mangrove swamp**, which gives way to **monsoon forests** in the central area and to **rainforests** in the mountains.

Population

The population is 90 per cent **Khmer**, with minorities of Vietnamese (five per cent) and **Cham** and **Chinese**. The majority (85 per cent) live in rural areas, and 95 per cent of Cambodians are **Buddhist**. Only 35 per cent can read and write.

As a result of the **war,** many unexploded landmines remain scattered across the country. The in-

Pol Pot
*Kompong Thom, 19.5.1928, † Anlong Veng, 15.4.1998
Originally a teacher, Pol Pot became the head of Cambodia's Communist Party in 1963 and led the Khmer Rouge in the 1970–1975 civil war. From 1976 to 1979 he was Prime Minister and introduced a kind of 'primitive Communism', murdering millions of his people, mainly intellectuals. After the Vietnamese invasion, he went underground and was condemned to death in his absence. He was leader of the Khmer Rouge until 1985.

adequate healthcare system and an absence of any social security structure, contribute to the country low life expectancy.

History and Politics

The ancient **Kingdom of the Khmer** was founded in the seventh century AD and collapsed in the seventeenth century after repeated attacks from neighbouring countries.

In 1867, the French occupied the region, defeating the Union of Indochina, and Cambodia did not regain **independence** until 1949. The French finally left Cambodia in 1954. The ruling **monarch** abdicated a year later and became president. The coup d'état in 1970 caused a **civil war**, which lasted for two years. The Communist **Khmer Rouge** emerged victorious and established a **reign of terror** that was brought down after an invasion by Vietnamese troops. After the Vietnamese withdrew in 1989, the State of Cambodia was proclaimed. An assembly charged with drawing up a constitution was voted for in 1993 under UN supervision. Cambodia became a constitutional monarchy and Prince Sihanouk became king once more. The last of the Khmer Rouge surrendered in 1998, and Cambodia became a member of ASEAN in 1999. The first free local elections took place in 2002. Sihanouk abdicated in October 2004 when he was replaced by his son, Norodom Sihamoni.

Ho Chi Minh
*Kim Lien, 19.5.1890, † Hanoi, 3.9.1969
In the 1920s, Ho Chi Minh organised the resistance to French colonial rule in Indochina. His Vietminh fought against the Japanese but after 1946, resumed the fight against the French. After the division of Vietnam, in 1954, he became the president of North Vietnam. He led the war against South Vietnam and became a symbolic figure for the student revolts in the West against the war.

Economy

Agriculture makes up one-third of GDP and this sector also employs some 80 per cent of the labour force. Rice is the main crop. Due to the absence of infrastructure, the **manufacturing sector** only contributes 28 per cent of GDP. Tourism is increasingly becoming an important growth factor and is sure to boost future exports.

Transport Infrastructure

The rail network connects the capital with Vietnam. Only part of the road network, that covers 603 km, is paved. Shipping on the **Mekong** is very important. There are international airports in **Phnom Penh** and **Angkor**.

Tourism

The main attraction is the temple city of Angkor Wat, north of the Tonle Sab.

Vietnam	
Area:	329,560 sq.km
Capital city:	Hanoi
Form of government:	
Socialist Republic	
Administrative divisions:	
7 regions; 52 provinces,	
3 municipalities	
Population:	
85 million	
(258 inhabitants/sq.km)	
Language:	Vietnamese
GDP per capita:	US$720
Currency:	
1 dong = 10 hào = 10 xu	

Natural Geography

Vietnam lies on the east coast of south-east Asia. **Tonking** is a region in the north containing the deltas of the Red and Black Rivers. South of this is the country's central region, the **Annam**, bordered by a long, jagged coastal stretch, which is only 40 km wide at its narrowest point. **Cochin-China** is in the south, and contains one of the largest river deltas on Earth, the mouth of the Mekong River, which covers an area of approximately 70,000 sq. km.

Climate

The coastal areas are affected by a **rainy season** which lasts from May to October and which sees large amounts of precipitation. The coastal regions in the south are covered in rainforest and mangroves. The climate in the north is more **sub-tropical**, with seasonal temperature variations. April is a particularly hot month with temperatures of up to 40°C.

*The tanks are abandoned but the ecological and economic cost of the **Vietnam War** is still very much in evidence today. The huge tunnel system of Cu Chi near Ho-Chi-Minh-City is one of the major memorials to the war in Vietnam.*

Temperatures in winter fall no lower than 17°C.

Population

Ninety per cent of the population is **Vietnamese**, but there are also minorities of **Chinese** (three per cent) and some **Thai** and **Khmer**. More than half the population are **Buddhist**.

History and Politics

In 1858, France occupied South Vietnam and incorporated it into its colony of **Indochina**. During World War II, the **Japanese** established a government for a short period of time, but this was abolished after their surrender. During the **Indo-Chinese War** of 1946 to 1954, the French colonial power succumbed to the Communist **Vietminh** guerrilas. The country was divided into the Communist North Vietnam and the Republic of South Vietnam. The north Vietnamese guerrillas aimed to reunite the country by force under Communist rule and this led in 1965 to an attack by the USA. The **Vietnam War** ended in 1975 with the capitulation of South Vietnam and the withdrawal of US forces. Vietnam has been reunited since 1976, but was not officially recognised by the United Nations until 1995. The **head of state** is chosen by the members of the National Assembly, who serve five-year terms of office.

Economy

Since 1986, Vietnam has been converting its economy from a socialist **state-run economy** to a **free-market economy** with some socialist orientation. **Agriculture,** which employs around 65 per cent of the labour force in the cultivation of rice, cereals, soya and coffee, has been successful and contributes 22 per cent of GDP. Vietnam is currently the second largest exporter of rice. The number of private companies in the **manufacturing sector** is continually rising and produces food, machinery and chemicals for export. Despite the economic successes of recent years, Vietnam is still an underdeveloped poor country. Large **areas of land** are still **contaminated** by the defoliants dropped by the

Americans and by land mines as a result of the long years of war.

Transport Infrastructure

Road and rail connects Ho-Chi-Minh-City with Hanoi. Only 25 per cent of the **road network** is surfaced. There are **International airports** in Hanoi and Ho-Chi-

Minh-City, which was once Saigon, the capital of South Vietnam.

Tourism

Vietnam offers natural wonders such as **Halong Bay**. **Ho-Chi-Minh City** and **the ancient capital of Hué** are among the important historical sites.

1 Daily life in Cambodia: Working elephants on the Siem Reap River near Angkor Wat

2 Extensive paddy-fields dominate the plains of the 70,000-sq.-km-large Mekong delta in Vietnam. Rice is cultivated here, yielding several harvests per year.

3 Women working in front of a pagoda in Soc Trang, Vietnam. The wide hat protects the shoulders from the burning sun.

4 Nature is reclaiming its territory: powerful tree roots wind around the walls in the Cambodian temple city Angkor Wat.

Malaysia

*One country, two worlds: while the indigenous peoples of **Borneo** still hunt with blow-pipes, the city of Kuala Lumpur has moved into virtual reality. Both worlds are located in Malaysia, but that may be the only similarity.*

Malaysia	
Area:	329 758 sq. km
Capital city:	Kuala Lumpur
Form of government:	
Constitutional Elective Monarchy within the Commonwealth	
Administrative divisions:	
13 federal states (including 9 Sultanates), 2 federal territories	
Population:	
25 million (75 inhabitants per sq. km)	
Languages:	
Bahasa Melayu (official), Chinese, Tamil, Iban, English	
GDP per capita:	US$5,700
Currency:	
1 Malayan ringgit = 100 sen	

Natural Geography

Malaysia consists of the southern part of the **Malay Peninsula** (West Malaysia) and – with the federal states of **Sabah** and **Sarawak** – the northern third of the **island of Borneo** (East Malaysia).

More than two-thirds of this predominantly mountainous country, with peaks of up to 2,000 m, is covered by a mighty **tropical rainforest**. Individual giant trees grow to a height of 60 m, with a circumference of 3 m.

West Malaysia is traversed north to south by a central **mountain range** 1,500–2,000 m in height on average, whose highest peak is **Mount Tahan** (2,190 m) in the state of Pahang. The south-east is has long **river valleys** and **alluvial plains**. The very flat

Kuala Lumpur: The Petronas Twin Towers are 452-m-high.

coastal areas are edged, especially in the east, by **kilometre-long white** sandy **beaches** and, in the west, by a long mangrove belt. East Malaysia's highest elevations are **Mount Murud** (2,422 m) in Sarawak and **Mount Kinabalu**, in northern Sabah, at 4,101 m the **highest mountain in south-east Asia**. Mangrove swamps predominate in the broad coastal plains. **Flora** and **fauna** are exceptionally varied. The largest flower in the world with a diameter of up to 1 m, the Rafflesia, grows only in Sabah.

Climate

Both parts of the country have a predominantly **moist tropical climate**, substantially determined by the **monsoons**. The average daytime temperature is 27°C, or 20°C in the uplands.

Population

Malaysia's population is composed of 64 per cent **Malays**, 27 per cent **Chinese**, and eight per cent **Indians**. The state religion is **Islam**; in addition there are Buddhists, Hindus and Christians. The official language is **Bahasa Melayu**.

History and Politics

The earliest evidence of human settlement in the area of present-day Malaysia comes from Sarawak: skull fragments from the **caves of Niah** date back 35,000 years. The Malay Peninsula was settled from the eighth to the second millenium BC by the **Orang Asli** and inhabited from the third millenium BC by **immigrants from South China**, particularly from the region of present-day **Yunnan**. The **Dayak** of Borneo are considered to be descendants of the original inhabitants, the Orang Asli.

During the first centuries AD a process of **'Indianisation'** took place in the peninsula, along with the founding of states. Up to the fourteenth century, various **Hindu** and **Buddhist** kingdoms dominated large parts of the region. The three most important of these were **Funan** (from the first century), **Srivijaya** (from the seventh century) and **Majapahit** (from the eleventh century).

Around 1400, the Malayan Prince Parameswara conquered the kingdom of **Malacca**. From this flourishing trade centre, at the time the largest city in south-east Asia, **Islam** began its triumphant advance through the ruling houses of Malaysia in the **fifteenth century**.

In 1511, the **Portuguese** conquered Malacca. The **Dutch** followed in 1641, and the **British** in the late eighteenth century. The British had already occupied North Borneo (now known as **Sabah**) in 1762, and leased Penang in 1786; they settled in **Singapore** in 1819, and took control of north-west Borneo (then known as **Sarawak**) in 1842. The **Straits Settlements**, Penang, Malacca and Singapore, became **British Crown Colonies** in 1867; in the Pangkor Treaty of 1874 the Malay sultanates subjected themselves to the British rule. The **Federation of Malay States** was founded in 1896, consisting of the sultanates of Perak, Selangor, Negri Sembilan and Pahang, with Kuala Lumpur as its capital. The **'non-federated Malay states'**, the sultanates of Kedah, Kelantan, Perlis and Trengganu in the north, were not ceded to the British by Thailand until 1909, and remained relatively autonomous, as did Johore in the south.

From 1941 to 1945, **Japan** occupied North Borneo and the Malay Peninsula. After Japan's surrender, the peninsula was at first ruled by a **British military government**, and Sarawak and Sabah became British colonies. In 1946, the sultanates under the British protectorate, the Crown Colonies of Penang, Malacca and Singapore (the last of which had meanwhile become self-governing) joined together to form the **Federation of Malaya** in 1948.

After a **guerrilla war** supported by the People's Republic of China, the Federation of Malaya was granted total **independence** under the **1956 constitution** on **31 August 1957**.

The state of Malaysia, proclaimed on **16 September 1963**, resulted from the union of the **Federation of Malaya**, Singapore (which left the Federation in 1965), **Sabah** and **Sarawak**; Singapore became independent in 1965.

According to the constitution – last changed in 1994 – the **king** is chosen every five years by the **council of rulers**, which consists of the **nine sultans**, from among their number. The monarch is the leader of the Islamic faith, of the military and government; he approves the **prime minister**

*Scenes from the Thaipusam Festival at the **Batu Caves** in Malaysia. Thousands of faithful climb the 272 steps to the caves to take part in the important Hindu festival. They test their faith in a trance by piercing themselves with needles.*

appointed by **parliament** and appoints some of the representatives of the **state assemblies**. Parliament is elected for a five-year term.

Economy

Malaysia is the **biggest producer of tin, rubber, palm oil** and **pepper**, as well as an important supplier of **tropical hardwoods** and of natural gas and petroleum.

The backbone of the economy, however, are the **high-tech** and **the automotive** industry. The **services sector** contributes 42 per cent of the country's GDP. The second largest source of income is **tourism**.

Transport Infrastructure

The well-developed, nationwide **road network** covers 93,975 km, of which 70,481 km are paved. **Buses**, **shared taxis** and **bicycle rickshaws** are important means of transport. Two **railway lines** run between Singapore and Thailand. Regular **flights and ferry routes** link the two parts of the country. The international airport, the **largest airport in Asia**, is at Kuala Lumpur.

Tourism

The cultural, economic and tourist centre of the country is the **capital**, Kuala Lumpur, which also proclaims its status with its 452-m-high **Petronas Twin Towers**. In addition it offers important museums and places of interest. On the coasts there are a number of seaside resorts with many opportunities for **water sports**. The most interesting of the **national parks** are the Taman Negara national park, the Gunung Mulu national park and the Sepilok Orang-Utan reserve, where tourists can explore the jungle and watch these fascinating primates. The local food is a great attraction in the cities.

Singapore

Area:	692 sq. km
Capital city:	Singapore
Form of government:	
Republic in the Commonwealth	
Administrative divisions:	
5 districts	
Population: 4.5 million	
(6,500 inhabitants per sq km)	
Languages:	
Malayan, English, Chinese, Tamil	
(all official)	
GDP per capita:	US$30,000
Currency:	
1 Singapore dollar = 100 cents	

Natural Geography

The group of islands on the **Malacca Straits** at the southern tip of the Malay Peninsula includes the rolling hills of the **main island of Singapore** and some **54 smaller islands**. A mere 5.5 per cent of the total land mass lies more than 31 m above sea level.

The native **fauna** and **flora** have been severely affected by human overpopulation.

Climate

Proximity to the equator ensures only **minor fluctuations in temperature** between 24°C and 31°C throughout the year.

The heavy **rainfall** of the **southwest monsoon** is concentrated between November and January.

Population

The population is 76.4 per cent **Chinese**, 14.9 per cent **Malay**, 6.4 per cent **Indian** and 2.4 per cent other ethnic groups. Singapore has **four official and teaching languages**, Chinese (Mandarin), Malay, Tamil and English. Apart from **Buddhists** and **Muslims** there is a also large **Christian** community.

History and Politics

In **1819,** a member of the British East India Company, **Sir Thomas Stamford Raffles**, acquired Singapore from a Malay sultan. In 1867 it became a **British Crown Colony**. From 1942 to 1945 Singapore was occupied by the **Japanese**. In 1946, it became a British Crown Colony with **self-government** and became a member of the **Malay Union**, and then joined the **Malay Federation** in 1948, from which it separated in 1950. In **1959**, Singapore was granted the status of an **autonomous state** and became **independent** in 1963 within the **Federation of Malaysia**. It finally became an **independent republic** in 1965. The head of state is the **president**, who, since 1991, has been directly elected; the **unicameral parliament** is elected every five years.

Economy

As one of the **leading centres of industry and services** in Asia, Singapore has a highly **export-oriented economy**, which continues to record high levels of growth. Thirty-five per cent of GDP is contributed by industry and 65 per cent by services.

Transport Infrastructure

The 2,686 km **road network** is well developed. A rail and road causeway links the main island with the Malay Peninsula. The **deepwater port** has one of the world's highest turnovers of shipping. Singapore has two **international airports** and is an important **air transport hub**.

Tourism

In addition to the attractions of the great modern city, Singapore is a model of cleanliness due to

*The immense crude oil and natural gas reserves have made the **Sultan of Brunei** one of the richest men in the world. His wealth increases by over US$ one billion a year – and he will get richer as the prices of oil and gas continue to soar.*

strictly enforced legislation. The 'fusion food' of south-east Asia is a big attraction in the cities. The offshore islands offer ideal **opportunities for scuba-diving and swimming** among the palm-fringed beaches and coral reefs.

Brunei

Area: 5,765 sq. km
Capital city:
Bandar Seri Begawan
Form of government: Sultanate
Administrative divisions:
4 districts
Population:
370,000 (64 inhabitants/sq. km)
Languages:
Malay (official), English
GDP per capita: US$30,600
Currency:
1 Brunei dollar = 100 cents

Natural Geography

Two unconnected land areas on the north-west coast of Borneo, surrounded by the **Sarawak Mountains**, form the country of Brunei. **Tropical rainforest** covers 60 per cent of the land.
The coast consists mainly of **alluvial soil** with **mangrove swamps**, interspersed with **sandy coral beaches**. The **hill country** in the interior is home to a **variety of wildlife**.

Climate

Brunei has a **wet equatorial climate**; temperatures range from 24°C to 30°C and there is high humidity.

Population

The population, the majority of which consists of Malays at 64 per cent with **Indians and Chinese** at 20 per cent, benefits from a comprehensive social security system as a result of the country's enormous wealth. The citizens pay no taxes, and healthcare and education are absolutely free.
Islam, the state religion, is that of 64 per cent of the population, while only about 14 per cent are **Buddhists** and ten per cent **Christian**.

History and Politics

Trade relations with **China** in the sixth century and with the **Javanese kingdoms** in the thirteenth to the fifteenth centuries led to early **Buddhist** and **Hindu** influences. In the fifteenth century, **Islamicised** Malays founded the **Sultanate of Brunei**. When the Portuguese explorer, **Magellan,** landed on the coast of Brunei in 1521, the fifth sultan ruled over large areas of Borneo, the neighbouring islands and the Sulu archipelago. In 1888, Brunei became a **British protectorate**.
After the **Japanese** occupation from 1941 to 1945 the Sultanate again became a **British colony** until the **1959 constitution**, which established the country's sovereignty.
In 1984, Brunei finally became **independent**. The Sultan, enthroned in 1967, took over the running of the state in 1973, and has ruled since 1984 as an **absolute monarch**, supported by a **council**. There is no right to vote and there are no political parties.

Economy

In this small country whose ruler is one of the richest men in the world, the **economy** is of little importance. Most foodstuffs are imported. Of the country's GDP, 60 per cent derives from **petroleum and natural gas**. With its rich reserves, Brunei is one of the **largest oil exporters** in the Pacific region.

Transport Infrastructure

Brunei has a well-developed **road network**. The two parts of the country are linked only by a ferry. The capital city has an

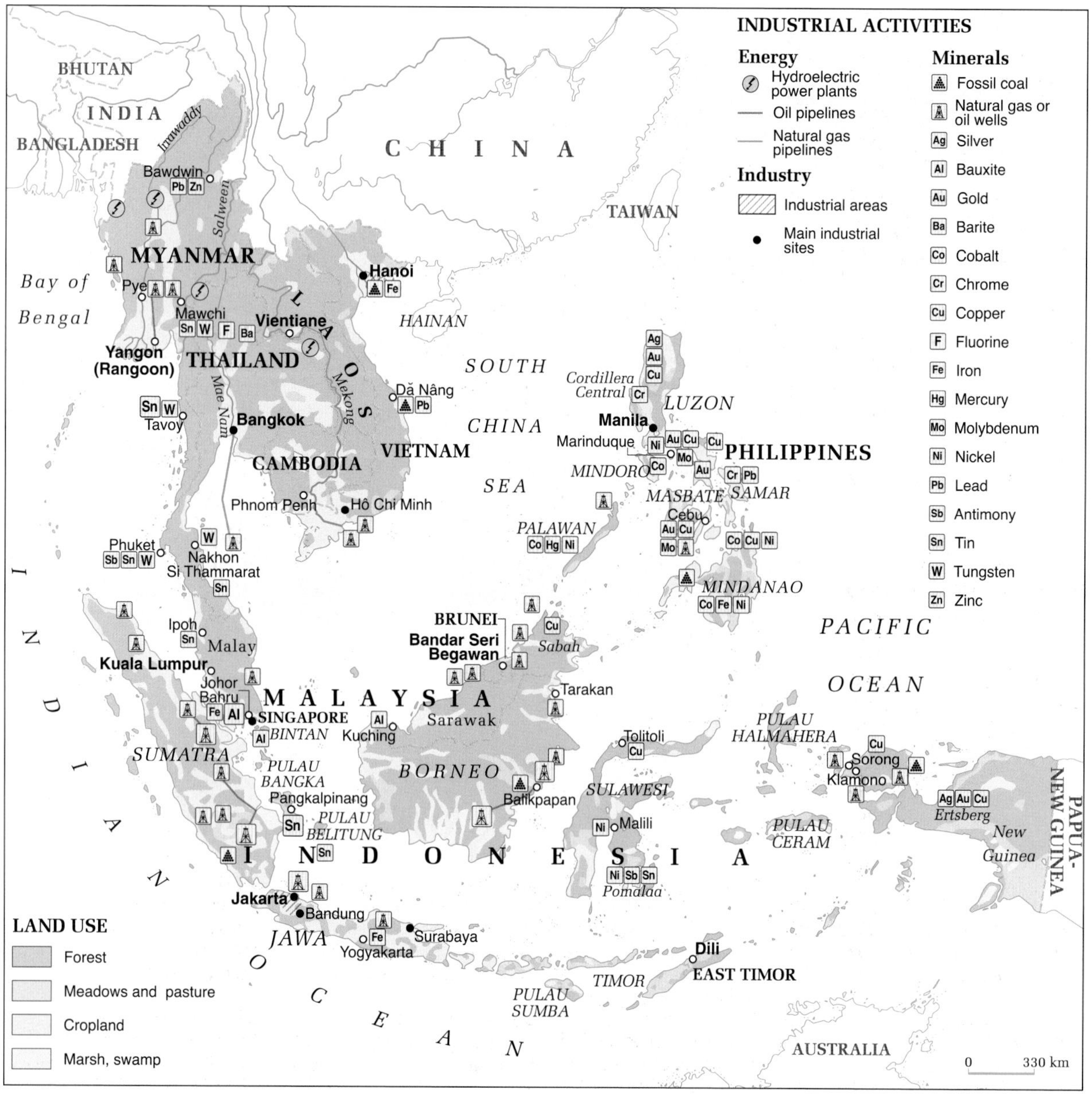
INDUSTRIAL ACTIVITIES
Energy
Hydroelectric power plants
Oil pipelines
Natural gas pipelines
Industry
Industrial areas
Main industrial sites
Minerals
Fossil coal
Natural gas or oil wells
Ag Silver
Al Bauxite
Au Gold
Ba Barite
Co Cobalt
Cr Chrome
Cu Copper
F Fluorine
Fe Iron
Hg Mercury
Mo Molybdenum
Ni Nickel
Pb Lead
Sb Antimony
Sn Tin
W Tungsten
Zn Zinc
LAND USE
Forest
Meadows and pasture
Cropland
Marsh, swamp
BHUTAN
INDIA
BANGLADESH
C H I N A
TAIWAN
MYANMAR
Bay of Bengal
Hanoi
HAINAN
Vientiane
LAOS
THAILAND
Yangon (Rangoon)
Bangkok
CAMBODIA
VIETNAM
Phnom Penh
Hô Chi Minh
SOUTH CHINA SEA
LUZON
Manila
PHILIPPINES
MINDORO
MASBATE
SAMAR
PALAWAN
Cebu
MINDANAO
PACIFIC OCEAN
BRUNEI
Bandar Seri Begawan
Sabah
Kuala Lumpur
MALAYSIA
SINGAPORE
Sarawak
Kuching
BORNEO
SUMATRA
SULAWESI
I N D O N E S I A
Jakarta
Bandung
JAWA
Surabaya
Yogyakarta
Dili
EAST TIMOR
TIMOR
AUSTRALIA
PAPUA-NEW GUINEA
New Guinea
INDIAN OCEAN
0 330 km

Ahmed Sukarno

*Surabaya, 6.6.1901,
†Jakarta, 21.6.1970

The founder of the Indonesian National Party (PNI) led the independence struggle against the Dutch colonial powers even before World War II. In 1945, he proclaimed the Republic of Indonesia, which was recognised by the Netherlands in 1949. He remained president until his official resignation in 1967, but from 1965 onwards was gradually disempowered by Suharto, his successor.

Bali's Kecak Dance tells the 2,000-year-old story of the kidnap of Princess Sita, who was rescued by Prince Rama with the help of a powerful army of monkeys. Narrative dances and other forms of story-telling, such as the shadow puppet theatre, are very important in Bali. The great wealth of Hindu mythology is brought to life by numerous performances and rituals. The island has more than 20,000 religious shrines.

international airport; the most important **deepwater port** and oil terminal is at Muara.

Tourism

Brunei has **no developed tourism**, but the capital with its old city, mosque and sultan's palace and the unspoiled jungle are major attractions.

Indonesia	
Area:	1,919,440 sq. km
Capital city:	Jakarta
Form of government: Presidential Republic	
Administrative divisions: 27 provinces, 3 provinces with special status	
Population: 230 million (120 inhabitants per sq. km)	
Languages: Indonesian (official), Javanese	
GDP per capita:	US$1,640
Currency:	1 rupiah = 100 sen

Natural Geography

More than **13,600 islands**, half of which are inhabited, extend in a curve more than 5,000 km long on either side of the equator. **Chains of volcanoes** run through western Sumatra and the Maluku (Molucca) islands; the highest of the **70 or so active volcanoes** is Kerinci on Sumatra at 3,805 m. The highest peak at 5,020 m is **Puncak Jaya** in the Maoke mountains of New Guinea.
More than half the land area is covered by **tropical rainforest**; in the wide **lowlands** of Sumatra and Borneo there are extensive **wetlands and freshwater swamp jungles**.
In December 2004, a violent tsunami inflicted devastating damage, particularly on Sumatra.

Climate

In the **moist tropical climate**, temperatures hardly vary throughout the year, at around 26°C.

Population

Indonesia is predominantly inhabited by **Malayan Indonesians**, of whom 45 per cent are **Javanese**, 14 per cent **Sundanese**, 7.5 per cent **Madurese** and there are other minorities. The largest groups of aborigines are the **Dayak** in West Kalimantan, the **Papua** in Irian Jaya and the **Balinese**. In addition there are a great number of **Chinese**, **Arabs**, **Indians** and **Pakistanis**. Some **250** different **languages** and **dialects** are spoken, of which **Javanese** predominates. The official language is **Bahasa Indonesia**, which, like English and Dutch acts as a channel of communication within this multilingual country. The **Islamic** faith is professed by 87 per cent of In-

donesians, with minority groups of **Catholics**, **Protestants**, **Hindus** and **Buddhists**.

History and Politics

As early as 1000 BC, **Protomalays** emigrated from the Asian mainland to become the earliest inhabitants of Indonesia. Through of trade with **China**, beginning in the early Christian era, and later with **India**, **Buddhist** and **Hindu** influences reached Indonesia.
From the ninth to the thirteenth century the kingdom of **Srivijaya** ruled the Malay Peninsula, western Java and Sumatra. In the late twelfth century, it was separated from the Javanese kingdom of **Majapahit**, which Islamicised the country from the thirteenth to the fifteenth century. The exception was **Bali** which remained Hindu.
In 1511, **Portuguese sailors** first landed on the Maluku Islands, known as the Spice Islands or the Moluccas. They were followed by the **Spanish**, **Dutch** and **British**, who had no problem playing off the local princelings against each other. Representatives of the **Dutch East India Company**, using **Batavia** as a base, conquered the whole archipelago within three centuries, took control of the lucrative spice trade and ruled the **colony of the Dutch**

1 High-rise offices dominate the skyline of Singapore. The city has become famous for its strict laws and has lost almost all of its historic quarters.

2 The Kek Lok Si Temple on the Penang peninsula is one of the largest and most attractive Buddhist temples in Malaysia.

3 Great contrasts in Jakarta: alongside the sparkling skyscrapers of the Kuningan district, the city's slums are constantly expanding.

4 The curving terraced rice fields blend harmoniously into the hillside, a common feature of the landscape in Bali.

Rice forms the staple diet in south, east and south-east Asia. Rice farmers reap the highest yields through shallow flooding irrigation – a process in which rice seedlings are propagated and replanted in a flooded field for cultivation. The top rice producing countries are China, India, Indonesia, Vietnam and

Thailand. On the left, you can see a patchwork of rice terraces laid out in the landscape of Longsheng in the Chinese Province of Guangxi Zhuangzu; on the right, rice farmers harvest their crop in Laos (top) and the production of rice cakes in a rice mill in Vietnam (bottom).

Indonesia, East Timor, Philippines

Rice is the staple food of south-east Asia, but its cultivation remains hard work. The rice has to be planted and harvested by hand. Ducks are used to eat the weeds that, if allowed to grow, would choke the crop.

East Indies until 1954, with short interruptions from 1811 to 1816 and 1942 to 1945 when it was occupied by the Japanese. As early as 1927, the **Partei Nasional** was founded, whose leader was **Sukarno**. He became president when Indonesia proclaimed its independence in 1945 although the colony had been returned to the Netherlands. The **Republic of Indonesia** was finally granted **independence** in **1949**, and five years later the union treaty with the Netherlands was dissolved.

Military coups, **uprisings**, and politically and religiously motivated unrest have since repeatedly troubled the country. The **presidential administration** of 1945 provides for a **unicameral parliament**, whose members are elected every five years. A proportion of the seats is reserved for **military personnel**, who are appointed directly by the president. The **People's Consultative Assembly**, which meets every five years, chooses the president and lays down policy guidelines. The **president** is both head of state and head of government.

Economy

Forty-four per cent the population works in **agriculture**. Rice, maize, cassava and sweet potatoes are the main crops for domestic use. Coffee, cocoa, tea and rubber are **exported**. Tropical hardwoods, rattan and copal are other important exports. More than 59 per cent of GDP is generated by agriculture and industry. The extremely rich supplies of petroleum and natural gas, coal, metals and minerals are the basis for the country's **highly developed heavy industry**, which produces exclusively for export.

Transport Infrastructure

There is **rail transport** on Sumatra and Java; the network, consisting mostly of narrow-gauge railway lines, is 6,458 km long. Half of the **393,000-km-long road network** is paved. The inland waterways are important arteries. Indonesia possesses a significant **merchant fleet** as well as more than 127 international ports. The domestic flight network is extensive and there are eight **international airports**.

Tourism

In addition to the sandy beaches that stretch for miles, Indonesia boasts has a plethora of outstanding cultural and historical sites. The Buddhist temple complex of **Borobodur** is considered the most important in Indian art, while the shrine of **Prambanan** is Indonesia's largest Hindu temple complex; both are on Java. Java is famous for its unique culture.

The Kutai National Park in southern Borneo is one of the **largest rainforests** in the world. The Gunung Leuser National Park in Sumatra contains countless species of birds and reptiles, as well as gibbons and **orangutans**. The island of Komodo is famous for the largest and most lethal reptile in the world, the **Komodo dragon.** The unspoiled island of Sulawesi is also famous for its jungles and wildlife.

East Timor

Area:	15,007 sq. km
Capital city:	Dili
Form of government:	Republic
Administrative divisions:	
13 districts	
Population:	
1m (67 inhabitants per sq. km)	
Languages:	
Portuguese and Tetum (official), Indonesian, English	
GDP per capita:	US$350
Currency:	
1 US dollar =100 cents	

Natural Geography

This republic covers the eastern half of Timor, one of the **Lesser Sundanese Islands**. The central mountain range includes the 2,960-m-high **Mount Ramelan**. The original vegetation has been destroyed except for some jungle.

Climate

East Timor has a **tropical monsoon** climate with a short rainy

season (December to March) and a dry period (May to October).

Population

The population consists predominantly of **Malays**, who are almost exclusively Roman Catholics, a relic of Portuguese colonisation.

History and Politics

East Timor was a **Portuguese colony** from 1695. The west of the island was **Dutch territory**. After World War II, the **western part** of the island was assigned to **Indonesia**. After the retreat of the Portuguese from 1975 a **civil war** broke out, and the victorious Fretilin party declared **independence**. In 1975/1976 **Indonesia annexed East Timor**. The Fretilin continued the battle against the Indonesian troops. Some 200,000 people died as a result of the Indonesian annexation policy.

In 1999, the majority of the population voted for **independence**. Indonesian troops and militias then destroyed the entire infrastructure of the country. In the autumn of 1999 the United Nations sent in a peacekeeping force and set up a caretaker government. On 20 May 2002, East Timor became independent. The Fretilin leader, **J. A. Gusmão**, was elected its first president.

Economy

The basis of the economy is the cultivation of **coffee**, rice, **manioc** and **coconut palms**. There are hopes of finding **petroleum and natural gas** in the Timor Sea. The economy is gradually recovering from the Indonesian occupation.

Philippines

Area:	300,000 sq. km
Capital city:	Manila
Form of government:	
Presidential Republic	
Administrative divisions:	
13 regions, 73 provinces	
Population: 90 million	
(300 inhabitants per sq. km)	
Languages:	
Filipino (official), Spanish, English	
GDP per capita:	US$1,350
Currency:	
1 Philippine peso = 100 centavos	

RAINFOREST

| | Present extension |
| | Deforested areas |

POPULATION DENSITY (People/km²)

	below 10
	10-100
	above 100

*The **Sulu Islands** in the Philippines are home to several completely different peoples. As a result, the Badjao on the island of Bongao have been able to preserve their wedding rituals. The bridesmaids paint their faces white before accompanying the bride to the marriage ceremony. Life is less peaceful on other islands in the group and some are in a state of war, sadly brought to the world's attention by the taking of hostages by the Abu Sayyaf islamicist rebels.*

Natural Geography

The Philippines constitute the north-eastern part of the Malay Archipelago. The country consists of some **7,100 islands**. The largest island, **Luzon**, in the north and the second largest, **Mindanao**, in the south, are separated by the **Visayas** islands, the largest of which is **Negros**. These mountainous islands are often subject to earthquakes and volcanic eruptions. Some 50 per cent of the land mass is covered with **tropical rainforest**.

Climate

The Philippines have a **dry tropical climate**; average temperatures all year round are between 25°C and 28°C.

Population

The population is composed of four per cent new Malay Filipinos (Bisayas, Tagalog, Bicol, Ilocano), 30 per cent Indonesians and Polynesians, ten per cent old Malayans (Igorots, among others) and Negritos (Aetas), ten per cent Chinese and five per cent Indians. Some 92 per cent of Filipinos are **Christian**, five per cent are **Muslim**, and in addition there are **Buddhists** and **animists**.

History and Politics

Trade relations with **China** and **India** are recorded from about 1000 AD. Islam probably began to spread only after the **arrival** of the Portuguese explorer, **Magellan**, in 1521, especially on Mindanao. **Spanish colonial rule** from the end of the sixteenth century caused almost the entire population to convert to **Roman Catholicism**. The **opening up of trade** from 1830 and economic growth led to **efforts to gain independence** in 1896, which were ruthlessly suppressed by Spanish troops. After the **victory** of the USA in the Spanish-American War of 1898, the area came under **American rule**. In 1935, the **Commonwealth of the Philippines** was founded in preparation for independence, but freedom was won only after liberation from the **Japanese occupation** of the Philippines that occurred between 1941 and 1945.

In 1946, the area was declared a **republic**, with the **USA** securing extensive rights to construct military bases. The **dictatorship** that followed, lasting more than thirty years, which destroyed the country in both economic and social terms, only ended in 1986 when President Ferdinand. Marcos was deposed in a popular uprising.

Economy

Farming is the only source of income for 37 per cent of the population, who cultivate grain and fruit as well as cash crops such as coconut palms and copra. This has enabled the country to become the **largest producer of coconuts and related products**. The **copper** and **nickel** deposits as well as **oil wells** form the basis of industry. The main export income is derived from the sale of **electronics** and **telecommunications** equipment.

Transport Infrastructure

The main mode of transport other than the roads is the domestic flight network with **more than 300 airfields** and there are also good ferry links between the islands. There are nine **international airports**. The only **railway line** operates on Luzon. The **road network** covering 200,000 km is largely unpaved.

Tourism

The centre of the country is the capital city, Manila, with its interesting colonial buildings. In the north of Luzon there are the **rice**-growing **terraces** of Banaue, one of the many scenic beauties of the country. Popular **leisure resorts** and **beaches** are found on Cebu, Mactan, Bohol, Boracay and Negros in the Visayas group of islands. Mindanao was popular for its jungle, but has been less frequented recently due to its militant Islamic minority.

1 A sampang, a typical boat in the Philippines, floating in El Nido Bay, surrounded by the hilly landscape.

2 Farmers from the surrounding area selling their wares in a vegetable market in Jakarta. The slim profits are barely sufficient for day-to-day survival.

3 The city of Cebu is an important trading centre in the Philippines. Even after dark, the market is bustling.

4 The famous Chocolate Hills on the island of Bohol are a collection of some 1,268 conical limestone hills 40 m high.

The famous Kecak dancers in
Bali appear with expressive
make-up and splendid costumes.

The Peoples of Asia

*In 1900 the population of the world's largest
continent was just over 800 million; 50 years
later it had already reached around 1.3 billion.
The population in most Asian countries has
since undergone an explosive growth. At a*

A folk-theatre performance in Western China.

*total of 4 billion people, approximately two-
thirds of the world's population lived in Asia at
the turn of the century, with China, India,
Indonesia and Japan among the most populous
countries, and the Indians and Chinese combining to make up more than a third of the
world's population.*

*With its diverse landscapes and cultures
embracing several millennia, Asia is home to
the widest range of peoples and ethnic groups.
The spectrum extends from city populations
living in modern, urban environments, such as
the Japanese or the Han in China, through to
what are still very traditional ethnic groups,
such as the Dayak or Batak in Indonesia.*

The almost 1 million Druze belong to a religious community formed in Cairo at the start of the eleventh century and alleged to derive from a branch of Shiite Islam. The majority of Druze, whose encrypted esotericism is accessible only to the initiated and who know no hierarchical distinction between men and women, live in Syria and Lebanon, with a minority population in Israel.

The Turks

Around 50 million ethnic **Turks** form part of the group of south-western **Turkic peoples**, whose origins are presumed to lie in the Mongolian **Altai region**. This group of Turkic peoples also included the **Seljuks**, who advanced as far as **Anatolia** in the eleventh century and played a major role in the spread of Islam. The mighty **Ottoman** empire evolved in around 1300, its domain embracing the whole of the **Balkans** and extending as far as **Africa** and **Palestine** in the sixteenth and seventeenth centuries. It was only in the 1920s, under **Ataturk**, that political reforms led to the separation of state and religion. Today, the rural population accounts for no more than about a third of Turkey's overall inhabitants. Traditional handicrafts (silver work, embroidery, carpets) play an important role in the lives of inhabitants in rural areas.

of the Kurds, whose country (Kurdistan) was divided up between Turkey, Iraq and Iran in the nineteenth century, belongs to the west Iranian sub-group of **Indo-Germanic languages**. The Kurds' traditional livelihood is based on agriculture and livestock breeding, with handicrafts – and carpet making in particular – also playing an important role. The Kurds are divided into larger **tribal groups (ashirets)** and their social order is based on close family relationships. However, women do enjoy greater freedom than those in strict Islamic societies and can even take the place of the male head of the family following his death.

In addition to the largely Muslim Kurds there is also the Yazidi community in Iraq and Iran, their religion containing elements of both the archaic Iranian and the Christian faiths. The Kurds in Turkey and Iraq have suffered persecution and violence for many years due to their attempts to gain autonomy.

a third of the area of Armenia is used for growing wheat, tobacco, vegetables, fruit and cotton, with livestock breeding also a key activity. Armenia, the first place in the world where **Christianity** was declared the official state religion (in around 300), was subject to **Persian, Arab, Mongolian, Turkish** and **Russian** rule for centuries. Over a million people lost their lives during the expulsion of the Armenians by the Turks during World War I. However, an independent culture has managed to develop under the significant influence of the autonomous Armenian Church, with literature in particular playing an important role, along with architecture.

The Georgians

Georgia, along with **Armenia** and **Azerbaijan**, is one of the Transcaucasian countries and comprises the autonomous casian languages; most Georgians are Georgian Orthodox, while the majority of the around 500,000 Adjarians are Muslims.

Following the Christianisation of Georgia in the fourth century, the country became subject to the alternating rule of the **Persians, Arabs** and **Turks**, until being largely destroyed by the **Mongolians** in the fourteenth century. The eastern part then fell to the Persians and the west to Turkey, with the Russians seizing power in 1801. Despite these numerous foreign influences Georgia has managed to develop a rich culture that survives today, particularly in the rural areas, and comprises music and art traditions as well as pre-Christian religious ceremonies.

The Chechens

Only around three-quarters of the approximately 1 million ethnic **Chechens** (indigenous name:

today. The Islamisation of the Chechens in the eighteenth century took place relatively late, as can still be seen from the remains of the old pre-Islamic tombs and stone ornaments. The Chechens – to whom the **Itchkeri, Kists** and **Galgans** belong, among others – are closely related to the Ingush people; traditionally they live in large families numbering between 40 and 50 members, many of whom amalgamate to form larger clans.

The Darginians

The area settled by the **Darginians** covers parts of **Azerbaijan** and **Kalmykian** reaching as far as the autonomous **Republic of Dagestan** in the North-East Caucasus, home to some 35 peoples and more than 70 different languages and/or dialects, also including the Avars (Turkish for 'wanderers'), **Laks, Kumyks** (Caucasus Tatars), **Lezgins,**

The Caucasus Peoples

In terms of language, the peoples of the Caucasus can be divided into three main groups. First there are the Indo-Germanic-speaking Armenians, Ossetians, Tatars and Talysh, then the Turkic-speaking Azerbaijanis, Kumyks, Karachays, Balkars and mountain Tatars and finally the Caucasian-speaking Georgians, Lezgins, Chechens, Cherkess, Abkhazians and Ingush. Violent secessionist struggles have flared up repeatedly since the 1990s, such as that between Chechnya and Russia.

In Turkey the production of fine faience painting is largely the task of women.

The Palestinians

'Palestinian' is the indigenous designation for all Arabic-speaking inhabitants of the former British Mandate of Palestine, the majority of whom are Muslims. Of a total of 7 million Palestinians, about 1 million live in Israel and almost 3 million in the autonomous and/or Israeli-occupied territories. About 1 million are accommodated in refugee camps in Egypt, Lebanon and in Syria. A further 1.5 million live in Jordan, which is the only Arab country to grant them citizenship.

The Kurds

The area settled by the almost 30 million **Kurds** covers southeast **Turkey, Iraq, Iran, Syria, Armenia** and **Georgia**; minority populations also live in **Lebanon**, as well as in **Jordan, Pakistan** and **Afghanistan**, with around 600,000 refugees residing in European countries. The language

The Armenians

About half of the around 7 million **Armenians**, whose name is of Persian origin, live **abroad**, especially in **Lebanon, Syria, France** and the **USA**. Their language belongs to the **Indo-European** group of languages and has its own alphabet, comprising thirty-eight letters. About

Republics of **Abkhazia** and **Adjaria** as well as the autonomous **South Ossetia**. It has a population of around 5 million people, only approximately 70 per cent of whom are **Georgians** (Grusinians), followed by **Armenians, Azerbaijanis, Russians, Abkhazians, Greeks, Kurds, Ossetians** and **Ukrainians**. The Georgian language (Kartuli) belongs to the branch of Cau-

Nokhchii, meaning 'people') live in the autonomous Republic of Chechnya, which declared its independence in 1991. The rest have settled largely in **Dagestan** and **Kazakhstan**, with a smaller number in Turkey. Their language belongs to the East Caucasian family of languages; it was originally written using the Arabic and later the Latin alphabet, with the Cyrillic alphabet still used

Nogais, Tabasarans and **Tats**, who belong to the Dagestan group of peoples encompassing about 1.5 million people, largely of the Muslim faith.

In addition to farming – mainly wheat, maize and sunflowers are cultivated, using terraced farming – the Darginian economy is largely based on handicrafts, particularly carpet making and wrought iron work. The Dagestan

As is the case throughout the Near and Middle East, tea is the most important beverage in Yemen, where it is always freshly poured and served hot in small glasses at any time of the day. The men meet to drink tea, exchange news and chat in the many public tea houses that replace the 'corner bar' in Islamic countries, where the Koran forbids the drinking of alcohol in any form.

peoples share a relatively similar cultural tradition.

The old epic songs performed by three singers (aschug) and accompanied by a triangular lute (agatsch komuz) remain universally popular, as do folk dances such as the Lezginka, enjoyed throughout the Caucasus.

The Azerbaijanis

About 20 per cent of the approximately 30 million **Azerbaijanis** live in Azerbaijan, the most populous country in the Caucasus. About 7 million of them have settled in the CIS states and around 15 million Azerbaijanis live in Iran, where they make up 25 per cent of the overall population. Their official language (Azeri) belongs to the group of **Turkic languages** and used to be written alternatively in the Arabic, Latin and Cyrillic alphabets. Today the Latin alphabet is once again in force.

Almost half the population of Azerbaijan still live in the countryside, their livelihood based largely on growing vegetables, cotton, wheat, fruit, tea, rice, tobacco, olives and mulberries, and on breeding livestock (sheep, goats, cattle). Handicrafts – in particular carpet making, along with brazing, gold work, woodcarving and **silkworm breeding** – form other sources of income.

Azerbaijan was conquered by the Arabs in the seventh century and then by the Mongolians in the thirteenth century; it fell to the Persians in the seventeenth century, who then ceded the north to the Russians in the nineteenth century, with the south remaining an Iranian province.

The Jews

The designation 'Jew' refers to all members of the Jewish religion and their descendants. The Tora and the Talmud are the most important religious sources and Jerusalem is their religious base. The key festivals are the Jewish New Year (Rosh Hashana), the Day of Atonement (Yom Kippur), the Feast of Tabernacles (Sukkot), the Festival of Lights (Hanukka)

and Passover. The first Jewish diaspora occurred as far back as 722 BC following the conquest of the Jewish heartland, Palestine, by the Assyrians and the abduction of Jews to Mesopotamia. The Jews have been subjected to repeated persecution and expulsion throughout the course of history, with Jewish communities developing in Europe and North Africa, as well as in the Near and Middle East. In Europe the distinction was made between Jews from the east (Ashkenasim) and the west (Sephardim). The national Jewish movement, Zionism, developed at the end of

the nineteenth century as part of the reaction to the recurrent anti-Semitic pogroms; it lead in 1948 to the founding of the state of Israel as the homeland of all Jews and had been preceded by what was the culmination of anti-Semitism, namely the mass murder of 6 million European Jews by the National Socialists in Germany. This almost completely wiped out the Jews of Eastern Europe. Only a fraction of European Jews were able to escape to the USA. There are 100,000 Jews living in Germany today, and approximately 15 million worldwide. Around 5 million Jews live in **Israel**, founded on **Palestinian territory**, together with around 1 million **Palestinians** of Arab descent. Palestine has been the scene of (civil) war/conflict between the Palestinians and the Jews since 1948, with the founding of a Palestinian nation and the granting of land and settlement rights for both peoples the central issues.

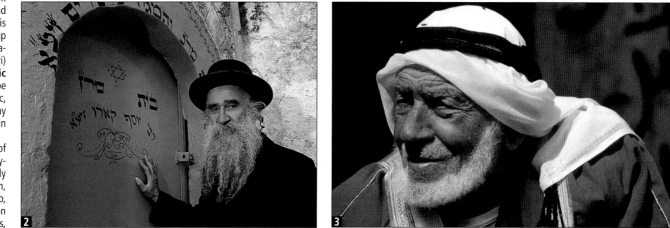

The Arabs

The term '**Arab**' embraces all populations of Arabian descent and/or Arab-speaking groups in the countries of **North Africa**, the **Near** and **Middle East** and the **Arabian Peninsula**. Today, there are over 150 million Arabs,

1 A familiar sight in all Eastern countries: the leisurely smoking of the narghile, here in Cairo.

2 Strict adherence to the commandments of the Tora and the Talmud has characterised the everyday life of Orthodox Jews for more than 2,000 years.

3 As a result of the conflict with Israel, many of the around 7 million Palestinians live in exile or are housed in camps.

4 In Yemen the curved daggers worn openly on the belt continue to be a prominent symbol of courage, pride and manhood.

The members of the Dervish order, whose whirling dances came to be known in the West, are followers of the Islamic mystics also known as Sufis. Sufism as a means of attaining the goals of devotion and adherence to the love of God (Tariqat) developed in northern Iran in the eighth century, spreading to all Islamic countries via the Dervishes. Famous Sufis included Rabia al-Adawiya, a female Iraqi mystic, the Egyptian Dhu'n-Nun and the Persians Al Ghazali and Djelalledin Rumi.

approximately 95 per cent of whom are **Muslim**, with the balance being largely **Christian** and **Druze**. Due to the common Islamic influence shared by all Arab peoples, there is a largely similar social order despite what are sometimes significant ethnic differences. The Arab language belongs to the **south-west Semitic family of languages** and is divided into a northern and a southern sub-group.

The Persians

Around 30 million **Persians** make up approximately half the population of Iran, their name being attributed to the Ancient Persian **Arynam** ('Land of the Aryans'). They are the descendants of **Indo-European peoples** (Medes, Persians, Parthians) from southern Russia. They are thought to have settled in the area in around 1600 BC and it is from their language that modern-day **Persian** (Farsi) derives, having adopted numerous Arab words following the Arab conquest of Persia in 632 and the subsequent **Islamisation**.

Today around two-thirds of the Iranian population live in urban areas, and the livelihood of the rural population is based on cultivating tea or fruit, depending on the climate of the region. The Persians formed a link between the Near East and Central Asia, their empire, which in the sixth century BC also comprised **Babylon**, **Palestine**, **Syria** and **Asia Minor** and which was conquered by the **Greeks** (Alexander the Great), the **Turks**, the **Mongolians**, the **Afghans** and the **Russians** during the course of history, making contact with numerous other cultural elements.

The population of Iran is almost entirely **Muslim**, of whom about 90 per cent are followers of the Shiite faith, which is also the state religion; around eight per cent are Sunni Muslims and a further, smaller group is made up of the **Zoroastrians**, whose religion originally derived from the prophet **Zoroaster** in the sixth century BC. Zoroastrians were persecuted in their homeland because of their faith, and many fled to India in the thirteenth century, where they live today as **Parsees** ('Persians') mainly in the area around the city of **Bombay**.

The Bachtiaris

The 700,000 **Bachtiaris**, who belong to the Iranian family of languages and peoples and who are members of the Islamic Shiite faith, inhabit south-west Iran. Until approximately 50 years ago they were the most politically influential group in the country next to the **Qashqai**.

Living as seasonal or semi-nomads in the past, the Bachtiari were traditionally divided into two large groups (taifa), which were themselves then subdivided into several sub-groups led by a local tribal leader (khan). The **khans** were headed up by a central ruler (ilkhan), whose power came to an end only under the rule of the first Persian **Shah** (1925–41). The majority of Bachtiaris were consequently forced to give up their nomadic lifestyles.

The Lors

The area settled by the around 600,000 **Lors** covers the **mountain regions** of the province of **Lorestan** in south-west Iran. The Lors speak partly **Kurdish** and partly **Lori**, which belongs to the **south-west Iranian family of languages** and is closely related to the Bachtiari language. The Lors are members of the **Schiite faith** and live as seasonal nomads, largely making their living from livestock farming. They used to be considered a warlike people whose culture and way

Camel racing is a popular Arab pastime.

of life resembled that of the adjoining Kurds. Like the Bachtiari, the Lors are traditionally divided into numerous tribes and sub-tribes (tirah), each of which is subject to a tribal prince (khan).

The Qashqai

Around 700,000 Qashqai, whose language belongs to the **West-Turkic family of languages**, live in the **province of Fars in south-west Iran**. Their forefathers are thought to have come to **Persia** from **Turkestan** in the fourteenth century. Next to the Bachtiaris, they were among the largest and most politically influential nomadic tribes in Iran up until approximately 40 years ago. Their economic livelihood is based mainly on livestock farming, and a further important source of their income comes from the production of their highly elaborate **Shiraz carpets**. The extended family forms the Qashqai's most important social unit and their possessions are shared equally among family members. Islam played only a relatively minor role among the Qashqai for a long time, as a result of which women could hold important positions within the community in the past.

The Bani Lam

The small **Bani Lam** ('descendants of Lam') ethnic group belongs to **Iran**'s Arab population, which makes up about one per cent of the country's overall inhabitants. The name of the Bani Lam people, who live in the north-west of **Iran** and who are members of the Shiite faith, derives from the famous **Lam Ben Harita**, leader of the **Quahan** tribe on the **Arabian Peninsula**.

The Quahans controlled the pilgrim routes to **Medina** until they were expelled in the fifteenth century, initially settling in **Iraq** and later in **Persia**. Today the Bani Lam, who used to live as nomadic livestock farmers, are largely settled crop farmers.

The Balochs

Of today's around 4.5 million **Balochs**, approximately 1 million of them live in **East-Iranian** and 2.5 million in **West-Pakistani Balochistan**, with minority populations to be found in **Afghanistan**, **Turkmenistan** and **Oman**. The Balochs, the majority of whom are **Sunni Muslims**, belong to the Iranian group of peoples and their language (**Balochi**) is closely related to **Persian**.

They live either as farmers or seasonal nomads (cattle, goats, sheep, camels), depending on the region, and are thought to have settled originally in **Northern Iran** from where they were ousted by the Turkic **Seljuks** in the eleventh century and later by the Mongolians in the thirteenth century.

Today the Balochs, who can trace their descent back to a common twelfth-century ancestor, have a social order still largely determined by the traditional tribal structures, with the different tribes (Bollak, Tuman) ruled by a tribal leader (sadar). In Europe the Balochs are known primarily for their **Baloch carpets**, which are also produced by the nomadic **Aimaq** in **Afghanistan**.

The Turkmen

In addition to the **Republic of Turkmenistan**, the settlement area of the approximately 5 million **Turkmen** nowadays also embraces **Syria**, **Iraq**, **Iran** (700,000), **Afghanistan** (500,000) and the Transcaucasian countries as well as **Turkey**. The Turkmen are the descendants of an **Oghuz Turkic people** who originally came from **Mongolia**, their language belonging to the **western group of Turkic languages**. The Turkmen used to be nomadic livestock farmers and the men in particular were known for their striking lambskin hats, but nowadays the majority live as settled farmers breeding livestock (Karakul sheep, camels, horses, cattle) and silkworms; they are also crop farmers (corn, vegetables, cotton, fruit).

Today the Turkmen's traditional social structure is still based on classification into numerous tribes; they largely follow the Muslim faith but still retain a number of customs from the pre-Islamic era such as **shamanism** and **ancestor worship**, for example.

In addition to handicrafts – their silver jewellery and knotted carpets merit special mention – Turkmen cultural tradition also comprises folk literature, some of which is passed on via an oral tradition.

Islam

Islam, the world's second largest religion after Christianity, has more than a billion followers, of which some 700 million live in Asia, 270 million in Africa, 35 million in Europe and 5 million in America. Islam has also been declared the state religion in around 40 African and Asian countries.

Islam derives from the Prophet Mohammed (*c.* AD 570–632), originally a merchant from Mecca, who witnessed a revelation in a cave near Mecca in 610. According to the revelation, Mohammed preached that there is only one God who will prevail over the world on Judgement Day. This was in contradiction to the prevalent polytheistic religious traditions of the time and hostility from his fellow citizens forced Mohammed to flee to Medina in 622, the start of the Islamic calendar.

Following the conquest of Mecca in 630, in the aftermath of which he ordered the former images of deity to be destroyed,

Mohammed gained ever more followers, and Islam evolved and spread rapidly through Africa and Asia. Mohammed himself recorded the revelations imparted to him between 610 and 632 in Arabic in the Koran, the holy book of Islam, divided into 114 chapters (sura). In addition to biblical stories these sura also contain the description, in verse, of God's seven heavens and the horror of hell awaiting humans after death depending on the life they have led, along with numerous commandments. The sura also include the five holy obligations that every believer has to fulfil: the first being Shahada, the profession

of faith, and the second being the duty of prayer (Salat), which has to be performed five times a day in the direction of Mecca. The muezzin calls the faithful to

prayer from the minaret of the mosque, the prerequisites for prayer including ritual washing and a clean place to pray, symbolised by a prayer mat. The third obligation is Sawm, which requires fasting in the ninth month of the lunar year (Ramadan), when the daily fasting period lasts from dawn to dusk, during which nothing may be

eaten or drunk. The fourth and fifth obligations are the giving of alms to the needy (Zakat) and the pilgrimage (Hajjh) to the holy sites in Medina and to the Kaaba in Mecca, which every Muslim is expected to make once in his lifetime. Every year around 2 million people from throughout the world make this journey.

Large image: South Yemeni women with the burka (veil) prevalent in the region.

Top left: In Bandarabas (Iran), too, only heavily veiled women are seen on the streets.

Top right: A believer immersed in the Koran in front of the large mosque in Peshawar.

Below: Thousands worship at Friday prayers in Teheran.

Central Asia

Samarkand in Uzbekistan, one of the oldest cities in Central Asia, founded in the fourth century BC, is a symbol of the glorious oriental past. With its strategic central position on the trade route between the Mediterranean and the Far East (the Silk Route), it was in ancient times an important trans-shipment base for goods of every kind. Today its inhabitants make their livelihood mainly from trading vegetables, fruit and tea, and from tourism.

The Uzbeks

The modern-day settlement area of the approximately 20 million Sunni Muslim **Uzbeks** (indigenous name: O'zbek) covers **Uzbekistan**, **Kazakhstan**, **Tajikstan** and **Afghanistan**, with a small minority also living in **China**. Their original homeland is thought to have been in southeast **Mongolia**, with their name deriving from Ozbek, a powerful fourteenth-century ruler of the Golden Horde. The distinction is made between the 'real' Uzbeks and the descendants of the initially **Persian**, and later **Turkic-speaking**, indigenous inhabitants of Uzbekistan.

In addition to agriculture (rice, vegetables, fruit, cotton, tobacco) and silkworm breeding, the livelihood of the Uzbeks is based mainly on trade and handicrafts, which include the production of silk fabrics (ikat) and embroidered cloths (susani), as well as brazing and woodcarving.

The Dalai Lama

Until the occupation of Tibet, the current 14th Dalai Lama – whose lineage extends back to the fourteenth century and who is considered the reincarnation of Buddha – was the absolute religious and political leader of all Tibetans; the seat of his government was the Potala Monastery in Lhasa. In 1959 he fled on foot over the Himalayas to Dharamsala in Northern India where he has since lived in exile. According to the Tibetan spiritual tradition, namely Mahayana Buddhism, the Dalai Lama will be reincarnated as a child after death.

The Kazakhs

Of the almost 10 million **Kazakhs** (indigenous name: Qazaq – the independent), about 8 million live in **Kazakhstan**, which was known as Kirghizia until 1924, and the balance live in adjoining **China**. They are the descendants of **Turkic-Mongolian peoples** who entered the modern-day settlement area of the Kazakhs about a thousand years ago. Their language belongs to the north-western group of **Turkic languages**.

The Kazakhs are among the largest group of **nomadic peoples in Central Asia**, crossing the wide, open steppe and the desert regions of Kazakhstan with their herds of livestock (sheep, horses, camels, yaks, cattle, goats) and their easily transported yurts (traditional tents). Nowadays, however, many Kazakhs also make their living from trade and handicrafts – especially felt embroidery, wooden and leather goods – while others have settled as farmers and make their livelihood from agriculture (millet, wheat).

Due to their nomadic lifestyle, Islam, which was only introduced in the nineteenth century, has made only superficial progress and the Kazakhs still retain many customs from the pre-Islamic era, such as **shamanism** and **ancestor worship** (avrak).

The Kirghiz

There are around 3 million Kirghiz and they originally came from the **Mongolian Altai region**. Their language belongs to the **Turkic languages** and their territory covers **Kirghizistan**, **Uzbekistan**, **Tajiikstan** and **China** as far as **Northern Afghanistan**. Following the destruction in the thirteenth century of their former empire by the **Mongolians**, the Kirghiz settled in the area that they inhabit today, living as nomadic livestock farmers in traditional **felt tents** (yurts) until the early twentieth century. Most now live in adobe or stone houses and make their living from livestock farming (sheep, cattle) and crops, including corn, potatoes, vegetables, fruit, tobacco and poppies.

The Kirghiz social order is based on membership of one of forty tribes, each of which has a **chief** (**manap**) who is selected according to his possessions. The extended family is the smallest social unit, with several families with a common ancestor usually combining to form an economic unit. Some Kirghiz men still wear the traditional white felt hat and some of the women wear white or dyed headscarves. The Kirghiz have been Muslim since the nineteenth century but many customs from the pre-Islamic era have been retained, including

The Kholi settlement area is Pakistan's Indus Valley.

shamanism, the **belief in spirits** and **ancestor worship**, and the typically **monumental Kirghiz tombs** also derive from this period.

The Tajiks

The territory of the **Tajiks**, of whom there are around 10 million, today covers **Tajikistan** and Afghanistan, where they make up roughly 25 per cent of the population. There are minority populations living in **Uzbekistan**, **China** and **Northern Pakistan**. They belong to the **Iranian group of peoples** and their language (Dari), which is also the lingua franca in Afghanistan, is based on an **Ancient Persian dialect**. The majority of Tajiks are either **Sunni** or **Ismaili Muslims**. The economic livelihood of the Tajiks, whose traditional social order has no tribal divisions, is based on farming, livestock breeding, handicrafts and trade.

The Hazara

Today there are around 4 million Hazara; they form **Afghanistan**'s fourth largest population group, although many live as refugees in the adjoining countries of **Iran** and **Pakistan** due to the political situation. The Hazara are descendants of Mongolian **nomads** who reached their current settlement area in the thirteenth and fourteenth centuries. Their language (Hazaragi) belongs to the **Western-Iranian group of languages** and is a Persian dialect with many words borrowed from Mongolian. The Hazara, largely **Shia Muslims**, live primarily from livestock breeding (sheep, goats) and terraced farming. They are also considered skilled craftspeople and are known for their felt and woven carpets (kelims). Due both to the lack of land for pasture in their settlement area and the takeover of the fertile areas by the Paschtuns, many Hazaras have been forced to migrate to the towns as hired hands.

The Pashtuns

Of the 20 to 25 million largely **Sunni Pashtuns** (Pathans – ethnic Afghans), who make up 40 per cent of the population of **Afghanistan**, several million live as refugees in **Iran**, **Pakistan** and **India**. Their language, Pashto, belongs to the **Iranian group of languages** and is the second official language in Afghanistan after Dari. The Pashtuns are considered a proud people and with the Tajiks they have played a state-supporting role since the founding of Afghanistan in 1747, a country that today comprises numerous population groups speaking **45 different languages**. They are divided into several **tribes** (Quaum, Taifa) and **clans** (Khel) ruled by a chief (khan, malik). Conflicts and differences of opinions between the **tribes** and the clans are settled in the **council meetings** (djirga), and the traditional **code of values** (pashtunweli), which contains generous guest and asylum rights, plays an important role. The Pashtuns' livelihood is based on crop and livestock farming, as well as trade and handicrafts, particularly in the towns. Afghanistan's infrastructure has been largely destroyed as a result of the lengthy war against the occupying Russian forces, the **Taliban** rule and the offensive by the USA in 2002. It is now to be rebuilt under international supervision.

The Sindhi

The territory of the approximately 7 million **Muslim Sindhi** embraces the Pakistani province of **Sindh** and Western **India**; their language (Sindhi) belongs to the group of **Indo-Aryan languages** and has been the official language in **Pakistan** since 1973. The Pakistani Sindhi are competent traders but have encountered competition in recent decades from immigrant Indian merchants. Sindhi men can usually be recognised by their blue or red turbans (ajrak), which are wound from metre-long strips of fabric; the women wear the harem pants (salvar) common throughout the region under their knee-length dresses (kamiz).

The Tibetans

Almost 50 per cent of the approximately 5 million **Tibetans**, whose language belongs to the Tibeto-Burman branch of the

About 80,000 Sherpa ('Eastern People') live in Nepal's mountain regions as well as in the capital Kathmandu. Originating from the East-Tibetan province of Kham, they settled south of the Himalayas in the fourteenth century and grow potatoes, maize and corn in fields at an altitude of almost 5,000 m, also earning a living through livestock farming (yaks) and trading. The Sherpa are renowned as porters and mountain guides for Himalayan expeditions.

Tibetan family of languages, today live outside Tibet as refugees, mostly in **northern India**. Their religious leader is the **Dalai Lama** ('Lama' meaning teacher), who was also their secular ruler until the **Chinese** occupation of the country in 1950.

The majority of Tibetans live traditionally as nomads or semi-nomads from livestock farming (cattle, yaks, horses, sheep, goats) and from growing crops such as barley, wheat, millet and buckwheat, along with fruit and vegetables in the lower-lying areas, while in the towns handicrafts and trade are important activities.

Today Tibetan society, in which women traditionally enjoy equal rights, is still largely characterised by **Buddhism**. The monasteries, in which music and literature together with the arts of handicrafts, printing and painting (thangkas) were fostered, used to be the cultural hubs. Some of them were also bases for **Tibetan medicine**. About 6,000 of the monasteries were destroyed during the course of the Chinese occupation and tens of thousands of monks and nuns expelled, arrested and murdered.

The Mongolians

Some 2.3 million of the approximately 7.5 million **Mongolians** live in the Republic of **Mongolia** with around 5 million in the **Mongol autonomous region** or **Inner Mongolia** in China, and minorities in **Tibet** and **Northern Afghanistan**. The Mongolians also include other smaller or larger groups of peoples, such as the **Burjats** and **Kalmyks** (Kalmykians). Their language is divided into eastern and western branches and belongs to the **Altaic** family of languages.

During the Middle Ages the Mongolians were a much-feared equestrian people known as the Golden Horde. Led by their legendary ruler **Genghis Khan** in the early thirteenth century, and then by his descendants, including **Kublai Khan**, over the next 300 years the Mongolians extended their vast empire until at times it embraced the whole of **China** and

Russia, **Iran**, **India**, the **Caucasus** and **Turkey** as far as the **Baltic Sea** to **Silesia**, as well as reaching the **Adriatic** to the south. Today many Mongolians still live as seasonal or semi-nomads livestock farmers, seeking out pastures often at huge distances from each other with their large herds (horses, yaks, cattle, sheep, goats) and their traditional **yurts** (tents) as accommodation. A further important source of their income comes from crop farming, primarily barley and millet. However, the slowly expanding industrial sector now plays an increasingly important role.

The Mongolians are **Lamaist Buddhists** but also practise **shaman rituals**; they have a traditional social order based primarily on the extended family, with a number of families sharing a common ancestor usually amalgamating to form large clans.

The Buryats

The **South Siberian Buryats**, along with the 350,000 Buryats in the autonomous **Buryat** Republic in Russia, also live as minority populations in **Irkutsk**, **Chita** and **Mongolia**. They are descended from the Khori, a Mongolian people mentioned in the *Secret History of the Mongols* (thirteenth-century) who interbred with Turkic tribes. Their language belongs to the **East Mongolian group**. The Buryats are divided into the **West** and the **East Buryats**, depending on their settlement area. Apart from a Christian minority, they are

Tibetan Buddhists and also practise **shamanism**. The Buryats live traditionally as nomads from livestock farming or as settled farmers from crop growing, with fur hunting providing a further source of income. Their social order is based on family clans, each of which is headed by the eldest male family member.

1 For decades the governments of Central Asia have tried in vain to persuade the nomads to adopt a settled way of life.

2 Very different peoples with their own culture and language live in the small nation of Nepal at the foot of the Himalayas between Tibet and India.

3 Nepalese women contribute to the family's livelihood with their sewing work.

4 Yurts are the typical form of housing among the Mongolian nomads. These stable, round tents provide enough space for the extended family and are easy to transport.

Eastern Asia

Since their subjugation by the Japanese in the fifteenth century, the approximately 20,000 Ainu (meaning 'person') – Japan's indigenous inhabitants – have lived mainly on the island of Hokkaido. Their language defies allocation to any language group and is rarely spoken today.

The Han

The **People's Republic of China** is made up of **57 nationalities** to date. Since the majority of the population belongs to the **Han** ethnic group, the other 56 groups are designated as national minorities. The Han number about 1.2 billion in East Asia, roughly 90 per cent of whom live in China. Many Han live as foreign Chinese in South-East Asia, particularly in **Thailand** (5 million), **Malaysia** (5 million), **Indonesia** (4 million) and **Singapore** (2 million). **Han** is the name of several **dynasties** in China who ruled the country over a long period of time. The old

The Japanese Tea Ceremony

The traditional Japanese tea ceremony, known as sado or chado, was strongly influenced by Zen Buddhism and its origins date back to the sixteenth century.
In addition to the precisely prescribed equipment, including a bamboo whisk (chasen) with which the bitter green matcha tea is stirred, the classic tea ceremony involves a complicated and equally detailed sequence of steps, during which the host prepares and serves the tea in the presence of guests. The time and concentration required induce a meditative state of mind, bringing relaxation to all who are involved.

custom of binding the feet of wealthy Chinese women so that they became crippled as the famous 'lily feet' derives from this ruling caste.
The Chinese minority populations such as the **Hezhen, She, Dai, Li, Gaoshan** and **Wa** also include 7 million people comprising the **Uyghur**, a Turkic people in **Sinkiang** in the north-west of China, which is also home to the **Hui**, as well as 10 million Chinese Muslims, who have repeatedly tried to shake off Chinese rule.

The Zhuang

Numbering 18 million, the **Zhuang** are the second largest population group in China. They practise a **polytheistic** faith, belong to the **Tai peoples** and speak their own **Zhuang language**.

The Manchu

Today's approximately 10 million **Manchu** are the third largest population group in **China** after the **Han** and the **Zhuang**. About three-quarters of them live in **Manchuria in north-eastern**

The geishas and maikos are the ultimate Japanese symbol of grace.

China. Their language (Manchu) belongs to the **Manchu-Tungusic languages within the Altaic family of languages**, and their script is based on the Mongolian alphabet. The approximately 200,000 **Xibe** are close relatives of the Manchu and live in **north-eastern China** as a nationally recognised minority; their language (Xibe) derives from a **Manchurian dialect**. Today the Manchu, originally a nomadic equestrian and hunting people, are largely settled and make their living as farmers from crop grow-

ing and livestock breeding, as well as from fishing and hunting. The production and sale of ginseng is also an important source of income.
The Manchu and the Xibe are followers of **Buddhist-shamanist religious practices** with the veneration of numerous gods as well as the belief in spirits and ancestor worship playing a major role.

The Taiwanese

In addition to the **Taiwanese of Chinese descent**, about twenty population groups of **Malay-Polynesian** origin live in **Taiwan** (Chinese: 'terraced land'), formerly called **Formosa** (Portuguese: Ilha Formosa = wonderful island) but today officially designated part of the **Republic of China**. Those of Malay-Polynesian descent are considered the indigenous inhabitants of the island and number about 350,000. They include the Ami on the **east coast**, the largest group in terms of numbers, and the **Atayal, Paywan, Bunun, Puyuma, Rukai** and **Tsou**, who live in the inaccessible mountain regions of **Eastern Taiwan** and

were feared as headhunters until approximately 80 years ago. Their languages belong to the Austronesian family.
While the **Ami** live mainly from fishing, the other population groups are primarily slash and burn farmers (potatoes, millet) and hunters, with the breeding of small animals also providing an source of income.
In contrast to the other indigenous Taiwanese population groups with traditionally patrilineal social orders, the Amis had a **matrilineal** structure. With the exception of the **Paiwan** and the **Rukai**, whose village communities were ruled by chiefs, there was no centralised tribal organization, but a council of elders instead.

The Koreans

Along with about 70 million **Koreans**, two-thirds of whom live in **South Korea** and almost one-third in **North Korea**, there are also larger Korean groups on the Japanese island of **Sachalin** together with minorities in **Kazakhstan, Uzbekistan** and on the island of **Hawaii**. Their language belongs to the **Altaic group** but, like Japanese, it has borrowed numerous words from **Chinese**, which spread via Korea as far as Japan after the third century. On the other hand, the Korean alphabet (Hangul) managed to retain its independence before being superseded by the normal, complicated Chinese alphabet at the beginning of the twentieth century.
The traditional economic basis of the Korean's livelihood is agriculture, with fishing and **silkworm breeding** also providing an important source of income. However, following the division of the country into the communist-ruled north and the western-influenced industrialised south, the proportion of farmers in South Korea today is only about ten per cent, with around one-third of them living in North Korea. The majority of South Koreans are **Christians** (25 per cent), **Confucians** or **Buddhists**. More than two-thirds of the North Koreans are non-denominational.

The Japanese

At a total of 125 million people, almost 80 per cent of whom live in the towns and cities, the ethnic **Japanese** today make up more than 99 per cent of their country's overall population, with another 1.5 million Japanese in **North and South America** as well as on **Hawaii**. Their language, the origins of which are unknown, was subjected to significant Chinese influence after the third century BC with the result that about half of modern-day **Japanese** comprises Chinese words, the pronunciation of which has changed substantially over the centuries. The Japanese alphabet is also derived from the Chinese alphabet adopted in the fourth and fifth centuries, from which an **independent syllabary** (hiragana) developed in the eighth century and was then later supplemented by a simplified system (katakana) in the twelfth century. This lettering, together with **hiragana** and about 2,000 'real' Chinese characters, has since been used throughout Japan.
The Japanese state religion is **Shinto** ('The Way of the Gods'), which comprises more than eighty different orientations. In addition to ancestor worship it is based on the belief in a variety of spirits (kami) and natural gods, who are venerated at shrines and are the subject of an elaborate mythology, according to which, for example, the grandson of the Sun goddess **Amaterasu** is considered the direct ancestor of the **Japanese emperor** (tenno). In 538 **Buddhism** reached **Japan** via **Korea**, along with numerous orientations, including Zen Buddhism. Today it is the second most important religion. With its strict standards, such as the fulfilment of duty, simplicity, self-control, the ethics of the '**true heart**' and the classic warrior's virtues (bu-shido), **Shinto**, together with Buddhism, developed to form the basis of Japanese culture. This also includes the classic martial arts of **karate, kendo** (swordplay) or **jiu-jitsu** and the **Samurai** tradition, along with architecture, landscape gardening, theatre (Noh, Kabuki), music and dance.

Multifaceted India

The land of the Hindu Brahmans and mendicants was also the home of Prince Siddhartha who later, as Gautama Buddha, changed the culture of many Asian countries. Along with Egypt, Mesopotamia and China, India – whose holy texts (vedas) evolved about 3,500 years ago – is one of the oldest advanced civilizations.

These women in Rajasthan provide livelihoods for their families with handicrafts.

Gurus (teachers) and sadhus (spiritual ascetics) are highly respected in India. Their caste is indicated by the markings on their forehead.

Every seven years the religious festival known as Kumbh Mela takes place in India. Millions of people gather from all over the world to take part.

More than 70 per cent of the approximately 1 billion Indians, more than one-third of whom live below the poverty line, subsist as farmers (growing mainly rice, grain, vegetables, sugar cane, tea, coffee, legumes, bananas, mangos, peanuts, spices, rubber and cotton), or from livestock farming (buffaloes, horses, donkeys, camels, cattle, sheep, goats). India is also one of the most important industrial nations, with an important and constantly expanding software industry (particularly in Bangalore in Southern India), along with countless small and medium-sized family companies, particularly in the textile production sector.

Around three-quarters of the Indian population speaks one of the northern Indo-Aryan languages, primarily Hindi (40 per cent), the official language, together with Bengali, Bihari, Punjabi, Gujarati, Assami, Kashmiri, Nepali or Urdu. Sanskrit also has Indo-Aryan roots but is today used for religious ceremonies only. In the south, however, the Dravidian languages (including Tamil and Telugu) predominate, while the languages of the Manipuri and Naga in Northern India belong to the Sino-Tibetan family.

Approximately 80 per cent of all Indians are Hindus, followed by the Muslims at about 12 per cent, and the Christian, Sikh, Jaina, Buddhist and Parsee (Zoroastrian) minorities. Indian cultural roots are based in the spiritual traditions of Hinduism and its many gods, such as Krishna, Vishnu or Kali, as well as the ancient holy texts (vedas), which include the Baghavadgita among others. Hinduism is based on the belief in an eternal, universal order (dharma), which human beings have to live up to through the fulfilment of their tasks in order to comply with the karma law of cause and effect and to evade eternal rebirth (reincarnation). The individual's tasks derive from membership of one of the four castes (varnas), which

comprise numerous sub-castes (jatis) and determine the Indian social order. The individual is born into a caste according to his karma in the context of the Hindu faith. The highest caste is the Brahman (priests) group, to which about five per cent of all Indians belong, followed by the Kshatriyas (warriors) at around 40 per cent and the Vaishyas (merchants, livestock farmers) as well as the Shudras (workers, farmers) at about 33 per cent. The so-called 'untouchables' (or dalits, meaning 'broken') comprise approximately 160 million people or some 15 per cent and they are outside the caste system, and therefore at the lowest

level of society, as are India's indigenous inhabitants (or adivasis, meaning 'the first in the country') with around 300 minority groups making up about seven per cent of the overall population. They live mainly in the northern and central Indian forest and mountain areas. The abolition of the centuries-long social discrimination of the lower castes, such as the prohibition of marriage between members of other castes and the discrimination of the 'untouchables', referred to by Mahatma Gandhi as 'harijans' ('the children of God'), has long been legislated but is being implemented only very slowly.

The livelihood of the 2.8 million Balinese is based primarily on terraced farming (rice, sugar cane, coffee, fruit, vegetables) and livestock breeding, as well as on tourism. The mainly Hindu Balinese are renowned for their handicrafts (woodcarving, silver and gold work), their fine fabrics, often incorporating gold and silver thread in the weaving, and their embroidery work, as well as for their music (gamelan) and dance.

The Indians

The approximately 1 billion **Indians** differ greatly among themselves both in external appearance and culture. In addition to the highly sophisticated North Indians, the **Sikhs, Rajputs** and the coastal people of Western and Southern India, and the dark-skinned **Tamils** (60 million), there are slash and burn farmers such as the **Munda people** (around 10 million) or the extremely culturally diverse **Gond** living in the interior of the subcontinent. **Sikhs** (Hindi for 'followers') is the name given to the followers of the **Sikhism** reform movement, which rejects the Hindu caste system. Demands for an independent **Sikh nation** escalated in 1984 with the murder of the then prime minister **Indira Gandhi.** The 120 million **Rajputs** (Sanskrit: 'son of a king') also include many of North India's princely families. The **Gujar** (2 million) belong to a tribal caste in Western India. The Tibeto-Burman-speaking **Naga**, a group of Mongol mountain tribes, live along the border with Burma.

The Sinhalese

The name of the 15 million **Sinhalese** who, ahead of the **Tamils**, today make up approximately 75 per cent of the overall population of **Sri Lanka** (formerly Ceylon), derives from the word **Simha** ('lion'), a mythical ancestor. According to their 'Great Chronicle' (Mahavamsa), the history of the Sinhalese, whose language (Sinhala) belongs to the **Indo-Aryan group of languages**, dates back to the fourth century BC. According to this history, their ancestors originated from **India's Bengal** and forced Sri Lanka's indigenous peoples, the **Vedda**, back into the mountains when they settled in the country.
The Sinhalese are **Buddhists**, the religion having begun to expand to Sri Lanka after the third century BC. The numerous monumental **Buddha statues**, as well as the mighty temple complexes (dagoba), are testimony to the ancient Buddhist **Theravada**

culture. The Sinhalese social order is based on caste membership. The most prestigious are the members of the **Goyigama caste**, property owners and independent farmers, while the fishermen and artisans belong to the lowest caste, the **Karava**.

The Bengalis

More than 95 per cent of the population of **Bangladesh** is made up of **Bengalis**, with a further 1.5 million belonging to the Indian **Bihari.** Two-thirds of Bengalis are illiterate since there is no compulsory education in Bangladesh. At over 85 per cent, the Muslims are in the majority, followed by the Hindus at ten per cent. The majority of Bengalis earn their livelihoods from agri-

culture. Bangladesh is repeatedly the victim of natural disasters (parts of the country lie below sea level).

The Chittagong

The **Chittagong peoples**, who embrace some 12 ethnic groups with different languages, live

reclusively in the **Chittagong Mountains** in south-eastern **Bangladesh.** Today their numbers are estimated to be around 500,000.
The largest of the groups include the **Mogh** (Marma), closely related to the Burmese, and the **Chakma**, whose languages belong to the **Sino-Tibetan family of languages.** There are also small groups such as the **Murung** (Mru), **Lushai** or **Panko**, who are among the earliest inhabitants of the Chittagong mountain region and who inhabit the autonomous districts of **Chakma, Mru** and **Mogh**, each with their own chief (rajas).
While the Buddhist **Chakma** and **Mogh** have largely adapted to the **Bengali** way of life, the other Chittagong peoples have remained relatively untouched by outside influences to date.

The Padaung are a minority group in Myanmar.

The Veddas

The **indigenous inhabitants of Sri Lanka (Ceylon),** the **Veddas**, who belong to the Dravidian group of peoples, are the oldest population group in South Asia. Following partial interbreeding with the Singhalese and Tamil populations, as a result of which they gave up their language in

favour of that of their respective adjacent peoples, only small groups of the original **Veddas** (mountain Veddas) now live in the remote mountainous jungle on the eastern side of the island.

The Burmese

In addition to the approximately 30 million **Burmese**, who make up almost 70 per cent of the overall population of **Myanmar** (formerly Burma), several large minority groups also live in autonomous regions, speaking their own language and enjoying their own culture. The largest minority groups include the **Shan** and the **Karen**, who settled primarily in the mountain regions and originate from China, together with the **Mon**, the **Chin**, immigrants from India's Assam, the **Kachin** and the **Rohingya**. The language of the largely **Buddhist Burmese** belongs to the **Tibeto-Burmese** group of the **Sino-Tibetan** family of languages, with their alphabet based on a modified form of the **Pali alphabet** and also encompassing the ancient Buddhist lettering. Almost three-quarters of the Burmese still live in the countryside in both small and large village communities, most of which consist of **pile dwellings** roofed with palm leaves. Their living is based on **irrigated cultivation** (rice) and market gardening, along with fishing and livestock farming.

The Shan

With around 4 million people, the **Shan**, who belong to the **Thai group of peoples**, are among the largest of the autonomous minority groups in **Myanmar.** Their alphabet displays many similarities to the **Burmese alphabet**, while their language, Thai, is closely related to the **Thai** spoken in Thailand; the **Shan** are often referred to by the Thailanders as the **Thai-Yai** ('tall Thai'). The history of the Shan starts in the eleventh century when some of the Thai peoples from Southern China and North Vietnam settled in the north of

Myanmar, among other places, and founded numerous principalities, each headed by a prince (Saohpa).
Today the Shan are largely followers of the **Theravada Buddhist** faith, which originated from **Sri Lanka** (Ceylon) but which has also become interspersed with numerous pre-Buddhist religious concepts, including the belief in **natural spirits** and **ancestor worship.**

The Thai

Today's approximately 50 million **Thai** (formerly the Siamese), like the **Lao** and the **Shan**, belong to the Thai group of peoples and make up the **largest population group in Thailand** at around 80 per cent. Thailand is the only south-east Asian nation never to have been subjected to foreign colonial rule. Almost 80 per cent of the Thai, whose language (Thai) belongs to the **Sino-Tibetan group of languages**, live in the countryside, with the cultivation of rice a key activity.
The ancestors of the present day Thai, who came from Southern China in a number of waves after the eighth century, settled in their current territory, gradually expelling the ruling **Mon-Khmer peoples** and founding their first united empire in the thirteenth century. The Thai adopted the **Theravada Buddhist** religion, among other things, from the indigenous Mon, and this has had a sustained influence on their culture.
The large **temple complexes** (Wats) in **Bangkok** and the numerous **statues of Buddha**, which derive from the Chinese and Burmese influences as well as those of the **Khmer**, are famous throughout the world. **Ramakien**, a version of the Indian **Ramayana epic**, is the greatest of Thailand's national epics, on which both music and dance are also based.

The Lisu

The settlement area of today's around 600,000 **Lisu** covers the inaccessible **mountain regions**

Mass events such as this gymnastics competition in the capital Pyongyang, with no fewer than 50,000 people participating, are characteristic of communist ruled North Korea. This is a symbolic demonstration of a longstanding tradition among many East Asian peoples, namely the subordination of the individual to the community, which contrasts sharply with the western emphasis upon the individual.

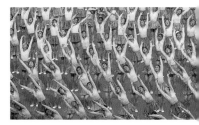

of Thailand, **Myanmar** and **Southern China** and their language belongs to the **Tibeto-Burmese group of Sino-Tibetan languages**. In addition to hunting and livestock farming, their livelihood is primarily based on rice and millet, with poppies also being grown for opium in Thailand.

The Lisu are traditionally divided into larger clans, each possessing a tribal chief elected by the council of elders. Depending on the region, they are either **Buddhist** (Thailand, Myanmar) or **Taoist** (China), but have also largely retained their traditional beliefs.

The Miao (Meo)

The majority of the approximately 6 million **Miao** (Hmong – 'person'), who are divided into numerous sub-groups, live in **South-West China**, with the balance spread over the **north of Thailand, Laos** and **Vietnam**. Their language belongs to the **Miao-Yao branch of the Sino-Tibetan group of languages**. The Miao traditionally make a living from crop farming (mainly rice and maize, alternating seasonally with poppies for opium), livestock breeding (cattle, pigs, chickens) and also from handicrafts (especially cotton and hemp textiles, as well as batik fabrics).

While the Miao living in Thailand managed to resist national attempts at forced resettlement forty years ago, many of the Miao in Laos, who had fought on the side of the government in the civil war, were forced to emigrate after the war, mainly to North America, where larger groups now live.

The Khmer

Today's approximately 11 million **Khmer** make up around 90 per cent of the overall population of **Cambodia**. More than 1 million people lost their lives during the Khmer Rouge's reign of terror between 1975 and 1979.

Their language, Khmer, belongs to the large group of **Mon-**

Khmer languages. More than 85 per cent of the Khmer people live in the countryside, their livelihood based mainly on rice, fruit and vegetables, fishing and handicrafts (weaving, pottery, metalwork).

The Khmer are largely followers of **Indian Theravada Buddhism**, which has had a major influence on the culture and lifestyle of the people. For instance, it used to be common practice for every man to spend time as a monk in a monastery. The first **Khmer empire** was established in AD 802 and was ruled for the next 300 years by

the mighty **Angkor dynasty** led by a god king, followed by the aristocratic Brahmans and their officials. The magnificent **temple complex of Angkor Wat** was built between 1113 and 1150 during their reign, which at times extended as far as Thailand and South Vietnam.

The Vietnamese

Around 80 per cent of the approximately 70 million **Vietnamese**, who are closely related to the **Chinese** and whose language belongs to the **Mon-Khmer group of languages**,

live in rural areas, with about 70 per cent being employed in agricultural collectives. The main crops are rice, vegetables and tropical fruit, as well as spices.

The Vietnamese culture was extensively influenced by the Chinese rule that lasted more than a thousand years (111

BC–AD 939); the first division into a northern and southern empire came in the sixteenth and seventeenth centuries. About half of all Vietnamese are **Buddhist**, followed by adherents of the Chinese **Confucian** and **Taoist** faiths. A minority of people also belong to a Christian denomination.

1 In addition to the Tsou, Paiwan and Atayal, the small group of Ami people also lives on the island of Taiwan.

2 Among the Badjao on the Philippine island of Bongao, both the bride and the bridegroom wear particularly elaborate wedding outfits.

3 For the Thai Buddhist monks, the major religious festivals – such as the annual Flower Festival – provide a welcome change from the daily routine of life in the monastery. As is common in Asia, these Buddhist monks are always clothed in orange robes.

Ethnologists consider all the indigenous ethnic groups of the Malaysian archipelago to be Indonesians in the truest sense, their oldest traces dating back around 4,000 years. In addition to the large ethnic groups, such as the Javanese, Balinese, Malays and Filipinos, these also include around 150 small groups and tribes such as the Drau or Nono – often with little more than 1,000 members – who have developed an independent language and culture.

The Akha

The settlement area of today's approximately 400,000 **Akha**, one of the **Lolo peoples** whose language belongs to the **Tibeto-Burmese family of languages**, covers **Southern China, Myanmar, Northern Thailand, Laos** and **Vietnam**. They live in the higher mountain regions above 1,000 m, largely as slash and burn farmers growing dry rice, millet and maize for their own subsistence needs, and cultivating poppies as the raw material for opium production. They are also highly talented craftspeople, especially in iron work.

The Akha are divided into numerous clans and the women are striking in their bright traditional dress, different hues of felt fabrics and silver jewellery. The Akha generally live as extended families in grass-roofed pile dwellings made from bamboo, with two 'spirits gates' traditionally placed in front of each settlement to protect the village community against evil spirits from the primeval forest. In addition to the shaman priests, who are responsible for the **ancestor worship**, **female shamans** are responsible for the healing rituals.

The Malays

Numbering around 30 million, the **Malays**, whose indigenous name is Orang Melayu, are the second largest group in **South-East Asia** after the Javanese. In addition to **Malaysia**, their settlement area covers mainly **East Sumatra, Borneo** and many of the smaller Indonesian islands. Their language, Malay, contains many words borrowed from Indian and Arabic languages and forms the basis for **Indonesia's official language** (Bahasa Indonesia).

As seafaring merchants and pirates, the Malays were the most well known peoples of the south-east Asian archipelago for centuries. Their history goes back 2,000 years to when the ancestors of the modern-day Malays were already engaged in brisk maritime trade. During the first century their territory at the time

– **the Malaysian Peninsula and East Sumatra** – was subject to Indian influences; from the sixth to the twelfth centuries their kingdom, which was based on the Indian example and became the heart of **Indian Mahayana Buddhism**, controlled the maritime trade between Indonesian islands and also maintained contacts with the Chinese empire and the Indian principalities. Although the majority of today's Malays are **Muslims** – the Malaysian Peninsula was Islamised after AD 1450 – they still retain a number of pre-Islamic traditions, such as the **belief in spirits** and many **magic rituals**.

The Batak

Batak is a collective term for a number of ancient Indonesian peoples in **Northern Sumatra** (Batak land), whose numbers today are estimated to be around 4 million. These peoples include the **Mandailing, Simalungun, Angkola, Pakpak** (Dairi) and the **Karo** as well as the largest group, the **Toba**.

Despite Islamization (Angkola, Mandailing), Christianization (Toba) and the strong Hindu-Indonesian influences (Simalungun, Karo), the Batak have largely managed to retain their traditional culture. The **priests** play an important role with necromancy and the interpretation of oracles assigning them the status of intermediaries between man and the creator deity. The social order of the **Toba** – who, like the other Batak peoples, live mainly from crop farming (rice, yams, taro, potatoes, tobacco, cinnamon) and livestock breeding – is based on **exogamous family clans** (marga); among the **Karo** up to 16 extended families live under one roof. The Batak are known in the West for their large, overhanging **pile dwellings** with elaborately carved gable facades in their fortified village complexes.

The Minangkabau

About 6 million **Minangkabau** (indigenous name: Urang Padang)

live mainly in the central **highlands** and on the **west coast of Sumatra**. Their language is closely related to Malay. Their livelihood is mostly centred on terraced farming (vegetables, rice, fruit, tobacco, cinnamon) and they are also renowned as very talented craftsmen (woodcarving, basketry, silver work and the production of Songkhat fabrics).

Although the Minangkabau have been Islamised since the eighteenth century, their social order retains a strictly matrilineal structure today. Accordingly, lineage is determined solely by the female ancestors (sabuah parui – 'from a womb'). After marriage the women live together with their children in the large **clan home** along with the mother, grandmother and aunts; the husband enjoys visiting rights only, while the women's brothers or other male relatives adopt the role of father for their children.

Life in Hanoi largely takes place on the street.

The Dayak

Dayak is a collective term for numerous groups of peoples on the **island of Borneo**, encompassing a total of about 3 million people who differ from one another in both language and culture. The Dayak include several dozen tribes, each with about 300 further sub-tribes that are relatively loosely connected to one another and usually comprise several extended families. The villages of the Dayak, who are mainly farmers living from rice farming, traditionally consist of just a single so-called **longhouse**. This is a pile dwelling, often several hundred metres long, and can accommodate over 300 people. Each family has their own section in the longhouse, with communal life taking place on the external veranda.

The Dayak used to be feared as headhunters and performed ritual human sacrifices; they

are largely **Christianised** or Islamised but have retained many of their religious traditions with an elaborate mythology, distinct ancestor worship and death cult practices.

The Acehnese (Achinese)

What has been the autonomous settlement area since 1949 of the approximately 3.5 million **Acehnese** – a mixed people comprising **Malays, Javanese, Batak, Indians** and **Arabs** – covers the flat coastal areas of **north-western Sumatra**. The Acehnese live mainly from agriculture (rice, sugar cane, maize, pepper, coconuts, rubber trees, tobacco) and fishing. They are also talented armourers and are known for their gold and silver work.

Unlike any other Indonesian peoples the Acehnese, whose first empire was established in the sixteenth century and which, in addition to north Sumatra, encompassed large areas of present day Malaysia in the seventeenth century, are **devout Muslims**. The women used to enjoy considerably more influence than their counterparts in other Muslim societies, and four **female sultans** held power during the seventeenth century. Towards the end of the seventeenth century the empire broke into several smaller states whose rule was broken only in the early twentieth century by the colonial policies of the Dutch.

The Nias

Today's approximately 500,000 **Nias** belong to the **ancient Indonesian peoples** who settled mainly on the **island of Nias**, as well as on the Batu Islands west of Sumatra.

The Nias' livelihood is based on rice farming as well as livestock breeding, mostly of pigs. The Nias are now largely Christianised and are known principally for their megalith culture, with giant **menhirs** having represented an important component of their traditional religion. This traditional religion also included a

Totalling around 85 million people the Javanese, whose language belongs to the Austronesian family of languages, are the largest population group in Indonesia. The majority of Javanese are Muslims, and only a few ethnic groups, such as the

Tengger in Eastern Java's Tengger Mountains for instance, have retained their pre-Islamic (fifteenth-century) rural culture with its Indian Hindu influences and their religious customs, including the annual festival of sacrifice to their gods.

strong leaning towards **ancestor worship**, with elaborately carved **spirit** and **god figures** playing an important role, as did **headhunting** and **ritual human sacrifices** in the past.

The Nias in the south of the island traditionally live in large villages, most of which are situated on hills and comprise numerous pile dwellings, with pathways paved with large stone slabs running between them. The **pile dwellings** belonging to the village chiefs are built on large tree trunks, with steep roofs often up to 20 m in height, and are particularly striking. The villages of the northern Nias are smaller and comprise oval pile dwellings.

The Toraja

Toraja ('mountain people') is a collective term for some 60 **indigenous ancient Indonesian ethnic groups** comprising a total of about 3 million people who inhabit the mountain regions of the **Indonesian island of Sulawesi** (Celebes). There is a distinction made between the ethnic groups in Southern Sulawesi and the inhabitants in the west and east of the island: the latter are often also included among the **Alfur** people as a result of their close contacts to the **Moluccans**.

In addition to the growing of rice, taro, yams and maize, the Toraja's livelihood is largely based on livestock farming (water buffalo, pigs), with animals used solely for ritual purposes.

Although the Toraja have been largely Christianised for about a hundred years, they have retained a number of features from their traditional culture. A special role is played by the many ceremonies that accompany the **death rituals** of the **southern Toraja** (Sadang), according to which the dead laid to rest in the burial cliffs are guarded by life-sized wooden dolls. Other cultural characteristics of the Toraja include their pile dwellings, which are elaborately decorated with geometric ornaments, and their handicraft skills, including basketry, weaving and metalwork.

The Filipinos

The term **Filipinos** refers to the modern and ancient Malay Christian peoples settled in the Philippines who, at a total of almost 70 million, today make up about 90 per cent of the overall population. The largest ethnic group is formed by the **Bisaya**, to whom around 25 million people belong, while today's almost 20 million **Tagal** are the most influential group politically, their language (Filipino) being the **official language of the Philippines** with its around

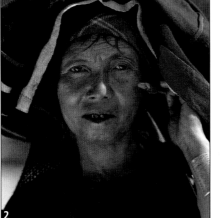

7,100 islands. These are followed by the **Ilokano** with 9 million, the **Bicol** with around 6.5 million people, as well as the smaller **Pampagan, Pangasinan, Sambal** and **Cagayan** (Ibanag) ethnic groups, whose different languages belong to the western group of the **Austronesian family of languages.**

The Filipino's original homeland is in **Southern China,** from where their forefathers migrated to the **Philippines** via **Taiwan** in the second century BC, expelling the indigenous population (Aeta, Igorot). The first states were founded in around 1000; contacts with the **Hinduist Javanese** and the **Buddhist kingdom of Sumatra** existed even then and had a sustained influence on the Philippine culture, including both the alphabet and the spoken language (especially Tagal and Bisaya). The Malay influence brought about a short-lived Islamization in the fifteenth century, superseded by Christianization at the hands of

the Spanish colonists after the sixteenth century. Today more than 90 per cent of all Filipinos are **Christians**, whereas the **Moros** on **Mindanao** and the **Samal** remain Muslim. Nevertheless, a number of indigenous religious traditions, such as the belief in spirits, have been retained in the rural areas.

1 Vietnam is the home of the Flower Hmong people.

2 Myanmar's mountain peoples have retained many of their traditions.

3 Female shaman enjoy considerable prestige among the Akha due to their healing skills.

4 The Pa-o in Myanmar originate from the eastern mountain regions of Tibet.

5 The Malay social order was influenced by Indian Hinduism for more than a thousand years. Islam has been the determining social factor since the fifteenth century.

Africa

With an area of 30.4 million sq. km – roughly one-fifth of the total surface of the Earth – and approximately 900 million inhabitants, Africa is the third largest continent, after Asia and America. It is dominated by the Sahara, the World's largest desert, the Kalahari desert, the river valleys of Chad, the Congo and the Zambezi. At 5,895 m, Mount Kilimanjaro is the continent's highest mountain, and Lake Victoria is Africa's largest lake. The world's longest river, the Nile, 6,671 km in length, flows south to north through Africa. Central Africa close to the equator is covered with hot and humid rain forests, bordered to the north and south first by broad savannahs, and desert areas in the lattitudes of the tropics of Cancer and Capricorn. Africa's rich wildlife is more or less confined to the extensive national parks.

Egypt has one of the oldest cultures in the world, and archaeological finds have shown that human life first emerged in sub-Saharan Africa.

Africa, physical

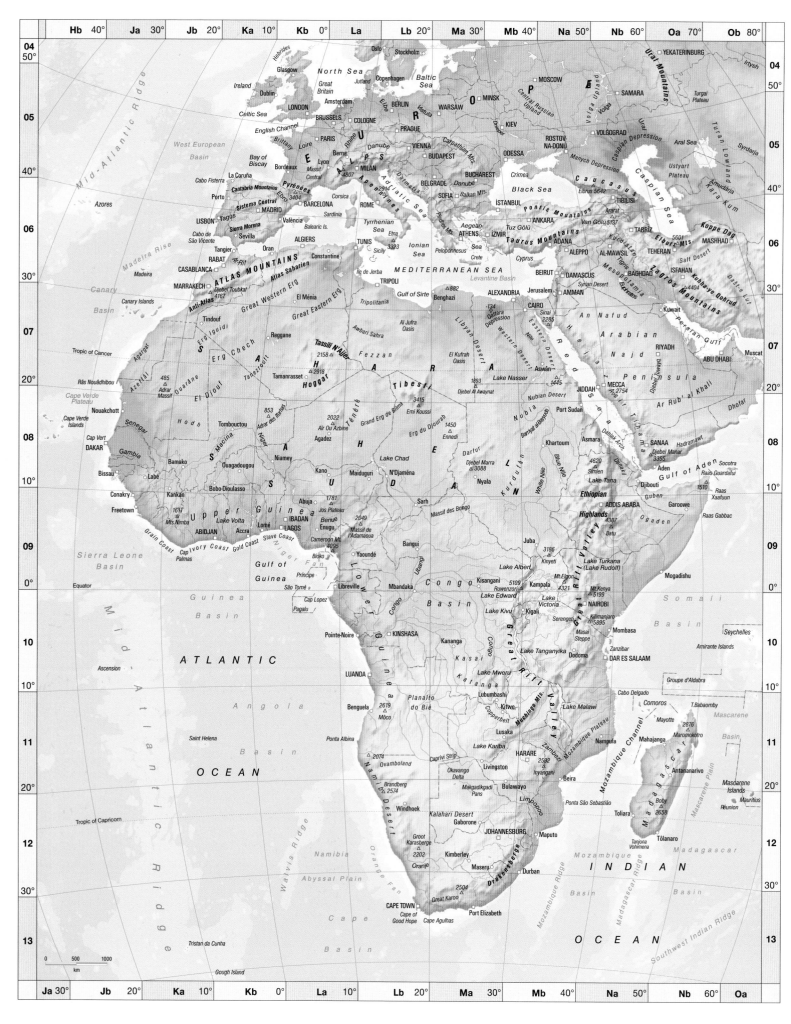

Africa, political

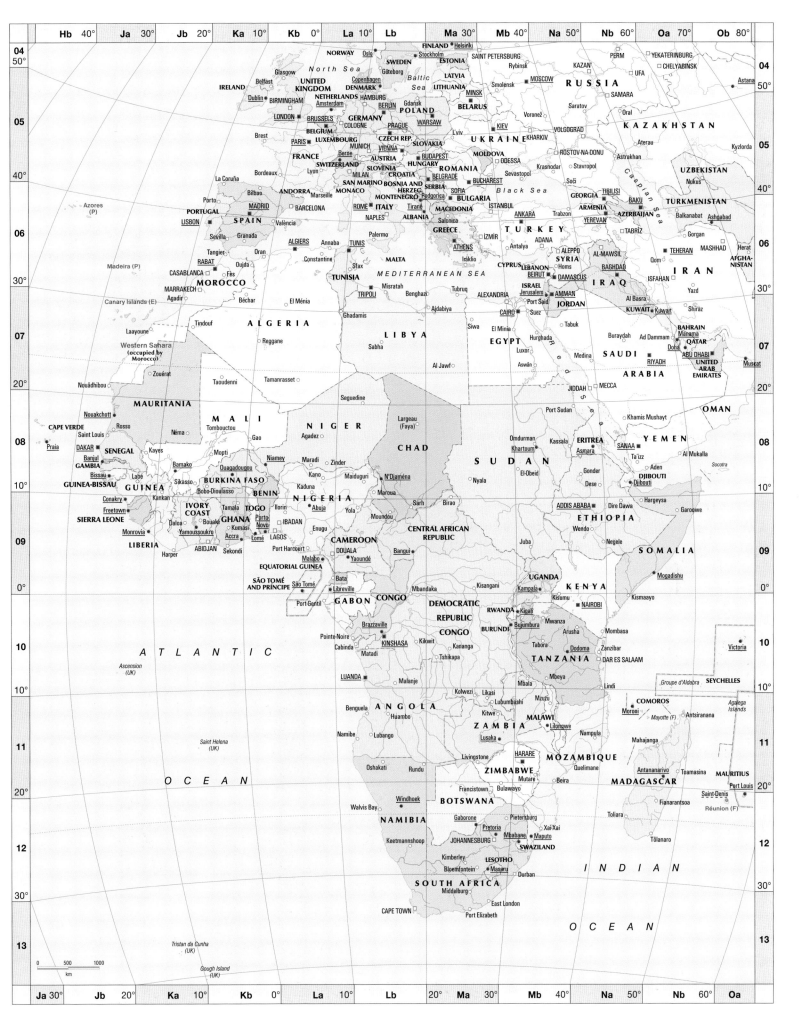

A show of power: four huge seated statues of Pharaoh Rameses II guard the entrance to the great temple at Abu Simbel. Rameses II (1279–1213 BC) built a large number of monuments in Ancient Egypt.

The History of Africa

The 'Dark Continent' is the cradle of mankind. It was from here that Homo sapiens spread out to settle the entire globe. One of the first great cultures developed in Egypt, but remains of other early civilisations have been discovered

The civil war in Liberia turned millions into refugees.

south of the Sahara, for example in Greater Zimbabwe. The south coast of the Mediterranean was inhabited in turn by the Phoenicians, Romans, Byzantines, Vandals and finally the Arabs, who spread Islam throughout large parts of Africa. The arrival of European explorers saw the beginning of the colonial period when most of Africa was under foreign domination. Colonialism was at its height in the nineteenth century, most African sovereign states only being established after World War II. Natural disasters, civil wars, epidemics and crop failures have also shaped the continent.

Early African History

*Sudan: Kushite Kings were buried in the pyramids at **Meroe**, the capital city of the Kingdom of Kush, in imitation of the ancient Egyptian practice. The golden age of this sub-Saharan civilisation lasted from about 300 BC to 350 AD.*

Early history

Homo sapiens is believed to have emerged in Africa more than 200,000 years ago. The species lived as hunter-gatherers, used simple stone tools and eventually spread throughout the continent as nomads or bushmen.

The growing population became differentiated into various races some 12,000 years ago, while the agrarian cultures pushed the nomads ever further into the more inhospitable regions. Bantu-speaking people came to dominate wide expanses of central and southern Africa. For the most part, the original population was organised into clans, but later great kingdoms came into being in western and central Africa.

North Africa

The first major civilisation emerged in ca. 5000 BC in the Nile delta, where the regular flooding of the river created the right conditions for an effective system of agriculture. For more than 4,000 years the Egyptian kingdom of the Pharaohs influenced world history. Its mining and smelting of iron and its forms of political organisation and administration spread to the tropical regions of Africa in the eighth century BC.

Ancient Egyptian history is divided into various kingdoms. The Old Kingdom lasted from 2755 to 2255 BC. It was during this period that the pyramids of Giza were built. These monuments are a testimony in stone to the unlimited power of the kings who ruled a well-organised theocratic state. After the collapse of the Old Kingdom, Egypt experienced a revival during the Middle Kingdom era, beginning with the twelfth dynasty in 1991 BC, but ending again with the thirteenth dynasty. Most ancient Egyptian buildings that still stand date from the New Kingdom, whose most important rulers were Sethos I and Ramses II. Impressive monuments, such as the temples of Karnak, Luxor and West Thebes, still stand. After the death of Ramses III the Egyptian kingdom fell into decline and came under the rule of various foreign monarchs including the Hyksos who devasted the country.

The foreign rule of the Persians from the twenty-eigth to the thirtieth dynasty was shaken off from time to time, but the kings of the third dynasty were the very last Egyptian Pharaohs. In 332 BC, Alexander the Great conquered Egypt and created Alexandria, named after himself, turning it into an intellectual and political capital. The last dynasty, that of the Ptolemies, ended with the defeat of Queen Cleopatra at the battle of Actium. From 30 BC to 395 AD the land of the Nile was a Roman province.

The Phoenicians set up trading posts along the Mediterranean

The Egyptian King Tutankhamun (1347–1339 BC) and his wife.

coast, which eventually developed into the mighty trading and naval power of Carthage. After the Third Punic War against the Carthaginians, the Romans gained a foothold in present-day Tunisia in 146 BC, which now became part of the Roman Empire as the province of Africa. By the first century BC they had conquered the whole of North Africa, and by the fourth century the regions west of twhat is now

Libya were added to the Western Roman Empire, while those to the east of it became part of the Eastern Roman Empire.

After the downfall of the Western Roman Empire in the fifth century, the Vandals, a Germanic tribe, became the dominant power on the Mediterranean coast, until they were ousted again by the Byzantines. Soon after the death of the Prophet Muhammad, in 632 AD the Arabs invaded Egypt and csubsequently onquered Morocco. The population was converted to Islam, only the states of Alodia and Makuria in the Sudan were able to remain Christian for another 600 years. Caravan trade through the Sahara led to the Islamisation of further parts of the continent; Muslim conquerors from the Yemen conquered Aksum, part of what is now Ethiopia, and founded Adal and Harar.

The triumphal progress of Islam seemed unstoppable and the conquest of the Iberian peninsula posed a serious threat to Christian Europe. The Mamlukes, who con-

quered the Christian areas of the Sudan in the fourteenth century, became the ruling Muslim power. From the advent of the Ottoman Turks until Napoleon's Egyptian campaign in 1798 the Mamelukes ruled Egypt. In 1542, an initially successful attack on Christian Ethiopia by the Sultanate of Adal was beaten off with the assistance of Portugal.

The kingdoms of West Africa

Trade in slaves, gold, salt, cloth and household goods via the Sahara favoured the rise of larger kingdoms. The kingdom of Ghana was founded whose capital city was Kumbi Saleh zone was founded ca. 400 in what is now western Sudan. Until the eleventh century it controlled the trade routes between Morocco and the coastal forests of West Africa. The Arabs from the north became increasingly powerful, until the Almoravids, under Yusuf ibn Tashfin, gained supremacy in a Holy War in the late eleventh century. They were followed in the twelfth century by the Soso, who themselves were driven out in 1240 by the Mali people.

The kingdom of Mali was founded in the eleventh century by the Malinke and flourished in the fourteenth century under King Mansa Musa. This ruler is known to have made a pilgrimage to Mecca, Islam having been adopted earlier by the kingdom. After 1400, the Songhai empire followed that of Mali, reaching its zenith under Askia Mohammed. The capital city of Gao was conquered in 1591 by the troops of Al-Mansur from Morocco. The kingdoms that followed, Macina, Gonja Ségou and Kaarta, were unable to develop any lasting political and economic structures.

The city states of the Hausa, such as Biram, Daura, Katsina, Zaria, Kano, Rano and Gobir, in the region between the river Niger and Lake Chad became powerful in the tenth century, due to shift in e the great trading routes. North and east of Lake Chad, the kingdom of Kanem-Bornu established itself, continuing until 1846.

While Islam in West Africa was at first confined to the cities, the systematic advance of Islam began in the fifteenth century, and the ordinary population became

converted. The first to proselytise were the Kunta Arabs, followed in the sixteenth century by the Qadiriyyah order and later the Fulbe. In the early nineteenth century, the Hausa states were conquered by the Fulbe and theocracies ruled by a monarch, such as Macina, were founded.

The kingdoms of East Africa

Relatively little is known about the early history of East Africa. Bantu peoples settled in the interior, while the coastal regions were soon controlled by Arab traders, who in the thirteenth century founded the Zenj city states and traded in gold, slaves and ivory. Between Lake Victoria and Lake Edward some well-organised states emerged in the fourteenth century, under the rule of the Bachwezi. They lasted until about 1500, when they were conquered by invaders from the Sudan. Other states joined them, of which Bunyoro was the most important until the mid-eighteenth century, succeded by Buganda.

The kingdoms of Central Africa

Although little reliable information exists about the early communities in Central Africa, political formations probably existed as early as the ninth century, trading in copper and ivory. In the fourteenth century, the kingdom of Congo was founded, around 1500 the Luba kingdom and about one hundred years later the Lunda kingdom. The Karanga, a Bantu people, formed the kingdom of Mwene Mutapa, which flourished due to its rich reserves of gold. In the fifteenth century it stretched from the Zambezi across the Kalahari desert, as far as the Indian Ocean and the Limpopo river.

The kingdoms of South Africa

In South Africa, by the early nineteenth century, the Bushmen had been largely driven out of the land into the enclave of the Kalahari desert by the Bantu peoples. The incursions of the Zulus, a warrior nation, triggered extensive demographic changes in southern Africa. The Ndwandwe kingdom, the kingdom of Swazi and that of the Ngoni emerged

*Kidnapping: until well into the nineteenth century the **slave trade** flourished in Africa. The European buyers had their 'goods' shipped from the west coast of Africa to plantations in the USA, Brazil and the Carribean.*

though the last soon split into five parts. In the south of what is now Mozambique, the state of Gaza developed in 1830, and a short time later, in present-day Zimbabwe, a kingdom was created in Matabeleland.

Arrival of the Europeans

In the fifteenth century, the Portuguese navigators succeeded in circumventing the trade routes controlled by the Muslims and established trading posts on the west coast. Thus the coastal regions acquired even more importance in relation to the interior. At first, textiles, metalwares and firearms were exchanged for ivory and gold, but soon the slave trade took on greater significance. Spaniards, Portuguese, British and French purchased labour for their mines and plantations in the New World. The Europeans did not usually capture the slaves directly, but made use of Arab and African intermediaries, leading to the foundation of prosperous kingdoms whose basis was the slave trade. The first of these was Benin, in the western part of present-day Nigeria. At the end of the seventeenth century the kingdoms of Dahomey and Oyo took up the dominant position, to be replaced from the eighteenth century as the great power in West Africa by the Ashanti. Prisoners captured in the many civil wars, which continued until the end of the nineteenth century, were profitably sold to the Europeans.

After the loss of its North American colonies, the relationship of Great Britain to the slave trade changed. Slavery was now outlawed, and a special colony for freed slaves was to be set up. After a failed attempt in St George's Bay, Freetown in Sierra Leone, which became a British Crown Colony in 1808, was used as a British merchant naval base in its fight against the international slave trade. In 1822 freed slaves from the USA founded the first Black African republic, Liberia.

The British fight against slavery, was not founded on purely humanitarian motives. The British crown was concerned about sovereignty on the high seas, and the capture of Spanish and Portuguese slave-ships had the useful side-effect of weakening its

sea-faring rivals on the pretext of a fight for human rights.

This policy also brought Britain into conflict with the African nations who relied on trade in human merchandise. Thus, in the mid-nineteenth century, The British fought many skirmishes against the Africans, during which they subjugated the Ashanti and some of the peoples of the Niger delta, such as the Calabar, Bonny and Brass. In 1861, the British formally took control of the island Lagos, until recently the capital of Niger.

The British campaign against the slave trade in East Africa was not quite so successful. Since the

seventeenth century, the Portuguese had fought for supremacy against indigenous Islamic rulers. Ethiopia was able to maintain its independence with Portuguese support, but by the end of the eighteenth century the Portuguese had to abandon their positions in northern East Africa. Despite the provisions forbidding slavery in agreements with Britain, it continued in this region for quite some time to come. Even to this day, a form of the slave trade persists, largely between African and the countries of the Arabian peninsula. At the Cape of Good Hope, the Dutch had been setting up bases for their trade with Indochina since 1652. The most important of these was Cape Town, at the southern tip of the continent. The Boers (Dutch for 'farmer') descendents of the original Dutch settlers, pushed ever further into the interior in search of grazing land and arable land, driving out the original inhabitants, the Bantu and the Khoikhoin.

Imperialism

From the late eighteenth century the European powers began the systematic exploration of the Dark Continent and its incorporation into their colonial empires. The continuing reconnaissance of the interior was vital to European interests.

1 A wealth of elegant historical buildings are a reminder of the former glory of the Moroccan royal city, Marrakesh.

2 The pillars of Aksum, the royal city of the Ethiopian rulers, date from the fourth century, when Ethiopia became Christian under the king Ezana.

3 Djenné was an important Islamic cultural centre which in the fourteenth century became the main trading centre in the kingdom of Mali.

4 Elmina castle, built by the Portuguese in 1482, was the first slave-trading post exporting slaves from West Africa.

Modern Africa

Gamal Abd el-Nasser, the Egyptian dictator who ruled from 1954 till 1970. In 1958, he created a temporary union with Syria, known as the United Arab Republic, which soon collapsed in 1961. The Libyan leader Muammar al Gaddafi was at one time working on plans to unify Libya with other Arab and African states.

In 1770 the British explorer James Bruce reached the source of the Blue Nile. Another British explorer, Mungo Park, followed the course of the Niger in the early nineteenth century, and the German Heinrich Barth discovered Muslim western Sudan for the Europeans. David Livingstone explored the Zambezi and in 1855 discovered the Victoria Falls. In 1863, the source of the Nile was found by John Hanning Speke, James August Grant and Samuel White Baker.

In parallel with these discoveries the great European nations competed in a frenzied imperialist race to acquire as much territory as possible to add to their colonies. The driving force was national prestige and the prospect of great gain from the exploitation of natural resources and later from the building of railways.

In 1830, France conquered Algeria, and with the occupation of Tunisia in 1881 it acquired a large contiguous colonial empire in western and equatorial Africa. In 1895, it conquered the island of Madagascar and in 1911 Morocco, thus controlling the whole of the three countries (Tunisia, Morocco and Algeria) along the south coast of the Mediterranean known collectively as the Maghreb.

Disputes over the division of Africa frequently brought the European nations to the brink of war. In 1908 and 1911, the French were able to assert themselves against German gunboat diplomacy in Morocco, but had to abandon their advance into the upper Nile region in the Fashoda incident of 1898–1899 as a result of energetic British resistance. In 1806–1814, Great Britain seized the Cape Colony from the Dutch and thus began to build a major colonial dominion in South Africa. In 1843, they added Natal, in 1866–1879 Caffraria (later the Eastern Cape). The fought the first fierce battle against the Dutch in 1880–1881, capturing the Orange Free State, in 1885 added Bechuanaland and in 1890 Rhodesia. The Boer War (1899–1902) was won by the British who conquered the Dutch states along the Vaal river. In 1910, the British consolidated their possessions in South Africa to form the Union of South Africa.

In 1882, The British occupied Egypt and from there conquered the eastern Sudan in 1896–1899 after a war with forces of the Mahdi, the Muslim ruler. In 1887–1890 they acquired Kenya, Uganda and Tanganyika in East Africa. In exchange for Heligoland, the former German island colony of Zanzibar also became British. The Portuguese extended their coastal possessions in the west to include Angola, and in the west to Mozambique. The Congo Free State, founded in 1881–1885, which was more or less the private possession of the King of the Belgians, became Belgian Congo in 1908. The German Empire acquired Togo, Cameroon, German South-west Africa and German East Africa in 1884 to 1885. Spain retained small areas of Morocco and Western Sahara. Italy, the last colonial power in Africa, conquered Libya from the Ottomans in 1911–1912 and Abyssinia (Ethiopia) in 1936, but lost both during World War II.

Following the decisions of the Treaty of Versailles in 1919 the German colonies became man-dates of the League of Nations in 1919. The Berlin Congo conference of 1884–1885, in which the German Chancellor Bismarck, had acted as an 'honest broker', achieved a balance of interests for the imperialist powers, but was not finally able to eliminate their rivalries. Navigation rights for the Congo and Niger rivers were defined, and each of the signatory powers undertook to inform the others if it wanted to acquire new territories or take over a protectorate.

Liberation movements

Political policy in Africa was determined by the European rulers; the indigenous population was not involved in decision-making. The needs of the Europeans also had significant consequences for the traditional social system of the indigenous population.

Not everyone was prepared to bow unresistingly to foreign rule. In 1870, there was an uprising in Algeria against the French, who also encountered significant resistance in western Sudan. The British suppressed armed uprisings in Matabeleland, the Ashanti region of Nigeria, the Fulbe states, Sokoto and Sierra Leone. The Germans fought from 1904 to 1908 against the Herero of south-west Africa and against the Maji Maji Rebellion in Tanganyika from 1905 to 1907.

The only successful uprising was in Ethiopia which was able to defend itself against Italian attempts at conquest in the battle of Adowa in 1896.

After World War I, the exploitation of Africa continued apace. Several colonies such as Algeria, South Rhodesia and Kenya, which had significant populations of white settlers acquired a large measure of self-rule, but the indigenous population had no voting rights or say in government. On the eve of World War II, African nationalist movements existed, but were only well-organised in Algeria and Egypt.

The new Africa

World War II led gave a boost to African self-confidence. The British and French made extensive concessions, which hastened the organisation of nationalist movements. A Pan-African Movement was founded, headed by intellectuals such as Kwame Nkrumah and Jomo Kenyatta.

Everywhere in Africa, political parties and trades unions were founded. In most places, the transition to independence was peaceful, even though the Mau-Mau, the Kikuyu guerillas in Kenya aimed to bomb their way to freedom. Ghana was the first Black African state to become independent in 1957; Guinea followed a year later. In the 'African year' of 1960, seventeen sovereign African nations came into being: Cameroon, Congo-Brazzaville, Gabon, Chad, the Central African Republic, Togo, Ivory Coast, Dahomey, Upper Volta, Niger, Nigeria, Senegal, Mali, Madagascar, Somalia, Mauritania and Congo-Léopoldville. Sierra Leone and Tanganyika followed in 1961. Tanganyika and Zanzibar united in 1964 to form Tanzania. In 1962, Uganda, Burundi and Rwanda, in 1963 Kenya and in 1965-66 Gambia declared their independence.

The white settlers of Rhodesia declared unilateral independence in 1965. Only the Europeans had political rights, leading to the country being boycotted by the UN. South Africa's apartheid policy resulted in international protests and boycotts. The black opposition united in the African National Congress.

King Mohammed V of Morocco was able to declare independence from France in 1956 and Tunisia under President Habib Bourguiba became a sovereign state in the same year, Algeria's situation was different, since it was considered a part of metropolitan France and had a huge European population. The Algerian War was fought between 1954 and 1962. In 1958, a military coup which started in Algiers toppled the fourth French republic, and France's new strong man, Charles de Gaulle, attempted a settlement, but it was not until 1962 that the People's Democratic Algerian Republic was proclaimed. The neighbouring state of Libya was under UN trusteeship and became independent in 1951 under King Mohammed

1 Democratic steps like this village court are overshadowed by **2** armed conflicts and civil wars such as those in Ethiopia. **3** Liberia is not the only country affected by hundreds of people fleeing from the war. **4** With the first free elections in 1994 democracy was introduced in South Africa.

In the 1950s, the African states began to gain independence from the European colonialists. Among the most prominent black African politicians were (from left to right) **Patrice Lumumba** (Belgian-Congo), **Julius Nyerere** (Tansania), **Ahmed Sékou Touré** (Guinea) and **Kwame Nkrumah** (Ghana).

Idris I. He was toppled by a military coup in 1969. Since then, the country has been ruled by the 'Leader of the Revolution' the dictator Muammar Ghaddafi.

The Belgian Congo was granted independence in 1960 and its duly elected president Patrice Lumumba took office. Immediately, the provinces of Katanga (under Moîse Tshombe) and South Kasai attempted to secede, starting a brutal civil war, involving foreign powers and white mercenaries, that lasted until 1964. In the end Colonel Mobutu Sese Seko gained power in a coup d'état, supported by the West which suspected Lumumba of being too friendly with the communists.

By the end of the 1970s, almost the whole of Africa was independent. After the end of the dictatorship in Portugal, the wars in Mozambique and Angola ended, and Guinea-Bissau and Cape Verde also achieved independence. Nevertheless, these former Portuguese possessions were not to attain peace. Angola and Mozambique were granted independence in 1974 and 1975 respectively when Portugal overthrew its dictator, Salazar. However, in both countries civil war broke out as various warring factions, supported by the West and the communists with help for the former from South Africa, battled each other in a bloody struggle for power. The Angolan war lasted from 1974 to 1991 and the Mozambique war from 1975 to 1994. Both countries are still recovering from the damage and there have been setbacks in Angola due to severe flooding in recent years.

In 1975, French rule ended over the Comoro Islands, and a year later Djibouti gained independence. In 1976, Spain withdrew from its overseas province of Western Sahara, which was claimed by both Mauritania and Morocco. Mauritania withdrew its troops in 1979, but Morocco continued the war against the Polisario Front which championed a separate Sahara state. In 1992, a peace agreement provided for a referendum under UN supervision, but this has since been delayed by Morocco. Algeria has been riven by civil war after the fundamental Islamicist party the

FIS were denied power in 1991. The war broke out in 1992.

In 1980, Southern Rhodesia formally achieved independence under the name of Zimbabwe. In 1990, following the resolutions of the so-called Turnhalle Conference, Namibia, until then governed from South Africa, also became independent.

The young African states faced a whole series of major problems. The national borders ran along arbitrary colonial lines with no regard for ethnic and cultural affinities, thus hindering the establishment of genuine nation-states. Many countries replaced

democratic parliamentary constitutions with one-party systems and dictatorships. The USSR iencouraged this form of rule, and both West and East tried to extend their influence in Africa and conducted several 'proxy wars'. One bright spot was the end of apartheid in South Africa and the election of the winner of the Nobel Peace Prize, Nelson Mandela, as the country's president. Yet even today, many Africa countries are mired in strife. Ethnic conflicts, military coups and wars are still the order of the day. Among the worst were the massacres in Burundi and Rwanda in 1994. Civil wars prevail in Liberia, Sierra Leone, the Democratic Republic of Congo, Chad, Uganda, Guinea-Bissau, Somalia, the Ivory Coast and Nigeria. After Eritrea split from Ethiopia in 1993, border conflicts led to a war that ended in 2000 with the defeat of Eritrea. The border has since then been policed by UN forces. A civil war rages in Sudan against the

tribal people of the south conducted by the Janjaweed Islamic militia. Most African countries are in a state of economic depression due massive debt. Their inadequate healthcare systems are unable to cope with epidemics such as AIDS, malaria and ebola, droughts and floods. The future for Africa looks grim.

1 In the Western Sahara the Polisario Front fights against the Moroccan army for a sovereign state.

2 Fifty covered ox-wagons in the town of Dundee in South Africa commemorate the Battle of Blood River in 1838 between the Boers and the Zulus.

3 Confident of victory, ANC leader Nelson Mandela speaks during his election campaign in Durban in spring 1994.

4 In the early 1990s, more than 50,000 were killed and a further 300,000 died of famine in the civil war in Somalia.

Preserving their culture has some negative aspects for the children of the Masai. Young girls are often engaged to be married at birth and are subject to the genital mutilation known as 'female circumcision'.

The Countries of Africa

Africa, the third largest continent in the world after Asia and America, stretches from the Mediterranean in the north to the Cape of Good Hope in the south and lies between the Atlantic and Indian Oceans. The Sahara divides

A traditional method of carrying water in many African regions.

the continent into two completely different regions. The north is populate by light-skinned Arabs and Berbers, the dark-skinned peoples, Bushmen, Khoikhoi and Pygmies live in the south. There is also a great difference in flora and fauna. The Mediterranean north has a desert landscape with few animal species, while the rainforests and savannahs of the south have a rich plant and animal life. Even now that they have gained their independence, most of the young African nations struggle with natural disasters, famine, poverty, disease, civil wars and ethnic conflicts.

Casablanca is the largest city and the economic centre of Morocco. The port began to prosper in the Middle Ages, and has been repeatedly destroyed and rebuilt. After the withdrawal of the French, *Morocco experienced economic difficulties, but Casablanca has recovered. An expression of the city's new self-confidence is the Grande Mosque de Hassan II with its 200-m-high minaret, which opened in 1993.*

Morocco	
Area:	446,550 sq. km
Capital city:	Rabat
Form of government:	
Constitutional Monarchy	
Administrative divisions:	
16 regions	
Population:	33.7 million
(75 inhabitants/sq. km)	
Languages:	
Arabic (official), French,	
Berber dialects	
GDP per capita:	US$2,100
Currency:	
1 dirham = 100 centimes	

Natural Geography

The Mediterranean coast is 475 km long and lined with steep cliffs. It is bordered by a flat coastal plain which stretches for 1,050 km. A broad coastal plain then develops into the Moroccan Meseta, an area of high plains with an altitude of up to 450 m. The plains are flanked in the south and east by the **High and Middle Atlas Mountains**. The High Atlas extend 700 km, of which the highest point is the 4,165-m-high Jebel Toubkal. The Middle Atlas has peaks of up to 3,240 m in height and the Ante-Atlas in the southwest is an area of plateaus up to 2,000 m above sea level. In the north of the country, parallel to the Mediterranean coast, are the **Rif Mountains**, a range of fold mountains with peaks of up to 2,456 m. High plains in the east mark the border with Algeria. The semi-desert area below the coastal plain is known as the bled.

Climate

The Atlas mountains form a barrier between the Mediterranean climate of the north-west and the Saharan-continental climate in the south and south-east. In the dry, hot summers of the northwest the temperature can rise to 29°C, and winters have high precipitation, with average temperatures of 12°C. This part of Morocco receives between 200 and 900 mm of rain per year. The **continental climate** of the south means that temperatures can range between 0°C in winter and up to 45°C in summer. Precipitation is below 250 mm. High altitude regions receive 1,000 mm of precipitation, but above 1,000 m most of this falls as snow. A **desert climate,** with precipitation below 200 mm, predominates on the Saharan fringes.

Population

Half of the inhabitants are Arabianised Berbers, and about 40 per cent are Berbers. Malaki Sunnis represent 89 per cent of religious affiliation. Average life expectancy is 71 years and the literacy rate is 44 per cent. There are minorities of Christians and Jews.

Morocco: carpets shops in the souqs of the Medina of Marrakesh.

History and Politics

In the twelfth century BC, the **Phoenicians** established trading posts on the north-west African coast. The Berber kingdom of Mauritania was established in the fourth century BC in the interior of the country. After the final defeat of **Carthage**, whose centre had been close to modern Tunis, the **Romans** began to exert influence over the region. After the collapse of the Western Roman Empire, the **Vandals** claimed it in the fifth century AD From the seventh century onwards, the **Arabs** continued to tighten their grip on Morocco, and together with allied Berber tribes conquered the Iberian peninsula, which had been occupied by the Visigoths. Islamic rule changed from the the Idrisids in the eleventh century to the Almoravids, who 100 years later gave way to the Almohads. These in turn fell to the Merinids in the thirteenth century, and finally the Wattasids in 1420. Under the Reconquista in 1492, Spain was recaptured from the North African Moors and henceforward, the Arab empires of North Africa came under increasing European influence. Initially, the Spanish and Portuguese controlled all the most important ports, until the Alawite Dynasty, which still rules today, recaptured these cities in ca. 1670. Only Melilla, Ifni and Ceuta remained Spanish. In 1830, France attempted to bring Morocco under its influence. This resulted in a war, ending in 1844 with Moroccan defeat. The French and the Spanish divided Morocco between them in two protectorates.

Morocco gained full **independence** in 1956, except for the enclaves of Ceuta and Melilla; until 1969, Sidi Ifni remained Spanish. Sultan Mohammed V became King and was succeeded by his son Hassan II in 1961 as the head of a constitutional monarchy. In terms of foreign policy, Hassan followed a pro-European course. He died in 1999. His eldest son was then crowned Mohammed VI. The occupation by Morocco of the former Spanish colony of the Western Sahara in 1975 has developed into a long-term conflict. The most recent UN interventions failed. In 2002, there was conflict with Spain arose when Moroccan police occupied the island of Perejil in the Mediterranean. The constitution was last amended in 1996 and provides for a **bicameral parliament** with a National Assembly and a Senate.

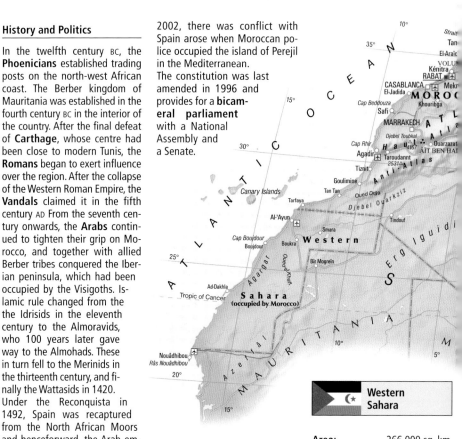

Economy

In 2006, Morocco had a GDP of 66 billion US dollars. Of this, 14 per cent derived from **agriculture,** 33 per cent from **manufacturing** and 53 per cent from the **services sector**. The most important exports are phosphate, the sale of fishing licenses and tourism. Morocco imports raw materials, machine tools and vehicles, foodstuffs and finished products. Exports include fertilisers, foodstuffs and manufactured goods.

Transport Infrastructure

The **rail network** is 1,907 km long, and the road network covers 60,513 km. International **airports** are at Rabat, Tangiers, Marrakesh, Agadir and Casablanca, where the most important **ports** are located.

Tourism

The old royal cities of Casablanca and Marrakesh and the Mediterranean beaches are Morocco's main attractions.

Western Sahara	
Area:	266,000 sq. km
Capital city:	El Aaiún
Form of government: Republic/	
annexed by Morocco since 1979	
Population:	
380,000 (1 inhabitant/sq. km)	
Languages:	Arabic, Spanish
GDP per capita:	
no data available	
Currency: virtual currency 1 Moroccan dirham= 100 centimes	

Natural Geography

The country is almost uninhabited and consists mainly of **desert and semi-desert** with stony desert in the north, and sandy desert in the south.

Climate

The extremely **arid climate** yields an average temperature of 22°C all year round. Rainfall is limited to a couple of days a year.

Population

The small population of the Western Saha is mainly **Sahrawi**, a mixed race with Arab, Berber and black African roots. 90 per cent profess Sunni Islam.

Marrakesh was founded in 1063 by the Almoravid Dynasty. It was also the capital city of the Almohads until the end of the thirteenth century. It is one of the four Moroccan royal cities, the others being Meknes, Fés and Rabat, and possesses important examples of Islamic architecture. The Jemaa-el-Fna is the centre of one of the most beautiful souqs (markets) in Morocco. The medina of Marrakesh is a UNESCO World Heritage Site.

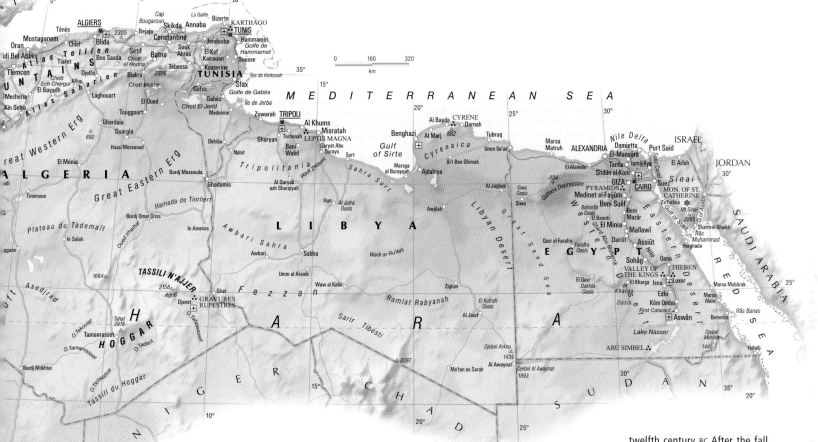

History and Politics

Since the eleventh century, the territory has been part of the Islamic empire which today rules Morocco. In 1885, the territory became Spanish, as Spanish Morocco and was declared the overseas province of Spanish Sahara in 1958. In 1973, the **Polisario Front**, a liberation movement, was established. Spain withdrew from the area in 1975 and Morocco and Mauritania were left to govern the country. Mauritania abandoned its claims to the land in 1979 in favour of the Polisario, and the land was then annexed by Morocco.

After a UN peace initiative, the Polisario and Morocco agreed to a ceasefire in 1991, to be followed by a referendum. So far, neither side can agree on how the process should continue. In 2002, the Security Council requested a UN mandate. In 2003, the UN made a new proposal, but as yet only the Polisario has agreed to it. Under the proposal, the region must enter a transitional phase with considerable autonomy, followed by a referendum in 2008. The Democratic Arab Republic of Sahara (UN name: Western Sahara) is recognised by 29 OAU states and 77 states worldwide.

Economy

The country has **phosphate reserves** and **fish stocks** in the coastal waters. Oasis agriculture and livestock-rearing is sufficient for the country's population.

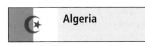

Algeria

Area:	2,381,741 sq. km
Capital city:	Algiers
Form of government:	
Presidential Republic	
Administrative divisions:	
48 districts	
Population:	
33.3 million	
(13 inhabitants/sq. km)	
Language:	Arabic

GDP per capita:
US$3,400

Currency: 1 Algerian dinar = 100 centimes

Natural Geography

The country consists of a narrow coastal plain with numerous bays on the Mediterranean Sea. The hinterland consists of the **Atlas Mountains** with peaks of up to 2,308 m. In the south the mountains form a plateau at an altitude of between 800 and 1,000 m, dominated by salt marshes called the 'chotts'. South of this is the **Saharan Atlas**, reaching an altitude of 2,328 m and bordering the **Sahara Desert**. The Sahara covers 80 per cent of Algeria's land mass and, apart from a narrow strip of rolling hills, the land is sandy desert with almost no vegetation. The volcanic **Ahaggar Mountains** in the southwest rise to a height of 2,918 m.

Climate

The coast and the northern slopes of the Atlas Mountains have a Mediterranean climate, with an average rainfall of 500 to 1,000 mm. The damp winter **steppe climate** of the chotts produces temperatures of 0°C in winter and 30°C in summer, with precipitation of approximately 350 mm per year. Air temperatures in the Sahara can vary by up to 20°C throughout the course of the day, with a winter average of 0°C and a summer average of more than 40°C. In summer, the area is affected by the dry **Sirocco** wind.

Population

The Algerian population is 70 per cent **Arab** and approximately 30 per cent **Berber (Kabyle)**, with a small French minority. With the exception of a few Christians, the population is almost exclusively Muslim.

History and Politics

The land was originally ruled by Berber and Moorish tribes until the **Phoenicians** established their first settlements in the twelfth century BC After the fall of **Carthage** in 149 BC, the **Romans** conquered the land in 46 BC along with the kingdom of Numidia; Numidia-Mauritania was a Roman province until the invasion of the Vandals in 429. From the seventh century onwards, several Berber and Arab kingdoms were established, until the deys, elected by the Turkish Janissaries of Algiers, took power in 1600. The Spanish, Dutch, British and French were held back until the **French** occupied Algiers in 1830 and extended their sphere of influence ever further south. In 1947, all Algerians were granted French citizenship, but this did not stop the formation of a **resistance movement**. The FLN ('Front de Libération Nationale'), under the leadership of **Ben Bella**, initiated a war against the French in 1954, until France was finally forced to recognise Algeria's **independence** in 1962. Ben Bella became the first Prime Minister of Algeria and, in 1963, the country's first President, until he was overthrown in a coup d'état by the chief-of-staff, Houari Boumedienne, in 1965.

Algeria, Tunisia

The **Sahara** covers more than 80 per cent of Algeria's land area. The Tuareg used to control the trade routes and participated in caravanserai trade. Today, it is very difficult for them to practice their traditional nomadic economy.

Since the early 1990s, the conflict between the government and the **Front Islamique du Salut (FIS)** has caused severe problems. An unparalleled terror campaign has cost in excess of 80,000 lives, but it is unclear who is responsible for the massacres – the Islamic fundamentalists or the military. The constitution of 1996 provides for a freely elected bicameral parliament, and although a new National Assembly was elected in 1997, an end to the violence is not in sight. In 2001, there was unrest among the Kabyles, who demanded equality and cultural autonomy. As a result, the Berber language, Tamazight, was introduced as a second official language.

Economy

In 2006, Algeria's gross national product was US$114 billion. Of this, **agriculture** contributed ten per cent, **manufacturing** 60 per cent and the **service sector** 30 per cent. Main exports are crude oil and natural gas. Algeria imports food, machine parts and motorised vehicles.

Transport Infrastructure

The **rail network** covers 4,772 km, and the road network extends for 102,424 km, of which 70,650 km is surfaced. There are international **airports** in Algiers and Oran. These cities are also the main **sea ports**.

Tourism

Tourist numbers have fallen significantly due to the terrorism of the Islamic fundamentalists. The situation is improving, however.

	Tunisia

Area:	163,610 sq. km
Capital city:	Tunis
Form of government:	
Presidential Republic	
Administrative divisions:	
23 provinces	
Population:	
10.2 million (62 inhabitants/sq. km)	
Languages:	
Arabic (official), French	
GDP per capita:	US$3,000

Currency:

1 Tunisian dinar = 1000 millimes

Natural Geography

In the north, undulating steppes cover the foothills of the **Atlas Mountains**. The foothills of the Saharan Atlas Mountains, whose peaks rise to 1,590 m, extend as far as the coastal plains around Sfax. To the south lie salt marshes, which eventually give way to the desert dunes of the **Great Eastern Erg**, which are bordered in the east by salt marshes and the **Ksour Massif**. The north of the country has a steep coastline, but the coast in the south is sandy, with numerous lagoons. The island of **Djerba** is located off-shore in the Gulf of Sirte.

Climate

The north of the country has a **Mediterranean climate**. Precipitation is between 500 and 1,000 mm on the north coast and approximately 1,500 mm in the mountains. Average temperatures are 10°C in January and 26°C in August. The **desert climate** of the Atlas results in temperatures of up to 45°C, and precipitation of a maximum 200 mm per year.

Population

Tunisia's population is 98 per cent **Arab** and Muslim Berbers. There are also 1.3 per cent tribal **Berbers** and a minority of Europeans – mainly French. Islam is the state religion, and 98 per cent of Muslims are Sunni. In addition, there are also Jewish, Catholic and Protestant minorities. Average life expectancy is 75, and adult literacy rate is 70 per cent.

History and Politics

The region was first settled by Berber peoples, but the **Phoenicians** established trading posts in around 1100 BC The empire of **Carthage** ruled the western Mediterranean until the **Romans** succeeded in obtaining a foothold in North Africa after the Third Punic War in 149 BC The region was conquered by the **Vandals** in 439, who ruled for over 100 years, followed by the **Arabs**. The Habsburgs ruled for a short period from 1535, followed in 1574 by the Turks, who incorporated Tunisia into the **Ottoman Empire**.

In 1881, the French made Tunisia a protectorate. Tunisia gained full national **independence** in 1956 and, after a short period as a monarchy, became a republic in 1957. The first President, **Habib Bourguiba,** held office until 1987. His successor, **Ben Ali,** who followed a liberal path. Ben Ali retained his post as President in elections in 1994, 1999 and 2004. The constitution dates from 1959 and was last amended in 1994. It provides for election of the parliament every five years and the direct election of the President.

Economy

In 2006, GDP was US$31 billion, of which 16 per cent derived from **agriculture**, 28 per cent from **manufacturing** and 56 per cent from **services**. Main exports are textiles and leather, phosphates, heavy industry, energy and foodstuffs. Main imports are raw

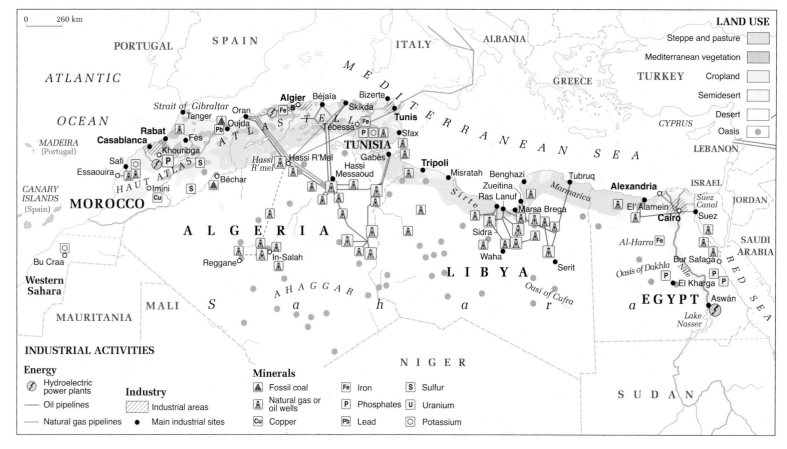

LAND USE

- Steppe and pasture
- Mediterranean vegetation
- Cropland
- Semidesert
- Desert
- Oasis

INDUSTRIAL ACTIVITIES

Energy
- Hydroelectric power plants
- Oil pipelines
- Natural gas pipelines

Industry
- Industrial areas
- Main industrial sites

Minerals
- Fossil coal
- Natural gas or oil wells
- Copper
- Iron
- Phosphates
- Lead
- Sulfur
- Uranium
- Potassium

Tunis was established by the Phoenicians in the sixth century BC, but only gained importance under the Hafsid Dynasty. Its importance increased under the Spanish Moors from the thirteenth to the seventeenth centuries. Many examples of Islamic architecture can be seen in the medina. The Great Mosque of Tunis was founded in 732, and reconstructed between the thirteenth and fifteenth centuries. The minaret was renovated in 1894.

materials and semi-manufactured products, machinery, vehicles and manufactured goods.

Transport Infrastructure

The **rail network** is approximately 2,260 km long, with some additional narrow-gauge sections for the transport of phosphates. The road network covers 20,830 km, of which 15,832 km are surfaced. There are International **airports** in Tunis, Sfax, Monastir, Tozeur, Djerba and Tabarka. Main **sea ports** are in Tunis La Goulette, Gabès and Bizerta.

Tourism

In 2004, Tunisia welcomed 6 million foreign visitors, bringing US$1.605 billion into the country. The excellent infrastructure and varied tourist attractions, including ruins from the Phoenician and Roman periods, as well as mosques and religious buildings make Tunisia an attractive country. Tunisians are also famous for their cuisine, considered to be the best in the Maghreb.

Libya

Area:	1,759,540 sq. km
Capital city:	Tripoli
Form of government:	
Islamic People's Republic	
Administrative divisions:	
3 provinces, 10 governorates	
Population:	
6 million (3 inhabitants/sq. km)	
Languages:	
Arabic (official), Berber dialects	
GDP per capita:	US$8,400
Currency:	
1 Libyan dinar = 1000 dirham	

Natural Geography

Tripolitania in the north-west consists of the coastal plains and the Al Hamadah al Hamra plateaus at an altitude of 968 m. The Sirte Basin region includes the volcanic **Al-Haruj al-Aswad** mountain (1,200 m) and has massive crude oil reserves. The **Fezzan** is an area of the hinterland consisting of sand, gravel and stony desert. **Cyrenaica** in the north-east is dominated by **Al Jabal al Akhdar** karst mountains, which descend steeply to the coast and which become the steppes of **Marmarica** in the east and the Libyan desert in the south. With 2,286 m, Picco Bette is Libya's highest mountain, one of the northern foothills of the **Tibesti** on the border with Chad.

Climate

Almost 85 per cent of Libya's land mass is **desert** without significant precipitation, but the temperatures vary from around 0°C in winter to over 50°C in summer. On the Mediterranean coast, the average January temperature is 12°C and the average temperature in August is 26°C. Average precipitation is 300 mm. The flora and fauna of the coast are typically Mediterranean. This changes to steppe vegetation further inland, before completely disappearing in the barren desert. The most common animal species are hyenas, jackals, desert foxes and jerboa, birds of prey, snakes, scorpions, wild asses, hares and baboons.

Population

Libya's population is 97 per cent **Arab** and Muslim **Berbers**. There are minorities of Tuareg, Nilo-Saharans, Egyptians and black Africans. Islam is the state religion and that of 97 per cent of the population. There are small minorities of Catholics, Copts and other religions. Average life expectancy is 76 years.

History and Politics

In pre-Christian times, the **Phoenicians, Greeks**, and **Cartha-** ginians established settlements on the Libyan coast until the **Romans** occupied the area in the first century BC When the Roman Empire divided in two, Tripolitania became part of the Western Roman Empire, and Cyrenaica was ruled by Byzantium. The **Vandals, who succeeded the Romans** ruled for some hundred

 Adrar is the main town in the Touat Oasis in Algeria and is an important centre of local trade.

2 **Ghardaia**, the main town of the Algerian oasis region Mzab. It forms a pentapolis with four other towns. Houses with terraced rooves are very typical.

3 **Taghit** is a typical oasis settlement on the edge of the Great Western Erg in Algeria.

4 Tunisia: The Sidi Okba Mosque or Great Mosque in Kairouan was reconstructed in the ninth century and stands out due to its marble and porphyry columns.

Erg is the Arabic word for a wide desert of sand-dunes such as the Libyan desert. A stony, rocky desert is called a hamada, a serir is a desert plain covered in pebbles and gravel, and fesh-fesh are deserts of fine golden sand.

years, until the **Byzantine Empire** was able to reconquer the land in the sixth century.

In 644, the **Arabs** controlled the region and converted the Berbers to Islam. In the sixteenth century, Libya became a part of the **Ottoman Empire**, and remained so until the Italo-Turkish War of 1911–1912. Italy declared Libya an Italian colony in 1934. The Sanussi, who had ruled hitherto, **resisted** the colonial rulers. In World War II, Italian and German troops fought heavy battles against the Allies on Libyan soil.

In 1945, Libya was occupied by the British and French until the UN declared the country an independent, united kingdom in 1951. King Idris al-Senussi was toppled from power in 1969 by a military coup led by **Muammar al Ghaddafi**. Although Colonel Ghaddafi no longer officially holds office, he continues to exert a strong influence on Libyan policy.

Congress is the nation's highest policy-making body.

The government consists of a General Secretariat of seven members. Political parties are not permitted. The voting age is 18.

Economy

GDP in 2006 totalled US$50 billion, of which **agriculture** accounted for seven per cent, **manufacturing** 44 per cent and the **services sector** 49 per cent. The main products are crude oil and natural gas, which represent 90 per cent of exports. Libya imports industrial finished products, machinery and transport equipment, chemicals, foodstuffs, luxury items and livestock.

Transport Infrastructure

The country's **road network** has a total length of some 19,189 km, more than half of which is

Egypt

Area:	1,001,450 sq. km
Capital city:	Cairo
Form of government:	Presidential Republic
Administrative divisions:	26 provinces
Population:	80 million (68 inhabitants/sq. km)
Language:	Arabic
GDP per capita:	US$1,500
Currency:	1 Egyptian pound = 100 piastres

Natural Geography

The **Nile** is Egypt's wellspring of life. In Upper Egypt, the river has eroded a course through the limestone bedrock of the desert. Between Lake Nasser and the beginning of the delta region north of Cairo, the Nile forms a stretch of fertile land approximately

The Mediterranean coast has a flat, dune-covered landscape.

Climate

Only the area north of Cairo has a Mediterranean climate, with a rainfall of between 100 and 200 mm per annum. In the south it hardly ever rains and temperatures fluctuate greatly. In the north, average temperatures vary between 20°C in winter and 35°C in summer. In Aswan, temperatures range between 24°C and 41°C. In the spring, the **Khamsin**, a hot, dry sandstorm, blows across the country.

Most of the country is almost devoid of vegetation, with the exception of some tough grasses, acacia and thorn bushes. Various varieties of reed, bamboo and lotus grow on the banks of the Nile. The animal species include typical desert animals, such as the jerboa, scorpions, jackals and

History and Politics

The legendary **King Menes** united the kingdoms of Upper and Lower Egypt in around 2900 BC Hieroglyphic writing, the Egyptian calendar, a distinctive cult of the dead and a polytheistic religion had already developed by the end of the first of a total of 30 Egyptian dynasties. **Ancient Egyptian** culture experienced its first golden age under the pharoahs of the fourth dynasty. The pyramids of Snofru, Cheops, Khafra and Mykerinos remain today as examples of this great civilisation.

After the collapse of the Old Kingdom between 2134 and 1991 BC there was a phase of instability, which ended when the Princes of Thebes caused Egypt to flourish once more in the **Middle Kingdom**. Foreign rule by the Hyksos lasted from 1650 until 1544 BC, followed by the es-

---

Muammar al Gaddafi

*Sirte, Sept. 1942

In 1969, Colonel Ghaddafi led a group of military officers and toppled King Idris of Libya. He has since determined the country's policies under several guises. In his 'Green Book' he promoted the main elements for the establishment of an Islamic Socialist Republic. His nationalisation of the oil industry and support for Islamic terror organisations lisolated Libya on the global stage. His policies have now changed.

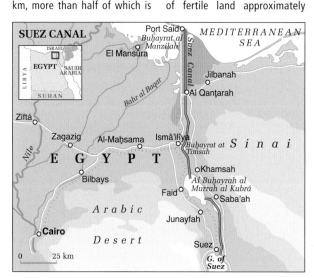

Gamal Abdel Nasser

*Beni Mor, 15.1.1918, †Cairo, 28.9.1970

Nasser assisted General Naguib in overthrowing King Farouk in 1952. In 1954, he seized power from Neguib, becoming President. He soon aligned himself with the Eastern Bloc, although Communists were persecuted in Egypt. His rule saw the construction of the Aswan Dam, the nationalisation of the Suez Canal and the Six-Day War of 1967 against Israel, in which Egypt was resoundly defeated.

Mohammed Anwar Sadat

*Mit Abu al-Kaum, 25.12.1918, †Cairo, 6.10.1981

As a founder of the 'Free Officers Movement', Sadat played a decisive role in the fall of King Farouk. He became Nasser's successor and led Egypt in the Yom Kippur War against Israel in 1973. In 1979, Sadat was the first Arab leader to make peace with Israel. He was thus able to recover Sinai and reopen the Suez Canal but his moderate stance caused him to be assassinated by an extremist.

During Ghaddafi's rule, planned unions with Islamic 'brother states' have failed and the nationalisation of the oil industry and the banks have caused conflict between the Libyan ruler and the Western world. This tension was increased by direct military engagement in Chad and Libyan support of Islamic **terror organisations** abroad.

Libya was even suspected of producing chemical weapons. In recent years, all this has changed and Ghaddafi is now considered a moderate in the Arab world. Under the terms of the 1977 constitution, the General People's

surfaced. Important **sea ports** are Tripoli, Bengazi and Misurata. There are international **airports** for the main cities, Tripoli and Bengazi.

Tourism

Due to the political situation, tourism in Libya is relatively under-developed. The country is visited by 140,000 visitors per year, who spend around US$220 million. This is a pity, as there are some spectacular Roman and Carthaginian remains and other attractions. In recent years, tourism has been encouraged.

25 km wide. North of Cairo, the delta covers roughly 23,000 sq. km, and includes tributaries, canals and irrigation systems.

West of the Nile, the **Libyan Desert**, has a monotonous sand-dune landscape broken only by a few scattered oases. The **Arabian Desert** east of the Nile is dominated by a line of mountains up to 2,000 m high, dissected by numerous wadis (dry river beds). Egypt's highest point is the 2,637 m Jabal Katrina (St Catherine's Mount), in the **Sinai** peninsula. The **Red Sea** coast contains many coral reefs and the mountains descend right to the sea.

hyenas. There are just under 200 species of fish in the Nile, and a few crocodiles. The variety of birds is comparatively large.

Population

Egypt has a relatively homogeneous population, descended from the **Ancient Egyptians** and **Arabs**. There are also minorities of Sudanese, Syrians, Bedouin, Nubians, Palestinians, Berbers, Beja and Europeans. Some 90 per cent are Muslim, mostly Sunni, and the rest are Coptic, Greek Orthodox, Catholic, Protestant and Jewish. Average life expectancy is 71.

tablishment of the **New Kingdom**, under Amenophis Thutmosis. The New Kingdom had its age of glory in the nineteenth dynasty under Seti I and Ramses II. Most of the great Egyptian monuments date from this era.

The collapse of the kingdom began in the twenty-first dynasty when it was conquered by Ethiopians, Assyrians and, in 525 BC, by the Persians, who formed the twenty-eighth, twenty-nineth and thirtieth dynasties. The rule of the Hellenistic **Ptolemaics** began in 332 BC under Alexander the Great. This dynasty lasted until the fateful battle of

Mulid is one of the most important Islamic festivals. During the festival, people illuminate their houses with decorative lights, sing songs and collect in the mosques to remember the birth of the prophet Muhammad. The celebrations do not follow a special liturgy, but instead, people pray as normal. On this festival, all the mosques in the Islamic world, such as this one, the Hussein Mosque in Fostat, the old part of Cairo, are particularly busy.

Actium in 30 BC, which Cleopatra VII and Mark Antony lost to Octavian. Egypt remained a **Roman province** until the collapse of the Roman Empire in 395, and then became part of **Byzantium**.

After a short period of occupation by the Persians, Arabs converted the country to Islam in 640 and it became part of the **Caliphate ruled from Baghdad**. The Egyptian Mamelukes seized power in 1250 and ruled until Egypt became part of the **Ottoman Empire** in 1517. Between 1798–1801, Napoleon led an unsuccessful campaign to conquer Egypt. In the aftermath, the Turkish governor Mehmet Ali was able to stabilise the situation, but in the mid-nineteenth century, as the Ottoman Empire declined Egypt fell increasingly under British and French influence, mainly due to the construction of the **Suez canal**.

From 1914 to 1922, Egypt was officially a **British protectorate**, and then an independent constitutional monarchy under Fuad I. In 1936, the British officially withdrew altogether under pressure from King Farouk, but they continued to maintain control of the Canal Zone.

Egypt's first attack on the newly established state of **Israel** in 1948 ended in a ceasefire. **Gamal Abdel Nasser** became President of the Republic of Egypt after a military coup. He followed his own path of 'Arabic socialism', oriented towards the Soviet Union. His effort to unite Arab nations failed in 1961 with the dissolution of the **United Arab Republic**, of which Egypt, Syria and the Yemen were members. The second war launched against Israel was the **Six Day War** of 1967. Israel captured the Sinai peninsula and the Gaza Strip from Egypt. The third attack on Israel, the Yom Kippur War of 1973, launched by Nasser's successor **Mohammed Anwar Sadat** was more successful. Sadat was the first Arab leader to make peace with Israel. Egypt was temporarily isolated within the Arab world and Sadat paid for the peace with his life in 1981 when he was assassinated by a Muslim fanatic. Under his successor, **Mohammed Hosni Mubarak,** Sinai was restored to Egypt in 1981 and the head

office of the Arab League was moved back to Cairo in 1990. On a domestic level, attacks by Islamic fundamentalists on tourists are a repeated source of unrest.

The constitution of 1971 was limited in 1981 by an emergency law. Of the 454, members of parliament, 444 are elected for five-year terms, and ten are named by the President. The advisory board, the Shoura, consists of 210 members, 57 of whom are chosen by the President. The head of state is directly elected every six years upon the recommendation of the parliament. The voting age is 18.

Economy

Gross Domestic Product in 2006 was US$108 billion, to which **agriculture** contributed 15 per cent, **manufacturing** 35 per cent and the **services sector** 50 per cent. Half of all export income derives from oil and gas. Cotton, textiles, metal products and foodstuffs are also exported. Important imports are machinery, foodstuffs, iron, steel and also cars. After the Suez canal, tourism is the main source of income in Egypt.

Transport Infrastructure

Africa's oldest **rail network** covers a total length of 4,751 km, but much of the rolling stock is outdated. Some 30 per cent of the 50,000-km-long **road network** is surfaced. The most important **sea ports** are Alexandria, Port Said and Suez. There are international **airports** at Cairo, Luxor and Alexandria. The

Suez Canal links the Mediterranean to the Red Sea.

Tourism

In 2004, 5 million foreign visitors spent approximately US$6.3 billion in Egypt. The best time to visit Upper Egypt is in the cooler months, from October to April.

1 Egypt: the camel remains an important form of transport – here a camel market in the Souq al-Jamaal in Cairo.

2 Cairo has more than 500 mosques, some of which date from the ninth century. The Sultan Hassan Mosque is the most beautiful in the city.

3 Fostat, the old town of Cairo, with its narrow alleys, mosques and bazaars, is a UNESCO World Heritage Site.

4 The Isis Temple and Trajan's Kiosk on the Island of Philae were moved to the island of Agilkia during the construction of Aswan Dam.

Mauritania

*Mali's agriculture is constantly subject to devastating periods of **drought**. Dams and irrigation systems are designed to expand the area of cultivable land and transform desert areas into farmland.*

Mauritania

Area:	1,030,700 sq. km
Capital city:	Nouakchott

Form of government:
Islamic Presidential Republic

Administrative divisions:
13 regions

Population:
3.2 million (3 inhabitants/sq. km)

Languages:
Arabic (official) and languages of Niger and the Congo

GDP per capita:	US$930

Currency:
1 ouguiya = 5 khoums

Natural Geography

Desert covers 47 per cent of the country's surface area and the coastal area is lined with sand dunes. Inland, lowland sand and rocky desert forms the Western edge of the **Sahara**.

In the central part of the country is a series of sandstone plateaus 300 to 500 m above sea level; the highest peak, **Kédia d'Idjil**, has an altitude of 915 m. In the eastern part of the country, the flat stony desert turns into the sandy desert valley of **El Djouf**. Agriculture is only possible in the south of the country, on approximately one per

Climate

Practically the whole country has a dry, hot desert climate with temperatures averaging 20 to 24°C in January and 30 to 34°C in July. The average rainfall is less than 100 mm in the North, and between 300 and 400 mm annually in the South.

The **desert steppe** and the **arid savannah** of the Sahel contain grassand and shrubs; date palms grow only in the **oases**. The banks antelopes. Ostriches, leopards and wart-hogs roam the desert steppes.

Population

Arabs and Berber Moors account for 81 per cent of the population. The **black Africans** consist of seven per cent Wolofs and there are five per cent Tou-

Islam is the state religion; there is a small minority of Christians. Due to the adverse conditions of terrain and climate and lack of natural re-

History and Politics

When the Portuguese landed on the coast of Mauritania in the early fifteenth century, the once-powerful Islamic Almoravid

Moktar Ould Daddah

***20.12.1924,
†Paris 14.10.2003**

The leader of the Parti du Peuple became the ruler after Mauritania gained its independence from France in 1960 and its first president in 1961. In 1964, he established an authoritarian one-party system and was confirmed in his office three times in elections. After unsuccessfully trying to take over the former Spanish Western Sahara in 1976, the country suffered a serious economic crisis. Daddah was overthrown in a military coup in 1978.

Mauritanian women are gaining self-confidence and independence in this Islamic state.

Moussa Traoré

*Kayes 12.9.1936

Traoré gained power through a military coup staged in Mali in 1968 and established a brutal regime of terror. In foreign policy, he was dependent on the Western, receiving support mainly from France, especially after the catastrophic droughts of the early 1970s. In 1991, he was overthrown himself in an army coup and imprisoned. After seven years, he was tried and sentenced to death, together with his wife, for abuse of power. He was subsequently pardoned.

cent of the country's surface area. The Senegal is the only river that contains water all year round and constitutes the most favourable area for human settlement.

of the Senegal are covered with baobab trees, raffia (raphia) palms and bamboo.
The savannah provides a habitat for elephants, lions, hyenas and

couleurs, three per cent Soninkes and one per cent Fulbes, Bambaras, Sarakolés and other ethnic groups. There are around 5,000 Europeans in the country.

sources, 31.4 per cent of Mauritanians live below the poverty line. The average life expectancy is only 53 years and the illiteracy rate is 49 per cent.

kingdom which extended as far as Spain had been defunct for 300 years. Due to the country's inhospitable terrain, the colonial powers showed little interest in

*Masks play an important role in the lives of the **Dogon** in Mali. There are a 100 different designs of the imaginative masks, symbolising ancestors, animals and spirits. Myths and stories are performed in rituals and dance.*

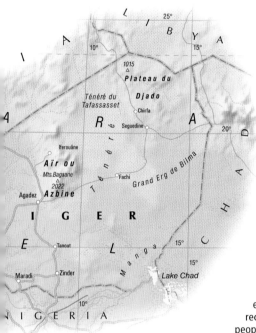

it; consequently, Moorish sultans reigned until the end of the nineteenth century. Not until 1903 did the French declare Mauritania a protectorate and in 1920 they finally made it into a colony.

After gaining **independence** in 1960, Morocco renounced its claims to the area but these were not surrendered until 1970. Following the retreat of the Spaniards from the Western Sahara, Mauritania occupied the south and Morocco the north of this former Spanish colony. Both powers subsequently embarked in a war, supported by France, against the **Polisario National Front** independence movement . During the clashes, Mauretania's armed forces revolted and in 1979 Mauritania waived all claims to the Western Sahara.

Several coups d'état and government reshuffles ensued which resulted in a turbulent period. Tensions with Senegal led to the respective expulsions of citizens. Since 1991 a new constitution has been in place which stipulates that Islamic sharia law is now to be enforced. In 1992, the first multi-party elections were held and good relations with Senegal were restored.

The national assembly is re-elected every five years and the members of parliament, the supreme court and the head of state are elected directly by the people every six years. Voting rights are granted to those aged over 18. Although opposition parties are permitted, elections have allegedly been manipulated to ensure the ruling party wins.

Economy

The Gross Domestic Product was US$2.7 billion in 2001. **Agriculture** accounted for 19 per cent of this amount, **industry** for 30 per cent and the **services sector** for 51 per cent.

The main exports are fish, fish products and raw materials, especially iron ore and gypsum. The main imports include foodstuffs, machinery, vehicles, oil and gas and chemicals.

Transport

Of the 8,900 km of **roads** only 1,700 km are surfaced. The only stretch of **railway track**, which is 675 km long, runs from Zouîrât to Nouadhibou and is predominantly used for transporting iron ore. There are **international airports** and **sea ports** in Nouakchott and Nouâdhibou.

Tourism

Tourism in Mauritania is extremely under-developed. Several oases and the remains of ancient Islamic architecture are worth a visit. The best time to visit is between November and March.

	Mali
Area:	1,240,192 sq. km
Capital city:	Bamako
Form of government: Presidential Republic	
Administrative divisions: 8 regions and a capital district	

1 The Dogon in Mali build their villages on the steep slopes of the Bandiagara Highlands in a loop of Niger river. The thatched buildings serve as granaries.

2 In the market of Bamako, the capital of Mali, the wares on offer include convenience foods, grain, fish and spices. Many shoppers still practise barter.

3 From 1907 until 1909 the great mosque of Djenné was restored, modelled on the orginal fifteenth-century design that had been destroyed.

Fulbe: they are probably the largest language group in West Africa, divided into several branches, widely varied in economic, cultural and religious terms. The Bororo are nomadic cattle herdsmen living in Niger and are not as influenced by Islam as the sedentary Fulbe tribes, who often live in small communities as farmers. The Bororo men are famous for their elaborate face painting.

Population: 12 million
(9 inhabitants/sq. km)
Languages: French (official language), Bamakan, other Mandé languages
GDP per capita: US$500
Currency:
1 CFA franc = 100 centimes

Natural Geography

The country is mainly desert, being covered by the **Sahara**, the **Sahel** and the **Sudan**. The desert in the north is flanked by the Adra mountains, rising to an altitude of up to 853 m. The river Niger flows through the south and floods vast areas on a regular basis. The highest elevation is the 1155-m-high Hombori Tondo south of the Niger Bend. The tableland of the southwest is characterised by the valleys of the Senegal river and its tributaries.

Climate

The climate outside the desert areas is **humid and tropical**, whilst a **desert climate** prevails in the areas covered by the Sahara. Average temperatures range between 25 and 30°C in the south and 18 and 36°C in the Sahara. During the rainy season, precipitation is between 1000 and 1500 mm in the south, whilst it often does not rain for years in the Sahara. The grassland savannah and gallery forests of the south adjoin dry savannah and thornbush savannah as one heads northwards. These finally turn into semi-desert and finally full desert. This is the habitat of lions, hyenas, leopards, monkeys, elephants, crocodiles, gazelles, buffalos, giraffes, hippopotamuses and many types of birds and snakes.

Population

The population comprises 32 per cent **Bambaras**, 14 per cent **Fulbes**, 12 per cent **Senufos**, nine per cent **Soninkés**, seven per cent **Tuaregs**, seven per cent **Songhais**, six per cent Malinkés and smaller individual groups. Muslims account for 80 per cent of the population, 18 per cent are followers of natural religions and just over one per cent is Christian. The average life expectancy is only 50 years and the illiteracy rate is 61 per cent.

History and Politics

Following the demise of several great empires the country broke off into smaller political units in the sixteenth century and was a French colony from 1895 to 1960. Following a failed attempt at a confederation of French Sudan and Senegal, Mali proclaimed its **independence** on 22 September 1960. After a revolt, a military dictatorship followed the first Socialist government. There has been a democratic constitution since 1992. The parliament and the head of state are elected directly every five years. Citizens over the age of 21 have the right to vote.

Economy

The Gross Domestic Product was US$6,200 million in 2006. **Agriculture** accounted for 46 per cent of this amount, **industry** for 17 per cent and the **services sector** for 37 per cent. The main imports are machinery, vehicles, petroleum and foodstuffs. Exports include cotton and gold.

Transport Infrastructure

The **road network** is approximately 13,000 km long, although only around 1,800 km is paved. The majority of the roads are in the south. The **rail network** is 650 km long. The rivers Niger and Senegal are navigable at times. There is an international **airport** in Sénou.

Tourism

The infrastructure is still underdeveloped. Mali is the site of the legendary city of Timbuktu (Timbuctoo), once the centre of a flourishing empire, which is its main attraction. Bamako has interesting markets and the national museum. The best time to visit is between November and February.

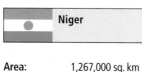

Niger

Area:	1,267,000 sq. km
Capital city:	Niamey
Form of government:	
Presidential Republic	
Administrative divisions:	
8 départements	
Population:	12.8 million
(10 inhabitants/sq. km)
Languages: French (official), Hausa and other tribal languages
GDP per capita.: US$280
Currency:
1 CFA franc = 100 centimes

Natural Geography

The **Aïr** volcanic mountain range dominates the centre of the country, rising to 2000 m and surrounded by the Central Sahara Basin on three sides. It adjoins the **Ahaggar Massif** to the North and the **Djado Plateau** and the **Tibesti Ridge** to the north-east. Numerous wadis criss-cross the **desert**. Only the River Niger and the Komadugu Yobe contain water all year round.

Climate

In the Sahara region a **desert climate** prevails, with temperatures between 17 and 34°C; precipitation is less than 50 mm. In the Sahel, temperatures range from 22°C in January to 34°C in June. Over half of the 400 to 700 mm precipitation falls in August. Grassland dotted with clumps of trees is characteristic of the savannahs of the south, whilst in the desert vegetation is confined to the oases. Desert foxes, lizards and desert rats (jerboa) are typical desert creatures. Ostriches, elephants, buffaloes, warthogs, lions, gazelles, antelopes and hyenas live in the savannah, in addition to numerous species of birds and snakes. Crocodiles and hippopotamuses live in the rivers.

Population

Hausas account for 53.6 per cent of the inhabitants of Niger. **Djermas** and **Songhays** account for 21 per cent, **Fulbes** for 10.4 per cent, **Tuaregs** for 9.2 per cent and **Kanouris** for 4.3 per cent. Tubus, Arabs and Europeans form small minorities.

80 per cent of the population is Muslim, approximately 15 per cent are animists and a minority are Christians. Life expectancy is extremely low at 44 years and the illiteracy rate is exceedingly high at 86 per cent, despite the fact that primary school is compulsory.

History and Politics

Before Europeans explored the country in the late eighteenth century, several great empires and city-states existed in what is now Niger and these were converted to Islam at an early stage. The colonial powers took no interest in the country until the late nineteenth century. Niger became a French colony in 1921, an overseas territory in 1946 and an autonomous republic in 1958.

After France granted Niger **independence** in 1960, several military dictatorships suceeded the first civilian government. The first free elections took place in 1993. In 1999, there was another coup d'état led by the army. Today the country has become a **democratic presidential republic** again. In accordance with the 1999 constitution, the Parliament is elected every five years. The head of state is also elected through direct elections every five years. The right to vote is granted at 18.

Economy

The GDP was almost US$3.6 thousand million in 2001. **Agriculture** accounted for 40 per cent of this sum, **industry** for 18 per cent and the **service sector** for 42 per cent. The main imports are consumer goods, partially processed and capital goods. Uranium, peanuts, gum arabic and livestock are exported. Niger recently hit the world headlines due the possibility that the country provided the former Iraqi dictator, Saddam Hussein, with uranium for bomb-making. The lasting drought has produced a prolonged economic crisis.

Transport Infrastructure

The length of the **road network** is only approximately 9,700 km,

Despite catastrophic economic conditions there is a rich offer in the markets of Cape Verde.

*Long period of drought and extreme temperatures are common in Niger. The sand and rock desert of **Ténéré** in the north of the republic is sparsely populated due to its unforgiving surroundings. However archaeological finds show that there was a thriving hunting and herding culture in the area between 7,000 and 3,000 BC, when the climate was considerably been milder. Djado is one of the few settlements in this region, consisting of traditional mud huts.*

of which only 3,200 km are paved. There is an international **airport** at Niamey. The river Niger is partially navigable.

Tourism

The main tourist attractions are the **'W'-National Park** and the **Aïr** and **Ténéré National Nature Reserves**. Only around 17,000 tourists visited the country in 1996. The best time to visit Niger is between November and March.

Cape Verde

Area:	4,033 sq. km
Capital city:	Praia
Form of government:	Republic
Administrative divisions: 15 districts	
Population: 420,000 (104 inhabitants/sq. km)	
Languages: Portuguese (official), Creole	
GDP per capita:	US$2,400
Currency: 1 Cape-Verde escudo = 100 centavos	

Natural Geography

Only ten of the 18 islands within a distance of 630 km of the West African coastline are inhabited. Whilst **Sal**, **Boa Vista** and **Maio** are relatively flat and characterised by sand dunes and salt marshes, the remaining islands are mountainous with a rocky coast. Pico, an extinct volcano is the highest elevation on Fogo Island, at an altitude of 2829 m.

Climate

The passat wind, blowing from the north-east produces a **tropical climate** with temperatures ranging from 22°C in February to 27°C in September. The precipitation of 250 mm on the coast and 1000 mm at altitudes only occurs during the south-west monsoon season from August to October. In some years, however, there is no rain at all. Brushwood and thorn bushes have replaced the original vegetation which has almost completely disappeared due to bush fires and overgrazing. While the sea offers a unique variety of species of fish, only wild goats and a few

species of lizards and rodents survive on dry land, in addition to approximately 100 species of birds.

Population

71 per cent of the inhabitants of Cape Verde are **mixes race**, 28 per cent are **black** and one per cent white. Catholics account for 96.3 per cent of the population, one per cent are Anglicans and a minority are followers of animist religions. The average life expectancy is 71 years and the illiteracy rate is 24 per cent.

History and Politics

In around 1460, explorers took possession of the island for the Portuguese crown. With the end of the slave trade, the colony lost its economic significance. In July 1975 the Cape Verde islands gained **independence**. Attempts at unification with Guinea-Bissau finally collapsed in 1980. Until 1991, the system of government was of a non-aligned one-party state. When this was abolished, the first **free elections** were held. The 1992 constitution stipulates that parliament is elected every five years and that the president is directly elected every five years. The voting age is 18.

Economy

The Gross Domestic Product was US$1,100 million in 2006. **Agriculture** accounted for 11 per cent of this amount, **industry** for 17 per cent and the **services sector** for 72 per cent. The trade balance is in deficit, but thanks to good rates of growth, Cape Verde hopes to emerge from being one of the world's least developed states in economic terms in 2008. Machinery, vehicles and foodstuffs are imported, while fish products and shoes are exported. One of the most important sources of foreign currency for the country are the funds sent home by expatriate Cape Verdians, of whom there are approximately 700,000, mainly in Portugal.

Transport Infrastructure

The country's **road network** is 2,250 km in length. Only one hundred kilometres are surfaced. Motor boats and small airlines

link the various islands. There is an international **airport** on Sal.

Tourism

The long, sandy beaches and the good scuba-diving, as well as the welcoming environment, make the Cape Verde Islands popular with tourists.

1 For hundreds of years camel caravans have been crossing the Sahara in the Republic of Niger, below the Aïr mountains.

2 The river Niger forms an approximately 40,000 sq. km delta in central Mali, with a labyrinth of creeks, lakes and swamps. It has a rich flora, including the typical doum palm and the baobab.

3 There are only few settlements in the Ténéré desert in the Republic of Niger. The oasis of Iferouane is located in the shadow of the Aïr mountains.

In the sahelian zone, the transition zone between the Sahara and the African savannah, a long-lasting drought occurs every few years resulting in catastrophic hunger. The amount of annual rainfall has been decreasing since the mid-twentieth century so the desert continues to expand.

Increasing desertification is accelerated by intensive livestock breeding and overgrazing of the resultant sparse vegetation. Civil wars have additionally increased the suffering of the people. The picture shows images from Burkina Faso, Southern Sudan and Mali.

In recent years, the situation of **women in the Gambia** has improved significantly. Most of the population are Sunni Muslims. The number of women in work is rising. In spite of the questionable nature of the democratic reforms introduced in the 1996 constitution, women have become more self-confident. They are increasingly banding together in small cooperatives, running enterprises such as bakeries.

Senegal	
Area:	196,722 sq. km
Capital City:	Dakar
Form of government:	
Presidential Republic	
Administrative divisions:	
10 regions	
Population:	
12 million (60 persons/sq. km)	
Languages:	French, Wolof
GDP per inhabitant:	US$770
Currency:	
1 CFA-franc = 100 centimes	

Natural Geography

Most of the country is covered by the Senegal and Gambian coastal lowlands. In the east, there is the mountainous region of Fouta Djallon, the source of the head-waters of the rivers of Senegal. The coastal plain is flat with the exception of the Cape Verde Peninsula, which is the result of volcanic activity on the islands.

Climate

Senegal's tropical climate is extremely dry in the north, which is often affected by **droughts**, and has an average rainfall of only 300 mm. In the south up to 1,500 mm of rain falls between April and November. The average temperature fluctuates between 27°C inland and 24.5°C on the coast.

In the coastal region, there are mangrove swamps; inland, a tropical jungle predominates, which changes into tree savannah, bush savannah and finally dry savannah to the north. The **Niokolo-Koba National Park** contains a wealth of flora and fauna, including antelopes, monkeys, hyenas, hippopotamuses, leopards, lions, elephants and buffaloes.

Population

44 per cent of the Senegalese are **Wolof**, 15 per cent **Sérer**, 11 per cent **Toucouleurs** and five per cent **Diola**. There are also minorities of Mandinka, Soninka, Malinké, Fulani, Moors, Lebanese, Syrians, French and other groups. As regards religion, 94.5 per cent are Sunni Muslims, five per cent Christians and a minority follow animist religions. The average life expectancy is only 59 years. The literacy rate is 37 per cent. More than half the population lives below the poverty line and 44 per cent live in cities.

Senegal: 78 per cent of the working population lives from farming.

History and Politics

After the Portuguese discovered the mouth of Senegal River in 1444, the Dutch, French and British traded along it in gold, ivory and, above all, slaves.

In the nineteenth century, today's Senegal became a **French colony**. Soon afterwards, the Africans living in Senegal were granted French citizenship, before the country achieved **independence** on 4 April 1960. The first president was Léopold Senghor, an author whose work was extensively published in France.

An attempted federation with French Sudan (now Mali) failed in 1959, just before independence. A federation with the Gambia, known as Senegambia, lasted from 1982 to 1989.

Today, Senegal is a relatively stable democratic presidential republic. The President is elected directly every five years; parliament is also elected every five years. The voting age is 18.

Economy

In 2006, GDP amounted to US$9.2 billion of which 18 per cent derived from **agriculture**, 27 per cent from **industry** and 55 per cent from the **services sector**. Semi-manufactured products, foodstuffs, machinery, oil and vehicles are imported. Exports include fish, fish meal, peanuts and chemicals, mainly phosphates.

Transport Infrastructure

Only 3,600 km of the 14,000 km **road network** is paved. The **rail network** covers 1,200 km. Dakar is an important **sea port** and has an international **airport**.

Tourism

Although the tourist infrastructure is still being developed, around 360,000 tourists visit Senegal annually. Cultural centres are Dakar and Saint Louis.

Gambia	
Area:	11,295 sq. km
Capital city:	Banjul
Form of government:	
Presidential Republic	
Administrative divisions:	
6 regions, 35 districts	
Population:	1.6 million
	(141 inhabitants/sq. km)
Languages:	
English (official), Mandinka, Wolof, other local languages	
GDP per inhabitant:	US$220
Currency:	
1 dalasi = 100 butut	

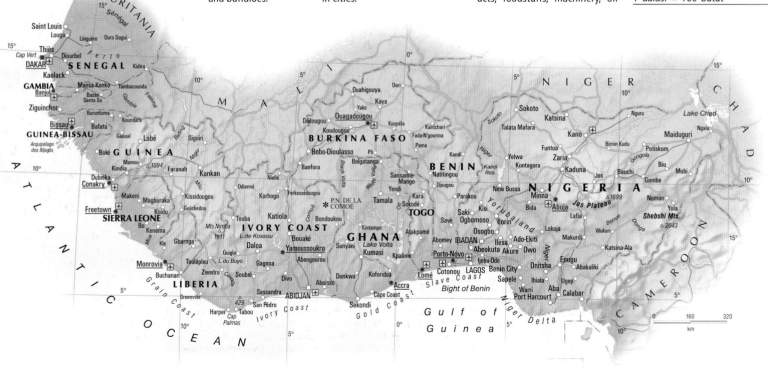

Bidjogo: The kinsmen of this small ethnic group on the coast of Guinea-Bissau, are known to be excellent fishermen, boat-builders and makers of handicrafts. Thus along with masks, they also produce cult objects, spirit containers,

fertility dolls and ancestor figures, as well as naturally styled bull masks. These are worn together with hippopotamus or colourful bird masks, during inititation ceremonies or rites of passage.

Natural Geography

The Gambia is surrounded on three sides by **Senegal**. It is a small country running beside the length of the river Gambia for 375 km from the Atlantic into the African hinterland; in parts it is only 24 km wide. The river landscape of Gambia changes from an alluvial plain to low hills and finally to a plateau which reaches a height of 200 m.

Climate

The **tropical climate** produces average temperatures of 23°C in January and 28°C in July. During the rainy season, between June and October, rainfall is 1,300 mm on the coast and 1,000 mm inland. The area at the mouth of the river Gambia is covered in mangrove swamp. In the central reaches of the river there is wet savannah and in the east dry savannah. Both major areas of the country contain large numbers of the big animals, especially in the national parks. Typical species are crocodiles, hippopotamuses, monkeys, antelopes, wart-hogs, hyenas, jackals, leopards and many species of birds.

Population

The many ethnic groups include the **Mandinka**, the largest at 44 per cent. There are also 17.5 per cent **Fulani**, 12.3 per cent **Wolof**, seven per cent **Diola**, seven per cent **Soninke** as well as smaller minorities. 85 per cent are Muslim, ten per cent Christians and a minority of followers of natural religions. The average life expectancy is only 53 years. The literacy rate is 39 per cent.

History and Politics

Portuguese explorers first discovered the Gambia in the mid-fifteenth century but handed over the trading rights to England as early as 1588. Soon trading posts were founded along the Gambia River. In 1816, the British purchased Saint Mary's Island from a local chief and established Bathurst, now the capital Banjul. This city was important early on especially for its use as a buffer against the slave trade. The Gambia was important for the trade in

gold, ivory and ebony. In 1889, the official borders were established between British Gambia and French Senegal, and they still apply today.

After **independence** in 1965, Dawda K. Jawara ruled until the military coup by Yahyah Jammeh, the current president. Attempts at reunification with Senegal failed. In keeping with the 1997 constitution, 45 members of the parliament are elected directly and four members of the assembly are appointed by the president who is elected every five years. The voting age is 18 years.

Economy

In 2006, GDP was US$350 million of which 36 per cent came from **agriculture**, 12 per cent from **industry** and 52 per cent from the **services sector**. The balance of trade is alarmingly in deficit. Imports include foodstuffs, industrial goods, machinery, fuel and vehicles. Livestock, mainly cattle, peanuts, fish, skins and furs are exported.

Transport Infrastructure

Around 500 km of the 3,100 km **road network** is paved. The river Gambia is navigeable and river transport is important. Bajul has an international **airport**.

Tourism

The Atlantic beaches are attracting more and more tourists. The best time to travel is between November and May.

Guinea-Bissau	
Area:	36,125 sq. km
Capital City:	Bissau
Form of government: Presidential Republic	
Administrative divisions: 3 provinces, 8 regions, 1 district (capital city)	
Population: 1.5 million (41 inhabitants/sq. km)	
Languages: Portuguese (official), Creole, dialects	
GDP per inhabitant:	US$200
Currency: 1 CFA-franc = 100 centimes	

Natural Geography

The Bijagos Archipelago, lies off the ragged coastline and are part of the Guinea-Bissau national territory. In the undulating hinterland, which reaches a height of 300 m, there are numerous meandering rivers, which flood large parts of the country during the rainy season.

1 The smallest socio-economic unit in Senegal is the extended family, which encompasses a large group of relatives and which is presided over by a male elder.

2 Traditionally, the most important decisions of the

village community are made by the elder. This important institution has preserved its role among all the ethnic groups of Senegal.

3 Local produce is sold in the numerous markets of Senegal, though the selcetion is often rather limited.

Around 85 per cent of Guinea's labour force is employed in **agriculture**, which still only contributes 24 per cent of GDP. Manioc, rice, plantains, palm kernels, bananas and pineapples constitute the main crops. The land is not very fertile, due to widespread slash-and-burn practices and primitive cultivation methods. Unfortunately, children are still widely used in the labour force, so only around 30 per cent of them attend school.

Climate

The humid and dry tropical climates produce average temperatures of 26°C. During the rainy season, between May and October, average rainfall in the north is around 1,200 mm and 3,000 mm in the west.
The coastal vegetation consists of mangrove forests and swamps; the coastal flats and the islands are covered in evergreen rainforest. Inland, there are dry forests, which turn into tree and shrub savannah in the east. Typical fauna of the savannah are elephants, hyenas, buffaloes, antelopes and leopards. Many types of birds live on the coast, as well as crocodiles and hippopotamuses.

Population

25 per cent of the inhabitants are **Balanta**, 20 per cent **Fulani**, 12 per cent **Mandinka**, 11 per cent **Manjak** and ten per cent **Papel**. There are also other groups, including a white minority.
Over 50 per cent are followers of animist religions, 38 per cent are Muslims and eight per cent Christians – mostly Catholics. The average life expectancy is 47 years. The literacy rate is 55 per cent.

History and Politics

In 1446, the Portuguese took possession of the country, calling Portuguese Guinea, and organising a lucrative **slave trade**. Portuguese rule lasted until in 1961, resistance formed against the rulers in Lisbon and a protracted liberation war began, ending in independence after the revolution of 1974 in Portugal, toppling the dictator Antonio Salazar. Repeated efforts at unification with neighbouring Cape Verde, also a former Portuguese colony, failed, leading to a series of military incursions and virtual civil war. After unsuccessful military coups in 2000 and 2003, the new start to democracy is now running into difficulties. The National Assembly and Head of State are elected directly every five years. The voting age is 18 years.

Economy

GDP was US$300m in 2006. Of this, 69 per cent derived from **agriculture**, 13 per cent from **industry** and 18 per cent from the services sector. Guinea-Bissau currently has enormous foreign debts and a very negative balance of trade. This is due to political unrest, coupled with the fact that the country is too small and underdeveloped to be economically viable. Food, machinery, vehicles, oil and petroleum products are imported. Cashew nuts are the most important crop contributing to 85 per cent of exports. Other exports are timber from the tropical forests, fish, coconuts and rice.

Transport Infrastructure

Only 300 km of the **road network** which stretches over a total length of around 5,000 km is paved. There is no rail network. The capital city, Bissau, possesses an important **sea port** and an international **airport**.

Tourism

Due the unsettled political situation, all foreigners living in the country in 1998 were evacuated. Tourism is still not possible.
For climatic reasons, the best time to travel would be between December and April.

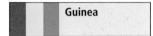

Guinea	
Area:	245,857 sq. km
Capital city:	Conakry
Form of government:	Republic
Administrative divisions: 4 super-regions, 30 regions, 1 district (capital city)	
Population: 10 million (40 inhabitants/sq. km)	
Languages: French (official), tribal languages	
GDP per inhabitant:	US$330
Currency: 1 Guinea-franc = 100 centimes	

Natural Geography

The coast, which has many bays, is dotted with offshore islands. The coastal plane is 50–90 km wide in places. The **Fouta Djallon** plateau, which adjoins the coastal plain reaches a height of up to 1,500 m. Here lie the sources of the river Gambia and the river Senegal, as well as other rivers.
The tablelands in the east are between 400 and 500 m high and are intersected by the Upper Niger and its tributaries. The highest peak of the island mountains to the south is the Mount Nimba at 1,752 m.

Climate

The tropical wet/dry climate results in average temperatures ranging from 25°C to 28°C. During the rainy season, in which there are often tremendous storms, the rainfall in the south east and on the coast reaches up to 4,000 mm, while inland only 1,300–2,000 mm.
The unspoiled **rainforest vegetation** has only been maintained in large areas of the south-east. Deforestation has produced a **moist savannah** in the west and **dry savannah** in the north-east. The coast is lined with mangrove swamps.
The once rich wildlife has only been preserved in the Nimba Reserve. The typical animals here include elephants, leopards, lions, antelopes, buffaloes, monkeys, hyenas, crocodiles, snakes, hippopotamuses, manatee and many species of birds.

Population

There are numerous ethnic groups of which the **Malinké** and **Fulani** with 30 per cent each are the most numerous. There are 15 per cent **Susu**, 6.5 per cent **Kissi** and 4.8 per cent **Kpelle**. 95 per cent of the population is Muslim and there are 1.5 per cent Christians as well as followers of various animist religions. The average life expectancy is 50 years. The literacy rate is 30 per cent.

History and Politics

By the time the Portuguese founded their first trading posts on the part of the coast of West Africa known as the Guinea Coast for its rich gold reserves, in the late the fifteenth century, the Islamic Empire of Mali, which experienced its heyday in the fourteenth century under Mansa Musa, had long been destroyed.
The other European colonial powers became involved in the area only in the nineteenth century. The French, who were able to assert their claim over that of the British, had a long struggle against the resistance of the local population. From 1893, Guinea was a French

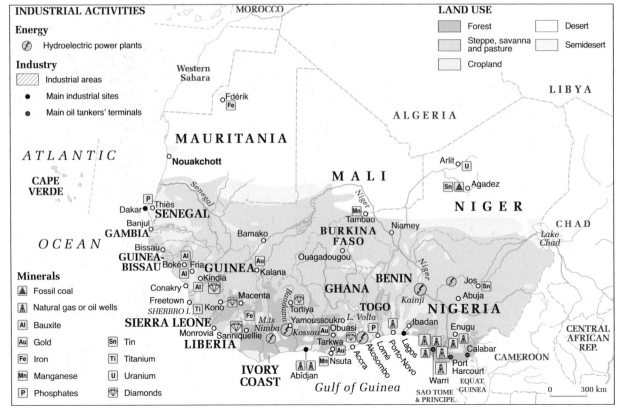

INDUSTRIAL ACTIVITIES

Energy
- ⊘ Hydroelectric power plants

Industry
- ▨ Industrial areas
- ● Main industrial sites
- ● Main oil tankers' terminals

Minerals
- ⬚ Fossil coal
- ⬚ Natural gas or oil wells
- Al Bauxite
- Au Gold
- Fe Iron
- Mn Manganese
- P Phosphates
- Sn Tin
- Ti Titanium
- U Uranium
- ▽ Diamonds

LAND USE
- Forest
- Steppe, savanna and pasture
- Cropland
- Desert
- Semidesert

*The **Temne**, a farming people, account for a third of Sierra Leon's population and are organised around into chiefdoms, each chief usually governing several surrounding villages. Alliances and relationships within each chiefdom are of great importance to the Temne. The organisation of religious festivities is entrusted to local men's and women's associations.*

colony under the name of French Guinea (Guinée française).

After Guinea was granted **independence** in 1958, under the dictator Ahmed Sekou Touré, all opposition was brutally suppressed and two million citizens fled the country. Relations were warmest with the Soviet Union. After the death of Touré in 1984, the army staged a coup d'etat.

The new head of state, Colonel Lansana Conté, promised to introduce a multi-party system and free elections, but Guinea remains a one-party state. There are known to be human rights violations and election manipulation. The 1991 constitution provides for the election of parliament every four years and the direct election of the head of state, the president, every five years. The voting age is 18 years.

Economy

In 2006, the GDP was US$3.2 billion of which 24 per cent derived from **agriculture**, 31 per cent from **industry** and 45 per cent from the **services sector**. In spite of the great potential of the country for agricultural development and the rich deposits of bauxite, diamonds, gold and iron ore, Guinea is still dependent on international aid. Engines, machines, vehicles, consumer goods, oil and oil products and foodstuffs are all imported; coffee, rice, palm kernels, alumina, bauxite, gold and diamonds are amongst the main exports. Despite its vast natural resources, Guinea remains a very underdeveloped country.

Transport Infrastructure

Only one sixth of the 30,270 km long **road network** is paved. In addition to the private railway lines that are used exclusively for freight transport, there is a 660 km long state **rail link** from Conakry to Kankan. There are **sea ports** at Kamsar and Conakry and Conakry also has an international **airport**.

Tourism

Tourism is virtually non-existent. One reason is that the rulers of Guinea have agreed to allow foreign toxic waste to be dumped in their territory. The climate is at its most bearable between December and March.

Sierra Leone	
Area:	71,740 sq. km
Capital city:	Freetown
Form of government: Republic in the Commonwealth	
Administrative divisions: 4 provinces, 1 municipality, 147 chiefdoms	
Population: 6 million (84 inhabitants/sq. km)	
Languages: English (official), Creole	
GDP per inhabitant:	US$250
Currency: 1 leone = 100 cents	

Natural Geography

The coastal plains are lined with mangrove swamps and are about 40 km wide with offshore islands, estuaries and sand banks. The partly mountainous peninsula of Sierra Leone (meaning 'lion mountain') reaches heights of up to 890 m. The plains inland border the Guinea highlands in the east, dominated by the Loma Mountains. The highest mountain is the Loma Mansa, which reaches a height of 1,948 m.

Climate

The wet/dry **tropical climate** produces temperatures between 25 and 28°C in the coastal area. During the dry season, the hot dry wind known as the **Harmattan** blows south from the Sahara. The rainfall on the Sierra Leone peninsula can amount to 5,000 mm per annum. In the east, it is 3,000 mm and in the north only 2,000 mm annually.

The tropical rainforest gives way to many cultivated land and scrub. The rivers are lined with forests and in the north the savannah predominates. In addition to countless species of birds and insects, crocodiles and hippopotamuses live in the rivers. Monkeys live in the forests and antelopes and buffaloes live in the savannah.

1 Play of colours: in the market of Mamou, a small town in Guinea, the local farmers sell their wares.

2 Blood diamonds: both government and the rebels in Sierra Leone have used precious stones to finance arms and mercenaries.

3 In addition to bauxite and gold, diamonds also play an important role in the Guinea economy.

4 Mobile office: because of the high illiteracy rate, professional scribes with 'offices' in the streets, have plenty of work in Freetown.

Sierra Leone, Liberia, Burkina Faso

The agricultural sector in Burkina Faso has been consistently supported by foreign aid since the 1980s. The country's biggest asset is its **livestock**. Cattle, sheep, pigs, donkeys and poultry are reared. The supply of livestock to the capital Ouagadougou from the surrounding area is more than adequate and some traders even become wealthy enough to bring their wares to market on a motor-bike.

Population

Among the many ethnic groups, the Mendes with 34.6 per cent and the Temnes with 31.7 per cent are the most frequently represented. In addition, there are 8.4 per cent Limba, 3.5 per cent Kuranko as well as minorities of Europeans, Asians and Lebanese. In addition to followers of local religions, 39 per cent profess Islam and eight per cent Christianity.

History and Politics

After the country's discovery by the Portuguese, the Dutch and British also founded trading settlements, from where the lucrative trade in slaves, gold and diamonds was conducted in the eighteenth century. Sierra Leone became a British colony in 1808 and the first colony of freed slaves, which is why the capital is called Freetown. For a long time these Creoles dominated the country due to their better education. It was declared a British protectorate in 1896. After **independence** in 1961, conflicts broke out between the Creoles and the native population. In 1971, the status of a dominion within the Commonwealth was granted and a **Republic** declared. After a succession of military regimes, the Temnes-Group All-People's Congress assumed power in 1978, suppressing all opposition. From 1990, a civil war broke out against rebels from the Revolutionary United Front (RUF), originated from Liberia. The 1991 Constitution promised democratisation but this never happened due to another military coup. Following the intervention of the West African peace-keeping force ECOMOG in 1998, President Ahmad Tejan Kabbah, first elected in 1996, returned to power, This caused the rebels to respond with further attacks. In 1999, with the aid of British forces, a peace treaty was signed and the UN stationed a peace-keeping force in the country. In May 2002 Kabbah was once more elected President. Since then, security has improved.

Economy

In 2006 the GDP was US$1.5 billion, of which 53 per cent derived from **agriculture**, 31 per cent from **industry** and 16 per cent from the **services sector**. There are rich deposits of titanium, gold, diamonds, iron ore and bauxite but they are not well developed. The gemstone trade, mainly diamonds, principally serves the financing of the war. The agricultural sector remains weak and the arbitrary and ruthless clearing of the rainforests has led to catastrophic **environmental damage**. Machinery, vehicles, timber and foodstuffs are imported; rutile, diamonds, bauxite and cocoa are exported.

Transport Infrastructure

Only around 1,200 km of the **road network** which covers 7,500 km is paved. The single **railway** line extends 84 km between Pepel and Marampa. The rivers are only navigable during the rainy season. In Freetown there is a **seaport** and somewhat further north there is an international **airport**.

Tourism

The constant civil wars and virtual absence of infrastructure make tourism almost impossible. The swampland encourages malaria which is why this part of the coast of West Africa, the Guinea Coast, was traditionally known as 'the white man's grave'. Nevertheless, if the unrest is quelled and a stable form of government achieved, the higher land of the 'lion mountain' can be relatively pleasant. Between November and March, the weather is at its best.

Liberia	
Area:	111,369 sq. km
Capital city:	Monrovia
Form of government:	
Presidential Republic	
Administrative divisions:	
11 districts, 4 territories	
Population:	
3.2 million (29 inhabitants/sq. km)	
Languages:	
English (official), tribal languages	
GDP per inhabitant:	US$180
Currency:	
1 Liberian dollar = 100 cents	

Natural Geography

The 600-km-long coast is characterised by numerous sand banks, spits and lagoons as well as in parts by a rocky shoreline. A plateau landscape, which reaches heights of up to 400 m, adjoins the 10–50 km wide marshy, coastal plain. In the north, there are mountains, such as the Nimba Range, including the 1,384 m high Guest House Hill.

Climate

The **tropical, rainy climate** produces average temperatures of 24 °C to 27°C on the coast and from 22°C to 28°C inland. On the coast the rainfall is 4,500 mm, inland 2,000 mm and in the mountains 3,000 mm. In summer, the **Harmattan** desert wind produces a hot, dry spell. A third of the country's area is covered by tropical rainforests, though these have been reduced by almost half due to massive deforestation and the sale of timber. On the coast, there are mangrove swamps and savannahs.

Population

Liberia contains 16 different ethnic groups. The largest are the **Kpelle** at 20 per cent, the **Bassa** at 14 per cent, the **Grebo** at nine per cent, the **Kru** at eight per cent, the **Mandinka** at six per cent and the **Loma** at six per cent. 70 per cent of the inhabitants follow animist religions, 20 per cent are Muslims and ten per cent Christians of various denominations.

History and Politics

After the Portuguese occupied the Pepper Coast in 1461, several European nations founded trading posts to sell slaves and exotic woods. Nevertheless, the country remained of little interest to the colonial powers. In 1816, US philanthropists purchased a costal strip of land from the Kru tribes and from 1822 freed American slaves settled there. In 1847, Liberia became the first independent African **Republic** with a constitution based on the US model. Under President Wilson Tubman, who ruled between 1944 and 1971 the country was once again open for foreign investors. Liberia is one of the countries that operates as a 'flag of convenience' for merchant shipping, and it became nominal port for the world's largest merchant fleet. Tubman's death was followed by several brutal **military dictatorships**. A civil war broke out that was temporarily ended in 1996. In 1997, the rebel leader, Charles Taylor, staged a coup and made himself president. In 2000, civil war broke out between government troops and the Liberian United for Reconciliation and Democracy (LURD). LURD was able to bring large parts of Liberia under its control. The fighting lasted until 2003. In August 2003, Taylor resigned and went into exile to Nigeria. With US support the West African peacekeeping force, ECOMIL, managed to stabilise the situation. In October 2003, the businessman Gyude Bryant, became head of a transitional government. In 2005, former UN Diplomat Ellen Johnson-Sirleaf was elected Head of State.

Economy

In 2006, GDP was US$ 600 million, of which 42 per cent came from **agriculture**, seven per cent from **industry** and 51 per cent from **services**.

Transport Infrastructure

Only around 750 km of the 10,000 km **road network** is paved. The **rail network** is around 520 km long and is used mainly to carry iron ore. There is an international **airport** near Monrovia.

Tourism

Liberia's tourist trade is scarcely developed. The best time to travel is between November and March.

Burkina Faso	
Area:	274,200 sq. km
Capital City:	Ouagadougou
Form of government: Republic	
Administrative divisions:	
45 provinces	
Population:	
14 m (50 inhabitants/sq. km)	
Languages:	
French (official), Fulani, Moorish	
and other tribal languages	

The mosques in Burkina Faso are made of clay, which is a typical West African construction material.

*Under president Félix Houphouët-Boigny grandiose building projects were implemented. In 1990 the **Notre-Dame-de-la-Paix** basilica, that can contain up to 18,000 people, was opened in the capital Yamoussoukro.*

GDP per inhabitant: US$450
Currency:
1 CFA franc = 100 centimes

Natural Geography

A large part of the country's land mass consists of a 250–350 m high plateau and individual mountain ranges. The highest peak is the 749 m Tenakourou. The sandstone tablelands in the south-west of the country are the source of the Black Volta.

Climate

In the north-east, a dry **tropical climate** predominates; rainfall of less than 500 mm falls between June and August. The **south-west monsoon** causes rainfall of up to 1,200 mm in the south and centre of the country.
The average temperatures are 27°C to 30°C; in the north, the temperature can rise to 44°C on occasion. In the dry season, the dry hot **Harmattan** wind blows from the Sahara in the north.
In the south, moist savannahs predominate with jungle lining the rivers. In the north, there are only thorny savannahs and steppes. The national parks are well-stocked with birds, buffaloes, hippopotamuses, lions, jackals, monkeys and crocodiles.

Population

Burkina Faso has around 160 ethnic groups, including 48 per cent **Mossi**, ten per cent **Fulani** and seven per cent **Dagara** and **Lobi**. There are also groups of **Mende** as well as a European minority. Half of the population professes various animist religions, 43 per cent are Sunni Muslim and 12 per cent Christians, most of them Roman Catholic. The literacy rate is 25 per cent. The average life expectancy is only 49 years.

History and Politics

Europeans first began to explore the region in the early nineteenth century. Under Mossi rule, the country largely remained without foreign influence until the French claimed the region for themselves at the end of the nineteenth century. The country, under its former name of Upper Volta (Haute Volta) was declared a self-govening

republic within the French community in 1958. After **independence** in 1960, Maurice Yaméogo became president, but he was soon overthrown in a military coup by Colonel Laminaza. One brutal dictator followed another. In addition to terror, corruption and political assassinations, a ruinous financial and economic policy resulted in a catastrophic situation. Since 1991, the former dictator Blaise Compaoré has ruled as elected head of state and has been able to achieve moderate economic advances.
The constitution was finally changed in 1997. Parliament is now directly elected every five yeas and the head of state, the president, every seven years. The voting age is 18.

Economy

In 2006, GDP was US$6 billion; of this, 35 per cent derived from **agriculture**, 17 per cent from **industry** and 48 per cent from the **service sector**.
The country has natural resources, including gold, zinc, silver, lead, nickel and manganese. Ony the gold is fully exploited. Industrial goods, food, fuel, machinery and vehicles are all imported; the most important exports are gold, cotton, peanuts, hides and skins. The economy is not helped by the fact that the country is small and landlocked. The economy is improving thanks to modernisation that has encouraged investment.

Transport Infrastructure

Only 1,100 km of the 16,500 km **road network** is fixed. There is a 517-km-long **railway stretch** and two international airports in the capital city and in Bobo Dioulasso.

Tourism

Tourism is developing very slowly. The best time to travel is between December and February.

	Ivory Coast

Area:	322,462 sq. km
Capital City:	Yamoussoukro
Form of government:	
Presidential Republic	

Administrative divisions:
49 departments
Population:
18m (55 inhabitants/sq. km)
Languages:
French (official), Dioula and other languages
GDP per inhabitant: US$1,000
Currency:
1 CFA-franc = 100 centimes

1 The vicinity of Dori in the north-east of Burkina Faso is inhabited by nomadic tribes, still building their huts the traditional way.

2 The Abron belong to the Akan people of western Ghana and the eastern Ivory Coast.

3 Cotton, cocoa and wood are important exports for the Ivory Coast. There is increasing demand for other crops, especially pineapples, and although modern growing techniques are used, transport methods are often primitive, as seen here.

*The **Ashanti** are Ghana's largest ethnic group. Until the nineteenth century they dominated a vast empire in West Africa. They are organised into a theocracy, in which the dignity of the ruler is emphasised by the amount of gold he wears.*

Natural Geography

The coast is characterised by rocky cliffs in the west and lagoons in the east. A 60-km-wide coastal plain is backed by a hilly plateau. In the north and northwest, the **Nimba mountains** reach a height of 1,752 m.

Climate

In the north, a hot dry **desert climate** predominates with rainfall of 1,200–1,400 mm; in the south it is humid. Up to 2,300 mm rain falls in the mountains; 1,500 to 2,000 mm on the coast. The average temperatures range between 25°C and 28°C. Slash-and-burn forestry clearance and overgrazing have destroyed the jungle and left clearances of poor soil. Coconut palms and mangroves grow along the coast, inland, there are tropical rainforests and jungles. To the north, the moist savannah turns into a dry savannah.

Population

The population is composed of over 60 ethnic groups. In addition to 23 per cent **Baule**, 18 per cent **Bete**, 15 per cent **Senufo**, 14 per cent **Agni-Ashanti**, 11 per cent **Malinké**, ten per cent **Kru** and **Mande**, there are Dan Gouro, Kuoa, Fulani and other groups. 60 per cent are followers of animist eligions, 27 per cent are Muslims and 20 per cent are Christian, mostly Catholic.

History and Politics

The Portuguese in the fifteenth century and the French in the seventeenth set up trading posts along on the coast, from which they operated a flourishing trade in **ivory** and **slaves**. In the nineteenth century, the French controlled additional inland areas and operated plantations. In 1895, the Ivory Coast became part of French West Africa. Following **independence** in 1960 Félix Houphouët-Boigny took power, and remained head of state for 33 years. In 1986, he changed the official name of the country to Côte d'Ivoire. He was resented by the population for his grandiose building projects at the expense of the national economy. His successor was overthrown by

a military coup d'état in 1999. In 2000, Laurent Gbagbo became president. The Ivory Coast was once considered the only stable country in the region but in September 2002, an anti-government uprising of Muslim rebels developed from a military revolt. French troops prevented the taking of Abidjan, the former capital, and the new capital, Yamoussoukro. They also supervised an armistice. The rebels were granted a share in government in the subsequent peace deal agreed in Paris in 2003. However, even the deployment of a United Nations peace-keeping force has brought no lasting stability.

Economy

In 2006, GDP was almost US$18 billion. Of this, 31 per cent was derived from **agriculture**, 20 per cent from **industry** and 50 per cent from the **services sector**.

Women in Togo carrying goods on their heads.

There are large reserves of iron, nickel, copper and some oil. Foodstuffs, machinery and medicines are imported. Important exports include cocoa (the Ivory Coast is the world's largest producer), coffee, pineapples, wood and cotton.

Transport Infrastructure

Only 3,800 km of the 54,000 km road network is paved. The rail network is 665 km long. the major sea ports are Abidjan and San Pédro. The international airport is at Abidjan.

Tourism

The sandy beaches around Abidjan are increasingly popular with tourists, but political unrest has hampered expansion.

Ghana	
Area:	239,460 sq. km
Capital city:	Accra
Form of government:	
Presidential Republic	
Administrative divisions:	
10 regions, 110 districts	
Population:	
22 m (92 inhabitants/sq. km)	
Languages:	
English (official), over 70 other languages and dialects	
GDP per inhabitant:	US$600
Currency:	
1 cedi = 100 pesewas	

Natural Geography

The hinterland from the coast consists of a 20–100 km wide lowland plain which joins on to the Ashanti plateau at an altitutde of 700 m.

In the huge Volta river valley contains the 8,500 sq. km **Lake Volta**, one of the largest dams in the world. The **Volta** flows through a narrow gorge in the **Akwapim-Togo mountain range**, which runs along the border with Togo; the highest peak is the 885 m high Afadjoto.

Climate

The **Harmattan**, the hot dry wind that blows south from the Sahara, and the wet **monsoon**, determine the climate of the inland tropical convergence zone. There is a rainy season between May and September, limited by the savannah climate in the north. Precipitation is between 1,100 and 1,270 mm annually. In the south there are two rainy seasons. The south-west has a rainfall of 1,250–2,100 mm annually but in the lee of the Akwapim-Togo mountain range, rainfall is only 750 mm.

Average temperatures are between 26°C and 29°C in the south; in the north, they can reach up to 43°C. Slash-and-burn deforestation, over-grazing and commercially driven timber-harvesting have led to a massive decline in the original rainforest. It has been replaced by secondary afforestation, which turns into savannah towards the north. Jungle continues to line the rivers, however. There are wild game sanctuaries in both parts of the country, populated by monkeys, antelopes, lions, leopards, buffaloes, elephants, hippopotamuses, crocodiles and many species of birds.

Population

Ghana has over 100 different population groups, the largest of which, at 52.4 per cent, are **Ashanti** and **Fanti**. There are 11.9 per cent **Ewe**, 7.8 per cent **Ga** and **Ga-Adangbe**, 1.3 per cent **Yoruba**, 15.8 per cent **Mossi**, 11.9 per cent **Guan** and 3.3 per cent **Gurma**. There are also Manda Haussa, Fulani and Europeans. As for religion, 40 per cent are Protestants, 20 per cent Catholics, 35 per cent followers of local religions and five per cent Muslim. The average life expectancy is 59 years. The literacy rate is 64 per cent.

History and Politics

In 1471, Portuguese sailors landed on the Gold Coast and from then on, the Europeans traded in gold and slaves. In 1874, the Gold Coast became a British colony and in 1957 became the first country in Black Africa to gain its **independence**. At that time, the country changed its name to Ghana. The socialist course taken

by the first prime minister **Kwame Nkrumah** led the country into economic ruin. The situation did not improve under the subsequent military dictatorships. One of the most important figures of recent history is Flight-lieutenant Jerry Rawlings, who served as the country's president several times. In 1991, he began democratic reforms and in 1992, a new constitution was voted in. In the presidential elections, Rawlings was confirmed in office. In 2001, the leader of the opposition, John Agyekum Kufuor, was elected President.

Economy

GDP for 2006 was US$13 billion of which 36 per cent derived from **agriculture**, 25 per cent from **industry** and 39 per cent from the **services sector**. The principal exports are gold, cocoa, manganese, bauxite and timber. Machinery, crude oil and finshed products are amongst the main imports. Ghana is now the world's second-largest producer of cocoa. The beans were introduced by the British. Cocoa production has fallen as the trees are cut down for fuel and it takes 15 years for a tree to start producing beans.

Transport Infrastructure

The **rail network** covers around 1000 km and the **road network** 37,561 km, of which 9,535 km are paved. There is an international **airport** at Kotoka.

Tourism

In 1996, 300,000 tourists contributed US$248 m in foreign currency. The best times to travel are between July and September and December and March.

Togo	
Area:	56,785 sq. km
Capital city:	Lomé
Form of government:	
Presidential Republic	
Administrative divisions:	
5 Regions	
Population:	
around 6 million (105 inhabitants/sq. km)	

Once known as the Slave Coast, togo took its name from a small town on Lake togo (today Togoville). In the language of the Ewe, the biggest ethnic group, 'To' means water and 'Go' shore. The handwashing women at the river may seem romantic, yet their cheerful goings should not delude as to the otherwise miserable living conditions. The majority of Togo's population lives below the poverty line.

Languages:
French (official), Kabyé, Ewe

GDP per inhabitant: US$360

Currency:
1 CFA franc = 100 centimes

Natural Geography

The coastline is ragged, with lagoons and bays and is only 5 km long in total. The hinterland is both flat and hilly and almost 200 km wide. Mount Agou (formerly known as Mount Baumann) is the highest mountain in Togo at 986 m. North-west of the mountains, the Oti plains forms the border area with Burkina Faso.

Climate

The south is dominated by a **savannah climate** with two rainy seasons, which last from March until June and from September until October. The north only has one rainy season, from April to October. On the coastal plains, the average rainfall is 600 to 700 mm; inland it is 1,500 mm and in the north it is 1,200 mm. On the coast, the average temperatures are 27°C, and inland in the north it rises to 30°C.

Savannahs of wide grasslands with a few clumps of trees are the characteristic landscape of Togo. Mangrove swamps grow along the coast and there are palm-fringed sandy beaches. The tropical rainforest has only been preserved in the south-west Togolese mountains. In the national parks and in the game reserves, the original fauna has been able to survive. Typical animals include buffaloes, lions, leopards, hyenas, antelopes, hippopotamuses, crocodiles and a wide variety of birds and reptiles. The homes of thousands of Keto were destroyed due to coastal erosion due to the building of the Volta dam.

Population

The inhabitants belong to 40 ethnic groups. The **Ewe** are the most strongly represented with around 46 per cent. There are also **Temba, Mopa, Gurma, Kabyé, Losso, Hausa, Fulani** as well as Lebanese and French minorities. 50 per cent profess various animist religions, 35 per cent are Christians (almost exclusively Roman Catholic) and 15 per cent

Sunni Muslims. The average life expectancy is 56 years. The literacy rate 52 per cent.

History and Politics

The Portuguese discovered the coast of Togo in the fifteenth century. They traded slaves from there, later being joined by the Danes. When slavery ended, the British and French founded trading posts. Nevertheless, large parts of the country remained under African rule, including the kingdom of **Dahomey** in the east and the **Ashanti-kingdom** in the west. German involvement began

with Gustav Nachtigal and in 1884, Togo became a German colony. After World War I, France and Great Britain divided the region, which in 1922 was officially made into a mandated territory by the League of Nations. In 1946 this was reorganised into a British mandated territory in the east (British Togoland and French mandated territory in the west). In 1956 the British mandated area was annexed to Ghana and became known as the Volta region. The French mandated Togo became an **autonomous republic** on 27 April 1960.

The first president, Sylvanus Olympio, was murdered in 1963. In 1967 Etienne Gnassingbé Eyadéma overthrew the government in a bloodless coup. In spite of permitting opposition parties and a democratic constitution, he ruled the country as a dictator. After his death in 2005, his son Faure Gnassingbé became the new head of state. The parliament is directly elected every five years, as is the president.

Economy

In 2000, GNP was US$2.2 bn, of which 35 per cent derived from agriculture, 23 per cent from industry and 42 per cent from the services sector. Machinery, foodstuffs and fuel are imported. Calcium phosphate, cotton, cocoa and coffee are exported.

1 Elmina was founded in 1482 by the Portugese in the Gold Coast. The fortress is a reminder of the former slave trade.

2 A Lobi woman burning pots to make millet beer. The Lobi are ethnic Gurs, a group consisting of several million people living in West Africa.

3 In an Ashanti village near Kumasi in southern Ghana. Traditional ceremonies to honour the chiefs are still held.

4 Near Bolgatanga in northern Ghana, the old architectural style of the Mossiv people has been preserved unchanged for centuries.

Togo, Benin, Nigeria

*Most of the Beninese are followers of indigenous religions. A prevalent **ancestor cult** is based upon the belief that the ancestors must be consulted before important decisions are taken.*

Transport Infrastructure

The **rail network** covers 525 km and the **road network** 7,519 km, of which 2,376 km are paved. Lomé has a **major sea port** and an international **airport**.

Tourism

Tourism in Togo is barely developed. In 2003, 61,000 tourists visited the country. This is despite the beautiful scenery and hospitable people. This is because the political situation continues to give cause for concern. The best time to travel is between November and April when there is little rain.

Area: 112,622 sq. km
Capital City: Porto Novo
Form of government: Presidential Republic
Administrative divisions: 6 provinces, 78 districts
Population: 8 million

Wole Soyinka

*Abeokuta 13.7.1934

The playwright, poet, novelist and screenplay writer received the Nobel Prize for Literature in 1986. In his work, he attempts a synthesis of African mythology and the realities of modern life. He was engaged in the fight against military dictatorship in Nigeria and as a resutl was subject to constant persecution. He fled the country and was accused in absentia of treason in 1997. He returned to Nigeria from exile in 1998.

(70 inhabitants/sq. km)
Languages: French (official), Fon, Yoruba and other tribal languages
GDP per inhabitant: US$620
Currency:
1 CFA franc = 10 centimes

Natural Geography

The sandy coastline turns into a lagoon area and mangrove swamps towards the north. This is replaced by the 'terre de barre', adjoining a semi-arid plateau up to 500 m high. In the north-west, the high mountainous region of **Atacora** rises to 641 m. A steep, 300-m-high escarpment adjoins the **Pendjari lowlands**. In the north-east, the plateau falls gradually away to the Niger river valley.

Climate

In the humid savannah climate of the south, average temperatures of 27.5°C dominate; these can climb to over 40°C at times. In both the rainy seasons from March to July and from September to November, the average rainfall is 1,000–1,500 mm. In the north, on the other hand, rainfall is no more than 500 mm during the rainy season between May and September. In the dry season, the **Harmattan**, the hot Sahara wind replaces the damp **south-west monsoon**.
The largest part of the country is covered by savannah grassland with isolated clumps of trees. Of the once vast rainforest, only traces remain along the courses of the rivers and in the south-east of the country. The interesting and varied fauna is protected in nature reserves. In these areas, common species include elephants, buffaloes, antelopes, lions, monkeys, crocodiles and numerous species of birds and snakes.

Population

Of the 60 or so ethnic groups, **Kwa, Fon, Yoruba, Adja, Bariba, Som**-ba and **Gun** make up around 80 per cent. There are also Fulani, Hausa and European minorities. 60 per cent of the inhabitants of Benin are followers of various animist religions, 20.4 per cent belong to the Catholic church, the rest are divided between Islam and the Methodist church.
The average life expectancy is 53 years. The literacy rate is 40 per cent. 39 per cent of the inhabitants of Benin live in the cities. Although Porto Novo is the official capital, Cotonou, the former capital, remains the most important city.

History and Politics

Since the fifteenth century, firstly the Portuguese, and then the French operated a lucrative **slave trade** from their coastal trading posts. Most of the slaves from what is now Benin were sent to Haiti. When the slave trade ended, the main focus of French activity shifted to trading in palm oil and cotton. It was only towards the end of the nineteenth century, that the French succeeded in conquering the smaller African kingdoms. Under French rule, Benin was known as **Dahomey**. In 1904, Dahomey became part of French West Africa. After **independence** in 1960 eight military and civil governments followed each other in succession, until finally, in 1972, a Communist government came to power and the country was renamed Benin in 1975.

In 1989, Communism was officially abandoned. A liberal constitution was introduced in 1990, which has provided for the election of parliament every four years and the direct election of the President every five years. The voting age is 18 years.

Economy

In 2006, GDP was US$4.8 bn, of which 36 per cent derived from **agriculture**, 15 per cent from **industry** and 49 per cent from the **services sector**.
Principal imports are industrial goods, food, machines, transport equipment and fuel. Exports include cotton, oilseed, petroleum, cement, fish products and palm oil.

Transport Infrastructure

Only one third of the 7,400-km-long **road network** is passable all year round. The **rail network** covers 580 km. Cotonou has a **sea port** and an international **airport**. Ships ply between the ports on the West African coast.

Lagos is both an industrial centre and Nigeria's major port. It covers four islands.

Tourism

There are many museums and royal palaces in the country. The oral traditions of Benin are a unique cultural treasure, including those of the Gèlèdè people, which were declared an Oral Heritage of Humanity in May 2001. The Ouidah Slave Route is an important attraction for tourists.

Area: 923,768 sq. km
Capital City: Abuja
Form of government: Presidential Federal Republic
Administrative divisions: 36 Federal States, capital city-territory
Population: 135 million (146 inhabitants/sq. km)
Languages: English (official), Arabic, tribal languages
GDP per inhabitant: US$800
Currency: 1 naira = 100 kobo

Natural Geography

Dominated by the basins of the Niger and Benue rivers, Nigeria can be divided into four distinct geographic regions. Most of the coastline is dominated by the Niger delta, lagoons and marshes, while in the south-east it is rocky. The **coastal plain,** which is around 150 km wide, turns inland into the **Yoruba Plateau** west of the Niger, the **Oban** and the **Udi Hills** and in a southerly direction into the **Benue Plateau** east of the Niger. The Gotel and Shebshi Mountains (Dimlang 2,042 m.) lie along the border with Cameroon. The central plateau is around 1,200 m high and in the Jos Plateau rises to 1,752 m. In the north-west, the plateau sinks to the plains of Sokoto and in the north-east it leads into the alluvial plain of **Lake Chad**.

Climate

The tropical climate produces temperatures between 26°C and 29°C on the coast, from 23°C to 33°C in the north and between 21°C and 26°C in the central plateau.
In the south, the rainy season lasts from April to November; average rainfall on the coast is up to 4,000 mm. The rainy season in the north lasts from May to October; where precipitation is just under 700 mm. In the dry season, the **Harmattan,** the hot Sahara wind, determines the climate. In the north-east, which is part of the Sahel, there is semi-arid savannah. The Sudan zone, which adjoins this zone in a southerly direction consists of dry savan-

Benin is the cradle of **Voodoo** – a religion that spread through slaves and was further developed, mainly in Haiti. It is said to have some 50 million followers worldwide. The religion, based upon rituals rather than written scriptures, has found an avid following in West Africa. In the former royal palace of Abomey, numerous ceremonial items are displayed. Cult objects such as these iron fetishes were produced in the forge.

nah with thorn bushes and isolated baobab trees.

The Guinea zone is characterised by deciduous forests and savannah dotted with clumps of trees, while in the coastal region mangrove swamps predominate.

The rich variety of mammalian fauna and reptiles is seriously endangered. Only in the game reserves of Borgu and Yankari are there significant numbers of elephants, hippopotamuses, giraffes, buffaloes, lions, antelopes as well as numerous types of birds. The number of manatees in coastal waters has declined significantly.

Population

A total of 434 ethnic groups live in Nigeria, including Hausa, Fulani, Hamitic and Chad peoples, Ibo, Ibibio, Yoruba, Fulani as well as a European minority. Just under half are Christians of different persuasions, 45 per cent are Muslim. In addition, there are numerous followers of animist religions. Average life expectancy is 47 years. The literacy rate is 57 per cent. 40 per cent of Nigerians live in the cities.

History and Politics

Important cultures have been established in Nigeria for 2000 years. From the eleventh century AD, the **Hausa** in the north had created their own city-states with a unique culture. Islam was soon adopted by a large percentage of the population and was already firmly established when the Portuguese discovered the Kingdom of Benin in 1472. Europeans then operated a flourishing **slave trade** with the New World until 1807. This led to wars among the different tribes as well as to extremely high population losses.

In the mid-nineteenth century, Britain declared Nigeria to be a colony, though leaving some of the traditional ruling structures in place. After the final conquest of the kingdom of Benin in 1897, the British protectorates of South and North Nigeria came into being and these merged into the Colony and Protectorate of Nigeria in 1914, Britain's largest African possession.

In 1960, Nigeria was granted its **independence** and in 1963 it became a republic within the British Commonwealth. The recent governance of the country has been characterised by coups d'état and political murders.

The Ibo region, which is predominantly Christian, attempted to break away, declared its own state, named Biafra. In 1967, a civil war broke out. By 1970, the war had cost one million lives. Biafra lost the war and was again incorporated into Nigeria.

Different military regimes have made huge profits from the rich natural resources, without allowing benefit to the population. The regime of the late General Sani Abacha was especially brutal and corrupt. The regime suffered stiff opposition by pro-democracy activists but Abacha was protected by international oil concerns, attracting strong criticism against the Shell company in particular. Even after Abacha'sdaeth in a plane crash in 1998, the promised return to **democracy** did not happen. The 1999 elections under international supervision were an important step towards democracy, however. In the same year, a new constitution came into force. The widespread corruption and unrest between Christians and Muslims, which continued under the new President Olusegun Obasanjo has hindered development. In 2007, Umaru Musa Yar'Adua was elected the new head of state and government.

Economy

In 2006, GDP stood at US$115 bn, of which 30 per cent derived from **agriculture**, 45 per cent from **industry** and 25 per cent from **services**. Nigeria's wealth is based on oil which accounts for 93 per cent of total exports. Machinery, chemicals, vehicles and consumer goods are imported.

Transport Infrastructure

The national **rail network** covers 3,557 km, the **road network** 32,105 km, of which 26,005 km is paved. There are five international **airports**. The major **sea ports** are at Lagos, the former capital, Calabar and Warri. Bonny and Burutu are oil terminals. The ports are very busy and merchant ships have to wait for days to get into harbour.

Tourism

Only 887,000 visitors came to the country in 2003; however they brought in foreign currency to the value of US$263 million. The best time to travel is between October and March. Tourism is being developed around Lagos and Kano and in the national parks.

1 In the eighteenth century, villages were erected on poles in Lac Nokoué in Benin, which could only be reached by boat. This construction protected the inhabitants from their enemies.

2 The traditional kingdom of Abomey still flourishes in Benin. Some kings who, like other members of the royal family, are allowed to have several wives, continue to be important members of society.

3 The Niger delta covers an area of 25,000 sq. km, and is the largest in Africa. Its rich fish stocks provide subsistence for the local inhabitants.

Chad

Chad is one of the poorest countries in the world. 85 per cent of the population lives from agriculture. The relatively abundant supply of cattle in the market at the Faya-Largeau oasis cannot conceal widespread shortages in the region.

	Chad

Area 1,284,000 sq. km

Capital city: N'Djamena

Form of government:
Presidential Republic

Administrative divisions:
8 prefectures

Population: 9.8 million
(8 inhabitants/sq. km)

Languages:
French, Arabic (both official)

GDP per inhabitant:
US$680

Currency: 1 CFA franc =
100 centimes

Natural Geography

The West and the interior of consist of the Chad Basin which is flanked in the North by the **Tibesti-Massif** which is some 3,415 m in altitude, in the

South by the North Equatorial Ridge and in the east and west by the Enedi and Quadaï plateaus. Lake Chad is in the west.

Climate

In the north, the desert climate of the Sahara prevails. It is responsi-

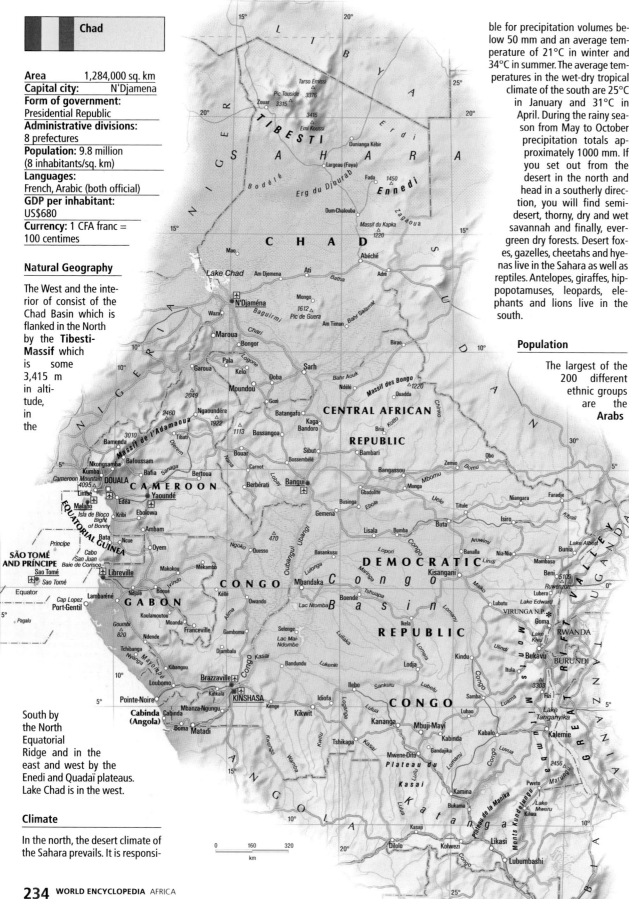

ble for precipitation volumes below 50 mm and an average temperature of 21°C in winter and 34°C in summer. The average temperatures in the wet-dry tropical climate of the south are 25°C in January and 31°C in April. During the rainy season from May to October precipitation totals approximately 1000 mm. If you set out from the desert in the north and head in a southerly direction, you will find semi-desert, thorny, dry and wet savannah and finally, evergreen dry forests. Desert foxes, gazelles, cheetahs and hyenas live in the Sahara as well as reptiles. Antelopes, giraffes, hippopotamuses, leopards, elephants and lions live in the south.

Population

The largest of the 200 different ethnic groups are the **Arabs** who account for 15 per cent and **arabised peoples** account for 38 per cent, while Sara and **Tibbu Daza** comprise 30 per cent of the population. **Fulbes**, **Hausas** and others make up the remainder. Approximately half the population are Muslim, 30 per cent Christian and 20 per cent animist. The average life expectancy is 48 years and the illiteracy rate is 52 per cent.

History and Politics

From medieval times onwards, three powerful Islamic empires existed in the region, operating a lucrative slave trade. In the late nineteenth century, Chad became a French colony, and became part of French **Equatorial Africa** in 1910.

Following independence in 1960, President Tombalbayé pursued a pro-French course. However, he was only able to maintain his rule by employing dictatorial measures. He was assassinated in 1975. The traditional north-south conflict finally culminated in a bloody civil war in which Libya took the side of the Islamic north and France the side of the Christian south. The 1996 constitution has not yet been fully put into action. However, the domestic situation is now relatively stable.

Economy

GDP was US$6.5 billion in 2006. **Agriculture** accounted for 46 per cent of this figure, **industry** for 14 per cent and the **services sector** for 40 per cent. Chad's agriculture aims to be self-sufficient but is unable to meet local demand. The exploitation of oil reserves looks very promising. In 2003, a pipeline to the Atlantic coast in Cameroon was put into operation. Cotton, meat, livestock, hides and skins are also exported.

Transport Infrastructure

Except for the approximately 200-km-long **network of roads** which are surfaced, there are only cart tracks and paths. Yaoundé has an international **airport**. Chad is landlocked.

*There are more than 200 ethnic groups in **Cameroon**. The south is populated by Bantu-speaking people, the north mainly by Muslims and a range of Sudanese tribes. On the far right, a marabout – a Muslim sage.*

Tourism

The National Museum in N'jamena has collections of the Sarh culture dating back to the ninth century. Lake Chad was once the center of Africa's lucrative salt trade but is now shrinking (literally). The lake is best seen during the August to December period, when the water level is highest and the occasional hippo or crocodile can be spotted.

Cameroon	
Area:	475,442 sq. km
Capital city:	Yaoundé
Form of government:	
Presidential Republic	
Administrative divisions:	
10 provinces	
Population:	
18 million (38 inhabitants/sq. km)	
Languages:	
French, English (both official languages), Bantu languages	
GDP per capita:	US$1,000
Currency:	
1 CFA franc = 100 centimes	

Natural Geography

To the west of a narrow lowland line called the Cameroon Line, there is the Cameroon Mountain a volcano which reaches altitudes of up to 4,000 m, west of the Adamawa mountains. These mountains rise to a height of 2,500 m and drop down in a northerly direction to Lake Chad. Several offshore islands are also of volcanic origin. The marshy coastal plain is replaced by a low-lying plateau landscape in the south which turns into the Congo Basin.

Climate

In the south, a wet-dry tropical climate prevails with precipitation volumes of 4,000 to 5,000 mm. On the coast, the average temperature is 26°C. The region surrounding Cameroon Mountain is one of the **rainiest areas** on earth with precipitation of over 10,000 mm. In the north only 500 mm of rain falls during a comparatively short rainy season and the average temperatures vary from 10°C to 40°C. In the central highlands the average temperature is

22°C and the precipitation volume is 1,500 mm. Marshes and mangrove swamps cover the coastline and the south is covered in tropical rainforest. Central Cameroon is characterised by savannah. There are many different species of the savannah in the national parks, such as baboons, giraffes, rhinoceroses, lions, elephants and buffalo. Anthropoid apes and numerous species of birds live in the rainforests.

Population

Approximately 200 ethnic groups live in Cameroon. **Bantu-speaking minority** account for 40 per cent of the population, **Semibantus** and **Adamawas** for 20 per cent. Additionally, there are Hausas, **Fulbes**, **Pygmies** and a minority of Europeans. 53 per cent of the population is Christian, 22 per cent Muslim and there are many followers of animist religions. Average life expectancy is 51 years and the illiteracy rate is 37 per cent.

History and Politics

In addition to the **Portuguese** who landed in Cameroon around 1470, the Scandinavians, the Dutch and the British also operated a flourishing slave trade from here for over 300 years. In 1884, Cameroon became a **German colony**. Following World War I, the British and French divided the country up between themselves.

French Cameroon, as it was known, gained **independence** in 1960 and the British Cameroons followed in 1961. Cameroon was reunited, with the exception of a small area which became part of Nigeria. In the post-colonial era the country was ruled by President **Ahmadou Ahidjos** who favoured a centralist policy. Following his resignation in 1982, his successor **Paul Biya** attempted to carry through seemingly democratic reforms. As a result of the 1972 constitution, the parliament and head of state are elected every five years. Citizens have the right to vote from the age of 20.

Economy

In spite of a considerable north-south cultural and linguistic divide, which has the potential for

conflict, Cameroon is one of the richest states of sub-Saharan Africa. The country's GDP in 2006 was US$18 billion. **Agriculture** accounted for 39 per cent of this figure, industry accounted for 23 per cent and the **services sector** accounted for 38 per cent. The foreign trade balance is positive. Oil, coffee, wood, bananas,

1 Chad: like its neighbours, agriculture and livestock breeding suffered from the two disastrous droughts in the 1970s and 1980s in the Sahel.

2 The north of Cameroon is inhabited by semi-nomadic shepherds. Their

houses and grain stores are mostly built in a round shape from clay and stones.

3 The Arabic Tubu people live in the north and east of Chad. In the Ennedi plateau the oldest African cave paintings have been discovered.

*The rare African **forest elephant** lives in the rainforests of West and Central Africa and reaches maximum height of 2.3 m. The extremely shy animals were only discovered in 1899. They differ from the Savannah elephants by having five toes on their front feet and four on the hind feet. Furthermore the four subspecies have round ear form rather than triangular. Their number is being estimated at only 200,000 specimen.*

cotton, timber and cocoa are the main exports.

Transport Infrastructure

A mere 2,800 km of Cameroon's total **road network** of 71,000 km is surfaced. The **rail network** has a length of 1,115 km. The most important **port** and **airport** are at Douala.

Tourism

The tourism infrastructure is developing slowly. Yaoundé, has the Musée des Bénédictins, a collection of traditional arts and crafts housed in a Benedictine Monastery on Mont Fébé, and the newer National Museum of Yaoundé.The best time to visit is between November and April.

⚑	**Central African Republic**
Area:	622,984 sq. km
Capital city:	Bangui
Form of government:	
Presidential Republic	
Administrative divisions:	
16 prefectures, capital city	
Population:	

4.3 million (7 inhabitants/sq. km)
Languages:
French, Sangho (both official), Bantu and Sudan languages
GDP per capita: US$350
Currency:
1 CFA franc = 100 centimes

Natural geography

Between the Chad Basin in the North and the Congo Basin, a tropical lowland line in the South, stretches the **North Equatorial Ridge**, hilly country with an altitude of 500 to 1,000 m which also contains the headwaters for numerous rivers. In the north-west and north-east there are two mountain ranges, the Massif du Yadé and the Massif de Bongo. The Ubangi river rises by 6 m in the rainy season (June to November).

Climate

The wet-dry tropical climate is responsible for a precipitation of just under 900 mm in the north and for average temperatures of 22°C to 30°C which may rise to 40°C in summer. The average temperatures in the south range between 24°C and 28°C and the precipitation ranges between 1,500 mm and 1,800 mm. The dry savannah adjoins wet savannah in the south. Gallery forests grow along the riverbanks and evergreen tropical rainforests can be found in the extreme south. Elephants, rhinoceroses, hyenas and antelopes number roam the savannah. The forests also contain many species of primates.

Jean-Bédel Bokassa

*Bobangui 22.2.1921,
†Bangui 3.11.1996

The former general commander-in-chief of the Central African Republic became president after staging a coup in 1966. He was an unpredictable dictator. In 1972 he declared himself a President-for-life and in 1977 appointed himself the Emperor Bokassa I. His reign of terror ended in 1979 when he fled the country. He returned, was tried and sentenced to death, but this was commuted to a life sentence.

Population

The largest ethnic groups include the **Bandas** (30 per cent), the **Gbayas** (24 per cent), the **Gbandis** (11 per cent), and the **Azandes** (ten per cent). In addition to **Yakomas**, **Bantus** and other peoples, there is a minority of Europeans. 57 per cent are followers of animalist religions, 35 per cent are Christians and eight per cent Muslims. Average life expectancy is 49 years and the illiteracy rate is 40 per cent.

History and Politics

The original population was obliterated to a great extent in the eighteenth and nineteenth century through the slave trade. From the late nineteenth century onwards, the French established their **colonial rule** in the area of the present-day Central African Republic which was part of French Equatorial Africa.
Following formal **independence** in 1960, one military dictatorship replaced another. In 1966, Colonel **Jean-Bédel Bokassa** took power in a military coup and had himself crowned emperor in 1977. With France's assistance, he established a brutal terror regime before being overthrown in 1979. The country has been repeatedly plagued by military conflicts over power and resources ever since independence. In March 2003, the elected president, Félix Patassé, who was disliked by the people due to his political repression and poor governance was overthrown by the former General Chief of Staff François Bozizé.

Economy

In 2006 Gross Domestic Product totalled US$1,500 million. **Agriculture** accounted for 60 per cent of this sum, **industry**, 25 per cent and the **services sector**, 15 per cent. Coffee, wood, cotton and, above all, diamonds are the principle exports.

Transport Infrastructure

5,000 km of the country's 24,000-km-long **road network** are passable all year round. The Ubangi river is navigable and is an important artery. The capital city, Bangui, has the only international **airport**.

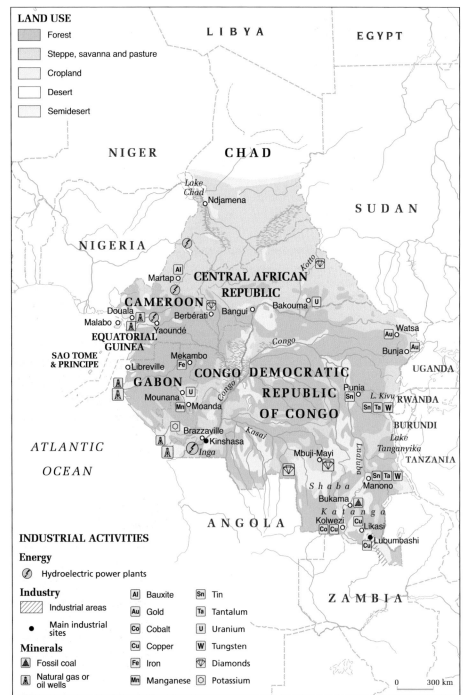

LAND USE

- Forest
- Steppe, savanna and pasture
- Cropland
- Desert
- Semidesert

INDUSTRIAL ACTIVITIES

Energy
- ⚡ Hydroelectric power plants

Industry
- Industrial areas
- ● Main industrial sites

Al	Bauxite	Sn	Tin
Au	Gold	Ta	Tantalum
Co	Cobalt	U	Uranium
Cu	Copper	W	Tungsten

Minerals
⛏	Fossil coal	Fe	Iron
⛏	Natural gas or oil wells	Mn	Manganese
		▽	Diamonds
		O	Potassium

0   300 km

*The African **pygmies** were among the first to settle in the Congo basin. Usually less than 1.5 m tall, they are the shortest people in the world. There are between 150,000 and 300,000 of them left now.*

Tourism

Tourism is extremely underdeveloped. The country's great natural diversity could be the basis for future development of the industry.

★ ★	São Tomé and Príncipe

Area: 1,001 sq. km
Capital city: São Tomé
Form of government: Republic
Administrative divisions: District of São Tomé, Príncipe Island (autonomous status)
Population: 180,000 (180 inhabitants/sq. km)
Languages: Portuguese (official), Creole
GDP per capita: US$750
Currency: 1 dobra = 100 centimes

Natural geography

Both of the main islands of São Tomé and Príncipe and the smaller, uninhabited islands belonging to the state are of volcanic origin. The **Pico de São Tomé** is 2,024 m high and the main summit of Príncipe is 948 m high.

Climate

The tropical, hot **rainy climate** is responsible for average temperatures of 25°C to 30°C which decrease to 20°C above 800 m. On average, 4,000 to 5,000 m of precipitation falls in the south-west during the rainy season which lasts from October to April. There is only 1,000 mm of precipitation in the north, however. With the exception of the areas cleared for cocoa plantations in the north, the evergreen **rainforest** is still preserved to a large extent.

Population

At the time that the country was discovered by the Europeans the islands were uninhabited. Consequently, the population consists principally of the **descendants of former slaves** originating from all over Africa, of **people of mixes race** and a few Portuguese. 93 per cent of the population are Catholics and three per cent Protestants. There are also smaller groups of followers of various animist religions. Average life expectancy is 67 years and the illiteracy rate is 40 per cent.

History and Politics

After the Portuguese discovered the islands in around 1470, they planted cocoa bushes which were cultivated by slaves. Cocoa remained the main economic factor following independence from Portugal in 1975. Since the 1990 constitution, the parliament has been directly elected every four years and the country's president every five years. Voting begins at 18.

Economy

The country is dependent to a large extent on the global market price for cocoa and payments from the donor countries of Portugal and France. The Gross Domestic Product was US$125 million in 2006. **Agriculture** accounted for 17 per cent of this figure, industry for 15 per cent and the **services sector** for 68 per cent.

Transport Infrastructure

The road network is approximately 300 km long in total. A regular connecting ferry service is in operation between the two main islands. An international **airport** is situated in close proximity to the capital city.

Tourism

There are relatively few foreign visitors to the country. The best time to visit is between June and August.

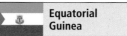

	Equatorial Guinea

Area: 28,051 sq. km
Capital city: Malabo
Form of government: Presidential Republic
Administrative divisions: 7 provinces

1 The main fuel in Equatorial Guinea is still wood.

2 Cameroon's main cash crops are coffee, cocoa, cotton and bananas.

3 Agriculture in the Central African Repulic provides for the country's needs and it supplies major exports such as coffee, cotton, cattle and tobacco.

4 The Ubangi river in the south of the Central African Republic is the border with the Democratic Republic of Congo.

Equatorial Guinea, Gabon, Congo

*A medicine man talks to a **fetish**. A fetish is an object considered to have supernatural powers. Fetishes are widespread in West and Central Africa. Powerful ancestors are supposed to communicate through them.*

The practices of medicine men are based on the assumption that supernatural energies are active everywhere and men are both dependent on them and able to make use of them for their own purposes.

Population:
550,000 (20 inhabitants/sq. km)
Languages:
Spanish (official), Pidgin English, Bantu languages
GDP per capita:
US$15,500–30,000
Currency:
1 CFA franc = 100 centimes

Natural Geography

The name of the country is misleading as it lies approximately 200 km north of the Equator. The mainland province of **Mbini** consists of a coastal plain and an inland plateau at an altitude of up to 1,200 m. The islands of **Bioko** and **Pagalu** are mountainous and together form the island province of Bioko in the Gulf of Guinea.

Climate

The tropical **rainy climate** is responsible for an average annual temperature of 25°C and an average precipitation of 2,000 mm which can, however, reach 4,000 in some regions of the country. The mangrove swamps of the coastal region are replaced by tropical rainforest inland and by savannah at higher altitude.

Population

Bantu-speaking groups account for 80 per cent of the population, **Bubis** for ten per cent and a minority are **mixed race** or white. 99 per cent of the population is **Catholic**, although in 1978, Roman Catholicism was banned. Average life expectancy is 50 years and the illiteracy rate is 50 per cent.

History and Politics

Portuguese rule began in 1472 and did not come to an end until 1778. It was ended by the Spaniards who, in the mid-twentieth century, united Bioko with the mainland region of the Spanish colony of Río Muni which the Spanish acquired in 1900. Following **independence, Francisco Macías Nguema** ruled the country using terror and oppression. After being overthrown and executed in 1979, his nephew, Lieutenant-Commander **Teodoro Obiang Nguema Mbasogo**, promised liberal reforms. However, he also proved to be a power-obsessed dictator. In

2002, he was reinstated in office for seven years. In accordance with the 1991 constitution, parliament is elected every five years and the head of state every seven years. Citizens 21 years of age and over have the right to vote.

Economy

The economy of Equatorial Guinea is today determined by its oil reserves. In the last few years, large deposits have been discovered on the coast and the mainland. Rates of growth have sometimes reached 30 per cent, which is a world record. The oil economy accounted for 90 per cent of GDP.

A market women in Congo sells oil in rather strange bottles.

Despite this fact, approximately two-thirds of the population still live below the poverty line.

Transport

The **road network** is only 180 km long on Bioko and 1,500 km long on the mainland. Regular connecting **sea** and **air services** are in operation between the islands. The **sea ports** and **airports** are at Malabo and Bata.

Tourism Infrastructure

Tourism is practically non-existent. The best time to visit the country is between December and February.

Gabon	

Area:	267,667 sq. km
Capital city:	
Libreville	
Form of government:	
Presidential Republic	
Administrative divisions:	
9 provinces	

valleys and gorges of a **plateau** that is part of the African Shield formation. The coastal lowland, which is up to 200 km wide, ascends to the foothills of the Lower Guinea Ridge at an altitude of 890 m. At 1,575 m, **Mont Iboundi** in the central Massif du Chaillu is the country's highest mountain. The 800-km-long coastline consists of lagoons and spits of land in the south. In the north, it is sub-divided into deltas, bays and river estuaries.

Climate

The wet-hot **tropical climate** causes only slight variations in temperature. The average monthly temperatures are approximately 26°C on the coast and 24°C inland. There are two rainy seasons, lasting from October to December and January to May respectively. In the north-west, the average precipitation is 4,000 mm. In the southerly coastal zone it is 2,500 mm and approximately 1,700 mm inland. Three-quarters of the country is covered in **tropical rainforest**. Tree-felling has, in places, transformed the once thick vegetation into secondary forest. On the coast and in the river valleys there are vast areas of **grassland**. Various species of monkeys and birds, elephants, antelopes, buffalos, crocodiles and hippopotamuses inhabit Gabon.

Population

Approximately 40 different ethnic groups live in Gabon. 52 per cent are Catholics, 40 per cent followers of traditional religions and eight per cent Protestants. Average life expectancy is 55 years and the illiteracy rate is 37 per cent.

History and Politics

Following discovery by the Portuguese, various European **colonial powers** operated a flourishing trade in exotic timber, ivory and slaves on the coast and along the navigable waterways. In 1886, Gabon became a French colony and in 1910 it became part of French Equatorial Africa. Even after gaining **independence** in 1960, the country's wealth remained to a great extent in foreign hands. Omar Bongo has been head of state since 1967.

Gabon enjoys a relatively high degree of political stability. The one-party state was transformed into a multi-party democracy by the 1991 constitution which was amended in 1995. The national assembly, the senate and the head of state are directly elected every five years. Citizens can vote at 21 years of age.

Economy

Gross Domestic Product was US$9.5 billion in 2006. **Agriculture** accounted for seven per cent of this figure, **industry** for 55 per cent and the **service sector** for 38 per cent. The most significant economic factor is the exploitation of the **oil fields**, which at 88 per cent make up the lion's share of export revenue. The export of tropical timber and manganese also make a significant contribution.

Transport Infrastructure

Only approximately 600 km of the 7,500-km-long **road network** is surfaced. A 648-km-long **rail connection** links Libreville with Franceville. There are international **airports** in Port-Gentil and in Libreville.

Tourism

Gabon has underdeveloped tourism. The Lopé national park right in the centre of the country covers an area of 5,360 sq. km and is a promising destination for safaris and ecotourists. Another important site is the Schweitzer Hospital at Lambaréné. The best time to visit is between July and December.

Congo	

Area:	342,000 sq. km
Capital city:	Brazzaville
Form of government:	
Republic	
Administrative divisions:	
9 regions and 4 urban districts	
Population:	3.5 million
	(10 inhabitants/sq. km)
Languages:	
French (official) and various Bantu languages	
GDP per capita:	US$2,200
Currency:	
1 CFA franc = 100 centimes	

Population:
1.4 million (5 inhabitants/sq. km)
Languages:
French (official), Bantu languages
GDP per capita: US$6,800
Currency:
1 CFA-franc = 100 centimes

Natural Geography

The country is characterised by the Ogooué and its tributaries which wend their way through

*In **Ituri primeval forest** of the Democratic Republic of Congo, ancient rituals are preserved. These Epulu women paint parts of their faces white for menstruating ceremonies. The Ngodi-Ngodi paint themselves with slaked lime and kohl.*

Natural Geography

The coastline which is approximately 50 km wide is sandy in the north and marshy in the south. The Mayombé mountainous region reaches altitudes of up to 800 m and turns into the **Batéké Plateau** after Niari Valley which is flanked by the Monts de la Lékéti which are over 1,000 m high. The **Congo Basin** in the north-east occupies the majority of the country's surface area. The Congo and its tributaries form a floodplain here which is approximately 100,000 sq. km in area.

Climate

In the north, a tropical wet climate prevails with a virtually constant average temperature of 25°C and precipitation volumes of between 1,500 mm and 1,900 mm which are attained during the two rainy seasons from January to May and October to December. In the South, temperatures vary between 22°C and 27°C. The average precipitation of 1,300 mm falls predominantly in March and November. Mangroves grow on the coast. Wet savannah can be found in the mountains and the highlands and there are frequent floods north of the Alima. The Congo Basin is the largest **rainforest region** in Africa. Gorillas and chimpanzees inhabit the rainforest, whilst antelopes, elephants, leopards and giraffes live in the savannah.

Population

The population consists mainly of **Bantu-speaking** groups. 52 per cent are **Ba-** and **Vili-Congos**, 24 per cent are **Batekes** and **Bavilis** and 12 per cent are **M'Boshis**. In addition, there are minorities of Tékés, Sangas, pygmies, Ubangi groups and Europeans. Average life expectancy is 51 years and the illiteracy rate is 25 per cent. Half of the Congolese are Catholics and the remainder are followers of various animist religions.

History and Politics

When the Portuguese discovered the estuary of the Congo river in 1482, the interior was ruled by the kingdoms of **Congo** and **Loango** which played a part in the slave trade, assisting the European colonial powers. In 1880, the explorer **Pierre Savorgnan de Brazza** journeyed through the central Congo region and brought it under French control. Following **independence** in 1960, one military government replaced another. In 1970, **Marien Ngouabi** declared the country to be the People's Republic of Congo, a Marxist-Leninist state. Following his assassination, a military junta seized power in 1977. In 1991, the official name was changed back to the Republic of Congo.

Following the adoption of a new constitution, presidential elections were held in August 1992. These were won by **Pascal Lissouba** who also won the parliamentary elections in 1993. Following armed clashes between government troops and opposing militia, Lissouba was overthrown in 1997 by the followers of **Denis Sassou-Nguessos**. The new president succeeded in consolidating his power. Opposition candidates were not permitted to take part in the election. Sassou-Nguesso was therefore able to gain over 89 per cent of the vote for himself in the March 2002 presidential election. In the same year, there were constant clashes with rebels. In March 2003, government and militia were united, ensuring their immunity from prosecution. In October 2003, the unrest flared up again. The country is usually referred to as Congo Brazzaville, so as to avoid confusion with its neighbour, which was formerly known as the Belgian Congo, under colonial rule, then Zaïre and is now called the Democratic Republic of Congo.

Economy

Gross Domestic Product amounted to US$7.7 billion in 2006. **Agriculture** accounted for seven per cent of this sum, **industry** for 62 per cent and the **services sector** for 31 per cent. Crude oil is both the main economic factor and the most important export.

1 The widest section of the Congo river runs through the rain forest of the Congo basin.

2 Congo: apart from coffee, cocoa, manioc, rice, palm kernels, sugar cane and peanuts, and fishing are important to the economy.

3 Between Kisangani and Kinshasa the Congo river is an important navigable waterway.

4 The economy of the Congo has not yet recovered from the crisis in the 1980s. The local markets still have precious little to sell.

*The African **rainforests** are preserved in isolated areas scattered across Central Africa. They were often cleared for agricultural use. To this day many precious hardwood trees are being cut for wood processing.*

The unscrupulous deforestation also has a lasting impact on the animal kingdom. Many species once widespread in the rainforests, were deprived of living space and are now in danger of extinction.

Transport Infrastructure

Only approximately 550 km of the 11,000-km-long **road network** is surfaced. The two **railway lines** have a total length of 800 km. The 2,600 km of **waterways** which are navigable year round are important transport links. There are international **airports** at Pointe Noire and Brazzaville.

Tourism

The political situation has hindered significant tourism until now. The tourism infrastructure is therefore very poorly developed. The best time to visit is between June and September. However, the country is ripe for safari tourism.

Congo, Democratic Republic of	
Area:	2,345 410 sq. km
Capital city:	Kinshasa
Form of government: Presidential Republic	
Administrative divisions: 10 regions, 1 district (capital city)	
Population:	

Sese Seko Mobutu

*Lisala 14.10.1930,
†Rabat 7.9.1997

In 1960 the general commander in chief of the Force Publique assumed power in a military coup in the former Zaïre. After the reappointment of Kasavubu, he retained the supreme command of the army and became a dictator after another coup in 1965, until he was deposed in 1997, after a long and bloody civil war.

60 million (26 inhabitants/sq. km)	
Language:	French
GDP per capita:	US$140
Currency:	
1 Congo franc = 100 centimes	

Natural geography

The relatively small coastal plain which is characterised by the estuary of the Congo follows a narrow line which links the interior of the country with the Atlantic. The majority of the country consists of the **Congo Basin** which is covered in rainforest. In the north, there are vast tracts of grassy savannah. The eastern border and **Lake Tanganjika** form volcanic mountains (the Ruwenzori reaches an altitude of 5,119 m in the Margherita).

Climate

In the north, the tropical climate produces average temperatures of around 25°C which remain constant all year round and there is a precipitation volume of 2,000 mm.

Thatched huts on the slopes of Ruwenzori mountains.

In the south, the temperatures are more variable and rainfall varies between 1,200 mm and 1,500 mm, predominantly between September and May. Typical **rainforest flora** can be found in the Congo Basin along with fauna in a relatively original state. Eight to ten thousand types of plants flourish here in a complicated **ecosystem** which has hitherto only degenerated to

secondary forest in small areas due to the commercial tree-felling. for timber. Among the 600 types of wood, there are numerous **valuable tropical woods**. Today, baobabs, mahogany trees, African walnut trees and limba trees still continue to flourish. Western red cedars, iroko and sable palms also grow. As the distance from the equator increases, the landscape turns into grassland savannah. In the **mountainous regions** of the east mountain, there are mountainous forests on the slopers; the flood plains are alluvial and **marshy**.

The rich wildlife is protected predominantly in the seven great **national parks**. Okapis, gorillas and chimpanzees are some of the rainforest's inhabitants. Zebras, lions, elephants, buffaloes, rhinoceroses and giraffes live in the savannah and hippopotamuses, crocodiles and numerous fish, especially cichlids, live in the freshwater envionment. There is an especially great number of species of bird.

Population

Of roughly 250 ethnic groups, **Bantu-speaking groups** are the **majority**. 18 per cent are **Lubas**, 16 per cent **Congolese**, 13 per cent **Mongos** and ten per cent **Rwandans**. There are also Sudanese groups, Pygmies and Europeans. As far as religion is concerned, 42 per cent are Catholics, 25 per cent Protestants and 15 per cent are followers of other Christian denominations. Another two per cent are Muslims or followers of animist religions. Average life expectancy is 53 years and the illiteracy rate is 33 per cent.

History and Politics

Although the **Portuguese** discovered the area of present-day Congo in 1482, the African empires of the Congo, Luba, Cuba and Lunda remained stable until the mid-nineteenth century. In 1885, the Independent Congo State was created following the Congo Conference in Berlin. The Congo became the private fiefdom of the Belgian **King Leopold II**. The slave trade was abolished. In 1908, the area finally became a Belgian colony. During World War I, Congolese troops conquered the Rwanda-Urundi area for the Allies which was granted to Belgium in 1919. Following independence from Belgium in 1960, revolts, politically motivated murders, recurring secession attempts by Katanga province and corruption affected all areas of political and economic life. In 1965, **Sese Seko Mobutu** was finally able to prevail against all adversaries and establish an authoritative, corrupt terror regime. Large sections of the population lived in poverty, and still do, despite the country's wealth. His most prominent opponent **Patrice Lumumba** who was murdered on 12 February 1961 in circumstances that remain unclear. The perpetrator has never been identified. Mobutu renamed the country **Zaïre** and ruled for over 30 years. Following a very long civil war **Laurent-Désiré Kabila** overthrew the sick dictator in 1997 and made Zaïre into the Democratic Republic of the Congo. Kabila requested that a constitution be drawn up modelled on the constitution of the USA but the promised democratisation did not

happen. Politically motivated murders, corruption and armed clashes between the various tribal militia were the order of the day. In 2001, Kabila was assassinated. Shortly afterwards, his son Joseph Kabila assumed power. In 2003, a transitional constitution which the conflicting parties had agreed upon came into force. The transitional government prepared the country for free elections which were held in 2006. Kabila was confirmed in office as a result. The elections were monitored by EU troops.

Economy

Despite extensive **mineral resources** the country is one of the world's poorest. Currency reform and privatisation and cooperation plans have not been implemented. A budget acceptable to foreign investors does not even exist. The Gross Domestic Product amounted to US$8.5 billion in 2006. Fifty-nine per cent derived from **agriculture** which is little developed thus far, 15 per cent was derived from **industry** and 26 per cent from the **services sector**. Machinery, semi-finished goods, foodstuffs and fuel are imported and diamonds, crude oil, copper, cobalt and coffee are some of the main exports.

Transport Infrastructure

The country's **rail network** is 5,138 km long, although only 858 km is electrified. 2,500 km of the country's 145,000 km **road network** is surfaced. There are international **airports** in Kinshasa, Lumbumbashi, Bukavu, Goma and Kisangani.

Tourism

Due to the political situation the tourist infrastructure is practically non-existent. However, the extraordinary wealth of wildlife and especially the gorilla colonies deep n the rainforest are promising for ecotourism. Many scientific expeditions visit the country to explore the medicinal potential of the various plant species in the rainforest. The best time to visit the area north of the equator is from December to January and for the area south of the Equator June and July.

Today's South Africa is well on its way towards transforming itself in to a modern, multi-cultural society. Yet even in the flashy urban canyons of the boomtowns the language of the masks is understood and has not been forgotten.

Although the Democratic Republic of Congo holds the greatest of Africa's natural wealth, it is one of the poorest countries in the world, and is in decline due to mismanagement, corruption and civil wars. Almost two-thirds of the population work on the land. The picture on the left shows a quinine tree

plantation, used for the production of quinine. The most important branch of industry is mining, extracting copper, gold, silver, cobalt, manganese and diamonds. The image on the right shows mine workers in Eastern Congo, searching for gold using simple manual tools.

Sudan, Eritrea

A camel caravan transports salt blocks from **Lake Assal** in Djibouti. The salt lake is situated 155 m below sea level and is the lowest point of Africa. Djibouti's salt pans are among the largest on earth.

Sudan

Area:	2,505 813 sq. km
Capital city:	Khartoum
Form of government:	Republic
Administrative divisions:	
26 provinces	
Population: 40 million	
(16 inhabitants per sq. km)	
Languages:	
Arabic (official), English, as well as Hamitic and Nilotic languages	
GDP per capita:	US$1,000
Currency:	
1 Sudanese pound = 100 piastres	

Natural geography

Sudan is the largest country in Africa. It has a flat valley landscape, interrupted only by a few isolated mountains. The highest elevation is represented by Kinyeti (3,187 m) in the south. The great Sudd swamp, a flood plain of the **White Nile**, separates the north and south of the country. Almost 60 per cent of the population lives in the Nile valley which has the best farmland. Almost one third of the country consists of sandy desert, bordered to the south by savannah and grass steppe. Rainforests are found in the mountainous regions of the south.

Climate

The climate is largely continental-tropical turning to desert in the north. At the Red Sea, temperatures of over 50°C are regularly recorded. The Khartoum region has the highest average annual temperature (32°C).

Population

Of the Sudanese population 52 per cent are predominantly **Nilotic**, falling into more than 500 different ethnic groups, while 39 per cent of the population are of **Arab origin**. Some 70 per cent are adherents of Islam, living mainly in the north of the country, while the Christians, who live mainly in the south and in Khartoum, make up only ten per cent of the population. One quarter of Sudanese are adherents of animist religions. The official language, Arabic, is the mother tongue of 50 per cent of the population, while the other half speak more than 100 languages, of mainly Nilotic origin.

History and Politics

The history of what now constitutes the Sudan dates back millennia, when, as Nubia, it was part of the Egyptian empire. It was not until 1000 BC that the independent kingdom of Kush came into being. It was replaced in the sixth century BC by the Kingdom of Meroe whose rulers and converted to Christianity, and which lasted until 325 AD. The kingdom of Axum, now Ethiopia, then conquered the land. Arab tribes followed in the late thirteenth century and Islamised the country. Britain and Egypt ruled the Sudan jointly from 1820. In 1881 a bloodthirsty revolt was led by Mohammed Ahmad, the so-called 'Mad Mahdi' – the Mahdi being the renewer of faith awaited by Islam, who would restore divine order. General

Sudan: the El-Sheik Deffa Allah Mosque koranic school, Omdurman.

George Gordon quelled the revolt in 1899, since when he was known as Gordon of Khartoum. In 1956, Sudan declared its **independence** from the joint Anglo-Egyptian rule, and disputes broke out between north and south. As early as 1958 a military regime took over. In 1971, Colonel Ghaafar Numeri ruled a one-party state. In 1983, open **civil war** broke out between north and south. The war produced a prolonged **famine**, due partly to the centuries-old religious and political clashes between the Christian African south and the Islam-dominated north but aggravated by drought conditions. Even the parliamentary constitution of 1998 could not change this, since a state of emergency had been declared. A cease-fire declared in 2002 was ignored by both the military regime and the rebels. The United Nations has tried to intervene in Darfur, where the Janjaweed government-backed militia is persecuting the Christian and animist minority but without success.

Economy

Some 58 per cent of the labour force is engaged in agriculture, largely a **subsistence economy**. The main exports are cotton, peanuts, sesame and oil seeds, as well as some 80 per cent of the worldwide production of gum arabic. The nomadic populations breed cattle.

In 2006, GDP was US$ 38 billion, of which 39 per cent came from **agriculture**, 25 per cent from **industry** and 36 per cent derived from **services**.

Transport

The 11,610-km-long **road network** consists mainly of dirt roads, which do not allow all-year-round connections to the neighbouring countries. The Nile **waterways** are important transport routes, inland navigation being possible for 5,310 km of the river's length. The major **port** is at Port Sudan, and the only international **airport** is at Khartoum.

Tourism

Tourists rarely visit this crisis area. Sites of cultural and historical interest include Dongulah and Karimah from the Nubian empire and the mosques of Khartoum.

Eritrea

Area:	121,320 sq. km
Capital city:	Asmara
Form of government:	Republic
Administrative divisions:	
40 provinces	
Population: 4.8 million.	
(40 inhabitants per sq. km)	
Languages:	
Arabic, Tigrinya (both official)	
GDP per capita:	US$250
Currency: 1 nafka = 100 cents	

Natural geography

This small republic is bordered to the north-east by the **Red Sea**. The narrow coastal plain expands in the north into the **Abyssinian Highlands**, where the highest point of the country, Soira (3013 m), is found, and which also includes the main settlement area as a result of its rich natural resources and cooler climate. The southern lowland at the foot of the Danakil mountains is largely desert. The Dahlak islands in the Red Sea are also part of the territory of Eritrea.

Climate

The narrow coastal strip along the Red Sea is among the hottest regions on earth, but in general a continental-tropical climate prevails. In the highlands above 1,000 m a pleasantly temperate climate prevails. Temperatures in the capital are about 15°C in January, 22°C in July.

Population

The population of Eritrea consists of 50 per cent **Tigrinyans**, 40 per cent **Tigre** and **Kunama**, four per cent **Afar** (nomads) and three per cent **Saho**. 50 per cent of the population are Sunni Muslems and 50 per cent Eritrean Christians. In this under-developed country, 80 per cent of the population is illiterate.

History and Politics

From 1890 to 1941, the area of present-day Eritrea was **Italian sovereign territory**, but it was captured by Great Britain during World War II and ruled by Britain until 1952. For ten years, Eritrea remained an autonomous area within Ethiopia, but it was then **annexed** as a fourteenth province, which caused an uprising. After a thirty-year struggle for freedom, Eritrea gained its **independence** as a republic in 1993. The 1997 constitution has not yet come into force. In 2002, Parliament decided against the introduction of a multi-party system. In 1998, Eritrea entered a border war against Ethiopia, in which it incurred heavy losses. A cease-fire was declared in 2000. A buffer zone has so far been guarded by UN forces. In 2002, both countries agreed to the proposals of a border commission. However, in 2003 Ethiopia rejected this decision.

Economy

In 2006, GDP was US$ 1.4 billion, of which 15 per cent came from **agriculture**, 24 per cent from **industry** and 61 per cent from **services**. Eritrea continues to be reliant on foreign aid due to military conflict with Ethiopia, frequent drought, a high rate of militarisation and a restrictive planned economy.

Transport

The entire infrastructure is in a state of redevelopment. This applies both to the **rail network**, which was taken out of service in 1978, and to the **road network**, which consists mainly of dirt roads. The most important **port** is at Massawa; there is an international **airport** at Asmara.

Tourism

The tourist sector is inadequately developed; the main travel destinations, apart from Asmara and

Eritrea's economy was heavily marred by droughts, famine and the war with Ethiopia. When the country declared its independence in 1993, much of its flora had been destroyed and most of the farmland was lying idle.

Famine was only averted because of international aid. A number of development projects have been initiated to strengthen the agricultural sector. Fode is now a center for vegetable farming.

History and Politics

In 1884, it was part of several French protectorates on the Gulf of Aden which became French Somaliland. In 1967, the name was changed to Territory of the Afars and the Issas. As **Djibouti**, it became an **independent republic** in 1977. Rivalry between the two largest ethnic groups holds potential for future conflict.

services sector generates some 82 per cent of GDP.

Transport

A **railway line** links this small country with Ethiopia. The most important place of transshipment and also the only international **airport** is in the capital city, Djibouti.

Tourism

The tourist centres are the cities of Djibouti and Tadjoura and the sandy beaches.

Cohaito, include the colonial architecture of Asmara and Massawa and impressive mosques. Tourism is unlikely to develop in any scale in the near future, due to the political situation and the ongoing dispute with Ethiopia.

The coasts are popular with scuba-divers. The oasis town of Dikhil is the starting point for trips to the Bara national park. The famous alkaline Lake Abbé is visited by huge flocks of flamingos.

Natural geography

The **Tadjoura basin**, which is among the hottest regions on Earth, is succeeded in the interior of the country by sand and stone deserts (Lake Asal is 155 m below sea level), as well as steppes, which occupy 95 per cent of the land area. Abundant vegetation is found only at heights above 1,200 m in the northern foothills of the Danakil Mountains. Throughout the country there are hot springs and active volcanoes, and earthquakes are frequent.

Climate

Djibouti has an extremely hot climate with very high humidity.

Temperatures in the capital city are around 26°C in January, and average 36°C in July.

Population

The Issa, a Somali people, living mainly in the south of the country, constitute 60 per cent of the population, the **Afar** in the north about 35 per cent.
Two-thirds , who are 94 per cent Muslim and six per cent Christian, live in the capital, and the rest are nomadic shepherds. Health care is inadequate and infant mortality is correspondingly high, so that average life expectancy is only 51 years for men.

Economy

Because of the nature of the country as well as regularly recurring droughts, agriculture only accounts for four per cent of GDP. Most foodstuffs have to be imported. The **processing industry** contributes 14 per cent to GDP. The economy is based on the country's strategic position as the route for Ethiopian exports and its position on the great international navigation routes through Africa, as well as its status as a free trade area. The

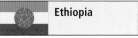

★	Djibouti

Area:	23,200 sq. km
Capital city:	Djibouti
Form of government:	Republic
Administrative divisions: 4 districts	
Population: 800,000 (34 inhabitants per sq. km)	
Languages: French, Arabic (both official), Kushite languages	
GDP per capita:	US$1,000
Currency: 1 Djibouti franc = 100 centimes	

	Ethiopia

Area:	1,127,127 sq. km
Capital city:	Addis Ababa
Form of government: Federal Republic	
Administrative divisions: 9 regions, capital city	
Population: 75 million (66 inhabitants per sq. km)	
Languages: Amharic (official), 70 other languages and dialects	

*The south-west of **Somalia** is dominated by a dry Savannah. Most agriculture consists of livestock-rearing, mainly in the river valleys of Juba and Webe Shebele. The latter disappears into the 10–50 km wide dune stripe on the south coast.*

GDP per capita:	US$180

Currency:
1 birr = 100 cents

Natural geography

Ethiopia consists of high mountains with elevations of up to 4,620 m (Ras Dashen); its plateau is shared by the **East African Rift Valley**, which leads in the north into the Danakil Depression (125 m above sea level). Here there are lakes and a few volcanoes which are still active today. Towards Sudan the mountains drop steeply away.

Climate

The northern landscape of the country consists of deserts and dry savannahs, the south-west is covered in rainforest containing many of the large mammals (rhinoceroses, elephants, buffaloes, numerous bird and reptile species). Temperatures in the capital city of Addis Ababa are only 10°C to 21°C due to its high altitude.

Population

The Ethiopians are composed of some 80 different ethnic groups, the largest of which are the **Oromo** at 40 per cent, and the **Amhara** and **Tigray-Tigrinya** at 32 per cent. Muslims make up 45 per cent of the population, 40 per cent are Ethiopian Christian, and the rest consist of other minorities. Because of the lack of healthcare, average life expectancy is only 50 years for men, while infant mortality is very high.

History and Politics

The first legendary kingdom of the **Queen of Sheba** was followed in the first century by the powerful **Aksum**, an empire that lasted for more than a thousand years, became Christian as early as the fourth century and resisted all attempts at Islamisation in the period that followed. It was not until after the end of the kingdom of the **Neguses** in the nineteenth century that a mighty state formed again, which successfully resisted European colonisation. After the last emperor, Heile Selassie, was forced to abdicate in 1974, a socialist people's republic was established, whose leader was toppled in 1991. In 1993, after a thirty-year war, the former coastal province of **Eritrea** became independent. In 1995, a parliamentary-pluralistic constitution came into force in Ethiopia. After border disputes with Eritrea, a border war began in May 2000, which was settled in June with a cease-fire agreement. In December 2000, a peace treaty was signed. The president since 2001 has been Girma Wolde Giorgis. Catastrophic drought conditions have repeatedly caused famine among the population.

Economy

Agriculture, which provides about half of the country's GDP (46 per cent) and offers basic subsistence to 85 per cent of the population, can however hardly deliver the most basic needs in grain and pulses. Ethiopia is regularly beset by droughts and famines. The most important export is coffee. Underdeveloped industry serves the domestic market and relies on agricultural produce; an additional complication is that the largest enterprises are still state-owned.

Transport

The only **railway line** runs from Djibouti to Addis Ababa. The **road network** which covers most of Ethiopia is barely asphalted. Access to the sea, for this landlocked country is via the **ports** of Eritrea. Ther are international **airports** in Addis Ababa and Dire Dawa.

Tourism

Apart from the landscape and the wildlife in the national parks (such as that at Awash) the ruins of old Aksum and the Christian sites in Adis Ababa, at Lake Tana and in Lalibela are among the main attractions. Tourists are gradually returning to Ethiopia.

★	**Somalia**

Area:	637,657 sq. km
Capital city:	Mogadishu
Form of government:	Republic

Administrative divisions:
18 provinces

Population: 9 million
(14 inhabitants per sq. km)

Languages: Somali (official), Arabic, English, Italian

GDP per capita:	US$200

Currency: 1 Somali shilling = 100 centesimi

Natural geography

Somalia, which covers the **Horn of Africa**, has a 3000-km-long coastline, mainly steeply sloping and rocky at the Gulf of Aden and the Indian Ocean. The highest elevation is the 2,416-m-high **Mount Shimbiris** close to the **Gulf of Aden**. Along the flat southern coast, edged by a dune belt 10 to 50 km wide, lies a chain of coral reefs. The two largest rivers, the

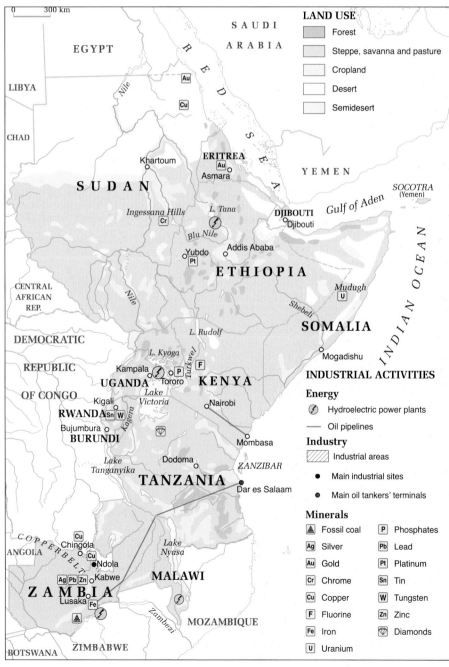

LAND USE
- Forest
- Steppe, savanna and pasture
- Cropland
- Desert
- Semidesert

INDUSTRIAL ACTIVITIES

Energy
- Hydroelectric power plants
- Oil pipelines

Industry
- Industrial areas
- Main industrial sites
- Main oil tankers' terminals

Minerals

Fossil coal		Phosphates	
Silver		Lead	
Gold		Platinum	
Chrome		Tin	
Copper		Tungsten	
Fluorine		Zinc	
Iron		Diamonds	
Uranium			

Haile Selassie

Ras Tafari Makonnen
*Ejersa Goro 23.7.1892,
†Addis Ababa 27.8.1975

Heir to the throne since 1916, the grandson of Menelik proclaimed himself Negus (king) of Ethiopia in 1928. As emperor, he gave the country its first consitution in1931. He went into exile in England during the Italian occupation and reclaimed his throne in 1941. In 1974 he was deposed by a provisional military government.

*The famous rock temples were built at the end of the twelfth century at heights of 2,600 m, on the initiative of King **Lalibela** in the Ethiopian city named after him. The eight churches were carved directly into the tufa rock and are linked to each other through a system of passages and tunnels. The church of St George, built in the shape of a cross, is considered the most beautiful. It is constructed inside a shaft 12 m deep and is only accessible through a gallery.*

Jubba and the Shebelle, form large swamps at their mouths, but only the Jubba contains water all year round. The destruction of trees for fuel and by heavy grazing has caused the desert area to expand.

Climate

In the north-east of Somalia the climate is responsible for a desert landscape and temperatures of up to 45°C; otherwise the alternation of north-east and south-west monsoon causes seasonal climate fluctuations. Rain falls mainly from April to June, when non-irrigated crops can be grown. Temperatures in the capital city average 26°C.

Population

Various **Somali groups** make up 85 per cent of the population; in addition there are **Bantu-speaking groups** and a small number of **Arabs**. However, exact figures are hard to obtain, for the civil war has resulted in lasting changes to the country. There is no organised health care system, life expectancy is low and infant mortality is high. The collapse of the infrastructure is responsible for famine.

History and Politics

After the first Muslim settlements in the seventh century, as well as Portuguese and Turkish influences in the sixteenth century, the **Sultans of Oman** ruled the region from the seventeenth to the nineteenth centuries.

From 1875 to 1884 the colonial regions of **French Somaliland** and **British Somaliland** were founded on the Gulf of Aden, followed from 1889 to 1908 by **Italian Somaliland** on the Indian Ocean.

In 1960, the **Republic of Somalia** was established. The military dictatorship of Major-General Mohammed Siad Barré.which had ruled since 1969 was toppled in 1991 after violent clashes, and Barré fled. The **civil war** which has prevailed since then between various tribal militias caused the north-east of the country to declare independence in 1991 as the **Republic of Somaliland** in the territory of the former British Somaliland. In 1992, the United States marines tried to restore order but were unable to do so and suffered heavy casualties inflicted

by the forces of the various Somali warlords. The United Nations tried to intervene as mediator in the country, where no political system currently exists. In 1995, the UN abandoned its mission having achieved nothing. In the east of the country, Puntland was declared an autonomous region in 1998. A peace conference began in the autumn of 2002. In 2003 the participants signed an agreement providing for a caretaker parliament. In 2006, Ethiopian troops marched into Mogadishu and expelled the Union of Islamic Courts, which had previously taken over large areas of the country.

Economy

Somalia is one of the poorest in the world. Cattle-breeding and agriculture are among the main branches of the economy. In 2006, GDP was roughly US$2 billion, of which 65 per cent came from agriculture, 10 per cent from industry and 25 per cent from services. As a result of the civil war and catastrophic droughts, the population suffers from a chronic lack of adequate food supplies, water and medical care. Economic life has shifted to the black market, smuggling and barter. Only in the breakaway province of Somaliland are conditions somewhat more stable.

Transport

The country's **road network** outside the larger cities consists of dirt roads, there are hardly any paved roads. There is no railway line, and national **air transport** is irregular. Mogadishu and Berbera are the major **ports**.

Tourism

There is no tourism due to the political situation. The capital, Mogadishu has suffered heavy damage. There are ten game reserves; the beaches on the Indian Ocean are protected by a very long coral reef and are among the longest in the world.

1 The selection offered in the markets of Hargeisa is impressive, despite the severe economic crisis in Somalia.

2 Ethiopia: in the treasure chamber of the St Mary of Zion church in Aksum, part of its treasure is on display, including the emperor's crowns.

3 The church of Debre Berhan Selassie was founded by Emperor Yasu the Great in Gondar. It is still an important place of worship for Ethiopians.

4 Rashaida are nomads of Arab origin. They constitute 0.3 per cent of the population of Eritrea.

Kenya, Uganda

*The **Turkana** are one of the East Nile ethnic groups living in north-western Kenya. The approximately 200,000 Turkana breed cattle, camels, goats and sheep. Blood and milk are the basis of their diet. The cattle herds are significant both in economic and social terms. There is a fishing industry on Lake Turkana. The Turkana people are famous for their silver jewellery.*

Kenya	
Area:	582,646 sq. km
Capital City	Nairobi
Form of government:	Presidential Republic
Administrative division: 7 provinces,1 district (capital city)	
Population: 35 million (60 inhabitants/sq. km)	
Languages: Kiswahili (official), English and tribal languages	
GDP per capita:	US$670
Currency: 1 Kenyan-shilling = 100 cents	

Natural geography

Kenya is on the east coast of Africa lying directly on the **equator** and comprises four main landscapes: dry savannah with thornbush vegetation in the north-

Jomo Kenyatta

*Ichaweri 10.10.1891,
†Mombassa 22.8.1978

The chairman of the Kenyan African National Union was sentced to seven years in prison by the British colonial rulers for his leadership of the Mau-Mau-uprising. In 1960, he became its leader again and in 1963 the first prime minister of Kenya. In 1964 Kenyatta became the president – an ofice he was to hold until his death. He rejected a multi-party system because he feared divisions along ethnic lines.

east, barren mountain foothills in the north-west around Lake Turkana, tree and thornbush savannah in the south-east and a plateau which reaches altitudes of over 3,000 m.
The savannah and vast parts of the highlands are populated with great herds of wild animals (elephants, rhinoceroses, zebras, antelopes, buffaloes and giraffes) and predators (lions, cheetahs).

Climate

The climate is tropical, hot and humid, but those parts of the country visited by the monsoon also have long dry periods. The relatively mild west of the country contains most of its population. Average temperatures are approximately 20°C in Nairobi which stands at an altitude of 1670 m.

Population

Kenya's population consists of roughly 40 Bantu-speaking groups and Nilotic tribes; the most important of these are the **Kikuyus** (who account for 22 per cent of the population), the **Luhyas** (who account for 14 per cent of the population), the **Luos** (13 per cent), the **Kalenjins** (12 per cent), the **Kambas** (11 per cent) and the **Kisiis** and the **Merus** who each account for six per cent. Over 60 per cent of Kenyans are Christians and approximately 25 per cent followers of animist religions. There are also minorities of Jews, Hindus and Muslims.

Nairobi is the economic and administrative centre of Kenya.

Average life expectancy is 50 years. The HIV/AIDS infection rate is high at ten per cent. Approximately 40 per cent of the population is illiterate.

History and Politics

In 1963, the former British colony gained **independence** and declared itself a republic. **Jomo Kenyatta**, the first president, held office until 1978. A one-party system was subsequently introduced. However, in 1982 other political parties were permitted and due to pressure from foreign countries providing development aid. In 1992, the first free elections were held since 1978. In 2002, Mwai Kibaki was elected president. The parliament is elected every five years and the head of state is elected every five years through direct elections.

Economy

In the enormously productive **agricultural** sector (27 per cent of GDP), tea, coffee, sisal, sugar cane, fresh vegetables, legumes, cashew nuts and pineapples are the main exports. Cattle rearing also accounts for a sizeable proportion of the favourable foreign trade balance. In the **manufacturing sector**, 17 per cent of GDP is generated from the processing of foodstuffs and oil. Tourism is the country's second most important foreign currency earner after agriculture, generating some 56 per cent of GDP.

Transport

A **railway line** traverses the country. Of the 63,800-km-long **road network** 8,800 km is surfaced. National air traffic is buoyant and includes charter flights for safaris. Three of the 29 **airports** offer connections to international airports. Nairobi is the hub of East Africa.

Tourism

Kenya's main attractions are the **national game reserves** The best known are the Masai Mara, the Amboseli and the Meru national reserves. Nairobi is the nation's centre. The port of Mombasa has an old town with Arab-influenced architecture which is worth a visit. Further tourist destinations include Lake Victoria and the Lamu Archipelago. The Olduvai Gorge where the first remains of homo sapiens were found is in Kenya.

Uganda	
Area:	236,040 sq. km
Capital City	Kampala
Form of government: Presidential Republic within the Commonwealth	
Administrative division: 38 districts	
Population: 30 million (127 inhabitants/sq. km)	
Languages: Kiswahili, English (both official), Luganda	

Idi Amin Dada

*Koboco 1925,
†Jeddah 16.8.2003

This former army officer became deputy chief-of-staff in 1964 and subsequently Supreme Commander of the Armed Forces of Uganda in 1966. In 1971 he overthrew President Milton Obote and established a brutal dictatorship. Around 300,000 Ugandans fell victim to his regime. After his overthrow through Tanzanian troups in 1979, he went into exile in Saudi Arabia.

GDP per capita:	US$320
Currency: 1 Uganda shilling = 100 cents	

Natural geography

The majority of the landlocked African country of Uganda which lies on the equator forms a plateau of approximately 1,000 to 3,000 m in altitude. The plateau contains the large mounds known as monadnocks.
The highest elevations in this savannah landscape are the 4,322 m Mount Elgon in the east and the 5,109 m **Ruwenzori Massif** in the west. In the south-east, half of the large **Lake Victoria** lies in Uganda. The country also possesses vast lakes and marshes such as Lake Kioga and Lake Salisbury. In contrast, the rainforests and mountain forests are dwindling. Whilst the landscape in the north is characterised by thornbush savannah, wet savannah predominates in the south.

Climate

The hot and humid tropical climate is strongly attenuated by the country's altitude. The temperatures in the capital city are approximately 22°C all year round.

Population

A total of 45 ethnic groups live in this multi-national state. **Bantu-speaking groups** constitute the majority of the population with a 50 per cent share (of which 28 per cent are Gandas). There are also Nilotic and Sudanese ethnic groups and Indian and Arabic minorities. The majority of Ugandans are Christians, 16 per cent are followers of Islam and 18 per cent believe in animistic religions.

History and Politics

A series of central African realms existed in the region of Uganda for centuries when the British conquered the country and made it into a **British protectorate** in 1894. After Uganda gained its **independence** in 1962, its fortunes were determined in the 1970s and the 1980s by conflicts between various factions fighting a civil war and the dictatorships of Idi **Amin** and Milton **Obote**, which were almost as bloodthirsty as each other. The political situation stabilised somewhat in the 1990s. The introduction of a new constitution in 1995 still failed to provide Uganda with a **multi-party democratic system**. Although political parties are now permitted, they do not as yet have the right to participate in elections. Yoweri Kaguta Museveni has been president of the country since 1986. The situation in Northern Uganda is problematical as government troops advance against the rebel movement which calls itself Lord's Resistance Army. The Ugandan army intervened in the civil war in the Democratic Republic of Congo.

The Nilotic tribes in Kenya live nomadic lives of cattlebreeders in the savannahs and have preserved their customs and traditional clothes, which is particularly true for the Samburu, who pay a lot of attention to body ornaments .

Economy

Agriculture is the most important branch of the economy and the country's greatest earner of foreign currency. Coffee is the main export. It has hitherto generated approximately 70 per cent of export revenue. Fish from Lake Victoria have become the second most important export in recent years. Tea, cotton and tobacco are also exported. As in the 1990s, Uganda was recently able to show rates of growth of 5–6 per cent, but despite this around 40 per cent of the population remain poor. Roughly 40 per cent of the national budget is financed by donor countries. In 2006, GDP was US$ 9.5 billion, of which 32 per cent came from agriculture, 22 per cent from industry and 46 per cent from services.

Transport

The **roads** are in a poor overall condition. Only a quarter of them are passable all year round. Consequently, the 1,240-km-long **rail network** is being extended further. Domestic flights and connections by sea to neighbouring countries are also irregular. There is an international **airport** in Entebbe.

Tourism

The country's most significant sites worth visiting include both lakes and the Ruwenzori National Reserve, a paradise for rockclimbers. Part of the Virunga National Reserve belongs to Uganda; the Bwindi National Reserve is has extensive flora and local African mammalian fauna. Entebbe has a wonderful botanical gardens started in colonial times, and the spectacular Lake Victoria is dotted with lovely islands.

Rwanda

Area:	26,338 sq. km
Capital City	Kigali
Form of government:	Presidential Republic
Administrative division:	11 prefectures
Population:	c. 9.5 million (360 inhabitants/sq. km)
Languages:	Kinyarwanda, French (both offical), Kiswahili, English

GDP per capita: US$270
Currency:
1 Rwanda franc = 100 centimes

Natural geography

The highest elevations of this predominantly mountainous country are located in the west where they reach altitudes of up to 4,507 m in the **Virunga Volcanoes**. In central and eastern Rwanda, hilly plateaus of around 1500 m predominate.

Climate

Rainforests and wet savannah predominate up to an altitude of 2,500 m in the tropical climate which is attenuated by the altitude (average temperatures range from 19°C to 21°C). Rainforests and wet savannah turn into bamboo forests on the higher mountains. There is a wealth of animal species including lions, leopards, hippopotamuses, rhinoceroses, crocodiles and monkeys, especially in the game reserves.

Population

80 per cent of the inhabitants of this densely populated country are Hutus and 19 per cent are **Tutsis**. The country is largely reliant on foreign aid for the reconstruction of its infrastructure, the maintenance of its health service and the provision of foodstuffs. Average life expectancy is just 45 years – one of the world's lowest.

History and Politics

In the fifteenth century, the Tutsi people arrived in the region populated by the Hutus and established a feudal system.
This power structure was consolidated under German rule which began in 1885 with the charter founding German East Africa. In 1916, Rwanda came under **Belgian colonial rule**. When the Belgians left the country, the Tutsis dominant position was threatened by Hutu rebellions from 1955 onwards. As a result, conflicts arose between the two groups in Rwanda and in the neighbouring country of Burundi. These culminated in a terrible genocide in 1994. in which the Hutu massacred the Tutsis, following decades of combat.

According to official estimates, 800,000
people were killed from both factions. After 1997, those who had been expelled or fled in their masses returned. They had become refugees in neighbouring countries which also rejected them. In spite of a peace agreement and mediation attempts on the part of the United Nations the unrest continues.
Paul Kagame became president in 2000 and was confirmed in office in 2003. There are tensions with neighbour-ing Uganda and also the Democratic Republic of Congo, since Rwanda gave military support to the rebels challenging Congo's president Laurent Kabila.

Economy

Rwanda's economy which was completely ruined by civil war has been reconstructed since 1996 thanks to massve international assistance. The most important export is coffee, followed by tea, pyrethrum, beans, maize and bananas. In 2006, GDP was US$ 2.5 billion, of which 41 per cent came from **agriculture**, 22 per cent from **industry** and 37 per cent from **services**.

Transport

The infrastructure was severely affected by the civil war. However, the main roads are in comparatively good condition. The international airport is located in Kigali.

Tourism

Due to the permanent unrest, Rwanda is still not considered safe to visit. One of the last few colonies of mountain gorillas live in the Virunga National Reserve.

Burundi

Area:	27,834 sq. km
Capital City	Bujumbura

Form of government:
Presidential Republic
Administrative division:
15 Provinces
Population: c. 8 million
(285 inhabitants/sq. km)
Languages:
Kirundi, French
(both official), Kiswahili
GDP per capita: US$120
Currency:
1 Burundi franc = 100 centimes

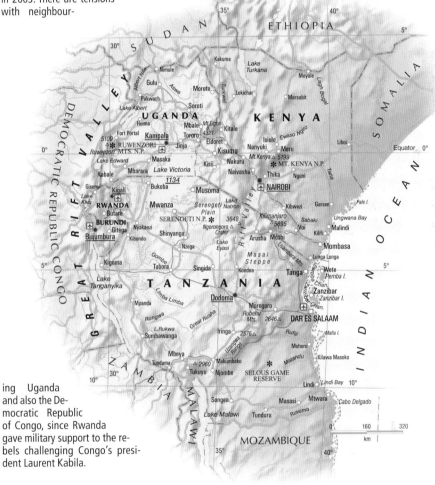

Natural geography

Lake Tanganyika constitutes the south-western border of Burundi. North-east of the lake, there are highlands with wet savannah. The country's interior forms a plateau with an average altitude of 1,500 m which is dominated by grass savannah straddling the watershed of the Congo and the Nile. There is rainforest in the north-east.

Photo safaris are an important source of income for Tanzania. Tourists can watch lions at the Ngorongoro Crater in the northern Tanzanian highland or elephants roaming wild in the Serengeti national park near Lake Victoria.

Climate

The equatorial climate is attenuated by altitude. Average temperatures range from 17°C to 22°C.

Population

The **Hutus** account for the majority of the population at 85 per cent, whilst the **Tutsis** account for 14 per cent. Both groups converse in related languages and have very similar animist religions.

History and Politics

In the fifteenth century, Tutsi tribes came from the north to settle in the area of present-day Burundi occupied by Hutu tribes. The Tutsis established a **feudalist system** which socially disadvantaged the **Hutus**.
In 1890, the country, along with Rwanda, became part of the Ger-

Julius Kambarage Nyerere

*March 1922,
†14.10.1999

As founder of the Tanganyika African National Union, he led Tanganyika to independence and became the first prime minister. After the unification of Tanganyika and Zanzibar, he became the President of the new state Tanzania. He was an advocate of a self-confident Africa and actively supported the Organisation for African Unity. In 1985, he stepped down as the President of Tanzania but continued as the chairman of the OAU. He continued to lead his party until 1990.

man colony of East Africa which was later governed by Belgium as Rwanda-Urundi. In 1962, Burundi gained **independence**. The country's situation has been determined by continually erupting conflicts between the two groups ever since. It was envisaged that the 1992 constitution would promote the resolution of ethnic conflicts, but instead it led to the bloodiest war in the country's history, resulting in hundreds of thousands of deaths and the flight of more than

one million inhabitants to neighbouring countries. Although peace has officially reigned since 2000, civil war flares up continually. In 2001, a transitional constitution and a government composed of Tutsi and Hutu ministers were created. The peace process is repeatedly endangered due to constant violations.

Economy

Burundi is one of the world's poorest countries. Hunger and poverty-related illnesses are widespread. One of the country's problems is the reintegration of approximately 1.2 million refugees. The majority of the population is dependent on the cultivation of crops (Hutus) and cattle rearing (Tutsis) for their livelihood. Women are responsible for 70 per cent of agricultural production. Coffee is the main export. In 2006, GDP was over US$ 900 million, of which 50 per cent came from agriculture, 20 per cent from industry and 30 per cent from services. Eighty to ninety per cent of inhabitants survive on less than one US dollar per week.

Transport

Very little of the **road network** is surfaced. **Sea** and **air connections** exist only in neighbouring countries. The capital city has an international **airport**.

Tourism

The region surrounding the capital city is the country's tourist centre and the starting point for safaris to the two national game reserves where mountain gorillas and African big game species are protected. However, tourism has come to a complete standstill due to the ongoing civil unrest.

Tanzania	
Area:	945,087 sq. km
Capital City Dodoma (Seat of government: Dar es Salaam)	
Form of government: Federal Presidential Republic	
Administrative division: 25 regions	
Population: 39 million (41 inhabitants/sq. km)	
Language:	Swahili
GDP per capita	US$330
Currency: 1 Tanzania shilling = 100 cents	

Natural geography

Tanzania, on the **Indian Ocean**, is characterised by plateaus and mountainous country formed by tectonic fractures such as the eastern and central African rifts and volcanoes. **Mount Kilimanjaro** is Africa's highest mountain at 5,895 m. Three great lakes are located at the country's borders (Lake Victoria, Lake Malawi and Lake Tanganyika). The islands of Zanzibar, Pemba and Mafia also belong to the country.

Climate

While the climate is tropically hot and humid in coastal areas, a moderate tropical climate prevails in the highlands. Temperatures range from 19°C to 24°C in the capital city, Dar es Salaam.

Population

Bantu tribes who are, in turn, subdivided into **130 different ethnic groups** account for 95 per cent of the inhabitants.
45 per cent of the population are Christians, 35 per cent are Muslims and 20 per cent followers of local religions. The population of the island of **Zanzibar** is of Arabic-African descent and is 99 per cent Muslem.

History and Politics

After the Portuguese occupied the coast in the early fifteenth century, **Tanganyika** became the main component of the colony of **German East Africa**. In 1920, Kenya was assigned to Great Britain under a mandate of the League of Nations and was ruled as a confederation with Uganda and Tanganyika. In 1946, it was converted to a UN trust region. The country gained independence in 1962.
In 1964, Tanzania emerged as a federal presidential republic from the **union of Tanganyika** with the British protectorate of **Zanzibar,** which had gained independence in 1963. Following an attack by Uganda, Tanzanian troops occupied Uganda in 1979 and overthrew the dictator Idi Amin. The constitution drawn up in 1977 envisaged a one-party state but this was replaced by a multi-party system in 1992. Benjamin Mkapa, who had been in office since 1995, was replaced as head of state in 2005 by Jakaya Kikwete.

Economy

Tanzania is still one of Africa's poorest countries, but at the same time it is also one of the fastest growing national economies in Africa (at 6.4 per cent on average since 2000). In 2006, GDP was US$ 12.8 billion, of which around 45 per cent came from agriculture, 17 per cent from industry and 39 per cent from services. Tanzania is well able to supply itself with food. The **manufacturing sector** plays an increasingly important role and the economic significance of the services sector, especially tourism, is also on the increase.

Transport

The **road network** is impassable to a great extent in the rainy season. Consequently, the **railways** have a key role to play.
The domestic flight network and the ferries to neighbouring countries offer a good service. There is an international **airport** in Dar es Salaam.

Tourism

Tanzania possesses some uniquely beautiful natural sites, including Kilimanjaro, Lake Tanganyika and the Ngorongoro crater. The old town of Bagamoyo and the island of Zanzibar are also extremely picturesque. Kilimanjaro is a favourite with mountain-climbers. The best time to visit is between June and September.

The Ngorongoro caldera has a diameter of 22 km and 700-m-high walls.

Approximately half a million elephants live in the African savannah, in the Serengeti in Tanzania for instance. These large mammals are no longer as threatened as they were by poachers after their ivory tusks.

Nairobi was founded towards the end of the nineteenth century as a British camp for railway workers. Due to its relatively moderate climate and in particular to its prominence as a business centre, the number of inhabitants grew from 11,000 in 1905 to 2.75 million in 2005. Many hundreds of

thousands of immigrants have settled on the edge of town in the very poorest conditions. Seen here are images from the slum settlement of Kibera, where illnesses such as tuberculosis are rife. However, a modest economic infrastructure is developing, primarily through small workshops

*Salisbury was established in 1890 as a military settlement of the British South African pioneer colony, and from 1899 onwards developed into an important trading centre, as a result of the rail connection with Beira. In 1923, it became the capital of the British colony of Southern Rhodesia, and from 1953 to 1963 was capital of the Federation of Rhodesia and Nyasaland. In 1982, when White rule ended, the city was renamed **Harare**. It remains the capital of Zimbabwe.*

Angola

Area:	1,246,700 sq. km
Capital city:	Luanda
Form of government:	Republic

Administrative divisions:
18 provinces

Population:
c. 15 million
(12 inhabitants/sq. km)

Languages:
Portuguese (official),
Bantu languages

GDP per capita:	US$2,900

Currency:
1 kwanza = 100 iwei

Natural Geography

To the west of the country there is a narrow coastal strip covered in rainforest. In the east, this coastal stretch meets the **Luanda Ridge** (highest point: Morro de Moco: 2,620 m) where it rises steeply to form an upland area, criss-crossed by numerous rivers. The broad steppes and humid savannahs extend to the far south-west to the fringes of the Namib Desert. The national territory also includes the northern exclave of Cabinda.

Climate

The areas in the south and along the coast have a semi-desert climate. In the capital city, average temperatures range between 21°C and 26°C. The tropical climate in the interior is milder at higher altitudes.

Population

Angola is inhabited by over 100 ethnic groups, the majority of whom are Bantu-speaking peoples. The **Ovimbundu** (37 per cent), the **Mbunda** (22 per cent) and the **Kongo** (13 per cent) are the largest groups.

History and Politics

The Portuguese explorer Diego Cão became the first European to land in the country in 1483. Portugal founded the settlement of **Luanda** in 1576 and made the country into a Portuguese colony. From 1961 onwards, various **liberation organisations** fought for sovereignty, until Angola was granted **independence** in 1975,

after the fall of the dictator Antonio Salazar in Lisbon. In the very same year, a **civil war** erupted in the country and this lasted for 27 years. The MPLA emerged victorious, with the help of Cuban troops, and proclaimed the People's Republic of Angola. The first President was Antonio Agostinho Neto. After his death in 1979, José Eduardo dos Santos took over the office of President. UNITA began its guerrilla activities. In 1990, the country's name was changed from the People's Republic to the Democratic Republic of Angola, but this did not bring an end to the conflict, because UNITA did not want to hand over its diamond-rich region in the north of Angola to the government. Hundreds of thousands of civilians fled from the disputed regions. Large areas of the country were covered in landmines. In February 2002, UNITA leader Jonas Savimbi died in battle. After this, the rebels and

the government started to negotiate and a peace treaty was signed in April 2002.

Economy

Angola's economy has been severely damaged by the prolonged civil war, and the population is largely dependent on foreign aid. In 2006, GDP was about US$ 45 billion, of which 9 per cent

came from **agriculture**, 58 per cent from **industry** and 33 per cent from **services**. The country has large reserves of **diamonds**, which were used as currency and 'blood diamonds' during the civil war, as well as **crude oil** and **iron ore**, but the economy is completely dependent on crude oil. Ninety per cent of export income comes from the petroleum industry, which in turn represents 80 per cent of the national budget.

Transport Infrastructure

The whole transport infrastructure has been largely destroyed by the civil war: more than 80 per cent of the 72,000 km of **roads** are damaged and the **rail network** only operates with great restrictions, due to large numbers of landmines. The only international **airport** and the most important **port** are in Luanda. Malongo in oil-rich Cabinda is the main oil terminal.

At the Victoria Falls, the Zambezi drops 110 m into a crevasse.

Tourism

Angola is not currently a tourist destination because the collapsed infrastructure makes travel outside the capital impossible. The country has many attractions from the colonial era, such as the São Miguel Fortress and was once a playground for rich South Africans. The best time to visit is between May and September.

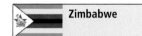

Zimbabwe

Area:	390,580 sq. km
Capital city:	Harare

Form of government:
Presidential Republic

Administrative divisions:
8 provinces

Population:
12 million
(30 inhabitants/sq. km)

Languages:
English (official), Bantu languages

GDP per capita:
US$470

Currency:
1 Zimbabwe dollar = 100 cents

Natural Geography

The land mass is defined by the Zambezi in the north and the Limpopo basin in the south. It consists mainly of a highland region which forms part of the fringes of the Kalahari depression. In the

Robert Gabriel Mugabe

*Kutama, 21.2.1924

In 1963, Mugabe founded the Zimbabwe African National Union (ZANU). After the resignation of the last White head of state, Ian Smith, Mugabe took over as Prime Minister in the renamed Zimbabwe, holding office from 1980–1987. In 1981 he split with his rival, Joshua Nkomo. He became President in 1987 and again in 1990, 1996 and 2002 in elections boycotted by the opposition. In 2008 he won an uncontested election. His increasingly authoritarian leadership, which is leading the country to ruin, is subject to international protest.

east, the land rises to form the **Inyanga Mountains** with peaks of up to 2,592 m. The uplands in the interior of the country form an undulating plain with isolated hills and savannah vegetation.

Climate

The climate is defined by Zimbabwe's position on the Tropic of Capricorn; from May to October it

is the dry season. Average temperatures in the capital, Harare, range between 14°C and 21°C.

Population

The population is up to 98 per cent Bantu people, of whom the **Shona** (77 per cent) and the **Ndebele** (17 per cent) form the largest groups. Half the population adheres to syncretistic beliefs, 25 per cent are Christian, 25 per cent follow animist religions.

History and Politics

Zimbabwe first became an independent state in 1980 as the result of a long conflict over the British colony of **Rhodesia**, which had been a British protectorate since 1891 and an autonomous colony since 1923. In 1930/1931, the country was divided in two, known as Rhodesia and Nyasaland, a European and an African region, much to the advantage of the Europeans.

In 1966, **ZANU** (Zimbabwe African National Union), began a guerrilla campaign against the White minority government. In 1979, talks were held in London between all parties involved and a constitution was agreed that limited the privileges of the White minority, but granted them 'protective rights'. In 1980, the country became **independent** and the name changed to Zimbabwe. In 1987, the seats reserved for Whites in parliament were abolished and the presidential system was introduced. Robert Mugabe was elected state President with executive powers. In 2000, the population voted against a law that would have enabled the government to remove land from the owners of large farms, most of whom were white, without compensation. Following this, the farms were occupied anyway and violence broke out against members of the opposition. This unrest led to an economic crisis and damaged foreign relations. As part of a land reform policy in 2002, approximately 2,600 white farmers were forcibly removed from their land. Zimbabwe left the Commonwealth in 2003.

Economy

Zimbabwe's **agriculture** is geared towards export. Its natural reserves

*Even though only a small minority follow Islam, very few tribes in Zambia keep **pigs** for use as meat. The animals are mainly used for maintaining public hygiene, as they eat all waste and keep the villages clean.*

(gold, copper, nickel, coal) and diversified manufacturing sector once made Zimbabwe one of the richest countries in Africa. Today, the nation is almost bankrupt. The economy has shrunk dramatically since 1998. In 2006, GDP was US$ 5.5 billion, of which 18 per cent came from agriculture, 23 per cent from industry and 59 per cent from services.

Transport Infrastructure

The country has good **rail** and **road networks**. The domestic flight network is good. Harare has the only international **airport**.

Tourism

The main attractions in the country are the Victoria Falls on the border with Zambia, and the fourteenth century ruined city of Great Zimbabwe.

	Zambia

Area: 752,614 sq. km
Capital city: Lusaka
Form of government:
Presidential Republic in the Commonwealth
Administrative divisions:
9 provinces
Population:
11.5 million (15 inhabitants/sq. km)

Languages:

English (official), Bantu languages
GDP per capita: US$950
Currency:
1 kwacha = 100 ngwee

Natural Geography

Zambia lies in an area of high plains at an average height of between 1000 and 1500 m above sea level. The plains rise gradually from south to north and some individual peaks are as high as 2,300 m.

Lakes and marsh areas define the landscape in the flats of the Zambezi and Kafue rivers. The Victoria Falls are a spectacular feature and the Kariba Dam is a man-made wonder. The north-east of the country is part of Africa's **Great Rift Valley**.

Climate

The tropical climate is made slightly milder by the country's altitude and, with the exception of the hot and humid months from December to April, the savannah of the uplands is mainly arid and has suffered from severe drought.

Average temperatures in the capital city, Lusaka, are 16°C in July and 21°C in January. In the river valleys and lake areas that are covered with dense deciduous forests the climate is hot and humid year-round.

Population

Africans from 73 different ethnic groups make up 98 per cent of the population. The most widely spoken of the more than 80 languages are **Bemba**, **Nyanja**, **Kaonda** and **Lunda**. More than 50 per cent of Zambians are Christian, but there are also Sunni Muslims, small groups of Hindus, and one per cent adhere to native religions.

History and Politics

Modern-day Zambia is a republic within the British Commonwealth of Nations. The country used to be part of **Northern Rhodesia**, a British protectorate created north of the Zambezi in 1911. In 1923, Northern Rhodesia became a protectorate under direct British colonial rule. Zambia gained independence and changed its name in 1964. In 1972/73, the first President, Kenneth (Kamuzu) Kaunda, created a one-party system. Internal and external pressure for democratisation finally paid off in 1990 when opposition parties were permitted.

In 1991, Frederick Chiluba became president after elections. The new constitution guarantees a **multiparty system** and provides for simultaneous presidential and parliamentary elections. In 2002, L.P. Mwanawasa was elected President. He was re-elected in 2006.

Economy

Zambia's economy is based on the extraction and export of the largest copper reserves on Earth. The **agricultural sector** contributes 21 per cent of GDP and employs 80 per cent of the population. Privatisation and greater diversification should create greater opportunities in the future, and the influx of the forcibly ejected farmers from Zimbabwe may also prove an economic advantage.

Transport Infrastructure

The **road and rail systems** are well constructed. The 891 km-long Tazara Line connects the country to the coast. There is also a dense network of domestic flights. International **airports** are located in Lusaka and Ndola. Mpulungu on Lake Tanganyika is the most important **port**.

Tourism

The main attractions are the magnificent Victoria Fall on the Zambezi, the man-made Lake Kariba covering an area of 5,000 sq. km, created by the construction of a dam and Lake Tanganyika. The large national parks are also of great interest for safaris. Zambia advertises itself as the safest tourist destination in Africa.

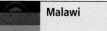

	Malawi

Area: 118,484 sq. km
Capital city: Lilongwe
Form of government:
Presidential Republic in the Commonwealth
Administrative divisions:
3 regions
Population:
13 million
(110 inhabitants/sq. km)
Languages:
Chichewa, English (both official), Tumbuka, other Bantu languages
GDP per capita: US$240
Currency:
1 Malawi kwacha =
100 tambala

Malawi, Mozambique, Botswana

*Mozambique: The 160-m-high and 330-m-long **Cabora Bassa** dam blocks the Zambezi. This has created an immense lake with an area of 2,700 sq. km and a volume of 160 billion cu. m. The aim is to prevent the annual flood disasters and to irrigate 1.5 million ha of land. The dam has also made 500 km of the Zambezi navigable. The power station that forms part of the dam was sabotaged many times during the course of the civil war.*

Natural Geography

A large part of the country is taken up by **Lake Malawi**, extending for 550 km from north to south. The land to the west and south of the lake is mountainous, with peaks of up to 3,002 m in height (highest point: Mount Mlanje, also known as Sapitwa). Open grassland and scrub form the main vegetation. The mountain regions have areas of dense woodland. The country once had a wide range of animal life (antelopes, zebras, elephants, rhinoceros), but this is now restricted to the four protected national parks.

Climate

The climate is tropical in the north but becomes drier further south. The rainy season lasts from November to April. In Lilongwe, average temperatures are 23°C in summer and 16°C in winter.

Population

99 per cent of the population belong to **Bantu-speaking peoples**, and 58 per cent of these are **Malawi**. There are also small minorities of Arabs and Europeans. 75 per cent are Christian – mostly Protestant – but some 20 per cent are followers of native religions. The adult literacy rate is 55 per cent. Roughly one sixth of the adult population is infected with HIV positive.

History and Politics

In 1891, the region around the Lake Nyasa became a British protectorate and was joined to Rhodesia under the name of Nyasaland in 1907. Malawi gained its **independence** in 1964. The constitution of 1966 gave the President comprehensive powers, but these were restricted in 1993 after a referendum which was held due to pressure from credit-lending countries. The first free elections took place in 1994.

Economy

Malawi today remains an agricultural country: 85 per cent of the population live from **agriculture** and contribute 40 per cent of GDP. The country's self-sufficiency is repeatedly threatened by drought. A large proportion of exports derive from the sale of coffee. Other export goods are tea, sugar and tobacco. The fishing industry is sufficiently developed to fulfill domestic demand.
Manufacturing industry is centred in the southern part of the country and processes domestic crops and products (tea, beer, cigarettes, textiles, shoes) for export. The tourism sector has become relatively well-developed and the service sector in total makes up 43 per cent of GDP.

Transport Infrastructure

The **road network** is 28,400 km long but mainly covers the south of the country and consists of the whole of dirt tracks. The **rail network** is 789 km long and connects Malawi to the international

Lake Malawi is famous for its plentiful fish stocks.

port of Beira in Mozambique. Of great importance to transport is Lake Malawi. Lilongwe has an international **airport**.

Tourism

Malawi has an extraordinary wealth of natural attractions. The main tourist centres are Lake Malawi – a lake that contains the greatest variety of fish species in the world – and Blantyre, the former colonial capital of Nyasaland, with its spectacular setting. Elephants and rhinoceros are among the animals that inhabit the Nyika and Kasungu National Parks.

Mozambique	
Area:	801,590 sq. km
Capital city:	Maputo
Form of government: Republic	
Administrative divisions: 10 provinces, Capital city	
Population: 20 million (25 inhabitants/sq. km)	
Languages: Portuguese (official), Bantu languages	
GDP per capita:	US$390
Currency: 1 metical = 100 centavos	

Natural Geography

The Indian Ocean coast has a large number of coves and bays with offshore coral reefs. Inland from the coast lie broad areas of savannah and scrubland. In the north, the land rises steeply to form a mountainous region (highest point: Monte Binga, 2,436 m). Mangrove swamps predominate in the marshes of the river deltas. The original African fauna (antelopes, gazelles, elephants and leopards) have been decimated by big game hunting.

Climate

The tropical climate is defined by heavy summer monsoon rains. Average temperatures in Maputo, the capital range between 22°C and 26°C.

Population

The population consists of Bantu peoples, of which the **Shangaan**, **Chokwe**, **Manyika** and **Sena** form the largest ethnic groups. 50 per cent follow native religions, 30 per cent are Christian and 20 per cent are Muslim.

History and Politics

The country was discovered in 1498 and occupied by the Portuguese in the sixteenth century. After a long guerrilla war, Mozambique gained **independence** from the Portuguese colonial rulers in 1975.
The liberation movement proclaimed a people's republic in the same year, and this became a parliamentary democracy with a new constitution in 1990. After a long and bloody **civil war**, a peace treaty between the right-wing rebels and the government was concluded in 1992. Free presidential and parliamentary elections were held in 1994 under the scrutiny of UN observers.

Economy

Agriculture and **fishing** contribute 35 per cent of GDP. Over half the exports income comes from the sale of crabs and prawns, which are processed by the **manufacturing industry** (13 per cent of GDP). The rich natural resources (precious and semi-precious stones, iron ore, minerals and metals) have scarcely been exploited. The wide-ranging privatisation programme in place since the 1990s has mainly been to the advantage of the **services sector** (52 per cent of GDP). The country's international ports also handle exports for neighbouring countries.

Transport Infrastructure

The 30,400-km-long **road network** is largely unpaved and the use of the roads is also further restricted by the large number of landmines placed on them during the civil war. Of great importance for the transport of goods to and from neighbouring countries are the 3,200-km-long **rail network** and the 3,750-km-long inland waterways. Mozambique has three international **airports** at Maputo, Beira and Nampula.

Tourism

In addition to nature reserves and the many beaches, the old trading posts and colonial cities of Maputo and Beira are also of interest to tourists. Mozambique was popular with tourists from neighbouring African countries before the civil war.

Botswana	
Area:	600,370 sq. km
Capital city:	Gaborone
Form of government: Republic	
Administrative divisions: 11 districts	
Population: 1.6 million (3 inhabitants/sq. km)	
Languages: Tswana, English (both official)	
GDP per capita:	US$6,700
Currency: 1 pula = 100 thebe	

Natural Geography

The semi-desert terrain of the **Kalahari** covers approximately 80 per cent of the country. Land suitable for the cultivation of crops can only be found in small areas in the south-east. The northern edge of the Kalahari is defined by the Okavango, an inland delta region with marsh and reed-covered areas. The north-east of the country adjoins the Makgadikgadi Pans, a large area of salt lakes.

Climate

The country has a very dry,, sub-tropical climate with summer temperatures reaching a high of 40°C, while winter lows can sink to 6°C. Temperatures in the capital city range between 13°C in July and 26°C in January.

Population

Up to 75 per cent of the population comes from one of eight **Bantu-speaking peoples** who speak the same language – Tswana. 12 per cent of the population are **Shona**. Small, nomadic ethnic groups live an isolated existence in the Kalahari Desert. Despite great efforts on the part of the government and interna-

*The **Okavango** rises in the uplands of Angola and ends in an outlet-free basin in Botswana. The marsh delta is very rich in animal life. The river constantly changes its path through the delta region.*

... tional organisations, Botswana has the highest HIV infection rate in the world (38.8 per cent).

History and Politics

Missionaries from Great Britain began visiting Botswana in 1820, and the country, which had hitherto been inhospitable to foreign interests, became part of the British Empire as the protectorate of **Bechuanaland** in 1885, because of its strategically important position north of the Boer region and east of German South West Africa.

Until 1964, the country was ruled by British ambassadors in South Africa, and became **independent** as the Republic of Botswana in 1966. The parliament consists of a National Assembly and a 15-seat House of Chiefs as an advisory institution.

Economy

80 per cent of the population lives from **agriculture** in a subsistence economy, mainly growing cereals and keeping livestock. Despite this, Botswana is only able to grow about 50 per cent of its own food requirements, and agriculture only contributes three per cent of GDP. The backbone of the economy is the rich mineral reserves discovered in the 1970s. Diamond-mining in the Kalahari Desert alone contributes 70 per cent of the country's income. There are also large reserves of iron ore and coal. In 2006, GDP was US$ 10.7 billion, of which 3 per cent came from agriculture, 51 per cent from industry and 46 per cent from services.

Transport Infrastructure

The populated areas of the country are well connected by **rail** and **road networks**. Gaborone is connected to the trans-African railway. The capital city also has an international **airport**.

Tourism

The range of animals in the national parks and the Kalahari Desert, inhabited by the famous Kalahari Bushmen, are attracting growing numbers of tourists. In 2003, the tourism industry contributed over US$300 million.

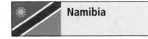

Namibia	
Area:	825,418 sq. km
Capital city:	Windhoek
Form of government: Republic in the Commonwealth	
Administrative divisions: 13 regions	
Population: 2 million (2 inhabitants/sq. km)	
Languages: English (official), Afrikaans, German	
GDP per capita:	US$3,100
Currency: 1 Namibian dollar = 100 cents	

Natural Geography

The sand and rocky regions of the **Namib Desert** extend parallel to the coast. The steep terrace of the Brandberg Massif (highest point, 2,579 m) leads to an undulating upland area to the country's interior, which falls in the east to join the **Kalahari basin** at an altitude of 1,000 m. In the north, in the Ovamboland region at an altitude of 1,050 m, lies the unique **Etosha Pan**, one of the largest salt water depressions in Africa. In the northeast lies the Caprivi Strip, stretching for 450 km to the Zambesi, and which is just 90 km wide at its broadest point.

Climate

The country has a sub-tropical climate with dry winters and hot summers. Temperatures at higher altitudes are milder, and the capital city remains approximately the same temperature year-round at 22°C. The main form of vegetation is thorny savannah.

Population

The **Ovambo** form more than 50 per cent of the population and are the largest group. Other ethnic groups in the country include the **Kavango** with nine per cent, and the **Herero** and **Damara**, each with seven per cent. People of European origin form seven per cent of the Namibian population. 86 per cent are Christians. The official language, English, is only spoken by seven per cent of the population; Afrikaans and German are the most common languages, and Oshivambo, Herero and Nama are also spoken.

History and Politics

The first contact with white traders and missionaries took place in the mid-nineteenth century, and the region was declared the colony of **German South West Africa** in 1884. After several uprisings, the most significant German colony received the right to self-government in 1907. After the occupation by South Africa in 1915, South West Africa was transferred to South Africa by the League of Nations in 1920, which governed the country until 1966.

From 1959 onwards, resistance formed against the governing powers, and the bloody **guerrilla war** was brought to an end in 1989 with a ceasefire. **Independence** was won in 1990, and was followed by a democratic constitution. The **SWAPO** (South West African People's Organisation), founded in 1957, who had led the resistance from the very beginning, remains today the most influential political power. SWAPO candidate Hifikepunye Pohamba has been president since 2004.

Economy

In 2006, GDP was US$ 6.3 billion, of which 10 per cent came from agriculture, 32 per cent from industry and 58 per cent from services. The country's biggest employer is the **agricultural sector**, which employs more than 70 per cent of the population and which produces enough food for the country's needs. Livestock rearing produces the country's most important export, beef. Despite set backs, the **fishing industry** has a lot of potential. The mainstay of the economy is **mining**, which brings in great profits, thanks to rich natural reserves (diamonds, uranium, copper, zinc and gold). The country has close economic links with South Africa.

Transport Infrastructure

Namibia has well constructed **rail** and **road networks** as well as a relatively dense domestic **flight network**. There is an international **airport** in Windhoek, and the country's **main trade port** is in Walvis Bay.

Tourism

The Namib Desert, the Etosha Pan and the national parks offer natural attractions. Those from the colonial period include the lake resorts of Lüderitz, Swakopmund and Walvis Bay.

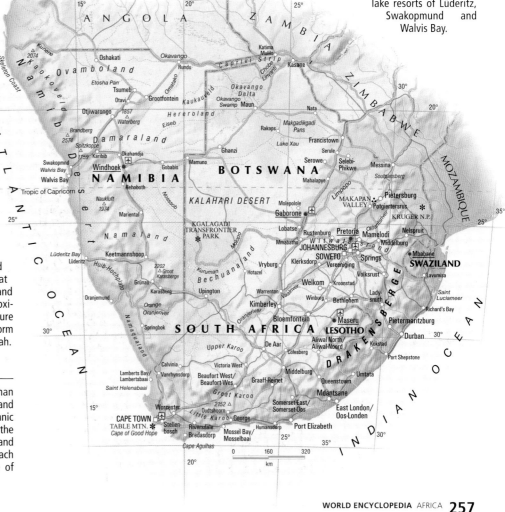

Cities of Africa

Cairo

The capital of Egypt, Cairo lies on the Nile Delta in eastern North Africa. It is the continent's largest city. The seat of government and the parliament are located in Cairo, which is also one of the most important seats of Islam. The old town of Cairo is a UNESCO World Heritage Site. Formerly an Ancient Egyptian settlement, the city found itself at the heart of the Islamic world under the Mamelukes in the thirteenth century. After the Ottomans conquered Egypt in 1517, Cairo's population fell dramatically. It was not until the end of the nineteenth century that it began its meteoric rise to become one of the largest cities in the world today.

Area:
214 sq. km (city)
Inhabitants:
7,950,000 (city, 2008)
16,100,000 (conurbation, 2008)
Population density:
37,150 inhabitants/sq. km (city)

Egypt's capital grew in just a few decades from 3 million to over 20 million inhabitants.

Lagos

Lagos, in West Africa, lies on the Gulf of Guinea. It is the largest city in Nigeria and the most important industrial and trading base in the country. Thousands of people from the country's interior and abroad streamed into Lagos during the economic boom in the 1970s, but this uncontrolled influx resulted in the large slum areas that today rub shoulders with the city's modern skyscrapers. The village of Lagos was established in the seventeenth century on Lagos Island, which had been discovered by the Portuguese. It developed into a base for the slave trade in the eighteenth century, and from 1906 belonged to the British Protectorate of Southern Nigeria.

Area:
300 sq. km (city)
Inhabitants:
9,360,000 (city, 2008)
About 12,520,000 (conurbation, 2008)
Population density:
31,200 inhabitants/sq. km (city)

People, trucks, market stalls – the bustling scene that is Oshodi Market in Lagos.

Cape Town

Cape Town is the largest city in South Africa and the country's seat of parliament. It lies to the south of Table Bay near the Cape of Good Hope on the Atlantic Ocean. The symbol of the city is Table Mountain, 1,086 m high. Cape Town is the cultural and scientific hub of the country, a dioscesan and university city. With its port and the Cape Town international airport, the city is an increasingly significant industrial and trading location. It was founded in 1652 as a way-station for ships of the Dutch East India Company on their way to the Dutch East Indies. From 1806 until 1910, it was the capital of the British Cape colony.

Area:
1,644 sq. km (city)
Inhabitants:
3,430,000 (city, 2008)
Population density:
2,086 inhabitants/sq. km (city)

The Victoria & Alfred Waterfront: A popular tourist destination, full of shops and leisure attractions.

Johannesburg

Johannesburg lies in the northeast of South Africa on the edge of the Witwatersrand mountain range. It is South Africa's trade, finance and industrial hub and, with 2.13 million inhabitants (in 2008), it is also Africa's third largest city. If Soweto, the residential area for blacks to the south-west of Johannesburg, is also included, the city's inhabitants total almost 4 million. Johannesburg's international airport is the largest in southern Africa. The layout of the city, founded in 1866 as a gold-diggers' settlement, resembles a chess board. Only a few historic buildings have been retained from its foundation, and the modern skyline is dominated by skyscrapers.

Area:
1,664 sq. km (city)
Inhabitants:
2,130,000 (city, 2008)
3,960,000 (conurbation, 2008)
Population density:
1,280 inhabitants/sq. km (city)

The gold-diggers' shanties have been replaced by skyscrapers: The Johannesburg skyline.

Abstract patterns and rainbow colours: these are the stark tones that distinguish the wall painting, the body decoration and traditional wear of the Ndebele women. In former times they painted with natural, earthen colours; today modern acryl tones are mixed with clay for effect.

*The **Herero** have long been a cattle-herding people. They arrived in the region around Windhoek from northeast Africa in the seventeenth and eighteenth centuries. The 1904 Herero Wars which were fought against former German colonists reduced the original population of 80,000 to just 20,000. Today, most of the Herero are Christian, and their language, a Bantu language, is taught in Namibian schools.*

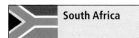

South Africa	
Area:	1,219,912 sq. km
Capital city:	Pretoria
Form of government: Republic	
Administrative divisions:	
9 provinces	
Population: 47 million	
(38 inhabitants/sq. km)	
Languages:	
English, Afrikaans, Zulu,	
Bantu languages (all official)	
GDP per capita:	US$5,400
Currency:	1 rand = 100 cents

Natural Geography

South Africa's landscape can be divided into three areas: the interior plateau, the Great Escarpment and the coastal seam. The extensive upland area in the country's interior, the **Karoo,** lies at an altitude of 1,000 to 1,800 m and is divided by isolated mountains. This region is bordered by the Great Escarpment, dominated in the east by the **Drakensberg Mountains**. The region contains South Africa's highest peak, Njesuthi (3,408 m). The Great Escarpment is in turn bordered by the coastal strip, which is mainly narrow and moderately craggy.

Climate

The climate is typical of the warm **sub-tropics**. In Pretoria, average temperatures are 11°C in July and 21°C in January.

Population

Three quarters of South Africans belong to the **Zulu, Xhosa, Pedi, Sotho,Tswana, Tsonga, Swazi, Ndebele** and **Venda** ethnic groups, while 13.6 per cent are of European origin. There are also nine per cent mixed race people known as coloureds (people of half-European, half-African descent) and 2.6 per cent Asians. There are a total of 11 official languages and numerous regional dialects. The HIV infection rate is 20 per cent.

History and Politics

Black settlement of South Africa dates back to the second and third centuries AD, but a Dutch Cape Colony was not established until 1652. Great Britain conquered the country in 1795, bringing many settlers to the country. From this time on, there were many conflicts between the Dutch **Boers** and the British. The Boer republics of **Transvaal** and the **Orange Free State** and the British crown colony of Natal were established as a result, but these regions came under full British rule after the defeat of the Dutch in the Boer War in 1901/1902. Brought together under the Union of South Africa in 1910, the colonies gained **independence** between 1926 and 1931.

The Black population suffered under the racist apartheid policies. Deeply angered, they began armed resistance in 1960, led by the African National Congress (**ANC**). In 1989, a process of protracted negotiations began between the government and the ANC, which finally ended in 1993 with the abolition of **racial discrimination**. Free elections were held place in 1994, the ANC being the clear winners. Nelson Mandela became president. The **homelands** were abolished and integrated into newly created provinces. South Africa became a member of the OAU. A new constitution was adopted in 1996. The parliament elected Thabo Mbeki as president in 1999.

Economy

In 2006, GDP was US$ 255 billion, of which three per cent came from agriculture, 32 per cent from industry and 65 per cent from services. **Agriculture** makes a relatively small contribution, although this sector, together with mining, make up most of the country's export income. South Africa is the world's leading source of gold and platinum. Serious problems exist, however, due to the high rate of unemployment, running at about 40 per cent, as well as the high rate of HIV infection.

Transport Infrastructure

South Africa has a good infrastructure and three international **airports**. The major sea **ports** are Durban, Cape Town and Port Elizabeth.

Tourism

South Africa is one of the most popular holiday destinations in the world and has a wealth of natural attractions. The country has many national parks, the most famous of which is the enormous Kruger National Park, which is an excellent game resort, offering great safaris. The Garden Route from Cape Town to Port Elizabeth is a favourite tour.

1 The Himba in Namibia occupy the so-called Kaokoland, a dry, mountainous area. They keep cattle, goats and sheep and cultivate maize and gourds.

2 The Namib Desert stretches along the Atlantic coast of Namibia. The interior of the country receives rainfall of less than 20 mm a year. Low temperatures and cloud formation are distinctive features of this coastal desert.

3 Camps Bay in Cape Town, South Africa, directly beneath the 'Twelve Apostles' mountains. The beach promenade is very popular.

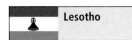 **Lesotho**

The **Ndebele** mainly live in Zimbabwe, but the ethnic group can also be found in South Africa. Ndebele women are famous for the brightly coloured works of art with which they decorate their houses.

Area:	30,355 sq. km
Capital city:	Maseru
Form of government:	
Constitutional Monarchy in the Commonwealth	
Administrative divisions:	
10 districts	
Population:	
2.1 million (69 inhabitants/sq. km)	
Languages:	Sesotho, English
GDP per capita:	c. US$700
Currency: 1 loti = 100 lisente	

Natural Geography

The central region of the country and the eastern section includes part of the Drakensberg Mountains, a high mountainous region (highest point: Thabana Ntlenyana, 3,482 m). The western region lies at an altitude of between 1,000 and 1,500 m. There are almost no trees and shrubs and the main flora is grassland savannah and mountain meadows.

Climate

Lesotho has a temperate sub-tropical climate and average temperatures in the capital city are 25°C in summer and 15°C in winter. In summer, the country suffers from long, heavy periods of rainfall.

Population

The population is up to 99.7 per cent **Basotho**, with small European and Asian groups. 80 per cent of the Lesotho people are Christian and 20 per cent follow native religions. One third of the adult population is HIV positive.

History and Politics

The kingdom of the **Basutho** was established in the nineteenth century. Its ruler appealed to Queen Victoria for British protection in 1868. The British protectorate ended in 1966, and the country was granted **independence**.

Since 1993, the country has been a constitutional monarchy. The ruler – Letsie III – only has ceremonial functions. The country has a tradition of close relations with South Africa in areas ranging from the economy to foreign policy. After a period of domestic turmoil, South African troops intervened in 1998 in order to support the government. New elections were held in 2007, and these endorsed the government.

Economy

In 2006, GDP was US$ 1.5 billion, of which 19 per cent came from agriculture, 40 per cent from industry and 42 per cent from services. The **agricultural sector** is poorly developed due to a lack of usable land and recurrent droughts. Main agricultural activities are the cultivation of cereals and livestock -breading. The country has almost no natural resources. The most important domestic economic factor is the **processing industry**, mainly textiles and leather processing. With the aid of foreign investment, this branch of the economy is currently being developed to make it suitable for producing exports.

Transport Infrastructure

The **road network** extends for a total of just under 5,000 km and consists mainly of dirt tracks. The capital city, Maseru, has good **rail** connections and **flight connections** to South Africa.

Tourism

The tourist centre of the country is the capital city, Maseru, with its numerous casinos and large hotels. The surrounding mountainous countryside is a well-kept secret by keen hikers. Most of the tourism is currently from neighbouring South Africa.

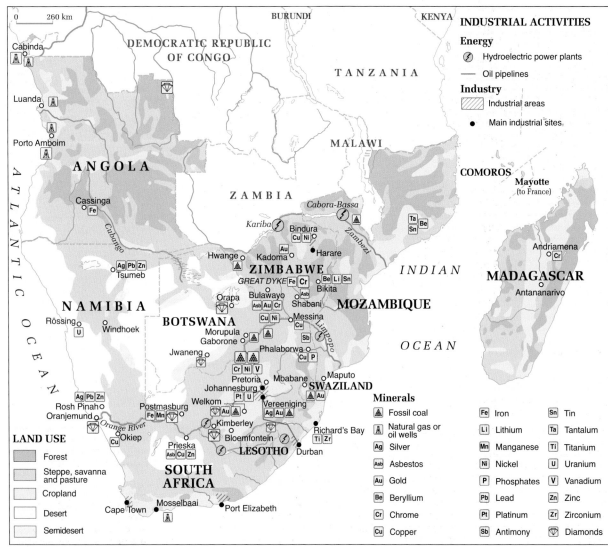

INDUSTRIAL ACTIVITIES

Energy
- Hydroelectric power plants
— Oil pipelines

Industry
- Industrial areas
- Main industrial sites

LAND USE
- Forest
- Steppe, savanna and pasture
- Cropland
- Desert
- Semidesert

Minerals

⛏	Fossil coal	Fe	Iron	Sn	Tin
⛽	Natural gas or oil wells	Li	Lithium	Ta	Tantalum
Ag	Silver	Mn	Manganese	Ti	Titanium
Asb	Asbestos	Ni	Nickel	U	Uranium
Au	Gold	P	Phosphates	V	Vanadium
Be	Beryllium	Pb	Lead	Zn	Zinc
Cr	Chrome	Pt	Platinum	Zr	Zirconium
Cu	Copper	Sb	Antimony	◊	Diamonds

Nelson Rohlilahla Mandela

*Qunu, 18.7.1918

The ANC leader was forced to go underground after the organisation was outlawed in 1961, but he continued to organise resistance to the apartheid system in South Africa. He was sentenced to life imprisonment in 1964 and only released in 1990 due to international pressure. After the first free elections, Mandela, winner of the Nobel Peace Prize, was elected South African President in 1994. He did not stand for a second term.

Desmond Mpilo Tutu

*Klerksdorp, 7.10.1931

The Anglican minister was Bishop of Lesotho from 1976 to 1978, and from 1979 to 1984 he was primate of the Church of the Province of Southern Africa, which he founded. He was Bishop of Johannesburg from 1984 to 1986, and from 1986 to 1996 Archbishop of Cape Town. Since 1987, he has led the African bishops. He received the Nobel Peace Prize in 1984 for his work against apartheid. From 1996 to 1998, he chaired the Truth and Reconciliation Commission.

Sangoma are medicine men or female healers among the Zulu and the related Swazi people, who make up to 85 per cent of the population of Swaziland. They are specialists in religious rituals and are said to cure illnesses using supernatural powers. Illness is a sign of scorn from the gods and can be caused by witchcraft and magic. The healers use herbs and massages as well as spiritual techniques.

Swaziland	
Area:	17,363 sq. km
Capital city:	Mbabane
Form of government:	
Constitutional Monarchy in the Commonwealth	
Administrative divisions:	
273 tribal areas, 55 traditional councils	
Population:	
1.1 million (64 inhabitants/sq. km)	
Languages:	
English, Siswati (both official)	
GDP per capita:	US$2,300
Currency: 1 lilangeni = 100 cents	

Natural Geography

The landlocked country lies between South Africa and Mozambique on the eastern slopes of the **Drakensberg Mountains.** Swaziland can be divided into four geographical areas: in the western uplands, the **Highveld,** there are plateaus and valleys at a height of between 1,000 and 1,800 m, covered in forest plantations. The **Midveld** lies at an altitude of 500 to 1,000 m and has grass and thorn bush savannah used for cereal cultivation and livestock-rearing. The Lowveld in the east is a lowland area at an altitude of 150 to 500 m and is also used for agriculture. The region is bordered by the mountainous **Lebombo Plateau** at between 500 and 800 m in altitude.

Climate

The west has a moderate, subtropical climate with high precipitation, but the east is hotter and drier. In the capital city, Mbabane, average temperatures are 12°C in July and 29°C in January.

Population

Up to 97 per cent of the population is **Swazi**. 60 per cent are Christian and 40 per cent belong to native religions. The country is troubled by an HIV infection rate of 33.4 per cent.

History and Politics

The region has been settled by the Bantu people, the Swazi, since the mid-eighteenth century. They founded their kingdom in 1815.

The first Boers entered the country in 1868, and greater numbers of British began entering the region from 1877 onwards. Swaziland was named a British protectorate in 1903 and regained its **independence** in 1968. The constitution of 1978 gave the king, Mswati III, extensive executive powers, which, despite great pressure for democratisation and an amendment to the constitution in 1992, remain largely unrestricted to this day.

Economy

The economy of Swaziland is traditionally dominated by the

processing of agricultural and forestry products and further processing for the export-oriented **manufacturing industry** is becoming increasingly important. As a result of structural change, manufacturing now contribute 46 per cent of GDP. The proportion contributed by the **services sector** is 42 per cent. The importance of mining (iron ore, asbestos) has greatly reduced, but the tourism industry has potential for growth.

Transport Infrastructure

The **rail network** is only 224 km long and is mainly used to transport goods to Mozambique. The **road network** has a length of 2,885 km but is only well developed between the main centres. The rest of the roads are mainly dirt tracks.

The **air strip** in Mbabane only has connections to international destinations via Johannesburg airport in South Africa.

Tourism

Entertainment districts have developed in the capital city, which attract many tourists from South Africa. In terms of landscape, the most attractive regions are the mountains and the large wild game reserves of Mlilwane, Malolotja and Hlane.

1 Basotho men ride across a river valley in Makhaleng, Lesotho – they are members of an ethnic group that arrived in the eighteenth century.

2 The South African metropolis of Durban has an impressive skyline, great beaches and a yachting marina.

3 From Table Mountain there is a breath-taking view of Cape Town, a city in one of the best locations in the world.

4 Many Sotho, one of the Bantu-speaking people who make up most of the population of Lesotho, live in huts constructed in traditional style.

South Africa now ranks first above all other African countries in terms of economy. In the last few years, its GNP has been rising by between two and three per cent, not least through the exploitation of its rich mineral resources. However, this upswing has been restricted to the white regions and the

areas around the large metropolises. In the former homelands, the unemployment rate is almost 40 per cent. The pictures on the left show diamond divers off the Atlantic coast and gold smelters; the pictures on the right show a worker in front of a factory near Johannesburg and a street trader's stand.

Madagascar, Comoros, Mauritius

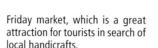

*The population of **Madagascar** is very different from that of the African mainland. Most inhabitants are descendants of Indonesian settlers who arrived 2,000 years ago, bringing with them rice cultivation.*

Madagascar

Area:	587,041 sq. km
Capital city:	Antananarivo
Form of government:	Republic
Administrative divisions:	
28 regions	
Population:	
19 million	
(32 inhabitants/sq. km)	
Languages:	
Malagasy, French (both official), Howa	
GDP per capita:	US$290
Currency:	
1 Madagascan franc = 100 centimes	

Natural Geography

Madagascar is the fourth-largest island in the world, and most of its land mass, apart from the coastal plains in the west, is taken up by a mountain which rises gradually to a height of 2,876 m. The summit is located to the west of a central upland area.

Climate

The country has a tropical climate with great variations in the amount of precipitation. The eastern side, bordering the Indian Ocean, has high precipitation and is typified by lush tropical rainforest. The unique flora and fauna is threatened by slash-and-burn deforestation, cyclones, spring floods and earthquakes.

Population

The majority of the **Malay-Indonesian** inhabitants, half of whom are Christian and half of whom practice native religions, belong to one of more than 20 clans. The social and health systems are deficient, as are basic food supplies.

History and Politics

The island was settled early on by south Asians but was discovered by the Portuguese in 1500, who settled on the coast, along with the French. The native population successfully resisted attempts at colonisation until 1896. The French colony became **independent** in 1960, when it called itself Malgache. It reverted to the name of Madagascar in 1975. The constitution of 1992 provides for a bicameral parliament. In 2002, civil unrest was provoked by vote-rigging during the elections.

Economy

In 2006, GDP was about US$ 5.5 billion, of which 30 per cent came from agriculture, 15 per cent from industry and 55 per cent from services.
The most important **exports** are coffee, vanilla, cloves, cotton, sisal hemp, peanuts and tobacco. The manufacturing industry is poorly developed but it is linked to the fishing industry, processing prawns, tuna and lobster for export. Madagascar's **natural reserves** are not insignificant, but are not yet fully exploited.

Transport Infrastructure

Only ten per cent of the **roads** are surfaced and many cross-country roads can become impassable. The main form of transport is the

Friday mosque in Mutsumudu on the Comoros island of Anjouan.

rail network. The domestic flight network is one of the most dense in the southern hemisphere.

Tourism

In addition to the many nature parks which are home to lemurs, numerous unique species of reptile and amphibian (frogs, chameleons) and civet cats, the capital city, Antananarivo has a large Friday market, which is a great attraction for tourists in search of local handicrafts.

Comoros

Area:	1,861 sq. km
Capital city:	Moroni
Form of government:	
Islamic Presidential Republic	
Administrative divisions:	
3 island districts	
Population:	
c. 650,000	
(350 inhabitants/sq. km)	
Languages:	
Comoran, French (both official), minority languages	
GDP per capita:	US$600
Currency:	
1 Comoran franc = 100 centimes	

Natural Geography

The national territory consists of the three larger islands **Njazidja** (Grande Comore), **Mwali (Mohéli)** and **Nzwani (Anjouan)** and further small islands off the coast of East Africa. These are largely of volcanic origin. The highest volcano is Le Karthala (2,361 m), which is still active.
In the upper regions of the craggy mountains, the tropical rainforest is replaced by savannah. The narrow coast has mangrove swamps and coral reefs.

Climate

The tropical climate results in high levels of precipitation. The average temperature is 25°C.

Population

The **mixed population** consists of African, Arab, Indian and Madagascan settlers. The low standard of education means that half of the population can neither read nor write. The health and social systems are also completely inadequate for the needs of the inhabitants.

History and Politics

The islands were ruled by the Persians and the Arabs in the sixteenth century. The French **colony** founded on the neighbouring island of Mayotte in 1843 was expanded to include the Comoros in 1912. The Comoros declared its **independence** in 1975. After years of instability, the foundation of an Islamic Republic in 1997 caused the two islands of Mwali and Nzwani to declare themselves independent. Colonel Azali Assoumani took power in a military coup in 1999. In 2001, a peace agreement was reached with those islands that had broken away. A new federal constitution in the same year created the Union of the Comoros.

Economy

Agriculture employs 80 per cent of the population, yet the subsistence economy does not grow enough food to adequately supply the population. Large sections of agricultural land are used for the cultivation of the main exports, vanilla, cloves, coconuts and ylang-ylang, a rich perfume. Gross domestic product in 2006 was US$400 million. Agriculture contributed 41 per cent, manufacturing 12 Muslim and the services sector 47 per cent.

Transport Infrastructure

Due to the island's landscape, it has very few **roads** and no **rail network**. Ferry and flight connections run between the islands at irregular intervals, although the transport network is improving, in order to attract tourists. There is an international **airport** in the capital Moroni.

Tourism

Tourism suffers from a lack of infrastructure, but this is being renovated. The Comoros are home to some rare and unique species of fauna, including the mongoose lemur. In addition to the capital city Moroni, with its wealth of Arabic architecture and mosques, the crater lakes and palm-fringed sub-tropical beaches attract many tourists, especially from the rest of Africa.

Mauritius

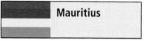

Area:	2,040 sq. km
Capital city:	Port Louis
Form of government:	Republic
Administrative divisions:	
9 districts, 3 dependencies	
Population:	
1.2 million	
(590 inhabitants/sq. km))	
Languages:	
English (official), Creole, Hindi, Urdu	
GDP per capita:	US$5,000
Currency:	
1 Mauritian rupee = 100 cents	

Natural Geography

The island is of volcanic origin. Its highest point is the Piton de la Rivière Noire at a height of 882 m. The coastline boasts many white sand beaches and numerous coves, with off-shore coral reefs. The territory also includes Rodrigues Island, the Agalega Islands and the Cargados Carajos Shoals.

Climate

The climate is sub-tropical, humid and warm. The rainy season lasts from May to October. Temperatures remain constant year-round at an average of 25°C. The original luxuriant rainforest vegetation has only been preserved in a few conservation areas.

Population

The ethnic and cultural composition of the population is very varied: 68 per cent are the descendants of **Indian plantation**

*The breath-taking natural beauty of the island nations of **Mauritius** and the **Seychelles** are of great importance for their economies. Magical beaches, amazing diving locations and good infrastructure attract large numbers of tourists.*

workers and 27 per cent are **Creole**. Hindus are the largest religious group, representing some 52 per cent of the population, but there are also a good number of Christians (29 per cent) and Muslims (17 per cent).

History and Politics

The island had already been discovered by early settlers in the tenth century but was occupied by the Dutch in the sixteenth century, who established a plantation there. It was at this time that the island received its current name, which derived from Prince Maurice of Nassau. In the eighteenth century, the French took over the colony and imported African slaves to the island to work on the plantations. Under British colonial rule, which began in 1810 and lasted until **independence** in 1968, Indian indentured labour was brought to the islands to work the plantations. In 1992, Mauritius ended its status as a constitutional monarchy under the rule of the British crown. The country became a republic with a president as head of state, but remained part of the Commonwealth.

Economy

In 2006, GDP was US$ 6.3 billion, of which six per cent came from **agriculture**, 22 per cent from **industry** and 72 per cent from **services**. The **manufacturing sector** is very much geared towards export. Main sectors include the processing of textiles, wool and sugar. The tourism industry today forms a significant part of the growing **services sector**, and employs 20 per cent of the working population.

Transport Infrastructure

The **road network** is well constructed. Port Louis has an international **airport**.

Tourism

The centre of the well-developed tourist industry is focussed on the capital city, Port Louis. The Black River Gorges and the Ile aux Aigrettes national parks, home to fruit-bats and numerous species of exotic birds, are also

well worth a visit. Extensive paradise beaches and diving spots can also be found on the other islands.

	Seychelles
Area:	454 sq. km
Capital city:	Victoria
Form of government:	
Republic in the Commonwealth	
Administrative divisions:	
23 districts	
Population:	
80,000 (177 inhabitants/sq. km)	
Languages:	
English, French, Creole	
GDP per capita:	US$9,400
Currency:	
1 Seychelles rupee = 100 cents	

Natural Geography

The archipelago lies in the western Indian Ocean, 1600 km off the coast of East Africa. Fewer than half the islands are inhabited. Many of them are coral atolls (with a total area of 210 sq. km), but the main islands of **Mahé**, **Praslin**, **Silhouette** and **La Digue** are mountainous. On the largest island, Mahé (area: 158 sq. km), the mountains reach a height of up to 905 m and have only sparse vegetation.

Climate

The tropical-oceanic climate divides the year into a relatively cool period with little precipitation (May to September) and the north-west monsoon period (December to March) with hot temperatures and a lot of rain.

Population

The population is 98 per cent Christian, and has Asian, African and European origins. Due to the

large number of tourists, the inhabitants of the Seychelles have the highest per capita income of any African country.
Ninety per cent of the population live on Mahé.

History and Politics

The uninhabited group of 115 islands was first discovered by the Portuguese Vasco da Gama in 1501 and became a French colony in 1756. The islands became a British colony between 1794 and 1811. From 1903, the Syechelles has had the status of an autonomous British crown colony.

Independence in 1976 was followed by years of political instability, during which the original constitution was abandoned as the result of a coup. The presidential constitution of 1979 gives the President extensive powers.

Economy

In 2006, GDP was US$ 770 billion, of which three per cent came from **agriculture**, 28 per cent from **industry** and 69 per cent from **services**.

Transport Infrastructure

The Seychelles have a very well-constructed infrastructure:

ships and planes connect the smaller and larger islands to each other.

Tourism

The Seychelles are well known to holiday-makers as a tropical paradise, with palm-fringed beaches and white sand. Mahé is an island which boasts powdery white sands and lush vegetation, rising through plantations of coconut palms and cinnamon trees to forested peaks that afford wonderful views of neighboring islands.
Other tourist attractions include the nature reserves on Praslin and Silhouette islands and the local Creole food.

A Kikuyu from Kenya decorated
with impressive ceremonial
make-up.

Peoples of Africa

*Today approximately one-eighth of the world's
population lives in Africa, the third largest
continent after Asia and America. Almost
40 per cent of Africa is covered by barren
desert and around 20 per cent with tropical*

This Maasai woman sports elaborate earrings.

*rainforest. More than 3,000 ethnic groups –
from the light-skinned Berbers in North Africa
and the proud Maasai people in East Africa
through to the small-statured bushmen in the
south of the continent – are spread across
54 nations, their borders drawn up largely on
the arbitrary basis of the colonial regimes
established by the English, French, Belgians,
Portuguese, Spanish, Italians and Germans.
Despite the tremendous European influence
that spread Christianity to almost every corner
of the continent, with the exception of the
Islamic north and eastern African states, and
despite massive urbanisation – almost one in
five Africans now lives in the towns – Africa still
retains an impressive cultural diversity.*

Northern Africa

A settled life in the Sahara has only ever been viable at the few oases, with the fortified villages (ksar) serving as protection for the residents from marauding nomads in the past. The abundance of water at the oases enables the cultivation of date palms and field crops, as well as livestock farming. The honeycomb-like dwellings in the clay brick Ksar Ouled protect their inhabitants against the sandstorms that regularly fill the wells with sand.

The Berbers

Today's approximately 7 million Muslim **Berbers** (their indigenous name, 'Amazigh', means 'free man') are the Hamitic inhabitants of north-west Africa and also include, among others, the **Beraber**, **Rifkabyle**, **Kabyle**, **Shluh** and **Tekna** ethnic groups. The settlement area of the Berbers extends from **Morocco** – where they account for almost half of the population – across the whole of **North Africa** as far as **Egypt**.

As settled crop farmers and semi-nomadic stock farmers, the Berbers live mostly in extended families, each one with the eldest male at its head; the families often combine to form larger communities, which are in turn subject to an elected leader (Amghar). The Berber culture is heavily influenced by Islam but has nevertheless developed its own traits.

More than 1 million **Shluh** (Shilh) inhabit **central** and **south-western Morocco** and make up one of the largest ethnic groups; it is subdivided into numerous tribes who live mainly from crop farming. Another significant Berber tribe, with around 1 million members, is the **Kabyle** in eastern Algeria, whose name derives from the Arabian **Qabila** ('tribal members'). They live largely from the farming of grain crops and from cultivating wine, olives and cork trees.

The Tuareg

The settlement area of the approximately 500,000 **Tuareg** ('highwaymen'), who refer to themselves as the Imuhagh and belong to the Berbers, today encompasses **Algeria**, **Libya**, **Niger**, **Burkina Faso** and **Mali**. Less than ten per cent of the Tuareg population live in the Algerian-Libyan desert, with the remainder residing at the oases and in the Sahel region.

The social order of the Muslim Tuareg, among whom only the men wear veils (**litham**), is strictly hierarchical. First come the powerful nobility comprising the warlike **Imuhar**, the only ones allowed to breed camels. Then come the **marabouts** or **ineslemen**, scribes and Koran initiates who also enjoy a great deal of prestige as the bearers of God's blessing (baraka). The largest group comprises the **Kel Ulli** ('goat people'), referred to as the Imrad ('ruffians') by the Imuhar, who live as livestock breeders and caravan escorts. Further down the social ladder are the dependants (**izzagaren**) and slaves (**iklan**) who often work as servants, herdsmen or gardeners for members of the higher class. The blacksmiths (**ineden**), with their own secret language, constitute a special group of artisans within the Tuareg, producing not only silver jewellery along with wooden and metal handicrafts, but also playing an important role as healers, musicians and singers.

The Toubou (Tibbu, Teda)

There are around 200,000 Muslim **Toubou**. Their name derives from the Arabic **Tu-bu** ('rock person') and their settlement area encompasses approximately 1.7 million sq. km extending from the mid-Sahara as far as Sudan. Only the Toubou men, like their

Only Tuareg men wear a veil, which is blue.

Tuareg counterparts, wear veils. The Toubou live as semi-nomads in wooden huts (ferrig) with roofs made of loose palm-leaf mats. They grow millet, wheat, barley, vegetables, fruit (dates), tobacco and cotton around the widely scattered oases, and the breeding and trading of livestock plays an important role in their economy. Like the Tuareg, the blacksmiths (assa) also play a special role among the Toubou as singers and dancers.

The Oromo (Galla)

At 40 per cent, the almost 25 million **Oromo** population group is Ethiopia's largest; their earlier name **Galla** (meaning 'roaming land seekers') was given to them by the **Amhara**. The Oromo are divided into more than 200 tribes, their territories extending from **southern Ethiopia** as far as **Sudan** and **Kenya**. The northern tribes are Coptic Christians, while the southern tribes are Muslim. Some of the tribes have a hierarchy based on age (gadas), with each male passing through five stages, each eight years in length, and the respective transition rituals performed by a high priest. The end of each level is marked by a test of courage comprising the killing of dangerous animals, for example, or the liberation of imprisoned tribal members, thereby procuring social prestige.

Following their repression by the Amhara in the nineteenth century, the Oromo have mainly made their livelihoods as crop farmers growing grain and coffee, as well as breeding livestock.

The Amhara

With more than 12 million people, the **Amhara**, who migrated to Ethiopia from southern Arabia more than 2,000 years ago, make up the country's ruling class. They belong to the Ethiopian Orthodox Church, headed by the **Negus**, and speak the Semitic (Cushitic)

Amharic language (Amarinya), which is today the country's official language. The Amhara live in the highlands of Ethiopia where their livelihood is based on the cultivation of millet (teff), barley, wheat and legumes, together with livestock farming (cattle, sheep, goats).

As proud warriors in a powerful feudal empire – the lineage of the former Amharic king **Menelik II** is said to extend as far back as Solomon and the Queen of Sheba – they subjugated numerous tribes (Oromo, Hahiya, Sidama and Kaffa) until the early twentieth century and had an influential elite of aristocrats and priests with dependent tenant farmers; the elite constituted the ruling class until the revolution in 1974.

The Tigray

There are about 6 million **Tigray** (Tigrinya) in Ethiopia and Eritrea; they are the descendants of Semitic immigrants from Yemen, who settled in North Africa some 2,000 years ago and, as members of a sophisticated civilisation, introduced the plough and terraced farming to the higher altitude areas, along with their own alphabet. Traditionally the Tigray live in patrilineal family groups (enda) with communal land possession; the tanners, potters, blacksmiths and weavers constitute a lower social class. In the rural areas the Tigray live mainly from growing grain, legumes and spices, while in the towns they belong to the ruling class, together with the **Amhara**.

The Nuba

The collective term Nuba refers to the approximately 1 million people living in groups in the Nuba Mountains of Southern Kordofan (the Republic of Sudan). They live as crop farmers growing millet and are also livestock breeders. The Nuba have largely retained their culture and their traditional religion without being a national unit, although they are strongly fragmented in terms of language. Tall, agile and elegant, they stage exhibition skirmishes and dance festivals, and are renowned for their unusual body painting.

The Nubians

Today, around 2.5 million **Nubians** embrace numerous ethnic groups in the Upper Nile areas of **Sudan** and **Egypt**, including the **Kenuzi**, **Mahat**, **Sukkot** and **Danagla**, along with many sub-tribes, such as the **Nyima**, **Birket**, **Midobit** or **Dilling**, who speak a common or similar language (Nubian). The Nubians settled along the Nile and live mainly from growing millet, barley, wheat, dates and figs, crops that are farmed in a strip about 2 km wide along the river. Away from the Nile oasis, their livelihood is largely based on livestock breeding.

The history of the Nubians dates back to the fourth century BC when the first tribes settled in the Nile valley. From about 2500 BC the Nubian culture became increasingly subject to Egyptian influence, with the Egyptians also adopting many aspects of the Nubian culture. The tribes were initially Christianised in the fourth century AD, and Islamised after the sixteenth century as a result of the Bedouin influence.

The Somalis

Today 6.7 million of a total of some 8 million **Somalis**, who are divided into several large tribal groups (including the Hawiya, Dir, Ishak, Darod), live in the country that is named after them, Somalia. About 1 million live in **Ethiopia**, with 300,000 in **Djibouti** (Issa Somalis) and 100,000 in **Kenya**. The Somalis speak a Cushitic language and were Islamised as early as the twelfth century. However, they retained pre-Islamic customs, including the belief in natural spirits (zar), expressed by the women as a state of ecstasy and by the men as the obligation to undergo a test of courage before marriage. The settlement area of the Somalis is largely made up of dry savannah, as a result of which most of them live as nomadic livestock herders.

Bedouins – The Desert Nomads

The Bedouins do not constitute their own ethnic group. Their name derives from the Arabic 'Badw' ('desert inhabitants') and is the collective term for all nomadic peoples of Arabic descent in the deserts and steppe areas of North Africa and the Middle East. They have been living as nomads for the last 3,000 years.

Semi-nomadic tribes, such as the Akkader, lived in south-west Asia as early as the middle of the third century BC, but it was the domestication after the twelfth century BC of the camel – which is capable of surviving long periods in the desert without water – as working animals, beasts of burden and mounts, that enabled the lengthy migrations of Bedouin tribes such as the Beni Hilal and Beni Sulaim from the region that forms modern-day Syria, first to the Arabian countries, and from there through the Egyptian desert as far as north-west Africa after 1050.

On their journey, the feared nomads took over the farmlands of the Fellachs, an agricultural, largely Muslim rural population, as pasture for their animals, overgrazing the lands and subsequently turning them into semi-desert. As caravan leaders, merchants and guardians of the trade routes, they also facilitated an economic and cultural exchange that led to the rapid spread of Islam in North Africa and south-west Asia after the seventh century.

According to current estimates, between only five and ten per cent of Bedouins can still be described as true nomads, sheltering in their black tents made from goat or camel hair and living mainly off the meat and milk products supplied by their camels. The majority live as settled farmers or semi-nomads on the edge of the oases in more or less established settlements, with livestock breeding playing an important role, along with the farming of grain and dates.

The social system of the Bedouins, who are divided into numerous tribes (qabila) and sub-tribes, is based on the patrilineal extended family, each of which is headed by the eldest male member of the family and whose social standing depends on both their lineage and their respective possessions, with the camel breeders enjoying the highest prestige.

The tribes' legitimation derives from their descent from a common ancestor, indicated by the designation Aulad ('descendent of ...') or Ben ('son of ...') preceding the man's name. The sheik is the head of the tribe, with the sleb or sulaba, the disdained artisan or hunter, being at the other end of the social ladder.

Top: Camels are the Bedouins' means of transport and their food supply.

Middle: Bedouin women enjoy great prestige and live in the women's section of the tents.

Bottom: The children are also active as herdsmen.

Western Africa

Today around 420,000 of the Portuguese-speaking Cape Verdeans live on the nine islands of the Republic of Cape Verde, located in the Atlantic some 600 km off the West African coast. They are descendants of West African slaves brought to the formerly deserted islands by the Portuguese after 1462. Today's population comprises around 70 per cent people of mixed blood (due to interbreeding with the European settlers), almost 30 per cent blacks and just one per cent whites.

The Wolof

At around 3.5 million, the **Wolof** make up the largest population group in **Senegal**, with a small minority living in adjoining **Gambia**. The Wolof, who are Islamic, live in small village communities, which comprise thatched huts grouped around a central village square. In addition to growing crops such as rice, peanuts and millet, their livelihood is mainly based on livestock farming (horses, cattle), and – unlike the majority of other West African peoples – they also make use of the milk and milk products from their animals. The Wolof are also exceptionally skilled at working with gold.

The history of the Wolof dates back to the fourteenth century with the founding of their first empire, headed by a god king and a retinue of powerful aristocratic and warrior classes. The next level of the hierarchy is made up of farmers and craftsmen, with the slaves at the lowest level.

Following a vigorous slave trade conducted during the fifteenth and sixteenth centuries with the **Portuguese**, who needed the slaves for their colonies, the Wolof's access to the coast became cut off by immigrant tribes, leading both to their economic and their political decline.

The Bambara

The **Bambara** form the largest ethnic group in Mali, with around 3.5 million people. They belong to the West African **Malinke** in terms of both their culture and their language. The Bambara's livelihood is largely based on agriculture (maize, millet and rice), but they have no system of private ownership, as a result of which the land belongs to the village community and only the usage rights are passed on.

The Bambara also live from hunting, as well as from trading in cotton fabrics dyed with locally produced indigo, and from the sale of their metalwork and woodcarving artefacts (including their antelope masks, used in dances and rituals), most of which portray religious motifs.

The Bambara live in small settlements and villages, each one subject to an earth priest as the descendant of the respective village founder. His influence is largely based on the traditional religion still practised today and retained despite the many attempts at Islamization. In addition to secret male societies, within which the blacksmiths play an important role, this also includes ancestor worship and the belief in spirits.

The Dogon

The **Dogon** ethnic group (indigenous name: Habe) lives in **southern Mali** and **Burkina Faso** and encompasses about 250,000 people; their language belongs to the **Gur**. They live in small villages, mainly in the highlands, and their livelihood is based primarily on terraced farming (millet, rice, maize), with the breeding of small animals, hunting and fishing playing only a minimal role. The Dogon are also considered to be talented wood carvers (masks and cult figures).

comprise several families forming an economic community, with all key decisions made by the family elders.

In the West the Dogon are known mainly for their ceremonies, during which witches and spirits play a significant role, not only within the context of ancestor worship (nommo) but also in the mask festival (sigi), which takes place only once every 60 years. The festival includes the re-enactment of mythological motifs, according to which Amma, the god of creation, made the world, with the primeval blacksmith having given man fire and lessons in crop growing.

The Hausa

Today over 20 million **Hausa** live mainly in north-western Nigeria, where they make up the largest population group, and in the south-west of **Niger**. Their language (Hausa) contains numerous Arabic elements and is also used by other West African peoples as a language of trade and as a lingua franca. The Hausa live

some of the most prosperous merchants in West Africa; their travels contributed to the exchange of many cultural elements from north and east African countries, such as instruments, weapons or clothing. Although they have been largely Muslim since the fourteenth century, the Hausa have retained some elements of their pre-Islamic culture. These include, for example, the women's **Bori cult**, its rhythmic dancing evoking the spirits of the ancestors.

The Ewe

The **Ewe** comprise a population of around 2 million people living in the east of **Ghana** as well as in southern **Togo** and whose language (Gbe) encompasses a variety of dialects.

The **Ewe** live mainly from rotating crop farming (yams, maize, cassava), followed by the breeding of small livestock, fishing and hunting; these activities are reserved for specific social classes, however. Handicrafts and trade also play a role.

The social order of the Ewe has a patrilineal structure and is divided into numerous chiefs' clans, with the majority of the material possessions being common property. The Ewe also have a sophisticated legal system as well as ancient tribal traditions,

which are passed down through the generations in a number of texts.

Although approximately half of the Ewe people are Christians, the majority continue to believe in a **god of creation** (Mawu) as well as in a predetermined fate (dzodzome). Ancestor and spirit worship is also important, with the ancestors (togbenoliwo) representing the helpful spirits and the unpredictable ones the **voduwo** and **trowo** spirits, originating from a threatening environment and from the elements. The ancestors must be evoked in ecstatic dance rituals, during which the dancers become intermediaries between the physical and invisible worlds.

The Igbo

The settlement area of today's approximately 20 million **Igbo** (formerly Ibo), the majority of whom are Christians, covers the savannah and rainforest regions of south-eastern **Nigeria**. Their language (Igbo) belongs to the **Kwa group of languages.**

Along with crop farming (yams, cassava, taro, maize) and fishing, the livelihood of the Igbo, one of the largest population groups in Nigeria after the **Yoruba** and **Hausa**, is largely based on trade and handicrafts.

The traditional social order of the Igbo – who live in villages and settlements administered by a council of elders – is based on the patrilineal extended family, which is headed by the eldest family member.

The Igbo's religion features a superior god of creation, **Chi**, who – along with the earth goddess **Ala** – controls the earth's fertility. There are also numerous lesser gods and spirits who are venerated within the context of the traditional ancestor worship. Nigeria gained independence from the British colonial administration in 1960, and in 1967 the Igbo – whose numbers were decimated by the slave trade on the West African coast during the nineteenth century – declared eastern Nigeria as the independent state of **Biafra**, which was abolished in 1970 following three years' of civil war.

Among the Dogon, all important decisions are made by the council of elders and the Hogon.

Among the Dogon, the village community is traditionally run by a council of elders, headed by the **Hogon**, who is both religious leader and judge and whose insignia, consisting of a rod and a stone worn around the neck, are inherited. The villages usually

from agriculture (millet, maize, yams, tobacco, cotton), and in the towns mainly from handicrafts (dying, weaving, metalwork and leather work). Their beneficial geographic location to the south of the major **trans-Sahara trade route** helped the Hausa become

Like many African women, the Yoruba women pay a great deal of attention to their appearance. A distinctive feature of this West African people is their incidence of twin births. At an average of 45 per thousand births, the rate is four times higher than that of industrialised countries. According to Yoruba mythology, twins are known as the 'children of thunder' because they are considered to be direct descendants of the thunder god, Shango.

The Yoruba

The approximately 22 million **Yoruba**, whose settlement area covers **Nigeria**, **Benin** and **Togo**, make up about 20 per cent of the total current population of Nigeria. Their language (Yoruba) belongs to the large **Kwa group of languages**. The Yoruba living in the south are largely Christian, while the majority of the northern inhabitants are Muslims.

The Yoruba live mainly from the growing of yams, maize, bananas and millet, with cocoa grown for trade purposes. Both agriculture and the control of the overall marketing system is traditionally reserved for women. The men are mainly merchants or craftsmen whose carvings and bronze artefacts fetch high prices at today's international art auctions.

With the historical city of Ife in south-western Nigeria, the Yoruba already had a key trading base at least a thousand years ago. The city's links extended as far as the coast as well as into the interior of the country.

Following the substantial decimation of the population by the Portuguese slave trade in the fifteenth century, the powerful **Oyo** kingdom was established in the seventeenth century, disintegrating into numerous small city states 200 years later. These are still ruled by kings (Oba) today who, as god kings, also used to be bestowed with sacral tasks.

The Ashanti

The former empire of today's approximately 12 million **Ashanti**, the majority of whom live in **Ghana** and **Ivory Coast**, is thought to have been established in about 1700 as a result of the merger of several principalities. The empire was ruled by a king (Asantehene), who was in charge of strictly organised warriors and dignitaries.

The economic success of the Ashanti was largely based on the extensive gold resources found within their settlement area, as portrayed by their national symbol, the sacred '**Golden Stool**', which represents the world of the ancestors and is reproduced in numerous articles of jewellery and ornaments made by goldsmiths. The Ashanti's famous gold weights – small figures made from brass castings and now exchanged for gold – are sought-after collectors' pieces.

Today the majority of the Ashanti, whose social order is largely matrilineal in structure, live from agriculture (including yams, maize, cassava, millet and fruit). The Ashanti are also known to be talented wood carvers, potters and textile manufacturers, especially with regard to their vibrant, printed **Adrinka** and woven **Kente fabrics**.

The Fulbe

The settlement area of the approximately 8 million **Fulbe**, who are also known as the **Fula**, **Fulani**, **Peul** or **Toucouleur**, extends from **Senegal** to **Mali**, **Guinea**, **Togo**, **Nigeria** and **Cameroon** as far as Chad. Their language is **Ful**, which, like the related Wolof language, belongs to the group of West-Atlantic languages that developed in Senegal about a thousand years ago.

The origins of the Fulbe have never been fully explained but it appears that, as a consequence of trans-Saharan trade, they are the descendants of a variety of ethnic groups, including North African peoples.

The Fulbe can be divided into four groups, which are based on their economic and cultural differences. These groups consist of the relatively light-skinned nomads, whose livelihood is based on livestock breeding and who are the least Islamised; the semi-nomadic herdsmen, who engage both in crop farming and cattle breeding; the settled farmers, who live solely from agriculture; and the dark-skinned Toucouleur who live as devout Muslims in the towns and villages of West Africa and constitute the religious and political elite in the respective regions.

1 Scenes from the mythical and colonial era are re-enacted by the Dogon from Mali in West Africa.

2 The faces of these young Bororo men are painted with impressive make-up. The Bororo are a sub-group of the Fulbe.

3 The surviving female family members have donned red dresses and their most valuable gold jewellery on the occasion of the death of a wealthy Ashanti in Kumasi in central Ghana. Mourners who are close friends of the family attend the funeral dressed in black.

Maasai women are proud and confident, playing an important role in the traditional economic order. They make glass bead jewellery, which they sell to tourists, and are also responsible for hut building and animal care.

In the event of physical abuse by her husband – who has to pay a bride price in the form of cattle upon marriage – a Maasai woman is entitled to demand a divorce (kitala) and may return to her family's kraal.

The Pangwe

The settlement area of the approximately 2 million **Pangwe**, also known as the **Mpangwe** and **Pahouin**, to which the **Beti**, **Bulu** and **Fang** tribes belong, covers northern **Gabon**, **Equatorial Guinea** and **southern Cameroon**. Their common language (Fang) belongs to the **Bantu** group and is today the lingua franca of **Gabon** and **Equatorial Guinea**.

The Pangwe live in small villages, each ruled by a village chief and the council of elders. They are characteristically crop farmers in the tropical rainforest and are considered to be exceptional blacksmiths who produced a kind of currency based on iron and copper bars in the pre-colonial

Warriors of the Savannah

Until the end of the nineteenth century the tall, slim Maasai – the personification of the proud African warrior in the West – still held sway over large parts of Kenya and northern Tanzania, but they were gradually driven ever further into infertile areas by the Europeans (Great Britain, Germany) during the course of colonisation, with the result that today they have access to only a fraction of their former territory. With their bright, distinctive clothing, their long spears and their abundance of vibrant, eye-catching jewellery, the striking Maasai warriors are frequently the subject of photographs taken by the safari tourists who flood the country every year.

era. The Pangwe also used to be renowned for their finely carved wooden and ivory sculptures and masks, the white masks of the famous Ngil secret society being especially valuable. The carved tree bark containers (bieri) decorated with wooden figures, which were originally used to store the mortal remains of the ancestors, are highly sought-after collectors' pieces today.

The Tutsi/Hutu

Today's around 2 million **Tutsi** (Tussi, Watussi), who belong to the **Bantu peoples** and are considered the world's tallest people on average, live as nomads with their herds of cattle (Watussi cattle) mainly in **Rwanda** and **Burundi**, as well as in the east of the Republic of the **Congo** and a small area of **Tanzania**. Although they make up only about 15 per cent of the overall population of Rwanda and Burundi, they dominate the **Hutu** (Bahutu), who today number over 12 million and are also a Bantu people living primarily from crop farming. The latter have been suppressed and ultimately subordinated since the fifteenth century by the immigrant Tutsi, who subsequently established a feudal kingdom with strict ethnic segregation and adopted the language of the Hutu (Kinyarwanda). The Hutu worked for the Tutsi as tenant farmers and herdsmen and were obliged to pay taxes to the king, to whom the entire country belonged. Severe ethnic feuds became a repeated occurrence following independence in 1962, ending in the bloody civil war of

1990 and 1994, which cost the lives of over 1 million people.

The Pygmies

The term **Pygmy** (Greek: 'dwarfish') is the collective term for the people, usually under 1.5 m in height, who live in the **tropical rainforests of Central Africa**; they are now estimated to total only about 150,000. The Pygmy peoples include the **Bambuti** tribe in the north-east of the Democratic Republic of the **Congo**, whose cultural features make them one of the most primordial Pygmy groups, the **Binga** in the west of the **Central African Republic**, the **Bongo** in **Gabon**, the **Bagielli** in **Cameroon** and the **Twa** (Batwa), who have interbred significantly with the Congoid peoples in the east of the Republic of **Congo** as well as in **Rwanda**, **Uganda** and **Burundi**; the tribes have adopted the language of the respective tribes in adjoining territories.

The Pygmies live in rainforest areas, mainly as hunter-gatherers. Small monogamous families are the norm, with the majority of families amalgamating to form

A warrior of the Sumburu, a Kenyan people related to the Massai.

small groups; they also maintain close economic ties with the settled farmers.

With the increasing restriction of their original territories, to which they have adapted extraordinarily well, many Pygmies have now moved into savannah regions, which are unsuitable both climatically and biologically. This has resulted in such a significant increase in illness and mortality that the Pygmy peoples seem likely to survive only for another few decades.

The Swahili

Today's approximately 600,000 **Swahili** people (formerly Suaheli, in Arabic 'sawahili' means 'coastal inhabitants') live in the East African coastal regions of **Somalia**, **Kenya**, **Tanzania** and **Mozambique**, as well as on the islands off the mainland. Their language, **Kiswahili** (Swahili), is a Bantu language, with many words borrowed from Arabic; it is one of the most important lingua francas in East Africa.

The modern-day Swahili are the descendants of southern Arabian and Persian merchants who settled on the East African coast in the eighth and ninth centuries, interbreeding with the indigenous Bantu peoples. The result was a Muslim mixed-blood population whose livelihood, in addition to fishing, crop farming and handicrafts, was mainly based on the trade with India that was already in existence in the third century. The most important merchandise included ivory, gold, iron and copper, with the slave trade gaining the upper hand in the eighteenth century, when slaves were exchanged for spices, carpets, fabrics or ironware.

The Azande

Today around 1 million **Azande**, who speak **Adamaua-Ubangi**, are spread across the humid savannah of the Democratic Republic of the **Congo**, the **Central African Republic** and **Sudan**, where they live as farmers on widely scattered plots of land, growing crops (cassava,

peanuts, rice, millet and sweet potatoes) and hunting, as well as breeding small livestock.

Ancestor worship and the belief in spirits play a major role in the Azande's traditional religion. Domestic problems, accidents, illness, failed harvests and death are often attributed to witchcraft, the culprit being identified with the help of the oracle and punished using corresponding counter spells.

The Azande became known mainly for their diverse musical skills and fine handicrafts. Their traditional musical instruments include a harp-like instrument and a stringed instrument similar to a mandolin.

Among the Azande, polygamy is permitted only within the aristocratic upper class, with girls often becoming engaged to nobles in their early childhood.

The Maasai

The settlement area of today's around 500,000 **Maasai** ('speakers of the Maa language') covers **southern Kenya** and **northern Tanzania**. Their twelve tribes are divided into larger clans such as the **Samburu**, **Laikipia**, **Kiangop**, **Kapiti** or **Kisongo**, who amalgamate under the leadership of a common chief to form groups of twos and threes.

The male Maasai are divided into three age groups – the warrior (ilmurran), older (ilmoruak) and eldest (iltasati). The warriors – young circumcised men who are aged between 15 and 20 – live in their own **kraals** (manyattas), each comprising 49 huts. Their main tasks include defending the women, settlements and herds from enemy attacks, as well as the conveying of messages. Their weapons consist of spears, daggers, clubs and buffalo-skin shields.

After about seven years the warriors are incorporated into the ilmoruak group during the **Eunoto ceremony**, and a second major ceremony (Olng'gescher) follows a further 14 to 20 years later to mark the entry into the eldest group, with the ritual shepherd's staff as their hallmark.

Since the Maasai do not have chiefs, the elders are responsible

A number of ethnic groups fall under the collective term *Nilots* and live in Ethiopia, Kenya, Uganda and Tanzania. The eastern and south-eastern Nilots, the so-called *Lotuko, Bari* and *Turkana* peoples (*Maasai, Nandi, Suk, Kramojo,* Tatoga*), are also referred to as *Nilohamites* because they speak a Hamitic language.
A further distinction is made between the western Nilots (*Nuer, Shilluk*) and the southern Nilots (*Nandi, Kipsigi*).

for all decisions relating to the well-being of the community. They also take the role of counsellors, judges and organisers of ceremonies, only now having permission to marry and start a family. The **Laibon** (leader) also comes from the older group and enjoys great prestige as fortune teller, healer and master of ceremonies. The eldest group is especially revered for their position as elders and counsellors. According to their tribal mythology, the Maasai consider themselves to be the legitimate owners of all cattle, with 50 animals indicative of only marginal prosperity and the wealthy members of the tribe able to possess up to a thousand cattle. Cow's milk is the staple food of the Maasai and cattle are slaughtered only for special occasions, such as religious ceremonies. Sheep and goats are also kept for bartering, while donkeys are used as a means of transport.

The Maasai worship the male-female god **Engai** who lives in the **Oldoinyo le Engai** mountain and is revealed as thunder and lightning. The warriors appeal to this god prior to the hunt in the **Olpul** cult festival, while the women hold their own cult rituals (Alamal Loonkituak).

An important role is played by the mothers who, during the ritual transition of their sons from warriors to the older group, cut their long hair as a symbol of their previously untrammelled lives. The ritual also involves the slaughter of an ox, and the women eat the meat to indicate that the young men have grown up and can now provide food for their mothers.

The Kikuyu

The approximately 5 million **Kikuyu**, who belong to the largest group of Bantu peoples, live mainly in the highlands of **Kenya**; they became famous throughout the world in the mid-twentieth century as the initiators of the **Mau-Mau rebellion** against British rule.

In addition to farming a variety of crops (beans, yams, cassava, sugar cane, sorghum, millet, potatoes, maize, bananas) and growing goods for export (coffee, tea, tobacco), the Kikuyu's livelihood is largely based on livestock breeding (cattle, goats, sheep), which also provides the measure of social prestige. The Kikuyu are also talented potters and blacksmiths.

Despite Christianization, the customary sacrificial rituals at the holy tree or shrines dedicated to the ancestors continue to play a major role in the traditional Kikuyu religion. The medicine men (mundu mugo and murogi) are just as important and, in addition to healing the sick, they are also responsible for carrying out the traditional rain rituals.

The Lunda

The settlement area of today's approximately 3.5 million **Lunda**, also known as the **Balunda** or the **Kalunda**, extends from the south of the Democratic Republic of the Congo as far as the adjoining countries of **Zambia** and **Angola**; their language (Cilunda) belongs to the group of **Bantu** languages. The Lunda today live in small village communities and make a livelihood mainly from crop farming and breeding small livestock. After around 1750 they were masters of a mighty empire, which, due to the strategically adept integration policies of the different Lunda clans, also included other tribes such as the **Yaka** or **Chokwe**, whose political leaders took on important functions in the Lunda system of government as '**lords of the earth**' but who were also obliged to pay tributes to the king. Their territory was conquered briefly by the

Chokwe in 1885 and after 1898 it became a province of the **Congo** Free State. In contrast to other African peoples, the Lunda lineage is determined both patrilineally and matrilineally. Thus, in addition to the king, for example, the '**mother of the Lunda**' or '**aunt of the Lunda**' also held important offices.

1 In the largely Islamic northern part of Chad, women appear in public only when wearing a veil.

2 One of the most popular photographic motifs for safari tourists in Kenya are the young Maasai who enjoy almost unlimited freedom as warriors.

3 With his ostrich-feather headdress, this Maasai warrior demonstrates that he has passed the test of courage.

4 These Tutsi dancers would have you forget that, only a few years ago, over 1 million people lost their lives in the war between the Hutu and Tutsi.

Southern Africa

*Of today's approximately 80,000 inhabitants of the **Seychelles**, some 90 per cent are the descendants of black slaves and their former French colonial masters. They enjoy one of the highest standards of living among the African nations.*

The Herero

Until the early twentieth century, the majority of the **Herero** (Ova-herero), who today total around 100,000, lived as nomads in the south-west of **Angola**, as well as in **central** and **northern Namibia**, where they settled in the seventeenth and eighteenth centuries after migrating from the north. Around 65,000 of the then 80,000 Herero lost their lives in the 1904 Herero uprising against their German colonial masters, who had expelled them from their original pasture areas; as a result their traditional lifestyle and culture have largely been lost. Today the majority of the Herero, whose language belongs to the Bantu languages and is one of the languages of instruction in Namibia, work as craftsmen and traders in Namibia's towns. The majority of Herero have long been Christianised so that the traditional ancestor worship plays very little part.

The Bantu

The term Bantu (ba-ntu = 'person') refers to some 200 tribes comprising more than 100 million people in Central, East and southern Africa. They speak over 400 languages; the most widespread, Swahili, is spoken by around 40 million people today. Due to the ethnic diversity, there are cultural differences as well as similarities, such as widespread polygamy and a social structure that is generally patrilineal.

The Ndebele

The Ndebele belong to the south-eastern Bantu tribe the Nguni. Originally from modern-day Natal, they fled north in 1820, as a result of warlike disputes, to the territory between the Zambezi and the Limpopo, where they founded the Matabele empire in 1836; it was subsequently destroyed in 1893 by British-South African troops.
The Ndebele women are famous for their brightly painted clay brick houses.

The Khoikhoi

The **Khoikhoi** (meaning 'person of the people') total around 100,000. They used to be referred to pejoratively as 'Hottentots' (Afrikaans: 'stutterer'). They are very light-skinned in comparison to the adjoining peoples, and are often no more than 1.5 m tall. They originate from northern **Botswana**, but today live mainly in **southern Namibia**. In terms of language and culture they are closely related to the adjoining San ('bushmen') – they speak a **Khoisan language**.

The Himba in northern Namibia belong to the Herero peoples.

The Khoikhoi used to live mainly as nomads (cattle and sheep), and were also hunter-gatherers. During the course of colonisation by the Boers during the eighteenth and nineteenth centuries, however, the **Lesser Nama** tribe in particular was absorbed by the other population groups in southern Africa, while other Khoikhoi groups were driven into the less fertile areas by the adjoining Bantu peoples and the Greater Nama tribe largely became settled livestock breeders. Today, the Khoikhoi, who are mainly Christians, live from either crop farming in the reserves or as paid workers in the towns.

The San

The approximately 60,000 **San** living in **Namibia**, **southern Angola** and **Botswana**, who were referred to as 'bushmen' by the first European settlers, are considered to be the direct descendants of southern Africa's original inhabitants. Only around five per cent of the San, who are somewhat smaller in stature than their relatives the **Khoikhoi**, still live as hunter-gatherers like their forebears, the rest of them working mainly as herdsmen.
In traditional San society, which consists of loosely associated groups of twenty to thirty family members without a hierarchical system, the men are responsible for hunting small animals while the women and children gather wild plants and fruit. In keeping with their nomadic way of life, the San live in simple grass huts and caves or use semi-circular mats as wind protection.

The Ovambo (Ambo)

Ovambo (Ambo) is the collective term for eight Bantu peoples with a population total of around 1 million, who live mainly in **southern Angola** and **northern**

The white Afrikaners

The approximately 3 million white Afrikaners are the descendants of the Boers (farmers), Dutch settlers who first set foot on African soil at the Cape of Good Hope in 1652 in order to farm the land. Their language, Afrikaans, is a mixture of Dutch and many words borrowed from English and the African languages. Conflict with the English over gold and diamonds led to the Boer War in 1899, won by the British in 1902. The policy of racial segregation (apartheid) was introduced in 1948 under the Afrikaner government and endured until the 1990s.
Under this system the blacks were prohibited from attending white schools and universities, nor were they allowed to settle in white areas; even public transport and buildings were segregated on the grounds of race for many years.

Namibia and make up about 50 per cent of Namibia's black African population.
The livelihood of the Ovambo, most of whom live in scattered individual settlements, is traditionally based on growing grain and vegetables (wheat, millet, maize) as well as livestock breeding (especially cattle, sheep, goats) and hunting. Many of them are also successful traders,

but today around 50 per cent of the men work in Namibia's mines and industrial sector.
Until the beginning of the twentieth century, some of the Ovambo peoples lived in their own small states headed by a hereditary priest king. Beneath these were the free people, the slaves being at the lowest level. Polygamy used to be customary, with each wife living in her own house with her children.

The Sotho-Tswana

After the **Nguni**, the 10 to 15 million **Sotho-Tswana** form the largest ethnic and linguistic group in southern Africa, also including the **northern** and **southern Sotho**, as well as the Bantu-speaking **Tswana**, who today number around 5 million and are probably among the oldest of southern Africa's immigrant groups; their settlement area covers **Namibia**, **Botswana**, **Zimbabwe** and the **Republic of South Africa**. Traditionally the Tswana livelihood is based on livestock breeding and crop farming (maize, millet, peanuts) but today the majority of the men are low-paid workers in the mines or are hired as seasonal workers in the large cities. Marriage between cousins used to be a widespread feature of the Tswana's traditional social order, the majority of whom have long been Christianised. The family clan is the most important social unit, with several related families living in close proximity to one another, headed by the eldest male family member.

The Xhosa

The approximately 3 million **Xhosa**, referred to pejoratively as '**kaffirs**' by the first white settlers, live in the Republic of South Africa and, like the Zulus, belong to the **Nguni** group.
Traditionally the Xhosa, among whom polygamy used to be common, are crop farmers (millet, maize), livestock breeders (cattle) and craftsmen. Today, however, almost half of the men are employed as migrant workers in the mines or in the industrial

*Although today many **Zulus** work in the cities, the mines or for the white farmers, their traditions remain very much alive. For instance, their ritual dances involve displaying weapons – especially spears and shields – and wearing the distinctive traditional dress. The range of costume extends from light fabric drapes to impressive loincloths made from goats' leather or from leopard skins, with intricately beaded belts.*

sector. On the one hand, the loss of their traditional values is the result of heavy casualties suffered during conflicts of the seventeenth and eighteenth centuries ('Kaffir Wars') against the **Boers** and the **English**, and on the other hand is due to the so-called **Xhosa cattle killings** of 1856–7. This crisis saw tens of thousands of people starve or become impoverished after the Xhosa slaughtered their entire cattle herds and ceased tilling their fields when their prophets predicted the recapture of former territories and the expulsion of the whites in return for such a sacrifice. Their traditional culture and the chiefs' dynasties disintegrated as a result, and the Xhosa were forced to work on the farms or in the mines. They later formed the core of the African National Congress (ANC) under Nelson Mandela.

The Zulus

Today's approximately 7.5 million **Zulus** who, like the **Swazi** and the **Xhosa**, belong to the **Nguni** group, live in the east of the Republic of South Africa as well as in Swaziland; their language (Zulu) belongs to the group of **Bantu languages**.
At the beginning of the nineteenth century the Zulus established a powerful kingdom based on strict military organisation; it was first weakened through colonisation by the **English** and the **Boers** and ultimately defeated in 1879 in the war against the English.
Traditionally the Zulus lived from crop farming (millet, maize), livestock breeding (cattle) as well as from handicrafts (dyed leather work, metalwork, basketry), but today they earn a living mainly as migrant workers. The villages comprise thatched mud huts arranged in a circle around the village square and fortified by dense thorn bushes. The village community is usually made up of several family clans headed by the eldest male member.
Ancestor worship is the most important feature of the traditional Zulu religion, with **Unkulunkulu**, the mythological forefather, to whom homage is paid in numerous rituals and ceremonies.

The Swazi

The approximately 1 million **Swazi**, whose settlement area covers **Swaziland** and **Mozambique** as far as the Republic of South Africa, belong to the **Nguni** group and speak **Siswati**, a Bantu language that also contains **Khoisan** elements.
The Swazi are traditionally crop and livestock farmers, although today only about 20 per cent of them can make a living from farming alone, with the rest forced to supplement their income as migrant workers.

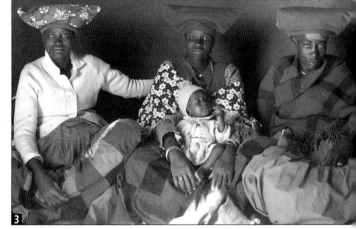

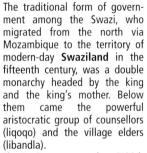

The traditional form of government among the Swazi, who migrated from the north via Mozambique to the territory of modern-day **Swaziland** in the fifteenth century, was a double monarchy headed by the king and the king's mother. Below them came the powerful aristocratic group of counsellors (liqoqo) and the village elders (libandla).
The territory was made a British protectorate at the end of the nineteenth century, entailing few restrictions for the monarchs but with the loss of two-thirds of the land to white settlers. The introduction of the so-called hut tax in 1915 also forced many Swazis to become workers for the white large property owners. Swaziland became independent in 1968 with the founding of a parliamentary monarchy. However, the parliament was abolished by **King Sobhuza II** in 1977 and today the country is ruled by his grandson **Mswati III**.

Polygamy is common practice among the Swazi; however, only the king is allowed to have more than ten wives. The homesteads where the head of the family lives with his wives and children, together with the married sons and their families, form the basic economic and social units among the Swazi.

1 Like many South African peoples, Zulu women like to wear bright clothing and striking headgear.

2 The seemingly old-fashioned ceremonial outfits of many Herero women are based on fashions of the Victorians in the nineteenth century.

3 The self-confidence of these proud Herero women is also based on their economic independence.

4 The Ndebele of the Republic of South Africa are famous for their bright, clay brick houses, which are elaborately decorated by the Ndebele women.

Australia and Oceania

With a surface area of 7.6 million sq. km, Australia is the smallest continent. It was first discovered by Europeans in the early seventeenth century, and was gradually settled by British colonists. The indigenous Australians, the Aborigines, were forcibly resettled into reservations as a result. Central Australia consists of deserts with scattered mountain ranges and isolated mountains, the most famous of them being Uluru (formerly known as Ayers Rock), a massive monolith rising out of the sand. Just off the coast lies the Great Barrier Reef, the largest coral reef on Earth. The flora and fauna of Australia are unique, including kangaroos, duckbilled platypuses, koalas, eucalyptus (gum) trees and mimosa bushes.

Oceania consists of 10,000 islands with a total land mass of some 800,000 sq. km. The islands of Melanesia, Micronesia, Polynesia, New Zealand and Hawaii cover a vast area of 70 million sq. km. Palm-fringed beaches and blue lagoons make the islands a tropical paradise.

Australia and Oceania, physical

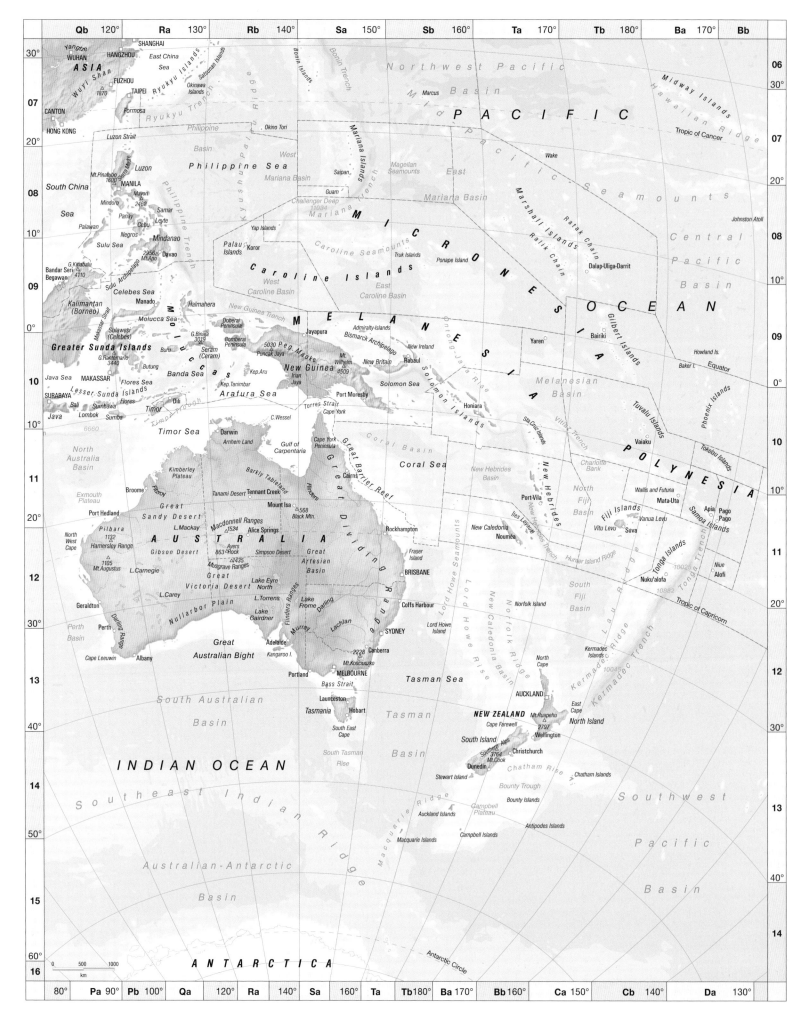

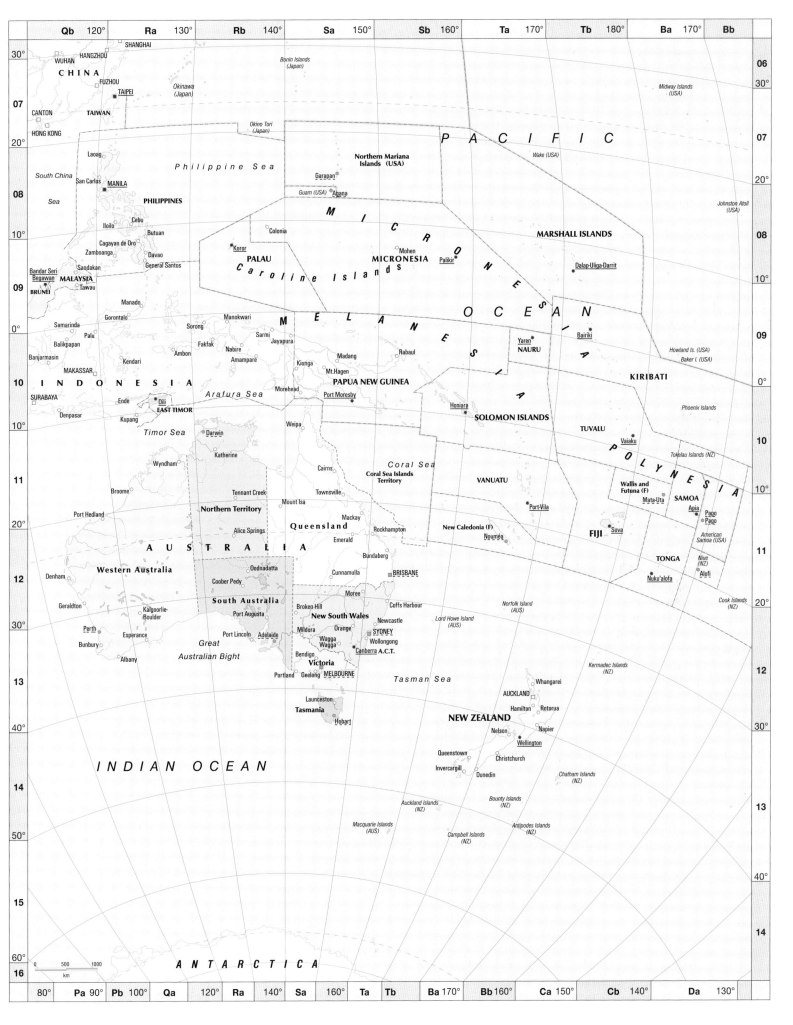

The Corroboree is the name of an Aboriginal ritual song and dance. The Aborigines believe that by performing songs they can gain a connection to the mythological 'dreamtime'.

The History of Australia and Oceania

The fifth continent and the Pacific islands were discovered in the sixteenth century by European seafarers, but this remote region did not interest the colonial powers for long. It was not until the late eighteenth century that the

Polynesia: carving of the god Tiki on the Marquesas Islands.

British began to use Australia as a prison colony. At the start of the nineteenth century, Australia and New Zealand became independent, but other regions of Oceania remained under European rule. Japanese expansion before and during World War II was a great threat to this dominance. After 1945, US influence increased, and the region was now regarded as part of its sphere of interest. It was only relatively recently that many of the islands were able to assert their independence. The indigenous peoples and their cultures had been almost completely suppressed. Only since the mid-twentieth century has the attitude of the descendants of the settlers changed towards them.

The History of Australia and Oceania

*Ancient rituals are still performed by the Maoris, New Zealand's indigenous people, in the village of **Whakarewarewa** in the district of Rotorua on the North Island. Since the 1980s, movements to revive Maori culture have been in the ascendant.*

Australia

As the remotest part of the world, from the European point of view, Australia was for a long time unknown to the West, but from the late Middle Ages it played an important theoretical role, since the existence was assumed of a so-called southland, terra australis incognita, as a counterpart to the northern land mass. Admittedly Spaniards and Portuguese reached the area as early as the sixteenth century, but it was not until later that the continent was recognised as a contiguous land mass.

The Aborigines, the original inhabitants of Australia, settled the continent some 60,000 years ago, and presumably it was before the arrival of the Europeans that they began to make contacts with traders from present-day Indonesia and New Guinea. They lived as hunter-gatherers and developed a complex social structure as well as a complicated mythological world of the imagination which encompassed all areas of life.

History of discovery

From the fifteenth century onwards, the Portuguese engaged in a flourishing trade with India from the west coast of Africa, which strengthened interest in the discovery of the legendary terra australis. Enthusiasm for pushing further south-east soon waned, however, since wind conditions were not conducive to voyages of reconnaissance. After the discovery of the Solomon Islands in 1567 the Spaniards hoped to take possession of gold and great territories for the Spanish crown by means of two expeditions from South America, in 1595 and 1605, but these two voyages of discovery ended in failure.

The real story of exploration first begins with the Dutch. In 1606, Willem Janzon reached the Torres Straits between the Australian mainland and New Guinea, and sighted the north coast of Australia. The Dutch governor-generals in Batavia equipped further expeditions, and in 1616 Europeans first trod on Australian soil, under the command of Dirk Hartog. Further discoveries followed, in which Abel Janzoon Tasman played the most important role. In 1642 he circumnavigated

Australia, discovering Tasmania and New Zealand in the process. On a second voyage, in 1644, he explored the north coast. Although the newly discovered land was called New Holland, the Dutch made no territorial claims to it, and soon stopped visiting the new continent.

The first British voyages of discovery proceeded in a similar manner. The descriptions by the English pirate William Dampier, who explored the west coast on two expeditions in the early eighteenth century, failed to arouse the interest of the British in further voyages. It was only the three journeys of James Cook that led to British claims to the continent. In 1770, Cook discovered Botany Bay

James Cook claimed Australia and New Zealand for Great Britain.

and took possession of the area for the British crown at Possession Island, naming it New South Wales. His second voyage, in 1772–1775, destroyed the notions of a southland and finally provided evidence of an island continent. Also in 1772, the French made an appearance, when Marion Dufresne prepared maps and other French navigators explored the south coast. No one was prepared to challenge British supremacy, but it was not until the

early nineteenth century that the Australian coasts were completely explored. Between 1801 and 1803 Matthew Flinders circumnavigated the entire continent for the first time, having first proved in 1798 with the help of the naval doctor George Bass that Tasmania was an island. At Flinders' suggestion, the continent was officially named Australia in 1817, as an allusion to the long-sought terra australis.

Colonisation

In spite of Australia's supposed unattractiveness, towards the end of the eighteenth century the country acquired a new and special socio-economic, significance for the British. After Britain's defeat in the American War of Independence it was no longer possible to transport convicts from the mother country's overcrowded prisons. So the plan was conceived in 1786 to build a penal colony at Botany Bay. In early 1788, Arthur Phillip arrived in Botany Bay with a first group of convicts, and on 26 January he founded – somewhat further north, the first permanent European settlement – Sydney.

By 1867, prisoners had continued to be deported to Australia,

forming the driving force of the early settlement. By 1852, as many as 150,000 people had been deported to New South Wales and the colony of Tasmania that had been founded in 1803. But from 1793, the first voluntary settlers began to arrive, creating the basis of the Australian economy by sheep-rearing. The conquest of the Blue Mountains by Gregory Blaxland and William Charles Wentworth, as well as the further opening up of the interior, now allowed large herds of cattle to be kept on extended areas of grazing land.

Around 1820, stock-breeder pushed forward into Victoria and southern Queensland; the penal colony of Western Australia was founded in 1829, and South Australia in 1837. In 1851, the colony of Victoria, with its capital, Melbourne, split off from New South Wales and, in 1859, Queensland also separated from New South Wales. A gold rush in the mid-nineteenth century ensured a further great influx of immigrants.

The conflicts of interest between stock-breeder and farmers, as well as the liberal socialist views of the new urban population triggered the development of political institutions in the mid-nineteenth century. Free trade was introduced and the eastern colonies were granted new constitutions in 1850, which allowed them extensive self-determination and self-government. Free gifts of land were replaced by the regular sale of property, and governments had to answer to elected parliaments. In formal terms British colonial policy regarded the Aborigines as equals, but in practice the sheep-farmers conducted an inhumane and brutal campaign against the natives. The few survivors were finally herded together in reservations. It was not until the mid-twentieth century that the indigenous population of Australia was able to regain its original size.

The federated state

The rapid increase in population and the rapid growth of the cities led in the mid-nineteenth century to the formation of an individual Australian culture, the foundation of universities, the building of railways and a strengthening of the workers' movement. In spite of the cultural similarities between

the six colonies, their relationship was marked by fierce rivalry. The Labour Party, in particular, pursued a resolute policy of national union. The positive outcomes of referenda in all six colonies finally led to the creation of the Commonwealth of Australia, which was confirmed by the British parliament in 1900 and came into force on 1 January 1901. The new constitution consisted of a mixture of British and American elements. In order to strengthen the concept of federation, in 1908, the capital was moved from Melbourne to the newly founded Canberra. Even before the start of World War I, comprehensive social welfare legislation and general conscription were introduced.

In World War I, Australia sent about 330,000 volunteers to fight on the Allied side in the European theatres of war and confront the German colonial troops in the Pacific. In 1919, Australia received a mandate from the League of Nations to govern the former German overseas territories of Kaiser-Wilhelmsland (now part of Papua New Guinea), the Bismarck Archipelago, the Solomon Islands and Nauru.

The outbreak of World War II meant cutting the cord that connected Australia to the mother country. Since Britain was not able to protect Australia effectively against the threat of Japanese invasion, a military alliance was concluded with the USA. This did not prevent the Australians from fighting bravely in all the theatres of war, but especially against the Japanese. Fortunately, the Australian forces were able to prevent a Japanese invasion of Australia. Australia also performed a valuable role during and after World War II in supply Great Britain with desperately needed food supplies.

After 1945, the country was transformed into a highly industrialised nation of growing importance in terms of foreign policy. Emotional attachment to the British Crown continued to dwindle, even though the 'White Australia Policy', banning non-white immigration despite the fact that the country was, and still is, underpopulated, was not officially abandoned until 1973. Immigrants to Australia are still predominantly of British and Irish

*In 1808, a settlement of white colonists was discovered on **Pitcairn Island** in the South Pacific. It had been founded by nine mutineers of the famous HMS Bounty, along with six men and twelve women from modern-day Tahiti. John Adams, the last mutineer, died in 1829, and his gravestone can still be seen. The small colony was later annexed by Great Britain. The mutiny against the infamous Captain William Bligh has been the subject of several novels and three films.*

origin, with a substantial number from Italy, Greece, Cyprus.

New Zealand

When, in 1642, the Dutch seafarer Tasman became the first European to reach the west coast of the south island, New Zealand had some 125,000 inhabitants, who had immigrated from Polynesia from the ninth century onwards. In 1769, James Cook realised that it consisted of two islands, and claimed them for the British crown. Soon afterwards, British missionaries and whalers founded the first settlements, and systematic immigration began around 1840 under the auspices of the New Zealand Company.

In 1840, in the Waitangi Agreement with more than 550 Maori chieftains, Captain William Hobson secured British sovereignty and in return granted the Maoris rights of possession and British citizenship. In 1841, New Zealand became a British Crown Colony with Auckland as its capital.

High levels of immigration led in 1845–1848 and 1860–1872 to armed conflict between settlers and the Maori population, the latter being decimated in the battles. Gold-mining and sheep-breeding formed the main sources of income and ensured a steady influx of immigrants. In 1852 a first constitution was adopted, and in 1893 New Zealand became the first country in the world to introduce women's suffrage. In 1907, New Zealand was officially declared a dominion in the British Commonwealth.

In the 1970s, under a Labour government, the country ended its military involvement in Indochina and intensified its contacts with its Asian neighbours.

The main concern of post-war home affairs was relations with the Maoris, to whom 50,000 ha of land, unlawfully taken from them, were restored. In addition, programmes for the preservation of the art and culture of the Maoris have been set up.

Oceania

Most of the Pacific islands, after being discovered by white settlers, were subjected to frequent changes in foreign rule, which ended comparatively recently.

Palau, for example, became a presidential republic in 1947, with strong connections to the USA. Papua New Guinea was an Australian mandated territory until 1975. Since 1980, Micronesia and the Marshall Islands since 1990 have both been a republic with a Compact of Free Association with the USA. Nauru was liberated in 1968 from the trusteeship of the UN, and Kiribati from British rule in 1979. In 1978, the British Protectorate over the Solomon Islands and Tuvalu came to an end. Fiji declared independence in 1979, as did Vanuatu in 1980, Samoa in 1962, Tonga in 1970 and Palau in 1994.

1 The Sydney Opera House – designed by the architect Jörn Utzon – one of the city's tourist highlights, along with an accurate reconstruction of the legendary 'Bounty'.

2 Melbourne, the capital city from 1901 to 1911, has a population of just under 3 million, making it the second largest city in Australia. It is situated at the mouth of the Yarra river in Port Phillip Bay.

3 The Parliament building in the Australian capital city of Canberra was completed in 1988, a striking example of modern Australian architecture.

The Caroline Islands are the largest island group in Micronesia and consist of 963 islands and atolls, mostly of volcanic origin. Archaeological finds indicate early settlements.

The Countries of Australia and Oceania

Australia is the smallest continent and is situated between the Indian and Pacific Oceans in the southern hemisphere. Australia is often considered to include the islands of Oceania, which are scattered over an area of

Australia: Sidney Harbour Bridge a famous landmark on the skyline.

70 million sq. km. The Australian mainland is one of uniform terrain, mainly consisting of desert, including the ancient dried-up sea in what is known as the Centre. The continent's isolated position means that it has developed unique flora and fauna, many of which have been endangered by species imported from Europe. New Zealand, on the other hand, has a hugely varied landscape, reminiscent of almost every type of European landscape. Before the arrival of the Europeans, the bird life was varied but there were no land mammals. Oceania consists of some 10,000 coral atolls or islands of volcanic origin. The climate is hot and humid.

Australia

Australia

Area:	7,686,850 sq. km
Capital city:	Canberra

Form of government:
Parliamentary Monarchy and Federal State

Administrative divisions:
6 states, 2 territories

External territories:
Christmas Island, Cocos Islands, Norfolk Island, Lord Howe Island, Coral Sea Islands Territory, Ashmore and Cartier Islands, Heard Island, McDonald Islands

Population:
20.4 million
(3 inhabitants/sq. km)

Languages:
English, minority languages

GDP per capita:	US$36,600

Currency:
1 Australian dollar = 100 cents

Natural Geography

Australia is the smallest continent and the world's sixth largest country in terms of area. It measures 3,680 km from north to south, and 4,000 km from east to west. The average elevation is 300 m, and the land is approximately 70 per cent desert or semi-desert, mainly in the west and centre of the country. These regions are covered in arid grassland and are largely uninhabited. The populated areas are concentrated in the south and southeast coastal regions, which have a milder climate. Western Australia is dominated by a plateau, which includes the **Great Sandy Desert**, the **Gibson Desert** and the **Great Victoria Desert**. This tableland also contains several monadnocks, for example the famous **Uluru** (Ayers Rock), a 600 million-year-old monolith.

The central Australian basin is an arid region devoid of rivers which extends from the Gulf of Carpenteria in the north, through the Simpson Desert and as far as **Lake Eyre** (16 m below sea-level), a salt lake on the south coast and the lowest point on the continent. Hundreds more salt lakes of varying sizes can be found on the **Nullarbor Plain** in the southern part of the **Great Victoria Desert**.

The **Great Dividing Range** runs parallel to the east coast for a total distance of some 3000 km, and joins the foothills of the **Snowy Mountains** in the south. The **Great Barrier Reef** is located in Australian waters just off the mainland, and stretches 2,000 km, connecting in the north to the Torres Strait Islands. This is the largest coral reef on Earth, and with 1,500 varieties of fish, 400 different corals and more than 4,000 species of mollusc, it is also has the greatest variety of sea life.

The north of the country is only sparsely populated. It has tropical vegetation and grass savannahs, which towards the coast turn into mangrove swamps and rainforests. There are few significant water courses, those that there are include the Murray and Darling Rivers in the south. The interior of the country is extremely dry and most of the larger lakes are usually dry except after periods of heavy rainfall.

South-east of the mainland, separated by the Bass Strait, lies the island of **Tasmania** (67,800 sq. km), which has large areas of cool rainforest in the south-west. One fifth of this sparsely inhabited, mountainous island (highest point: Mount Ossa 1,617 m) is a nature conservation area.

Australia's unique plant and animal kingdoms have developed as a result of almost 50 million years of isolated evolution. All native Australian mammals are **marsupials**, of which there are a total of 300 species, including 60 different species of kangaroo. Other animals characteristic of the country include the koala and the emu. Australia also has large numbers of insects (such as compass termites), reptiles (including freshwater and saltwater crocodiles) and the birds range from parrots, cockatoos, and budgerigars. There are some very odd animal species, for example the egg-laying duck-billed platypus and the Tasmanian devil. The country is also home to a many poisonous spiders and snakes. Almost all the trees are eucalyptus, Australia contains some 95 per cent of this tree variety.

Climate

In general, Australia has a desert to semi-desert climate. In the south and east of the country, the climate is more maritime, while the extreme north has a tropical climate with heavy rainfall. The precipitation declines rapidly inland from the coast, where it averages more than 1,400 mm per annum. Storms can be extremely powerful and torrential, particularly in the north and north-west of the country where the rainy season lasts from November to the end of March. Average maximum temperatures in central Australia around the Tropic of Capricorn can rise to over 50°C. In the region around Canberra, winter temperatures can fall to 2°C, and maximum summer temperatures can be over 40°C.

The damage to the ozone layer over large areas of the Antarctic is a serious environmental problem, the effects of which can be felt in Australia and New Zealand in terms of high ultra-violet radiation and increased **risk of skin cancer.** Bush fires, droughts, heavy storms and flash-floods are relatively common.

Population

Ninety-two per cent of Australians are of European descent, of which the majority have **British** and **Irish** heritage. Of the remaining population, seven per cent are of **Asian** origin, while the **Aborigines** and the even smaller group of Torres Strait Islanders have minority status, making up just two per cent of the population. Some 75 per cent of Australians are Christians, but there are also minorities of Jews, Muslims, Buddhists and Hindus. Just under half the total population lives in one of the three big cities, Sydney, Melbourne and Brisbane, while large areas of the country are uninhabited. Australia's population density of 3 inhabitants/sq. km is one of the lowest on Earth. The numerous outlying farms and homesteads are located relatively close to the few main long-distance roads which cross-cross the continent. The standard of living is high, and the social and health systems are highly developed. The education system is also very well organised, and many children, particularly in the outback, receive long-distance lessons via the radio. There are several **universities**, the most famous being in Melbourne, Sydney and Canberra.

The unique culture of Australia's indigenous people remains threatened, but attempts are being made to integrate the native people into mainstream Australian life.

Melbourne: modern skyscrapers behind the Victorian Flinders Street Station on the banks of the Yarra.

PAPUA NEW GUINEA

Arafura Sea

Torres Strait

Melville I.
C.Croker
Goulburn Is.
C.Wessel
Marchinbar I.
Eastern Fields
Prince of Wales
Cape York

Bathurst I.
Beagle Gulf
Van Diemen Gulf
Wessel Islands
Albatross Bay
Weipa
Lockhart River

Cartier Is.
Darwin
Jabiru
Maningrida
Gove Pen.
Nhulunbuy (Gove)
Cape York
Princess Charlotte Bay
C.Melville
Silver Plains
Osprey Reef

Cape Londonderry
✲ KAKADU N.P.
Bickerton I.
Cooktown
C.Flattery

Kalumburu
Adelaide River
Arnhem Land
Groote Eylandt
Mossman
Coral Sea Islands Territory

Kununurra
Pine Creek
Katherine
Limmen Bight
Maria I.
Edward River
Peninsula
Cairns
1612△
Babinda
Flinders Reef
Lihou Reefs and Cays

Mt.Hann 779△
Wyndham
Mataranka
Larrimah
Sir Edward Pellew Group
Wellesley Islands
Gununa
Mornington I.
Mitchell
Ingham
Hinchinbrook I.
GREAT BARRIER REEF MARINE PARK

KIMBERLEY PLATEAU
936△ Mt.Ord
Derby
Timber Creek
Top Springs
Daly Waters
Borroloola
Karumba
Normanton
✲ WET TROPICS OF QUEENSLAND
Halifax Bay
Townsville
Marion Reef

King Leopold Ranges
✲ PURNULULU N.P.
Halls Creek
Kalkaringi
Elliott
Burketown
Croyden
Forsayth
Ayr

Fitzroy Crossing
Bungle Bungle Ranges
Barkly Tableland
Camooweal
Charters Towers
Proserpine

Fitzroy
Sturt
Tanami Desert
Barkly Homestead Roadhouse
Mount Isa
Cloncurry
Julia Creek
Richmond
Hughenden
1277△
Mackay
Broad Sound
Swain Reefs

Great Sandy Desert
Tennant Creek
Northern Territory
Black Mtn. 568△
Dajarra
Queensland
Sarina
Saumarez Reef

Percival Lakes
L.White
Lander
Wauchope
Winton
Muttaburra
Longreach
Clermont
Marlborough
Yeppoon
Wreck Reef

L.Mackay
Sandover
Boulia
Jericho 823△
Emerald
Rockhampton
Curtis I.
Cato Island

L.MacDonald
L.Hopkins
Mt.Liebig 1524△
Mt.Zeil 1511△
Alice Springs
Macdonnell Ranges
Hale
Barcaldine
Blackall
Springsure
Gladstone
Tropic of Capricorn

ppointment
A U S T R A L I A
Diamantina
Great
Tambo
Monto
Hervey Bay
Bundaberg

son Desert
L.Amadeus
Yulara
Ayers Rock
Erldunda
Simpson Desert
Windorah
Quilpie
Charleville
Injune
Taroom
Maryborough
Fraser I.

tralia
Mt.Olga 1066△ 863△
ULURU N.P.
Mt.Woodroffe 1435△
Kulgera
Finke
Peera Peera Poolanna L.
L.Yamma Yamma
Morven
Roma
Miles
Gympie

L.Carnegie
Tomkinson Ranges
Musgrave Ranges
Mt.Sir Thomas 772△
Marla
Artesian
Basin
Wandoan
Bollon
Moonie
Darling Downs
Toowoomba
Kingaroy
Caloundra

L.Wells
Oodnadatta
Macumba
Basin
Sturt Stony Desert
Thargomindah
Cunnamulla
St.George
Warwick
Moreton I.
BRISBANE
Gold Coast

Great Victoria Desert
Coober Pedy
Lake Eyre North -16
Marree
L.Blanche
Grey Range
Paroo
Dirranbandi
Goondiwindi
Ipswich
Lismore

Yeo Lake
Cosmo Newbery Mission
Jubilee L.
Lake Eyre South
Milparinka
Bourke
Brewarrina
Mungindi
Moree
Casino 1524△
Ballina

Laverton
Plumridge Lakes
L.Maurice
South Australia
Leigh Creek
1083△
White Cliffs
Louth
Walgett
Coonamble
Narrabri
Glen Innes
Grafton

L.Minigwal
Maralinga
Lake Frome
Wilcannia
Cobar
Nyngan
Coonabarabran
Tamworth
CENTRAL EASTERN RAINFOREST RESERVES
Coffs Harbour

Rebecca
Nullarbor Plain
Tarcoola
L.Torrens
Kingoonya
Pimba
Woomera
Broken Hill
Menindee
Darling
New South Wales
1555△
Armidale
Port Macquarie

goorlie-oulder
Rawlinna
Deakin
Eucla Basin
L.Everard
Lake Gairdner
1180△
Olary
Wilcannia
Ivanhoe
Roto
Dubbo
Mudgee
Singleton
C.Hawke

L.Cowan
Belladonia Motel
Head of Bight
Penong
Coorabie
Ceduna
Port Augusta
Iron Knob
Flinders Ranges
Cobar
Forbes
Orange
West Wyalong
Cowra
Bathurst
Maitland
Newcastle

Norseman
L.Dundas
Eucla Motels
Streaky Bay
Kimba
Whyalla
Port Pirie
Menindee
Lake Cargelligo
Griffith
Lithgow
SYDNEY

Esperance
C.Pasley
Anxious Bay
Kyancutta
Eyre Peninsula
Wallaroo
Port Wakefield
Murray River Basin
Wentworth
Booligal
Hay
Cootamundra
Wollongong

Israelite Bay
Twilight Cove
Pt.Culver
Flinders I.
Mount Hope
Spencer Gulf
Murray
Mildura
Balranald
Narrandera
Wagga Wagga
Goulburn

Archipelago of the Recherche
Port Lincoln
Inneston
Gulf St.Vincent
Adelaide
Renmark
Ouyen
Riverina
Albury
A.C.T.
Canberra
Batemans Bay

Great Australian Bight
C.Spencer St.Vincent
Tailem Bend
Swan Hill
Deniliquin
Wodonga
Mt.Kosciuszko 2228△
Cooma

Cape Borda
Kingscote
Victor Harbor
Keith
Pinnaroo
Lascelles
Charlton
Shepparton
Mooroopna
Wangaratta
Nimmitabel

Kangaroo I.
Kingston South East
Naracoorte
Horsham
Victoria
Bendigo
Sunbury
Great
Cann River
Eden

Beachport
Hamilton
Castlemaine
Ballarat
MELBOURNE
Orbost
C.Howe
Mallacoota Inlet

Mount Gambier
Portland
C.Nelson
Warrnambool
Geelong
Cranbourne
Sale
Bairnsdale

TWELVE APOSTLES ✲ C.Otway
Morwell
Port Welshpool
South East Point

King Island
Bass Strait
Currie
Kent Group
Flinders I.

Smithton
Somerset
Burnie
Devonport
Launceston
St.Marys
Cape Barren I.
Banks Strait
Tasman Sea

Tasmania
Rosebery
1617△
Queenstown
Tasmania
Hobart

TASMANIA WILDERNESS WORLD HERITAGE AREA ✲
L.Gordon
L.Pedder
Port Arthur
South West Cape
Bruny I.
Storm Bay
South East Cape

History and Politics

More than 50,000 years ago, a land bridge existed between Asia and Australia, and there were many waves of migration from Asia to the large island continent. Divided into several clans, they wandered in complete isolation, mainly across the northern areas, around the coasts of Australia and Tasmania.

From the Middle Ages onwards, European scholars speculated about a legendary 'unknown land of the south', the **Terra Australis Incognita**, which they thought must exist in the southern hemisphere. The Dutch sailor Willem Janszoon was the first European to find the continent in 1606, when he spied Australia's

north coast. Fellow Dutchman Abel Tasman circumnavigated the continent and explored the coast of an unknown island that he named 'Van Diemen's Land' in 1642 and 1644. This was the island now known as Tasmania, later renamed in his honour. In 1770, Captain James Cook took possession of New South Wales for Great Britain. The British first used the continent as a **penal colony**. The first British settlers landed in Botany Bay in 1788 and founded Port Jackson, the heart of modern-day **Sydney**. Other cities which originated as penal colonies include Newcastle (founded in 1804) and Brisbane (1824). The first free British

settlers appeared in 1793 and founded Perth (1829), Melbourne (1835) and Adelaide (1836). From 1788 to 1865, Great Britain deported 160,000 prisoners to the continent, which was renamed Australia in 1817 after the name was popularised by Matthew Flinders, the British

explorer who circumnavigated and explored the continent. From 1851 to 1859, the first **gold rush** attracted a great wave of migration, laying the foundations of the six modern states, which fought for a greater measure of autonomy. In 1901, the six British colonies united to form the **Commonwealth of Australia,** a dominion of the British Empire. At this time, 3.8 million Australians lived in the country, and were almost exclusively of British and Irish origin. In 1927, Parliament moved to the newly established capital city of

Australia

*Large **trucks** for a large country. Australia's road network runs for 913,000 km and massive lorries, like these on Stuart Highway in the Northern Territory, transport goods across long distances around the country.*

Canberra, although Australia did not become officially independent until 1942. Since the end of World War II, Australia's population has doubled as people from a total of 120 countries have made a new home there.

The **native inhabitants** (Aborigines) of Australia have only been recognised as equal citizens and have only had citizenship and the right to vote since 1967. Their numbers plummeted in the first 100 years of European settlement from around 700,000 to just 70,000, and in the 1930s they all but disappeared, but their number has since risen to around 200,000. In recent years, the tribes have gradually received compensation for the denial of their traditional land rights, and have also received the right of free access to their holy places, distributed throughout the continent. Finally, in 1992 the High Court of Australia, in the so-called **'Mabo Ruling'**, determined that Australia had not been an 'uninhabited land' (Terra nullius) when Great Britain had taken it over.

The Australian constitution that came into effect in 1901 provides for a **bicameral federal parliament**, consisting of the Senate (76 seats, 12 from each of the six states and two from each territory, half of which are elected every three years) and the House of Representatives (148 members, elected every three years). In addition, the six federal states and the two territories have their own parliaments.

The British monarch remains Australia's head of state and is represented by the governor-general, and the governor of each of the states. For several years, there have been discussions about a possible referendum to change Australia into a **republic**. Australia cooperates with the US and New Zealand armed forces under the ANZUS Security Treaty of 1951.

Lord Howe Island in the south Pacific and Macquarie Island, which along with some neighbouring islands belong to the Antarctic territory of Tasmania, are also part of Australian national territory. Other territories belonging to Australia include the Ashmore and Cartier Islands, which are completely protected and upon which it is forbidden to land, Christmas Island and the Cocos (Keeling) Islands in the Indian Ocean, the Coral Sea Islands and Torres Strait Islands, the uninhabited Heard Island, which is a UNESCO World Heritage Site, the McDonald Islands in the south Pacific and Norfolk Island.

Economy

In 2006, GDP was US$ 755 billion, of which five per cent came from agriculture, 25 per cent from industry and 70 per cent from services. Australia has achieved a stable rate of growth of almost four per cent over the last ten years, and is one of the top ten OECD (Organisation for Economic Co-operation and Development) countries, with the highest per capita income. The whole country is rich in natural resources. It produces significant amounts of agricultural produce, minerals, metals and fossil fuels, and is one of the **biggest exporting nations in the world**. The most important exports are natural gas and crude oil, coal, iron ore, uranium, nickel, gold, silver, zinc, copper, sapphires and opals. Australia is the biggest exporter of bauxite, lead and uncut diamonds for industrial use.

Australia produces has the largest number of **sheep** in the world and produces the most wool. The country is also the largest exporter of beef in the world and is a major producer of dairy foods and cereals. Sugar cane, fruit, cotton and vines are also cultivated.

Transport Infrastructure

Australia's **rail network** covers 38,563 km, of which 2,914 km is electrified. The rail network is concentrated in the southern part of the country. Although Australia has six rail companies, large areas of central and northern Australia have no rail service.

The **road network** has a total length of some 913,000 km, one third of which is surfaced. Large parts of the country can only be accessed by poorly maintained trails and tracks. During the rainy season in the north, many of these tracks are impassable. Australia's car ownership is 604 cars per 1000 inhabitants, making it one of the most motorised countries in the world.

Despite 8,368 km of waterways, mainly in the south-east, **inland navigation** is of minimal importance, because most stretches of river are only navigable for small, flat craft. Australia has a **merchant fleet** of more than 600 ships, and more than 60 industrial **ports**, the most important of which are Adelaide, Brisbane, Cairns, Darwin, Fremantle, Geelong, Mackay, Melbourne and Sydne. The Tasmanian ports of Hobart, Devonport and Launceston are also significant.

Air travel is of great importance, operating from more than 400 airports and partially unsurfaced runways. Australia has nine international airports.

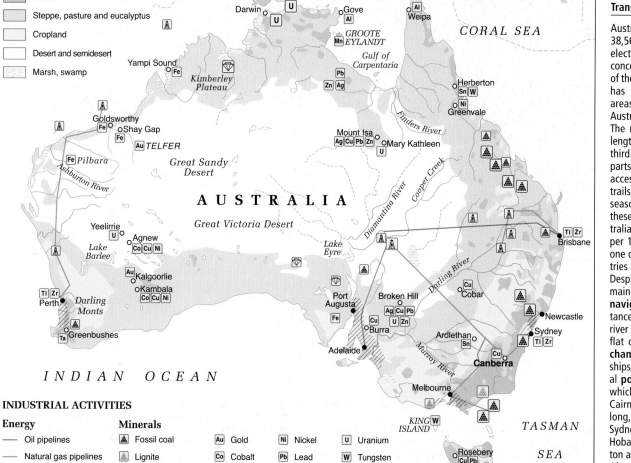

LAND USE

- Forest
- Steppe, pasture and eucalyptus
- Cropland
- Desert and semidesert
- Marsh, swamp

PAPUA-NEW GUINEA

CORAL SEA

Darwin · Gove · Weipa
GROOTE EYLANDT
Gulf of Carpentaria
Yampi Sound
Kimberley Plateau
Herberton
Greenvale
Goldsworthy · Shay Gap
TELFER
Mount Isa · Mary Kathleen
Pilbara
Ashburton River
Finders River
Great Sandy Desert
Cooper Creek
AUSTRALIA
Great Victoria Desert
Diamantina River
Yeelirrie
Agnew
Brisbane
Lake Barlee
Lake Eyre
Darling River
Kalgoorlie
Kambala
Cobar
Port Augusta
Broken Hill
Perth · Darling Monts
Newcastle
Greenbushes
Burra
Ardlethan · Sydney
Adelaide
Murray River
Canberra
INDIAN OCEAN
Melbourne
KING ISLAND
TASMAN
Rosebery
SEA
TASMANIA

INDUSTRIAL ACTIVITIES

Energy
— Oil pipelines
— Natural gas pipelines

Industry
- Industrial areas
- ● Main industrial sites

Minerals
- Fossil coal
- Lignite
- Natural gas or oil wells
- Ag Silver
- Al Bauxite
- Au Gold
- Co Cobalt
- Cu Copper
- Fe Iron
- Mn Manganese
- Ni Nickel
- Pb Lead
- Sn Tin
- Ta Tantalum
- Ti Titanium
- U Uranium
- W Tungsten
- Zn Zinc
- Zr Zirconium
- ◇ Diamonds

0   300 km

Australia is the world's largest producer and exporter of **wool**. When Europeans first settled there, they brought large numbers of Merino sheep, and sheep-farming quickly became a major occupation. Since then, the importance of wool has decreased. Today, wool exports contribute eight per cent of the total volume of exported goods, compared to 25 per cent 30 years ago. Almost half the wool comes from New South Wales and Western Australia.

Tourism

Millions of tourists visit Australia each year. The country has an amazing wealth of attractions, including endless sandy beaches, unparalleled natural beauty and great cities.

The focal point of the Northern Territory is the regional capital of Darwin. The city is a transport hub for flights to south-east Asia. The **Kakadu National Park** in Arnhem Land is one of Australia's greatest attractions. The cliff landscape contains indigenous cliff drawings which are thousands of years old. the landscape changes towards the coast to become a wetland full of natural wonders. The swamps contain rare plant and animal species. Uluru National Park lies in the south deep in the Outback. This is where the famous **Ayers Rock** and the **Olga Mountains**, called Kata Tjuta by the native inhabitants, are located. These are two of the most important holy sites for the Aborigines.

The densely populated coastal areas on the east coast are great centres for **watersports**. Brisbane is the capital of Queensland. The **Great Barrier Reef**, a chain of some 2,500 coral reefs and 500 islands is one of the most spectacular scuba-diving locations on Earth. Other popular holiday islands include Hinchinbrook Island, Orpheus Island, Heron Island, Hamilton Island and Fraser Island, which at 135 km long, is the largest desert island in the world.

The coast is lined with large tracts of rainforest, for example the **Daintree National Park** and the **Mount Spec National Park**, much of which is protected. Australia's interior is best explored by taking the Matilda Highway, which extends 1,500 km through the outback.

The heart of the state of New South Wales is the buzzing metropolis of **Sydney**, with its 40 beaches, numerous museums and parks and the world-famous Opera House. The most popular recreation area is the **Blue Mountains**, whose seemingly unreal colour is actually caused by large numbers of silvery-blue eucalyptus trees. The **Capital Territory** is dominated by the capital city of **Canberra**, which

contains the parliament and some interesting museums.

The centre of the southern state of Victoria is **Melbourne**, Australia's second largest city. In contrast to Sydney, Melbourne seems dignified and considers itself the continent's cultural centre. The city has several museums and spacious parks, as well as many theatres and hosts many festivals and sporting events.

Some of the most attractive winter sports locations are in the **Great Dividing Range** and include the region around Mount Kosciusko, the skiing areas around Beauty, Buffalo, Buller and the Baw Baw Mountains. The centre of the state of Southern

1 The Great Barrier Reef off the north coast of Australia is over 2,000 km long and comprises several islands and atolls, making it the largest coral reef on Earth.

2 The fascinating skyline of Sydney, the largest city in Australia, with modern skyscrapers, the spectacular Sydney Opera House and Sydney Harbour bridge, completed in 1932.

3 The Pinnacles are thousands of strange limestone pillars, up to 5 m high, rising out of the yellow sand in the Nambung National Park.

Australia, New Zealand

*Beneath the white lighthouse on **Cape Reinga** on New Zealand's North Island the Pacific Ocean joins the Tasman Sea. Maori mythology has it that the souls of the dead flee to this part of the far north.*

Australia is Adelaide, which has a cliff-lined coast and a famous **viticultural district**. **Flinders Range** is a popular hiking area. Australia's spectacular southern coasts have colonies of penguins. The nature conservation area of **Kangaroo Island** is home to several indigenous animal species, including kangaroos, emus and koalas. The island also has impressive sea-lion colonies. The whole western part of the state is covered by the Simpson Desert. The opal settlement of **Coober Pedy** in the middle of the outback is a truly unique wonder; due to the searing heat, all of the main buildings are located underground.

Perth is the regional capital of Australia's largest state, Western Australia, which occupies the entire western third of the country. The east is characterised by desert and semi-desert and is completely uninhabited. In the north lies the wood and bushland of **Kimberley Range**. The area contains interesting cliff formations, caves and gorges, especially the sandstone cone discovered in 1982 in **Purnululu (Bungle Bungle) National Park**, and known as Wave Rock, and the spectacular Pinnacles Desert in **Nambung National Park**. The 1,106-m-high **Mount Augustus**, Aus-

tralia's highest monolith, can be found in Hamersley Range.
The **Hamersley National Park** is popular with hikers. Eighty Mile Beach is an extension of the Great Sandy Desert and extends to the Indian Ocean.
The whole of the west coast is lined with salt marshes.
Hobart is the centre of **Tasmania**, and has a historic district that is well worth visiting. In addition to the great rainforest regions (giant ferns and eucalyptus trees up to 150 m high), which are accessible by trekking routes, Tasmania has many natural won-

ders, including limestone caves and waterfalls.
The most historic site is the ruins of the penal colony of Port Arthur, which was abandoned in 1877.

New Zealand	
Area:	268,676 sq. km
Capital city:	Wellington
Form of government: Constitutional Monarchy in the Commonwealth	
Administrative divisions: 90 counties, 3 municipalities	
External territories: Cook Islands, Niue, Tokelau	
Population: 4.1 million (15 inhabitants/sq. km)	
Languages: English, Maori	
GDP per capita: US$25,200	
Currency: 1 New Zealand dollar = 100 cents	

Natural Geography

New Zealand consists of two islands divided by the **Cook Strait**, which is just 38 km wide at its narrowest point. The islands are located 1,500 km south-east of Australia in the south-west Pacific. The Indo-Australian and Pacific plates join beneath the islands, and are defined by a chain of mountains.
The **North Island** has active volcanoes and large thermal areas with geysers and powerful hot springs. The island is also frequently affected by earthquakes. The South Island of New Zealand is dominated by the New Zealand Alps, a 300-km-long mountain chain which runs along the west coast. The mountains are very rugged in places. The highest point, at 3,764 m is Mount Cook, The mountains descend steeply towards the west coast, but in the east they flatten out to form extensive wide plains.
The Fiordland in the south-west contains a vast, inaccessible primeval forest. **Milford Sound,** one of the most beautiful fjords in the world, is in this area.
Stewart Island in the **Antarctic** is a little-explored, wooded island 1,746 sq km in area which is also part of New Zealand's national territory. New Zealand has further external territories in the south Pacific, namely the 15 Cook Islands, Niue (which is self-gov-

erned), the Chatham Islands, Tokelau (independent), the Kermadec Islands. Other islands, the Antipodes Islands, the Auckland Islands, Campbell Island and the Bounty Islands, are uninhabited.

Climate

Temperatures in Wellington in January average 19°C, and in the winter month of July, they fall to an average of 10°C. Only the south-east of the country and the interior of the South Island get significant winter snowfalls. The prevailing wind is normally from the west, and rainfall is heaviest in the west of the South Island.
The country was originally covered in dense primeval forest, but since the nineteenth century, much of this has been turned into grazing land. New Zealand has **unique fauna,** including a large variety of indigenous bird and animal species, some of which are endangered. The hole in the ozone layer over the Antarctic has caused excess exposure to UV rays. Both adults and especially children wear heads and neck protection when outdoors in summer.

Population

The population consists up to 78 per cent **European settlers** and their descendants. The proportion of **Maoris** is about 15 per cent. New Zealand is a popular **country of immigration**, and Asians and Pacific Islanders make up a further 12 per cent of the population. One in four New Zealanders lives in Auckland. The population density on the North Island is 24 inhabitants/sq. km in comparison to four inhabitants/sq. km on the South Island.
New Zealand's social and health systems are exemplary. The education system is heavily based on the British model, and is also very good. The country has seven **universities** and 25 institutions of higher education.

History and Politics

The islands were settled by the Maori in the ninth century, and were discovered by Europeans in 1642. Exploration by James Cook during the period 1769–1777 prepared the way for settlement, which began in 1792. Under the

*New Zealand was initially settled by the **Maoris,** who probably arrived from eastern or central Polynesia in around 900 AD They are famous for their elaborate facial and body tattoos. Sticking out the tongue is part of the war dance.*

Treaty of Waitangi, signed in 1840, the Maoris waived all sovereignty rights over the land, but this did not stop further land-grabbing by white settlers. In 1863, the Maoris were finally promised **land rights**, for which they are still fighting today. New Zealand was the first country in the world to introduce **women's suffrage.** The country became an independent dominion of the British Commonwealth in 1931. The **unicameral parliament**, whose members are elected for four-year terms, choose the prime minister. Five seats are reserved for Maori representatives. New Zealand's nominal head of state is the British monarch.

Economy

The **agricultural sector** is highly developed. Main products cultivated on the North Island are cereals and fruit. The South Island is dominated by sheep-rearing, and wool and milk production.

The **manufacturing sector** enjoys a similarly successful position. The main exports include electronics, chemicals and synthetics. In 2006, GDP was US$ 105 billion, of which eight per cent came from **agriculture**, 25 per cent from **industry** and 67 per cent from **services**. Large economic potential lies in the **generation of power** from hydro-electric and thermal sources.

Transport Infrastructure

The **road network** covers approximately 93,000 km, and bus travel is of great importance. There are ferry services between the two main islands, connecting the smaller islands to each other. The domestic **flight network** is also very important and links most of the larger towns and cities. Flying has become almost the main form of transport for New Zealanders. There are international airports in Auckland, Wellington and Christchurch. The **international sea ports** are located in Auckland, Wellington, Christchurch and Dunedin.

Tourism

New Zealand has a unique and, in some places, a largely undisturbed natural kingdom. The

country is very unpolluted, and contains numerous natural wonders. Almost one quarter of the land area is protected, ten per cent of which consists of the **124 national parks**. The Tongariro National Park was founded as far back as 1887 and is a popular skiing and hiking region in the shadow of the great extinct volcanoes.

The largest park is the Fjordland National Park on the South Island. Mount Cook National Park offers mountain and glacier tours. **Queenstown** in the Southern Alps is a major tourist centre and is famous as a base for adventure sports. The Coromandel Peninsula on North Island has beautiful beaches.

1 One of the most impressive sights in Westland National Park in the south-west of New Zealand's South Island is the 13-km-long Fox Glacier.

2 Lawn bowls, played beneath an open sky, is a popular sport in New Zealand. Competitions are held through-

out the country, as here in the spa and health resort of Rotorua.

3 New Zealand's landscape is extremely varied and is reminiscent of many parts of Europe. The country's scenery is often described as a 'miniature version of the Earth'.

Cities of Australia and Oceania

Sydney

The capital of New South Wales, Sydney is the oldest and largest city in Australia. It lies on the south-east of the Australian continent on Port Jackson on the Pacific Ocean. Sydney is the country's most important centre for tourism, business and finance. More than 4 million people live in the metropolitan region of Sydney. Built in 1957, the Opera House, with its façade resembling a series of sails, has become the symbol of the city, which can be traced back to the British penal colony established in 1788. Sydney developed into an affluent city in the nineteenth century. It was the venue of the summer Olympic Games in 2000.

Area:
1,664 sq. km (city)
Inhabitants:
3,641,000 (city, 2006)
4,120,000 (conurbation, 2006)
Population density:
2,188 inhabitants/sq. km (city)

The Sydney skyline, with the world-famous Opera House welcoming visitors to the city.

Melbourne

Melbourne lies at the eastern end of the south coast of Australia, where the Yarra River enters Port Phillip Bay. It is the capital of the state of Victoria. Almost three-quarters of the state's inhabitants live in the metropolitan area of Australia's second largest city. Founded in 1835 and named after British Prime Minister William Lamb (Viscount Melbourne), the city is the most important industrial base in the country and one of its largest ports. In 1956 it was the venue for the summer Olympic Games. The city's streets are laid out in grid formation. In the oldest part of the city many nineteenth-century English-style buildings lie in the shadows of modern high-rise constructions.

Area:
1,705 sq. km (city)
Inhabitants:
3,371,890 (city, 2006)
3,593,590 (conurbation, 2006)
Population density:
1,978 inhabitants/sq. km (city)

Skyscrapers with St Paul's Cathedral, the Princess Bridge and Flinders Street Station.

Brisbane

The Australian port of Brisbane lies on the east of the continent on the Brisbane River, about 30 km from its entry into the Pacific. Brisbane is the capital of the state of Queensland. Tourism is the main source of income for the region: the beaches on the Pacific Gold Coast are world famous. Brisbane is easily reached through an international airport. The streets of the inner city are laid out in a grid formation. Originally settled by the Turrbal Aboriginal people, the modern city evolved from a British penal colony in the nineteenth century when free settlers were also allowed into the area.

Area:
1,363 sq. km (city)
Inhabitants:
1,774,890 (city, 2003)
Population density:
1,302 inhabitants/sq. km (city)

A view over the Brisbane River, spanned by seven bridges, and downtown Brisbane.

Auckland

Radiating out from a narrow isthmus on the North Island, Auckland is the largest city in New Zealand. One-quarter of the population are Maoris and Polynesians and there are also large Asian and Pacific Islander communities, but the majority of the population are of European descent. With its port and New Zealand's largest international airport, Auckland is a significant trading base and an important transport hub. Icons of the city are the Harbour Bridge and the Sky Tower. Auckland was founded in 1840 and was one of the first European settlements. The seat of government of the British colony of New Zealand was based in Auckland from 1841 until 1865.

Area:
5,600 sq. km (conurbation)
Inhabitants:
1,199,000 (conurbation, 2003)
Population density:
214 inhabitants/sq. km (conurbation)

Auckland, 'City of Sails': At 328 m, the Sky Tower is the tallest tower in the southern hemisphere.

Papua New Guinea

Area:	462,840 sq. km
Capital city:	Port Moresby

Form of government:
Constitutional Monarchy in the Commonwealth

Administrative divisions:
19 provinces, 1 district (capital city)

Population: 5.8 million
(12 inhabitants/sq. km)

Languages:
English (official), Melanesian Pidgin English, Motu, other Papua languages

GDP per capita:	US$950
Currency:	1 kina = 100 toea

Natural Geography

The archipelago covers the eastern part of the Island of **New Guinea**, the **Bismarck Island group** as well as numerous smaller islands.

Climate

The wet, tropical climate has a year-round even temperature of roughly 27°C.

Population

The population consists mainly of **Melanesians**, but there are also **Papuan**, Micronesian and Polynesian minorities. Roughly 34 per cent of the population profess native religions, but the large majority are Christians.

History and Politics

The eastern part of New Guinea was annexed by Germany and Great Britain in 1884. After World War I, the land was ruled by Australia. Papua-New Guinea was finally granted its **independence** in 1975.

Economy

In 2006, GDP was US$ 5.6 billion, of which 29 per cent derived from agriculture, 42 per cent from industry and 29 per cent from services.

Tourism

Beautiful island tropical beaches and national parks are the country's main attractions.

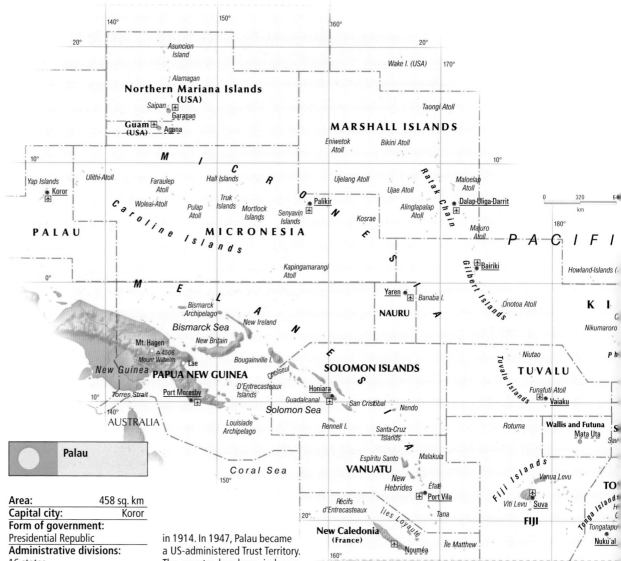

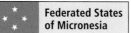
Palau

Area:	458 sq. km
Capital city:	Koror

Form of government:
Presidential Republic

Administrative divisions:
16 states

Population:
20,000 (44 inhabitants/sq. km)

Languages:
English, Palauan (both official), minority languages

GDP per capita:	US$8,500
Currency:	1 US dollar = 100 cents

Natural Geography

The 343 islands extend roughly in a line more than 200 km long in the south-west **Carolines**.

Climate

The country has a humid tropical climate, and temperatures remain in the region of 27°C year-round.

Population

The population is 84 per cent Palauan, with minorities of which the largest is **Filipino**. 33 per cent of the population profess the native religion, **Modekngei**, and 66 per cent are Christian.

History and Politics

The British controlled trade when the rich phosphate reserves attracted the interest of the Germans in 1899 and the Japanese in 1914. In 1947, Palau became a US-administered Trust Territory. The country has been independent since 1994.

Economy

In 2006, GDP was US$ 175 million, of which four per cent came from agriculture, 13 per cent from industry and 83 per cent from services.

Tourism

The large number of coral islands are a great attraction for divers from around the world.

Federated States of Micronesia

Area:	702 sq. km
Capital city:	Kolonia

Form of government:
Federal Republic

Administrative divisions:
4 states

Population:
108,000 (154 inhabitants/sq. km)

Languages:
English (official), 9 Micronesian and Polynesian languages

GDP per capita:	US$2,300
Currency:	

1 US dollar = 100 Cents

Natural Geography

The islands are partly of volcanic origin and partly coral atolls.

Climate

The country has a hot and humid climate with high precipitation and frequent, heavy tropical cyclones. Year-round temperatures are about 25°C.

Population

The population consists of nine Micronesian and Polynesian ethnic groups, the majority of whom are Christian.

History and Politics

The islands were discovered in 1520/21 and were claimed by the Spanish for several centuries before Germany captured them in 1899. After World War I, they became part of the Japanese mandate, and after World War II, this role was taken over by the USA. Micronesia became independent in 1990.

Economy

In 2006, GDP was US$ 250 million, of which 50 per cent came from **agriculture**, four per cent from **industry** and 46 per cent from **services**. The manufacturing industry processes tuna, copra and foodstuffs for export. **Tourism** contributes significantly to the economy.

Tourism

The ruined cities of Lele in Kosrae and Nan Mandol in Pohnpei are the main attractions, along with scuba-diving.

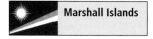
Marshall Islands

Area:	181 sq. km
Capital city:	Majuro
Form of government:	Republic

Administrative divisions:
24 districts

Population:
60,000 (332 inhabitants/sq. km)

*Due to the inaccessible landscape, many inhabitants of **Papua New Guinea** lived in complete isolation until the arrival of the Europeans. Although most of the indigenous inhabitants are today Christian, ancestor worship and occultism still play a large role. The 'Big Man' is an important and influential position within the tribe held only by men. Denoted by his striking body painting, the 'Big Man' needs to be eloquent and have a thorough knowledge of tribal mythology.*

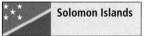

Form of government:
Parliamentary Republic in the British Commonwealth

Administrative divisions:
14 districts

Population:
13,000 (620 inhabitants/sq. km)

Languages:
English (official), Nauruan

GDP per capita: US$5,000

Currency:
1 Australian dollar = 100 cents

History and Politics

The island was discovered in 1798 by British whalers and became part of the **German protectorate** of the Marshall Islands in 1888. Japan and Australia ruled intermittently for a period until Nauru finally gained independence in 1968.

Economy

In 2005, GDP was about US$ 60 million. Nauru's economy is based on phosphate mining and export, which makes up three-quarters of economic output. The government is making efforts to diversify.

Tourism

Despite its magnficent beaches, Nauru has little tourism.

Population

The **Micronesian** population is 97 per cent Christian.

History and Politics

The island group was inhabited in prehistoric times, but was first discovered by Europeans in the nineteenth century. In 1892, the islands became part of a British protectorate along with the southern Ellice Islands, and were later part of the colony. After the detachment of the Ellice Islands in 1975, the territory became **independent** in 1979 it changed its name to Kiribati.

Economy

In 2006, the GDP of this poor island state was about US$ 70 million, of which 14 per cent came from **agriculture**, 11 per cent from **industry** and 75 per cent from **services**.

Tourism

The island of **Banaba** and the **Gilbert Island group** are the main tourist attractions.

Languages:
English (official), Marshallese

GDP per capita: US$2,300

Currency:
1 US dollar = 100 cents

Natural Geography

The republic covers two atoll groups, each 1,200 km long.

Climate

The Marshall Islands have a humid and hot tropical climate. Temperatures remain constant all year round at about 25°C.

Population

Most of the Micronesian population is Christian Protestant.

History and Politics

The island group was discovered in 1529 and became a German protectorate in 1884. Japan assumed the protectorate in 1920. The UN Trust Territory mandate, administered by the USA, ended in 1980.

Economy

In 2005, GDP was US$ 150 million, of which 14 per cent came from **agriculture**, 16 per cent from **industry** and 70 per cent from **services**. Coconuts, breadfruit, bananas, Taro and papaya are cultivated in a **subsistence economy**; livestock is also kept on the islands. The country has few natural resources; phosphate reserves are mined on one atoll.

Tourism

The island coral reefs provide some of the most spectacular scuba-diving experiences in the world.

Natural Geography

The small coral island is surrounded by a reef, that is exposed at low tide. A sandy beach circles the island, giving way to a strip of fertile land in the interior. The island's centre rises to a plateau 70 m high.

Climate

Nauru has a tropical climate with year-round stable temperatures of about 27°C. The rainy season lasts from November to February.

Population

The inhabitants, who speak Nauruan, are up to 60 per cent Nauruan, but there are also peoples from other Pacific islands and some immigrants from Australia, New Zealand and China.

	Nauru

Area: 21 sq. km
Capital city: Yaren

	Kiribati

Area: 811 sq. km
Capital city: Bairiki
Form of government: Presidential Republic
Administrative divisions: 3 administrative regions and 6 districts
Population: 100,000 (123 inhabitants/sq. km)
Languages: I-Kiribati, English (both official)
GDP per capita: US$700
Currency: 1 Australian dollar/Kiribati = 100 cents

Natural Geography

The national territory consists of 33 islands, distributed over an area of five million sq. km in the South Pacific Ocean.

Climate

The tropical climate means temperatures remain constant at 28°C. The weather is humid.

	Solomon Islands

Area: 28,450 sq. km
Capital city: Honiara
Form of government: Parliamentary Monarchy in a Commonwealth
Administrative divisions: 8 provinces, 1 district (capital city)
Population: 550,000 (19 inhabitants/sq. km)
Languages: English (official), Pidgin English
GDP per capita: c. US$600
Currency: 1 Solomon Islands dollar = 100 cents

Natural Geography

The Solomon Islands are located in the western Pacific Ocean and form a double chain of islands, stretching over a distance of 1,450 km.

Climate

The tropical rainy climate and average year-round temperatures of 27°C result in year-round precipi-

Samoa: on the islands of the Samoan archipelago you can find what might be the oldest of the Polynesian cultures. The precolonial social system consisted of a complex network of family and social ties: the head of a family was also member of the village council, which in turn sent a representative to the regional council. In modern Samoa, many of the old customs and traditional structures have been retained.

tation, which is heaviest in the period from November to April.

Population

The islands are mainly inhabited by **Melanesians**, but there are also some **Micronesian** and **Polynesian** inhabitants. In addition to the official languages, roughly 120 different languages and dialects are spoken.

History and Politics

Discovered by Spanish seafarers in 1568, the Solomon Islands became a British protectorate in the late nineteenth century. During World War II, the Japanese occupied the islands. Since independence in 1978, there have continued to be serious ethnic tensions. An intervention force under Australian command was sent to restore order in 2003.

Economy

In 2006, GDP was US$ 330 million, of which 46 per cent came from **agriculture** (primarily subsistence farming), seven per cent from **industry** and 47 per cent from **services**.

Tourism

Lagoons, waterfalls, excellent diving and sandy beaches are the main attractions for visitors. The tourist centre is the island of **Guadalcanal**.

Tuvalu	
Area:	26 sq. km
Capital city:	Vaiaku
Form of government:	
Constitutional Monarchy	
Administrative divisions:	
9 atolls	
Population:	
12,000 (460 inhabitants/sq. km)	
Languages: Tuvaluan, English	
GDP per capita:	US$1,600
Currency:	
1 Australian sollar = 100 cents	

Natural Geography

The island group consists of nine atolls and coral islands, dispersed over a distance of 560 km in the south-west Pacific. The islands are composed of coral limestone and many contain a central lagoon. Most of the islands are only a couple of metres above sea-level.

Climate

With an average year-round temperature of 29°C, the islands have tropical maritime climate.

Population

The population of the island group consists of up to 96 per cent **Polynesians**, with some Melanesians. It is almost entirely Protestant.

History and Politics

Great Britain established a Protectorate in Tuvalu in 1892 and in 1916 the island group was annexed as a crown colony. Even after gaining their independence in 1978, the islands have still remained a constitutional monarchy.

Economy

In 2002, GDP was some US$ 15 million, of which 16 per cent came from **agriculture**, 15 per cent from **industry** and 67 per cent from **services**, mainly raised from the sale of fishing rights and the licencing of the '.tv' internet domain suffix, popular because it also happens to be the abbreviation of 'television'.

Tourism

Tuvalu is a paradise for scuba-divers and lovers of the south seas.

Vanuatu	
Area:	12,190 sq. km
Capital city:	Port Vila
Form of government:	
Republic in a Commonwealth	
Administrative divisions:	
6 provinces	
Population:	
210,000	
(17 inhabitants/sq. km)	
Languages:	
English, French, Bislama and	
Melanesian languages	
GDP per capita:	US$1,800
Currency:	
1 vatu = 100 centimes	

More than 90 per cent of Vanuatuans are Melanesian.

Natural Geography

The republic is located 2,000 km east of Australia and consists of 12 main islands and 70 smaller ones, spread over a distance of 800km from north to south. Vanuatu consists of coral atolls and volcanic islands (some of which are still active) rising abruptly out of the ocean.

Climate

With the exception of the southern islands of Eromanga and Aneityum, which are mainly dry, the islands have a tropical rainy climate with temperatures of 25°C.

Population

The majority of the population is **Melanesian,** but there are also **Micronesian**, **Asian** and **European** inhabitants. Approximately 80 per cent are Christian.

History and Politics

The island group, formerly known as the New Hebrides, has been inhabited for at least 3000 years, and was discovered by the Portuguese in 1606. In 1906, Britain and France formed a joint administration. Vanuatu has been an independent **Republic** since 1980 and is a member of the Commonwealth. The 1980 constitution provides for a parliament of 50 members, elected every four years.

Economy

In 2006, GDP was US$ 380 million, of which 14 per cent came from **agriculture** (primarily subsistence farming), nine per cent from **industry** and 77 per cent from **services**. The main exports are coconut products, kava, wood and meat.

Tourism

The attractive tropical and volcanic landscapes and the beaches are the main attractions of the well developed tourist industry, whose centres are in **Malakula** and **Pentecost**.

Fiji	
Area:	18,270 sq. km
Capital city:	Suva
Form of government:	Republic
Administrative divisions:	
4 districts; 14 provinces	
Population:	
900,000 (49 inhabitants/sq. km)	
Languages:	
English, Fijian (both official),	
Hindi	
GDP per capita:	US$3,700
Currency:	
1 Fijian dollar = 100 cents	

Natural Geography

This archipelago consists of more than 320 islands, some of which are atolls and some of which are of volcanic origin. Only 110 of the islands are inhabited.

Climate

The country has a mild, maritime tropical climate with an average temperatures of 27°C in January and 23°C in July.

Population

The population is half **Melanesian** and half **Indian**, of which half are Christian and half Hindu. There is also a minority of Muslims. The Indians were all brought to the island by the British as indentured labourers in the nineteenth and early twentieth centuries.

History and Politics

Fiji has signs of early Polynesian settlement, but the islands were discovered by Abel Tasman in 1643. Captain James Cook's visit prepared the ground for British colonisation, which began in 1874. After gaining its independence in 1970, the country remained part of the Commonwealth until 1987 when it proclaimed itself a **republic** after a military coup. A House of Representatives and a Senate, consisting mainly of members appointed by the Great Council of Chiefs, share the governing of the country.

Economy

In 2006, GDP was US$ 3.2 billion, of which 16 per cent came from **agriculture** (primarily subsistence farming), 27 per cent from **industry** and 57 per cent from **services**. Apart from booming tourism and offshore banking business, Fiji's economy is mainly based on the export of sugar, gold, textiles, tropical woods and fish. Dependency on the 'classic' agricultural products of Fiji should be easing but investment has been lacking in recent times, particularly after political turbulence and natural disasters.

Tourism

The main destinations of the many tourists are the island resorts run by clubs , such as the **Mamanuca Islands** or the **Yasawa Islands**.

The modern-day inhabitants of **Polynesia** are not indigenous to the region, but instead moved there between 500 BC and 300 AD. Their exact origin is not known. The pre-colonial social structure has been retained, with the family unit (based on a patriarchal and sometimes polygamous structure) forming the backbone of society. Chiefs are selected by the elders in alternating succession.

Samoa

Area:	2,944 sq. km
Capital city:	Apia

Form of government:
Constitutional Monarchy

Administrative divisions:
11 districts

Population:
200,000 (67 inhabitants/sq. km)

Languages:
Samoan, English (both official)

GDP per capita:	US$1,900

Currency: 1 Tala = 100 sene

Natural Geography

Samoa consists of the two islands Savai'i and Upolu and seven other smaller ones. All volcanic in origin, the island interiors are covered in rainforest, with the coastal plains used for agriculture.

Climate

The country has an oceanic tropical climate with a cooler winter period from May to November (yearly average temperature: 27°C), year-round extensive periods of sunshine and short but heavy bursts of rain.

Population

The majority of the population is Protestant, and 99 per cent are indigenous **Polynesians**.

History and Politics

After early Polynesian settlement and discovery by the Dutch in 1721/1722, Samoa was in turn a British, German and American colony during the nineteenth century. In 1920, the islands came under the control of New Zealand and became a UN-Trust Territory after World War II. Samoa finally gained independence in 1961.

Economy

In 2006, GDP was US$ 370 million, of which 29 per cent came from **agriculture**, 42 per cent from **industry** and 29 per cent from **services**.

Tourism

Apart from the beaches and landscapes, a great attraction is the archaeological findings in **Letolo**, which are the most important in the Pacific area.

Tonga

Area:	748 sq. km
Capital city:	Nuku'alofa

Form of government:
Constitutional Monarchy within the Commonwealth

Administrative divisions:
5 areas

Population:
110,000 (147 inhabitants/sq. km)

Languages:
Tongan (official), English

GDP per capita:	US$2,100

Currency: Pa'anga = 100 seniti

Natural Geography

Tonga consists of a group of 172 islands in the South Pacific, which form two chains running from north to south. The islands to the west are mountainous and of volcanic origin, while those in the east are low coral islands.

Climate

With temperatures from 22°C to 26°C, Tonga has a tropical climate, influenced by the northwest trade winds. The rainy season lasts from December to April.

Population

The population of Tonga is very homogeneous, 98 per cent being indigenous **Polynesians.** The majority profess the Christian faith.

History and Politics

After Dutch and British expeditions in the seventeenth and eighteenth centuries, Tonga was converted to Christianity by British missionaries at the end of the eighteenth century. The islands were declared a British protectorate in 1900 and gained independence in 1970.

Economy

In 2006, GDP was US$ 225 million, of which 29 per cent came from **agriculture**, 15 per cent from **industry** and 56 per cent from **services**.

Tourism

The island of **Lifuka** and the **Ha'apai** island group are the main tourist centres. Tonga is unspoiled as it has not been invaded by mass tourism or by holiday clubs as have some of the better-known Polynesian Islands. The beaches are the main attraction.

1 Kayangel Island in North Palau is an atoll of volcanic origin, 2 km wide and 6 km long, surrounded by white sandy beaches.

2 The Caroline Islands are an archipelago in the western Pacific consisting of 963 small islands and atolls. In 1994, Palau became an independent state, and the other islands have since become part of Micronesia.

3 The islands of Samoa are one of the last untouched paradises. To preserve their own identity, the tourist infrastructure is barely developed.

Peoples of Australia and Oceania

Australia and many of the islands of Oceania were settled long before the arrival of the Europeans. Indeed, the Polynesians had distinguished themselves as skilled seafarers and

A mask is equivalent to face painting for this Papuan.

reached the Pacific islands from the west millennia ago. Metal tools were unknown to the Oceanian people but, on the other hand, the art of woodcarving flourished. Shell tools, flexible, perishable materials such as palm leaves and fronds, animal skins and tassels fashioned from human and animal hair are all still used today, both in daily life and on religious occasions. Oceanian art – whether in architecture (places of worship), in everyday design (decorated coconut shells) or in music (traditional dances) – always has a mythical and religious element. Masks and other figurative representations show spiritual beings.

Oceania

*The **Huli** probably established themselves in their current area of settlement in Papua New Guinea only 1,000 years ago. They had no contact with the outside world until well into the twentieth century and still live along traditional lines.*

Due to the mild climate, the men wear only a loincloth (dambale), holding a knife made from cassowary bone. Formerly, their everyday costume would also include wigs made of human hair decorated with flowers (manda).

The Micronesians

The inhabitants of the **Mariana, Marshall, Gilbert** and **Caroline Islands** are known as **Micronesians**. The largest archipelago in Micronesia is that of the **Caroline Islands**, which embraces more than 2,000 widely scattered islands, of which only 96 are inhabited; of these, only five cover an area greater than 100 sq. km. These are **Belau** (Palau), **Yap**, **Truk** (Chuuk), **Pohnpei** and **Kosrae**, and each island forms its own state or region, of which the surrounding smaller islands are part. Belau is known as the 'Republic of Belau' while the other islands are called the 'Federated States of Micronesia'. Research into the origins of the Micronesian peoples, as well as

The Marshall Islands

Micronesia also includes the Marshall Islands, made famous in Europe by the US atom bomb tests that were carried out on the Bikini atoll in the 1940s and 50s. Today, about 60,000 islanders still live here. They were converted to Christianity many years ago but formerly believed in their own gods. On the islands, their dwellings were considered sacred places, to which only priests and initiates had access. The traditional social order was based on matrilineal principles. Only men who were considered to be direct descendants of the gods and who thus had far-reaching authority could become chiefs.

that of the Melanesians and Polynesians, has revealed that they settled in the Pacific region in several waves of immigration from South-East Asia across the Indonesian-Malayan islands from the end of the ice age onwards. The immigrants formed three groups, each of which was very different from the others not only in appearance but also in linguistic and cultural terms. The **Melanesians** ('black islanders') have primarily **Negroid** features,

the **Polynesians** have mostly **Caucasian-Mongoloid** features and the **Micronesians** have predominantly **Mongoloid** features. There are also cultural differences between the Micronesian peoples. **Nine languages** are spoken on the islands – the inhabitants of the **Gilbert** and **Marshall Islands** and the **eastern Caroline Islands** speak **Austronesian languages**, while the inhabitants of the **western Caroline Islands**, the **Mariana Islands** and **Guam** (Chamorro) belong to the **Indonesian language family**.

The Micronesians have lived under the **colonial rule** or administration of Spain, Germany, Japan and the USA since their 'discovery' in the sixteenth century by the Portuguese, but the traditions of the inhabitants of the outer islands in particular, whose livelihoods are based on fishing and agriculture (taro, yams, coconut and sago), remain almost unchanged. The women on the island of Yap still wear **grass skirts** and the men **loincloths**, and their houses are made exclusively from local materials. An unusual currency in the form of '**stone money**' was once used on Yap. These were discs made from aragonite with a diameter of up to 4 m and a large hole in

the middle, through which a stick could be pushed to facilitate transportation. These stone coins now stand mostly outside the houses of the indigenous people as symbols of prestige. Only about 6,000 examples remain today but they were used in the past for large-scale business transactions, including dowries.

The Chamorro

Today, about 120,000 **Chamorro** people inhabit the Micronesian **Northern Mariana archipelago**, which belongs to the United States Commonwealth, and the island of **Guam**, which is under US administration.

Most of the Chamorro people, who enjoy Western lifestyles, are

Mud masks in Papua New Guinea protect against evil spirits.

the descendants of the former inhabitants of the islands, which were colonised by the Spanish about 150 years after their so-called '**discovery**' by the Portuguese seafarer **Fernando Magellan** in 1521. During the course of foreign rule and as a result of imported diseases, their numbers fell by the eighteenth century to about 4,000. Most of today's Chamorro have Spanish, Filipino or other Micronesian or US **ancestors**.

The Chamorro were the first of the Pacific islanders to cultivate **rice** for export; in addition, they were considered excellent **seafarers, fishermen, farmers** and **craftspeople**, with the men responsible primarily for fishing, horticulture and building houses and boats, and the women for **gathering plants** and for **craftwork** (pottery and weaving).

Originally, the **social organisation** of the Chamorro people was based on **family clans** with a **matrilineal structure**. Embedded within this structure was a complicated social **class system**, in which the women from the upper strata of society held particularly influential positions within the village community. Each of the family clans was led by a **council of elders**, which also administered the clan's jointly owned property.

Although the Chamorro were converted almost completely to **Christianity** in the seventeenth century, a few religious traditions from former times, such as ancestor worship, have been retained in the outer fringes.

The Abelam

The **Abelam** people, today numbering about 35,000, populate the **northern coastal region** of **Papua New Guinea**. Their economy is based mainly on **slash and burn agriculture** (yams, bananas, taro and sugar cane) and breeding livestock (pigs, chickens, dogs).

The Abelam live in village communities of between 500 and 800 people; the villages themselves consist of separate storage, living and cook houses. At the heart of each village is the **cult house**, its gabled walls – which measure up to 25 m – decorated with representations of the forefathers; cult objects and religious sculptures are kept within the building.

The Abelam, whose social order is patrilineal, are divided into numerous **clans**. Depending on their size, the clans are ruled by one or several chiefs, the **Big Men**, who are primarily responsible for social contacts with other clans in the form of complicated rituals of exchange.

One of the largest ceremonies of the Abelam people is the highly competitive **harvest festival**, an event for which the men cultivate giant yam roots measuring up to 4 m in length. According to their appearance, the yams are divided into male and female tubers and then decorated magnificently for the ceremony. Those who present the largest tubers are the winners and as such not only enjoy particularly high social prestige, but can also qualify for the office of a Big Man.

The Huli

Up in the **high mountainous regions** of **Papua New Guinea** live the members of the **Huli** tribe, whose population still numbers about 65,000 today. The Huli live from raising domestic livestock (pigs and chickens) but primarily from cultivating sweet potatoes, of which they grow more than 30 different varieties, as well as yams, bananas, taro and sugar cane.

Due to the frequent, heavy rainfall in the region, the Huli surround their fields with drainage ditches up to 4 m deep, which simultaneously mark the boundaries of family property and in former times would also serve as protective trenches against attacks by enemy tribes.

Unlike most of the other **Papuan people**, the Huli do not live in villages but instead live as extended families in widely distributed farmsteads, linked in loose **clans** (hamigini) and **subclans**, each of which is subject to a **tribal leader** (Big Man).

Under their usual social order, the Huli are governed by strict **gender segregation**. Accordingly, young men up to the age of around 25 are forbidden any contact with young girls. Marriage is not permitted until after thorough instruction in **tribal traditions**, completion of which is indicated externally through striking **body and head decorations**.

Even the work of the Huli is strictly divided by gender – men are responsible for **field work**, while women take care of the **home** and **bring up children**, as well as rearing pigs.

For many indigenous people, symbolic face and body painting and hairstyles, as well as other elements such as jewellery or clothing, indicate the personal status and circumstances of the wearer. In the case of this Papuan couple from the island of New Guinea, for example, the black face paint worn by the man signals a recent bereavement in his family, while the woman demonstrates her sympathy for her husband through the use of ochre face paint.

The Papua

New Guinea, which was colonised by the Dutch in 1828, is the **second largest island in the world** after Greenland. It consists of **Irian Jaya**, the western section, which has been part of Indonesia since 1963, and **Papua New Guinea**, the eastern section, which gained independence in 1975.

Today, with about 4.5 million people, the **Papua**, the **original inhabitants** of New Guinea who belong to the **Melanesian people**, make up about two-thirds of the total population. The Papua (in Moluccan papu-wa means 'curly hair') have a total of about **eight hundred ethnic groups** with almost as many **languages**; these are included in the **Proto-Austronesian languages** and differ from each other to such a great extent that the groups of Papua people are unable to understand each other. Different Papuan languages are also spoken outside New Guinea, such as by the **Sulka** on **Bougainville**; the **Baining, Arweae, Omengen** and **Nakanai** on the **New Britain archipelago**, and the **Buin**, who live on the northern **Solomon Islands**.

Traditionally, most Papuan people live from **fishing** and **agriculture**, and by keeping **small livestock**. They use plants that grow wild, such as the **sago palm**, and still employ simple **bone tools** to process them.

The **highland Papua** inhabit small villages comprising only 200 to 300 people; in the coastal regions, on the other hand, there are villages with up to 2,000 inhabitants. The **village leaders** of these communities with their strictly patriarchal structures, in which **polygamy** is still sometimes practised, are the so-called **Big Men**, who have made their name through possessing particular skills, and whose position cannot be inherited.

In the past, **bloody feuds** among the various Papuan tribes have led to **enemies** being killed and then partly eaten. However, this form of **cannibalism** was less widespread than the myth would have it appear.

The differences between Papuan tribes can be clearly seen in body

size: some tribal members reach an adult height of just 1.40 m, while others reach a height of over 2 m.

The Asmat

With about 40,000 people, the **Asmat** (meaning 'tree people') are one of the largest of the Papuan tribes. Their main area of settlement lies in the inaccessible swamp area in the **south-west** of **Irian Jaya**, the **Indonesian part of New Guinea**, where the Asmat people live primarily from

hunting and fishing, as well as from the starch collected from sago palms, which is a major staple food in the region. Since the Asmat did not come into close contact with Western civilisations until about 50 years ago, their original way of life has been largely retained.

The Asmat live in large villages comprising up to 2,000 people. Each village forms its own closed **economic** and **social unit**, and each family within the village lives in a **house built on stilts**, which provides protection against the regular flooding. In addition, each village has a large **community house**, in which the unmarried men live. At the same time, the community house serves as a cult house and a place of assembly; here, the **cult objects** (masks) used for religious ceremonies are stored.

The most important relics of the Asmat – who believe in the existence of a **creator** god who carved the first people from wood

– include the **ancestor poles** (mbis), measuring up to 8 m long, made from **mangrove wood**, which are always decorated with fresh leaves. These poles consist of elaborately carved figures, standing on top of one another to symbolise the line of **ancestors** and to act as a reminder of the great **creation myth**.

1 The complex facial decoration of this Papuan is not warpaint; he has painted his face for ritual reasons.

2 This man with his traditional head decoration comes from the island of Pohnpei, one of the Caroline Islands archipelago in Micronesia.

3 This man from the Vanuatu archipelago wears a leaf hat and clay make-up.

4 Leaf art is also a tradition for the Melanesians.

5 A magnificent Huli hairstyle from the mountainous regions of Papua New Guinea.

Oceania

*Still closely attached to their traditions are the inhabitants of the **island of Yap**, one of the 'Federated States of Micronesia', where the women still wear raffia skirts. Like all Micronesians, these islanders are also outstanding seafarers on the open sea, whose ancestors found their way from South-East Asia 4,000 years ago in their efficient boats using an astoundingly precise navigation system, so-called stick charts, on the long route to their current settlement area.*

The New Irelanders

The **New Irelanders**, numbering around 65,000, are the original Melanesian inhabitants of **New Ireland**, one of the islands belonging to the north-eastern **Bismarck Archipelago**, under the political jurisdiction of **Papua New Guinea**. The economy of the New Irelanders, who mainly live in small village communities, is based on fishing and the cultivation and processing of yams, bananas, taro and coconuts.

The New Irelanders belong to **twelve language groups** and live traditionally in **clans** distributed across several villages. In the past, there have frequently been military clashes between the different groups, in which **cannibalism** and **headhunting** also played a part.

The 'shark callers'

It was mainly Melanesians who settled on the largest of the heavily wooded islands of the Solomon Archipelago, which gained independence in 1978 as a parliamentary democracy. On the Solomon Island of Malaita, people have lived for generations on artificially created islands made from blocks of coral. This is also the home of the dying art of 'shark calling'. Shark callers are said to be able to summon and feed sharks without being attacked. Allegedly, the sharks will also rescue capsized seafarers, for which the islanders tradtiionally sacrifice a pig in thanks.

One particular cultural feature of the New Irelanders is their elaborately carved **masks** and **sculptures** (malanggan), based on mythological motifs, which were formerly an important part of their lavish **death ceremonies**. Each clan had its own particular motif, which was made by respected craftspeople out of sight of the public and burned after the ceremony. These **death and ancestor ceremonies**, in which magnificently costumed dancers presented scenes from the tribe's **creation myth**, generally lasted several days.

The Tannese

The **Tannese** are the Melanesian inhabitants of the island of **Tannu**, part of the **Vanuatu Archipelago** (formerly the New Hebrides and now the Republic of Vanuatu) comprising 83 islands and about 200,000 inhabitants in total. Like the other inhabitants of the archipelago, the Tannese live mostly from fishing and agriculture (taro, yams, cassavas, coconuts and bananas). The islands were discovered in 1606, and from 1906 fell successively under British and French **colonial rule**; Vanuatu has been an independent state since 1980.

During the course of their varied history, the Tannese people were attacked in their thousands in the nineteenth century by Australian seafarers – the so-called **Blackbirders** – and taken to Australia, the Fiji Islands and Samoa as slaves.

To a large extent, the Tannese have been able to maintain many of their old traditions (kastom) until today. These include the standard **assembly places** (nakamal) in each village, where ceremonies and **ritual dances** take place and where the male members of related families get together in the evenings (canoe). It is an old custom for young Tannese men to jump from towering wooden frameworks after the yam harvest, with only their feet secured to the tower by stems of the liana vine. **Tower-jumping** is both an initiation ritual and a symbolic request to the gods to provide a good harvest in the following year.

A **ritual** that dates from the nineteenth century, and which was temporarily banned and revived about 70 years ago, is the so-called **cargo cult**, which can be traced back to **male secret societies** (Dukduk, Iniet). A cargo cult is a movement in a tribal society arising from an encounter with a technologically advanced society. When the Tannese were confronted by Western consumer goods (i.e. cargo) during colonialisation, it gave rise to the belief that the colonial order would soon be overturned and the whites either enslaved or killed, and that their own ancestors would return to them, along with the Europeans' estates. Accordingly, the Tannese ravaged their plantations, since they would no longer be needed. These cargo cults were present not only on Tannu, but also among other Melanesian people.

On Hawaii, dances originally had a spiritual purpose.

To date, over 200 cargo cults have been identified in Melanesia.

The Solomon Islanders

Today, some 500,000 people live on the 990 **Solomon Islands**, which lie to the east of New Guinea. Discovered in 1568 by a Spanish navigator, the country began self-government in 1976 and became an autonomous Commonwealth state in 1978.

Most **Solomon Islanders** are of **Melanesian origin**; only the inhabitants of the Island of **Santa Cruz**, also part of the Solomon Islands, are **Polynesian**. In total, seventy different languages are spoken in Polynesia. In the past, frequent clashes have taken place between militants from the different groups.

Tattooing

Elaborate tattoos are a striking feature of the Maori people and are generally applied to the face and body in dramatic spiral-shaped patterns. The patterns were designed according to the social status of the person (anyone without a tattoo was regarded as having no status), and only specialist craftsmen were permitted to apply the tattoo. A full tattoo could often take up to several years to complete.

The word tattoo is of Tahitian origin: 'ta tatau' means 'hit' and refers to the technique of incorporating pigments in the skin by means of beating, burning and cutting.

The economy of the Solomon Islanders is based on coastal fishing as well as agriculture and keeping livestock. The cultural features of the islanders include their elaborately carved **longboats**, decorated with shell ornaments, which in former times would play an important part in religious ceremonies and in military clashes with other tribes.

In addition, the Solomon Islanders are considered to be outstanding **decorative smiths** and are famed for their fine jewellery. Unusual was the **feather money** formerly used on Santa Cruz, which was made from 9–11-m long, narrow plant strands, stuck with about 50,000 red feathers and rolled up for use as a method of payment.

The Trobrianders

There are currently about 15,000 **Trobrianders**, who speak one of the Papuan languages. They live on the volcanic island group of **Trobriand** to the east of **Papua New Guinea**. The islands were named by a French navigator, the first European to visit the islands, after his first lieutenant.

The livelihoods of the Trobrianders is based on fishing and keeping livestock (primarily pigs, both as a status symbol and for ceremonial occasions), along with the cultivation and processing of coconuts, yams, bananas, tapioca and taro. It is customary for two families to combine to form an economic unit.

The Trobrianders, who generally live in villages of 500 to 800 inhabitants, maintain a flourishing **barter trade** with tribes on surrounding islands. They used to cover hundreds of kilometres for this in lavishly decorated boats. On their trade routes, natural products were exchanged in a type of **ring system** (kula) for jewellery and other valuable objects such as necklaces or precious shells, and also pottery. The Trobrianders have traditional **tribal chiefs**, whose function is to lead religious ceremonies and who are materially supported by the other inhabitants of the villages. The tribal leaders reciprocate with festivals.

The New Caledonians (Kanaks)

The **New Caledonians** (or Kanaks, meaning 'people') today number around 80,000. They are the Melanesian inhabitants of the island of **New Caledonia**, which was settled about 6,000 years ago from South-East Asia and which has been under French territorial administration since the mid nineteenth century.

*On the 45 inhabited islands – along with over 100 uninhabited islands – of the **Tonga archipelago**, which belongs to Polynesia and lies about 2,000 km to the north-east of New Zealand, women traditionally enjoy a high social standing. This can also be seen in the way that male family members often rank below their sisters and their daughters. Tonga has been a constitutional monarchy since 1970, with a king as the head of state.*

The New Caledonian people are formed of numerous **clan tribes** among which **28 different languages** are spoken. They earn their living mainly from fishing and from agriculture (especially yams) and, according to ancient tradition, the ownership of their respective estates by individual clans cannot be changed through either sale or exchange but is passed down from one generation to the next.

The clans are the subjects of the supreme **tribal chief**, whose office is inherited by the eldest son. As an external sign of their rank, the chiefs wear bangles and high headbands, and at religious ceremonies they display elaborately crafted **battleaxes** made from nephrite.

The **circular houses** are traditionally built from bamboo, and the largest house in the heart of the village, whose door and gable are decorated with carved **figures of spirits and the ancestors**, is used as a **cult house** and **gathering place**. Even today, the **ancestor cult** and the **clan totem** continue to play an important role in the lives of the people of New Caledonia.

The Maori

Today, with more than 500,000 people, the **Maori** (meaning 'the locals') – the original inhabitants of **New Zealand** – still make up almost 15 per cent of the total population of the country.

The Maori were originally **Polynesians**, who apparently settled in New Zealand from **eastern Polynesia** in a number of immigrant waves during the first millennium BC. However, during the eighteenth century their existence became increasingly threatened by the arrival of the many English immigrants, and by the diseases that they brought with them; as a result of this, Maori population figures fell steeply from an initial 250,000 in the eighteenth century to around 40,000 by the end of the nineteenth century.

Like the Australian Aborigines, the early Maori population lived mainly by hunting the **flightless moa**, until this practice eventually led to the bird's extinction

during the twelfth century. Subsequently, the Maori became farmers (yams, sweet potatoes, flax and taro) and fishermen, as well as craftspeople (weaving and braiding).

Traditional Maori society is ordered in a hierarchical **three-class system**. Affiliation to one of these classes is determined either by birth or by adoption into a family at a different level. At the top level is the **nobility** (ariki), whose origin derived directly from the gods, then there are the **free people** (tutua), followed by the **subjects** (tau-rekareka) at the lowest level.

The traditional Maori way of life takes place in a village, and these are mainly located on hills, protected by earth walls or wooden palisades from enemy attack. In addition, each village has a large **cult and meeting house**, decorated with elaborately carved ornamentation (wharewahkairo), which symbolically represents an ancestor figure: the figure on the gable represents the head, while the roof symbolises the trunk, and the posts the arms and legs. The wood carving on the cult houses was carried out only by highly respected **carvers** (tohunga), who passed on their knowledge to their son, because the more magnificent such a cult house was, the greater the prestige for the respective village.

In the Western world, the Maoris have mostly become known for their outstanding skill and techniques in the fields of **jewellery** and **weapons manufacture**. Their jewellery – which included earrings, decorative combs and

amulets worn as necklaces (heitiki) – was generally decorated with ornaments or with symbolic human representations. It was made mostly of nephrite and jade and sometimes the teeth of sperm whales. Weapons such as axes and clubs, produced for purposes of prestige, were also made from nephrite and jade.

1 At markets on the islands of Tonga, numerous exotic fruits and spices are on offer, along with sweet potatoes, taro and cassavas.

2 These four young women from Samoa symbolise what is perceived to be the paradise of the South Sea islands.

3 These young Samoan farmers are the descendants of one of the oldest Polynesian peoples. Archaeological findings have shown that the islands – which are divided into independent West Samoa and American Samoa, administered by the USA – were already settled 6,000 years ago.

An Australian Aborigine with impressive face painting.

Aborigines – Dream Paths and Dream Time

Some 60,000 years ago, the first people migrated across a land bridge from Asia into northern Australia. The land bridge was subsequently destroyed by the rising sea level, and the Aborigines, one of the world's oldest people, were able to develop largely undisturbed for 40,000 years.

Enormous animals – now long extinct – confronted the first inhabitants of Australia. The animals included giant marsupials over 3 m in height, such as procoptodons, and emus (genyornis). These creatures were hunted using bushfires, which led over time to extreme changes in both the landscape and the animal kingdom.

Traditionally, the Aborigines lived as hunters and gatherers within nomadic family clans. The oldest men played the most important part within the group (council of elders). They were closely associated with certain animals and plants (totems). The Aborigines believe that they descended from a particular totem animal in mythical primeval times. This type of totemic kinship resulted in tribal rules, marriage laws and social regulations. The name for this early period is the same as that for dream and trance (dream time). Dream time has both a cult and a practical significance. Today, particularly talented Aboriginal representatives or medicine men can still understand and interpret through dreams what happened in primeval times, and work creatively using this knowledge. Waterholes can be located, for example, or medicinal knowledge passed on.

The creation myths (dream paths) of almost all Australian social associations are relatively uniform. The bringers of culture wandered through the world in primeval times; they combined animal and plant qualities within themselves, designed the country and left spiritual traces behind. Cult bases are located at these places, and even today people want to make a link to them through rituals.

The focus of Aboriginal ceremonial life is the cult retelling/narration of events in primeval times, through music and dance or the production of sacred objects (tjuringa), decorated with geometric patterns.

Sacred places such as Uluru (also referred to as Ayer's Rock), as well as totemic symbols made from ochre-hued clay, body painting, weapons and objects, have played an important part for thousands of years in dance and other forms of dream time expression. Knowledge was 'passed down' through listening and imitation. Initiation rituals in puberty, which could last for months, marked the transition into the adult world; particularly talented young people received special training to become medicine men or women. Failure to

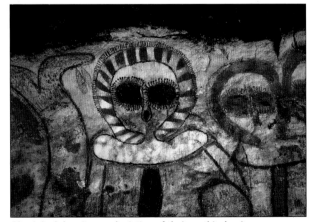

Aboriginal drawings: a depiction of their mythical universe.

Members of the Wanum Aboriginal group at the corroboree dance festival.

follow their recommendations was quickly avenged by the group, and some disputes were resolved by duels.

Due to the closeness of family relationships and the infrequent meeting of groups, the use of terms such as 'people' or 'tribal war' was unnecessary in the context of the Aboriginal way of life. Since there were around 600 different languages, the Aborigines often had to know several languages or make use of sign language in order to trade or barter with other families.

The Aborigines restricted themselves to essential, transportable items and had no interest in acquiring large quantities of food, clothing or personal property. When wandering, the women supplied the family by gathering plants and animal products, and were also responsible for the transportation of fire

in the form of a glowing ember. Cleverly camouflaged men with spears, boomerangs and stone slings went hunting or fished in coastal regions using canoes, nets, live clingfish or hooks made from bone and mother-of-pearl. The Aborigines, who rarely lived long in one place, generally slept outdoors between two small campfires, and built circular bark huts when the weather was wet or cold. Terms such as work, leisure, nature and art were unknown to them, and they usually spent a great deal of time telling stories, sleeping and playing. This way of life was largely destroyed by the British colonisers, who declared the Aborigines to be 'subhuman creatures' and described the Australia of 1788 as 'empty and uninhabited'.

Increased settlement after 1800 led to bloody clashes between the white settlers and the

Aborigines, who managed to defend themselves against expulsion but instead quickly fell victim to the imported diseases, racism and superior firepower of the whites, as a result of which their numbers fell by 75 per cent in just a few years.

In 1897, under the Aboriginal Protection and Restriction of the Sale of Opium Act, white protectors were appointed. Until the 1960s, the Aborigines had to obtain the approval of the administrators in matters of residence, work and marriage. Tens of thousands of Aboriginal children – now referred to as the 'stolen generations' – were forcibly separated from their parents and made to abandon the nomadic lifestyle and live in homes.

Only after decades of discrimination (and on the assumption that the extinction of the Aborigines was otherwise unavoidable)

were they finally granted citizenship in 1965. Between 1970 and 1996, a 33 per cent rise in the number of Aborigines brought the population up to about 200,000. Interest in their culture has increased, but although their

integration has greatly improved, a number of unresolved questions on land rights, accommodation and compensation have led to many problems. Today, 50,000 Aborigines still practise the rites of their ancestors.

Like her ancestors, this Tiwi woman has 'made herself up' according to ancient tradition.

A variety of hues and lines reflect mythical experiences of the dream time.

Oceania

*Today, the livelihood of Polynesian inhabitants of the **Cook Islands**, named after the famous English seafarer James Cook, relies mainly on tourism. Little remains of their own culture. However, indigenous people are also making attempts to revive their traditions and work against the kitsch romantic image of the South Seas, which for a long time has boosted foreign tourism.*

The Tongans

Some 100,000 people live in the **Kingdom of Tonga**, which has been an independent state since 1970. A further 30,000 Tongans have since migrated to New Zealand as a result of the poor economic conditions in their home country. The Tongan archipelago consists of more than 150 islands, of which 45 are inhabited. Some 70 per cent of the population is settled on the **main island of Tongatapu**.

The Tongans are the descendants of Polynesian immigrants, who landed about 3,000 years ago on the Tongan archipelago, and are the only Pacific people who have never been subjected to foreign colonial rule.

The **constitutional hereditary monarchy** has existed in its current form since 1845, and can be traced back to the conversion of the islanders to Christianity in the 1830s. In 1965, the current king, **Taufa'ahau Tupou IV**, took over the role of monarch from his mother, who had ruled the country for almost 50 years as **Queen Salote Tupou III**. Even today, Tonga still retains a strongly hierarchical social order with an influential **nobility**. Women have an important position, including within the political sphere, but they remain more in the background.

The livelihood of most Tongans is based on agriculture – the cultivation of cassavas, taro and sweet potatoes. Important export products include copra (the dried kernel of the coconut), coconut oil and fruit. **Fishing** also plays a part in the economy, and **crafts** were formerly an important source of income, with house and boat builders enjoying a particularly good reputation. The former way of life and culture of the Tongans (Fakatonga) was also characterised by Western influences (fakapalangi) during the course of **conversion to Christianity** in the nineteenth century. Today, traditions are generally still maintained only at weddings, christenings and deaths. On these special occasions, **tapa** are worn – wide lengths of fabric made from the bark of the **paper mulberry tree**, which are also used to decorate walls.

The Samoans

There are approximately 230,000 **Samoan** people in total, and today about 180,000 of these live on **Western Samoa**, which has been an independent state since 1962 and is divided into fourteen federal districts. The balance of the Samoan population has settled on the eastern archipelago, **American Samoa**, which has been under US administration since 1899. The economic basis of the West Samoans is primarily agriculture (taro, yams, bananas and coconut) and fishing.

Most of the islanders still live today in scattered villages, inhabiting oval huts (fales) which are open on all sides beneath a thatched roof. The Samoans' most important social unit is the **extended family**. The head of each family is granted automatic membership of the village council, whose **leader** (matai) represents the interests of the community in the Samoan parliament.

The social structure of the Samoans was formerly determined by a **two-class system**, consisting of a tier of nobility and one of ordinary people. But even non-noblemen and women had a political voice. A high-ranking title could be awarded or stripped on the basis of abilities and it was even possible for women with the right qualities to become the **supreme chief** (matai) or **war chief** (nafanua).

The wives, daughters and sisters of important men also formerly played a particular part in certain religious ceremonies, which are still practised today by groups of women (aulaluma). The sisters and daughters of a village chief were empowered to make decisions on women's matters within the village community.

Although the Samoans were **converted to Christianity** by the Europeans (Samoan: 'Papalagi') in the nineteenth century, some customs from their traditional religion have been maintained. Another ancient tradition, **tattooing**, came from Polynesia. Men have a **tatau**, which consists of intricate geometric patterns, while for women the **malu** is a simpler pattern.

In traditional dress: an inhabitant of the Solomon Islands.

The Tahitians

Five large archipelagos belong to **French Polynesia**, embracing a total of **121 islands** and today home to about 220,000 people. The most well known of these islands is **Tahiti**, the largest of the Society Islands, with a population of approximately 130,000. Until about a thousand years ago, the ancestors of the **Tahitians** belonged to the highly influential Polynesian people, whose culture had a widespread effect on other people in the Pacific island area.

The former social order of the Tahitians was based on a **three-class system**. At the top of the hierarchy was the hereditary **nobility** and **priest class**, whose members saw themselves as direct descendants of the gods, and in which women also had significant roles; then came the **landowners**, and finally the dependents. On the other hand, the religious cult community of the **Ariori** – who paid homage to **Oro**, the god of war, in their rituals – was relatively independent of class. Their members had to be unmarried, and the top ranks were reserved for the nobility.

Before their conversion to Christianity, the Tahitians, like the other peoples of the Pacific, believed in numerous gods, and **Huahine** and **Raiatea**, the islands adjacent to Tahiti, were considered the **spiritual heart of Eastern Polynesia**. Even today, the former sacred places of the Tahitians still exist, such as the **temple complex** of **Taputaputea Marae** (Raiatea); approximately 400 years old, it was formerly an important political base.

Tourism and industrialisation brought radical changes on Tahiti during the twentieth century. It has been under French administration since 1842 and is today used as an atomic test area and military base; the way of life of the islanders has changed so much that only fragments of the old traditions now remain.

The Easter Islanders

Of the approximately 2,700 inhabitants currently living on **Easter Island**, which belongs to Chile (known in Polynesian as Rapa Nui, in the indigenous language Te-Pito-Te-Henua, 'navel of the world'), about 2,000 are indigenous, with the balance of mixed race, with predominantly Chilean ancestors. At the time of the **discovery of Easter Island in 1722**, about 4,000 people lived here, but their numbers fell to just 111 in 1877 as a result of abduction, colonial rule and imported diseases.

The first inhabitants apparently came to Easter Island in the fourth century from the **Marquesas Islands** in Eastern Polynesia, and developed an astounding culture. The most famous evidence of this can still be seen today in the **monumental stone busts** (moia) carved from tuff, lined up in their thousands on sacred **ritual sites** (ahu) as memorials to their dead chiefs.

The Easter Islanders were also the only Polynesian population group to develop their **own script** (kohau rongorongo), which was scratched onto wooden boards. Their social order also included specialised professional groups, such as artisans and warriors, who were organised in a very precise and rigid hierarchy.

The Hawaiians

Today around 1.4 million **Hawaiians** live on one of the eight main islands of the archipelago, made up of a total of 120 islands. A little under 15 per cent of Hawaiian people are of Polynesian origin, and many of them have American, Korean, Japanese and European ancestors.

*An important branch of the economy on **Tahiti** and other French-Polynesian islands is pearl cultivation (see image, right). The pearls are processed by women into jewellery and then sold.*

Until their '**discovery**' in **1778** by **James Cook**, the Hawaiian islands were divided into four autonomous kingdoms, whose 350,000 inhabitants were ruled by powerful **male** or **female** **leaders** (ali'i), who also owned the land. Below them came the **priest classes** (kahunas), who were close to the king, and the **subjects**, who were obliged to pay **tribute** and whose relationships with the upper strata were strictly regulated by a complicated **taboo system** (tapu). At the lower end of the social hierarchy were the **outcasts** (kauwa). On the other hand, warriors, boat builders, astrologers, chroniclers, artisans, textile manufacturers and the religious **hula-kahiko** **dancers** and **musicians** enjoyed a high level of social prestige.

As soon as they were discovered, the islands became an important trade hub for both European and American **traders**. The old kingdoms broke down during the course of intensive **conversion** **to Christianity** and the massive **acquisition of land** by white plantation owners. Ancient traditions, including the Hawaiian language, were noticeably lost. Since then, however, efforts have been made to revive Hawaiian **customs** and today the language is taught in schools. The islands have been the fiftieth American federal state since 1959.

Population of Australia

Today, 95 per cent of the Australian population is of **British** or **Irish origin**, and 70 per cent are Christian. In addition, there are about 250,000 **Asians** and around 300,000 **indigenous people** (Aborigines). Approximately two-thirds of the population live in urban areas. The culture has Western characteristics, with British traditions and US habits prevailing.

The Aborigines

The indigenous people of Australia are known as Aborigines (from the Latin phrase 'ab origine' meaning 'from the beginning'). Since the settlement of

Australia by Europeans in the eighteenth century, the **indigenous people**, which at that time numbered around 500,000, were quickly decimated. Today there are approximately 200,000 Aborigines, a figure that corresponds to around two per cent of the total population of Australia.

It was not until the middle of the twentieth century that the lifestyle and cultural needs of the Aborigines were taken into account by the white majority, and since the 1980s their **art** and **culture** as well as their **medicinal knowledge** have become a considerable focus of interest.

Today, most Aborigines live in areas surrounding urban districts, and only a few live on **reservations** or on **mission stations**.

The Tasmanians

It is believed that the island of **Tasmania**, which lies off the south-east coast of Australia, was first populated about 35,000 years ago by Australian **Aborigines** who crossed via a land bridge that existed at that time. After separation from the Australian mainland by rising sea levels at the end of the **Wisconsin ice age** about 10,000 years ago, the **Tasmanians** developed their own culture, which differed strongly from that of their Australian cousins.

It is estimated that the population size at that time was somewhere between 2,000 and 5,000, which ensured the survival of the people but not the maintenance

of their original complex culture, knowledge of which only comes from the Australian Aborigines. After the **British** took possession of Tasmania in the early nineteenth century, the Tasmanian people were almost eradicated. Today, there is a population of only about 4,000 mixed-race Tasmanians living on the island.

1 Although it is the sixth largest country in the world, just under 20 million people live in Australia and 95 per cent of these are white people of European origin.

2 It is a Polynesian custom to welcome guests as they arrive with bright garlands of flowers.

3 The place of work is Queensland, not the American Wild West, for this Australian cowboy. A short distance inland is the start of the hot, dry Outback, which covers two-thirds of the continent. It is such an inhospitable environment that few people live there.

The Americas

The two continents of the Americas, including Greenland, stretch over an area of 42 million sq. km and have a population of more than 800 million. Mountain plateaus, such as the Grand Canyon, the Rocky Mountains and the Great Plains are typical of North America.

The Andes mountain chain (Aconcagua: 6,962 m), the Amazon basin containing the largest area of rainforest on Earth, as well as savannahs and steppes are typical of South America. The summits of the volcanic Cordillera reach heights of over 5,000 m. The paradise islands of the West Indies in the Caribbean are also of volcanic origin. Many large nature parks protect the monumental landscape and the unique flora and fauna, such as the Galapagos Islands off the west coast of South America. The original inhabitants of North America were the Native Americans who today mostly live in reservations. A mixed population has developed through immigration from Europe and Asia and the descendants of African slaves.

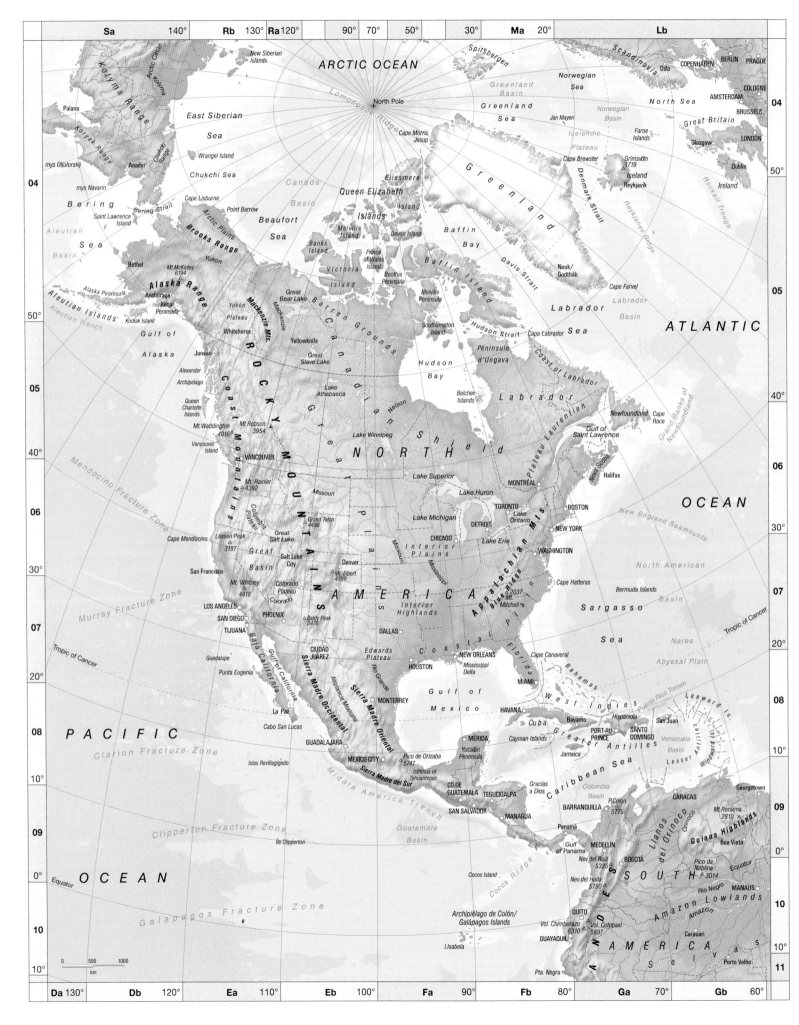

North America, physical

Sa 140° Rb 130° Ra 120° 90° 70° 50° 30° Ma 20° Lb

ARCTIC OCEAN
North Pole
Spitsbergen
Scandinavia
COPENHAGEN BERLIN PRAGUE
Oslo
AMSTERDAM COLOGNE
BRUSSELS
Great Britain
Glasgow LONDON
Dublin
Ireland

Kolyma Range
Arctic Circle
Palana
East Siberian Sea
Koryak Range
Chukchi Range
mys Oljutorskij
Anadyr'
mys Navarin
Wrangel Island
Chukchi Sea
Bering Strait
Point Barrow
Cape Lisburne
Bethel
Aleutian Islands
Saint Lawrence Island
Aleutian Trench
Bering Sea
Basin

Greenland Basin
Greenland Sea
Jan Mayen
Norwegian Basin
Faroe Islands
Icelandic Plateau
Grimsvötn 1719
Iceland
Reykjavik
Rockall Trough
Reykjanes Ridge

Cape Morris Jesup
Ellesmere Island
Queen Elizabeth Islands
Melville Island
Devon Island
Banks Island
Prince of Wales Island
Boothia Peninsula
Victoria Island
Baffin Bay
Baffin Island
Cape Brewster
Denmark Strait
Davis Strait
Nuuk/ Godthåb
Cape Farvel

Brooks Range
Arctic Plains
Beaufort Sea
Canada Basin
Yukon
Great Bear Lake
Mackenzie Mts
Mackenzie

Mt.McKinley 6194
Alaska Range
Anchorage
Kenai Peninsula
Kodiak Island
Gulf of Alaska
Juneau
Alexander Archipelago
Queen Charlotte Islands
Mt.Waddington 4016
Vancouver Island
Yukon Plateau
Whitehorse
Yellowknife
Great Slave Lake
Lake Athabasca
Mt.Robson 3954
VANCOUVER

Barren Grounds
Southampton Island
Melville Peninsula
Hudson Strait
Péninsule d'Ungava
Hudson Bay
Belcher Islands
Cape Labrador
Labrador Sea
Labrador Basin

ATLANTIC OCEAN

Coast of Labrador
Plateau Laurentien
Labrador
Newfoundland
Cape Race
Grand Banks of Newfoundland
Gulf of Saint Lawrence
Nova Scotia
Halifax
MONTRÉAL
TORONTO
Lake Ontario
BOSTON
DETROIT
NEW YORK
WASHINGTON
New England Seamounts

Mt.Rainier 4392
Columbia Plateau
Lassen Peak 3187
Cape Mendocino
Great Basin
Great Salt Lake
Salt Lake City
Grand Teton 4498
Mt.Elbert 4399
Denver
Colorado Plateau
Colorado
Mt.Whitney 4418
San Francisco
LOS ANGELES
SAN DIEGO
TIJUANA
PHOENIX
Baldy Peak 3476
DALLAS
Edwards Plateau
Rio Grande
Atlantide Mexicana
Sierra Madre Occidental
Sierra Madre Oriental
CIUDAD JUAREZ
Guadalupe
Punta Eugenia
La Paz
Cabo San Lucas
Gulf of California
Baja California

NORTH AMERICA
Great Plains
Missouri
Lake Superior
Lake Huron
Lake Michigan
Lake Erie
CHICAGO
Mississippi
Interior Plains
Interior Highlands
Appalachian Mts
Blue Ridge
Mt. Mitchell 2037
Cape Hatteras
Coastal Plain
Florida
NEW ORLEANS
HOUSTON
Mississippi Delta
Gulf of Mexico
MIAMI
Cape Canaveral
Bahamas
Bermuda Islands
North American Basin
Sargasso Sea
Nares
Abyssal Plain
Tropic of Cancer

PACIFIC OCEAN
Murray Fracture Zone
Clarion Fracture Zone
Clipperton Fracture Zone
Galapagos Fracture Zone
Mendocino Fracture Zone
Tropic of Cancer
Islas Revillagigedo
Île Clipperton
Archipiélago de Colón/ Galápagos Islands
I.Isabela
Equator
OCEAN

MONTERREY
GUADALAJARA
MEXICO CITY
Pico de Orizaba 5747
Sierra Madre del Sur
Isthmus of Tehuantepec
Yucatán Peninsula
MÉRIDA
CD.DE GUATEMALA
TEGUCIGALPA
SAN SALVADOR
MANAGUA
Panamá
HAVANA
Cuba
Cayman Islands
Jamaica
Gracias a Dios
Cocos Island
Cocos Ridge
Guatemala Basin

West Indies
Greater Antilles
PORT-AU-PRINCE
Hispaniola
SANTO DOMINGO
San Juan
Caribbean Sea
Puerto Rico Trench
Leeward Is.
Lesser Antilles
Windward Is.
Venezuela Basin
Colombia Basin
CARACAS
Mt.Roraima 2810
Georgetown
Guiana Highlands
Boa Vista
P.Colón 5775
BARRANQUILLA
Gulf of Panama
MEDELLÍN
Nev.del Ruiz 5325
BOGOTÁ
Pico da Neblina 3014
Nev.del Huila 5750
Llanos del Orinoco
Orinoco
SOUTH AMERICA
Rio Negro
MANAUS
Amazon Lowlands
Amazon
Carauari
Vol. Chimborazo 6310
Vol.Cotopaxi 5897
QUITO
GUAYAQUIL
Pta. Negra
ANDES
Porto Velho

Da 130° Db 120° Ea 110° Eb 100° Fa 90° Fb 80° Ga 70° Gb 60°

0 500 1000 km

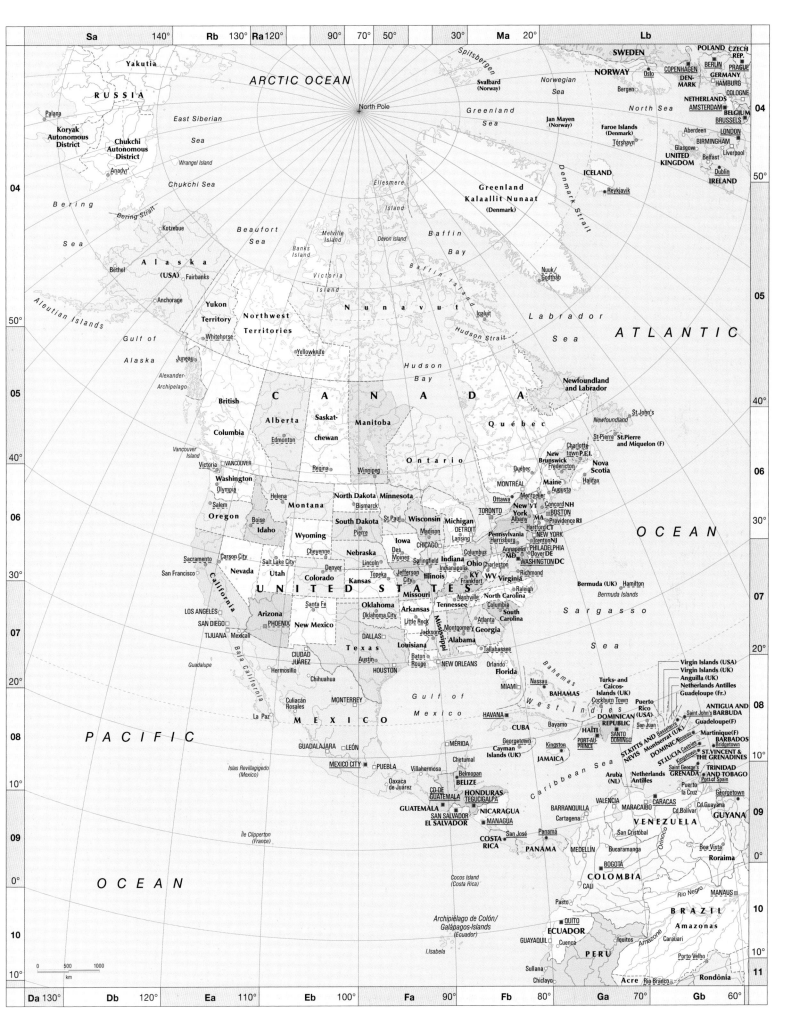

South America, physical

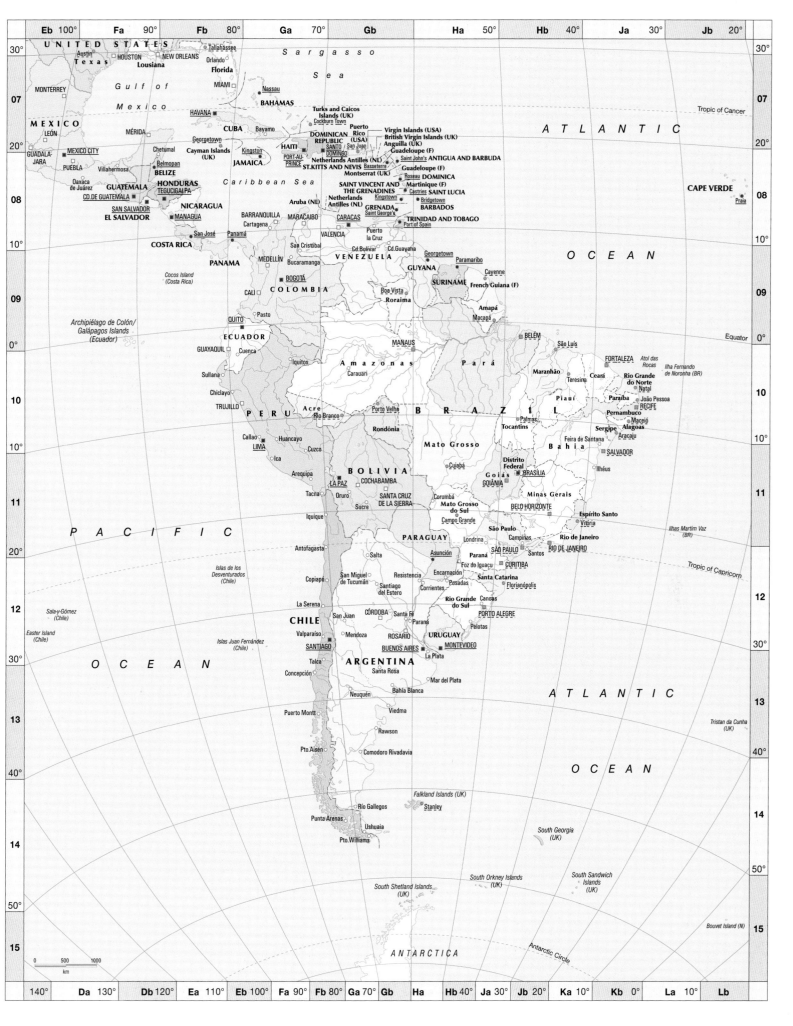

The Lincoln Memorial in Washington, D.C.: Behind the monumental portrait of the President, the 36 columns symbolise the 36 states united by Abraham Lincoln after the American Civil War.

The History of the Americas

It started as a mistake: the Genoese explorer Christopher Columbus set sail in 1492 to conquer India and discovered America, the 'New

The Mayan highlands: The Ruins of Chichén-Itzá in Yucatán.

World'. This proved to be a fitting name, for the 'old world' of America was destined to disappear almost without trace. The magnificent temples in the highlands of South and Central

A relict of the Spanish colonisation: the Fort El Morro in Puerto Rico.

America, some of which were thousands of years old, were flattened and replaced by churches that were no less imposing. Central and South America still suffer today from the legacy of the colonial era. By contrast, Canada and the USA emerged as wealthy democracies.

America as it was

*12 October 1492: This was the day on which the world changed. **Christopher Columbus** landed on Guanahani Island and America was 'discovered'. At the time, Columbus had no idea of the significance his discovery would have for world history. He believed he had arrived in the East Indies.*

The old empires

When European explorers landed in the New World at the end of the fifteenth century, it was a by no means 'primitive' population that they found. In Central America, a highly advanced culture, that of the Olmecs, who used a simple script and calendar system, had existed since 1500 BC.

Around 300, the Mayas succeeded the Olmecs as the rulers of Yucatán. The ruins of magnificent cities containing vast temples and the astronomical knowledge of these people bear witness to the high degree of civilisation of this Pre-Columbian culture. The Aztec empire which also originated in present-day Mexico, and the Inca empire in the Andes region are further examples of highly-developed social systems. The conquistadors and colonisers would not tolerate the co-existence of New and Old World cultures. The social structures of the original populations were therefore forcibly annihilated,

their natural environment systematically destroyed and the people exterminated on a massive scale.

Discovery of a continent

There has been much speculation as to whether Punic or Roman seafarers might have succeeded in sailing to the Americas in antiquity. It is certain, however, that the Vikings established a settlement in Newfoundland at the beginning of the eleventh century which they subsequently abandoned for reasons unknown. In the fifteenth century, the Portuguese funded many voyages of discovery to locate the sea route to the allegedly fabulously wealthy countries of the East. But it was a Genoese explorer in the service of Spain who was to discover America in 1492: Christopher Columbus. In the years that followed, the Spaniards continued their voyages of discovery. They reached Oregon on the west coast and Labrador on the east coast a mere 50 years later. However, it was not only the Span-

he decamped to Hispaniola where he founded the first Spanish stronghold in the New World, La Navidad. On three subsequent voyages he discovered the Lesser Antilles, Puerto Rico and Jamaica and set foot on the Central American mainland.

Spain and Portugal divided the New World between themselves as early as 1494 through the Treaty of Tordesillas. This treaty envisaged that Brazil, which had been discovered by Pedro Álvares Cabral, should become the prop-

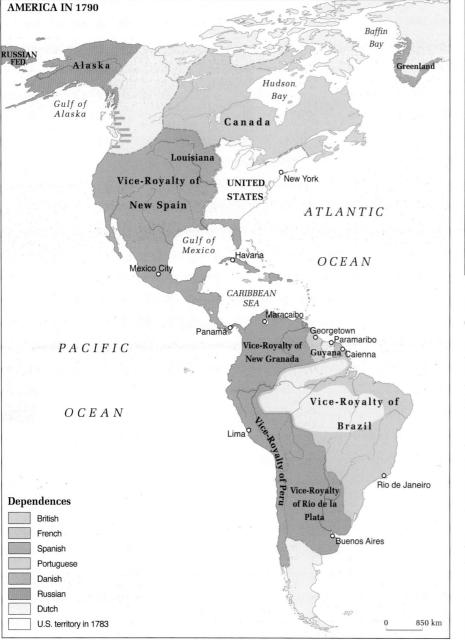

1 'Washington Crossing the Delaware' by E.G. Leutze.
2 The bitter battles fought during the American Civil War (1861–1865) cost a total of 623,000 lives.

ish and Portuguese who set sail for the New World. Commissioned by the English, John Cabot discovered Newfoundland in 1497 and Sir Humphrey Gilbert founded the first English settlement there in 1583. In 1524, Giovanni da Verrazano, a seafarer in French service, realised that America was a continent. In 1534–1535, the Frenchman Jacques Cartier sailed up the St Lawrence River to what is now Montreal. In 1608, Samuel de Champlain founded Quebec.

Colonisation of Latin America

America was discovered by Europeans on 12 October 1492, when Columbus set foot on land again after ten weeks at sea. He probably landed on the small Caribbean island of Guanahani (San Salvador). A few days later

erty of Portugal. The relatively accurate cartographic data circulated by Amerigo Vespucci to illustrate his discoveries, and his conviction that he had discovered a new continent, prompted the German cartographer Martin Waldseemüller to name the continent America.

The conquistadors

When the Spaniard Hernán Cortés landed on the Gulf Coast in 1519, accompanied by his small troop of followers, the Aztec empire was in its prime. Cortés was initially received courteously by Moctezuma II as it was believed that the Spaniards were the 'white gods' of prophecy. The conquest of the Aztec empire was ultimately made possible thanks to the psychological rather than the military

AMERICA IN 1790

Map of the Americas in 1790 showing:

Baffin Bay, Greenland, RUSSIAN FED., Alaska, Gulf of Alaska, Hudson Bay, Canada, Louisiana, Vice-Royalty of New Spain, UNITED STATES, New York, ATLANTIC OCEAN, Gulf of Mexico, Havana, Mexico City, CARIBBEAN SEA, Maracaibo, Panamá, Georgetown, Paramaribo, Vice-Royalty of New Granada, Guyana, Caienna, PACIFIC OCEAN, Vice-Royalty of Brazil, Lima, Vice-Royalty of Peru, Rio de Janeiro, Vice-Royalty of Rio de la Plata, Buenos Aires

Dependences
- British
- French
- Spanish
- Portuguese
- Danish
- Russian
- Dutch
- U.S. territory in 1783

0   850 km

America's indigenous inhabitants battled in vain: Atahualpa, the last Inca king, was executed by Pizarro in 1533. Even Sitting Bull was unable to stop the advance of the white man.

effects of their firearms, as well as through the infection of the Amerindians by pathogens that were harmless to Europeans.

The Inca Empire suffered a similar fate when it was weakened by internal conflicts upon the arrival of Francisco Pizarro's army. The Spaniards eventually succeeded in annihilating the Inca Empire in the mid-sixteenth century.

English vs. French in Canada

After French seafarers had taken possession of the region around the St Lawrence River, which they named 'New France', they extended their dominion to the Mississippi river. The conflict with the English colonies in Canada was decided in favour of the British and, in 1763, after the Seven Years War, the whole of Canada was surrendered. The Quebec Act of 1774 offered the Catholic French-Canadians full religious and cultural autonomy.

In 1791, two settlement areas were created which were different from a cultural and religious viewpoint: Upper Canada was dominated by the Anglo-Saxons and the province of Lower Canada was populated by the French. In 1841 they were united as a result of the Canada Union Act.

The arrival of the Pilgrim Fathers

The colonisation of the British area of North America began in 1620 with the landing of the Pilgrim Fathers on board the 'Mayflower'. Of these pious emigrants, 41 signed the 'Mayflower Compact', America's first governing document. The American colonists soon became discontented with the mother country due to a very unwise policy of severe taxation.

The United States is born

On 16 December 1773, 150 British settlers masquerading as Indians boarded three tea clippers which were anchored in Boston harbour and threw the cargo overboard in protest against unfair taxation and monopolisation of the tea trade. This was the prelude to the American Revolution. In 1776, the United States of America declared their independence. In 1789, Con-

gress met in New York for the first time and on 30 April 1789, George Washington became the first President of the United States.

His successor was John Adams (1797–1801) who was, in turn, succeeded in 1800 by the spiritual father of the Declaration of Independence, Thomas Jefferson. In 1803, Jefferson doubled the

young nation's territory through the Louisiana Purchase from France. Following the War of 1812 against England, which ended in a draw in 1815, the USA's self-confidence was further boosted. A foreign policy principle was subsequently formulated in 1823 by President James Monroe, with the Monroe Doctrine which rejected

1 17 years of work for eternity: Gutzon Berglum created the monumental portraits of Washington, Jefferson, Lincoln and Roosevelt in the Mount Rushmore National Monument.

2 Symbol of Christianisation: the Cathedral Metropolitana in Mexico City is the largest

cathedral on the continent. This is also the burial place of Mexico's bishops.

3 El Tajín, a great ruined city on the Gulf of Mexico, dominated by the so-called Niche Pyramid, named after the 365 niches that are decorated with stucco.

Modern America

Twentieth century US Presidents:
Democrat Franklin D. Roosevelt, 32nd President (1933–1945); Republican Dwight D. Eisenhower, 34the President (1953–1961); Democrat John F. Kennedy, 35the President (1961–1963); Republican Richard Nixon, 37the President (1969–1974); Republican Ronald W. Reagan, 40the President (1981–1989); Republican George Bush, 41st President (1989–1993); Democrat William J. Clinton, 42nd President (1993–2001).

European claims to American territory and advocated non-interference by the Americas in European policy matters.

Spanish and Portuguese interests in Latin America

The conquered regions of Central and South America were declared integral parts of the empire of Castile. The original inhabitants were considered to be free subjects of the Spanish crown. The Indian Council, which was resident in Spain and which ruled on financial, administrative, legal and religious affairs was an important administrative body. The Casa de la Contratación in Seville oversaw the transport of freight, goods, people and money to the colonies. Administrative units were established in Seville itself. These included Rio de la Plata, New Granada and the viceroyships of Mexico and Peru. The Portuguese established a feudal society in their South American colony, Brazil, which traded in timber, sugar and the slave trade. Brazil did not had its first gold rush in the late seventeenth century.

Colonial Christianisation

The conversion to Christianity of the indigenous people was an important component of Spanish colonial policy. While there were many forced baptisms, the Franciscans and Jesuits showed some interest in native American traditions. The Jesuit community that emerged during the seventeenth century in what is now Paraguay was an exception to this rule.

Independence in Central and South America

In 1825, Portugal was obliged to acknowledge the independence

of Brazil which became a constitutional monarchy. The demand for independence became more persistent in the Spanish territories. Under the leadership of Simón Bolívar and José de San Martin, the Spanish were expelled from the whole of South America in the 1820s. As a result of the Monroe Doctrine, the US supported these actions.

Central America was liberated from Spanish colonial rule in 1820. Mexico initially became an independent empire, then, 1823, a conservative republic.

New states of Latin America

New states emerged out of the former Spanish colonies from 1821 onwards. They formed alliances which sometimes disintegrated leading to war. Thus, the General Captaincy of Guatemala was initially part of the viceroyship of New Spain, before declaring its independence and joining the Empire of Mexico in 1822. Following the downfall of Augustin I, it seceded from Mexico and joined a Central American federation modelled on the United States, which became the first country in the Americas to abolish slavery. In 1839, the federation split into Guatemala, El Salvador, Honduras, Nicaragua and Costa Rica.

The federations and great empires of the South American continent only lasted a short time. In 1830, Bolívar's Gran Colombia disintegrated into the countries of Colombia, Venezuela and Ecuador. Paraguay, Bolivia, Uruguay. Argentina emerged from the united provinces of Rio de la Plata.

Expansion of the North American Federation

In 1846, the USA annexed Texas which had been independent

for ten years after a bitter battle with its ruling colonial power, Mexico. Mexico was further obliged to surrender California, New Mexico and parts of Arizona to the USA. In the mid-nineteenth century, the prospect of owning land and the discovery of gold mobilised millions of settlers to seek their fortunes in the 'Wild West'. The Native American population which had suffered greatly at the hands of the White Men in the past resisted the newcomers but were beaten in bitter fighting.

The War of Secession

The American Civil War which lasted from 1861 to 1865 was a true acid test. The conflict between the industrialised states of the North and the agricultural South had been smouldering for a long time. The cotton barons in the South viewed slavery as the basis of their economy but it had already been abolished in the North. South Carolina quit the union in December 1860, following the election of Abraham Lincoln. Six states followed, creating the Confederate States of America. Four further states left the union but, interestingly, the 'slave states' of Maryland, Delaware, Kentucky and Missouri remained in the union. Following the capitulation of the Confederacy, slavery was abolished throughout the USA under the thirteenth amendment to the Constitution.

Further territorial expansion

In 1867, Alaska was purchased from Russia and the Pacific islands of Hawaii, Samoa, Midway and the Philippines were acquired legally through secession and conquest. Guam and Puerto Rico came under US administration in 1898 after the United States won the Spanish-American War fought for the independence of Cuba. Washington ensured control of the Panama Canal by supporting Panama's attempts at independence from Colombia.

As the nineteenth century turned into the twentieth, the USA became a world player for the first time; Theodore Roosevelt acted as intermediary in the Russo-

1 These slaves, shipyard workers in Virginia photographed in 1861, were emancipated in 1865.

2 Millions of immigrants from Europe flooded America at the end of the nineteenth century.

3 The brutal regime of the Mexican dictator, Porfirio Díaz, who was supported by the United States, led to a bloody revolution in 1910.

4 The Great Depression: food distribution by the Red Cross to the needy in Arkansas during the economic crisis of the 'Hungry Thirties'.

5 Boomtown New York City: Since the late nineteenth century increasing numbers of skyscrapers have been constructed and now dominate the skyline. Here are a few builders taking a lunchbreak high over the city.

Japanese War of 1904–1905 and President Wilson took the US into World War I in 1917.

The Crash and World War II

The period of increasing prosperity was brought to an abrupt end in 1929 by 'Black Friday', the stock market crash. Unemployment and even hunger prevailed in the USA which had previously been so wealthy. The 'New Deal' policy introduced by President Franklin D. Roosevelt brought the United States out of the crisis. Following the 1941 surprise attack on Pearl Harbor by the Japanese, the USA entered World War II which they brought to a victorious end with the release of atomic bombs on Hiroshima and Nagasaki in August 1945.

All of a sudden, the USA became the most important player on the world stage. The Soviet Union, which also aimed for world domination, confronted the USA in the 'Cold War'. This determined American foreign policy for almost half a century.

Witch hunts and citizenship

The government resorted to drastic measures to deal with actual or supposed Communists at home during the post-war McCarthy era. The atmosphere became more liberal in the late 1950s and early 1960s, raising a question that had long been ignored: equality before the law for all ethnic groups. Racial segregation in public places was only finally outlawed under John F. Kennedy. When Kennedy was assassinated in 1963 by Lee Harvey Oswald, his successor, Lyndon B. Johnson, had to continue to bear the heavy burden of the Vietnam War.

A policy of strength

The confidence of the nation plummeted in the 1970s. Corruption, the political assassinations in 1968 of civil rights campaigner Martin Luther King and presidential candidate Robert Kennedy, the Watergate scandal and the failure to free the Americans taken hostage in the US Embassy in Tehran contributed to the depressed mood. Ronald Reagan, who was elected in 1980,

promised to return the USA to its former greatness. However, the break-up of the Soviet bloc made the policy of aggression obsolete and Reagan left behind a catastrophic budgetary situation.

The USA played the role of global policeman under George Bush. It imprisoned Noriega, the head of state of Panama and punished Saddam Hussein for the occupation of Kuwait with 'Operation Desert Storm'.

The economy stabilised under President William Clinton. During the Kosovan crisis, the USA participated in the aerial bombardment of Yugoslavia within the framework of NATO. In late 1999, the USA handed over the Panama Canal Zone to Panama. In January 2001, George W. Bush was sworn in as 43rd President of the United States. On 11 September 2001, the Islamic terrorists of al-Qaida destroyed the World Trade Center in New York and attacked the Pentagon in Washington. They demanded the extradition of Osama bin Laden, terrorist mastermind, who was supported by the Taliban regime in Afghanistan. In October 2001, the USA began a military offensive which led to the downfall of the Taliban though Al Qaida remained in hiding in Afghanistan. In 2002, the conflict with Iraq escalated when the US government accused the country of producing weapons of mass destruction. The USA commenced the 'Iraqi freedom' operation in 2003 with British and other European support. This pre-emptive strike against Iraq led to the collapse of Saddam Hussein's regime within weeks.

The USA views North Korea as a further security risk. In 2002, North Korea finally admitted to working to produce atomic weapons and carried out tests towards the end of 2006.

1 Juan Domingo and Evita Perón celebrating after his swearing-in as Argentinian President for a second term.

2 John F. Kennedy loved to be close to the people. This trust cost him his life in Dallas in 1963.

3 Fidel Castro and Nikita Khruschev, firm friends, in the Kremlin in 1963.

Canada in modern times

Despite a strong independence movement, Canada supported the British motherland in the Boer War and in World War I. Canada only gained independence as a dominion of the British Empire in 1931 thanks to the Statute of Westminster. It did not formally gain independence from the British crown until 1982, although the Queen remains head of state. Where home affairs are concerned, French-Canadian attempts at independence have produced tensions.

Latin America in the twenty-first century

The transition from liberal democracy to brutal military dictatorship gained a new dimension through the victory of Fidel Castro in Cuba in 1959. To protect the interests of the USA, President Kennedy dabbled in the well-tried policy of US intervention, but this time it failed miserably. The economic and political crises of the 1960s led to the downfall of many civilian governments which were replaced by military juntas. An attempt at Marxism, as practiced by Salvador Allende in Chile, was foiled by General Pinochet with US assistance. In 1973, Pinochet established a terror regime that cost the lives of many of his opponents. Since the 1980s, almost all of Latin America has been in civilian hands again and democratic constitutions have been introduced. But in oil-rich Venezuela, the election of Hugo Chavez in a landslide victory in 1998 has caused concern, with his increasingly radical Marxist policies. Despite formal democratisation, poverty and social inequality continue to provide great challenges. Also for this reason, South America has experienced a shift to the left in recent years.

4 Salvador Allende visiting a factory. The Marxist policy of the Chilean President ended abruptly in 1973, when he was assassinated in a coup.

5 The dream of freedom and equality for Afro-Americans was seriously threatened by the assassination black Civil Rights activist Reverend Martin Luther King in Atlanta in 1968.

Manhattan's skyscrapers symbolise for many the seemingly limitless possibilities that the United States of America offer.

The Countries of the Americas

From the Bering Straits in Alaska to Cape Horn at the southernmost tip of Chile, from north to south, the enormous expanse of the American continents links the Earth's two polar ice caps. A flight from west to east in North America

Rio de Janeiro, one of the most exciting cities in South America.

crosses eight time zones. The 42 million sq. km of the Americas encompasses more than a third of the Earth's land area.

With its tundra, salt deserts and tropical rainforests, The Americas are a land of variety and contrasts. This is not only true geographically: while the USA expands its political and economic supremacy, many inhabitants of the countries of Latin America live on the verge of subsistence. Their history is marked by military dictatorships and an often futile struggle for freedom and democracy.

Canada

Canada

Area:	9,984,670 sq. km
Capital city:	Ottawa
Form of government:	

Parliamentary Monarchy in the Commonwealth of Nations

Administrative divisions:
10 provinces, 2 administrative regions

Population:
33 million (3 inhabitants/sq. km)

Languages:
English, French (both official)

GDP per capita:	US$39,100

Currency:
1 Canadian dollar = 100 cents

Natural Geography

Canada is the world's second-largest country and, together with Alaska, occupies the entire northern section of the North American continent. The country stretches from the **Pacific** in the West to the **Atlantic** in the East, from the Great Lakes in the South to the islands of the North Pole.

Two great mountain chains run parallel to the coast in east and west. The **Cordillera** runs along the Pacific coast and continue into the South American Andes. The **Appalachians** in the east have been severely eroded in the course of the Earth's history and in some places are merely rolling hills. The **Canadian Shield** covers most of the country. It is a rocky plain 200 to 600 m above sea level which rises to 1,500 m in Labrador and is dotted with lakes. In the far north, the continent breaks up into a multitude of islands. The largest are **Baffin Island** with an area of 495,000 sq. km, **Victoria Island** with 212,000 sq. km and the **Queen Elizabeth Islands**. The **Canadian Archipelago** is permanently covered in snow and ice. The **Appalachians** and the **Notre Dame Mountains** which stretch to Newfoundland run parallel to the Atlantic coast.

Between the coast and the mountains there are broad **marshy plains** and deeply-cut **fjords**. The great St Lawrence Seaway cuts deep inland to the fertile **St Lawrence Lowland**.

Further west are the lowlands around the **Great Lakes**. Lakes Ontario, Erie, Huron and Superior share a border with the United States. The **Niagara Falls**, on the Niagara River between Lake Erie and Lake Ontario – one of the most spectacular natural sights in North America – are divided between Canada and the USA.

The **Canadian Shield** is the world's oldest **mountain range**, although it has lost a lot of height due to its age. The **Moraine Embankments** and the countless lakes are relics from the Ice Age.

In the west, they give way to a vast, flat landscape. The **Central Canadian chain of lakes** with Lake Winnipeg, Lake Athabasca, Great Slave Lake and Great Bear Lake form a transitional link to the **Great Plains**. The monotonous prairie landscape consists of debris and deposits from the Canadian Shield and contains enormous **deposits of coal, natural gas, crude oil and oil shale**.

Canada is bordered in the west by high mountains. The Northern **Rocky Mountains** are part of the same formation as the **foothills** of the **Columbia Mountains** although they divided from each other by the **Rocky Mountain Trench** through which the **Columbia River** and the **Fraser River** flow on their way to the Pacific Ocean.

The **Coastal Cordillera** runs parallel to the Pacific coast. Mount Logan, in this chain, is the highest mountain in Canada, rising a height of 5,951 m. The jagged coastline contains numerou fjords running parallel to the Atlantic coast. Between the mountain chains of the Coastal Cordillera and the Rocky Mountains there are wide areas of flat land such as the **Fraser Plateau** and the **Nechako**, **Stikine**, **Nisutin**, Yukon and Porcupine plateaus.

Climate

Canada as a whole is part of the Arctic and the sub-Arctic climate zones. Consequently, the average temperature is below 0°C in more than half of the country.

In the **permafrost regions**, on King William Island for example, the annual average temperature is -17°C, while on the southern

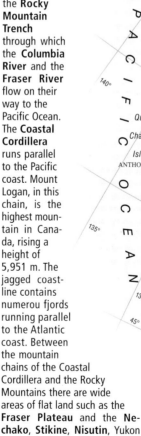

The St Lawrence River is the life blood of Quebec City.

Canada

edge of Hudson Bay, at the borderline between mixed woodland and tundra, the average temperature is a more bearable -6.6°C.

The climatic conditions only permit **year-round habitation** and agriculture in the southern parts of Canada. Whilst there is precipitation of 800 to 1,500 mm in the area of the Atlantic, the **precipitation** in the inner plains is only approximately 300 mm annually. The rainfall in the Arctic Archipelago is extremely low (just 60 mm), whilst rainfall on the western hillsides of the Coastal Cordillera can be as much as 6000 mm.

In the **tundra** of Upper Canada, moss, lichen and stunted bushes grow despite extreme climatic

there are **forests of cedars** and Douglas fir, red cedar and hemlock fir.

The **fauna**, of which there are many species, has been preserved especially in **nature reserves**. The largest national parks include the **Wood Buffalo National Park** south of the Great Slave Lake, the **Prince Albert National Park** in Saskatchewan and the **Banff** and the **Jasper National Parks** in the Rocky Mountains. **Caribou** and **musk-oxen** live in the Arctic regions, while **polar bears**, **seals** and **walruses** live along the coast.

The forests are roamed by **American elks**, **black bears** and various **species of deer**. **Grizzly bears**, **mountain goats** and **big horn sheep** live in the Cordilleras.

with 800,000 individuals, whilst European immigrants and their descendants predominate. These are **Anglo-Canadians** (28 per cent), **Franco-Canadians** (21 per cent) and Canadians of **Irish**, **German**, **Italian**, **Ukrainian**, **Dutch**, **Polish**, **Norwegian**, **Chinese** and South Asian origin. 45 per cent of Canadians are **Catholic** and 40 per cent **Protestant** belonging to a variety of denominations. The rest of the population is **Muslim**, **Orthodox**, **Jewish** or **Sikh**. **Schooling is compulsory** in Canada; this is regulated differently from province to province. The **illiteracy rate** is less than five per cent. There are 77 **universities**. **Medical provision** is exemplary; **average life ex-**

Cartier commenced the systematic reconnaissance and appropriation of the land for France in 1534. The first **French settlers** arrived in 1604 and in 1608 **Samuel de Champlain** founded the city of Quebec. From 1627 onwards, the country was annexed by the **Société de la Nouvelle France**, a trading company that operated a monopoly on the fur trade in particular. The land became the property of the French crown in 1674, so that French territory now stretched from Canada down to the Gulf of Mexico.

England disputed French supremacy at an early stage. The **Hudson's Bay Company**, which was formed in 1670, laid claim to all territories whose inland wa-

whole was awarded to the British crown. However, extensive cultural and religious autonomy was granted to the French settlers in the **Quebec Act** of 1774.

During the **American War of Independence**, the province of Quebec remained loyal to Great Britain. However, following the independence of the Thirteen colonies, the newly-formed **United States of America** raised claims to Quebec. The Forty-ninth Parallel was not formally acknowledged as a border until after the War of 1812–14.

The American Revolution led to a **migration movement** of loyalists from the former American colonies. A second **wave of immigration** – from Great Britain in particular – resulted in another significant increase in population in the mid-nineteenth century. Until 1840, the province of Quebec was divided into British-populated Upper Canada and French-populated Lower Canada as a result of the **Constitution Act** of 1791. The two predominantly autonomous administrative districts were subsequently united to form the Province of Canada. In 1887, the **Dominion of Canada** was created as a confederation of the provinces of Quebec, Ontario, New Brunswick and Nova Scotia. The regions which were controlled by the Hudson's Bay Company were annexed to the Dominion in 1869. **British Columbia** joined the federation in 1871, followed by Prince Edward Island in 1873 and Newfoundland in 1949.

An economic upturn and over-exploitation of raw materials commenced towards the end of the nineteenth century. In 1885, the transcontinental **Canadian Pacific Railway** was completed. On 16 August 1896, gold was discovered in Rabbit Creek, near Dawson, in the Yukon region. The creek was promptly renamed Bonanza Creek, and many of the locals started staking claims. Gold was found all over the place, and most of these early stakeholders became known as the 'Klondike Kings'. Since the Yukon was so remote, word spread slowly, but on 17 July, eleven months after the initial discovery, the steamship 'Portland' arrived in Seattle from Dawson carrying 'more than

Pierre Elliott Trudeau

*Montréal 18.10.1919
†Montréal 28.9.2000

This professor of constitutional and civil rights law was an MP for the Liberal Party from 1965 to 1984 and became its chairman in 1968. He was Prime Minister from 1968 until 1979 and from 1980 until 1984. The bi-lingual, charismatic politician is regarded as the architect of multi-cultural Canada thanks to his concept of bilingualism. He negotiated in the conflict between the Anglos and the French-Canadians and tried to prevent the separation of Quebec province from the rest of Canada.

Two Jack Lake, a magnificent lake in the Banff National Park in Alberta.

conditions. The **boreal coniferous forest** which extends as far as Lower Canada is almost 1000 km wide and stretches from west to east over the whole of Canada. Pines, firs and black and white spruce are the main species that grow here. **A belt of prairie** follows which alternates with mixed woodlands.

The original grassland and shrubs of the **prairies** have fallen victim to agriculture to a great extent. The **sugar maple** flourishes in the **hardwood forests** of the east. Its leaf has become the **national symbol** of Canada. In the high mountains of the west

Bison stocks have been severely reduced in the prairies and large herds can now be found only in the national parks. **Beaver**, **mink** and other fur-bearing animals can still be found almost anywhere. The varied **birdlife** is impressive, in Newfoundland and on the Gaspé Peninsula in particular. The rivers and lakes are full of **salmon**, **trout** and other species of fish.

Population

The original population, the **Native Americans**, **Inuits** and **Métis** are still in the minority

pectancy is 80 years. There is a fertility rate of 1.7 births per woman and, combined with a **minimal infant and child mortality rate**, the population growth is approximately one per cent. The **urban population** is 77 per cent. The most populous city is Toronto with around 4.3 million inhabitants.

History and Politics

The **Vikings** were the first Europeans to reach the east coast of Canada in approximately 1000 AD, but it was another 500 years or so before **Jacques**

ters flowed into Hudson's Bay. As a result of the **Spanish War of Succession**, Nova Scotia, New Brunswick, Newfoundland and the areas surrounding Hudson's Bay were awarded to England in the **Treaty of Utrecht** in 1713. The conflicts between the English and the French culminated in the **Seven Years War** fought in Europe between Brandenburg, Prussia and England on one side and Austria, France and Russia on the other. In 1760, the superior English fleet triumphed in the North American secondary theatre of war. Under the **Treaty of Paris** of 1763, New France as a

A ritually painted child of the **Algonquin** tribe performing a ritual dance. This tribe, that settled along the Ottawa river before the birth of Christ, now lives in poverty at the edge of Canada's capital. Ottawa's political importance, despite its remote location, is due to the fact that it lies at the border betwen the English- and French-speaking parts of Canada. Evidence of the Native American origins of the city are now confined to the Museum of Civilisation.

*A ritually painted child of the **Algonquin** tribe performing a ritual dance. This tribe, that settled along the Ottawa river before the birth of Christ, now lives in poverty at the edge of Canada's capital. Ottawa's political importance, despite its remote location, is due to the fact that it lies at the border betwen the English- and French-speaking parts of Canada. Evidence of the Native American origins of the city are now confined to the Museum of Civilisation.*

a ton of gold'. Within six months, approximately 100,000 gold-seekers set off for the Yukon. Many died or lost their enthusiasm. They had to walk most of the way, using pack animals or sleds to carry hundreds of pounds of supplies. The Canadian authorities required that all Klondikers bring a year's worth of provisions with them. Even so, starvation and malnutrition were serious problems along the trail. Cold was another serious problem. The Gold Rush eventually petered out when the rich seam of gold was depleted.

Canada's detachment process from the British motherland happened slowly and in several stages. Following World War I, in which Canada fought alongside the British, a separate Canadian delegation participated in the Versailles peace negotiations. In 1923, Canada concluded the first independent foreign trade agreement with the USA, the Halibut Treaty. However, it was not until eight years later that the subordination of the Canadian parliament to British institutions finally ended with the Statute of Westminster and the country gained **independence** as a dominion of the Commonwealth. **During World War II,** Canadian troops fought alongside the Allies and when the war ended Canada became one of the founder members of **NATO**. The constitutional law of 1982 meant final constitutional independence from Great Britain. In 1988, Canada and the USA agreed to establish a **free trade zone** which was extended to **NAFTA** in 1994 when Mexico entered into the agreement.

As far as home affairs are concerned, the dispute between the Anglo-Canadians and the Franco-Canadians has raged for decades. The French minority were granted greater **privileges** in 1969 and the French language was accorded the status of a **second official language** in 1974. Independence for Quebec province was rejected by a narrow majority in the **referendum** held in 1995.

Canada is a **parliamentary monarchy within** the British **Commonwealth** of Nations. The nominal **head of state** is **Queen Elizabeth II** who is represented by a local governor-general. The **Lower House** is re-elected every five years and 75 of the 301 seats are reserved for Quebec province. The **senate** has a maximum of 112 members who are appointed by the governor-general on the recommendation of the prime minister. The **right to vote** begins at 18.

Economy

Massive **deposits of raw materials**, **huge forests**, **modern industry** and efficient **agriculture** make Canada one of the world's richest countries. In 2006, Canada's **GDP** totalled

US$ 1.3 trillion. Agriculture accounted for two per cent of this figure, industry for 29 per cent and the services sector for 69 per cent. Four per cent of the working population is employed in **agriculture**, 23 per cent in **industry** and 73 per cent in the **services sector**. The balance of trade is positive. Major exports are motor vehicles, machinery, timber, wheat, mineral ores, aluminium, oil, natural gas and fish products. Significant **imports** include machinery, vehicles and manufactured goods. Canada's main trading partner is the USA.

Transport Infrastructure

The **rail network** spans **70,000 km**. In contrast to the north which is hardly opened up at all, the **road network** is well-developed along the US border. The St Lawrence Seaway is the longest river and is navigable, connecting the Atlantic coast with the Great Lakes.

Tourism

Canada has many tourist attractions, including **national parks** with magnificent scenery such as the Canadian side of the Niagara Falls and cosmopolitan cities such as **Quebec**, **Montreal** and **Vancouver** in British Columbia on the Pacific coast.

1 Ice floes drifting in Baffin Bay. Northern Canada is sparsely populated and barely developed.

2 Savoir-vivre: Montreal is a successful synthesis of tradition and modernity in architecture, lifestyle, art and culture.

3 The Moraine Lakes such as Ten Summits in Alberta, shown here, were formed in the Rocky Mountains during the Ice Age.

4 Toronto, the prosperous metropolis of the province of Ontario, Canada's answer to the Big Apple: almost 70 nationalities co-exist peacefully here.

United States of America

United States of America

Area:	9,826,630 sq. km
Capital city:	Washington, D.C.

Form of government:
Presidential Federal Republic
Administrative divisions:
50 federal states, 1 district
External territories:
Northern Mariana Islands, Puerto Rico, American Virgin Islands, American Samoa, Guam, 8 islands in the Pacific, 3 islands in the Caribbean
Population: 300 million
(30 inhabitants/sq. km)
Languages:
English (official), Spanish, Native American languages
GDP per capita: US$44,000
Currency :
1 US dollar = 100 cents

Natural Geography

The USA can be divided into four broad geographical areas, the **coastal plain** in the east, the **Appalachians**, the **Prairies** and the **Rocky Mountains** to the west. The Atlantic coastal plain extends from the 49th to the 24th parallel, that is from the mouth of the **Hudson River** in New York as far as the coastal plain at the **Gulf of Mexico** in Florida. In the west, the coastal plain is bordered by the **Appalachian** mountain range, which extends for about 2,500 km south-west to north-east from Georgia to Maine. The Appalachians, never more than 200 km in width, were formed in the Meso-zoic era and in geological terms are therefore considerably older than the **Rocky Mountains**.
The Appalachian mountain range is known by different names in different states, such as the **Great Smokies** in Tennessee and North Carolina, the **Catskills** in New York, the **White Mountains** in New Hampshire, the **Green Mountains** in Vermont, the **Blue Ridge Mountains** between West Virginia and Georgia, and the **Alleghenies** in Pennsylvania. This severely eroded rocky massif consists of ridges, valleys and plateaus The highest peak is Mount Mitchell (2,037 m) in the south.
The Missouri-Mississippi basin is the watershed of the two largest rivers in the USA and extends from the Canadian Shield in the north to the Gulf of Mexico in the south. This broad landscape reaches heights of about 400 m and slopes more steeply in the alluvial land of the **Mississippi**. The monotonous prairie landscape can be divided into four great lowlands, the Interior Plains, the Coastal Plains, the Great Plains and the Interior Highlands. The **Great Lakes** in the north form the US share of the Canadian Shield and are the largest contiguous lake district in the world. Lake Superior, Lake Michigan, Lake Huron, Lake Erie and Lake Ontario are linked to each other as well as to the Atlantic by the St Lawrence Seaway, consisting of the river and a network of canals. The Cordillera runs down the west coast and is up to 1500 km wide in places. The **Rocky Mountains** are a young folded mountain range consisting of individual chains, intersected by broad valleys. The mountains reach heights of 4,000 m and extend from the Arctic Ocean to the Mexican border.
The **Columbia plateau** in the north lies in the shadow of the Cordillera, traversed by the Columbia River, the Snake River and other smaller rivers. The **Great Basin** is the largest region of North America with no outlet to the sea and is characterised by inhospitable deserts such as **Death Valley** and the salt lakes. The Colorado plateau is semi-desert tableland through which the Colorado River has carved the **Grand Canyon** to a depth of up to 1,800 m. Further west is the Pacific Mountain System, beginning in the north with the snow-capped Cascades that rise to a height of 4,000 m.

In the south lies the **Sierra Nevada** with an average height of 3,000 m. Mount Whitney, at 4,418 m is the highest mountain in the contiguous United States. Only Mount McKinley in Alaska, at 6,194 m, is higher.
The **Coastal Ranges** are only 1,500–2,000 m high and are separated by the 700 km length of the Great Valley and by the Puget-Willamette Trough.

Climate

Because of the vast size of the country and its diverse geography, including several large mountain ranges, the United States runs the gamut of climates. In the north, conditions are cool to temperate and in the interior the **continental climate** ensures sharp contrasts between summer and winter. In the Deep South, the climate is **sub-tropical** and it is **tropical** in southern Florida. In the Pacific Northwest, the states

The Capitol dominates the skyline in Washington D.C.

*The monumental **Capitol building** is where Congress, the legislative power of the USA, sits in session. The rotunda, crowned by a statue of liberty, accommodates both chambers of Congress. The 79 m-high cupola was completed in 1863 and is the second-highest building in the city after the Washington Monument.*

manatees disport themselves along the coasts, which are rich in fish. The survival of endangered species prized for their fur is to some extent ensured by the **national parks**.

Population

The USA is the classic example of a multi-cultural society, whose population is composed of ethnic groups from almost all over the globe. The native population of **Native Americans**, **Eskimos** and **Aleuts** now accounts for only one per cent of he population, while 74 per cent are **white**, 13 per cent **black**, ten per cent **Hispanic** and four per cent of **Asian** origin. While in the nineteenth century and the first half of the twentieth century the majority of immigrants came from Europe, the main countries of origin of non-native citizens today are Mexico, the Philippines, China, Cuba, India and Vietnam. The population of the USA is composed of 26 per cent **Catholics**, 16 per cent **Baptists**, six per cent **Methodists**, 3.7 per cent **Lutherans**, 2.6 per cent **Jews**, 1.1 per cent **Episcopalians**, 1.5 per cent **Orthodox Christians**, 1.8 per cent **Muslims** and 1.8 per cent **Presbyterians**. In addition there are sizeable minorities of **Sikhs**, **Bahai** and **Buddhists** as well as adherents of various **sects**. Average life expectancy is 78 years. The education system is regulated by the individual states, but generally speaking education is compulsory between 7 and 16 years old. The illiteracy rate is less than five per cent. The USA has a total of some 3,700 **universities and colleges**. With 240 Nobel prizes, the USA tops the number of prize winners, though many of the laureates were foreign-born and educated outside the US. Apart from the very highly educated elite, a large number of school-leavers have inadequate spelling and basic arithmetic.

Of the US population, 76 per cent live in the cities, 22 per cent are under 15 years old and 13 per cent over 65. The average age is just 35 years, and the annual rate of population growth is one per cent.

History and Politics

The **Vikings** were the first Europeans to reach North America, but

than 40°C (Texas). Degrees of precipitation vary between 550 mm in the north and 800 mm in southern Texas. In the eastern states precipitation over the entire year amounts to between 760 mm and 1,270 mm. Summer temperatures often reach 30°C. In Florida, the summer weather is hot and sultry.

The contrasts in atmospheric pressure and temperature in the **Great Plains** often result in **tornadoes** and on the **Gulf Coast** in **hurricanes**, which regularly inflict severe damage. The extreme north-east (Vermont, New Hampshire) is covered in coniferous forest, which changes to mixed and deciduous forest further south. Spruce, fir, beech, maple, hickory and oak are the characteristic trees. In the dry interior, wide flat **prairies** extend with varying densities of vegetation. **Desert landscapes** predominate in the southwest (Arizona, New Mexico) and tropical vegetation with **mangrove swamps** in Florida.

The mountains in the west are wooded, and **Alaska** has a share of the boreal coniferous forest and tundra. There is a multiplicity of fauna. The typical inhabitants of the prairies include bison which, even after mass slaughter, even in the national parks, are now once again increasing in numbers. The national bird, the bald eagle, has become rare. In Florida, there are crocodiles and alligators, and in the north, grizzly, brown and black bears. Whales, dolphins and

of Oregon and Washington to the crest of the Cascade Mountains, there is up to 3,800 mm of precipitation a year, falling as rain and snow. In summer, temperatures average over 30°C. In the central Pacific region, the Rocky Mountains and the states of California, Idaho, Montana, Wyoming and Colorado, temperatures vary from

over 45°C in summer on the coast to as low as -20°C in winter in **Yellowstone National Park**. Southern California, Nevada, Utah, Arizona, New Mexico and south-west Texas have only about 250 mm of precipitation. In winter, temperatures rarely fall below freezing point, but in the summer they may rise to more

than 40°C. In the mid-western states of North and South Dakota, and from Minnesota to central Texas, the thermometer in winter often shows -10°C (North Dakota) and in summer it rises to more

United States of America

'Lady Liberty': For millions of immigrants, the **Statue of Liberty** at the entrance to New York harbour symbolised a dream come true. It is the work of the French sculptor, Frédéric-Auguste Bartholdi. The steel structure was built by Gustave Eiffel. The 46-metre-tall Statue stands on a 47-metre-high granite pedestal and was a gift from wealthy French citizens to the USA as a symbol of liberty. It was placed on the Liberty Island in 1886.

were not able to maintain their settlements in the long term. There is evidence of **settlements** at least 12,000 years ago. After the discovery of America by **Columbus** in 1492, it was another 73 years before the Spanish started the colonisation of North America with the foundation of St Augustine in Florida.

After the English defeated the Spanish Armada in 1588, their only rivals were the French and Dutch. The French founded **Quebec** in 1608, and the Dutch founded **New Amsterdam**, the present-day New York, around 1625. In 1607, the first British colony was established with the foundation of Jamestown in Virginia, followed by other settlements in the course of the sixteenth and seventeenth centuries. British colonisation continued on a larger scale after 1620 when the **Pilgrim Fathers** landed at Plymouth Rock in what is now New England. Hardships at home, political unrest and religious persecution of the Puritans led to an endless stream of settlers.

Three main British colonies were founded. The economy of the South (Maryland, North and South Carolina, Virginia, Georgia) was based mainly on large **plantations** using **slave labour** for the growing of cotton, indigo and tobacco.

The **New England colonies** engaged in trading and had fishing industries and a merchant fleet, while the Mid-Atlantic colonies were particularly attractive to settlers from Ireland, Scotland, Germany and the Netherlands with their cultural attractions, a high degree of religious freedom and flourishing trade. The British colonial power was able to secure supplies of raw materials and markets for its own manufactured goods and the British army and navy protected the settlers from attack by the Spanish, French, Native Americans and pirates.

In the **French and Indian War**, which became part of the **Seven-Years War**, the British established their claims, but the settlers' increasing self-confidence was displayed in 1773 at the **Boston Tea Party**. This was the start of the American **War of Independence** also known as the American Revolution of 1778. In 1789, the United States constitution came into being, and **George Washington** became the country's first president. In 1800, his successor John Adams moved into the White House in the **District of Columbia**, on land seceded from Maryland, which was now separate from the state of Virginia. Under the third president, **Thomas Jefferson**, US territory expanded by 140 per cent when **Napoleon** was paid US$15 million for the 2.1 million sq. km of land between Mississippi and the Rocky Mountains, now known as the Louisiana Purchase. A further war with England, the War of 1812, ended in a deadlock in 1815, but confirmed the territorial integrity and **independence** of the USA.

In the early nineteenth century, the US extended its borders to the south, south-west and north-west. After **Texas** broke away from Mexico in 1845 a war began with **Mexico**, which ended in 1848 with the acquisition of the land north of the Rio Grande.

The discovery of gold in California in 1849 and the prospect of fertile land resulted in the westward migration of millions of settlers. Native Americans who resisted the appropriation of their land were ruthlessly suppressed and forced on long treks into small, inhospitable reservations far from their homelands. Foreign policy was formulated in 1823 through the Monroe Doctrine, which claimed hegemony for Washington on the North American continent against all European claims west of the Atlantic. Social and economic

Franklin Delano Roosevelt

*Hyde Park, 30.1.1882,
†Warm Springs, 12.4.1945

After an electoral victory over President Hoover in 1932, Roosevelt tried to steer the US out of the terrible slump that followed the Wall Street Crash. Central points of his 'New Deal' were further state help for the poor and a job creation programme. Abandoning the isolationist policies of his predecessors, he brought the United States into World War II after the Japanese attack on Pearl Harbor in 1941. This popular politician was elected for an unprecedented third term in 1940 and a fourth term in 1944.

Dwight David Eisenhower

*Denison, 14.10.1890,
†Washington, D.C., 28.3.1969

The commander-in-chief of Allied Forces Europe in World War II, was elected 34th President in 1952 (1953–61). Despite the aggressive policies of his Secretary of State, John Foster Dulles, his policy towards the USSR during the Suez and Hungarian crises was more defensive. With the 'Eisenhower doctrine' of 1957 he secured support for self-rule for the Arab countries which led to an intervention in Lebanon in 1958. On the home front he expanded the social system known as Modern Republicanism.

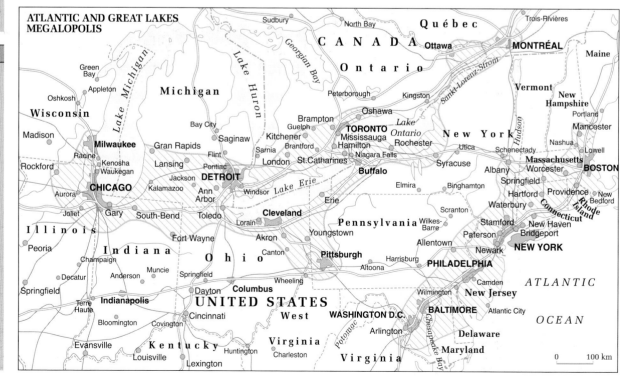

*The **Old State House** in **Boston** once served as the British Governor's office. Nowadays it is a museum of the city's history. The Georgian-style building is one of the stops on the 'Freedom Trail' a history of US Independence.*

It is here, on Boston Common that the first shots were fired in the War of Independence. Boston continues to be a centre of intellectual activity: several prestigious 'Ivy League' universities such as Harvard, are close by.

development was very variable and depended on the regions of the new federal state. While the farmers of New England and the industrialists and capitalists of the north favoured emancipation of slaves, the cotton barons of the Deep South wanted to retain **slavery**. The **antagonism** between the advocates of **slavery** and the **abolitionists** intensified, culminating in 1861 in the secession of eleven states, led by South Carolina, and their union as the Confederated States. The civil war that followed lasted four years and cost the lives of 623,000 soldiers. When the Confederacy surrendered in 1865, unity was restored and slavery abolished under the **Thirteenth Amendment** to the Constitution. **Reconstruction** was not completed until 1877, though the full emancipation of the Afro-Americans had by no means been achieved. On the contrary, a militant racism developed and the **Ku Klux Klan** came into being.

Streams of settlers from the Old World continued to decimate the native population. The extinction of the mighty herds of bison through the construction of the trans-continental railways took away the livelihoods of the native dwellers on the prairies. Occasional successes such as the rout of General Custer's cavalry at the Battle of **Little Big Horn River** in 1876 made no difference to the fate of the native population. After the defeat of the Apaches under their chief Geronimo in 1886 and the massacre of the Sioux at **Wounded Knee** in 1890, their resistance was finally broken.

The sudden rise of the USA to the status of a **world power** began around 1900. With Alaska, bought from Russians in 1867 for 7.2 million gold dollars, and the annexation of Guam, Hawaii, Samoa, Puerto Rico, Midway and the Philippines, the USA extended its claims in the Caribbean and Pacific. An explosion on an American warship in the port of Havana served as an excuse for **the Spanish-American War**, which ended in 1898 and was followed by Cuba's independence in 1902. The USA now claimed worldwide authority and operated imperialist policies in the Americas, intervening in Venezuela from 1902 to 1904 securing control, disputed under international law, of the

Panama Canal zone. President **Theodore Roosevelt** entered the world diplomatic stage as a mediator in the Treaty of Portsmouth, which ended the Russo-Japanese war, and at the conferences at Algeciras and the Hague. In World War I, the US at first declared neutrality, but in 1917, after the resumption of submarine warfare

by Germany, it entered the war on the side of the Allies.

Wilson's **Fourteen Point programme** for a democratic reconstruction of Europe was not implemented at the peace conferences of 1919. The USA did not join the **League of Nations** although it had been proposed by President Wilson. During

1 Midtown Manhattan: the architect Le Corbusier once described New York as a 'vertical city'. The buildings have to be narrow at the top for light to penetrate to street level.

2 The state of Maine is known for its spectacular coastline. The rugged rocks are topped with

old lighthouses such as this one dating from 1827.

3 Brightly illuminated Boston radiates a serene elegance, even by night. The capital of New England has around 600,000 inhabitants, small in comparison with other big cities in the US.

United States of America

During Prohibition, Mafia clans ruled in **Chicago**. Nowadays, it is the stockbrokers who rule the city. Chicago is one of the world's major trading centres and has the second most important commodities and futures market.

isolationism, women's suffrage and Prohibition were introduced. The ban on alcohol led to brisk smuggling and the rise of organised crime. The ban on alcohol was not lifted until 1933. The economy seemed to be booming, until the Stock Market Crash of 25 October 1929, known as **Black Friday.** President Hoover was unable to deal with the starvation and misery that resulted in the 1930s, and it was only the **New Deal** devised by his successor, Franklin D. Roosevelt, that slowly led the country back from disaster. The USA finally entered World War II after the Japanese attack on **Pearl Harbor** on 7 December

1941 and contributed substantially to the surrender of Nazi Germany on 8 May 1945. After the war, the USA abandoned its traditional foreign policy of nonintervention and became involved as an active world power. This role was imposed by the **East-West conflict,** which was to characterise world politics for more than forty years. The Marshall Plan, instigated and funded by the United States, for the reconstruction of Europe was introduced in 1947, and at the same time the **arms race** began with the Soviet Union. The USA took the leading role in the defence organisations of

NATO, SEATO and **CENTO** and reacted energetically to provocation such as the Berlin blockade and the Korean crisis. Stalin's death in 1953 seemed to usher in a phase of detente, but the political climate was intensified by the **Suez Crisis** and the failed Hungarian Revolution, both in 1956. The Berlin crisis at the end of 1958 and the conflict between Taiwan and the People's Republic of China followed. From 1950, the USSR had its own **atom bomb,** and from 1953, the **hydrogen bomb.** The shooting down of a U2 reconnaissance aircraft over the USSR and the successful Communist Revolution in Cuba in 1959

shattered the myth of American invincibility. At home, the McCarthy era brought a witch-hunt for real or supposed Communists, and the **Civil Rights movement** protests emerged to fight discrimination against African-Americans. The election victory of **John F. Kennedy** aroused great hopes, although his fame is to be sought in the legend of his vision of breaking through of new frontiers rather than in his actual success. Only by deploying federal troops was Kennedy able to end **racial segregation** in schools, already declared unconstitutional in 1954. From the point of view of foreign policy, the picture was

also somewhat negative. The attempted Bay of Pigs invasion by exiled Cubans in 1961, supported by the US government, was a miserable failed. Meanwhile, the Western world was forced to accept the building of the Berlin Wall. The **Cuban Missile Crisis** of 1962 led the world to the edge of global nuclear war, but was dispelled by the end of the year. After the **assassination of Kennedy** on 22 November 1963 in Dallas, Vice-president Johnson took over, inheriting a heavy burden. The **Vietnam War** and the civil rights movement, as well as the dependence of the USA on Arab oil imports, which became

John Fitzgerald Kennedy

*Brookline, 29.5.1917,
†Dallas, 22.11.1963

In 1960 the Democrat senator from Massachusetts won the presidential elections. His concept of the 'New Frontier' – an improvement of the social network, space programme and equal rights for Afro-Americans, appealed mainly to the younger generations. With regard to foreign affairs, the failed landing on Bay of Pig, the Cuban crisis and the Vietnam war fell into his responsibilty. The 35th President was assassinated in 1963 in Dallas.

Martin Luther King

*Atlanta, 15.1.1929,
†Memphis, Tenn., 4.4.1968

His sermons quickly made the Baptist priest into a symbol of peaceful resistance against the race discrimination in the USA. He was the chairman of several civil rights organisations and served repeated prison sentences as a reult. In 1964 he received the Nobel Prize for Peace. He was the target of several failed attempts on his life before he was tragically assasinated in 1968.

*From the **Kennedy Space Center** on Cape Canaveral in Florida a shuttle takes off on a space mission. The United States maintains the most ambitious and spectacular space programmes in the world, despite massive budget cuts. Shuttles are mainly deployed as they can be re-used. One of the most interesting space missions in recent years were the expeditions to Mars, which impressive the first pictures of Mars' surface.*

evident after the Six-Day War of 1967, impelled him to decline further candidacy in 1968. The new president, **Richard Nixon**, made efforts to normalise relations with China and to reach agreements on arms limitations (the SALT talks) with the Soviet Union. Despite the massive bombing of North Vietnam and Laos, the Americans finally withdrew in defeat in 1973. Two years later, South Vietnam collapsed. Although Secretary of State **Kissinger** received the **Nobel Peace Prize**, the myth of an invincible America was shattered. As many as 57,000 Americans lost their lives in Vietnam. On the domestic front, too, trust in the government was severely shaken when in 1974, two years after Nixon's re-election, the **Watergate affair** forced the president to resign.

Under **Gerald Ford**, the policy of disarmament continued and the Conference for Security and Cooperation in Europe was created. The foreign policy aim of President **Jimmy Carter** was to improve human rights abroad. His peace mediation between Egypt and Israel and the signing of two agreements on the Panama Canal were successful. But after the invasion of Afghanistan by the Soviet Union and the botched liberation of hostages in the US embassy in Tehran, the Republican opposition called for a return to **power politics**.

The former actor **Ronald Reagan**, who succeeded Carter in office in 1981 had the backing of the neo-conservative Republicans. The strength of America was to be renewed by a massive rearmament programme, including a plan for a new space defence system (the so-called 'Star Wars') and the deployment of new medium-range missiles in western Europe. Support for anti-communist regimes, regardless of their human rights record, was another aspect of Reagan's policy. The sending of US troops to **Lebanon**, the occupation of Grenada in 1983 and military strikes against the Libyan head of state **Ghaddafi** were calculated to boost American self-confidence. In President Reagan's second term of office, which was overshadowed by the **Iran-Contra affair**, there was a rapprochement with the Soviet Union,

which announced unilateral steps towards disarmament under **Mikhail Gorbachev**. The end of the Cold War was ushered in by the **START (Strategic Arms Reduction Treaty) discussions**. When **George Bush** moved into the White House in 1989, the USA was the only remaining superpower and self-confidently took on the role of **world policeman**. In 1989, for example, US troops marched into **Panama** and took General Noriega prisoner. Later, he was sentenced to 40 years in jail for drug-dealing in the USA. In 1991, the USA led the military **offensive** in an international alliance against the Iraqi aggressor **Saddam Hussein**, who was forced to reverse Iraq's occupation of Kuwait. The military mission in Somalia to secure UN assistance however remained without result. The economic policy of '**Reaganomics**', continued by President George Bush, introducing a period of high **unemployment**, a significant foreign trade deficit and an extremely high national debt. Not least as a result of the disastrous economic situation, the Democratic challenger William J. (Bill) **Clinton** succeeded in winning the presidential election of 1992. Clinton reduced the national debt, achieved almost full employment and strengthened the competitiveness of the economy. In terms of foreign affairs, he was able to gain international esteem through his peace negotiations between **Israel** and the **PLO** in 1993. In spite of Clinton's popularity, the Republicans pressed for his impeachment due to a **sexual scandal**, though this was averted after an embarrassing investigation. In the spring of 1999, NATO, under the military leadership of the USA, embarked on **bombing raids** on the former Yugoslavia, in order to prevent 'ethnic cleansing' in the semi-autonomous **Kosovo** region. In June 1999 Serbian units withdrew from Kosovo and international KFOR **peace-keeping** troops moved in.

1 The waters of Lake Erie reflect the clear-cut, elegant skyline of Cleveland, Ohio.

2 The palm-fringed boardwalk of Miami's South Beach oozes sunshine-state flair. The state has become a haven for retirees from the north seeking winter sunshine.

3 The picture of the traditional Mississippi paddlesteamer is inseparable from the image of longest river in the USA.

4 An old water-mill in West Virginia. The state is still very rural despite its coal mines.

United States of America

*The **Pueblo Indians** of Arizona and New Mexico are one of many Native American communities in the south-west. In 1680, they fought against subjugation by Catholic missionaries and won. The self-confident Pueblo Indians, so-called because they farmed and lived in villages, still practice their own religion: it is based on harmony between all beings and is also expressed in arts and crafts. Many Pueblo artists are renowned world-wide.*

In 2001 George W. Bush, son of George Bush, was sworn in as 43rd president. On **11 September 2001**, suicide bombers piloting hijacked aircraft destroyed the World Trade Center in New York and attacked the Pentagon in Washington. The result was a **military offensive against Afghanistan**, whose Taliban regime was sheltering the Al Qaida terrorist organisation. The war ended with the fall of the Taliban. A further result of 11 September was the **war against Iraq**, whom the USA accused of producing weapons of mass destruction and maintaining a worldwide terrorist network. The war began in the spring of 2003 and ended Saddam Hussein's rule. At home, Bush came under pressure after no weapons of mass destruction were found, and in Iraq, terrorist attacks were being carried out daily on the US forces.

The **constitution of 1789**, last amended in 1992, provides for a bicameral Congress. The 435 members of the **House of Rep-** resentatives are directly elected every two years, and the 100 **Senators** every six years, one-third being elected every two years. The president's serves for four years, with the option of one additional term. The head of state is not elected directly, but by an electoral college of 538 delegates. The voting age is 18 years.

Economy

The US economy is the largest in the world. In 2006, the GDP was US$13.2 trillion. This included **agriculture** at one per cent, **industry** at 22 per cent and the service sector at 77 per cent.

The area of land which is usable for agriculture amounts to some 47 per cent of the total land mass. The **enormous ranches,** averaging 190 ha, are used for breeding poultry, cattle, pigs and sheep. All kinds of fruits, vegetables and cereals are cultivated as well as tobacco. There are vineyards in the East and West. The USA is the world's largest exporter of wheat and the third largest of rice. The country's industry produces virtually every product imaginable, the most important categories being motor vehicles, electronics, chemicals, foodstuffs and metal-processing. The chief **imports** are capital goods, motor vehicles, luxury items and oil. The main **exports** are machinery and transport equipment, raw materials, consumer goods, motor vehicles and agricultural products. The most important **natural resources** are petroleum, natural gas, anthracite and brown coal, zinc, lead and gold.

Transport Infrastructure

The importance of the **railways** continues to decrease. The remaining 406,000 km of track are mainly used by private companies to transport freight. Passenger transport accounts for only 0.7 per cent of rail transport. Of a network of some 6,261,200 km of roads, 60 per cent is asphalted. The **Interstate Highways** link almost all the states and there are many freeways or parkways (motorways) inside the large cities, including New York, Chicago and Los Angeles, to

Two worlds in Nevada: Navajo shepherds and the glitz and glitter of Las Vegas are only kilometres apart.

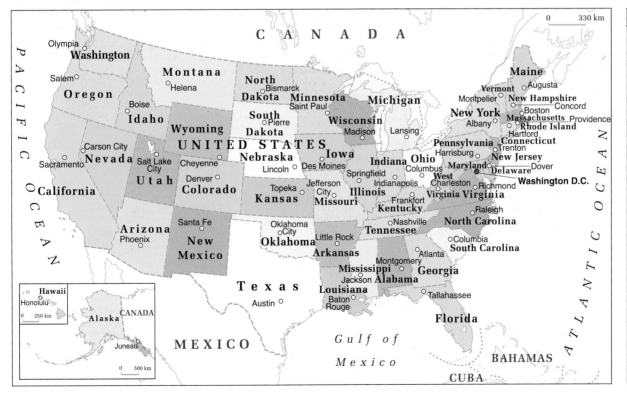

*The stuff that dreams are made of is produced in **Hollywood**: a day pretending to be movie star Mae West is in high demand as well as the ever popular Mickey and Minnie Mouse. Studio tours and theme parks are big attractions.*

aid the flow of traffic. However, due to the fact that public road transport has long been neglected in favour of the private car, there still tends to be massive road congestion in the cities. The public transport network is gradually being improved, with the construction of additional subway (underground) lines in cities such as Washington, D.C. and Los Angeles, but the problem still persists.

There are 13,400 airports in the USA. Of the 180 international airports, **Chicago O'Hare**, with 70 million passengers per year, is the largest in the world. The most important **seaports** are New Orleans, Houston, New York, Baltimore, Baton Rouge, Boston, Honolulu, Jacksonville, Los Angeles, Pittsburgh, Savannah, Seattle, Tampa and Toledo. **Inland navigation** is possible on 41,009 km of waterways.

Tourism

The **beaches** of Florida and California, the **surfing** spots of Hawaii, the impressive great cities, as well as the stunning landscapes, above all in the **national parks**, attracted 46.1 million tourists to the USA in 2004. In addition there is a strongly developed **domestic tourist industry**. In 2004, tourism brought in US$113 billion. The USA is a popular travel destination all year round; the **Indian summer** and autumn (fall) considered the most beautiful time of year, especially in New England.

New England

The name New England was coined in 1614 by the English captain John Smith. **Puritans** began to settle here from the early seventeenth century, followed by Scots and Irish. New York was at first a Dutch colony called New Amsterdam. The United States of America emerged from the earlier **New England Confederation**. Today, New England, with **Harvard University** and **MIT**, is one of the two intellectual centres of the USA, the other being Cali-

fornia. Agriculture, including livestock-rearing and the cultivation of fruit and vegetables, continue to be an important economic factor, as are fishing, timber and shipbuilding.

The Southern states

The Southern states are generally considered to be **conservative** in character and with an agriculture-based economy. The former cotton monoculture has given way to more diversified crops. In Virginia, despite massive anti-smoking campaigns, **tobacco-growing** remains important; Kentucky and

Tennessee have the most famous bourbon and rye **whiskey distilleries**, and **Cape Canaveral in Florida** is the launch site for the US space programme, under the control of Houston, Texas. The Florida **Everglades** offer breathtaking wonders of nature.

Great Lakes

The Great Lakes extend to the Canadian border and are linked by the **St Lawrence river** and numerous canals, so that giant ocean-going vessels can penetrate deep into the interior. Chicago O'Hare is the largest airport in the world and the automobile industry is centred in Detroit.

Midwest

The Midwest includes the states of Montana, North and South Dakota, Iowa, Missouri, Oklahoma, Kansas, Nebraska, Wyoming and Idaho. This area is chiefly agricultural. Of particular interest to

tourists is Wyoming, where the **Grand Teton National Park** and the **rodeos** attract many visitors. North-west of Montana lies the Glacier National Park. In South Dakota, there are the **Badlands National Park** and the Custer State Park. The Wild West is still alive near **Rapid City**, where the Indian chiefs **Crazy Horse** and

1 Denver: oil wells and an average of 300 days of sunshine a year attract newcomers to the 'mile-high' city.

2 The 2.7-km-long Golden Gate Bridge spans the San Francisco Bay, connecting

San Francisco with the famous wine-growing Sonoma Valley.

3 The vastness of Monument Valley in Arizona is legendary. The whole area is dotted with typical red sandstone outcrops called mesas and tumbleweed. This is Navajo Indian territory.

United States of America

Puerto Rico's capital city San Juan has preserved the character of its Spanish colonial past. Yet the picturesque views surrounding Fort Aleza conceals Puerto Rico's past when the indigenous people fought bitter battles against the Spanish colonists. The local people's defeat and their subsequent colonialisation were only possible due to the African slaves the Spanish brought in to fight alongside them. Puerto Rico is now a commonwealth of the USA.

Sitting Bull were based, and where the US cavalry lost General Custer's units at the Battle of Little Big Horn. This is where the conflicts with Native Americans ended with their massacre at the Battle of **Wounded Knee**. Near Keystone, five US presidents have been immortalised in stone by monumental likenesses carved into Mount Rushmore.

South-west

The states of Arizona, New Mexico, Nevada and Utah are sparsely populated due to the inhospitable landscape. Here, too, the Wild West lives on. Abandoned ghost towns from pioneer days and the rock formations of **Monument Valley** are familiar locations in many Western films. The salt lakes can film industry, and San Francisco, with its famous **Golden Gate Bridge**, attracts tourists, as do the national parks of Yosemite, Sequoia, Kings Canyon, Joshua Tree and Death Valley, and the exclusive, resort of Malibu with its famous Getty Museum, built as a re-creation of the Roman Villa of the Scrolls in southern Italy.

The **Pacific Coast of Oregon**, with its lovely mountains, waterfalls and forests has hardly been discovered by European tourists. Its attractions include the Crater Lake National Park, **Hell's Canyon** and old Portland. Apart from the busy city of Seattle, the embarkation port for Alaska, the state of Washington offers a number of impressive national parks and the beautiful Cascade Mountains, which includes Mount Hood, (3,426 m).

was sold to the USA in 1876. Before Alaska became the 49th state of the USA in 1959, it was a district until 1912, then a territory. Its main industries are fishing, logging and the processing of oil, natural gas, gold, iron, copper, tin, coal, asbestos and uranium. The capital is **Juneau**.

Hawaii

In 1798, James Cook discovered the **Sandwich Islands**, which cover an area of 28,313 sq. km and have 1.2 million inhabitants. Seven of the eight main islands are inhabited: Hawaii, Maui, Oahu, Kauai, Molokai, Lanai and Niihau. The Hawaiian state flag still features the union flag.

The capital is **Honolulu** on Oahu. In 1959, Hawaii became the 50th

came a protectorate of New Zealand after World War I, and gained independence in 1962. The **government** consists of a House of Representatives and a Senate as well as a US governor. The capital is **Pago Pago** on Tutuila. The main industry is **fishing**.

Guam

The largest of the Mariana islands at 541 sq. km is Guam, with some **160,000 inhabitants**, mostly Malayan Chamorros and Filipinos.

Missions to the island from Spain began in 1668. In 1889, the Spanish ceded Guam to the USA. The Japanese occupation, from 1941, ended in 1944 with the island's reconquest by the USA. Since 1982, Guam has had internal **au-**

From 1672, the region was colonised by Denmark, and St Croix was under French administration up to 1733. In 1917, Denmark sold the islands to the USA for US$25 million. Since 1927, the inhabitants have had US citizenship. The **government** consists of a 15-member parliament and a US governor. Almost all the income from the Virgin Islands derives from tourism.

US Commonwealth territories

Northern Marianas

Of these 16 volcanic and coral islands, with a total land area of 541 sq. km, only six are inhabited. The 52,284 inhabitants are predomi-

Richard Milhous Nixon

*Yorba Linda, 9.1.1913,
†Park Ridge, 22.4.1994

The former senator for California was elected the 37th President of the US in 1968. Together with Secretary of State Kissinger, he tried to de-escalate the Vietnam War, limit the arms race and normalise the relations with the People's Republic of China. The Watergate affair forced him to resign in 1974, two years after his re-election.

Waikiki Beach is the tourist centre of Hawaii, with an average of 80 hotels per sq. km.

of Utah, the **Grand Canyon**, the gambling city of Las Vegas and the national parks attract numbers of tourists, as do the mesas of New Mexico and Arizona, where many retirees come for the healthy climate. On account of the almost dust-free air, the **high-tech industry** has made its home here.

Pacific States

The states of California, Oregon and Washington are both agricultural and industrial, but tourism and, in California, the **computer industry**, play important roles. California is known as the Golden State due to its former gold rushes. **Hollywood**, a suburb of Los Angeles, is the centre of the Ameri-

States outside the continental United States

Alaska

Although Alaska has a land area of 1,700,138 sq. km, it only has some 669,000 inhabitants, including **Inuit**, **Native Americans**, Aleuts, Blacks, Asians, and 35,000 **members of the armed forces**. The **Alaska mountains** are in the south and include the 6,193-m-high Mount McKinley. There are fjords along the coast. The flat central plain, containing the **Yukon** and Kuskokwim rivers lies just south of the Arctic Circle. Alaska was discovered in 1741 and was a Russian possession until it

state of the USA. The main industry is **tourism**.

Overseas territories

American Samoa

This group of volcanic islands – Tutuila, Ta'u, Aunn'n, Olosega, Ofu and the atolls of Rose Island and Swains Island – cover a total land area of 194.8 sq. km. The population numbers **60,000 inhabitants** mainly of Polynesian descent. After its discovery by the Dutch, it was jointly ruled by Britain, Germany and the USA from 1889. Eastern Samoa became part of the USA in 1900, while Western Samoa be-

tonomy. The 15-member parliament is elected every two years, and the governor every four years. The capital is **Agana**. There is a US Army base on the island due to its **strategic importance**, and it is the main source of income. **Tourism** is also a big earner for the islands.

US Virgin Islands

The main islands, St Thomas, St Croix and St John, in this 348 sq. km island group in the **Caribbean**, have 97,120 inhabitants, of whom 80 per cent are **Black or mixed race** and 15 per cent **White**. When it was discovered by Columbus in 1493, it was inhabited by Caribs and Arawaks.

nantly Polynesian. They are US citizens but have no right to vote in US federal elections. The islands were discovered by **Magellan** in 1521 and were under Spanish rule until 1898. They were then sold to **Germany** and from 1920 they were a **Japanese mandated territory**. The Japanese used the islands as a strategic base during World War II. After 1945, the US Departments of Defense and the Interior took over the administration of the islands. In 1978, the islands adopted a constitution and in 1986 the UN trusteeship ended, and internal **autonomy** was proclaimed. Both chambers of the parliament are elected every two years, and the governor is elected every five years. The main source of income is **tourism**.

Puerto Rico

The islands of Puerto Rico, Mona, Vieques and Culebra have a total area of 8,959 sq. km. Of the 3.8 million inhabitants, 85 per cent are Spanish-speaking and 81 per cent are **Catholic**. After its discovery by Columbus in 1493, the Spanish colonised Puerto Rico, running **sugar-cane plantations** which were worked by slaves, and exploiting the mineral resources.

After the Spanish-American war in 1898, Puerto Rico was governed by the USA. In 1917, the inhabitants were granted limited US citizenship. In 1952, Puerto Rico was granted internal **autonomy**. In 1993, the population rejected both complete independence and also annexation by the USA as its 51st state. The government consists of a directly elected governor and a parliament. The inhabitants are US citizens, but have no voting rights in federal elections. Most of Puerto Rico's income is earned from tourism and from remitances sent home by those living in the US.

United States minor outlying islands in the Pacific

Baker Island

This 1.5 sq. km atoll is **uninhabited** and may only be accessed by scientists. The US Department of the Interior is responsible for its administration.

Howland Island

This 2.3 sq. km island is **uninhabited** and can be accessed for scientific purposes only. It is under the jurisdiction of the US Department of the Interior.

Jarvis Island

Only scientists can gain access to this 7.7 sq. km uninhabited island for research purposes. The US Department of the Interior is responsible for its administration.

Johnston Atoll

The north and east islands of this 2.6 sq. km atoll were a **test area for nuclear weapons** and are off limits up to the present day. The main island has a facility for disposing of chemical weapons. The atoll is being vacated and has been for sale since 2005.

Kingman Reef

This eight sq. km coral reef is **uninhabited** and is administered by the US Navy.

Midway Islands

This 5.2 sq. km coral atoll has been a US possession since 1867 and a **naval base** since 1903. In 1942, The Battle of Midway, one of the most famous sea battles in the war in the Pacific , was fought here. The 435 inhabitants all serve in the US Navy, which will shortly hand over the administration of the islands to the US Department of the Interior.

Palmyra

This six sq. km atoll is **private property**, but is administered by the US Department of the Interior.

Wake Island

The three coral islands, Wake, Wilkes and Peal, have a total area of 7.8 sq. km and about 200 inhabitants. They are administered by the **US Air Force**. The Republic of the Marshall Islands lays claim to the atoll.

United States minor outlying islands in the Caribbean

Navassa Island

This 5.2 sq. km island is **uninhabited** but serves as a base of yachtsmen and fishermen. It is administered by the US coastguard station.

Guantanamo Bay Naval Base

The 117 sq. km US naval base is on Cuban territory and has become notorious as the place in which suspected terrorists have been held without trial since 2002.

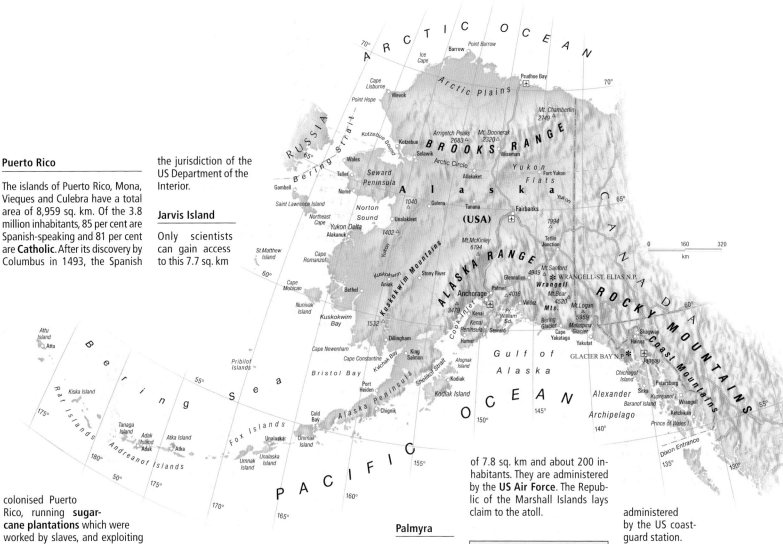

A bay surrounded by 16 glaciers: the Glacier National Park in south-eastern Alaska.

Since the end of World War II the USA has carried out many military actions, initially with the aim of stemming the rise of communist power (the Korean War, the Vietnam War). With the end of the Cold War, the Americans concentrated on securing important sources of raw materials, particularly in the

Arabian area (the Gulf War, the Iraq War). These images show US invasion troops in North Korea in 1950 (left, top), wounded US soldiers in South Vietnam in 1966 (left, below), US tanks in front of burning Kuwaiti oil wells in 1991 (right, top) and Marines in the desert near Baghdad in 2003 (right, below).

Cities of North America

San Francisco

San Francisco lies in the US state of California at the northern end of the peninsula between San Francisco Bay and the Pacific Ocean. The city's geographical location on the San Andreas fault caused the greatest catastrophe in its history: 80 per cent of the city was destroyed in 1906 in a devastating earthquake and the major fire that followed. San Francisco recovered quickly from this natural disaster. The Golden gate Bridge, a potent icon of the city completed in 1937 is symbolic of its recovery. San Francisco was the focus of American hippy culture in the 1960s and today still enjoys a reputation for liberalism, with a diverse and cosmopolitan population.

Area:
122 sq. km (city)
Inhabitants:
744,000 (city, 2006)
4,204,000 (conurbation, 2007)
Population density:
6,098 inhabitants/sq. km (city)

View through the Golden Gate Bridge to the pyramid of the Transamerica Building (left).

Los Angeles

The metropolitan area of the American city of Los Angeles is the second largest conurbation in the USA after New York. It includes towns such as Long Beach, Pasadena, Santa Monica, Beverly Hills and Malibu. Like San Francisco, Los Angeles lies on the San Andreas fault. The suburb of Hollywood forms the base of the US film industry. The city is a significant industrial and trading metropolis and home to the world's largest concentration of aeronautical and aerospace companies. Los Angeles can be traced back to a Spanish settlement founded in 1781. The summer Olympic Games took place here in 1932 and 1984.

Area:
1,200 sq. km (city)
Inhabitants:
3,850,000 (city, 2008)
12,950,000 (conurbation, 2001)
Population density:
3,208 inhabitants/sq. km (city)

Los Angeles: Freeways up to five lanes wide are the lifelines of this metropolis.

Chicago

The third largest city in the USA, Chicago lies in the US state of Illinois on the south-west bank of Lake Michigan. The city's position on the Great Lakes made it an important industrial and trading base from an early date. Grain was transhipped here and steel produced. Until the mid-twentieth century, Chicago was also a centre for the meat-packing industry with many slaughterhouses. However, the steel crisis in the 1970s had a very negative effect on the city's economic position. Chicago's first steel-framed skyscraper (the Home Insurance Building) was built in 1885 but demolished in 1931. The Sears Tower, which was completed in 1974, is one of the tallest buildings in the world at 442 m.

Area:
606 sq. km (city)
Inhabitants:
2,840,000 (city, 2006)
9,440,000 (conurbation, 2006)
Population density:
4,686 inhabitants/sq. km (city)

Chicago, the third largest city in the USA, has the world's largest river port.

New York

The largest city in the USA, New York lies in the Federal State of New York where the Hudson River enters the Atlantic. New York, 'the city that never sleeps', comprises five districts: Manhattan, the Bronx, Brooklyn, Queens and Staten Island. It houses the permanent headquarters of the United Nations and the New York Stock Exchange, located in Wall Street, the world's largest stock exchange in dollar volume. Founded in 1626 as New Amsterdam, its name was changed by the British after they won the colony from the Dutch in 1664. New York experienced one of the worst moments in its history on 11 September 2001 when Islamic terrorists flew two aircraft into the twin towers of the World Trade Center.

Area:
800 sq. km (city)
Inhabitants:
8,214,000 (city, 2006)
18,816,000 (conurbation, 2007)
Population density:
10,265 inhabitants/sq. km (city)

View over Manhattan, the island between the Hudson River, the East River and Harlem River.

Mexico

Area:	1,972,550 sq. km
Capital city:	Mexico City
Form of government:	
Federal Presidential Republic	
Administrative divisions:	
5 regions; 31 federal states,	
1 capital district	
Population:	
106 million	
(54 inhabitants/sq. km)	
Languages:	
Spanish (official),	
minority languages	
GDP per capita:	US$8, 000
Currency:	
1 Mexican peso = 100 centavos	

Natural Geography

North and central Mexico are covered by the **Meseta Central**, a highland plateau with elevations of 1,300 m in the south. The substrate of the high plain is characterised by **river basins**, **mountainous ridges** and **rift valleys** and is surrounded by massive, rugged mountain ranges extending about 1,200 km towards the

Basalt formations near Durango.

coast, by the **Sierra Madre Occidental** in the west with elevations up to 3,000 m and by the equally high **Sierra Madre Oriental** in the east. The southern central highland, the **Sistema Volcánica Transversal or Cordillera Neovolcánica**, consists of a volcanic belt in which Mexico's highest mountains are situated. These are the **Citlaltépetl** (5,700 m), **Popocatépetl** (5,452 m) and the **Iztaccíhuatl** (5,286 m). The mountain ridge of the **Sierra Mixteca** links the highland with the **Sierra Madre del Sur**, a

labyrinth of narrow mountain peaks and deep valleys, with summits reaching 3,000 m. The **Chiapas Highland** is connected to the **Isthmus of Tehuantepec**, the narrowest point in Mexico. Long beaches, marshes, sand banks and lagoons are typical of the Gulf coast. The lowland region reaches its widest point of 450 km at the limestone plain of the **Yucatán Peninsula**. In the north-west, the **Baja California** Peninsula, which is on average only 90 km wide, stretches over about 1,250 km, with elevations of up to 3,000 m. The most important rivers are the **Río Grande del Norte**, defining the northern border, the **Río Lerma**, which flows from its source in the Toluca high valley, feeding the **Lago de Chapala**, Mexico's largest inland lake, and emptying into the Pacific as the **Río Grande de Santiago**. In the north-eastern and Baja California deserts, the flora consists mainly of **succulents** and **cactuses**; in the southern highland steppe, there are **thorn bushes** and **agave plants**; in the evergreen tropical forest running along the coastal strip of the south-western Gulf of Mexico, there are **mangroves, bamboo, ferns** and **orchids**; the tropical rainforest in the southern Yucatán Peninsula contains **mahogany trees**, tropical **palms, chicle trees, epiphytes** and **kapok trees**.
The fauna is similarly varied. There are numerous **predators**, such as wolves, coyotes, black bears and lynxes, also **red deer and wild boars** as well as **capebaras** and various **reptiles** such as alligators,

rattle snakes and iguanas and many **species of bird and insect**.

Climate

Due to the enormous expanse of land from north to south and the numerous mountains, the country has a variety of different climates. The **sub-tropical areas** in the north have **hot dry summers** and

temperate winters, whereas the tropical **south** is hot and damp the whole year round. Central Mexico is roughly divided in terms of climate into the **Tierra caliente** (up to approximately 700 m above sea-level) with an average annual

temperature of over 25°C, the Tierra templada with temperatures of 18–25°C, the Tierra fría with temperatures of 12–18°C, at the upper limit of vegetation at 4,000–4,700 m, and the Tierra helada in the perpetual snow zone. South of the central high plains, average **annual rainfall**

is about 600 mm, but in many places in the north rainfall is only 250 mm. The **Baja California Peninsula** experiences similarly low levels of rainfall, whereas on average 1,000 mm falls on the Pacific coast, primarily between June and September. In the **trade winds** area on the Gulf of Mexico, rain falls evenly throughout the

The whole of Mexico celebrates 12 December as the day of the Virgin of **Guadalupe**. According to legend, the Virgin appeared on several occasions to the baptised Native American Juan Maria in 1531. The fervent celebrations on this day symbolise the deep piety in Mexico, especially among the native population. The culture of Aztecs and traditional animist beliefs have been syncretised with Catholicism.

year. This area is also within the **hurricane** belt. The highest precipitation of over 4,000 mm falls in the **Tabasco lowlands**. On the west coast, **tropical tornados** start in the **Gulf of Tehuantepec** and move northwards creating damage as far north as Southern California in the USA.

Population

Mexico's population is 60 per cent **mestiso (Spanish-Amerindian)**, 14 per cent **Amerindian** and nine per cent **white**. In addition, there are approximately **150,000 foreigners** who live permanently in the country. The urban population is 76 per cent. Average **life expectancy** is 75 years; the **illiteracy** rate is ten per cent; **infant mortality** is 2.7 per cent;

childhood **mortality** at 3.2 per cent and **population growth** at around 1.5 per cent. There are on average 2.2 births per woman. **Catholics** make up 89.7 per cent of the population, **Protestants** 4.9 per cent. The rest belong to the **Jewish**, **Baha'i** and **traditional religions**.

School attendance is compulsory for children aged between six and twelve years; secondary education lasts for up to six years and is voluntary; **school enrollment quota** is more or less 100 per cent. State primary schools are free of charge.

History and Politics

There is evidence of a **hunter-gatherer culture**. dating from about 22,000 years ago. In about 3000 BC., the first permanent settlements were founded and in 1100 BC, the **Olmecs** developed the first advanced civilisation whose centre was in **La Venta** . Between 200 and 600 AD, the **Teotihuacán** kingdom produced the first major examples of urban architecture. Their city had approximately 200,000

inhabitants. Trade and manufacturing guaranteed **relative prosperity**. The invasion of foreign peoples from the north determined Central Mexico's subsequent fate until the Spanish conquerors first made their appearance. In the twelfth century BC, the **Chicmecs** succeeded the the **Toltecs** as rulers. An advanced **Mayan** civilisation developed on the Yucatán Peninsula in 1200 BC. Between 400 BC and 300 AD, the Mayas developed a **written script** and a sophisticated **calendar system** which they were able to devise through astronomical predictions. During this period of prosperity, there were 110 religious and political centres lasted until the tenth century AD. There are varying theories concerning the decline of the Maya. The **Aztec's domination** of central Mexico began when **Tenochtitlán** was founded in 1370. In the mid-fifteenth century, King **Moctezuma I** created a

Mexico

*The cliffs of **Acapulco** rise to a height of 40 m and are rugged and magnificent. Several times a day young daredevils – the so-called 'Clavidistas' – leap from the highest rocks into La Quebrada bay. Acapulco is also famous for its night life, bars and luxury hotels. This port city in south-west Mexico was once an exclusive resort for the upper classes but it is now popular with tourists from around the world.*

territory that stretched from the Gulf to the Pacific coast. Under **Moctezuma II**, a **central administrative and legal system** was established along with a very tightly organised army. Aztec civilisation was doomed when in 1519 the Spanish explorer, **Hernán Cortez,** landed on the Gulf coast. The Spanish completely conquering the kingdom in 1547, aided by the psychological effects of **firearms** and a clever policy of alliances with **enemies of the Aztecs**. Tenochtitlán fell in 1521 and the new **capital of Mexico City** was created. In 1535, Spain appointed a viceroy to rule the colony of New Spain. More than 12 million Amerindians lost their lives in clashes with the colonists before 1570. Many of the deaths were due to **infections** and **diseases** that the Europeans brought with them. The colonial period lasted 300 years.

At the beginning of the nineteenth century **tensions** were mounting between the Spanish motherland and the colonial population. The ideas of liberty propagated by the French Revolution and the American colonists' War of Independence coupled with brutal economic exploitation of New Spain by the Spanish crown triggered the **Mexican War of Independence** in 1810, led by the priests **Miguel Hidalgo** and **José Maria Morelos**. **Augustín de Itúrbide**, who was crowned emperor of Mexico in 1822, renounced Spain, but was deposed two years later. The new republic was marked by extreme political and economic instability. By the end of the dictatorship in 1854/55, the government had changed 34 times.

The **USA** attacked the country in 1846-1847 due to unpaid debts and occupied half of the country under the Peace Treaty of Guadalupe Hidalgo. The **constitutional reform** implemented by **Benito Juárez**, Minister for Justice and later President, also failed to stabilise the political situation. In 1861, Mexico was occupied by **British**, **French** and **Spanish** troops. In 1864, the French appointed **Maximilian von Hapsburg** as emperor of Mexico. As **Napoleon III** of France withdrew, his troops under pressure from the USA, Juárez seized power and had Maximilian executed in 1867.

Although the dictatorship of Porfirio Díaz managed to put the economy back on its feet in the 35 years preceding 1911, he did not manage to end social tensions. The **Mexican revolution** began in 1910, led by **Pancho Villa** and **Emiliano Zapata**, and this led to the fall of Díaz in 1911.

After the civil war ended in 1920, the socialist maxims of the 1917 constitution caused owners of large land holdings to be dispossessed and mineral resources were placed under state control. In 1938, President **Lázaro Cárdenas** nationalised the oil industry and the railways. After World War II, there was a modest economic upturn, but this ended abruptly in 1982. From then on, the **Partido Revolucionario Institucional (PRI)**, which had ruled continually since 1929, gradually lost its position of power. In 1997, the PRI lost its absolute majority in Parliament and the mayor's post in Mexico City for the first time. There was a severe **economic crisis** in 1994 following the privatisation of the banks and entry into the NAFTA free trade zone. After the presidential elections in 2006, the winner Calderón was only able to assume office under conditions of protest similar to a general strike. Serious internal political concerns remain unsolved, such as: **corruption, nepotism, politically motivated homicides**, a powerful **drug mafia** and the armed struggle of the **Zapatista Army of National Liberation**, which fights for equal opportunities for the Amerindian population in the state of Chiapas.

Mexico is a **federal presidential republic** under a constitution, which has been altered several

Mexico city: the 'floating gardens' of Xochimilco.

On the Yucatán peninsula vendors sell tropical fruits.

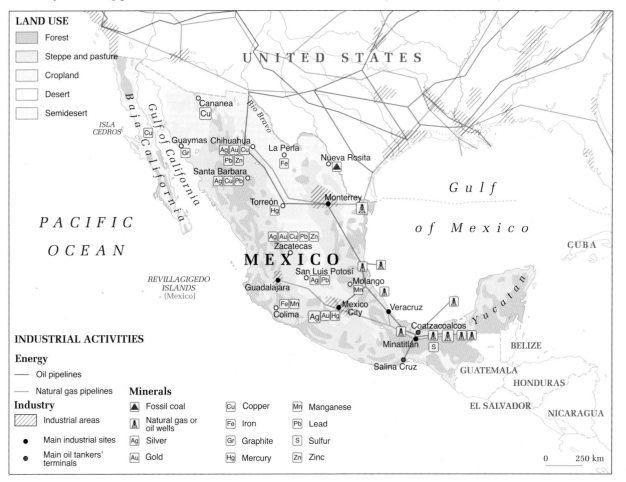

LAND USE

- Forest
- Steppe and pasture
- Cropland
- Desert
- Semidesert

INDUSTRIAL ACTIVITIES

Energy

— Oil pipelines
— Natural gas pipelines

Industry

- Industrial areas
- Main industrial sites
- Main oil tankers' terminals

Minerals

▲	Fossil coal	Cu	Copper	Mn	Manganese
▲	Natural gas or oil wells	Fe	Iron	Pb	Lead
Ag	Silver	Gr	Graphite	S	Sulfur
Au	Gold	Hg	Mercury	Zn	Zinc

0   250 km

*A Mexican woman making a tortilla in a special pan. The popular tortillas or tacos are eaten with spicy food in **Oaxaca**. Beans and sweetcorn are staple foods in Mexico. Cornmeal mush and thick soups as well as bread are made from slaked corn dough, known as masa harina. Cooking and raising children are women's work and in the countryside this strict Catholic division of roles has been preserved to this day.*

times since 1917. The 31 states (Estados) and the capital city's Federal District (Distrito Federal) have their own constitution and enjoy a relatively high degree of autonomy. The **President** is head of the government and commander-in-chief of the armed forces. He is elected directly for a six-year term. Citizens are **entitled to vote** from the age of 18. The **bicameral system** consists of a **House of Representatives** and a **Senate**. The Cámera Federal de Diputados has 500 members, of whom 300 are directly elected for a three-year term. The 128 senators are elected for six years.

Economy

In 2006, **GDP** was US$840 billion, to which **agriculture** contributed six per cent, **industry** 26 per cent and the **services sector** 68 per cent. **Unemployment** stood at four per cent and the **rate of inflation** 3.3 per cent. About a quarter of the labour force is employed in agriculture. The main crops are **maize**, **sugar cane**, **vegetables**, **coffee**, **cotton** and **cereals**. Further important contributors are **cattle-breeding**, **fishing** and the **timber and paper industries**.

Industry employs 22 per cent of the labour force. **Cars**, **textiles**, **electronics** and **chemicals** are produced. **Petroleum**, **natural gas**, **zinc**, **salt**, **copper**, **uranium**, **manganese**, **gold** and **silver** are also significant economic contributors. The tourism sector earned US$11.6 billion. The balance of trade is even. Manufactured goods are exported, of which the major components are 21 per cent **electrical devices**, 18 per cent **motor vehicles** and **parts**, 12 per cent **machinery**, ten per cent **oil** and four per cent **chemicals**.

The major **imports** are 51 per cent **machinery** and **vehicles**, 16 per cent **chemicals** and **plastics**, eight per cent **iron** and **steel** and four per cent **paper** and **printing products**. The USA is the major trade partner.

Pollution is becoming a serious problem in Mexico, due to the massive output of fumes from 130,000 factories and 2.5 million motor vehicles. Official laxity in this respect, in order to encourage foreign investment is likely to cause serious problems for the future and is a deterrent to tourism. There have been two serious gas explosions, one in 1984 in Mexico City and the other in 1992 in Guadalajara. Despite public outrage, little has been done to prevent future disasters.

Transport Infrastructure

Although the **transport network** has been expanded in recent times, some mountainous areas are still barely accessible. **Air transport** therefore plays an important role in travel. There are 33 national and 55 international airports, the largest of them in

Mexico City. The **road network** is 249,520 km long, of which 5,920 km are motorways or toll roads and 45,600 km federal highways. The remaining roads are only partly paved; the proportion of surfaced roads is around 37 per cent. The almost 21,000 km long **rail network** handles passenger and freight traffic. The 49 **seaports** on the Pacific and Caribbean coasts handle 85 per cent of exports.

Tourism

In 2004, there were 20.4 million foreign visitors to the beaches of **Acapulco**, **Puerto Vallarta** and the resorts of Cancún and the relics of pre-Columbian civilisation. Mexico City, built on a dried up crater lake, is the cultural centre of the country and has world-famous archaeological and art museums. Other notable buildings include the sixteenth-century cathedral and the Ministry of Education building which has murals by Mexico's most famous artist, Diego Rivera. Other cities that have interesting colonial architecture are Guadalajara and Monterrey. Due to its geographical location, Mexico City suffers from bad air pollution and traffic jams. The ideal **time to travel** to Mexico is between November and March when the weather is cooler.

1 The Pico de Orizaba National Park is situated between Vera Cruz and Pueblais around the Pico de Orizaba mountain peak (5,700 m).

2 Mexico City: The Zócalo in the centre of the capital is the site of the oldest cathedral in Latin America. Although it is 250 years old, it blends in well with the modern surroundings.

3 The 'street of the dead' and the sun pyramid. Teotihuacán was once a huge city but the founders remain unknown.

Honduras: The ruined city of Copán was only excavated in the nineteenth century. It is the biggest Mayan city discovered so far. The number of inhabitants has been estimated by experts at about 200,000, for whom Copán served as a ceremonial centre. Large stone figures from different eras fill the temple. The 'hieroglyphic stairs' are impressive, containing the longest known Mayan text.

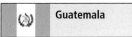 **Guatemala**

Area: 108,889 sq. km
Capital city: Guatemala City
Form of government: Presidential Republic
Administrative divisions: 22 departments
Population: 13 million (119 inhabitants/sq. km)
Languages: Spanish (official), Mayan-languages
GDP per inhabitant: US$2,300
Currency: 1 quetzal = 100 centavos

Natural Geography

The **Petén lowlands** in the north form part of the **Yucatán Peninsula**. The fertile Pacific coastline is up to 50 km wide. The **Cuchumatanes Mountains** and **Madre Mountains** are in the south. Of the 30 semi-active volcanoes, **Tajumulco volcano** at 4,220 m is the highest.

Climate

The lowlands have a **warm, humid climate** throughout the year, with average temperatures ranging between 25°C and 30°C. At altitudes between 600 m and 1500 m, the average temperature is 18°C, and at altitudes above 1,500 m it is 12°C. The **rainy season** lasts from May to October. Rainfall depends on the northeast trade wind. In the Caribbean lowlands and on the Pacific coast, precipitation is between 1,000 and 2,000 mm; in the mountains, it is up to 1,000 mm and in the plains and valleys, 6,000 mm.
The north and the Caribbean lowlands are covered with evergreen rain forests, which become tropical mountain forests, pinewoods, oak wood and mixed forest at higher elevations. On the Pacific Coast, there are dry forests and the Petén Lowlands are covered in savannah with pine scrub. Among the rich variety of fauna, there are pumas, manatee, jaguars, crocodiles, monkeys, tapirs and many types of birds.

Population

60 per cent of the population is **Amerindians**; 30 per cent is mestizo; **blacks**, **zambo** and **whites** constitute the remaining ten per cent. In addition to 80 per cent **Catholics** and 19 per cent **Protestants** there is a minority of **Bahai**. The average life expectancy is 69 years. The **literacy rate** is 60 per cent. Some 47 per cent of Guatemalans live in overcrowded city districts and over half live below the poverty line.

History and Politics

When **Pedro de Alvarado** conquered the country in 1524 for the Spanish Crown, the **Mayan** civilisation had been in decline for 600 years. In 1543, Guatemala became governed by the **Viceroy of New Spain**. After the withdrawal of the Spanish in 1821, the country came under Mexican administration and from 1823 until 1838, it was part of the **Central American Federation**. Guatemala became independent in 1847, and has since been ruled by a succession of dictators. Since the early twentieth century, most have been puppets of the powerful **United Fruit Company**. In 1944, a popular uprising, leading to a general election and democratic rule started what is known as 'The Ten Years of Spring', a period of free speech, political activity and proposed land reform under President Juan José Arévalo. In 1951, left-wing President **Arbenz Guzmán** initiated further reforms. All this ended in 1954 with the help of the CIA. Gen. Ydígoras Fuentes seized power in 1958 following the murder of Col. Castillo Armas. Left-wing guerrillas fought the government and the military, countered by extreme right-wing 'death squads'. The **civil war** lasted 36 years until the 1996 Peace Agreement with the loss of 200,000 lives. Guatemala is now a democratic presidential republic with a parliament elected every four years and a directly elected president. The voting age is 18.

Economy

In 2006 GDP was US$30 billion, of which 24 per cent derived from **agriculture**, 20 per cent from **industry** and 56 per cent from the **services sector**. Machinery, vehicles, consumer goods and raw materials are imported, coffee, sugar, bananas, cotton and timber are exported.

Transport Infrastructure

Guatemala has a 17,000-km-long **road network** and two **international airports**.

Tourism

Despite high levels of crime, in 2004, income from tourism amounted to almost US$800 million. Sites of special interest are Guatemala City, the Mayan centre of worship at **Tikal**, the colonial architecture of Antigua and Quetzaltenango and the national parks.

The Mask Temples of Tikal in Northern Guatemala.

 **Belize**

Area: 22,965 sq. km
Capital city: Belmopan
Form of government: Constitutional Monarchy within the Commonwealth
Administrative divisions: 6 districts
Population: 300,000 (13 inhabitants/sq. km)
Languages: English (official), Creole-English, Spanish, minority languages
GDP per inhabitant: US$4,000
Currency: 1 Belize dollar = 100 cents

Natural Geography

The green, flat hills in the northwest, change into humid, marshy coastal lowlands towards the Caribbean coast. A coral reef 250 km long parallel to the coast is divided into many **coral** atolls. At 1,122 m, Victoria Peak is the highest of the **Mayan Mountains**.

Climate

A **tropical humid climate** predominates. The average rainfall is 1,400 mm in the north and west, 2,500 mm on the slopes and up to 4,000 mm in the high altitudes. The average temperature is 26°C, while in the in the mountainous regions it is 24°C. The country is frequently afflicted by devastating **cyclones**. Almost half of Belize is covered with deciduous or evergreen **forests**. Belize also has **palm savannahs** and there are **mangrove swamps** on the coast. Jaguars, armadillos, tapirs and snakes, live in the forests and crocodiles and alligators live in the fresh and salt waters.

Population

The population of Belize consists of 43.6 per cent **mestizo**, 29.8 per cent **Creole**, 11 per cent **Amerindian** and 6.6 per cent **Garifuna**. 58 per cent of the population are Catholic and 28 per cent **Protestant**, there are also **Muslims**, **Hindus**, **Jews** and Bahai. Life expectancy is 68 years, only seven per cent of the population is illiterate.

History and Politics

Before **Columbus** discovered Belize in the early sixteenth century and Cortez turned it into a Spanish colony in 1524 and 1525, it was at the heart of the Mayan civilisation.
Around the mid-seventeenth century, **British pirates** came to Belize followed by settlers. In the subsequent period, the Spaniards and the British fought over the area. After the Spaniards were expelled from Central America in 1821, **Guatemala** imposed a turf war, whose effects are felt even today. In 1862, the colony of **British Honduras** was founded which became a Crown Colony in 1871. It was renamed **Belize** in 1973 and in 1981, it was granted **independence**. The British monarch, as head of state, is represented by a governor-general. The 1981 Constitution provides for a **bicameral parliament**. The congressmen are elected every five years, and senators are appointed every eight years by the governor-general. The voting age is 18 years.

Economy

In 2006, GDP was just US$1.2 billion, of which 20 per cent derived from **agriculture**, 23 per cent from **industry** and 57 per cent from the **services sector**. Machinery, consumer goods and raw materials are imported. Exports include timber, sugar, citrus fruits, bananas, fruit juices and fish and shellfish.

Transport Infrastructure

Around 1,600 km of the 2,000 km **road network** is passable throughout the year. Stanley Field is the major **airport**; the largest **sea ports** are at Belize City and Stann Creek.

Tourism

In 2002 over 250,000 tourists visited the ancient Mayan ruins, the coral atolls and the 17 national parks with their rich wildlife. The best time to travel is from November to April.

Guatemala: In Chichicastenango old Mayan and Catholic myths have been syncretised into a unique mixture. The city was founded on the ruins of a Mayan place of worship. Once a year, thousands of Guatemalans come here to celebrate Santo Tomás Day.

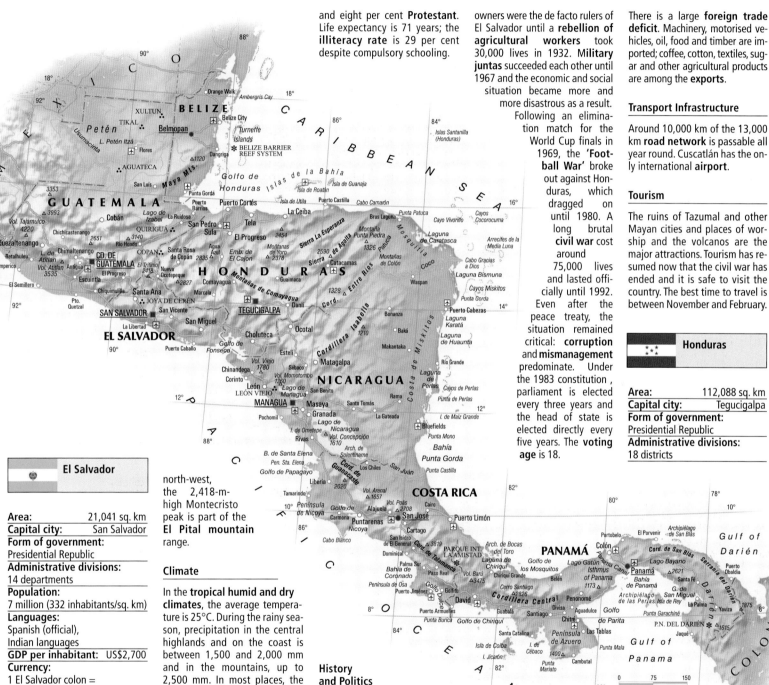

and eight per cent **Protestant**. Life expectancy is 71 years; the **illiteracy rate** is 29 per cent despite compulsory schooling.

owners were the de facto rulers of El Salvador until a **rebellion of agricultural workers** took 30,000 lives in 1932. **Military juntas** succeeded each other until 1967 and the economic and social situation became more and more disastrous as a result. Following an elimination match for the World Cup finals in 1969, the **'Football War'** broke out against Honduras, which dragged on until 1980. A long brutal **civil war** cost around 75,000 lives and lasted officially until 1992. Even after the peace treaty, the situation remained critical: **corruption** and **mismanagement** predominate. Under the 1983 constitution , parliament is elected every three years and the head of state is elected directly every five years. The **voting age** is 18.

There is a large **foreign trade deficit**. Machinery, motorised vehicles, oil, food and timber are imported; coffee, cotton, textiles, sugar and other agricultural products are among the **exports**.

Transport Infrastructure

Around 10,000 km of the 13,000 km **road network** is passable all year round. Cuscatlán has the only international **airport**.

Tourism

The ruins of Tazumal and other Mayan cities and places of worship and the volcanos are the major attractions. Tourism has resumed now that the civil war has ended and it is safe to visit the country. The best time to travel is between November and February.

Honduras	
Area:	112,088 sq. km
Capital city:	Tegucigalpa
Form of government: Presidential Republic	
Administrative divisions: 18 districts	

north-west, the 2,418-m-high Montecristo peak is part of the El Pital mountain range.

Climate

In the **tropical humid and dry climates**, the average temperature is 25°C. During the rainy season, precipitation in the central highlands and on the coast is between 1,500 and 2,000 mm and in the mountains, up to 2,500 mm. In most places, the tropical and savannah vegetation and mangrove swamps have been cleared for agriculture. As a result, the fauna has become depleted though there are many species of birds.

Population

The inhabitants consist of 89 per cent **mestizo**, ten per cent **Amerindian** and one per cent **white**. 92 per cent are **Catholics**

El Salvador	
Area:	21,041 sq. km
Capital city:	San Salvador
Form of government: Presidential Republic	
Administrative divisions: 14 departments	
Population: 7 million (332 inhabitants/sq. km)	
Languages: Spanish (official), Indian languages	
GDP per inhabitant:	US$2,700
Currency: 1 El Salvador colon = 100 centavos	

Natural Geography

Behind the narrow Pacific coastline, a **mountain chain** joins the **volcanoes**, some of which are around 2,000 m high and still active. The capital city, San Salvador, and **Lake Ilopango**, which is 250 m deep, lie in a depression. In the north, there is a plateau 400 to 1,000 m high; in the

History and Politics

El Salvador, conquered in 1526 by **Pedro de Alvarado** for Spain, remained part of the Kingdom of Guatemala (Also known as the Captaincy General of Guatemala) until 1821. After the Spanish defeat, the country fell first to **Mexico**, then from 1823 to 1839 it was part of the **Central American Federation**. In 1859, El Salvador became an independent **republic**. The plantation

Economy

In 2006, GDP was US$18.6 billion of which 12 per cent derived from **agriculture**, 24 per cent from **industry** and 64 per cent from the **services sector**. Unemployment is set to rise to at least 40 per cent.

Population: 7.5 million (66 inhabitants/sq. km)
Languages: Spanish (official), English, Indian languages
GDP per inhabitant: US$1,200
Currency: 1 lempira = 100 centavos

Honduras, Nicaragua

*The Indians of **Guatemala** are the descendants of Mayas. The legacy can still be found in the folklore art as well as on the many markets, not just for the tourists. Many Mayan women are masters at the art of weaving. The colourful textiles, skillfully combining creativity with tradition, are produced on a hand-loom.*

Natural Geography

The land mass stretches from the **Gulf of Honduras** on the Caribbean to the **Gulf of Fonseca** on the Pacific and consists of several mountain ranges of volcanic origin rising to up to 2,500 m. The Pacific coast is only 70 km long and very narrow. The Caribbean coast is characterised by estuaries, lagoons and marshes. The **Bahía Islands** and **Swan Islands** belong to the national territory.

Climate

On the side of the country facing the Pacific Ocean, a **dry, tropical climate** prevails in winter; the average temperature is 28°C; the average rainfall in the highlands is 1,000–2,000 mm. In the **permanently humid Caribbean lowlands** average temperatures of 25°C predominate.
The rainfall diminishes from north to the south. On the north coast, there are **cyclones** in the summer. The Caribbean lowlands are covered by **rainforest** up to a height of 1,500 m. The inland high plateau is covered with **dry savannah**, **pinewoods** and **mountain forests**. In the sheltered valleys, scrub and thorn savannahs dominate. The pacific plains are covered in **forest** while the coastline is covered in mangrove swamps. Bears, leopards, panthers and pumas road the tropical

rainforests which also have plenty of reptiles and insects.

Population

Of the population, 89.9 per cent are **mestizos**, 6.7 per cent **Amerindians**, 2.1 per cent **blacks** and 1.3 per cent whites. 90 per cent profess Roman Catholicism. The rest are Anglican, Baptist and Bahai. Life expectancy is 70 years; the illiteracy rate is 20 per cent. Some 44 per cent of Hondurans are concentrated in the overcrowded cities; 80 per cent live below the poverty line.

History and Politics

When Columbus landed in the area which is today's Honduras in 1502, the ancient Mayan culture had already declined to a large extent. Spanish rule ended in 1821; in 1823, Honduras became a part of the Central American Federation and in 1838 it gained its independence. It has a history of **military juntas**, with brief intervening periods of democracy. The true **rulers**, however, are to be found in the **USA**. The National Fruit Company ruled this **'banana republic'** in the back yard of the United States for centuries. In 1983, Honduras allowed the US backed right-wing **Nicaraguan contras** to operate land and sea military bases from which to attack Nicaragua. This unpopular policy

provoked a coup by junior officers. Today, the country is officially a democratic presidential republic. Parliament and President are elected directly every four years. The voting age is 18. The power of the **military** is considerable, although it has been restricted in recent years. Political assassinations are not uncommon.

Economy

In 2006, GDP was US$9 billion, of which 21 per cent derived from **agriculture**, 33 per cent from **industry** and 46 per cent from the **services sector**. Consumer goods, raw materials and textiles are imported, coffee, bananas and shellfish are exported as well

Belize: The 'Blue hole' in lighthouse riff.

as valuable tropical timber such as rosewood and mahogany.

Transport Infrastructure

Only one tenth of the total 18,000-km-long **road network** is paved. The major long-distance connection is the legendary **Pan-American Highway** that runs the length of the continent. There are three international **airports** and several national **airports**.

Tourism

In 2004, 670,000 tourists contributed US$400 million in foreign currency. The best-known

tourist destinations are the **Caribbean beaches** and relics of the Mayan culture, especially the **Copán ruins**. The best time to travel to Honduras is from December until May.

Nicaragua	
Area:	129,494 sq. km
Capital city:	Managua
Form of government:	Presidential Republic
Administrative divisions:	16 departments
Population:	5.7m (45 inhabitants/sq. km)
Languages:	Spanish (official), Chibcha
GDP per inhabitant:	US$900
Currency:	1 gold cordoba = 100 centavos

Natural Geography

Nicaragua is the largest country in central America and the most thinly populated. The **Cordillera mountain range** that includes the 2,107-m-high **Pico Mogotón** are in the north. The Caribbean lowlands contain many lagoons and marshes and are sparsely populated. In the east, they are up to 80 km wide. Many **sandbanks, islands** and **coral reefs** run parallel to the 480-km-long Caribbean coast. Lake Nicaragua, which has an area of 8,263 sq. km, and the smaller **Lake Managua** are in the Nicaragua Depression. A mountain range up to 1,800 m high containing active volcanoes runs parallel to the 346-km-long Pacific coast. Earthquakes and volcanic activity are a constant threat throughout the country.

Climate

The **tropical-humid** climate is only temperate on the Caribbean coast and in the mountainous regions. The temperatures fluctuate on average between 24°C and 28°C in the lowlands and between 17°C and 22°C in the mountainous regions. In the east, the average rainfall is 2,500–6,000 mm, in the west it is up to 2,000 mm and in the Nicaraguan Depression it is only 1,000 mm.

The **rainforest** of the Caribbean lowlands contains valuable tropical timber. In the north, there are vast pinewoods; on the Caribbean coast known as the Mosquito Coast, there are mangrove swamps and palms, while the Nicaraguan Depression contains the remains of a dry forest. **Coniferous mountain forest** begins at an altitude of 600 m; this turns into mixed woodland at an altitude of 800 m. The rich variety of **fauna** includes jaguars, pumas, monkeys, alligators, turtles, snakes and many species of birds.

Population

69 per cent of Nicaragua's population are **mestizo**, 14 per cent **whites**, nine per cent **blacks** and four per cent **Amerindians, mulattos** and **zambo**.
Some 89 per cent of the population is **Catholic**, five per cent **Protestant** and there are also followers of different natural religions. The life expectancy is 71 years; there is 24 per cent illiteracy. 63 per cent of Nicaraguans live in the cities and 44 per cent live below the poverty line.

History and Politics

In 1502, Columbus landed on the east coast of today's Nicaragua. In 1524, **Francisco de Hernández** conquered the country for the Spanish Crown. The **independence movement**, which started in 1811, expelled the Spaniards from Nicaragua in 1821. From 1823 until 1838 the country was a part of the Central American Federation. Interests of the **United Fruit Company** as well as a planned **canal** to link the two oceans placed Nicaragua increasingly in the US sphere of influence. From 1912 until 1937, the country was occupied by US troops. **Augusto Sandino** led the liberation movement that arose from the occupation. **Sandino** was murdered in 1934 by **Anastasio Somoza**. The **Somoza clan**, whose members largely acted in US interests, then ruled until 1979, exerting brutal dictatorial power. After the fall of the Somoza regime, the opposition, left-wing Sandinistas gained power under president **Daniel Ortega**. He implemented land reform and reformed the healthcare and education systems.

*Around 300 islands are scattered in the Central America's largest lake, **Lake Nicaragua**, 148 km long and 55 km wide. The Isla de Ometepe is the largest island. On the Isla de Solentiname, Ernesto Cardenal founded an artists' colony around the church.*

Democratic rights did not help the left wing junta on the road to success, due to the existence of the US-backed **contras,** a right-wing militia representing the vested interests of Nicaragua's landowners. After a long, bloody civil war, there was an **armistice** in 1988. In 1990, free elections were held for the first time, from which the centre-right opposition emerged victorious. In 2006, Daniel Ortega was re-elected as president. Under the 1987 constitution, last modified in 1995, the National Assembly is elected every five years. The period of office of the directly elected president is also five years. The **voting age is** 16 years.

Economy

In 2006, GDP was US$5.3 billion, of which 18 per cent came from **agriculture,** 26 per cent from **industry** and 56 per cent from the **services sector.** There is a serious **foreign trade deficit.** Industrial products, consumer goods and oil are imported. Exports are mainly timber, coffee, fish and shellfish, meat, sugar and bananas.

Transport Infrastructure

The 15,000-km-long road network is only well-developed in the west. The 384-km-long section of the **Pan-American Highway** as well as the only east–west road linking **Matagalpa** with **Puerto Cabezas** represent the most important highways. There is a 344-km-long railway network, as well as an international **airport** in Managua.

Tourism

Tourism is starting up again now that the fighting has ended. The Mosquito Coast, where many of the locals speak English, is popular. The best time to travel is between December and February.

	Costa Rica

Area: 51,100 sq. km
Capital city: San José
Form of government:
Presidential Republic
Administrative divisions:

7 provinces
Population:
4.1 million (80 inhabitants/sq. km)
Languages:
Spanish (official), English, Creole
GDP per inhabitant: US$4,900
Currency:
1 Costa Rica colon = 100 centimos

Natural Geography

In the north, the **Cordillera de Guanacaste** which reaches heights of 2,000 m, extends in a southerly direction. The **Cordillera Central**, which reaches heights of 3,000 m, adjoins the eastern side of the **Cordillera de**

Guanacaste. The **Central Valley** runs east-west in the centre of the country. South of the valley, the Cordillera's highest peak is the **Cerro Chirripó** (3,820 m). The Caribbean lowlands are characterised by a **coastline that contains many lagoons.** The mountains are volcanic and there is consequently frequent volcanic activity and earthquakes.

Climate

While the Atlantic coast has a **tropical climate** with an even temperature and rainfall of 3,000 to 4,000 mm, the **wet-dry Pacific coast** has only 2,000 to 2,500 mm of precipitation annually. In the Central Valley, the rainfall is under 2,000 mm and the average temperature is 20°C. The average annual temperature in the lowlands is 26°C, and at altitudes above 3,000 m it is on average less than 10°C. Most of the country is covered with **tropical rainforest** and in the mountain

regions there are **evergreen forests.** In the lagoons, there are mangrove swamps. The hinterland contains cabbage-palm swamps and on the Nicoya and Osa peninsula there are dry forests and savannahs. Tapirs, jaguars, pumas and monkeys are among the rich variety of **fauna.**

1 The impressive ruins of the Mayan city of Xunantunich stand on a mound overlooking the jungle in Belize. The temple city is one of the country's main attractions.

2 An important local market in Chichicastenango, northern Guatemala.

3 Guatemala: Antigua lies at the foot of three volcanos, including the Agua (3,766 m). The city has been destroyed several times in earthquakes.

4 Las Isletas: the beauty of the archipelago in Lake Nicaragua lake is deceptive, as the lake is highly polluted.

Costa Rica, Panama

Costa Rica: This small country has several active volcanos in a chain running from north to south. The Volcan Poás National Park surrounds the active volcano of that name which is 2,700 m high. The park contains a wealth of flora and fauna. The volcano is still active, belching steam and gas from its twin crater lakes.

Population

87 per cent of Costa Ricans are **white**, seven per cent **mestizo**, three per cent **black** and **mulatto**, two per cent **Asian** and one per cent **Native Americans**. 89 per cent of the population are Catholics, eight per cent Protestants and a minority are Bahai and Jewish. The life expectancy is 77 years and **illiteracy** is running at five per cent. Half of the Costa Ricans live in the cities; there is **compulsory education**.

History and Politics

The area was discovered by Columbus in 1502, and in 1520 it was seized by the Spanish Crown, finally becoming part of the **Kingdom of Guatemala** (also known as the Captaincy General of Guatemala). In 1821, the country separated from Spain and from 1823–29 it was part of the **Central America Federation**. After political and economic turbulence, the situation stabilised in the early twentieth century. Since 1889, the country has been a **republic**; the current constitution came into war after a brief civil war in 1949.

Costa Rica maintains no standing army and the country is regarded as **the most stable state** in the region. The civil war in Nicaragua however, had an adverse effect on northern Costa Rica. **Parliament** and the president are elected directly every four years.

Economy

The country is one of the wealthiest in **Latin America**. In 2006, GDP was US$21 billion of which nine per cent derived from **agriculture**, 29 per cent from **industry** and 62 per cent from the **services sector**. Raw materials, fuel and consumer goods are imported; exports include bananas, coffee, fish and shellfish, machinery, timber and tropical fruits.

Transport Infrastructure

Around 3,500 km of the 29,000 km **road network** is paved, however, only the central highlands are well developed in terms of infrastructure. The Juan Santamaria international **airport** is one of two airports in San José and there is a network of domestic airports.

Tourism

Tourism contributes considerably to the **economy**. Income from tourism represented US$1.6 billion in 2004. The Caribbean coast has long **sandy beaches**. The best time to travel is the between December and April.

Costa Rica: the Fortuna volcano looms over green hills

★	**Panama**

Area:	78,200 sq. km
Capital city:	Panama-City
Form of government: Presidential Republic	
Administrative divisions: 9 provinces, Panama Canal Zone	
Population: 3.2 million (41 inhabitants/sq. km)	
Languages: Spanish (official), English	
GDP per inhabitant: US$5,200	
Currency: 1 balboa = 100 centesimos	

Natural Geography

In the west of the country, the volcanic mountain range of the **Serrenía de Tabasará** includes the 3,478 m high **Chiriquí Mountain**, close to the border with Costa Rica. In the east, there are several smaller mountain ranges reaching heights of up to

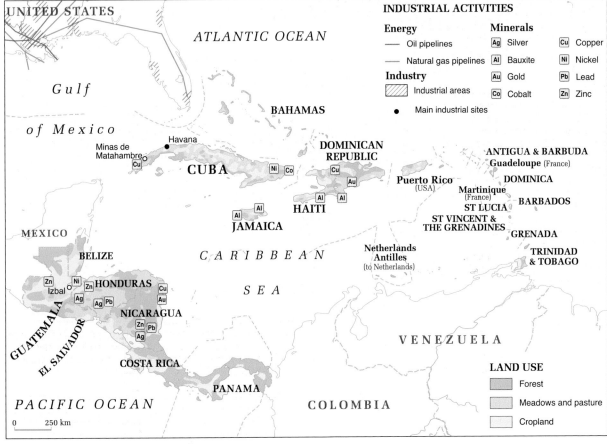

*Bananas are one of **Costa Rica's** major exports. Most of the plantations are situated on the Caribbean coast in the east of the country. A significant proportion of export income derives from bananas and coffee, which are sent mainly to the USA. Thanks to its stable political conditions Costa Rica has become a role model for governance in Central America. There is a good education and welfare system and the economy is booming.*

1,000 m. The open **Darien Lowlands**, which extend to the Caribbean Coast, are at the foot of these slopes. The isthmus of Panama at 46 km at its narrowest point between the Atlantic and Pacific oceans.

Climate

The **tropical climate** has constantly high temperatures and extremely high humidity. The average annual temperature is 27°C, in the mountain regions it is 20°C. The average annual rainfall is up to 4,500 mm on the Caribbean coast up to 2,000 mm on the Pacific Coast.
Evergreen **tropical rainforest** is found on the Caribbean Coast as well as on the Darien Lowlands. Cloud forest predominates at altitudes above 2,500 m. Savannahs and dry forests cover the lowlands on the Pacific cost, while the **Gulf of Panama** is covered in mangrove swamps. The fauna contains many species of birds, as well as crocodiles, alligators, pumas, ocelots, monkeys, jaguars and tapirs.

Population

Some 65 per cent of Panama's population are **mestizo**, 13 per cent are **black** and **mulatto**, ten per cent are **Creole**, 8.3 per cent are **Indian** and two per cent are **Asian**. Ninety-six per cent of the population are Roman Catholics, the remainder being Protestants and Muslims. Life expectancy is 75 years, and there is nine per cent rate of **illiteracy**. Some 65 per cent of the Panamanians live in cities.

History and Politics

After Panama's discovery by Columbus, **Vasco Núñez de Balboa** reached the Pacific Ocean by land in 1513. From 1542, Panama belonged to the **Viceroyalty of Peru**. After the 1821 war of liberation, it became a part of Greater Colombia and in 1903 it became a sovereign republic. Panama's **Independence** was supported by the United States. In this way, the US secured access to the **Panama Canal** which opened in 1914. Although the 16-km-wide Canal Zone was returned to Panama in

2000, the USA retains a **right of intervention**.
The period of constantly changing **military regimes** ended in 1990 through US intervention and the arrest of the dictator **Manuel Noriega**. The country's main problems are its failing economy and corruption in all areas of public life. In 2006, a decision was made through a referendum to extend the Panama Canal.
A presidential republic was created under the 1994 constitution. Parliament and the president are each elected for five-year terms. The voting age is 18.

Economy

In 2006, GDP was US$17 billion, of which eight per cent came from **agriculture**, 19 per cent from **industry** and 73 per cent from the **services sector**. The main **imports** are oil, capital goods and food; bananas, shellfish and coffee are exported. The most important economic factors by far are income from canal transport and the flag of convenience that makes Panama the owner of one of the **world's largest merchant fleets,** most of it foreign-owned. The Smithsonian Tropical Research Institute is located here.

Transport Infrastructure

One third of the 8,900 km **road network** is paved. The main transport artery is the Panama Canal. The Canal Zone has the most fully developed infrastructure of the country. The international **airport** of Tocumen is east of Panama City.

Tourism

In 2004, more than half a million tourists visited Panama and spent US$900 million. These were mainly **tourists on cruise ships**. The **Milaflores locks** are an amazing sight. The best time to travel is from December until April when the weather is cooler.

1 Costa Rica: The Valle Central near Cartago is dominated by the Irazú volcano (3,432 m), that has been dormant for the last 30 years.

2 In the interior of Panama there are many examples of colonial architecture such as this baroque church in Ocú.

3 Cartago in central Costa Rica is an important pilgrimage site: the basilica contains the shrine of the patron saint of Costa Rica.

4 Ocean-going ships passing through the Panama canal: the economy of Panama is heavily dependent on income from it.

Cuba

Havana: the capital of Cuba was the 'Paris of the Caribbean' until Fidel Castro took power. Poker games would run through the night, and ice-cold Cuba Libre would comfort lonely souls. The shows in the elegant 'Club Tropicana' bring this legendary atmosphere back to life – at least for the tourists.

Cuba

Area:	110,860 sq. km
Capital city:	Havana
Form of government:	
Socialist Republic	
Administrative divisions:	
14 provinces, 1 special administrative district	
Population: 11.4 million	
(103 inhabitants/sq. km)	
Language:	Spanish
GDP per capita:	US$3,500
Currency:	
1 Cuban peso = 100 centavos	

Natural Geography

The **main island** mainly consists of lowlands. In the south-east there are **Sierra Maestra** mountains that are often affected by earthquakes. The highest peak, Pico Turquino, reaches a height of almost 2,000 m. The Sierra Trinidad is a smaller range of mountains in the centre of the island, and the Cordillera de Guaniguanico lies in the west.
The Havana and Matanzas **highlands** are in the north. Numerous coral atolls and reefs are located off the **coasts**.

Climate

The **wet-dry climate** is affected by the north-east trade winds. Temperatures are between 22°C and 28°C. In the interior, annual precipitation, which is at its highest between June and October, is 1,000–1,500 mm. The natural

rainforests and mountain forests have largely given way to **cultivated land** and **palm savannahs**. The fauna is not very varied and consists mainly of insectivores, reptiles and rodents. By contrast, the coastal waters are well stocked with fish.

Population

Cuba's population is 51 per cent **mixed race**, 11 per cent black and 37 per cent white. 59 per cent of the population **profess no religion**, 39 per cent are **Catholic** and the rest a Protestant minority. The average Cuban **life expectancy** is 77, and **adult literacy rate** is just over 95 per cent. Schooling is compulsory. 76 per cent of the population lives in cities.

History and Politics

The island was discovered by **Columbus** in the year 1492 and

was subsequently occupied by the **Spanish.** Spain had to defend its new overseas territory constantly against pirates and colonial competitors. Towards the end of the nineteenth century, the **USA**

supported the independence movement and used this as a pretext to declare war on Spain in 1898. The island remained under US control until 1902. Guantánamo Bay was leased by the USA as a **military base in 1903** and today houses

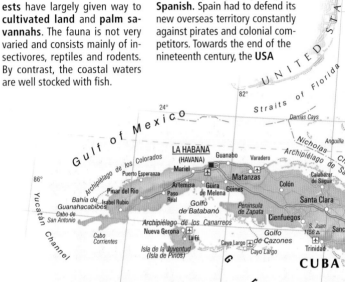

a camp for prisoners held without trial.
After an unstable period with several changes of government, **Fulgencio Batista** came to power in 1933, from when he ruled the country as a dictatorship until 1958. The revolution led by **Fidel Castro** resulted in a total reorganisation of the social system and the establishment of free health care and education for the masses.
Cuba's **socialist politics** and Castro's alignment with the **USSR** led to a permanent deterioration in the country's relations with the USA. A planned invasion of exiled Cubans at the Bay of Pigs, organised by the **CIA,** failed in 1961. Plans to station Soviet nuclear missiles on Cuba led to the **Cuban Missile Crisis** of

1962, which for a time threatened to escalate into a nuclear war. The crisis was resolved after concessions by Khrushchev were negociated, but the **embargoes** imposed on Cuba by the USA continue to cripple Cuban foreign trade to this day.
After the collapse of the Eastern Bloc, Cuba lost an important trading partner and as a result some of its economic power. Through improved **relations with Europe,** other countries in Latin America and the Catholic Church, Castro has made efforts to bring the country out of its isolation, without abandoning the principle of a socialist planned economy.

Fidel Castro

*Mayari, 13.8.1926

After the guerrilla war of 1956–59, Fidel Castro and a small liberation movement toppled dictator Juan Batista. Since then Cuba has been a one-party socialist republic. The exclusion of the old elite and the nationalisation of manufacturing and agriculture caused conflict with the USA which peaked during the Cuban Missile Crisis. Castro has recently tried to forge closer ties with the West. In 2006, due to illness, he transferred leadership to his brother Raúl.

The dome of the National Capitol dominates Havana's skyline.

Trinidad: 'Son' was Cuba's most popular musical sound in the 1920s and is still played today by the founding fathers from back in the day. Son is a mixture of solo and chorus singing, which later developed into salsa. Since the world-wide success of the Wim Wenders film 'Buena Vista Social Club', the melancholy music is once more well-known around the globe.

Economy

In 2006, Cuba had a GDP of US$19.4 billion, of which **agriculture** accounted for seven per cent, **manufacturing** 31 per cent, and the **services sector** 62 per cent. The trade deficit is *c.* US$3 billion. Main imports are machines, fossil fuels and transport equipment. Export products are tobacco, rice, bananas,

welcomed nearly two million tourists, who contributed some US$1.92 billion. The best time for travel is between November and April.

	Jamaica
Area:	10,990 sq. km
Capital city:	Kingston
Form of government:	
Constitutional Monarchy in the Commonwealth	
Administrative divisions:	
14 districts	
Population:	
2.7 million	
(245 inhabitants/sq. km)	

Climate

The north-east trade winds define the **warm, tropical climate**. Temperatures scarcely fluctuate from the average of 27°C. In the northern mountainous regions, annual rainfall is 2,500–5,000 mm, but in the south it is just 800 mm. Powerful **hurricanes** often strike the country in late summer. The limestone plateaus are dominated by **savannah vegetation**, and the mountain slopes are covered in evergreen **rainforest**. Higher regions have **mountain and cloud forest**. The country has many species of birds and reptiles, and is also home to mongooses and bats, though they are not native to the island.

Population

The population is 76 per cent **Black**, 15 per cent **mu-**

nous Carib population. In 1670, the **English** disputed Spain's claim to the island. The country was initially an infamous **pirate stronghold**, but sugar cane and cocoa plantations made Jamaica one of the richest colonies in the British Empire. Until slavery was finally abolished in 1838, large numbers of **African slaves** were brought to work on the plantations and sugar mills. After 1938, the government became increasingly autonomous, and Jamaica became **officially independent** in 1962. Since the 1970s, the country has fluctuated between a socialist and a market economy, following either a Cuba-friendly or USA-friendly course. The **House of Representatives** is elected every five years. The **voting age** is 18.

Economy

Gross national product in 2006 stood at US$10.4 billion, of which eight per cent was derived from **agriculture**, 34 per

country has two international **airports** and two **sea ports**.

Tourism

In 2004, just under 1.4 million tourists came to the country, spending US$1.73 billion. The best time for visiting Jamaica is between December and April.

	Haiti
Area:	27,750 sq. km
Capital city:	Port-au-Prince
Form of government:	
Presidential Republic	
Administrative divisions:	
9 départements	
Population:	
8.5 million	
(306 inhabitants/sq. km)	
Languages:	
French (official), Creole	
GDP per capita:	US$530
Currency:	
1 gourde = 100 centimes	

Natural Geography

Haiti covers the western third of the island of **Hispaniola** and consists of two large peninsulas around the **Gulf of Gonave**. The Massif du Nord and the Massif du Sud cover some 80 per cent of the country's land mass. Between these two mountain ranges lies the Plateau Central, the valley of the most important river, the Artibonite, and the Plaine du Cul-de-Sac which contains a salt lake, the Étang Saumâtre. Haiti is frequently struck by earthquakes.

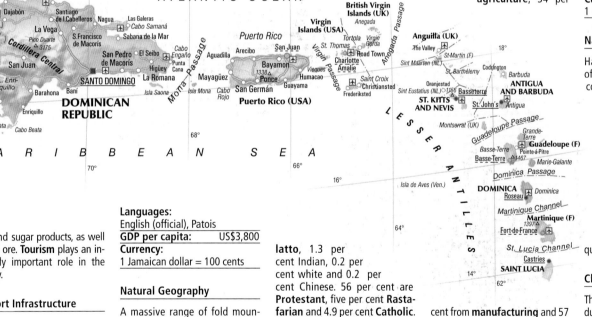

sugar and sugar products, as well as nickel ore. **Tourism** plays an increasingly important role in the economy.

Transport Infrastructure

The 4,677-km-long **rail network** is well constructed, as is the **road network**, which has a length of 27,100 km. There are five international **airports**.

Tourism

The main centres for foreign visitors are the cities of **La Habaña** (Havana), **Trinidad** and **Santiago de Cuba**, and the beaches of **Matanzas**. In 2003, the country

Languages:
English (official), Patois
GDP per capita:	US$3,800
Currency:	
1 Jamaican dollar = 100 cents	

Natural Geography

A massive range of fold mountains runs through the **island** from west to east. The highest mountain is **Blue Mountain Peak** with a maximum height of 2,256 m. Karstified limestone plateaus make up approximately two-thirds of the country's area. The narrow coastal strips are dominated by marshes in the south, and there are sandy beaches in the north. Much of the tropical rainforest has been cleared for cultivation.

latto, 1.3 per cent Indian, 0.2 per cent white and 0.2 per cent Chinese. 56 per cent are **Protestant**, five per cent **Rastafarian** and 4.9 per cent **Catholic**. There are also minorities of Baha'i, Jews and Muslims. Average life expectancy is 73, and the **adult literacy rate** is 80 per cent. Fifty-four per cent of the population lives in the cities.

History and Politics

The island was discovered by **Columbus**, and the Spanish settlement that followed almost completely eradicated the indige-

cent from **manufacturing** and 57 per cent came from the **service sector**. The most important imports are raw materials, consumer goods, semi-manufactured goods and food. Main exports are aluminium oxide, textiles, sugar, bauxite, bananas and coffee.

Transport Infrastructure

The **rail network** is 300 km long and a well constructed **road network** covers 17,000 km. The

Climate

The north-east trade winds produce a **tropical climate** and average temperatures of 25°C to 29°C. Temperatures are cooler in the uplands, where average precipitation is between 1,000 and 1,500 mm. On the plains, precipitation is just 500 mm. Powerful **hurricanes** are common in late summer.

Aggressive deforestation has meant that only ten per cent of the country is now covered in tropical **rainforest**. Cacti and thorn bushes grow on the mountain slopes, and dry or humid

Haiti, Dominican Republic

savannahs are found in the basins. Mangrove swamps grow along the coast. The country once had a rich variety of fauna, but all that remains today are some reptiles, rodents and bird species.

Population

Haiti's population is 60 per cent **black** and 35 per cent **mulatto**. Whites only represent a small minority of the population. Officially, 80 per cent are **Catholic** and ten per cent **Protestant,** but the traditional **Voodoo cult** and syncretic religions are widespread. Average **life expectancy** is just 53 years and more than half of the population of Haiti can neither read nor write. Only 32 per cent live in the cities.

History and Politics

After the island was discovered by **Columbus** in 1492, the **Spanish** struggled to establish themselves in the western region. Initially, Haiti was a **pirate stronghold,** but the French finally drove them out and became the nominal rulers in 1697.

Using **African slaves,** the colonists cultivated successful plantations and made Haiti into one of **France's** wealthiest colonies. In the aftermath of the French Revolution, the slaves demanded their right to freedom and broke away from France in 1804, under their leader Toussaint L'Ouverture. Haiti merged with the eastern part of the island, the Dominican Republic, but this union lasted for only 22 years, from 1822 to 1844.

After this, various **dictators** snatched power from each other in a series of coups, until the **USA** occupied the country in 1915. After the Americans left in 1935, Haiti remained under US financial control until 1947.

The dictatorships of François **Duvalier** and his son Jean-Claude ('Papa Doc' and 'Baby Doc') were infamous. Jean-Bertrand **Aristide** was elected President in 1990. Not long after Aristide gained power, he was overthrown by yet another military coup, and was only able to reclaim office in 1994, with the help of 20,000 US soldiers. Since 1996, there has once more been a freely elected civilian government, but Haiti remains the politically unstable and impoverished. The **bicameral parliament** is elected every four years, and the head of state every five years. The voting age is 18.

François Duvalier

*Port-au-Prince, 14.4.1907,
†Port-au-Prince, 21.4.1971

After his election to the post of President of Haiti in 1957 – supported by the military – 'Papa Doc', so-called because he had once been a doctor, became a dictator and named himself President for the rest of his life in 1964. During his office, the mulatto elite of the country was practically removed of all their powers. In 1971, he named his son, Jean-Claude, as successor. Known as 'Baby Doc', he was toppled in February 1986, despite attempts to reform, and went into exile in France.

A former presidential palace: the Museum of the Revolution, Havana.

Economy

In 2006, GDP stood at US$4.5 billion, of which 28 per cent was from **agriculture**, 20 per cent came from **manufacturing** and 52 per cent from the **service sector**. Unemployment stands at 60 per cent. The country has a huge foreign trade deficit. Main imports are consumer goods, machinery, food and fuel. Haiti exports light industry products, cocoa, coffee and sugar. Large numbers of Haitians work in the sugar cane plantations of the Dominican Republic; there is a huge emigré population, living mainly in the United States.

Transport Infrastructure

Only 600 km of the 4000-km-long **road network** is surfaced. The **railway** (600 km) is used for the transport of goods. The country has seven domestic **airports** and one international airport.

Tourism

Tourist numbers have reduced dramatically due to the high HIV/AIDS infection rate and significant levels of violent crime. Tourism remains an important economic factor however. The best time to travel is between December and March.

Dominican Republic

Area:	48,730 sq. km
Capital city:	Santo Domingo
Form of government:	
Presidential Republic	
Administrative divisions:	
26 provinces, Capital city district	
Population:	
9 million	
(185 inhabitants/sq. km)	
Language:	Spanish
GDP per capita:	US$3,600
Currency: 1 Dominican Peso =	
100 centavos	

Natural Geography

The national territory comprises two-thirds of the island of **Hispaniola**. Four parallel mountain chains traverse the island from north-west to south-east. The Pico Duarte in the Cordillera Central an altitude of 3,175 m, is the country's highest mountain. Extensive areas of lowland lie between the mountain ranges. The only substantial inland lake is the saltwater lake of Lago Enriquillo. The country is frequently struck by earthquakes.

Climate

The Dominican Republic has a **tropical climate**, the effects of which vary greatly depending on the region. In the area around the capital, temperatures range between 14°C and 27°C. Precipitation fluctuates between 2,000 mm in the mountains and 600 mm on the Hoya de Enriquillo, also known as the Cul-de-Sac Depression. The humid mountain slopes are covered in evergreen **rainforest**, and **mountain woodland** grows in the rain-sheltered areas of the Cordillera. In the **savannahs** of the plains, the flora mostly comprises thornbushes and cacti. There are many bird species, manatees, alligators and Hispaniolan hutia.

Population

60 per cent of the inhabitants of the Dominican Republic are **mulattos**, 28 per cent are **white** and 11.5 per cent **black**. **Catholics** make up 90 per cent of the population and the rest consist of Protestants, Jews and Baha'i.

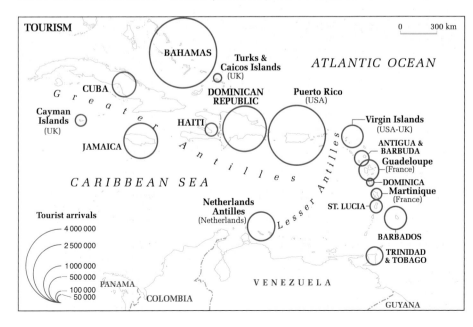

TOURISM

ATLANTIC OCEAN

BAHAMAS

Turks & Caicos Islands (UK)

CUBA

Greater

Cayman Islands (UK)

DOMINICAN REPUBLIC

Puerto Rico (USA)

HAITI

JAMAICA

Antilles

Virgin Islands (USA-UK)

ANTIGUA & BARBUDA

Guadeloupe (France)

DOMINICA

Martinique (France)

Lesser Antilles

ST. LUCIA

Netherlands Antilles (Netherlands)

CARIBBEAN SEA

BARBADOS

TRINIDAD & TOBAGO

Tourist arrivals

4 000 000
2 500 000
1 000 000
500 000
100 000
50 000

PANAMA

COLOMBIA

VENEZUELA

GUYANA

0   300 km

*The Hemingway Bar in **Havana** still pays tribute to the Nobel Prize winning writer, who often came to the bar, the 'Bodeguita del Medio', to enjoy different Mojito cocktails. Ernest Hemingway lived on the outskirts of Havana, and he made the drink famous throughout the world in 1939. The writer lived in **Cuba** for 20 years. His local bar, near the Catedral de San Cristobal de La Habana was his escape and his worst enemy: Hemingway was an alcoholic.*

Average **life expectancy** is 75 years and **adult literacy rate** is 82 per cent. 63 per cent of the population lives in cities.

History and Politics

After **Columbus** discovered the island of Hispaniola, the **Spanish** killed off the native Carib and Arawak population. Spain initially lost possession of the west of the island and ceded the east to the **French** in 1795. The country first became independent in 1804 and briefly united with Haiti, only to break away shortly after. The country once more came under Spanish control, and finally gained full **independence** in 1865. From 1916 to 1924, the Dominican Republic was occupied by the **USA**. A short-lived liberal phase ended in 1930 when the dictator **Trujillo Molina** came to power. His murder in 1961 was followed by a democratic government. A series of military coups and a civil war provoked new US intervention in 1965. Since then, the country has been a **republic**. Since 2000, the country has been ruled by the social democrat PRD. The bicameral parliament and head of state are directly elected every four years. Voting is compulsory starting at 18.

Economy

GDP in 2006 was US$32 billion, of which 13 per cent derived from **agriculture**, 32 per cent from **manufacturing** and 55 per cent came from the **services sector**. Important exports are gold, silver, nickel, sugar cane, coffee and cocoa. The Dominican Republic imports oil, machinery and consumer goods. **Tourism** brought in US$2.7 billion in 2002, and is a significant economic factor.

Transport Infrastructure

The **road network** covers 18,000 km and is well constructed. 30 per cent of the roads are paved. The international **airport** near Santo Domingo provides good flight connections to the US mainland and to other Caribbean islands.

Tourism

In 2004, some 3.4 million foreign tourists enjoyed the beaches of **Puerto Plata** and **La Romana**. The best time to visit is between November and April.

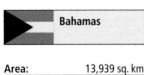

Bahamas

Area:	13,939 sq. km
Capital city:	Nassau
Form of government: Constitutional Monarchy in the Commonwealth	
Administrative divisions: 18 districts	
Population: 320,000 (22 inhabitants/sq. km)	
Language:	English
GDP per capita:	US$19,000
Currency: 1 Bahamian dollar = 100 cents	

Natural Geography

The **island kingdom** consists of 30 larger and 700 small tropical islands and some 2,000 atolls and cays, stretching over a distance of 1,200 km. Most of the flat islands have wide, palm-fringed beaches. The country has no highlands or large rivers. Only 30 islands are inhabited.

Climate

The **sub-tropical maritime climate** combined with the cooling effects of the **Gulf Stream** mean that the country has year-round pleasant temperatures of between 22°C and 28°C. In the north-west, annual levels of precipitation are 1,200 mm, compared with 1,000 mm in the south-east. In the latter half of the year, the islands are often hit by **hurricanes**. The Bahamas are covered in **savannahs**, and the north-west also contains **woodland**, salt marshes and mangrove swamps in the bays.

Population

The population of the Bahamas is 72 per cent **black**, 14 per cent

1 Cuba: Trinidad's emblem is the tower of the San Francisco Convent and Church.

2 Old American cars, such as this one in the city of Trinidad, are often driven in Cuba.

3 Cuba: The Plaza de la Catedral lies in the centre of Havana's old town. The colonial buildings in this part of the city are a tourist attraction.

4 The cultivation of sugar cane was once the main source of income for many Caribbean states. Tourism has now caused this activity to lose importance.

Dominican Republic: The beaches of the Caribbean island are a paradise for many tourists. Merengue musicians complete the tropical dream, which enchants ever more people each year. Since 1970, tourist numbers have increased by a factor of 50.

Catastrophes like Hurricane George in 1998 do not change the beauty of the region. The hurricane devastated large parts of the Dominican Republic. The government estimated the damage caused at US$1.2 billion.

mulatto and 12 per cent **white**. The majority belong to diverse **Protestant denominations**, and 16 per cent are members of the **Catholic** faith. There are also minorities of Muslims, Jews and followers of native religions. Average **life expectancy** is 66 years and the **literacy rate** is 95 per cent. The proportion of city-dwellers is 90 per cent.

History and Politics

Columbus first set foot on American soil in 1492 when he landed on the island of **San Salvador**, today also known as Watling Island. The **Spanish** carried off almost all of the native inhabitants as **slaves** to neighbouring islands. **English settlers** first arrived in 1648, but the settlement was constantly troubled by skirmishes with pirates until the islands were made a British colony and the British fleet was based in the Bahamas.

In 1973, the **crown colony** became **independent**. The Senate and the House of Representatives are elected every five years, and the 16 members of the Senate are appointed by the governor general. The voting age is 18.

Economy

In 2006, GDP was US$ 6.2 billion, of which three per cent came from **agriculture**, seven per cent from **industry** and 90 per cent from **services**. The major contributor to the economy is **tourism** which accounts for two-thirds of the income. There is also a flourishing invisibles sector because the particularly liberal **tax laws** attract foreign capital, making the Bahamas a trade and banking centre and the home of many 'accommodation addresses'. **Agriculture** and **manufacturing** are only partially developed.

Transport Infrastructure

The 22 inhabited islands are well served by a **road network** covering 4,100 km. There are regular **flights** between the islands, and Nassau and Freeport have international **air and sea ports**.

Tourism

The **paradise beaches** of Grand Bahama, Bimini, Cat Island and,

Rum Cay attract many visitors from the USA. The Blue Holes on the island of Andros are the world's longest and deepest submarine caves. In 2001, 4.2 million tourists spent US$1.75 billion.

St Kitts and Nevis

Area:	261 sq. km
Capital city:	Basseterre
Form of government: Federation/Constitutional Monarchy in the British Commonwealth	
Administrative divisions: 14 districts	
Population: 40,000 (153 inhabitants/sq. km)	
Language:	English
GDP per capita:	US$12,000
Currency: 1 Eastern Caribbean dollar = 100 cents	

Devon House in the Jamaican capital Kingston.

Natural Geography

St Kitts (area: 168 sq. km) and **Nevis** (area: 93 sq. km) belong to the **Lesser Antilles volcanic arc**. Mount Liamuiga (Mt Misery) on St Kitts is 1,137 m high and has a crater lake. The coasts are lined with black volcanic sands.The islands have sulphurous hot springs and are hit by earthquakes.

Climate

The **tropical climate** is affected by the trade winds. The coasts have relatively constant tempera-

tures of about 27°C. Average **precipitation** ranges from 750 mm in the west and 1,200–1,500 mm in the east, but can be as high as 3,000 mm in the mountains. The higher altitudes are covered with **rainforests and mountain cloud forests**. The lower slopes are used for **cultivation**. The fauna includes monkeys, mongooses and 60 species of bird.

Population

86 per cent of the population is **black**, 11 per cent **mulatto** and two per cent **white**. There are 40 different Christian denominations, including **Anglicans** (36 per cent), **Methodists** (32 per cent), **Catholics** (11 per cent) and **Moravians** (nine per cent). The other religious minorities are insignificant. Some 40 per cent of the population lives in the three main towns. Average **life expectancy** is 72 and the **literacy rate** is 90 per cent.

History and Politics

The island group, consisting of St Christopher, Nevis and Anguilla, were discovered by **Columbus**, and the **Spanish** then shipped the native population off to work in mines in Haiti. In the seventeenth and eighteenth centuries, the **English** and **French** fought over the islands, which became British in 1783. Both islands gained **independence** in 1983 and formed a **federation**, despite a strong separatist movement in Nevis. The islands have a joint national assembly, but Nevis

also has its own parliament and prime minister. The voting age is 18. The capital, Basseterre is on St Christopher Island; the main town on Nevis is Charlestown.

Economy

GDP in 2006 was US$490 million. **Agriculture** accounted for five per cent, 23 per cent came from **manufacturing** and 75 per cent derived from the **services sector**. Main exports are cars, sugar and sugar derivatives. Imports include machinery and foodstuffs.

Transport Infrastructure

There is a 300 km **road network** and an international **airport** and **deep sea port** in Basseterre. There are no direct flights to Nevis from outside the Caribbean.

Tourism

The main attractions are the beaches, hot springs and resort hotels. The largest hotel in the Eastern Caribbean was opened in 2003. The tourist season is between December and April.

Antigua and Barbuda

Area:	442 sq. km
Capital city:	St John's
Form of government: Constitutional Monarchy in the British Commonwealth	
Administrative divisions: 6 districts, 2 dependencies	
Population: 80,000 (180 inhabitants/sq. km)	
Languages: English (official), Creole English	
GDP per capita:	US$12,500
Currency: 1 Eastern Caribbean dollar = 100 cents	

Natural Geography

This small state in the Caribbean comprises the islands of **Antigua** (280 sq. km), **Barbuda** (161 sq. km) and the uninhabited **Redonda** (one sq. km) in the **Lesser Antilles**. The islands rest on layers of coral and have large areas of karstification. The Shirley Heights in south-west of Antigua are of volcanic origin. Barbuda has a

coastline with a large number of bays and coves and offshore coral reefs. The islands have no natural waterways.

Climate

The **mild tropical climate** reaches temperatures of 23°C to 28°C. Average **precipitation** is 900 mm. The woods contain wild boar and red deer (both imported) and various species of lizard, tortoise and bird.

Population

The inhabitants are 94.4 per cent **black**, 3.5 per cent **mulatto** and 1.3 per cent **white**. The majority are **Anglican**, but there are also some 14,500 **Catholics**. Average **life expectancy** is 72 and the **adult literacy rate** is 95 per cent. Only 36.2 per cent of the population lives in cities.

History and Politics

The islands were discovered by **Columbus** and the **Spanish** transported the native inhabitants as slaves to work in the mines of other colonies. Barbuda was settled by English colonists in 1628 and Antigua in 1632. In the seventeenth and eighteenth centuries, the **English** and **French** fought over the islands which later became a centre of the **slave trade**. From 1871–1956, Antigua and Barbuda were both British colonies. In World War II, the **USA** established marine and airforce bases on the islands which are very much resent by the inhabitants. This small state has been **independent** since 1981. The House of Representative is elected every five years, and the senators are appointed by the Governor-General who represents the head of state, Queen Elizabeth II. The voting age is 18.

Economy

In 2006, GDP was US$1 billion. **Agriculture** accounted for four per cent, **manufacturing** for 18 per cent and the **services sector** for 78 per cent. Agriculture and manufacturing are underdeveloped, the most important sector of the economy is **tourism**. Finished products, raw materials and foods are

*The simple art of **Haiti** fascinated the American DeWitt Peters so much that he founded the Centre d'Art in Port-au-Prince in 1944. The centre fosters Haitian art, which is characterised by optimistic paintings in bright colours. The paintings are exported to the United States and Europe where they are very popular. Many are also on sale in the art galleries of Haiti's capital city, **Port-au-Prince**.*

imported, and export goods include crude oil products, cotton and textiles.

Transport Infrastructure

The **road network** is some 1,000 km long and well constructed. There is an international **airport** in Coolidge and St John's has a **deep-sea port**.

Tourism

Some 200,000 foreigners visit the country every year for the white beaches of **Antigua** and the beautiful reefs of **Barbuda**. There are also an additional 250,000 **cruise visitors**. The high season is between December and April.

Dominica

Area:	750 sq. km
Capital city:	Roseau
Form of government:	
Republic in the Commonwealth	
Administrative divisions:	
10 districts	
Population:	
70,000 (93 inhabitants/sq. km)	
Languages:	
English (official), Patois, Cocoy	
GDP per capita:	US$3,500
Currency:	
1 Eastern Caribbean dollar = 100 cents	

Natural Geography

The mountainous **island** has continuous **volcanic activity**, as demonstrated by the crater lake known as Boiling Lake, discovered in 1922. There are numerous hot springs and fumaroles. Large parts of Dominica remain unexplored to this day. The mountains in the country's interior are up to 1,400 m high and have steep cliffs and ravines. The north coast has sheer cliffs some 200 m high.

Climate

The **tropical climate** is defined by the north-east trade wind that constantly blows across the region. Temperatures range between 25°C and 30°C. The coast has an annual **precipitation** of 1,800 mm, and in the mountains this can be as high as 6,500 mm.

The island is often affected by strong **hurricanes**. Almost the entire island is covered by tropical **rainforest**, which is home to many species of bird and various reptiles and rodents.

Population

91 per cent of the inhabitants are **black**, six per cent **mulatto** and **creole**, and 1.5 per cent **Indian**. There is also a small minority white population.

80 per cent are **Catholic** and 13 per cent **Protestant**. There are also minorities of Muslims, Hindus, Jews and Baha'i. Average

life expectancy is 75 years. The **adult literacy rate** is over 95 per cent, and 70 per cent live in the cities.

History and Politics

The island was discovered by **Columbus** on a Sunday ('Dominica' is Spanish for Sunday) in 1493, hence the name. The island's remote location meant that **European settlers** did not arrive until the seventeenth century. After a long period of dispute between the **British** and **French**, Dominica finally became British in 1814, and from 1967–1978 was a member of the West Indies Associated States. The country was granted **independence** in November 1978. The main towns are Portsmouth and Marigot.

Economy

In 2006, GDP was approximately US$250 million. Of this, some

18 per cent was derived from **agriculture**, 19 per cent from **manufacturing** and some 63 per cent from the **service sector**. Fossil fuels, consumer goods, machinery and chemicals are all imported; exports include agricultural produce (mainly bananas), cocoa, copra, coconuts and fruit juices.

 **1** The coral reefs of the Bahamas are a habitat for numerous species of flora and fauna. The Bahamas are coral islands.

2 In the Caribbean, people live at a leisurely pace. The local bar is a meeting place for sharing the latest gossip.

3 The markets in Haiti are very crowded. Many visitors come by bus from the more remote regions.

4 Sun, sea, palm trees: In Samana, a sleepy town in the Dominican Republic, you can experience an original tropical paradise.

*What is today a paradise for tourists was once a hell for the African slaves of the sugar cane plantations. The **Caribbean islands** used to be in the possession of the colonial powers, who maintained their power with violence. The descendants of these slaves now form the majority of the population in many of the Caribbean states, but most still live in terrible social conditions. Medical provisions are deficient, and poverty and hunger are widespread on many islands.*

Transport Infrastructure

The **road network** has a total length of ca. 800 km and is restricted to the coastal areas. Melville Hall is the international **airport**.

Tourism

The island's unspoiled **nature** attracts increasing numbers of tourists to the country. The best time to visit is between December and April.

St Lucia

Area:	616 sq. km
Capital city:	Castries
Form of government:	
Constitutional Monarchy in the British Commonwealth	
Administrative divisions:	
11 districts	
Population:	
170,000 (275 inhabitants/sq. km)	
Languages:	
English (official), French patois	
GDP per capita:	US$5,600
Currency: 1 Eastern Caribbean dollar = 100 cents	

Natural Geography

St Lucia belongs to the **Lesser Antilles** and is of volcanic origin, as demonstrated by the two 800-m-high conical volcanos, Gros Piton and Petit Piton in the southwest of the island. The south and west have white sandy beaches with offshore coral reefs. The interior is mountainous, with up to 950 m, and is traversed by numerous rivers and streams.

Climate

The north-east trade wind defines the **tropical wet-dry climate** and produces average temperatures of 25–30°C and precipitation of 1,200 mm on the coast and up to 3,500 mm inland. The original **rainforest** now only persists at higher altitudes. On the lower slopes, it has been replaced by cultivation. The rainforests contain a variety of bird species.

Population

The population of St Lucia is 90.3 per cent **black**, 5.5 per cent **mu-**latto, 3.2 per cent **Asian** and 0.8 per cent **white**. 77 per cent profess the **Catholic** faith and the rest belong to **Protestant** denominations. Average **life expectancy** is 74 years and the **literacy rate** is 82 per cent. The three largest towns account for 47 per cent of the population.

History and Politics

The island was discovered by **Columbus** but the **native inhabitants** successfully resisted attempts by European seafarers to conquer them until well into the seventeenth century. After a long dispute between **England** and **France**, the island became British in 1814, and became an **independent state in the Commonwealth** in 1979, although it still maintains its links to French culture and the local patois is based on French. St Lucia has a bicameral parliament based on the British system and Queen Elizabeth II is head of state. Compulsory voting is from the age of 21.

Economy

GDP in 2006 was approximately US$950 million, of which eight per cent derived from **agriculture**, 17 per cent from **manufacturing** and 75 per cent from the **service sector**. Main exports are agricultural products, including bananas, cocoa, sugar and citrus fruits. Imports include consumer goods, machinery, textiles and fertilisers. **Tourism**, mainly from the USA, is becoming increasingly important to the economy.

Transport Infrastructure

The 800 km-long **road network** is largely well-constructed. Two modern **ports** are being developed for foreign trade and **cruise ships**. An international **airport** is located near Vieux Fort.

Tourism

In 2002, the island welcomed more than 250,000 foreign visitors to the unspoiled countryside, including the volcanoes. The best time for travel is between mid-December and mid-April.

Palms, sand and deep blue sea: Sam Lord's Castle has one of the most beautiful beaches in Barbados.

St Vincent and the Grenadines

Area:	389 sq. km
Capital city:	Kingstown
Form of government:	
Constitutional Monarchy in the British Commonwealth	
Administrative divisions:	
6 districts	
Population: 117,000	
(300 inhabitants/sq. km)	
Language:	
English	
GDP per capita:	US$4,300
Currency:	
1 Eastern Caribbean dollar = 100 cents	

Natural Geography

To the north of the mountainous **main island of St Vincent** lies the **active volcano** of Soufrière (1,234 m). In the east of the country, the land becomes flatter towards the sea. The numerous smaller islands located to the south of St Vincent are called the **Grenadines** and are also of volcanic origin. These islands are largely uninhabited.

Climate

The country has a **tropical climate** with average temperatures between 25°C and 27°C. Mountainous regions have annual levels of precipitation of 3,500 mm; this is just 1,500 mm in the lowlands. The Grenadines are noticeably drier. In summer there are often strong **hurricanes**. The island's interior is covered in evergreen rainforest which is home to an amazing variety of bird species.

Population

The inhabitants of St Vincent and the Grenadines are 66 per cent **black**, 19 per cent **white**, 5.5 per cent **Indian** and two per cent **zambo** (mixed race with black and Indian parents). 75 per cent are **Protestant** and nine per cent are **Catholic**. Just under half of the population lives in cities. The average **life expectancy** is 74 years and the **literacy rate** is 82 per cent.

History and Politics

It is most likely that **St Vincent** was discovered by **Columbus** in 1493, but European seafarers were unable to conquer the warlike **native Caribs** and colonise the island until the seventeenth century. In the years prior to 1798 the colonial power switched between the **French** and **British** several times. From 1958–1962, the island group was part of the **West Indies Federation** and from 1969 it was an associated state in the British **Commonwealth**, before becoming **independent** in 1979. According to the 1979 constitution, part of the parliament is elected every five years and part is appointed by the Governor-General who represents Queen Elizabeth II. The voting age is 18.

Economy

GDP in 2006 was US$500 million, of which 12 per cent was derived from **agriculture**, 24 per cent from **manufacturing** and 64 per cent from the **services sector**. Main imports are machinery, consumer goods and foodstuffs. The country exports agricultural products, mainly bananas, arrowroot and cotton. **Tourism** is increasingly important to the economy.

Transport Infrastructure

Approximately half of the 400 km of **road** is well-constructed. Regional **flights** connect St Vincent with the international **airports** of neighbouring countries but there are no direct flights from outside the Caribbean.

Tourism

The island group, and especially Mustique, is popular with tourists. **Yachts** and **cruise ships** bring many of the 200,000 foreign visitors who arrive each year. The best time to visit is between January and May.

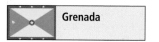

Grenada

Area:	344 sq. km
Capital city:	St George's
Form of government:	
Constitutional Monarchy	

*The sea is the most important source of protein for the people of the Caribbean. The **fish stocks** have been declining here for years, however, and it is ever harder to supply the increasing demand. A problem is the use of chemi-* *cals in fishing, for example the use of lead in crab fishing. This destroys the coral reef and the species living in it. The death of the smaller fish means that the larger predators also keep away from the reefs.*

Population:
c. 100,000 (290 inhabitants/sq. km)
Languages:
English (official), Patois
GDP per capita: US$5,000
Currency:
1 Eastern Caribbean dollar =
100 cents

Natural Geography

The **main island,** like the **Grenadines** to the south, is of volcanic origin. The interior of the island is mountainous, and the highest point is Mount Saint Catherine (840 m). Numerous crater lakes, sulphurous springs and earthquakes are all indications of volcanic activity. Grenada is the most southerly of the Windward Islands.

Climate

The **tropical climate** is made milder by the trade winds, and the country has an average temperature of 27°C. Annual precipitation on the coast is 1,500 mm, compared with up to 5,000 mm in more mountainous regions. The natural tropical **rainforest** has only been preserved in the mountains. The island is home to numerous species of birds, various reptiles, rodents and monkeys.

Population

The population is 82 per cent **black,** 13 per cent **mulatto,** three per cent Indian and one per cent white. 53 per cent are **Catholic** and 14 per cent **Anglican.** Seventh Day Adventists account for nine per cent of the population and seven per cent are members of the **Pentecostal Church.** Average **life expectancy** is 65, and the **literacy rate** is 91 per cent. Some 40 per cent of the population lives in cities.

History and Politics

The island was discovered by **Columbus** and was later settled by the **French,** who suppressed the indigenous people and used them, along with African **slaves,** to work their **plantations.** In 1762, Grenada was occupied by **Great Britain** and remained a Crown Colony until **independence** in 1974. Attempts at re-

form by premier **Maurice Bishop** ended in 1983 when he was murdered. The **USA** used this as an excuse to invade, but the actual reason behind the move was apparently to stop Grenada's improving relationship with the USSR. After the withdrawal of the US troops, the 1974 constitution was re-adopted with some alterations. Fifteen members of the House of representatives are directly elected, and 13 are appointed by the Governor-General. The voting age is 18.

Economy

GDP in 2006 was US$500 million. **Agriculture** accounted for ten per cent, **manufacturing** for 19 per cent, and the **services sector** for 71 per cent. The country has a serious foreign trade deficit. Imports include machinery, consumer goods, food and raw materials. Exports are based around nutmeg (25 per cent of world production), but also include cocoa, tropical fruits, rum and sugar. **Tourism** is becoming increasingly valuable to the economy.

Transport Infrastructure

The **road network** is 980 km long. There is an international **airport** at Point Saline.

Tourism

Grenada welcomes approximately 300,000 foreign visitors each year. By far the majority are **cruise ship passengers.** The best time to visit is between December and April.

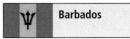
Barbados

Area:	431 sq. km
Capital city:	Bridgetown
Form of government:	
Constitutional Monarchy in the British Commonwealth	
Administrative divisions:	
11 districts	

1 The natural harbour, English Harbour, on Antigua also provides protection from hurricanes. This spot was once used to protect the British fleet.

2 An ancient sugar mill in Montpelier. On St Kitts and Nevis hardly any sugar cane is now cultivated. The tiny island lives off tourism.

3 The church of Soufrière stands directly on the beach. Space is short on Dominica, and the island has an area of just 751 sq. km.

4 The brilliant green bay is just one of the features that makes St George's, the capital of Grenada, one of the prettiest cities in the Caribbean.

Barbados, Trinidad and Tobago

The Mardi Gras carnival in **Trinidad** is the most important cultural event on the island. Every year, the dazzling parades through the streets offer a spectacle to rival that of Rio de Janeiro. The exuberance with which this Roman Catholic festival to mark the beginning of Lent is celebrated on Trinidad dates back to the the time of African slavery. The elaborate costumes, often consisting of huge wheels of tulle and flowers.

Population:
280,000 (650 inhabitants/sq. km)
Languages:
English (official), Bajan
GDP per capita: US$12,500
Currency:
1 Barbados dollar = 100 cents

Natural Geography

Barbados, the most easterly island of the West Indies, is of volcanic origin, and much of the surface consists of karst and coral limestone. The highest point is Mount Hillaby at 340 m. The east coast is dominated by cliffs but the south-east is relatively flat. The west and south coastlines are lined with broad, sandy beaches. **Coral reefs** surround most of the island.

Climate

The **tropical climate** is defined by the trade winds which constantly blow across the region. Average temperatures are a pleasant 24°C to 27°C. Average precipitation is 1,000–2,000 mm. **Hurricanes** are common in summer and autumn.
Extensive **agriculture** has eliminated all but small sections of the original **rainforest**. The country still has numerous species of birds, mongooses, monkeys and lizards. The waters are teaming with fish stocks.

Population

The population of Barbados is 92 per cent **black**, 3.2 per cent **white** and 2.6 per cent **mulatto**. **Catholics** make up five per cent of the population, and there are also minorities of Jews, Muslims and Hindus. The vast majority of the population belong to **Protestant** churches and sects.
Average **life expectancy** is 76 years and the **adult literacy rate** is more than 95 per cent. Bridgetown has a branch of the **University of the West Indies**. Just under half of the population live in cities.

History and Politics

Soon after discovering the country, the **Spanish** killed or deported the native inhabitants. When European settlers arrived in 1635, the country was uninhabit-ed. African **slaves** were brought in to work in the **plantations**. Until **independence** in 1966, Barbados was a **British colony**. The lower house of the bicameral parliament, the House of Assembly, is elected every five years and the Senate is appointed by the Governor-General. The voting age is 18.

Economy

GDP in 2006 stood at US$3.5 billion. **Agriculture** accounted for 6.4 per cent, **manufacturing** for 15.6 per cent, and the **services sector** for 78 per cent. Main imports are food, machinery, consumer goods, timber for construction, paper and crude oil.

Beaches of white sand make Barbados a holiday paradise.

Exports are predominately based on the island's monoculture, the cultivation of sugar cane. **Sugar**, **molasses**, **syrup** and **rum** are just some of the by-products of this branch of the economy. Diversification is finally taking place and cotton, textile, electronics and cement are now being exported. **Tourism** has become increasingly important and is the biggest earner.

Transport Infrastructure

The **road network** is 1,700 km long and is well constructed. There is a **sea port** and an international **airport** in the capital city, Bridgetown. The other towns – Speightstown, Holetown and Oistins – are linked by road.

Tourism

The country's sandy beaches are a great tourist attraction, as well as the fascinating flora and fauna and the impressive caves. The high season is from December to April.

Trinidad and Tobago	
Area:	5,128 sq. km
Capital city:	Port-of-Spain
Form of government:	
Presidential Republic in the Commonwealth	
Administrative divisions:	
8 counties, 3 municipalities, Tobago (autonomous)	
Population: 1.3 million (253 inhabitants/sq. km)	
Language:	English
GDP per capita:	US$14,000
Currency: 1 Trinidad and Tobago dollar = 100 cents	

Natural Geography

Approximately 8,000 years ago, these islands were connected to the South American mainland. On the island of **Trinidad**, three ranges of mountains extend from west to east. The El Cerro del Aripo at a height of 940 m is the highest point. Pitch Lake is the world's largest natural reserve of **asphalt**. The Maracas Falls and the Blue Basin waterfalls 91-m-high are remarkable. The landscape in the north and south is defined by a cliff-lined, steep coast, and the flat coasts in the east and west have many lagoons and mangrove swamps.
Tobago is dominated by a mountainous area up to 576 m high, the only flat strip of land being located in the south-west. With the exception of the cliffs in the north-east, the coast line consists of flat, sandy beaches. The country has many **coral reefs**, the most famous of which is Buccoo Reef.

Climate

The north-east trade wind gives the islands a **humid, tropical climate** with an average temperatures of between 24°C and 26°C. Most of the annual precipitation falls between July and December; amounts vary from 1,600 mm in the west to 3,800 mm in the east of Trinidad, and reaches 2,200 mm on Tobago.
Tobago is almost entirely covered by tropical **rainforest**, apart from the coastal regions. In the south and west of Trinidad there are also **savannahs** and **humid and dry woodland**.
The **animal kingdom** is very varied, including monkeys, bats, snakes, tortoises, alligators, raccoons, sloths, ocelots, peccaries, elk, the common agouti, armadillos and many species of birds and butterflies.

Population

The population is very diverse with 40.3 per cent **Indian ancestry**, 39.6 per cent **black** and 18.5 per cent **mulatto**. **Christians** account for 40.3 per cent, 23.8 per cent is **Hindu** and 5.8 per cent **Muslim**. Average **life expectancy** is 67 years and the **adult literacy rate** is higher than 95 per cent. Some 76 per cent of the population live in the towns, the capital Port-of-Spain, San Fernando, Arima as well as in Scarborough on Tobago.

History and Politics

Columbus discovered **Trinidad** on his third voyage in the year 1498. Until 1797, the **French, British, Dutch and pirates** of the Spanish Main challenged the Spanish governor for domination of the islands.
In 1802, the islands officially became a **British colony**, and finally gained **independence** in 1976. The European settlers who arrived in the seventeenth and eighteenth centuries brought **black African slaves** to the islands, and later also **Asian indentured labourers** to work on the plantations. This is the reason for the variety of ethnicities on both the islands.
The House of Representatives is elected for a maximum term of five years. Senators are also appointed and an Electoral College selects the president every five years. The voting age is 18.

Economy

GDP in 2006 was US$18.2 billion. **Agriculture** accounted for two per cent, **manufacturing** for 42 per cent, and the **services sector** for 56 per cent. The economy has experienced a five per cent rate of growth in recent years.
Natural reserves, including crude oil, natural gas and bitumen have made the islands rich. Exports include crude oil, natural gas, bitumen (Trinidad has the largest natural asphalt reserves on Earth in the 40-ha asphalt lake known as Pitch Lake), chemicals, sugar, rum, coffee and tobacco. The country imports raw materials, capital goods and consumer items.

Transport Infrastructure

Approximately 2,800 km of the total 6,400 km of **road** is surfaced, but much of it is in poor condition. The main **port** is found at Port-of-Spain, along with an international **airport**. Both islands are connected by a regular **ferry service**.

Tourism

Approximately 300,000 foreign tourists come to the islands each year, mainly attracted by the impressive **sandy beaches** and the natural wonders, such as the waterfalls and the unique Pitch Lake. The best time to visit is between January and May.

The Virgin Islands, part of the Lesser Antilles.

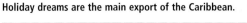

Holiday dreams are the main export of the Caribbean.

The Caribbean islands are popular with fans of water sports.

Caribbean Paradise

The island groups of the Greater and Lesser Antilles form a large arc, over more than 3,500 km, stretching from the coasts of Florida to Venezuela and enclosing the Caribbean Sea. The Caribbean island world offers endless sandy beaches, green hills, crystal clear waters and inhabitants who live life to the full.

The Caribbean has a tropical climate, which is perfect for abundant vegetation. Bromeliaceae grow along power lines and orchids grow on the walls of houses. The interior of many of the larger islands is covered in dense primeval rainforest, interspersed with expansive plantations growing traditional products such as bananas, tobacco, coffee and sugar cane. These plantations formed the economic basis of the islands for several centuries. Soon after the islands were discovered by Columbus, the first Europeans came to establish settlements and introduced the plantation economy. They brought millions of slaves from Africa into the region. The ancestors of these slaves now form the overwhelming majority of the Caribbean population.

In recent years, tourism has largely replaced traditional economic sectors. The unique way of life in the Caribbean, which varies from island to island depending on the mixture of African traditions and the cultural heritage of the European colonial powers, is one of the main attractions for many tourists.

The Greater Antilles are made up of Cuba, Jamaica, Hispaniola and Puerto Rico. The largest of the western Antilles is Cuba, famous for its cigars, rum and the amazing depth of musical tradition, which has the whole world on its feet dancing. The neighbouring island of Hispaniola is divided into two countries, Haiti and the Dominican Republic. Jamaica, the home of rum and Rastafarians, is approximately 150km south of Cuba. Jamaica's greatest export is Reggae, which spread from here across the whole world.

The Lesser Antilles comprise the Windward Islands and the Leeward Islands, which run parallel to the coast of Venezuela. The Windward Islands include Barbados, Trinidad and Tobago. The islands of the Lesser Antilles are part of a curve of volcanic islands at the edge of the Caribbean Plate, and, along with Montserrat, display much volcanic activity. Barbados is located to the east of the Caribbean arc of islands, and is made up of 80 per cent coral limestone. Some of the Caribbean islands are still overseas territories, including the British Crown Colony of the Cayman Islands and the Virgin Islands, which half belong to Great Britain and half to the USA. Martinique and Guadeloupe are French overseas Départements, and Montserrat belongs to Great Britain. St Kitts and Nevis, Antigua and Barbuda, Dominica, St Lucia and St Vincent and the Grenadines are independent states, as is Grenada, whose main export item, nutmeg, is proudly displayed on the nation's flag.

Colombia, Venezuela

*The mountainous landscape of **Colombia** makes road-building very difficult. Rivers, such as the Río Magdalena and its tributaries, have long been the traditional transport and trade routes.*

Floating markets have grown up at the main transport hubs, where traditional crops such as bananas, sugar cane and pineapples can be traded from boat to boat.

Colombia

Area:	1,138,910 sq. km
Capital city:	Bogotá
Form of government:	Republic
Administrative divisions:	
32 departments, capital city district	
Population:	
45 million (39 inhabitants/sq. km)	
Language:	Spanish
GDP per capita:	US$3,000
Currency:	
1 Colombian peso = 100 centavos	

Natural Geography

One third of the land mass is covered by part of the **Andes**. The Cordillera Occidental rises to a height of up to 4,000 m. The Cordillera Central, a mountain range containing many volcanoes, ends in the north in the **Sierra Nevada de Santa Marta**. These mountains include Colombia's highest peak, the 5,775-m-high **Pico Cristobál Colón**. Between the Cordillera Central and Oriental, the **Rio Magdalena** flows into the Caribbean Sea. The east is covered by lowland plains, extending into the **Amazonian Lowlands** in the extreme south-east.

Climate

Apart from its north Caribbean coast, Colombia lies in the **inner tropics**. Below 1,000 m, temperatures are constant at between 25°C and 30°C. At an altitude of up to 2,000 m, temperatures are about 18°C, and over 3,000 m, they drop to 10°C. There is great variation between day and night. The northern Pacific coast and the western side of the Andes has the highest rainfall, with an average 10,000 mm of annual precipitation, compared with just 300 mm on the eastern Caribbean coast. **Flora** and **fauna** vary greatly depending on altitude. Tropical rainforests can be found up to a height of 900 m, above which they are replaced by mountain and cloud forests. Above 2,500 m, the main vegetation is evergreen oaks, and above 3,200 m there is high steppe vegetation. The **snow line** is at 4,500 m. The flat plains known as 'llanos' are covered in humid or dry savannah, and towards the Pacific coast, marshy woodland is replaced by mangrove swamps. The **rainforest** contains a wide variety of flora and fauna including monkeys, anteaters, sloths, raccoons, jaguars and tapirs. The infamous piranha fish inhabit the rivers.

Population

Colombians are 58 per cent **mestizo** (of mixed Spanish and American heritage), 20 per cent **white**, 14 per cent **mulatto**, four per cent **black** and three per cent **zambo**. The literacy rate is 91 per cent, and life expectancy is 72 years. 95 per cent of the population is **Catholic**, and 73 per cent live in connurbations. Schooling is compulsory between the ages of six and twelve.

History and Politics

Alonso de Ojeda discovered the country in 1499, beginning a period of Spanish rule that only ended

Tunja: the Bolívar Monument in memory of the great national hero.

with the 1819 War of Liberation, led by **Simón Bolívar**. The national territory of the new Republic of Grand Colombia was gradually reduced, reaching its current size in 1903. Tensions between clerical and secular powers have defined the country's politics. The reforms of the 1930s ended in a civil war that cost a total of 200,000 lives between 1949 and 1958. Today, left-wing **guerrillas**, brutal attacks by the **military** and the **power of the drug cartels** maintain a wave of **violence** and **corruption**. The bicameral parliament and the state president are directly elected every four years. The voting age is 18.

Economy

In 2006, GDP was US$135 billion of which 11 per cent was derived from **agriculture**, 23 per cent from **manufacturing** and 56 per cent from the **services sector**. Exports include crude oil, coffee, coal and gold. Colombia is an importer of machinery, chemicals and food.

Transport Infrastructure

The **rail network** is 3,386 km long, and the **road network** covers 106,600 km. The country has three international **airports**. The **Pan-american Highway** is only well-maintained in some places.

Tourism

Approximately 800,000 foreign visitors bring in around US$1.3 billion annually. Attractions include Cartagena and Santa Cruz de Mompox, the Tieradentro and Los Katios **national parks**. The best time to visit is between December and March.

Venezuela

Area:	912,050 sq. km
Capital city:	Caracas
Form of government:	
Presidential Federal Republic	
Administrative divisions:	
22 federal states, 1 federal district (Capital city)	
Population:	
26 million (29 inhabitants/sq. km)	
Language:	Spanish
GDP per capita:	US$6,700
Currency:	
1 bolívar = 100 céntimos	

Natural Geography

Venezuela can be divided into three geographic areas: the **mountains of the Andes**, the **Orinoco Lowland** and the **Guiana Highlands**.
In the north-west lie the Maracaibo basin and Lake Maracaibo (13,300 sq. km), an area with rich crude oil reserves. This lowland area is bordered by the **Cordillera de Mérida**, a mountain chain which is home of the country's highest peak, the 5,002-m-high **Pico Bolívar**, and the Serrania del Perija. Southeast of this region lie the Orinoco Lowlands. This grassland is up to 400 km wide and is often flooded during the rainy season.
South of the Orinoco lie the Guiana Highlands, which cover almost half of Venezuela's land area. A number of **sandstone mesas** reach altitudes of around 3,000 m. The extreme south-west is part of the Amazonian basin.

Climate

Venezuela has a **tropical, wet-dry climate**. On the slopes of the Andes, annual precipitation is around 3,000 mm, but in the Orinoco Lowlands this is just 2,000 mm. The Guiana Highlands see approximately 3,000 mm of rain, the high basins of the mountains on the Caribbean coast, which are frequently struck by earthquakes, and some Andes valleys get up to 1,000 mm of precipitation, but on the north coast rainfall is just under 400 mm. At altitudes of up to 800 m, average annual temperatures reach between 25°C and 29°C. Up to the snow line at 2,000 m, temperatures are 15°C to 25°C, and on the coast and in the lowlands, they can climb as high as 38°C.

Population

Venezuela's population is 69 per cent **mulatto** and **mestizo**, 20 per cent **white**, nine per cent **black** and two per cent **Native American**. Life expectancy is 75 years and the literacy rate is 93 per cent. 93 per cent are **Catholic** and five per cent **Protestant**, but there are also minorities of Jews, Catholics, Orthodox and Muslims. Eighty-six per cent of the population live in the towns and cities. Schooling is compulsory between the ages of 5 and 15, with 15 per cent of the population living below the poverty line.

History and Politics

Columbus landed on the coast in 1498. After a short period of German rule, Venezuela became a Spanish colony in 1572. In 1777, the **Captaincy General of Venezuela** was established. The struggle for liberation, led by **Simón Bolívar,** ended in 1821 with victory over the Spanish. The newly created **Republic of Grand Colombia** collapsed just nine years later. Venezuela became an **independent republic** in 1830. The country was ruled by military dictators until World War II.
The mining of the country's rich natural reserves was mainly undertaken by foreign firms until 1976, but the subsequent nationalisation of the oil and iron ore industries did not bring economic and political stability. **Attempted coups** by the military, social unrest, **criminality** and **inflation** of almost 50 per cent are the norm. In 1998, the left-wing Hugo Chávez became President. The people voted for a new constitution in 1999, and the country became known as the Bolivarian Republic of Venezuela. The presidential elections of 2000 were won by Chávez, but his autocratic leadership attracted resistance from all levels of society. Despite a general strike, the opposition did not manage to affect a change in leadership at the start of 2003. The strike led to a huge economic crisis, as the oil industry was almost brought to a standstill. Chávez was re-elected in 2006. The parliament and president are directly elected every five years.

Economy

GDP in 2006 was US$180 billion. **Agriculture** accounted for four per cent, **manufacturing** 47 per cent, and the **service sector** 49 per cent. 80 per cent of exports are from crude oil and natural gas. Machinery and consumer goods are the main imports.

The small town of **Villa de Leyva** was declared a Colombian National Monument, due to the fact that almost all of the old colonial buildings have been preserved. Numerous churches, white-washed houses and the town hall around the 14,000-sq.-m Plaza Mayor are relics from the colonial age.

Transport Infrastructure

Venezuela has a good transport system, especially on the north coast. The **road network** is 82,700 km long, of which 32,501 km are surfaced. There is also 584 km of **railways** and seven international **airports**.

GDP per capita:	US$1,150
Currency:	
1 Guyana Dollar = 100 cents	

Natural Geography

The **Pakaraima Mountains** the highest peak being the 2,810-m-high Mount Roraima. These descend into a hilly landscape which adjoins the coastal lowlands, which are covered in dense mangrove woodland. The southwest of the country is 3,000 mm annual precipitation, but to the country's interior, this is just 1,500 mm. Almost 90 per cent of the land area consists of evergreen **rainforest**. The hills are covered in savannah vegetation, and the coastal region has **salt marshes** and mangrove swamp. The country has a wide range of **fauna,** including deer, jaguars, crocodiles, armadillos, tapirs, anteaters and ocelots, **poisonous spiders** and **piranhas** in the rivers.

South America. In 1814, the colonial powers divided the region into three. For 150 years, the west of Guyana was the colony of British Guyana. After the **abolition of slavery** in 1834, the region was in desperate need of workers, and **indentured labour** was brought over from **India**. In 1961, the British Crown Colony was granted autonomy, and five years later earned a place as an independent constitutional monarchy in the Commonwealth.

Since 1970, Guyana has been a presidential republic. The parliament is elected every five years; the

Tourism

More than 100,000 foreign visitors enter the country each year but Guyana's tourist infrastructure leaves a lot to be desired. The country is popular with trekkers, hikers, mountain-climbers and anglers. The main beauty spots are the Kaietur Falls in the Kaietur National Park.

	French Guiana

Area:	83,534 sq. km
Capital city: :	
Cayenne (seat of administration)	
Form of government:	
Département d'outre-mer (DOM) (French overseas region)	
Population:	
c. 200,000 (2 inhabitants/sq. km)	

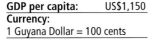

	Guyana

Area:	214,969 sq. km
Capital city:	Georgetown
Form of government:	
Presidential Republic in the Commonwealth	
Administrative divisions:	
10 regions	
Population:	
765,000 (3 inhabitants/sq. km)	
Languages: English (official), Hindi, Urdu	

Tourism

In 2004, 500,000 tourists brought approximately US$600 million into the country. The best time to travel is between December and April.

dominated by savannah vegetation. Since the seventeenth century, the sea has been held back to create areas suitable for agricultural use.

Climate

The climate is **tropical,** and the coast is influenced by the **trade winds**. The temperatures here remain constant, but temperatures on the Atlantic coast fluctuate between 24°C and 29°C. Coastal regions see between 2,000 and

Population

Indians constitute 51.4 per cent of the population, 30.5 per cent are **black**, 11 per cent **mulatto** and **mestizo**, and 5.3 per cent Native American.

Life expectancy is 66 and the literacy rate is over 95 per cent. **Protestants** constitute 34 per cent of the population, 33 per cent are **Hindu**, 20 per cent **Catholic** and eight per cent **Muslim**. The urban population is 36 per cent.

History and Politics

The British, **Dutch** and **French** all fought for the north-east corner of

winning party appoints the president. The voting age is 18.

Economy

In 2006, GDP was US$880 million, of which 31 per cent came from **agriculture**, 29 per cent from **manufacturing** and 40 per cent from the **service sector**. Guyana imports fuel and consumer goods. Main exports are gold, sugar, bauxite and rice.

Transport Infrastructure

The road network is approximately 5,000 km long, and only paved in the coastal regions. The major towns and cities are served by **regional air transport**.

Languages:
French (official), Creole

GDP per capita:	US$14,000
Currency:	1 euro = 100 cents

Natural Geography

A broad plain, 15–40 km wide, runs parallel to the coast. In the interior lie the Guiana Shield **hills**.

Climate

The yearly average temperature in this **humid and hot country** is 27°C. The rainy season lasts from December to July. The coastal strip consists of **savannah** and **mangrove swamps.** Most of the land is **tropical rainforest** with a wonderful range of wildlife.

French Guiana, Suriname

The **Yanomami** live in dense forest on the Venezuelan-Brazilian border. They are today one of the most threatened peoples in the the world. Land-grabbing and slash-and-burn deforestation is destroying their habitat. Many

Yanomami die from diseases that have been brought into the country which their immune systems cannot cope with. In Yanomami mythology, men and animals are inextricably linked by 'shadow souls' and both share the same fate.

Population

More than half of the population is **Creole**, but 30 per cent is **black**, ten per cent **white**, ten per cent **Asian** and Arawak Indian who live in the rainforests in relative isolation. A significant minority consists of Hmong people who are refugees from Laos, and who work mainly supplying and selling fruit and vegetables from their market

gardens. Some 78 per cent of the population are Roman Catholic. Education follows the French system and schooling is compulsory up to the age of 16.

History and Politics

The Spanish discovered what is now French Guiana in around 1500, but made no colonial claims. As a result, the **British**, **French**

and **Dutch** fought for the land until the borders were finally established in 1814. Since the mid-nineteenth century, **slaves from Africa** and later **indentured labour from Asia** were set to work on the plantations. From 1854 to 1938, Guiana was a **French penal colony**. The prison known as **Devil's Island**, one of the offshore islands in the Isles du Salut group, became famous as the

place to which Alfred Dreyfus was sent after being wrongly convicted of treason in France in 1894 and for the account of life there in the book 'Papillon' written by Henri Charrière, a former inmate. Since 1848, the French Guyanese have enjoyed **French citizenship**. The country has its own parliament, elected every six years, and also sends representatives to the National Assembly and the Senate in Paris.

Economy

In 2006, GDP was approximately US$ 2.8 billion (estimated). Half of the money spent in the country is related to the scientific work carried out at the **European Space Agency at Kourou**.
Coffee, rice, bananas, sugar cane and manioc are cultivated. Crab-fishing, the timber industry and gold-mining are also of economic importance. Consumer goods, machinery and vehicles are imported; exports are timber, helicopter parts, gold coins, crabs, coffee and rum. The economy is in general poorly developed and is dependent on French subsidies.

Transport Infrastructure

Of the 550-km-long **road network**, some 350 km of are surfaced. The interior can only be reached by **plane** or **riverboat**. There is an international airport and port at Cayenne.

Tourism

Tourism is restricted to the coastal region. The wildlife is spectacular and the countryside unspoiled, so the country is popular with trekkers and hikers. The best time to visit is between August and November.

INDUSTRIAL ACTIVITIES

Energy
- ⚡ Hydroelectric power plants
- — Oil pipelines
- — Natural gas pipelines

Industry
- ▨ Industrial areas
- • Main industrial sites
- • Main oil tankers' terminals

Minerals
- A Fossil coal
- A Gas and Oil wells
- Ag Silver
- Al Bauxite
- Asb Asbestos
- Au Gold
- Cr Chrome
- Cu Copper
- Fe Iron
- Mn Manganese
- Mo Molybdenum
- Nb Niobium

LAND USE
- Forest and woods
- Savanna, meadows and pasture
- Cropland
- Desert
- Semidesert and marsh, swamp
- Barren land

- Ni Nickel
- P Phosphates
- Pb Lead
- Pt Platinum
- Sb Antimony
- Sn Tin
- U Uranium
- W Tungsten
- Zn Zinc
- ▽ Diamonds

Suriname	
Area:	163,265 sq. km
Capital city:	Paramaribo
Form of government:	
Presidential Republic	
Administrative divisions:	
9 districts, capital city district	
Population:	
c. 480,000 (3 inhabitants/sq. km)	
Languages:	
Dutch (official),	
Hindustani, Javanese, English	
GDP per capita:	US$4,100
Currency:	
1 Suriname dollar = 100 cents	

Natural Geography

Surinam is mainly covered by a **high plateau containing many ravines**. The **Wilhelmina Mountains**, whose highest peak is the 1,230-m-high Julianatop lie in the interior. Near the Atlantic coast

San Agustín is the most significant archaeological site in Colombia. Between 650 BC and 1400 AD numerous tombs were constructed here – some simple and some hill-like burial mounds, decorated with puzzling figures. The stone sculptures are mythological beings, half animal and half human. San Agustín's origins remain unknown.

there is an area of hills and a coastal plain, between 20 and 100 km wide. This area is where 80 per cent of the population lives. It is the main agricultural area.

All of the country's rivers flow northwards; the two most important are the **Courantyne** and the **Maroni**. The **Suriname river** is dammed to form the Prof. Dr. Ir. W. J. van Blommesteinmeer (Brokopondo Reservoir).

Climate

Although temperatures in the mountains can fluctuate widely, the rest of the country has a constant **tropical temperature** of around 27°C. During the **rainy season,** up to 2,500 mm of rain can fall on the mountain slopes; the coastal region only receives 1,500 mm. 85 per cent of the country is covered in rainforest, parts of which are still unexplored. Towards the coast, savannah vegetation predominates, followed by mangrove swamp and marshes along the coast.

The tropical rainforests have a rich wildlife, including jaguars, tapir, monkeys and ocelots, numerous reptiles and many species of bird. The coastal waters contain manatees and turtles.

Population

The population consists of 34.2 per cent **Indians**, 33.5 per cent **Creole**, up to 17.8 per cent **Javanese**, 8.5 per cent **black** as well as minorities of **Native Americans, Europeans**, **Lebanese** and **Chinese**. Life expectancy is 69 years and the literacy rate is 93 per cent. 27 per cent of the population are **Hindu**, 23 per cent **Catholic**, 20 per cent **Muslims** and 19 per cent **Protestant**. Nearly half the population lives in the cities. Schooling is compulsory from 6 to 12.

History and Politics

Columbus landed in Guiana in 1498, when the country had already been settled by Native Americans for more than 2,500 years. Colonial wars and various treaties first brought the country under **French**, then **Dutch** and finally **British rule**. In 1814, what is now Suriname became a **Dutch colony** and in 1954, it became part of the Netherlands with equal rights and **a large measure of autonomy**.

Suriname was granted **independence** in 1975, but serious, ethnically motivated power struggles broke out. The resulting economic and political instability caused a **wave of emigration**. Since all inhabitants held a Dutch passport, one third of the population was able to move to the Netherlands. Under the 1987 constitution, the country is a presidential republic. The head of state and the bicameral parliament are elected every five years. All citizens over the age of 18 have the right to vote.

Economy

GDP in 2006 was US$2 billion. **Agriculture** accounted for 11 per cent, **manufacturing** for 20 per cent and the **services sector** for 69 per cent.

Despite an almost even trade balance, a large proportion of the population still lives in abject **poverty**. Many people can only survive by resorting to **black market dealing** and **smuggling**. The country's main imports are raw materials, processed goods and consumer products. The principal exports are aluminium, prawns and rice.

Transport Infrastructure

The only paved roads are to be found in coastal regions. The main cities, the capital Paramaribo, Nieuw Nickerie, Brokopondo and Nieuw Amsterdam, are connected by **domestic flights**. The rivers are the main form of transport.

Tourism

Tourism is expanding, and new facilities are opening up, including the Overbridge River Resort, popular with hikers and anglers. The colonial architecture of Paramaribo, including the cathedral, are also of interest. The best time of year to visit is from February to April.

1 In the Venezuelan Simón Bolívar National Park, people live at an altitude of 3,000 m. Venezuela's highest mountain Pico Bolívar (5,002 m) is in this region.

2 The east of Venezuela is largely uninhabited and rivers flow through endless jungle. The whole region around the Auyantepui (2,953 m) can only be reached by plane or boat.

3 Caracas is the political and economic centre of oil-rich Venezuela. Skyscrapers are typical of the city's skyline.

Cities of Central and South America

Mexico City

Mexico City, the capital of Mexico, is the largest city in the Americas with a conurbation of almost 23 million inhabitants. It is situated at a height of over 2,200 m at the southern end of a high-lying valley on a dried-up lake, Lake Texcoco. The city was founded by the Aztecs in 1325 as Tenochtitlán. It has been the capital city of Mexico since the country gained independence in 1821. One of the most striking buildings in Mexico City is the library of the national university (founded in 1551). Completed in 1953, the library's mosaic-clad façade by Juan O'Gorman displays a link with traditional Mesoamerican architecture.

Area:
1,499 sq. km (city)
Inhabitants:
8,720,000 (city, 2008)
22,730,000 (conurbation, 2008)
Population density:
5,817 inhabitants/sq. km (city)

The cathedral on the Plaza de Constitución (Zocalo) in the historic centre of the city.

São Paulo

São Paulo is the largest city in Brazil. It lies about 80 km inland from the Atlantic Ocean on the banks of the Rio Tiete. The conurbation of Greater São Paulo formed by São Paolo and a further 39 cities has over 19.5 million inhabitants. Uncontrolled growth in the 1960s/70s, when São Paolo was one of the fastest growing regions in South America, led to massive burdens on the infrastructure and the environment, but there are now plans for the decaying inner city to be revitalised. São Paolo was founded in 1554 by Portuguese missionaries. In the nineteenth century it became, and still is, a significant trading base for sugar and coffee.

Area:
1,509 sq. km (city)
Inhabitants:
10,886,000 (city, 2008)
19,560,000 (conurbation, 2008)
Population density:
7,214 inhabitants/sq. km (city)

View of the skyline of São Paolo: Its conurbation is home to almost 20 million people.

Lima

Lima, the capital city of Peru, lies close to the Pacific coast in the north-west of South America. About 8 million people live in its metropolitan area, almost one-third of the population of Peru. However, around half of Lima's inhabitants live in shanty towns and slums. Lima is the country's economic and cultural hub. Approximately 50 per cent of all of Peru's industrial companies are located here. The city was founded in 1535 by Francisco Pizarro as Ciudad de Los Reyes. It became affluent thanks to its ideal geographical position and the exploitation of natural resources such as silver and guano. Over the centuries, Lima has suffered significant damage due to repeated earthquakes.

Area:
2,672 sq. km (city)
Inhabitants:
6,954,580 (city, 2006)
8,190,000 (conurbation, 2005)
Population density:
2,603 inhabitants/sq. km (city)

The cathedral of Lima on the Plaza Mayor has been damaged many times by earthquakes.

Buenos Aires

The capital of Argentina, Buenos Aires lies almost 300 km inland from the Atlantic on the banks of the River Plate on the pampas. Buenos Aires is the second largest city in the southern hemisphere and is the cultural heart of South America. A popular destination for immigrants over the last two centuries, the city is a cultural melting pot. In the space of around 100 years, Buenos Aires grew from almost 290,000 inhabitants in 1880 to the 10 million or so who lived in the conurbation in the 1980s. Buenos Aires was founded in the sixteenth century by the Spanish. Its name is a shortened form of 'Puerto y Ciudad de Nuestra Señora Maria del Buen Ayre'.

Area:
203 sq. km (city)
Inhabitants:
2,970,000 (city, 2001)
13,800,000 (conurbation, 2001)
Population density:
14,631 inhabitants/sq. km (city)

Illuminated fountains on the Plaza del Congreso in Buenos Aires.

Brazil

Brazil

Area:	8,511,996 sq. km
Capital city:	Brasília

Form of government:
Federal Republic
Administrative divisions:
26 federal states
1 federal district (capital city)
Population:
185 million
(22 inhabitants/sq. km)
Languages:
Portuguese (official), regional
Indian languages

GDP per capita:	US$5,700

Currency:
1 real = 100 centavos

Natural Geography

The world's fifth largest country occupies almost half of the South American continent. It shares a border with all the countries of South America, with the exception of Chile and Ecuador. Some of the island groups in the west Atlantic also belong to Brazil.
Brazil is divided up into three large regions with very different landscapes: the **mountainous country of Guayana** in the north, the **Amazonas lowland** in the south and the **Brazilian mountain country** in the south-east.

The mountainous region of Guayana contains the country's highest mountain the **Pico da Neblina** (altitude: 3,014 m) which stands near the Venezuelan border. This mountain range is characterised by vast plains and isolated monadnocks. It ends very abruptly in the Amazon region.
The **Amazon the world's largest river** is up to 25 km wide and over 60 m deep at its lower reaches. It traverses the world's **largest tropical forest** (an area of 4 million sq. km). Its tributaries, of which there are over 1,000, are also exceptionally full of water but are not navigable, however, due to a large number of rapids.
The tributaries have some spectacular waterfalls, notably the 115-m-high **Guaira Falls**, the **Iguazu Falls** (72 m high) and the **Paulo Alfonso Falls** on the São Francisco River (81 m high).
Brazil's mountain region is approximately five million sq. km and occupies over half of the country's land mass. The mountain range is coated in sedimentary rock which was formed in the Palaeozoic and Mesozoic eras. In the south-east, it extends out to form the coastal mountain ranges of **Serra do Mar** and **Serra da Mantiqueira** before dropping steeply down to the Atlantic Coast. In the south and south-west, the uplands turn into coastal

terms of mineral resources. It possesses immense deposits of oil, iron, manganese, gold, gemstones, bauxite, magnesium, copper, tin, zinc, chrome, tungsten, nickel and uranium. The enormous resources in terms of **tropical timber** and **hydroelectric power** have become a significant economic factor.

Climate

In the Amazonas lowland of the north there is a **tropical rainforest climate** with temperatures of approximately 27°C and precipitation volumes of 2000 mm to 4000 mm.
In the mid-west and the mountainous Guayana region there is a **savannah climate** with a dry season in winter producing daytime temperatures of 17°C to 28°C. The average precipitation is approximately 1600 mm, producing deciduous forests and open grassland. There are large swamps in Pantanal.
A savannah climate, temperatures of 23°C to 30°C and precipitation of 1250 mm are typical of the **coastal region** to the south of the Amazon estuary. The vegetation is scrubland, stunted trees and succulents.
In the coastal area and in the south-east, a **tropical rainforest**

22°C and precipitation of 1330 mm favour a landscape of tall grasslands and coniferous forests. There are many cattle ranches in this area.
Recent climate problems have consisted of serious drought in

otters, monkeys, sloths and various species of birds and snakes. The Brazil has one third of the world's tropical rainforest, containing around 55,000 flowering plants,

---

Juscelino Kubitschek de Oliveira

*Diamantina 12. 9. 1902,
†Rio de Janeiro 22. 8. 1976

This medical doctor began his political career as governor of Minas Gerais from 1950 to 1954. In 1956, he was elected President of Brazil. He believed in boosting exports by improving the service sector and increasing Brazil's production of consumer goods and modernising the economy. This caused mounting inflation, however. During his term of office which ended in 1961 the new capital city of Brasilia was officially inaugurated in 1960. He was deposed in a military coup in 1964 and went into exile, before returning home in 1967.

The 395-m-high Sugarloaf Mountain dominates Guanabara bay and the skyline of Rio de Janeiro.

lowlands which are bordered by lagoons. The **Pantanal** Lagoon in the West is in the mountains of the **Mato Grosso**.
Although its geological indexing is only in its early stages, Brazil is one of the world's richest countries in

climate prevails with temperatures of between 18°C and 27°C and precipitation of 1460 mm. In the **sub-tropical wet**, **moderate climate** of the south the seasons are differentiated. Temperatures of between 14°C and

the north-east, the **El Niño** climate phenomenon and continued **deforestation**. Nevertheless, the Amazon jungle contains a wealth of **fauna**. Tapirs, wild boars, iguanas, jaguars, leopards, stags, racoons, anteaters, turtles,

the greatest variety in the world, many of which have not yet been classified, but due to deforestation, they are in danger of disappearing even before uses have been found for them.

*Splendid costumes and an exuberant lust for life: no country in the world celebrates the **Carnival** as lavishly as **Brazil**. The samba schools that lead the parades, are for the men and women from the favelas – the slums of Rio de Janeiro – a chance to escape the daily misery of their district, if only for one day.*

religions and **Afro-Brazilian cult**s. Many Brazilians belong to several religious denominations simultaneously! Consequently, it is impossible to compile accurate statistics. Average **life expectancy** is 72 years.

Health care is non-existent for large sections of the population in spite of continually improving healthcare and this affects the youngest members of society in particular. The **infant mortality rate** is just four per cent.

Although schooling is compulsory between the ages of seven and 14, the **illiteracy rate** is 13 per cent. 80 per cent of Brazilians live in cities. Although Brazil has the world's **eighth largest national economy**, in 2005, 22 per cent of the population were still living below the poverty line.

History and Politics

The Portuguese seafarer **Pedro Álvares Cabral** landed on the Brazilian coast on 22 April 1500 and seized the region for the Portuguese crown under the 1494 Treaty of Tordesillas. In order to protect the newly acquired regions from the claims of other colonial powers, Martim Alfonso **de Sousa** started systematically populating the region in 1532 by founding **São Vicente**. Portuguese aristocrats took possession of enormous estates. The Indians who lived there were systematically enslaved or slaughtered. African slaves were shipped in to work the large plantations. The seventeenth and eighteenth centuries were the time of the great **expeditions**:

Population

People of European ancestry account for 53 per cent of the population. They can be sub-divided as follows: 15 per cent of **Portuguese descent**, 11 per cent of **Italian descent**, ten per cent of **Spanish** descent and three per cent of **German descent**. Approximately 34 per cent of the population consists of people of **mixed races**, and 11 per cent are **black**.

There are approximately 300,000 **native Brazilians** belonging to approximately 200 ethnic groups. The **Japanese**, of which there are approximately one million, constitute a further minority. Roughly 75 per cent of Brazilians are **Catholic**, ten per cent are Protestant and members of alternative Christian denominations such as the Pentecostal Church. There are religious minorities of **Buddhists, Baha'is, Jews, Muslims**, followers of **natural**

Brazil

*The justice buliding and cathedrale in **Brasília**: the capital of Brazil was designed between 1956 and 1960 according to the at the time state of the art civil engineering concepts. Oscar Niemeyer was one of the main architects.*

Starting out from São Paulo, expeditions penetrated ever further into the interior of the country to capture Indians as slaves and capture fabulous treasures. The colonial area was constantly extended thanks to raids by these notorious **bandeirantes of São Paulo** – ruthless gold-seekers and slave-hunters. In 1763, the Portuguese colonial administration was relocated from São Salvador do Bahia (now known as Salvador) to **Rio de Janeiro**. Dutch and Spanish claims to the land were warded off.

The borders of modern Brazil were finally defined in the 1750 **Treaty of Madrid**. In 1789, the first revolt began against Portuguese supremacy which ended in defeat. The battle for autonomy continued for several more decades. In 1808, King Joaõ VI moved the Portuguese seat of government from Lisbon to Rio de Janeiro as Napoleonic troops had occupied Portugal. In 1821, the court returned to Lisbon.

Under the influence of the **Andrada de Silva** brothers, the king's son who had remained a prince regent and refused to acknowledge the renewed colonial status of Brazil declared the country's **independence** and was crowned Emperor **Pedro I** in 1822. Portugal finally granted Brazil its independence three years later.

The gradual emancipation of the slaves was proclaimed in the **'Golden Law'** of 1888. The monarchy was abolished and the Republic of Brazil proclaimed in 1889 through a **military coup**, facilitated by an **economic crisis** and **unrest** in the armed forces. The new rulers drew up a constitution modelled on that of the United States. In 1891, the United States of Brazil were founded. The first republican governments were despotic **military dictatorships**, but the political and economic situation stabilised from 1894 onwards.

The **export of coffee** and the stronger development of **industry** after the outbreak of **World War I** led to short-lived economic prosperity. The worldwide **postwar depression** also affected Brazil and the economic decline caused serious internal unrest which set Brazil's development back years.

In 1930, **Getulio Vargas** came to power. He used the global economic crisis to make himself an **absolute dictator** in 1937. Inspired by the fascist systems which then predominated in Europe, he abolished the constitution and all political parties.

Vargas' **role models** were undoubtedly **Mussolini** and **Hitler**. However, in 1942, under pressure from the USA, Vargas joined the coalition against Hitler. The **Estado Novo** ended in 1945 with Vargas' downfall but in 1950 he returned to power. Due to **maladministration** and **corruption** in his regime he came under greater pressure and eventually committed **suicide** in 1954.

Juscelino **Kubitschek de Oliveira** attempted to remedy the economic devastation that was Vargas' legacy by making a fresh start. His government operated an ambitious **industrialisation policy** from 1956 and he decided to found a new capital for the nation, the city of **Brasília deep in the interior**. This decision was symbolic. Kubitschek de Oliveira wanted to develop the Brazilian interior which was mostly underdeveloped. Although his economic policy led to increases in productivity, little benefit appeared to have been gained since this economic expansion had been funded by printing money, leading to crippling inflation. Purchasing power was seriously reduced and foreign debt reached record levels.

In 1963, President **João Goulart** attempted to push through **agrarian reform** for the benefit of landless farmers and attempted to nationalise the **oil industry**. His socialist ideals were opposed by a strong conservative opposition, supported by leading senior army officers. Eventually, there was a **military** coup in 1964, backed by the USA.

A state-regulated **two-party system** replaced the hitherto multiple political parties. The **opposition** was brutally suppressed. It was not until General Ernest **Geisel**, who served as president from 1974 to 1979, that the severe **repression** of the dictatorship was slightly relaxed.

In 1973, Brazil experienced an **economic upturn** with growth rates in double figures, but another depression followed soon afterwards. In 1985, the **military** finally exited the political stage and a gradual **process of democratisation** ensued but in 1990, inflation still stood at a staggering 1,795 per cent.

Since the mid-1990s the **economic reforms** of civilian governments have borne their first fruits, but the country still suffers from a deep **social divide** between the rich and the poor, marauding death squads, drug-dealing, corruption and immense foreign debt. Luiz Inácio Lula da Silvo, ('Lula') the current left-leaning Labour president who has been in power since 2003 can rely on the widespread support of all sections of society. He appears to be leading the country into a new era of democracy and prosperity. Since the 1988 constitution was last amended in 1997, Brazil has been governed by a bicameral **parliament** consisting of a house of representatives elected every four years, and a senate elected every eight years. The president, the **head of state**, is directly elected every four years and can only serve two terms. The **right to vote** begins at 16;

São Paulo: Skyscrapers dominate the skyline of the biggest city in South America. Almost ten million people live or just survive here.

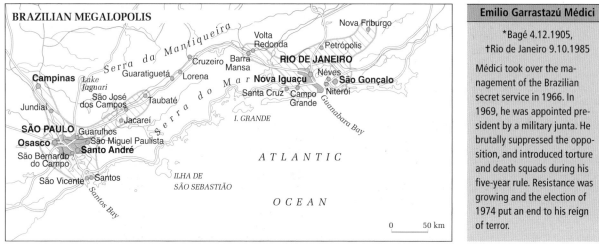

Emilio Garrastazú Médici

*Bagé 4.12.1905,
†Rio de Janeiro 9.10.1985

Médici took over the management of the Brazilian secret service in 1966. In 1969, he was appointed president by a military junta. He brutally suppressed the opposition, and introduced torture and death squads during his five-year rule. Resistance was growing and the election of 1974 put an end to his reign of terror.

*Chainsaws and slash-and-burn clearing methods are eating away at the **Brazilian rainforests**. Many Brazilians see no alternative to this. Around 10,000 sq. km of rainforest are cleared each year.*

Economy

In the last 25 years, Brazil has developed from an agrarian nation to an **emerging market country** thanks to massive **industrialisation**. The Brazilian **economic miracle** is extremely unevenly developed regionally and socially.

In 2006, **GDP** was US$1 trillion. **Agriculture** accounted for 15 per cent of this amount, **industry** for 20 per cent and the **services sector** for 75 per cent. Brazil's main trading partners are the USA and Argentina. The trade balance surplus amounted to US$14 billion in 2004.

The main imports are machinery, vehicles, fuel, electrical appliances and foodstuffs. The most important **exports** are metals and metal products, vehicles and vehicle parts, soya beans and soy products, chemicals, mineral ores, paper, coffee and sugar. 14 per cent of the agricultural land is used for **crop-growing** and approximately half the total area to **cattle-rearing**; the rest lies fallow. In the fertile south **soybeans, sugar cane, coffee** and **tobacco** are grown, and there is a thriving cattle trade. In the north, the cultivation of **tropical fruits, cocoa plantations** and **forestry products** plays an important role. The annual **clearance** of 25,544 sq. km of jungle is liable to seriously upset **the ecological balance**.

Brazil's energy resources are largely untapped. They consist of hydro-electric power (at present there are two large dams, Itaipú on the Paraná River and Tucuruí on the Tocantins River) and the possibility of using nuclear power fuelled by the considerable deposits of uranium ore.

Transport Infrastructure

The **rail network** which was **privatised** in 1997 extends for 27,400 km, only 2,200 km of which is electrified. 60 per cent of freight and 65 per cent of passenger traffic are transported by road. The road network extends over 1,939,000 km but only 178,400 km are paved. Projects such as the construction of the 5000-km-long Transamazónica Highway are intended to improve Brazil's road

infrastructure. **Rio de Janeiro** and **São Paulo** are the largest of the 22 international **airports**. Santos, Rio de Janeiro, Angra dos Reis, Praia Mole and Vitória are the largest of the 50 **sea ports**. Of the approximately 50,000 km of inland waterways, the Amazon accounts for 3,680 km. The largest inland port, **Manaus,** can be reached by large ocean-going vessels via the 1,600 km navigable stretch of the Amazon.

Tourism

Roughly 4.8 million foreign visitors came to Brazil in 2004 and

spent approximately US$4.8 billion. The most popular destinations are the coastal cities of **Rio de Janeiro, São Paulo, Salvador** and **Recife** and, in the interior, **Manaus** (whose famous opera house must count as the most remote in the world), **Brasilia** and the **Iguazu Falls**. The **Copacabana** Beach in Rio de Janeiro, the **Sugarloaf Mountain** and the samba spectacle in the **Carnaval do Brasil** number among the numerous tourist highlights. The Amazonian **rainforest,** with its fascinating and unique fauna and flora, makes Brazil a destination which is visited all year round. The country's tropical summer lasts from **April** to **October** and these are also the most pleasant months for visiting and touring the country.

Other attractions are Mount Roraima, Xingu National Park. Between December and May the entire Brazilian coast is warm enough for bathing.

1 The baroque coastal town of Olinda is one of Brazil's oldest and most beautiful cities. The Benedictine monastery of São Bento, surrounded by palms, is a masterpiece of late baroque architecture.

2 The Waira, an indigenous Amazon people have preserved

most of their rites and customs under the protection of the rainforest.

3 There is just one way to reach Belém and that is by boat on the Rio Pará. Almost all the wares on sale in the big market of Belém are transported via the river.

4 In Salvador de Bahia time seems to stand still. The beautiful colonial-style houses have been elaborately renovated with much attention to detail. Colourful baroque facades and splendidly-decorated church towers line the streets.

Ecuador

In the isolation of the **Galapagos Islands**, a unique ecosystem developed which helped Charles Darwin to explore the mechanisms of evolution. The 30 volcanic islands are inhabited by endemic, i.e. unique species such as these marine iguanas. The understandable fascination with the Galapagos is rather problematic: although tourism is already strictly limited, it still disrupts the fragile habitat.

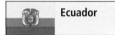

Ecuador

Area:	283,560 sq. km
Capital city:	Quito
Form of government:	
Presidential Republic	
Administrative divisions:	
20 provinces, Galapagos Islands and undefined areas	
Population:	
13.7m (48 inhabitants/sq. km)	
Languages:	
Spanish (official), Indian dialects	
GDP per inhabitant:	US$3,000
Currency: 1 US-dollar = 100 cents (since 2000)	

Natural Geography

The smallest country in the Andes is divided into three large regions. **Fertile lowlands** between 50 km and 150 km wide extend along the Pacific Coast. Two chains of the Andes mountains surround the **Sierra region**, which is up to 3,000 m high. The highland basins are separated from each other by ridges. The highest peak of the Cordillera Occidental is the extinct volcano Mt Chimborazo which is 6,310 m high. The 5,897-m-high Cotopaxi in the Cordillera Oriental is still active. This region is under constant threat from earthquakes. The **Amazon region** in the east is barely populated and crisscrossed by many tributaries of the great river.

José María Velasco Ibarra

*Quito 19.3.1893,
† Quito 30.3.1979

The lawyer was the dominating politician in Ecuador since 1934 and ruled altogether five times: 1934–1935, 1946 to 1947, 1952–1956, 1960–1961 and 1968 till 1972. However he could only survive one term without being overthrown by the military. In 1970 he suspended the Constitution, dissolved the parliament and ruled – supported by the conservative military – as a dictator. He was deposed in 1972.

Climate

The coastal region is characterised by a **tropical climate**; rainfall reduces towards the south. In the north, which has an annual rainfall of over 2,500 mm, there are vast **rainforests**, which turn to **thornbush and cactus savannah**. The average temperature in Guayaquil, the regional capital, is 25.5°C. The south, which is affected by the Humboldt Current, is extremely dry with less than 300 mm rainfall. In the highlands, rainfall is low, and the average temperature of 15°C remains constant all year round, though there are considerable fluctuations between day and night. In the Andes region, where the rainfall is up to 5,000 mm, there are mountain forests and cloud forests; above the tree line at 3,500 m this turns into mountain meadows. The **lowlands** in the east, which are sparsely populated, are characterised by evergreen rainforests. The climate phenomenon known as **El Niño** causes severe damage to agriculture, producing **flooding** in the coastal area and droughts inland.

Population

The population of Ecuador is composed of 35 per cent **mestizo**, 25 per cent **white**, 20 per cent **Indian**, 15 per cent **mulatto** and five per cent **black**. 93 per cent of the population profess the **Catholic faith**, the remainder are **Protestants**, **Baha'i**, **Jews** and followers of native natural religions. Life expectancy is 76 years; there is ten per cent illiteracy. 60 per cent of the population lives in the cities; 20 per cent live below the poverty line. Education is compulsory for ten years.

History and Politics

Before Pizarro's General **Sebastián de Benalcázar claimed** the country for the Spanish crown in 1533/1534, Ecuador was a part of the Inca Empire. The Quito Audiencia first belonged to the **Viceroyalty of Peru**, then, from the early eighteenth century, to the **Viceroyalty of New Granada**. The struggle for liberation from the Spanish ended victoriously for Bolívar's General **Antonio José de Sucre** in 1822, and Ecuador became **part of Greater Colombia**. Ecuador finally declared its **independence** in 1830. Its subsequent history is characterised by a large number of **coups** and **extreme political instability**. The republic was dedicated to the Sacred Heart of Jesus (by act of Congress) in 1873. The period 1925 to 1944 was one of extreme instability when no president was able to complete his term of office. **Josémaría Velasco Ibarra** was able to stabilise the situation in 1944, but after unrest and yet another economic crisis, he was overthrown in 1972. Two military juntas followed, until the introduction of a market economy and a democratisation process were achieved in 1978. Failed economic policies, reductions in the price of oil and the climate phenomenon known as El Niño led the country into **economic**

*During the colonial period, **Lima** was the most cultured and influential city in South America. In this 'pearl of the Pacific' Peru's biggest ecclesiastical complex, the abbey-church of San Francisco was founded in the shadow of the dreaded Inquisition. Its yellow front shines in the sun and is regarded the most beautiful church facade in Lima. The adjoining monastery buildings are impressive, built in the splendid Mudéjar architectural style of the Spanish Moors.*

crisis from 1998 to 2000, at the climax of which the American dollar was introduced to replace the sucre, the existing currency. Under President Gustavo Noboa and, since 2003, under Lucio Gutiérrez, the country has slowly been recovering and inflation has fallen from 90 to nine per cent. GDP increased in 2002 by 3.3 per cent. In 2006, the left-wing Rafael Correa was elected president. The 1978 **constitution**, which was last amended in 1998, provides for a parliament whose representatives are elected every four years; the president is elected directly for a period of four years. The voting age is 18 years.

Economy

In 2006, GDP was US$40 billion, of which seven per cent came from **agriculture**, 32 per cent from **industry** and 61 per cent from the **service sector**. 28 per cent of the labour forced work in agriculture, 18 per cent in industry and 53 per cent in the service sector. There is a considerable foreign debt of US$10.8 billion.
Raw materials, capital and consumer goods as well as fuel are the principal imports; crude oil, bananas, industrial products and shrimps are the main exports.

Transport Infrastructure

Only half the 37,000-km-long road network is passable all year round; the 1,392 km long Pan-American Highway is regarded as the most important arterial route. There is a rail network which is 1,000 km long and two international airports in Quito and Guayaquil. The major sea ports are Guayaquil, Esmeraldas, Balao, Manta and Puerto Bolívar.

Tourism

Tourism is not yet well developed on the mainland but by far the greatest place of interest is the **Galapagos** Islands which are part of the national territory. These islands are inhabited by species of fauna not seen elsewhere, such as the giant tortoises and were the inspiration for Charles Darwin's ground-breaking *Origin of the Species*. The best time to travel to mainland Ecuador is from June to October.

Peru

Area:	1,285,216 sq. km
Capital city:	Lima
Form of government:	
Presidential Republic	
Administrative divisions:	
25 regions	
Population:	
28 m (22 inhabitants/sq. km)	
Languages:	
Spanish, Quechua (both official), Aymará	
GDP per inhabitant:	US$3,300
Currency:	
1 new sol = 100 centimos	

Natural Geography

Peru is divided into three large regions. The coastline is 2,300 km long and 50–140 km wide and interior consists of deserts and savannah. The three main chains of the Andes running parallel to the coast, the **Sierra**s consist of the Cordillera Occidental whose highest peak is the 6,768 m Huascarán; the Cordillera Central and the Cordillera Oriental. **Lake Titicaca** is high in the mountains at an altitude of 3,812 m. The main rivers, the Marañón and the Ucayali, meet in the north-eastern **lowlands** of the Amazon. The Montaña region on the eastern slopes of the Andes contains the Amazon headwaters, known as the Selva.

Climate

Because of Peru's tropical location, the climate is relatively stable. In the coastal regions it is cooled by the **Humboldt Current** and on average there is only 45 mm of rainfall annually. The coastal desert continues far up the Andes slopes, where the vegetation consists mainly of cacti and thorn bushes. The montaña has a tropical hot climate with abundant rainfall. Here, and in the eastern lowlands, tropical rainfall predominates. In the Andes, rich forests of palms, tree ferns and Peruvian bark trees are found up to altitudes of 3,500 m. At up to 4,600 m, there are alpine meadows, grassland and moorland. At the higher altitudes, stone and rock outcrops, depleted of vegetation, predominate. As for the fauna, condors, alpacas, llamas and vicuñas live in the highlands; in the eastern lowlands, there are various species of monkeys, reptiles and birds as well as jaguars, peccaries, tapirs and sloths.

Population

The population consists of 47 per cent **Amerindians**, 32 per cent **mestizos**, 12 per cent **white** and small minorities of **Japanese**,

1 Like this farmer with his cabbages, one third of Ecuador's population lives from agriculture. They sell their produce in the local markets.

2 The Quechua Indians in Peru and Ecuador have a long tradition of Alpaca breeding.

Typically colourful blankets and pullovers are made from the wool, to protect the Quechua against the cold of the high Andes.

3 The Manú river winds its way into the Amazon basin. Manú national park covers over 18,000 sq. km.

Indigenous Bolivianss represent 71 per cent of the population. Although they have officially had equal rights since 1953, they still live a politically and culturally remote existence in Bolivia's highlands. Their diet consists of maize and sweet potatoes and they only visit the cities such as La Paz for the big, colourful markets in which they can sell their handicrafts, the ponchos, pottery and silver jewellery that are popular with tourists.

mulatto and **Chinese**. Some 89 per cent of the population are **Catholics** and three per cent are **Protestants**. There are also a number of Jews and followers of **natural religions**. Forty-nine per cent of the population live below the poverty line and 71 per cent live in the cities. Life expectancy is 70 years and there is 11 per cent **illiteracy**. Education is compulsory from six to 15 years, al-

Ernesto »Che« Guevara Serna

*Rosario 14.6.1928,
†Higueras 9.10.1967

The Argentinian doctor together with Castro liberated Cuba from Batista's dictatorship in 1959. As the minister of industry he was crucial in the revolutionary change of Cuba. The leading figure of the armed conflict against imperialism went eventually to Bolivia in 1966 in order to found a guerilla army. However he failed both politcially and in military terms. He was arrested in 1967 and killed without a court process.

though only 20 per cent of schoolchildren take their school-leaving examinations.

History and Politics

A civilisation had already been established in Peru by the second century BC. Between 1000 and 300 BC, **advanced civilisations** arose with monumental places of worship, such as the **Chavin de Huántar**. Between 200 and 600 AD, powerful urban centres developed which waged war against each other. The **Tiwanaku culture** was replaced by other regional cultures in around 1000 AD, of which the most powerful was the **Chimú** whose capital city was **Chan Chan**.
The **Inca culture** developed around 1200. It was brutally destroyed by the Spanish, first under Francisco Pizarro who landed in 1532/1533 and finally in 1572 by Francisco de Toledo, despite its obvious military superiority. In 1739, the **Viceroyship of New Granada** and in 1776 **the Vice-**

royship of **Río de la Plata** were detached from the **Viceroyship of Peru**.
Simón Bolívar's and José de Sanmartin's armies achieved **independence** in 1821, which was consolidated in 1824 after the victory of Antonio José de Sucre. The discovery of deposits of **salpetre** caused an **economic upswing** that lasted until the mid-nineteenth century but ended after the country lost the **Salpetre War** against Chile in 1884. The provinces of Tarapacá and Arica were awarded to Chile. Tacna was handed back to Peru in 1929. In the early twentieth century, the discovery of **rubber** trees and **oil reserves** once more improved the economic situation, though the majority of the population did not benefit. **Military dictatorships** ruined any plans for reform. The majority of the mineral resources were in foreign hands until the government nationalised the mines in 1973.
The 1980s were characterised by the civil war between the **Sindero Luminos (Shining Path) Marxist guerillas** and the military. President Alberto Fujimori, elected in 1990, introduced a strong **neoliberal economic system** but his **authoritarian** and corrupt **regime** met with increasing dis-

approval from the population. After accusations of bribery he fled in 2000. In 2001, Alejandro Toledo was elected president. He achieved democratic stabilisation and a strengthening of basic rights. In addition, he passed on to his successor Alan García an economy growing at almost seven per cent.
The unicameral parliament is elected every five years, as is the president. The voting age is 18.

Economy

In 2006, GDP was US$93 billion of which 12 per cent was derived from **agriculture**, 30 per cent from **industry** and 50 per cent from the **service sector**. Exports include lead. Other exports are coca, coffee, lama and vicuña wool, copper, iron and oil. Imports include machinery, vehicles and foodstuffs. The deposits of gold, silver and zinc iron remain to be exploited.

Transport Infrastructure

The **rail network** covers around 2,041 km and the **road network** covers 71,400 km, of which only 7,783 km is paved. There are **four international airports**.

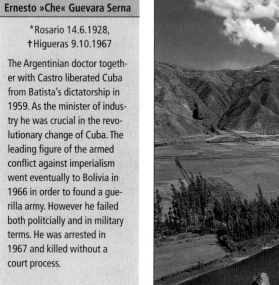

In the wide 'Holy Valley of the Incas' near Cuzco the Inca rulers finally rest in peace.

Tourism

The Inca ruins are the most popular attractions. The best time to travel is November to April.

	Bolivia

Area: 1,098,581 sq. km
Capital cities: Sucre, La Paz
Form of government:
Presidential Republic
Administrative divisions:
9 departments
Population:
9 million (8 inhabitants/sq. km)
Languages:
Spanish, Quechua, Aymará
(all official)
GDP per inhabitant: US$1,200
Currency:
1 boliviano = 100 centavos

Natural Geography

The 3,609–4,000-m-high **Altiplano de Bolivia (Andes highland**

POPULATION DENSITY (People/km²)

below 1
1-10
10-100
above 100

Brazil's Regions

0   550 km

Lake Titicaca (8300 sq. km) is situated between Peru and Bolivia. Taquile Island with its stone gateways lies in this 'Holy Sea of the Incas'. The Aymará live on islands in the Bolivian part. They build their boats of totora, a kind of bullrush.

plateau) forms the heartland of Bolivia. The west of the country is dominated by the Cordillera Occidental, and the north-east by the Cordillera Real including the 6,682-m-high Mount Illimani. In the south, the Cordillera Oriental and the Cordillera Central form the East Bolivian mountain range. The **lowlands** are in the east and the Chaco Boreal region is named after the river of the same name that runs through it.

Lake Titicaca and **Lake Poopó** are in the highlands. They are connected to each other by the Desaguadero river which has large salt flats at its estuary.

Climate

The climate is **tropical** throughout nearly the whole country, but the rainfall decreases from up to 2,000 mm in the north-east to 200 mm in the south-west. In the cool **Altiplano**, the rainfall, which is already low reduces further towards the south. Average temperatures fluctuate in La Paz from 8°C in July to 12°C in December. In the lowlands, savannahs and jungle predominate. The river valleys and mountainsides are covered in virgin rainforest.

Population

Around 71 per cent of the inhabitants are **Amerindians** and there are also **mestizos, whites** and **creoles**. As far as religion goes, 92,5 per cent of the population are Catholic, the remainder are Protestant and Baha'i. Life expectancy is 66 years; there is 17 per cent **illiteracy**.

History and Politics

Settlements have been found in Bolivia dating from 5,000 BC. From 200 to 800 AD, the **Aymará-Indians** developed an **advanced civilisation**. Between 1460 and 1475, the **Incas** conquered the region which the Spanish seized in 1538. Five years later, Bolivia joined the **Viceroyship of Peru** and in 1776 the **Spanish Viceroyship of the Río de La Plata**. Antonio José de Sucre led a war of liberation in 1809, which resulted in Bolivian **independence** in 1825. Since then, the country's history has been determined by wars and

domestic unrest. Since Bolivia was foundation, there have been around **200 governments**.

In several wars, Bolivia lost areas that were rich in raw materials, such as the Atacama Desert and the Gran Chaco. The **reform**s introduced by President Victor **Paz Estenssoro** came to a sudden end in 1964 after a **military coup** replaced him with a junta. The death of **Che Guevara** in battle in 1967, crushed the **left-wing Partisan movement**. There followed a succession of **military** coups. The reform policy, which **Gonzalo Sánchez de Lozada** introduced in 1993, seemed at first to stabilise the political situation, but the former **dictator Hugo Banzer** returned to power between 1997 and 2001. This time he was democratically elected, though in 2001 he resigned on health grounds. In 2002, Lozada was once more elected president. After demonstrations lasting for weeks against Lozada's neoliberal economic policy, he resigned in 2003. His successor was Carlos Mesa. Evo Morales won the presidential elections held in December 2005.

The parliament consists of a house of representatives and a senate both of which are elected every five years, as is the President, who is directly elected.

Economy

In 2006, GDP was US$11 billion of which 17 per cent derived from **agriculture**, 31 per cent from **industry** and 52 per cent from the **services sector**. The growth rate is one per cent. Of those employed, 44 per cent work in agriculture.

The main imports are capital goods, semi-processed products, raw materials, and consumer goods. The exports are mainly zinc, gold, soya, tin, timber, natural gas and silver; the importance of the **cocaine trade** should not be underestimated.

Transport Infrastructure

There is a 25,000-km-long road network, much of it in poor condition. There are 4,000 km of railway. There are international airports at **La Paz**, the seat of government (Sucre is the seat of the judiicary) and at **Santa Cruz**.

Tourism

In 2001, around 600,000 tourists contributed US$156 million to the Bolivian economy. The best time to visit is between April and October. Lake Titicaca, the Andes and the various remnants of Inca culture are among Bolivia's main attractions.

1 The skyscrapers in the skyline of La Paz look like matchboxes against the backdrop of the Andes.

2 The Incas built the giant fortress of Sacsayhuamán, in order to protect the riches of their former capital of Quito. The huge,

smooth stone blocks are almost seamlessly laid one upon the other.

3 Built on relics: Cuzco has been plundered and razed to the ground. The Plaza de Armas at the heart of the old city, and the cathedral stand on the ruins of Inca temples.

Argentina: Millions of farm animals graze the vast pastures of the Pampas. Cattle and sheep are driven by gauchos across ranches the size of Luxembourg. Every second farm animal lives in the Pampas and 90 per cent of Argentinian grain is produced here. The seemingly endless stretch between the Andes and the Atlantic is only interrupted by occasional clumps of trees.

	Paraguay

Area:	406,752 sq. km
Capital city:	Asunción
Form of government:	
Presidential Republic	
Administrative divisions:	
17 Departamentos	
Population:	
6 million (15 inhabitants/sq. km)	
Languages:	
Spanish, Guaraní (both official)	
GDP per capita:	US$1,600
Currency:	
1 guaraní = 100 céntimos	

Natural Geography

The eastern area, consisting of undulating **hills** and **plains** with elevations of up to 700 m, extends to the **Río Paraná**, the river bordering Brazil and Argentina. The west is part of the **Gran Chaco** lowlands.

Climate

The prevailing climate is **tropical** in the north and **sub-tropical** in the south. Rainfall is 2,000 mm in the east and 800 mm in the west. Sub-tropical, evergreen **rainforests** are typical of the **mountain regions** in the east. **Wet savannah** predominates in the northern lowlands of the **Oriente** region and prairie grasslands cover the southern lowlands. In the Gran Chaco, there are deciduous dry forests, quebracho forests, savannah and bush. Jaguars, vampire bats, various species of reptile, monkeys, red deer, wild boar and parrots are some of the very varied **fauna**.

Population

Paraguay's population is 90 per cent **mestizo (Spanish Amerindian)**, three per cent **Amerindian** and two per cent **Creole**. There is eight per cent illiteracy. Average life expectancy is 71 years. **Catholics** make up 94 per cent of the population and there are also **Protestants** and **Baha'i**. Some 53 per cent of the population live in the towns and cities.

History and Politics

The **Spanish first occupied** the country in 1535. In 1609, a Jesuit state was established, lasting until 1767. Following the end of Spanish colonial rule, a **free state** emerged under the dictator **Rodriguez de Francia**. The country was completely **isolated** politically and economically. In 1840, Paraguay started to open up under the rule of **Carlos Antonio López**.

During the regency of his son **Francisco Solano López**, Paraguay waged a **war** against **Uruguay**, **Brazil** and **Argentina**, which only a fraction of the population survived. The country only recovered from this blow after 1918. Although renewed hostilities with Bolivia over **oil fields** ended in victory for Paraguay, these oil reserves eventually did not prove to be worth exploiting. The country's political and economic situation rapidly became unstable. In 1954, **General Alfredo Stroessner** seized power and established a **military dictatorship** that lasted 35 years. Even since Stroessner's overthrow, subsequent governments have often found themselves facing allegations of **corruption** and **election** fraud. The **Head of State** is **elected directly** for a five-year period; the **parliament** consists of a Chamber of Deputies and a Senate. Citizens are entitled to vote from the age of 18 years.

Economy

In 2006, **GDP** was US$ 9.5 billion, to which **agriculture** contributed 27 per cent, **industry** 25 per cent and the **services sector** 48 per cent.

The relatively high **unemployment rate** remains constant at about 20 per cent due to lack of development. About 34 per cent of the labour force is employed in agriculture. Consumer goods, machinery, cars and trucks, fuel, raw materials and semi-processed products are **imported**. Cotton, soybeans, maté, vegetable oil and timber are the primary **exports**. There is a substantial **deficit in the balance of trade**.

important river harbour in this land-locked country.

Tourism

Paraguay is not a classic holiday destination. Most visitors come from the **neighbouring states** to buy cheap duty-free goods, as the trade in smuggled goods has assumed vast proportions.

Besides a lot of natural wonders, there are remains from the period when Paraguay was a **Jesuit state** on the Jesuit highway between Asunción and **Encarnación**. The best time to travel is between April and October.

	Uruguay

Area:	176,215 sq. km
Capital city:	Montevideo
Form of government:	
Presidential Republic	

POPULATION DENSITY
(People/km²)

below 1	
1-10	
10-100	
above 100	

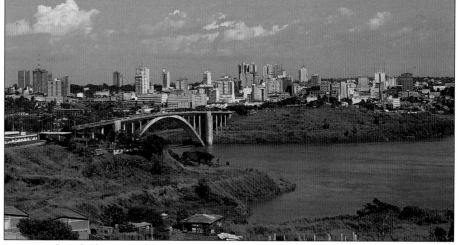

Paraguay: a large bridge across the Paraná leads to the Ciudad del Este.

Transport Infrastructure

The state railway consists of a 376-km-long **rail network** linking Asunción with Encarnación. The **road network** is approximately 13,000 km long, of which 705 km is part of the **Pan-American Highway**. Most of the roads are not paved.

River navigation plays an important role in the eastern region, which is almost completely surrounded by the country's river borders. Trade with neighbouring states is mainly possible via the waterways. Asunción is the most

Administrative divisions:	
19 Departamentos	
Population:	
3.3 million	
(19 inhabitants/sq. km)	
Language:	Spanish
GDP per capita:	US$5,900
Currency: 1 peso uruguayo =	
100 centésimos	

Natural Geography

Uruguay is a country of gently undulating **hills** between the **Río de la Plata**, the Uruguay river and the **Atlantic**. Barely ten per cent of the country is at an alti-

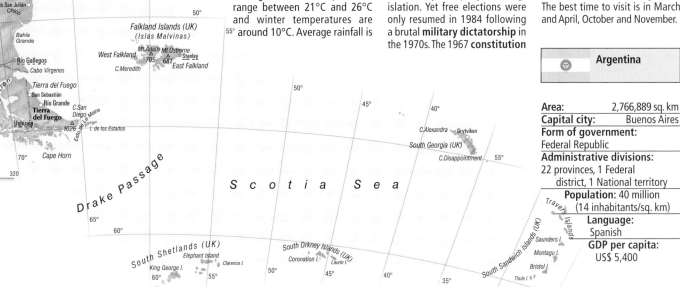

Uruguay: Punta del Este is a popular resort on South America's Atlantic coast. Fine sandy beaches, dunes and eucalyptus groves attract thousands of tourists to the small town during the holiday season.

1,000 mm. Uruguay's original wooded landscape has given way to vast **grassy meadows**. The **animal kingdom** has also lost a large part of its biodiversity. It is now rare to find the nandu or common rhea a flightless bird that grows to a height of 1.70 m. Jaguars, foxes, caimans, armadillos, red deer and pumas live in the north.

Population

Uruguay's population consists of 88 per cent whites, eight per cent mestizos (Spanish-Amerindian) and four per cent blacks. As many as 91 per cent live in the towns. **Life expectancy** is 76 years. Illiteracy stands at three per cent. **Catholics** make up 78 per cent of the population and there are 75,000 **Protestants** and 50,000 in the **Jewish community**. School is compulsory between the ages of six and 15.

History and Politics

tude higher than 200 m. The highest elevation is the **Cerro Catedral** at 501 m. The country lies on the **Brazilian Shield** with old crystalline rocks in the south and fertile loess soils and alluvial plains on the many lagoons of the **Atlantic coast**.

Climate

Cold air streams moving in from the Pampas occasionally affect the **sub-tropical**, **humid climate**. Average summer temperatures range between 21°C and 26°C and winter temperatures are around 10°C. Average rainfall is

In the eighteenth century, the Portuguese and Spanish occupied in name only the country that they had discovered in 1515, as a result of what they saw as its poor mineral resources and due to bitter resistance from the **native population**. Uruguay became part of the Spanish viceroyship of the **Río de la Plata** from 1777, then part of Brazil in 1817. After a war of liberation in 1828, it declared its independence.
From the beginning of the twentieth century until the 1960s, Uruguay's great prosperity was matched by exemplary social legislation. Yet free elections were only resumed in 1984 following a brutal **military dictatorship** in the 1970s. The 1967 **constitution**

provides for a bicameral parliamentary system. The head of state who is also the head of government is elected for a five-year-term. Citizens are **entitled to vote** from the age of 18.

Economy

Until the mid-twentieth century, Uruguay enjoyed relative affluence but was unable to safeguard it. In 2006, GDP was US$ 19.2 billion, of which 12 per cent came from **agriculture**, 28 per cent from **industry** and 60 per cent from **services**. After a serious crisis in 2002, the economy has again recovered and is on a path to growth (2005: six per cent). Forming 60 per cent of exports, agriculture (rice, maize, wheat, potatoes, cattle- and sheep-rearing) continues to play a key role. Also significant are the financial and insurance sectors and software production.

Transport Infrastructure

The 2,070-km-long **rail network** is in poor condition. Of the extensive 50,900-km-long **road network**, only 6,973 km is paved.
The only international **airport** is in Montevideo, which is also the major sea port.

Tourism

In 2004, revenue from tourism amounted to US$500 million. The **spas** and beaches on the coast and the capital city of **Montevideo** are the most popular destinations. Most visitors come from Argentina. The best time to visit is in March and April, October and November.

Argentina	
Area:	2,766,889 sq. km
Capital city:	Buenos Aires
Form of government:	
Federal Republic	
Administrative divisions:	
22 provinces, 1 Federal district, 1 National territory	
Population: 40 million (14 inhabitants/sq. km)	
Language: Spanish	
GDP per capita: US$ 5,400	

Argentina

Currency: 1 Argentinian peso = 100 centavos

Natural Geography

Argentina, the 'land of silver', stretches over an expanse of 3,700 km from north to south. The northern part of the Andes forms the vast highland of the **Puna Argentina** with 5,000 m high peaks and numerous salt marshes. The **Nevado Ojos del Salado** at 6,863 m is the highest of all the massive volcanoes. The main Cordillera begins south of the Puna with the Cerro Aconcagua, the highest mountain in South America at 6,960 m. The pre-Cordillera runs parallel to this in the east with the Pampas of the Sierra on the coast. The **Patagonian Cordillera** lies adjacent in the south and contains numerous lakes and rivers. The Tierra del Fuego Cordillera stretches south of this to Cape Horn.

The wide, level **steppe landscape** of the **Pampas** is characteristic of the natural scenery.

Climate

While the **north** is hot and humid with temperatures of over 30°C in the summer, the **Tierra del Fuego** is distinguished by a **subantarctic cold** climate, the lowest temperatures dropping to -30°C and below. A sub-tropical climate predominates in central Argentina: the average temperature of Buenos Aires ranges between 10°C in winter and 23.5°C in summer. Two-thirds of the country lies in a wide **dry zone**; the rainfall is only 500–1,000 mm on the eastern plains. Precipitation can be as much as 2,000 mm in the mountain region of Misiones, in the Tierra del Fuego, in the eastern descent of the Andes in the north-west and in part of the south Cordillera.

There is **savannah and woodland** in the **area between the rivers**, with swamp forests along the river banks. **Bush forests** grow south of this area and in Patagonia there are arid, semi-desert scrubland and steppes. There are **evergreen rainforests** in the mountains of Misiones and on the eastern slopes of the Sierra in the **north-west**.

Jaguars, howler monkeys, tapirs, caiman, swamp deer and numerous species of bird live in the forests and marshes of the north. The steppe fauna includes guanacos, nandus, armadillos and chinchillas, whereas the south Andes provide an environment for pumas, condors and guemal. On the coast of Patagonia there are colonies of penguins and seals.

Population

Some 90 per cent of Argentina's population is descended from **European immigrants** and five per cent are **mestizos** (Spanish-Amerindian). In addition, there are 35,000 **Amerindians** and 2.3 million **foreigners**. Catholics make up 91 per cent of the population and Protestants two per cent. Life expectancy is 76 years. **Illiteracy** is less than 3.8 per cent. **School is compulsory** between the ages of six and fourteen. 88 per cent of the population live in the cities.

History and Politics

Spanish rule over the country began when **Juan Díaz de Solís** sailed up the River Plate in 1516. In 1776, the viceroyalty of the **Río de la Plata** was created. In 1816, the **United Provinces of South America** broke away from Spain; the **civil war** that followed eventually led in 1853 to Argentina's first free **constitution**.

A military junta, supported by the rich cattle-breeders, ruled at this time. Military **conflicts** and internal **unrest** prevailed until the early twentieth century, when the economy began to expand. This upturn, which peaked in the early 1920s, led to a **wave of immigration** by European settlers. The growing **prosperity** of the country ended abruptly when the **worldwide economic crisis** hit in the 1930s.

The moderate, **democratic government** which was in power until 1930, was removed by a **military coup** followed by a **dictatorship**. The situation was unstable for over a decade.

In 1946, the people finally chose an authoritarian, neo-fascist, populist politician, President, **Juan Domingo Perón**. Both the president and his wife Maria Eva ('Evita') née Duarte enjoyed great popularity. She was almost worshipped as a saint. Evita, who had grown up in relative poverty was able to curry favour with the lower classes. She fought passionately for the poorest people in Argentina and for women's right to vote.

Perón was forced to leave the country in 1955, following his wife's death. From then on, the country alternated between **civilian** and **military regimes**. Under the military junta, which had ruled since 1976, Argentina occupied the Falkland Islands, a British Overseas Territory in 1982. The dictatorship of the generals ended in 1983, follow-

---

María Eva Duarte de Perón

*Los Toldos 7.5.1919,
†26.7.1952

The first wife of General Perón had a crucial impact on the the rise of her populist husband. Her unflinching support for the 'descamisados', the have-nots and the introduction of women's suffrage made this former actress incredibly popularity in Argentina. Coming herself from a modest back-ground, she was able to empathise with the common people. She continues to be revered as a saint in Argentina.

Juan Domingo Perón

*Lobos 8.10.1895,
†Buenos Aires 1.7.1974

The general played an important role in the various coups staged in 1942–1944. In 1943, he became Vice-president, Minister of War and later Secretary of labour. After his overthrow in 1945 he won the support of many social classes in Argentina and was elected president in 1946. His authoritarian rule led to his removal in 1955. After his return from exile in 1973 he was again elected president.

LAND USE

- Forest
- Steppe, meadows and pasture
- Cropland
- Desert
- Marsh, swamp
- Barren land

INDUSTRIAL ACTIVITIES

Energy
- ⊘ Hydroelectrics power plants
- — Oil pipelines
- — Natural gas pipelines

Industry
- ▨ Main industrial areas
- ● Main industrial sites
- ◉ Main oil tankers' terminals

Minerals
- ▲ Fossil coal
- ▲ Natural gas or oil wells
- Ag Silver
- Au Gold
- Cu Copper
- Fe Iron
- Hg Mercury
- Mo Molybdenum
- Pb Lead
- S Sulfur
- Sn Tin
- U Uranium
- Zn Zinc

Argentinian steaks are eaten all over the world. The meat of this country is of high quality as the cattle in the Argentinian Pampas offer optimal grazing conditions. Beef alone accounts for eight per cent of Argentina's total exports. Although the majority of livestock is for export, lamb and beef are traditionally an important part of the Argentinian diet.

ing Argentina's defeat in the war with Great Britain over the islands. In spite of a few **corruption scandals** and a long-ignored aversion to deal with the past, the **democracy** that was founded in the **1994 constitution** has appeared increasingly stable. The serious economic crisis in the late 1990s, which led the country to the brink of insolvency, acted as a severe test. The Peronists are the only significant political opposition, but they are split into several factions. In the presidential elections of 2003, Néstor Kirchner beat his opponent, former president Carlos Menem. Cristina Fernández de Kirchner followed him as head of state after a clear electoral victory in 2007.

Argentina is a **Federal Republic** consisting of 22 provinces, the **Buenos Aires district**, and the national territory of Tierra del Fuego. The bicameral **Parliament** consists of a chamber of deputies and a senate. The President is directly elected for a four-year term. Citizens are **entitled to vote** from the age of 18 years.

Economy

In 2006, GDP was US$212 billion, to which **agriculture** contributed nine per cent, **industry** 36 per cent and the **services sector** 55 per cent. Agriculture employs ten per cent of the labour force, industry 24 per cent and the services sector 66 per cent.

Since 2002, the Argentine economy has experienced something of a boom, with growth between seven per cent and nine per cent. The main imports are machinery, transport vehicles, consumer goods and chemical products, and the main exports are agricultural products.

Transport Infrastructure

Argentina has the best transport network in South America. Of the **216,100 km of road**, 61,598 km is paved, but is often in poor condition. The **rail network** stretches for 37,910 km.

There are nine international **airports** in addition to Buenos Aires and over 100 **sea ports**. Goods are also transported over the 11,000-km-long network of **inland waterways**.

Tourism

In 2004, Argentina had 3.4 million visitors. The **beaches** of the **Atlantic coast** are popular, as is the capital city **Buenos Aires**, the **skiing areas** and **national parks** in the Andes and the large **game reserves** in the Tierra del Fuego. The best **time to travel** to **central** Argentina is between February and May or September and November; the best time to visit the **sub-tropical regions** is between April and October. To visit the **south**, people mostly travel in the summer which lasts from December to February. The most important holiday month for Argentinians is January.

1 The Iguazú Falls are among the largest in the world. The noise is deafening: every second, almost two tonnes of water fall 74 m into the chasm.

2 The Plaza de la Republica by night. This is one of the most important squares in Buenos Aires. The 67-m-tall obelisk in the centre is a monument to the city's foundation in 1536.

3 Five hundred km of eternal ice: the Perito Moreno glacier in Patagonia is the main attraction in the Los Glaciares national park.

Chile

⭐	Chile

Area: 756,950 sq. km
Capital city: Santiago de Chile
Form of government:
Presidential Republic
Administrative divisions:
12 regions, capital city region
Population:
16 million (21 inhabitants/sq. km)
Language: Spanish
GDP per inhabitant: US$8,900
Currency:
1 Chilean peso = 100 centavos

Natural Geography

With a length of 4,230 km and an average width of only 176 km, the country extends along the western coast of South America.

Salvador Allende Gossens

*Valparaiso 26.7.1908,
†Santiago de Chile 11.9.1973

The Marxist politician was elected president in 1970 and enraged the landed oligarchy and the army with his nationalisation and social reforms. In 1973, the generals revolted in a coup led by Pinochet. Salvador Allende was murdered when the presidential palace was stormed. Allende was the first elected left-wing president in Latin America.

Augusto Pinochet

*Valparaíso 25.11.1915,
†Santiago de Chile 10.12.2006

Having led a military coup in 1973 against Marxist president Salvador Allende, Pinochet became president in 1974. He stepped down in 1990, ensuring his regime escaped prosecution for human rights violations. Arrested in the UK in 1998, he was released in 2000. Accused of conspiracy to murder, he lost his immunity in 2004. He was also accused of corruption and manipulation of foreign accounts.

Two mountain ranges run through the country from the north to the south. Parallel to the **coastal cordillera (Cordillera de la costa)** which is up to 2,500 m high, the Cordillera Principal extends in the east. In the broader north section, there are active **volcanoes** such as the 6,880 m high Ojos del Salado and the Llullaillaco at 6,723 m. In the south, the heavily glaciated **Patagonian Cordillera**, which extends beyond the Strait of Magellan into the **Cordillera in the Tierra del Fuego**, joins to this main ridge of the Andes. The longitudinal valley which lies in between is divided by ridges into several valleys. The Atacama desert, the driest on earth is in the north, but the central part of the country consists of a **fertile**, **undulating landscape** with many lakes and in the south the north-south valley sinks below sea level. There are frequent **earthquakes** due to continuous movement of the earth's tectonic plates and many of the volcanoes are still active.

Climate

From north to the south, Chile is split into five land formations that determine the climate. The **'great north'** consisting mainly of desert, has a rainfall of less than 100 mm annually and it is relatively cold because of the **Humboldt Current**, with an annual average temperature of 16–18°C. The sparse vegetation is characterised by succulents and dwarf shrubs. In the **'little north'**, south of the Huasco river with its dwarf shrubs and succulents, the rainfall is 100–250 mm. Between Illapel and Concepción a **temperate warm climate** predominates and the rainfall is 2,000 mm. With an average annual temperature of 13–15°C, plants that prefer a temperate climate flourish. Vast deciduous and coniferous forests cover the **'small south'** up to the Gulf of Ancud. In the cool temperate, moist climate, the average temperature is

Chile's capital city Santiago de Chile at dusk.

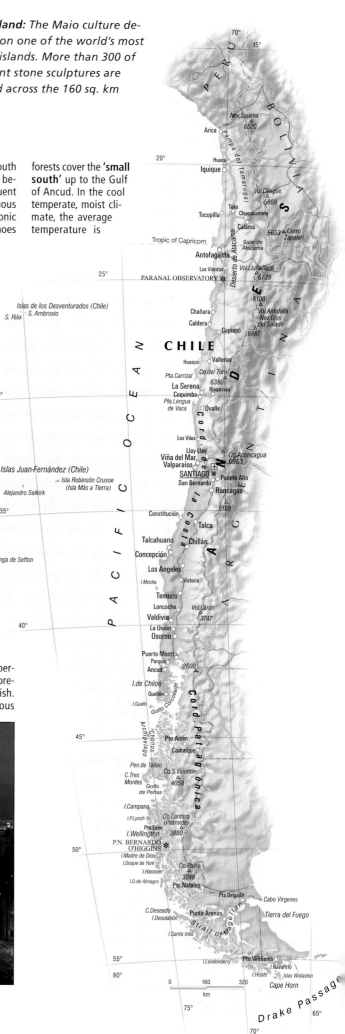

*The Valle Colchagua near Santa Cruz is one of **Chile's** famous wine-making regions. The even temperatures makes Chilean wine very low in acidity. The wine is mainly red, made from French Merlot or Cabernet vine stocks.*

12°C and average rainfall is 1,000 mm.

In the **'great south'**, on average, temperatures of 6°C to 8°C predominate and there is up to 3,000 mm rainfall. The evergreen **rainforest and cloud forest** is replaced in the far south by stunted trees and **sphagnum bogs**.

Population

The population – 84 per cent of whom live in the cities – is composed of 91.6 per cent **mestizo** and **white** and 6.8 per cent **Amerindian**. 77 per cent of Chileans are Catholic, 13 per cent Protestant. The life expectancy is 77 years. Around 15 per cent of Chile's population live below the **poverty line**.

History and Politics

In 1541, the country was conquered by the **Spaniards**. In 1778, Chile became the independent **Kingdom of Chile (also known as the Captaincy General of Chile)**, and in 1818 it became a sovereign state. The **'War of the Pacific'** which ended victoriously for Chile in 1883 and the exploitation of the rich **copper deposits** made Chile into an important exporter of raw materials. The domestic situation however was characterised by many changes of government. In 1918, the **saltpetre monopoly** was disbanded, a situation which led to economic decline and social tensions. Further crises followed a brief **upturn** after World War II. The socialist reforms of the **President Salvador Allende**, elected in 1970, ground to a halt in 1973 when he was assassinated in a **military coup**. Under the cruel dictatorship of General **Augusto Pinochet**, political opponents were persecuted and tortured and over 3,000 were murdered or 'disappeared'. In 1988, Pinochet authorised a referendum after domestic and overseas pressure, which resulted in the majority of voters rejecting an extension of his rule. In 1990, free elections were held for the first time. Under the leadership of Christian Democrats Patricio Aylwin and Eduardo Frei, Social Democrat Ricardo Lagos and Michelle Bachelet, since January 2006, Chile has developed once more into a country

with a stable democracy. Chile has been a **Presidential Republic** since 1925. The constitution, which was last amended in 2000, provides for a **bicameral parliament** and an obligation to vote from the age of 18 years.

Economy

Chile's economy is currently growing at about six per cent. In 2006, GDP was US$ 145 billion, of which four per cent came from **agriculture**, 45 per cent from **industry** and 51 per cent from **services**. For many years, copper was the only export product

(Chile was already a rich country in the nineteenth century thanks to precious metals and saltpetre) but its share in export volume was restricted to about 40 per cent. Agriculture provides wine, fruit and vegetables for export, and the fishing industry also plays an important role – no country exports more farmed salmon than Chile. In addition, forestry is also significant.

Transport Infrastructure

Of the 79,750 km of roads only 11,006 km are paved. The **rail network** covers around 6,782 km. There is a good **long-distance bus network**. The most important **airport** is in the capital Santiago de Chile. 90 per cent of foreign trade uses the well-developed sea routes.

Tourism

With around **1.8 million** tourists, tourism is only moderately devel-

oped in Chile. Popular tourist destinations are **Easter Island**, part of the national territory, the north Chile coast and the **lakes** around **Osorno**. Tierra del Fuego is an adventure holiday.

The **best time to travel** to **southern Chile** is January and February, for central Chile the best time to travel is from October to March.

1 Chile's 'Lake District' impresses with its snow-covered peaks and crystal clear lakes, so suitable for boat trips.

2 The port city of Valparaiso is of strategic importance to Chile. On the Plaza Sotomayor there is a monument to fallen soldiers.

3 Dirt roads cross the Atacama Desert, the most arid in the world. It is situated in Chile's 'Great North'.

4 The gigantic glaciers of Patagonia lure many tourists on take boat trips and helicopter flights.

Emperor penguins are the largest of the seven species of penguin in the Antarctica and grow to 115 cm tall. Like all penguins, they are ratites, flightless birds, protected from the cold with pads of fat and well adapted to life in icy waters.

Emperor penguins dive as deep as 260 m. They breed in colonies but do not make nests. They hold the single egg on their feet and warm it under a flap of skin. In the emperor penguins the male birds nurture the young.

The Arctic

Area: 26,000,000 sq. km
Territorial affinity:
Canada, Russia, USA, Denmark, Norway

Natural Geography

The Arctic covers the **Arctic Ocean**, the land mass and its surrounding islands. The central Arctic region consists of pack ice – compressed sea ice broken up into fragments – up to 40 m thick. In the summer months, the polar **pack ice** extends as far as northern **Spitzbergen** in Norway, **Severny Zemlya**, the **New Siberian Islands**, **Cape Barrow** in Alaska, the islands of the **Canadian Archipelago** and the **north coast of Greenland**.

The Polar ice cap extends further over the sea during the Arctic winter, covering the **Bear Islands** north of Iceland, across the southern tip of Greenland and over the **Newfoundland Reef** roughly as far south as Halifax in Canada, as well as over parts of the **Bering Sea**, the **Sea of Japan** and the **Sea of Okhotsk** off Siberia.

Climate

Only 40 per cent of the Arctic is permanently covered in ice. Average temperatures are around 0°C in summer and -30 to -35°C in winter. The **coldest region** in the world is **Yakutsk**, located in the Siberian Taiga. The Russian **Vostok** (eastern) **Research Station** in Antarctica holds the record for the world's lowest temperature, at -88°C.

The parts of the polar regions not covered in ice are covered in **permafrost**. So are the forests of Scandinavia, Canada and Siberia within the Arctic Circle and just below it. An average temperature significantly below 0°C is required before the sub-soil freezes permanently. The **boreal coniferous forest belt** include the Siberian Taiga and the Scandinavian and Canadian coniferous forests. If the average temperature during the warmest month does not exceed 10–12°C, normal tree growth is no longer possible. Consequently, only stunted, dwarf conifers and bushes grow in the **tree and bush tundra**. The permanently frozen ground of the **Arctic tundra** adjoining the Arctic circle is treeless, the only vegetation consisting of lichen, moss, club-moss and hardy grasses. In the **summer months**, the subsoil thaws to a depth of a few tens of centimetres for a month or so and plants grow. In the **winter** a severe frost prevails with temperatures as low as -50°C. Due to progressive warming of the climate, it is estimated that 10–15 per cent of the ice will have melted by 2100.

Population

Approximately two million people live in the Arctic. They consist of **northern Europeans** and **northern Asians** as well as **Inuits** (Eskimos), **Samis** (Lapps) and **Yakutians.**

History and Politics

The territory of the Arctic regions is shared between **Canada** (Arctic Archipelago), **Russia** (Siberia), **USA** (Alaska), **Denmark** (Greenland) and **Norway** (Spitzbergen, Jan Mayen Island and Bear Island). On 1 October 1996, the **Arctic Council** was formed. Due to the highly fragile nature of the Arctic eco-system, this body's purpose is to coordinate all **development plans** in the field of mineral resources, fishing and hunting. The member countries are **Denmark, Finland, Iceland, Russia, Norway, Sweden** and the **USA**. Also three **organisations of native inhabitants** have the right to have their say. From the fifteenth century onwards, **European seafarers** attempted to map out the Arctic Ocean. Their objective was to find a sea route to the Orient, the long-sought **north-west Passage**. Not until the nineteenth century did **scientific interest** also have a role to play. In 1827, the **expedition** of ships on runners led by **Sir Edward Parry** came within 900 km of the Pole. A costly rescue operation for **Sir John Franklin** who wanted to locate the **north-west Passage** in 1845 lasted 15 years and gleaned valuable geographical insights, although Parry and his crew were never found. Numerous other spectacular expeditions failed. The American **Robert E. Peary** claimed the honour of being the first person to step on to the North Pole on 6 April 1909. On 19 April 1968 the American **Ralph Plaisted** reached the North Pole on foot. In 1926, **Roald Amundsen, Lincoln Ellsworth** and **Umberto Nobile** flew over the Pole in a dirigeable airship. In 1958, the American nuclear submarine **Nautilus** dived underneath the Polar ice cap and the nuclear-powered Soviet ice-breaker 'Arctica' traversed the Pole on the surface of the water in 1977.

Economy

The economic significance of the North Pole lies in the **exploitation** of its **raw materials**. The USA is producing oil in Alaska. **Petroleum, natural gas, zinc, silver** and **gold** are present in the Canadian Arctic, there is **zinc** in Greenland, **coal** in Norway and Russia and **iron** in Norway; **apatite, petroleum, natural gas, non-ferrous metals, gold, diamonds** and **nickel** are all present in Russia. All the countries bordering the Arctic Ocean have **fishing industries**. The **breeding, hunting** and **trapping of fur-bearing animals**, such as fur seals and arctic foxes is of economic importance in Canada and Russia. Small groups of native peoples make a living from **hunting whales and seals**, though this traditional way of life is disappearing.

Antarctica

Area:
12,500,000 sq. km, 14 million sq. km including the polar ice cap.

Natural Geography

Antarctica was part of the original continent of **Gondwanaland** that split into **Antarctica, Africa, South America, Australia** and the **Near East** approximately 180 million years ago. With an average altitude of 2,040 m, the highest part of the continent lies below the Antarctic Circle. It has an area of 12.5 million sq. km – or 14 million sq. km including the **polar ice cap**. 90 per cent of the world's **freshwater ice** is stored here. This corresponds to 80 per cent of the world's total reserves of fresh water. The sea has an open link to the Atlantic and also to the Indian and Pacific Oceans. The **Ross Sea** and **Weddell Sea** divide the continent into two halves. In the

On the coasts of Antarctica there are very few ice-free zones.

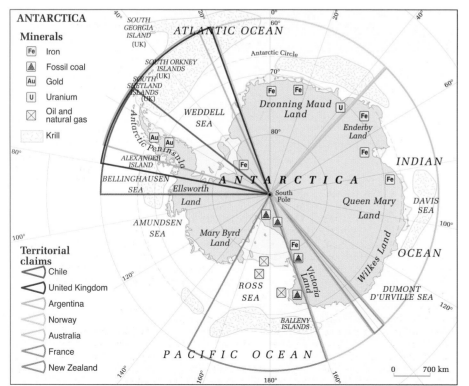

ANTARCTICA

Minerals

Fe	Iron
A	Fossil coal
Au	Gold
U	Uranium
⊠	Oil and natural gas
	Krill

Territorial claims

- Chile
- United Kingdom
- Argentina
- Norway
- Australia
- France
- New Zealand

Exploration of the Antarctic: *the Esperanza base is located in the Argentinian area of the Antarctic. The peninsula in the West extends the furthest into the Polar sea. Antarctica has been divided into claims but most countries do not recognise these divisions. However, the researchers have a common goal: the investigation of the importance of Antarctica for the world climate and the growing threat of a gap in the ozone layer.*

East, there is a high pleateau with an area of 10.4 million sq. km which is covered in ice sheets; in the West, the great **Antarctic peninsula** with an area of 2.69 million sq. km ends in numerous islands to the north.

Western Antarctica contains glaciated fold mountains of over 4,000 m in altitude. **Mount Erebus**, an active volcano rising to a height of 4,023 m, stands on **Ross Island** in the Ross Sea. Around the Pole the inland ice which is up to 2,500 m thick forms a **plateau** approximately 3,000 m above sea level. This turns into **glaciers** and finally into **icebergs** with **drift ice** around its edges.

Climate

Central Antarctica is an extremely **cold**, **dry desert** with an annual average precipitation of 30 to 70 mm and an average temperature of between -50°C and -60°C. The conditions at the coast are somewhat less extreme with a precipitation of 200 to 400 mm and temperatures ranging from -10°C to -20°C. The continent's **violent storms**, **lack of sunshine** and persistent fog are responsible for a natural environment that is equally hostile.

Population

Antarctica is **uninhabited** apart from the scientific personnel who live there temporarily at the **42 research stations**. Approximately 1,000 scientists live in the Antarctic in summer and 4,000 scientists in the Antarctic winter.

History and Politics

Although it was assumed that there was a 'terra incognita' in the southern polar region as early as Antiquity, the British seafarer **James Cook** first reached the Antarctic Circle in 1772 to 1775. Antarctica was sighted very soon afterwards, in 1820, by three explorers, the British Edward **Bransfield**, the American Nathaniel **Palmer** and the Russian Fabian von **Bellinghausen**. Scientific research into the region did not begin in earnest until the twentieth century. On 14 December 1911, the Norwegian Roald **Amundsen** was the first explorer to reach the South Pole, several weeks before the famous expedition of the Englishman Robert Falcon **Scott**. Numerous **expeditions** followed over land and by aeroplane. Seven countries have laid claim to approximately 80 per cent of the Antarctic region but they are not recognised in international law. Argentina claims the region it calls Antárdida Argentinia (1,231,064 sq. km), Australia the Australian Antarctic Territory (5,896,500 sq. km) and the area surrounding Heard and the McDonald Islands (359 sq. km), Chile, Antártida Chileña (1,205,000 sq. km), France, Adélieland (432,000 sq. km), Great Britain, the British Antarctic Territory (1,710,000 sq. km), New Zealand, the Ross Dependency (750,310 sq. km) and Norway, Queen Maud Land (2,500,000 sq. km).

On 1 December 1959, 12 states signed a treaty to regulate the economic exploitation and other interests of Antarctica. The **Antarctic Treaty** came into force on 23 June 1961. Since then, **43 countries** have signed the treaty, 26 with consultative status, i.e. with the obligation to maintain a scientific station. These 26 countries are Argentina, Australia, Belgium, Brazil, Chile, the People's Republic of China, Germany, Ecuador, Finland, France, Great Britain, India, Italy, Japan, South Korea, New Zealand, the Netherlands, Norway, Peru, Poland, Russia, Sweden, Spain, South Africa, Uruguay and the USA. The following countries have entered into the treaty **without consultative status**: Bulgaria, Denmark, Greece, Guatemala, Canada, Colombia, North Korea, Cuba, Austria, Papua New Guinea, Romania, Switzerland, Slovakia, the Czech Republic, Turkey, the Ukraine and Hungary. Under this treaty, all claims to regions south of the 60° latitude are illegitimate. **Administration** is via consultative conferences. Under this comprehensive treaty, the whole of Antarctica is demilitarised and nuclear testing is prohibited. Within the framework of amicable scientific research work, all the parties to the treaty have free access to the territory.

Supplementary treaties ensure the preservation of flora and fauna and prohibit exploitation of the mineral deposits. **The ozone layer** in the Antarctic has been **under observation** since 1957 and has developed a worrying hole.

Economy

The exploitation of **deposits of raw materials** is not permitted under the Antarctic Treaty and **fishing** is strictly controlled.

Tourism

Tourism exists but strict **ecological conditions** apply. Tourists can visit the **penguin colonies** or bathe in **volcanic inland waters**.

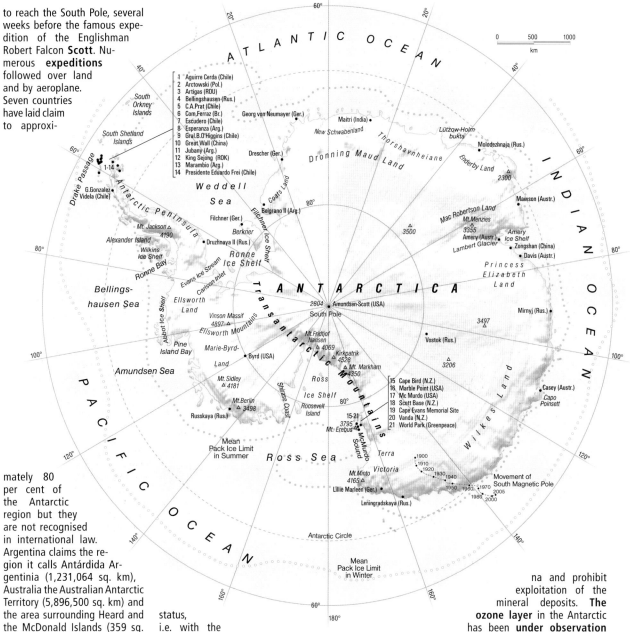

Peoples of America

The name 'America' derives from Amerigo Vespucci, who explored the east coast of South America. He was a contemporary of Christopher Columbus, who discovered the continent –

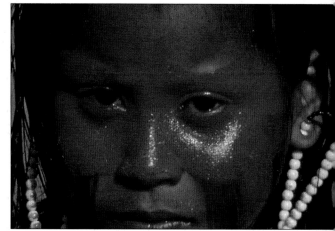

The Amazonian Indians have fought for survival for many years.

although it cannot be said to have been discovered in the true sense of the word, since America had been settled for many years. The original inhabitants were named 'Indians' by Columbus due to his mistaken belief that he was in fact in India. Some of the indigenous people formed highly developed civilisations, such as the Aztecs, Maya and Incas, many of whose culture was destroyed to a large extent during the Conquista – the conquering and religious conversion of Central and South America by the Spanish and Portuguese. The Native North Americans were subjected to a similar fate; their land was seized and settled from 1583, first by the English, then by white settlers and adventurers from various countries.

Northern America

*Around 65,000 **Inuit** live in Alaska and northern Canada, with another 30,000 in Greenland and several thousand in Siberia. They speak Inuktitut or Eskimo Aleutian. In order to survive in the extreme cold of the Arctic, the Inuit created the igloo lit by whale-oil lamps, built kayaks for travel by water and dressed in anoraks to keep out the cold and wet. In remote areas they still maintain their traditional existence, by hunting seals, sea lions and caribou.*

Population of North America

Today more than 330 million people live in the two countries of the North American continent: **Canada** and the **United States of America**, including Alaska. Few facts are known about how the first settlement came about. What is certain is that America is one of the most recently settled continents. In the period between 30,000 years ago and the end of the **ice age**, which occurred around 10,000 years ago, groups of hunters and gatherers probably migrated to the continent from Asia across the **Bering Strait**. These **Mongoloid peoples** were the precursors of the original population of North

just one per cent of the total population. Today, 70 per cent of the North American population is **white** and 12 per cent **black**. At 13 per cent, the **Hispanics** are now the largest minority group. The rest is made up of **Asians**.

The Inuit (Eskimos)

Approximately 100,000 **Inuit** people, the indigenous population of northern America, live in **Alaska**, the **Aleutian Islands** and **Canada**. A minority has settled in **Russia**, and there is a further group on **Greenland** that has interbred widely with the Danes. The Inuit were originally known as Eskimos (meaning

tents made of skin in summer and in snow huts (**igloos**) in the winter. For many years, fish, seals and whales formed their principal food source. **Reindeer breeding** began in the late nineteenth century. The Inuit used **kayaks** and **dog sleds** for transport and made their clothes from furs and skins.

Outside the family there are few tribal associations or distinct class differences and chiefs. The Inuit, who were converted to Christianity in the eighteenth century, use music for ritual purposes. The **shaman's drum**, the Inuit's only instrument, makes reference to their original religion – shamanism. According to Inuit belief, people have two souls, one of which enters the

The Whites

The white population currently living in North America is of European origin. Due to their 'British' character, the whites are known as **Anglo-American**; the French-speaking whites in Canada are called **French-Canadians**. The capital of the Dutch colony, **New Amsterdam**, founded in 1625, was renamed **New York** after being taken over by the English in 1664. This was the first port of entry for millions of hopeful immigrants from Europe. Those who did not receive an entry stamp offshore on **Ellis Island** had to return home. Many new arrivals stayed in New York and formed their own communities.

8 million Germans and 5.8 million Italians alone. Today, over 7 million people from a wide range of ethnic and religious origins live in **New York**, including almost 2 million blacks, 1.2 million Hispanics and 1.2 million Jews.

The African Americans

The second influential factor in the composition of the population of North America was the **importation** of thousands of slaves from **sub-Saharan Africa** from the early seventeenth century. Today, about 35 million **African Americans** live in the USA, about 12 per cent of the total population; on the other hand, only 200,000 live in

The Pilgrim Fathers

The Pilgrim Fathers were a group of about a hundred Puritans who split from the Church of England in order to preserve their religion. When they landed off the coast of Massachusetts ten years later, on 21 November 1620, these first Europeans realised their dream of a living in a country free from economic hardship and religious or political persecution, where everyone could be free. When the Pilgrim Fathers and their families stepped onto American soil, it was a big step towards the settlement of this vast country, which would develop into the greatest global power of non-indigenous peoples.

Many Americans are confirmed patriots and are proud of the pioneering feats of their ancestors.

Colonisation

In the seventeenth century, French traders settled in the interior of what is today Canada, while many English colonies grew up along the East Coast and on Hudson Bay. The result was a battle for power between the English and French. Under the 1763 Treaty of Paris, Canada and territories to the east of the Mississippi River were assigned to England. While Canada did not demand political autonomy until 1848, remaining part of the English Crown until that time, the 13 American colonies were able to separate from England on 4 July 1776, after a struggle for liberation that lasted three years.

America – the **Eskimos** (**Inuit**) and the Native North Americans. Following the discovery of America in 1492 by Europeans, they became increasingly marginalised. After prolonged territorial battles, settlers from **Spain, England, France, the Netherlands, Sweden** and **Russia** occupied their land and seriously decimated the original population, sometimes by military subjugation, sometimes through the diseases they brought with them. Almost **3 million Native North Americans** live in **Canada** and the **USA**, mostly on reservations –

'snowshoe netters'. In Siberia and Alaska they are now known as **Yuit** and, in Greenland, **Kaluait**. These originally Mongoloid polar people migrated from the **Asiatic Chukchi Peninsula**, across Alaska and along the Canadian coast of the Arctic Ocean to Greenland. Small in stature, with a yellowish-brown skin tone and straight, black hair, the Inuit have retained a more pronounced epicanthic fold than the Native North Americans as a result of their isolated location. At times they live a semi-nomadic existence, sheltering in

kingdom of the dead after death, with the other entering a child. As carvers, the Inuit produce original **works of art** (amulets) from walrus ivory, bones and soapstone. Contact with white people had an early influence on their traditional way of life. They were gradually robbed of their natural resources and forced back into reservations, which brought many social challenges for the indigenous inhabitants, who had once lived in harmony with nature. This is evident in the high rates of illiteracy, alcoholism and unemployment.

The new freedoms written into the American constitution under **George Washington** attracted millions of immigrants, who saw no economic, religious or political prospects in their own land. The two largest **waves of immigration** took place in the nineteenth and twentieth centuries. Before 1890, increasing numbers of English, Irish, German and Scandinavian immigrants arrived; between 1890 and 1910 they came mostly from **Southern** and **Eastern Europe**. Between 1890 and 1991, almost 60 million immigrants arrived from Europe, including

Canada. They are almost without exception descendants of those first Africans who stepped onto American soil from 1619 onwards as **slaves**. Until the ban on the **slave trade** in 1808, and including those slaves taken to **Central** and **South America**, approximately **10 million people** from Africa involuntarily entered the **'New World'**, about one fifth of whom did not survive the sea journey. Most slaves were from West Africa, often from the **Igbo, Wolof, Ewe** and **Bambara** tribes; initially they were officially supposed to be trained as servants,

*Compared to the eastern coast of the USA, and states such as **Florida** and **California**, the American Midwest is only relatively thinly populated. This is the home of country music, which has its roots in blues, Celtic music and folk music and tells the melancholy, romanticised stories of the lives of 'lonesome cowboys', the long-distance trucker, or the wronged wife – usually sung with a guitar accompaniment in equally melancholic style.*

but from 1660, and in Virginia and Maryland in particular, they were publicly declared unfree. Up until 1790, 20 per cent of the total population was African American, around 60 per cent of whom worked on the cotton plantations belonging to the whites. As a result, by 1850 cotton made up about 50 per cent of American exports, thereby forming the foundation of America's economic rise. At the start of the American **Civil War** in 1861, there were around 3.2 million slaves, who became free citizens for the first time when the **Union** was victorious, in 1865, under **Abraham Lincoln**. Due to the poor living conditions of the African Americans in the Southern States in the late nineteenth century, many migrated to the north and east. Until the 1960s, **racial segregation** was in force on public transport. The black **theologian** and **Nobel Peace Prize winner Martin Luther King** fought against **discrimination** and **racial taunting**, and was assassinated in 1968. Currently the rate of African American population growth is twice that of the white.

The Hispanics

The American 'melting pot' has been enriched in recent decades by **Latin American immigrants**, who came primarily from **Puerto Rico**, **Mexico** and **Cuba**. As a result **Spanish** is now the second most widely spoken language after **English**. The Latin American people in North America are known as **Hispanic**. Already partially mixed with **whites** or **blacks**, they have preserved their own Hispanic culture. The increased influx has led to the formation of slums in many cities in areas with a high Hispanic population. Identification and return transportation of illegal Latin American immigrants have since become one of the main tasks of the US border authorities.

The Asians

After two large **waves of Asian immigration** during the nineteenth and twentieth centuries,

an additional influx followed between 1980 and 1990, mainly to the **west coast** of **the USA** and to **Canada**. The majority of the new arrivals were **Chinese** and **Japanese**, followed by Filipinos. Large **Asian communities** have formed in **Toronto** (Canada), **San Francisco** and **New York** in particular.

The Amish

The original make-up of **ethnic groups** from **Germany** is preserved to a large extent in some

parts of the USA. These groups came to North America from Europe mainly for religious reasons, as was the case with the Amish, whose 150,000 members today live in **Pennsylvania** and **Ohio**. The Amish community's ancestors emigrated to North America from Germany some 300 years ago, goes back to a splinter group of the Mennonite Baptist community founded in 1694 by Jacob Ammann (another Baptist group was the **Hutterites**, which also left Europe due to religious persecution). Even today, most Amish still speak an old **Palatinate (north German) dialect**. They dress very simply, using only hooks and eyes instead of buttons.

The Amish, with their many children, live primarily as farmers and craftsmen and refuse to use any modern technology. State support is declined, and in cases of emergency the community or Amish relief organisations provide help. The holding of public

office, voting and military service is also forbidden among the Amish. According to statistics, they suffer less frequently from the illnesses caused by today's lifestyle. Their stable family life is based on the iron rule of lifelong partnerships, and their deep devoutness forms the basis for their everyday life.

1 Only a few Inuit in the extreme north of Canada still maintain the old traditions.

2 In Tennessee, whiskey has been distilled from malt for generations and is much more popular in the USA than the Scottish variant, whisky (with no 'e'), made from grain.

3 In the vast plains of the Midwest, most people farm or breed cattle.

4 The Williamsburg Museum contains reconstructed settlements showing the poor conditions under which the slaves lived in the eighteenth and nineteenth centuries.

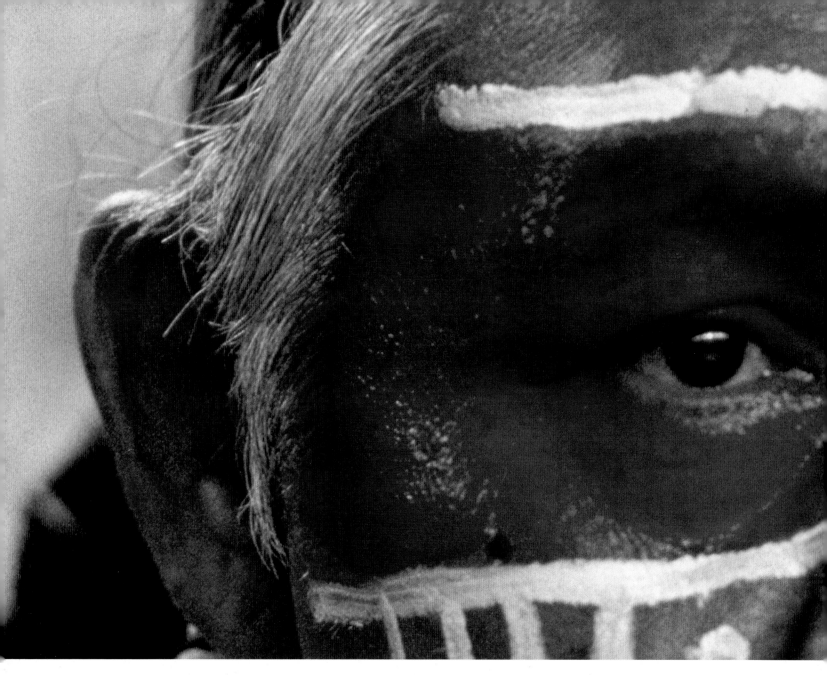

Native North American Reserves

Native North Americans make up just one per cent of the total North American population, and only three per cent of the land originally in their possession remains so today, spread over some 270 reserves. Their conditions have changed radically from their former existence as hunter-gatherers and farmers.

Face-painting was once widespread among Native North Americans – a tradition that is today principally practised at the powwow, a type of traditional folk festival.

When, in 1492, Christopher Columbus first set foot on the island now known as the Bahamas, he believed he had landed in the Indies (as Asia was known at the time), and consequently referred to the indigenous people as 'Indians', a term that was adopted for the whole of the continent. The ancestors of the 'Indians' had migrated from Asia across the Bering Strait 30,000 years ago, via a land bridge that disappeared 20,000 years later, and initially settled in North and then later in South America. According to widely differing estimates, they numbered between 15 and 100 million, spread out across the whole of America, before colonisation by the Europeans.

In 1990, there were just over 2 million Native North Americans in the USA, including 35,000 Inuit. Around 600,000 First Nations people and 30,000 Inuit live in Canada, although these figures can vary significantly according to the way the data is recorded. Some people consider themselves Native North Americans but are not entered in any tribal register and so not recognised as such. A case in point is the Cherokee Nation – more than 300,000 people claim tribal affiliation, a figure that would make the Cherokee the largest of the US Native North American Nations today, yet only around 70,000 members are entered in the tribal register.

Current statistics on life expectancy, as well as medical care, education, unemployment and living conditions, prove that Native North Americans living in the USA – the country with the highest gross national product in the world and the seventh richest industrial nation on earth – are the most discriminated against of the ethnic groups, with living conditions on reserves comparable to those in third-world countries. It has been shown that on

A dignified member of the Umatilla Tribe, proud to celebrate his tribal culture.

Right: Native North Americans today are confident in expressing their needs and interests.

many reserves up to 75 per cent of Native North Americans live below the poverty line. In some regions, up to 90 per cent are unemployed and reliant on state assistance. This is mainly due to there being no, or very little, industry to provide work, or because the industry that does exist is there because companies are unable to find any other site due to the environmental burden they impose or other risks they pose to the inhabitants. Approximately 80 per cent of all nuclear industry companies are located adjacent to reserves or in Native North American territories.

In spite of, or perhaps because of poor social, health and economic conditions, Native North Americans have retained and continue to cultivate rituals from their past. Powwows or large social gatherings continue to be held annually. Native North Americans lived in small, nomadic tribes, each protecting their own natural resources, and would congregate each year in a large gathering. The chiefs would discuss and settle tribal matters and establish political and trading links. The powwows were also an occasion for festivals and ceremonies, characterised by traditional rites such as the sun dance and adoption and name-giving ceremonies. Today, more than ever, Native North Americans seek to maintain links with their past by perpetuating the traditions that strengthen their sense of identity. In this context the powwow represents an important form of expression of their different cultures. It is a time for meeting people, for friendship and mutual respect, accompanied by symbolic music and ritualised dancing. The most important instrument here is the drum, which creates a link to the ancestors.

Nowadays, there is a distinction between three types of powwow. In the splendid competition powwows, the most beautiful costumes and the best dancers are presented with awards. Tourists can also attend these powwows, which therefore represent a useful source of income. Other powwows are more spiritual and religious in nature – different healing rituals are carried out and the spirits are consulted. The socio-cultural powwow is one where social and cultural interaction between different tribes takes place. Dance forms an important part of all three types of powwow and is a popular form of expression. During the sun dance – a day-long dance of purification in which the

Even members of the most geographically remote tribes would not miss a powwow.

dancers are exposed to pain, hunger and thirst, and exhaustion – asceticism is believed to induce visions that help in solving problems and provide a context for spiritual questions. Humility before nature and respect for the spirits are the goals of every powwow.

Northern America

*The roots of jazz lie in **New Orleans**, the city with the French-laced charm of the Old South. Jazz originated around the late nineteenth and early twentieth centuries, evolving from the traditional music of the African Americans – blues,*

gospel, spirituals and ragtime. Among its famous exponents were musicians such as Louis Armstrong and singer Billie Holiday, whose music made the bittersweet attitude towards life in the Southern States famous worldwide.

Native North Americans

Today Native North Americans represent almost one per cent of the population of the USA, while in Canada, where they are known as the First Nations, they represent around three per cent of the Canadian population in approximately 660 tribes and tribal groups. Despite an often romantic portrayal in books and films, their fight for survival has been hard, particularly after European colonisation.

The Tlingits

The **Tlingit** people, of whom there are around 100,000, and whose territory once extended

The Kwakiutl

The 5,000 **Kwakiutl** living in **British Columbia (Canada)** are a First Nations people of the **north-west coast** and comprise thirty tribes. They were expert woodworkers, producing objects such as finely carved and painted **totem poles**, **canoes** and **masks**. The southern Kwakiutl are particularly known for their **Tseyka dances** or winter ceremonies, in which stories of their ancestors are told. The dancers wear **bird masks**. The Native North Americans of the north-west coast were also known for the **potlatch festival**, during which wealth would be redistributed. In order to gain prestige, material goods were given away on what was at times a ruinous scale.

The Chippewa speak one of the **Algonquian** group of languages. They once lived in small, scattered settlements in **wigwams** (Algonquin: 'abode'), oval- or circular-shaped dwellings with a framework made from flexible beech or birch saplings.

Traditional hunting is still practised by the Chippewa, as is the production of maple syrup and the harvesting of wild rice. Secret societies of medicine men and women still take part in the **Midewin** ceremony, which lasts from two to five days.

The Crow

The **Crow** are one of the Plains Native North American peoples. Approximately 7,000 Crow (in

The Iroquois

The union of the six **Iroquois** nations of the **Mohawk**, **Cayuga**, **Seneca**, **Onondaga**, **Oneida** and **Tuscarora** in **Canada** and the **north-eastern USA** comprises some 600,000 people. The Onondaga territory in New York State has so far remained sovereign, and no US authority may cross the border without the agreement of the supreme chief (**Tadodaho**). Even today there is still a longhouse at the heart of the village in many communities, used for political and religious gatherings. The Iroquois nations were united in the **Iroquois Confederacy**, a political alliance that took place after long tribal feuds between 1400 and 1600, mostly before major European

speaking nations. 'Sioux' is an abbreviation of the Chippewa term 'Nadoweissiw' (little snakes), which was initially corrupted to become 'Nadouessioux', and later 'Sioux'. Their most important traditional ceremonies include rituals of spiritual cleansing, the **sun dance** at the annual **powwow** and **pipe ceremony**, where the smoke represents a link to the spiritual world.

The Blackfeet

There are about 20,000 **Blackfeet** (moccasins, black from prairie ash) living in the border area between **northern Montana** and **southern Alberta**, but they are quite separate from the **Blackfoot**, a **Lakota-Sioux** tribe.

Many African Americans live in poor conditions in the Southern States of the USA.

from **southern Alaska** to **northern California** and the islands offshore, are one of the peoples from the **north-west coast**, as are the Nootka and Haida. Still spoken by approximately 1,500 people in 1990, their language is one of the **Na-Déné** family of languages. A typical cultural feature of the Tlingits were their elaborately carved **totem poles**, up to 15 m tall and decorated with stylised animal motifs, which only master craftsmen were allowed to produce.

The Chippewa (Ojibwa)

One of the largest groups of Native North Americans/First Nations people is the **Chippewa** (also known as the Ojibwa). Of this group, about 60,000 have settled on reservations in the northern **USA** (**Montana, North Dakota, Minnesota, Wisconsin, Michigan**), while a further approximately 150,000 live in southern **Canada** (**Ontario, Manitoba, Saskatchewan**).

their own language: **Absaroka**) now live in reservations in **southern Montana**. As the Sioux's greatest enemy, in 1876 they fought with **General Custer** at the famous **Battle of the Little Bighorn** against the Sioux chief **Sitting Bull**.

The Crow have retained many of their ancient traditions, such as the annual **sun dance**, and **medicine men and women** still play a key role in the lives of the community. Many Crow still speak their own language.

contact – and their constitution became a model for the US.

The Sioux

The fourteen tribes of the **Lakota** (also **Dakota, Nakota**) which today number over 100,000, live primarily on reserves in **Minnesota, North** and **South Dakota, Nebraska** and **Montana**. They are the largest and best known of the **Sioux**-

The Blackfeet, once typical representatives of Plains Native North Americans who hunted bison, today gain an important part of their income through tourism.

The Cheyenne

The **Cheyenne** ('people of the foreign language'), today numbering about 50,000 together with the **Arapaho**, are divided into two groups, one living in the

*'Little Tokyo' in Los Angeles is just one of the districts found in many cities throughout the USA and Canada where immigrants from abroad have formed tightly cohesive ethnic communities – from **'Little Italy'** in New York to **'Little** Havana'**, the Cuban community in Florida, and the **'Chinatowns'** of San Francisco and Vancouver. Stepping into these vibrant pockets of culture is like being transported to another country or even continent.*

north in **Montana** and the other in the south in **Oklahoma**. They speak an **Algonquian** language. Once living as farmers in Minnesota, in the eighteenth century they migrated to the Great Plains where they hunted buffalo.

The Navajo

Around 160,000 of the 220,000 **Navajo** (also called Navaho; in their own language: Diné – 'people') are settled in reserves in **north-eastern Arizona**, **Colorado**, **Utah** and **New Mexico**, where they arrived in around 1400 from Canada. Today, the Navajo – who speak one of the **Athapaskan** languages – have their own schools and in 1969 gained their own university, in which the ancient traditions and the Navajo language are taught. The traditional knowledge of the **shamans** forms an important part of the teaching. Their healing ceremonies feature chanting and images drawn in sand that depict healing plants and mythical events.

The Apache

'Apache' is the collective term for six culturally related Native North American tribes (including the **Jicarilla**, **Mescalero** and **Kiowa**), who speak one of the **Athapaskan** languages. These former nomadic bison hunters put up successful long-term resistance under their legendary leaders **Cochise** and **Geronimo**, before they were forced onto reservations in **Arizona** in 1886, where around 25,000 of them still live today.

The Shoshone

The **Shoshone**, who speak a **Uto-Aztec** language, formerly lived in the mountains of **Wyoming** and **Montana**, as well as in **Utah**, **Nevada** and **Oregon**. The western Shoshone were once also known as **'Digger Indians'**, possibly after the practice of digging for roots. After adopting the use of the horse in around 1700, the

Shoshone, like their principal subgroup the **Comanche**, specialised in hunting bison and took on many of the cultural elements of the Plains Native North Americans. The **medicine men** and **shamans** played an important role, for instance in hunting rabbits and antelope. Today, 6,000 Shoshone and 5,000 Comanche live on reserves.

The Hopi

The Hopi (peace) today number around 10,000 and are the only

group of Native North Americans who never signed a treaty with the US government. They live in northern Arizona in adobe villages (pueblos) located in three areas called mesas, which together comprise the Hopi Reservation. The history of each tribe has been passed down orally. The oldest tribe, who also occupy the highest position in Hopi society, came from the region of the Anasazi people, to the north and east of what is today Hopi territory. Each tribe is responsible for maintaining a certain part of traditional ceremony, such as the Kachina dance.

The Cherokee

With 300,000 members, the **Cherokee** are one of the largest of the Native North American peoples in the USA and were once one of the **'Five Civilised Tribes'**. They speak an **Iroquois**

language and are subdivided into clans structured according to the matrilineal descent system. Today, the Cherokee live principally in **Oklahoma** and **North Carolina**. In 1824, the Cherokee **Sequoyah**, who worked as a silversmith, invented a script that contained 86 characters representing syllables.

1 Many Americans still feel an affinity with – and enjoy perpetuating – the traditional cowboy lifestyle.

2 The strict rejection by the Amish of the 'blessings' of modern civilisation have made them both a curiosity and a tourist attraction.

3 Because of their old-fashioned appearance, the Amish seem to be out of place in contemporary America.

4 Once an essential element of the Native North American way of life, wild horses are today caught by cowboys using a lasso.

*The 30,000 **Cuna** population is concentrated along the coast of **Panama** and on the San Blas islands. Cuna women still wear traditional nose rings, and when Cuna marry it is the man who moves into his bride's home.*

Peoples of Central America

Around 170 million people live in the Central American countries of **Mexico**, **Belize**, **Guatemala**, **Honduras**, **El Salvador**, **Nicaragua**, **Costa Rica** and **Panama**, as well as on the Caribbean islands that lie off their eastern shores.

The largest ethnic group in **Mexico** and **Central America** are the **mestizos** (of mixed white and indigenous Native American parentage); **Native Americans** are the largest group in **Guatemala**, and **whites** in **Costa Rica**. There are very few

Central America: as well as **mestizos** there are **mulattos** and **zambos**, (the offspring of one Native American and an African parent). 'Creole' was the term originally used to describe European migrants from Latin Europe to Latin America ('**white Creoles**'); however, in Brazil the term '**black Creoles**' is used to describe the descendants of slaves of African origin.

The Whites

In Spanish-speaking Central America, the white population is

influence of the **Spanish** and **Portuguese**: Panama was conquered in 1510, as were the Mexican Aztecs by the Spaniard **Hernan Cortés** in 1519–21. **Pedro de Alvarado** took Guatemala and El Salvador, while in South America **Francisco Pizarro** defeated the Peruvian Inca kingdom, and **Pedro de Valdivia** conquered what is today Chile. By 1500, **Pedro Cabral** had taken **Brazil** for **Portugal**, which, just like the other colonial powers, profited from the rich mineral resources found in its colonies. Their exploitation was, however, only possible through the work of African slaves, who

part of the Southern Mexican state of **Oaxaca**. They make their living primarily as farmers (coffee, sugar cane, wheat), as rural craftsmen (weavers, potters), or as merchants in the towns.

In around 500 BC, the Zapotecs, whose language is closely linked to Mixtec, founded a town on **Monte Albán** (Taniquiecache) in the heart of the Oaxaca valley, which became the cultural and political focus of Southern Mexico. Vestiges of its ancient culture include some 300 stone slabs bearing images of naked human figures in strange positions, known as '**dancers**' (danzantes), which are thought to represent prisoners being ritually slaughtered, as well as many blocks of stone bearing a hieroglyphic script, the earliest form of writing in Central America.

The Nahua

Numbering around 2 million, the **Nahua** (meaning 'speakers of clean language') represent the largest Native American group in Mexico. Their language, **Nahuatl** ('fine-sounding'), which includes several dialects, is spoken by 1.5 million people, and was the literary language of the **Aztecs** at the time of the **Conquista** – this can be seen from many documents that survive from the early colonial period.

Due to high levels of unemployment in modern times, many Nahua have since migrated to the towns, while those who are left in the country continue to live primarily from the cultivation of maize.

The Virgin of Guadalupe is particularly revered by the Nahua, as legend has it that she spoke Nahuatl when she appeared.

The Mixtecs

The **Mixtecs** number around 300,000 (in the Aztec language: 'people from the cloud country'; in their own language, Nuudzahui: 'people of the rain') and live in **northern and eastern Oaxaca**, as well as in the south of Puebla in Mexico. In addition to agriculture (maize, beans and

pumpkins), they survive by fishing and from their crafts (pottery, weaving and braiding). Today, many Mixtecs still wear their traditional costumes – women usually wear **long tunics** (huipil) and **shawls** (rebozos), and men wear white cotton trousers.

The Mixtecs can be traced back to AD 692 and the founding of their capital city, **Tilantongo**, to the north-west of **Monte Albán**. After seizing power over the Zapotecs in the eighth century, the **Mixteca-Puebla** culture flourished in the eleventh century, when large works of art were produced in the fields of painting, ceramics and gold work. Another feature of the Mixtec culture is their unusual **mosaic work**, examples of which were found in magnificent royal tombs in the Oaxaca valley. The Mixtecs left a record of their history from between 1000 and 1520 in eight **codices**, 'folded books' with decorative painted buckskin covers, which give an insight into the life of the ruling dynasties, including marriage contracts, military conflicts and religious ceremonies.

The Tarascan

Today, about 150,000 **Tarascan** people (in their own language: Purépecha) live in the mountainous volcanic regions of the western Mexican state of **Michoacán**. Their language (Tarascan) is not related to any other local languages, but does bear certain similarities to Quechua, which is spoken from **Ecuador** and **Columbia** to **Northern Argentina** and **Chile**, so the Tarascan people may have migrated from South America.

The only Mexican people never conquered by the **Aztecs**, today the Tarascan mainly live from agriculture (maize, pumpkin and beans), keeping small livestock, and crafts. To a large extent the people in the remote villages still maintain a traditional way of life.

The Otomi

The area settled by the **Otomí** (in their own language: Nahñu), today numbering around 350,000,

The Garifuna (Black Caribs)

Around 80,000 Garifuna live in Belize, Guatemala, Honduras, Nicaragua and the USA. They are the descendents of African slaves who, having escaped from their masters, mixed with Carib Native Americans on the Antillean island of St Vincent in the seventeenth century. Their language combines Native American Araucanian with the Yoruba, Swahili and Bantu languages of Africa, and also borrows from Spanish, English and French.

The Garifuna still subscribe to ancestor worship and possession rituals. They believe that illness, accident and death result from angering their ancestors' spirits. In African tradition, ancestor worship takes the form of a voodoo ritual. Rhythmic music puts the medicine man into a trance in which he is possessed by the spirits of the ancestors.

Fruit seller on the beach in Cartagena, Columbia.

indigenous inhabitants still living on the Central American islands, where the majority of the population is made up of **blacks** and **mulattos** (people of mixed black and white ancestry). Whites form the majority group in **Cuba** and **Puerto Rico**. Indians and Chinese have also settled in the Caribbean.

There are also many people of mixed-race descent living in

primarily descended from the Spanish who came from mainland Spain to colonise Central America, and also from **Europeans** (such as the British) and migrants who arrived from the **USA**.

While the majority of the settlers in North America, after its 'discovery', were principally **English** and **French**, at the beginning of the sixteenth century Central and South America came under the

were brought to the continent in huge numbers, while the original inhabitants were soon decimated.

The Zapotecs

Most of the **Zapotecs**, of whom there are around 500,000 (in their own language: Penizaa – 'cloud people') live in the eastern

*The term **Quechua** refers to the language and Native American population of the mountainous regions of Bolivia, Peru, northern Chile and northern Argentina. The Quechua call themselves and their language Runa Simi. Though the Quechua speak various dialects, they all share similar economic and cultural structures. In communities more than 4,000 m above sea level, the Quechuas' survival is entirely dependent on their livestock (alpacas, lamas and sheep).*

extends across the Mexican states of **Puebla and Hidalgo** and includes parts of **Mexico City**. They speak Otomí-Pame, a form of the **Oto-Mangue language**, but many Otomí now only speak Spanish, as is common among the modern Mexican rural population. Most Otomí live in scattered villages and small towns and work the land farming maize, beans, chilli, pumpkins, wheat and barley. In addition, they keep livestock (goats, sheep, pigs and chickens) and sell craft products (weaving, ceramics and basket making). In some villages, '**compradazgo**' is still a part of the social fabric, a relationship in which people take on a role similar to that of godparent at the birth of a child, pledging support between two families.

The Maya

The **Maya** comprise many diverse ethnic groups and today number 2.5 million people. The golden age of Mayan culture – considered to have been the most highly developed in the whole of the American continent – was between AD 200 and 900. Due to language and cultural differences, a differentiation is made between the **highland Maya**, who principally live in the Mexican Chiapas, in **Southern Guatemala** and western El Salvador (including the **Tzotzil**, **Mam**, **Kekchi**, **Quiché** and **Cakchiquel**), the **lowland Maya**, who include – with a special culture – the **Huaxtec** on the Gulf Coast of Mexico, as well as the **Mayeros**, **Macehuales** and **Lacandon** on the **Mexican Yucatan Peninsula**, who speak the Maya languages (Maya'tan), and the lowland Maya in **Belize**, in **northern Guatemala** and in **Honduras**. While the lowland Maya primarily live by slash and burn agriculture, the livelihood of the highland Maya is based on the cultivation of maize, beans and squash; they are additionally considered to be talented craftsmen and women (weaving, pottery), who even in early colonial times maintained many trading links with non-indigenous traders and craftsmen. Although they converted to Christianity

many years ago, in many highland Mayan villages elected brotherhoods (cofradias) are still responsible for religious festivals, characterised by many pre-Christian images, reflecting a belief in the supernatural.

Peoples of South America

The original Native Americans were driven back in great numbers, robbed of their natural resources and cruelly repressed by the Spanish and Portuguese conquerors who arrived in the southern half of the American continent in the sixteenth century. The introduction of African **slaves** soon followed.

Today, various ethnic groups have become intermingled throughout the South American continent. **Blacks** and **mulattos** are mainly found in **Brazil** and the tropical coastal areas. The populations of **Venezuela**, **Columbia**, **Ecuador**, **Paraguay** and **Chile** are very much of mixed descent. Only **Bolivia** and **Peru** still have a Native American majority. Today, it is whites who form the majority of the population in Brazil, Uruguay and Argentina. In the mid-nineteenth century, many Europeans migrated to the area, mainly from **Spain**, **Germany**, **Italy** and **Poland**, as well as **Asians** (Japanese and Indians). The number of people moving to the cities has led to increased urbanisation – in South America there are over **30 cities** of over one million people, ten of which are in **Brazil** alone.

Native South Americans

Today, the purest of the indigenous peoples of South America are found primarily in Columbia and the central and northern **Andean highlands** (in Ecuador, Peru and Bolivia), as well as in the **Amazon** rainforest.

1 Having migrated to the cities, many Native Americans are now small-scale traders.

2 On 12 December, the people of Mexico celebrate their country's patron saint, the Virgin of Guadalupe. The festival is a mix of both Christian and pre-Columbian traditions.

3 Bright, vivid hues are typical of the Virgin of St Guadalupe festivities.

4 Native Americans have had a strong influence on Guatemala. The bright, striped ponchos and headwear worn by the Nebaj Native Americans are typical of Central America.

The Yanomami – Survival in the Rainforest

For years, human rights and environmental groups have been fighting for the survival of the Yanomami people. The encroachment of economic forces upon the indigenous Yanomami's territory has made the risk of losing their homeland ever more tangible. Thanks to their unusual social structures and largely unchanged traditions and customs, the Yanomami have become one of the most studied Amazon Native American groups for both ethnologists and linguists.

The Yanomami are probably the most well-known people in the entire Amazon rainforest. They live in a mountainous border region between Venezuela and Brazil, roughly equivalent in size to Switzerland. There are about 10,000 Yanomami in the northern part of the Brazilian state of Amazonas and a similar number across the border in Venezuela, making them the most populous people of the Amazon rainforest. Venezuelan Yanomami ('house-dwellers') live in villages of around 250 people. Each village takes the form of a communal building called a shapono, built in a circular shape with a sloping roof. The Yanomami survive from hunting, fishing and gathering wild plants, and they also grow plantains and cassava. The ground in the rainforest cannot be cultivated for long periods, however, so the villagers have to move to a new location every three or four years.

In the 1950s, incursion on Yanomami territory from the outside world – in the form of buildings to house the government's authorities and the construction of a major highway – saw many Yanomami lose their lives to newly imported illnesses such as 'flu, tuberculosis, measles and malaria. Rates of malaria among the contemporary Yanomami range from 70 to 90 per cent of the population, depending on the area.

In the 1980s, gold, uranium and valuable minerals were discovered in the Brazilian Yanomami territories. Since that time, the Yanomami's land has been overrun by thousands of gold diggers (garimpeiros), who have not only driven away the game hunted by the Yanomami, but also polluted the region's rivers and ground water with mercury used to extract the gold.

According to the Yanomami's mythology and belief system, the life spirits (hekura) live within the shamans. Each spirit is associated with its own totem animal, responsible for life, accidents, illness and death. When a member of the tribe dies, the body is cremated and the ashes ground to a fine powder, which is then mixed with plantain soup and consumed by his surviving relatives. If the deceased fell victim to conflict, the Yanomani set about avenging his death.

Main picture: Due to the tropical climate, the Yanomami wear very little clothing.

Inset: Male Yanomami wear various items of impressive bead jewellery.

The festival of the pijiguao palm is a Yanomami tradition to which allied tribes are also invited. Often, it serves as an opportunity to launch an attack on hostile tribes, the aim being to abduct as many women as possible.

The Maká are one of the Gran Chaco Native American tribes. Together, the Gran Chaco encompass 19 peoples, some 100,000 individuals and seven different languages. Their settlements span the Gran Chaco steppe, from Paraguay to Argentina and Bolivia. The Maká survive from hunting, fishing and gathering wild fruits and plants. By contrast, the other Native American settlements in this area are primarily sustained through farming the land.

The Cauca

The 200,000 Cauca Native Americans are divided into the **Paez**, **Yanacona** and **Inga** groups, as well as the closely related **Guambiano**, **Coconúco** and **Totoró**. They live in the mountains of **south-west Columbia**. Since the 1970s, the Cauca have been one of the most active members of the Columbian Native American movement in the fight against the power of the white landowners. The Cauca keep their own animals (chickens, pigs, horses and cattle) and also grow their own potatoes and corn. At lower altitudes, the Cauca also cultivate wheat, cassavas, sugar cane, coffee and pineapples for sale on the commercial market. They generally farm the fields using a rotation system.

Though the Cauca speak different languages – **Quechua**, **Paez**, **Guambiano** and Spanish – their various cultures are closely related. In particular, they all believe in the existence of an underworld and upper world. According to the Cauca, the various gods are also present in some parts of the visible world, and must be paid due respect if harmony between man and the gods is to be preserved. Here, the medicine man plays an important role. Stimulated by the ritual chewing of **coca leaves**, the medicine man becomes an intermediary between the two worlds. He is the only person permitted to set foot in the sacred and otherwise closed-off districts, where he gathers plants used for healing and rituals.

The Guajíro

The **Guajíro Native American** population stands at around 130,000. They are settled in the Guajíro peninsula, most of which belongs to **Columbia** and the rest to **Venezuela**. The Guajíro live in disparate small settlements and lone farmsteads, surviving primarily from their own animals (cattle, horses, donkeys and sheep). It is the size of their herd that determines their social status. Agriculture also contributes to the Guajíros' survival (they grow corn, beans, cassava and pumpkins), although prolonged dry periods mean that farming is only possible for a few months of every year. As a result, many Guajíro have now migrated to the city (most of them to Maracaíbo).

Guajiro society is traditionally based around membership of one of thirty clans, each of which is associated with its own **totem animal** and represents a different social status. The **Jaguar clan** (Ulíana), for example, enjoys a particularly high social standing. **Polygamy** was once the norm in Guajíro society. Medicine men and women – who also act as priests and dream interpreters – play an important role in the life of the Guajíro.

The Saramaka

There are some 20,000 Saramaka people in the rainforests of Suriname and French Guyana. They are – alongside the Djuka, Auca, Boni, Matawai and Paramacca – just one of the peoples of the region of African descent, but are distinguished from other groups by both their language and culture. The Saramaka are descendants of African slaves who escaped from their masters' large plantations in the seventeenth and eighteenth centuries and fled into the rainforest. The remote and hard to reach location of their settlements has allowed the Saramaka people to maintain their independence.

In contrast to the black Creole descendents of liberated slaves, the Saramaka are – like the area's other peoples of African descent – classified as Maroons or Marrons. The Saramaka speak Saramakan Tongo (Deepi-Takhi), while the other Maroon groups speak Taki Taki dialects. The Taki Taki language is spoken throughout Suriname, and borrows many idioms from English.

1 In the Native American communities of Ecuador, children work out of economic necessity.

2 The samba is to Brazil what the tango is to Argentina – a fundamental part of the country's popular culture. Its rhythms are based on the music once played by West African slaves.

3 The Rio carnival is a spectacle of fantastic costumes whose parades and street festivals go on for days. The event attracts millions of tourists every year. For the samba schools, coming first in the competition for the best costumes is the culmination of a year's worth of ambition.

Southern America

*The festival of Inti Raymi, which takes place in the Peruvian city of **Cusco**, near Machu Picchu, is a reminder of the former glory of the Inca empire. The empire was the last great Andean high culture before the Spanish conquest.*

Rice cultivation and slash and burn farming provide the primary basis of the Saramakas' existence. Their village communities are matrilineal societies ruled by a chief called the Gran Man, who also fulfils the role of a priest. As such, his responsibilities include the guardianship of the so-called shrine of the earth mother and, above all, the preservation of the ancestor cult.

It is the Saramakas' religious conviction that witchcraft summons evil spirits, and its practice is therefore strictly forbidden.

The Xukuru

There are currently around 7,000 **Xukuru Native Americans** living in the north-eastern **Brazilian** state of **Pernambuco**. Their language is a member of the **Macro-Gê linguistic family**. Most Xukuru live in relatively small village communities, surviving from agriculture (beans, corn, sweet potatoes and maracujá) and animal breeding (cattle, pigs and goats). Many are also employed on the **fazendas** of the large landowners. At the same time, the Xukuru have for years been fighting for the return of at least some of their former land holdings.

Though the Xukuru have long since been Christianised, their traditional religious beliefs still exert significant influence. The Xukurus' most important god is Tupã, and they also believe in the earth mother Tamain, the goddesses of the forest, and the spirits. The ritual **toré dance** is performed in homage to both the Xukurus' gods and their ancestors. Dancers cover their entire bodies with body paint and wear special garments made from corn or palm straw and brightly decorated with lots of bird feathers. The shaman and the healer (Pajé) are also important figures.

The Gê

The Gê Native American settlements span the mountainous regions of several eastern Brazilian states. Their population comprises around 2,000 **Kayapó** and the fifteen sub-groups of the

Timbira (including around 1,000 **Canela**), as well as the Suyá, Xerente and Xavante groups. These different groups are bound together by their similar dialects and cultures.

The Gê people rely primarily on agriculture for their survival (cassava, sweet potatoes, corn, yam, pumpkin, beans, peanuts and Brazil nuts), but they also hunt using a bow and arrow.

The traditional villages of the Gê people are built in a circular shape. The villagers live in gabled houses, and there is always a men's house located at the heart of the settlement.

The Gê people have developed a form of social organisation in which they are split into two groups, and the villages are often divided into halves, each with its own chief.

The freedom associated with the gaucho way of life is the subject of many songs.

The Gauchos

The term 'gaucho' was coined in the Rio de la Plata plain of Argentina, Uruguay and Brazil. In the Mapuche and Quechua languages, it means 'orphan', but the word may also derive from the phrase 'guahu-che' ('people who sing sadly'). Around a million gaucho seasonal workers live in Argentina, spread between the pampa around Buenos Aires, the Argentinian part of Patagonia in the south of the country and the northern province of Corrientes. Descendants of part-Spanish mestizos, the gauchos are now synonymous with the idea of freedom, but in the seventeenth century they were still regarded as contemptible animal thieves,

riding through the pampa on horseback and rustling the semi-wild cattle herds that provided a valuable source of meat, leather and fat. When the pampa was settled in the late eighteenth century, the white farmers (estancieros) employed the gauchos to do jobs that could only be accomplished on horseback. In the early nineteenth century, the gauchos' extensive local knowledge saw them play a significant role in the Argentine War of Independence. The traditional life of the gaucho began to change with the invention of refrigeration systems. These made it possible to preserve and sell meat, attracting town-dwellers to the pampa for the first time.

The Tukano

The **Tukano** live in south-east **Columbia** and north-west **Brazil**. They are a large group comprising more than twenty different tribes, among them some 12,000 members of the Winá (Desana), Baniwa and Tariana peoples, as well as the Tukano proper. The latter, who call themselves

The Xingu

Established in 1961, the 'Parque Indigéna do Xingu' (Xingu Indigenous Park) lies along the upper reaches of the Xingu river. Its formation brought together the territories of 16 different indigenous Native American tribes, who, fleeing from settlers, had established themselves in the Xingu region over the centuries. Epidemic illnesses made heavy claims on the Xingu population, which now stands at around just 2,500. They have, however, preserved their traditional tribal social structure, and their contact with the outside world is limited. One of their ceremonies is the 'Kwarup', held in respect of the dead.

Dakséa, are the biggest group. Though the various groups speak different languages, their culture is similar. They survive mainly through slash and burn farming (cassava), as well as from hunting, fishing and gathering wild plants. The **medicine man** (yai) is the spiritual leader of the Tukano. In religious ceremonies, he acts as an intermediary between man, plants and animals. Drugs also figure prominently in Tukano religious ceremonies.

The Munduruku

Up until a hundred years ago, the **Munduruku** population stood at some 40,000. As a result of newly introduced illnesses, however, that figure now stands at around just 1,500. The Munduruku are spread between a number of villages of the **Mato Grosso high plateau** of central Brazil. Their language is a member of the Tupí linguistic family. Alongside cassava, the Munduruku grow a wide range of **plants**, some of them **medicinal**. They also survive from hunting, fishing and trading rubber and animal furs. Until the beginning of the twentieth century, the Munduruku were revered as fearsome warriors possessed of a tightly organised **military machine**.

Having initially engaged in bitter conflict with their European occupiers, the Munduruku joined forces with the Portuguese towards the end of the eighteenth century. In return for Portuguese assurances of their traditional territorial rights, the Munduruku, allied with other **Native American** groups, set about **capturing slaves** from hostile tribes.

The Caraya

The approximately 2,000-strong **Caraya** population lives on the world's largest known inland river island, **Bananal**, in the **Rio Araguaia** river of central Brazil. The Caraya (whose own name for themselves is Yña, meaning 'person') have their own language, which does not belong to any of the region's linguistic families. As a river people, their survival

*The **Yagua** people live in the rainforest around the upper reaches of the Amazon and its tributaries. They belong to one of Latin America's largest and most spread-out linguistic groups, the Caribs. Today, there is a total Carib population of approximately 25,000, divided into some 20 tribes. Although they traditionally survive by hunting and gathering wild plants, a significant number of Carib have also started to work for white 'Padrones'.*

rests primarily on catching fish and turtles, as well as collecting turtle eggs, mussels and crabs. Gifted craftsmen, the Caraya also sell their handiwork to tourists. The big **clay figurines** (Litjoko) made by Caraya women and the large wooden masks used in the Carayas' traditional **masked dances** are particularly popular.

The Jívaro

The **Jívaro** comprise five tribal groups: the **Jívaro** (who call themselves the Shuar), the **Achuar**, the **Aguaruna**, the **Huambisa** and the **Mayan**. Their various languages and cultures are closely related, and their total population stands at around 70,000. They live in the tropical rainforest on the eastern slopes of the Ecuadorian and Peruvian Andes, surviving both from agriculture and from hunting small animals. They still hunt with blowguns and arrows poisoned with curare.
As late as the 1950s, **shrunken head trophies** were still an important part of traditional Jívaro culture. The tradition was rooted in the belief that serious illness, accidents and sudden deaths were the result of witchcraft, and any practitioner would be killed in order that his **avenging spirit** (Muisak) – which would leave his body upon his death – could be trapped in the preprepared shrunken head (Tsantsa).

The Chiriguano

Today, there are some 40,000 **Chiriguano** (who call themselves Guaraní). Their settlements span **south-east Bolivia**, **northern Argentina** and **northern Paraguay**. Chiriguano is one of the **Tupí-Guaraní languages**. The Chiriguano are considered to be the best corn farmers in the **Andes**, and they also survive from rearing animals (sheep, chickens, horses and cattle). They are well known for their skilled craftwork, especially for hammocks, textiles and ceramics. The latter – prized for their unique shapes and bright decoration – are among **Latin America**'s finest. Difficult economic conditions have, however, led many Chrigiuano to migrate to the cities or find seasonal work on the haciendas owned by the large landowners.

Aymara

Totalling around 1.2 million, the **Aymara** make up about 20 per cent of the **Bolivian population**. There are approximately a further 800,000 Aymara in Peru, most of them in the highlands around **Lake Titicaca**, which belongs to

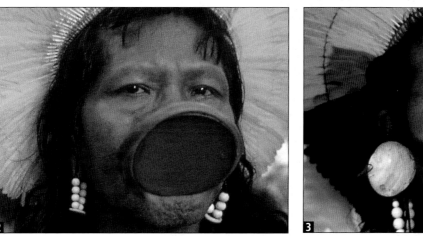

both countries. The Aymara may be subdivided into rural and urban groups, separated not only by location but also by their differing social structures. The Aymara of the Andean Altiplano grow potatoes, barley and other crops, cultivated at altitudes up to 4,000 m. They also keep lamas, alpacas and sheep.

The Mapuche

The **Mapuche** ('people of the land') are also known as **Araucanians**, **Huiliche** or **Picunche**. The majority of the Mapuche population (about 500,000) is found south of the city of **Concepción**, **Chile**, but there are also 20,000 Mapuche in **southern Argentina**. The Mapuche resisted Inca invasion of their original settlements around **Santiago de Chile** in the fifteenth century, but, faced with growing Spanish power, emigrated to **Argentina**

in the sixteenth century. There, the Mapuche's status as both legendary **mounted warriors** and excellent **animal breeders** secured them great influence over the local Indian population. It was the end of the nineteenth century before the Mapuche finally succumbed to Argentina's far superior military power.

1 In the barren mountainous regions of Peru, 4,000 m above sea level, life for the Quechua is hard.

2 In Amazon Native American communities, a lip plate like the one worn here by Raoni, chief of the Brazilan Kayapo tribe, is a traditional sign of beauty.

3 Indigenous South American peoples use face painting to signify a person's social status within their tribe.

4 In the central Brazilian Mato Grosso, the warrior-like appearance of the male Suya is designed to provoke both fear and respect.

Index of Topics

Picture credits

This edition is published on behalf of APA Publications GmbH & Co. Verlag KG, Singapore Branch, Singapore by Verlag Wolfgang Kunth GmbH & Co KG, Munich, Germany

Distribution of this edition:

GeoCenter International Ltd
Meridian House, Churchill Way West
Basingstoke, Hampshire RG21 6YR
Great Britain
Tel.: (44) 1256 817 987
Fax: (44) 1256 817 988
sales@geocenter.co.uk
www.insightguides.com

Original edition:
© 2008 Verlag Wolfgang Kunth GmbH & Co. KG, Munich
Königinstr. 11
80539 Munich
Ph: +49.89.45 80 20-0
Fax: +49.89.45 80 20-21
www.kunth-verlag.de

English edition:
Copyright © 2008 Verlag Wolfgang Kunth GmbH & Co. KG
© Cartography: GeoGraphic Publishers GmbH & Co. KG

Printed in Slovakia

Translation: American Pie Translation, London; JMS LLP, Somerset, UK
Printed in Slovakia

The information and facts presented in this book have been extensively researched and edited for accuracy. The publishers, authors, and editors, cannot, however, guarantee that all of the information in the book is entirely accurate or up to date at the time of publication. The publishers are grateful for any suggestions or corrections that would improve the content of this book.